The Kael Index

The Kael Index
A Guide to a Movie Critic's Work,
1954-1991

William J. Slattery
Claire Dorton
Rosemary Enright

1993
LIBRARIES UNLIMITED, INC.
Englewood, Colorado

To Pauline

Copyright © 1993 William J. Slattery
All Rights Reserved
Printed in the United States of America

No part of this publication may be reproduced, stored in a retrieval system, or transmitted, in any form or by any means, electronic, mechanical, photocopying, recording, or otherwise, without the prior written permission of the publisher.

LIBRARIES UNLIMITED, INC.
P.O. Box 6633
Englewood, CO 80155-6633

Library of Congress Cataloging-in-Publication Data

Slattery, William J., 1930-
    The Kael index : a guide to a movie critic's work, 1954-1991 / by
William J. Slattery, Claire Dorton, Rosemary Enright.
    viii, 287 p. 22x28 cm.
    Includes bibliographical references.
    ISBN 1-56308-119-9
    1. Motion pictures--Reviews--Indexes. 2. Kael, Pauline--Indexes.
I. Dorton, Claire. II. Enright, Rosemary, 1940-   . III. Title.
PN1998.3.K34S63 or PN1995.K22556   1993
016.79143'75--dc20   93-11821
                                                              CIP

Contents

Introduction vi
Books by Pauline Kael and Code Key to *The Kael Index* vii
Sample Entries viii

INDEX 1

Introduction to a Selected Bibliography 283
A Selected Bibliography 284

Introduction

In July 1992, I visited Pauline Kael, author and former film critic at *The New Yorker* (1968-1991), in the small Massachusetts town where she lives. After lunch at a little Japanese place she likes, we went to Kael's grand, old Victorian house and poked around upstairs in a small storeroom where she keeps the newspaper and magazine clippings she has collected about herself over the years. After I expressed an interest in them, Kael said, "I'll lend you a suitcase for you to take them home in."

I have no idea how many clippings I came away with. Certainly there were more than 5,000. They seemed to weigh hundreds of pounds and filled three very large suitcases plus two shopping bags. Kael's friend, the writer Steve Vineberg, recently came to my house for dinner and was momentarily rendered speechless by the sheer volume of these clippings.

Many of my friends have suspected for some time that one day my mind would snap. Many of them, upon observing these piles of clippings, conclude that "nutso day" has finally arrived. Kael herself thinks I'm a little mad for wanting to look at all of these clippings about her. Perhaps I am. But in my opinion, these clippings are, in aggregate, of inestimable value. They represent a look into the life and opinions of one of America's most respected film critics.

Pauline Kael was born June 19, 1919, in Petaluma, California. She attended the University of California from 1936-1940, and has since accumulated a number of honorary doctorate degrees. Prior to *The New Yorker*, Kael contributed to several magazines including *Film Quarterly, McCall's, Life, The New Republic, Vogue, Atlantic,* and *Holiday.* Her books include *I Lost It at the Movies*, 1965; *Kiss Kiss Bang Bang*, 1968; *Going Steady*, 1970; *Deeper into Movies*, 1973 (which won the National Book Award, 1974); *Reeling*, 1976; *When the Lights Go Down*, 1980; *5001 Nights at the Movies*, 1982; *Taking It All In*, 1984; *State of the Art*, 1985; *Hooked*, 1989; and her latest, *Movie Love: Complete Reviews, 1988-1991*, 1991. Kael lists herself as a contributing author of *The Citizen Kane Book*, 1971 (a book that included the actual movie script, and a lengthy analysis of the script and the film and their impact). Among her awards are the George Polk Memorial Award in 1970 and the Front Page Award given by the Newswomen's Club of New York in 1974 and again in 1983.

With the kind of reputation Pauline Kael has earned during her years of commenting on members of the film industry, it only made sense to publish an index to her work. I made this suggestion to her during a conversation last year. I commented that an index of her books would be a helpful and interesting reference for scholars and film enthusiasts. She informed me that one was already being compiled; however, progress on the book had slowed and eventually had been discontinued due to an illness in the author's family.

Fortunately, the author, Claire Dorton, had completed approximately seventy percent of her index to Kael's books. At that point, my wife, Rosemary Enright, took over Claire's project and after several months' work, completed what Claire had begun. Both women have demanding full-time jobs. That this index got done at all borders on the miraculous. My literary agent, Neil G. McCluskey of the Westchester Literary Agency, found a publisher for the index. All of us are friends of Pauline's who was generous with her time and gave us access to her papers.

This book indexes Kael's work, beginning in 1954, and provides the reader—whether a film enthusiast, critic, scholar, or student—with a single source for finding out what and who in the movies has been reviewed where. The entries in the index are categorized by movie titles; names of actors, directors, and screenwriters; and names of entities, such as the American Broadcasting Company. Film schools and programs, libraries, and movie buffs will find the index an indispensable addition to their reference collections.

William J. Slattery

Books by Pauline Kael and Code Key to The Kael Index

5001   *5001 Nights at the Movies*. 2d ed., New York: Henry Holt, 1991.

DIM   *Deeper into Movies*. Boston: Atlantic-Little, Brown, 1973.

GS   *Going Steady*. Boston: Atlantic-Little, Brown, 1970.

H   *Hooked*. New York: A William Abrahams Book, E. P. Dutton, 1989.

ILIATM   *I Lost It at the Movies*. Boston: Atlantic-Little, Brown, 1965.

KKBB   *Kiss Kiss Bang Bang*. Boston: Atlantic-Little, Brown, 1968.

R   *Reeling*. Boston: Atlantic-Little, Brown, 1976.

SOTA   *State of the Art*. New York: A William Abrahams Book, E. P. Dutton, 1985.

TIAI   *Taking It All In*. New York: Holt, Rinehart & Winston, 1984.

WTLGD   *When the Lights Go Down*. New York: Holt, Rinehart & Winston, 1980.

Sample Entries

The Kael Index lists names of people and groups interspersed with the names of movies, or other works, and all are in alphabetical order sorted by word. The index includes listings for movies, books, plays, articles, essays, music, television shows, actors, directors, authors, and even alternate titles for the same work.

Following the index listing is the code for the Pauline Kael book referenced. The code is the acronym for the title of that particular Pauline Kael book. (The code key is on page vii.) Following the code is the page number of the Kael book where the listing is discussed. For director listings, the name of the director is indexed alphabetically, and is followed by the book code, the abbreviation "dir." indicating director, the name of the movie he or she directed, and the page number in the referenced book where the director or movie is discussed. The following are sample entries from *The Kael Index* that depict some of the above:

Death of a Cyclist (Muerte de un Ciclista;
      also known as *Age of Infidelity)*
    5001

(index lists 3 different titles)

(5001 = 5001 Nights at the Movies
- alpha listings, no pp. nec)

"Death of a Playmate" (article)
    SOTA 91

(SOTA = State of the Art, p. 91)

Death of a Salesman (play)
    R 117, 157, 224-226
    H 200, 351

(R = Reeling, pp. 117,157,224-226)
(H = Hooked, pp. 200,351)

Death of a Salesman
    ILIATM 70
    KKBB 203, 361

(movie)
(ILIATM = I Lost It at the Movies, p. 70)
(KKBB = Kiss Kiss Bang Bang, pp. 203,361)

Death on the Nile
    WTLGD 462-466
    5001

(movie)
(WTLGD = When the Lights Go Down, pp. 462-466)
(5001 = 5001 Nights at the Movies - alpha listings, no pp. nec)

It should be noted that only the second edition of *5001 Nights at the Movies* is indexed. Since the reviews in *5001* are in alphabetical order by movie title, page numbers in *The Kael Index* are given for references to individuals, but not for movies. A "2nd ed" listing following the "*5001*" reference to a particular movie indicates that the review appears only in that edition. The following is an example of this:

Educating Rita
    SOTA 83-85
    5001 (2nd ed)

(movie)
(SOTA = State of the Art, pp. 83-85)
(5001 = 5001 Nights at the Movies,
second edition - alpha listings no pp. nec)

A

À bout de souffle, see *Breathless*
A Ciascuno il Suo, see *We Still Kill the Old Way*
À double tour, see *Léda*
À nos amours
    H 151
À nous la liberté
    ILIATM 282
    KKBB 140-141, 311, 320
    5001
A tout prendre
    R 172
"A-Team, The" (TV)
    SOTA 217
A.I.P., see American International Pictures
Aaron, Caroline
    5001 162
Abbess of Crewe, The
    WTLGD 262-266
Abbott & Costello Meet Frankenstein
    R 404
Abbott, Bruce
    H 68
    5001 618
Abbott, Bud
    ILIATM 307
    GS 186
    DIM 180
    TIAI 108, 467
    H 155
    5001 631
Abbott, Diahnne
    WTLGD 285
    TIAI 458, 459
    SOTA 46
    H 145
    5001 381, 396, 521, 745
Abbott, George
    KKBB 231
    5001 18, 97, 831
Abbott, John
    WTLGD 123
    5001 28, 76, 182, 276, 285, 345, 446, 469,
        654, 672
ABC "Movie of the Week" (TV)
    WTLGD 120, 446
ABC, see American Broadcasting Company
Abdication, The
    R 345-347
    WTLGD 205
    5001
Abdul-Jabbar, Kareem
    5001 12, 251
Abe, Yutaka
    SOTA 327
    5001 454
Abel, Alan
    DIM 324, 326; dir., *Is There Sex After Death?*,
        324-326
    5001 371

Abel, Alfred
    5001 477
Abel, Jeanne
    DIM 324, 326; dir., *Is There Sex After
        Death?*, 324-326
    5001 371
Abel, Walter
    5001 170, 273, 306, 527, 614, 760
Aberdein, Keith
    SOTA 244
    5001 810
Abie's Irish Rose
    RK 13
    TIAI 91
About Last Night...
    H 176-179
    5001 (2nd ed)
Abraham, F. Murray
    WTLGD 468
    SOTA 101, 102, 249, 253
    ML 316
    5001 21, 70, 658
Abrahams, Jim
    TIAI 50-51; co-dir., *Airplane!*, 50-51, 367
    H 179-180, 483-485; co-dir., *Airplane!* 154,
        179, 484; *Ruthless People*, 179-180, 484;
        dir., *Big Business*, 483-485; co-dir., *Top
        Secret!* 484
    5001 12, 68, 648
Abril, Victoria
    SOTA 46, 47
    5001 495
Abroms, Edward
    TIAI 486
    5001 87
Absence of Malice
    TIAI 288-290, 441
    SOTA 78
    5001
Absolute Beginners
    H 157-161, 389
    5001 (2nd ed)
Accatone
    KKBB 253
Accident
    KKBB 105-109
    R 220, 235, 343
    5001
    H 45
Accidental Tourist, The
    ML 67-71
    5001 (2nd ed)
Accomplices to the Crime
    TIAI 21, 24
Ace, The, see *The Great Santini*
Ace in the Hole (also known as *The Big Carnival*)
    ILIATM 153
    5001
Achard, Marcel

    5001 209
Acheson, Dean
    ILIATM 327
Acheson, James
    5001 171, 408
Acker, Sharon
    5001 768
Ackerman, Thomas
    5001 61
Ackland, Joss
    R 389
    WTLGD 50
    5001 221
Ackridge, Bill
    5001 680
Across the Bridge
    5001
Across the Pacific
    ILIATM 299
    5001
Across the River and Into the Trees
    WTLGD 280
Act of the Heart
    DIM 205-206
    5001
Actor's Revenge, An
    SOTA 327
Actress, The
    ILIATM 305
    5001
Acuff, Eddie
    5001 578
Adabachian, Alexander
    5001 172
"Adagio for Strings" (music)
    TIAI 84
    H 251
Adair, Jean
    KKBB 232
    5001 35
Adalen 31
    DIM 41-42, 104
    5001
Adam, Ken
    GS 227
    DIM 389
    WTLGD 190
    TIAI 276, 277, 278
    5001 53, 495, 574, 667, 703, 857
Adam's Rib
    KKBB 228:n, 330
    H 173
    5001
"Adam's Rib" (TV)
    WTLGD 47
Adams, Brooke
    WTLGD 521-522
    5001 177, 368
Adams, Casey, see Showalter, Max

Adams, Dorothy
  5001 413
Adams, Edie
  WTLGD 449
  5001 65, 339, 441, 554, 808
Adams, Frank R.
  5001 786
Adams, India
  5001 50
Adams, Jill
  KKBB 277
  5001 306
Adams, Joe
  5001 120
Adams, Julie (Julia)
  5001 160, 409
Adams, Lee
  GS 237
  5001 111, 528
Adams, Mason
  5001 274
Adams, Maud
  SOTA 4
  5001 462, 539
Adams, Nick
  5001 488, 618
Adams, Samuel Hopkins
  5001 373
Adamson, Ewart
  5001 30
Addams, Charles
  ILIATM 86
Addams, Dawn
  5001 395
Addie, Robert
  TIAI 186
Addison, John
  5001 244
Addy, Wesley
  KKBB 238
  DIM 147
  SOTA 210
  5001 71, 94, 663, 813
Adele, Jan
  H 433, 434
  5001 333
Adjani, Isabelle
  WTLGD 55-58, 145, 153
  SOTA 368
  H 310, 311
  ML 90
  5001 204, 371, 685, 717
Adkinson, Suzanne
  5001 610
Adler, Buddy
  5001 269, 627
Adler, Hans
  5001 254, 751
Adler, Larry
  KKBB 270
  5001 281, 765
Adler, Lou
  WTLGD 448-450
  5001 808
Adler, Luther
  GS 244, 247
  TIAI 290

  5001 2, 123, 819
Adler, Stella
  5001 669
Admirable Crichton, The, see Paradise Lagoon
Admiral's Daughter, The
  H 74
Adolphe, Hylette
  5001 240
Adorf, Mario
  KKBB 258, 340
  5001 187, 643
Adrian
  5001 75, 84, 153, 194, 259, 266, 300, 407,
    447, 465, 580, 736, 845, 865
Adrian, Iris
  KKBB 341
  GS 116
  5001 289, 405, 645, 647
Adrian, Max
  DIM 380, 382
  5001 96, 328, 398, 504
Adventure of Sherlock Holmes' Smarter Brother,
    The
  WTLGD 98-101
  5001
Adventurers, The
  DIM 132-136, 148, 420
  5001
Adventures of a Young Man, see Hemingway's
    Adventures of a Young Man
Adventures of Baron Munchausen, The
  ML 106-11
  5001 (2nd ed)
Adventures of Buckaroo Banzai, The
  SOTA 217-220
  ML 25
  5001 (2nd ed)
Adventures of Don Juan
  5001
Adventures of Robin Hood, The (1938)
  KKBB 180, 184, 228:n
  TIAI 483
  ML 132
  5001
Adventures of Robinson Crusoe, The
  KKBB 228-229:n
  ML 117
  5001
Adventures of Tom Sawyer, The
  5001
Adventuress, The, see I See a Dark Stranger
Advise and Consent
  ILIATM 294, 306
  GS 207
  5001
Aeneid
  WTLGD 300
Affair in Kamakura
  KKBB 271
Africa Addio
  R 66
African Lion, The
  KKBB 180, 184
African Queen, The
  ILIATM 24, 299
  KKBB 131, 180, 229:n
  R 317

  WTLGD 62-63, 275, 281, 508
  H 364-366
  5001
After Hours
  H 38-41, 226
  ML 151
  5001 (2nd ed)
After the Fall (stage)
  R 153, 157-158
After the Fox
  GS 158
  R 69
  5001
After the Rehearsal
  H 430
After the Thin Man
  5001 (2nd ed)
Against All Odds
  SOTA 145-147, 158
  5001 (2nd ed)
Agar, John
  5001 259, 396, 672
Agatha
  WTLGD 551-554
  TIAI 159
  5001
Age and Scarpelli
  5001 69, 584, 729
Age d'or, L'
  KKBB 43
  DIM 336
  5001
Age of Infidelity, see Death of a Cyclist
Agee, James
  ILIATM 19, 26, 114, 295
  KKBB 142, 229, 289, 317
  GS 49-50
  RK 51
  DIM 133
  R 5, 143
  TIAI 438
  5001 9, 19, 101, 526, 835
Agee on Film (book)
  WTLGD 330
Ager, Cecelia
  RK 44
Aghayan, Ray
  R 460
Agnes of God
  H 243
Agnew, Spiro
  DIM 100, 420
  WTLGD 62
Agony and the Ecstasy, The
  5001
Aguirre, the Wrath of God
  TIAI 401, 402, 405, 406
  SOTA 199
Agutter, Jenny
  5001 223, 706
Ah, Wilderness!
  KKBB 285
  DIM 76
  5001
Aherne, Brian
  WTLGD 7
  5001 349, 384, 510, 694, 738, 774, 815, 829, 830

Ahlberg, Mac
  5001 618
Ahlstedt, Börje
  TIAI 487
  5001 236
Aidman, Charles
  5001 402
Aiello, Danny
  TIAI 153
  SOTA 339
  H 277, 371, 423
  5001 259, 290, 496, 581, 604, 610
Aierra, Iñaki
  TIAI 409
  5001 735
Aigle à deux têtes, L', see *The Eagle with Two Heads*
Aimée, Anouk
  KKBB 126, 333
  GS 263, 264
  TIAI 89, 313, 419, 420
  H 469
  5001 213, 382, 415, 429, 441, 456, 490, 593, 787
Ainley, Henry
  5001 36
Ainley, Richard
  5001 36, 349, 833
Air Force
  5001
Airplane!
  TIAI 50-51, 367
  H 154, 179, 484
  5001
Airport
  DIM 132, 136-137, 147, 173, 220, 233, 294
  R 53, 72, 137, 364, 432
  5001 (2nd ed)
Airport 1975
  R 363-365, 385
  5001
Ajaye, Franklyn
  WTLGD 188
  5001 118, 155
Akers, Karen
  SOTA 337
  H 190
  5001 325, 604
Akins, Claude
  5001 301
Akins, Zoë
  DIM 341
  5001 116, 136, 305, 498, 542, 864
Akst, Harry
  5001 547
Akutagawa, Ryonosuke
  KKBB 337
  5001 616
Alaimo, Marc
  WTLGD 545
Alamo Bay
  H 50
Albano, Captain Lou
  H 153
  5001 842
Albeck, Andy

H 22
Albee, Edward
  KKBB 21, 106, 108, 212
  TIAI 127
  5001 66
Alberghetti, Anna Maria
  KKBB 308
  5001 473
Alberni, Luis
  5001 157, 210, 253, 359, 439, 734, 792
Albers, Hans
  WTLGD 177
  5001 85, 813
Albert, Eddie
  KKBB 185
  R 70, 276, 353-354
  WTLGD 125-126
  TIAI 11
  SOTA 231
  5001 122, 203, 324, 346, 357, 433, 445, 552, 636, 688, 745
Albert, Edward
  SOTA 277
  5001 260
Albert, Katherine
  5001 706
Albertazzi, Georgio
  5001 412
Alberti, Guido
  5001 213
Albertina Rasch Ballet
  5001 337
Albertson, Frank
  KKBB 230
  5001 11, 15, 44, 273, 387, 640, 675
Albertson, Jack
  5001 441, 458, 840
Albertson, Mabel
  DIM 432
  5001 52, 244. 831
Albright, Hardie
  5001 112, 694
Albright, Ivan
  5001 581
Albright, Lola
  KKBB 249, 299
  GS 127
  WTLGD 210, 491
  5001 145, 210, 435
Albright, Zsissly
  5001 581
Alcaine, José Luis
  5001 848
Alcott, John
  WTLGD 482
  SOTA 73, 148
  5001 53, 308, 532. 800, 805, 836
Alcott, Louisa May
  TIAI 61
  5001 428
Alda, Alan
  WTLGD 505-507, 529-530, 532
  TIAI 19, 208, 379: dir., *The Four Seasons*, 207, 208, 415
  H 161-164; dir., *Sweet Liberty*. 161-164, 167
  ML 201-202; dir.. *The Four Seasons* 201

  5001 115, 162, 469, 651, 735
Alda, Robert
  WTLGD 147
  5001 352, 457
Alda, Rutanya
  TIAI 236
  5001 78, 183, 492, 610
Alda, Ruth
  5001 330
Alden Robinson, Phil, see Robinson, Phil Alden
Alderson, Brooke
  TIAI 31
  5001 361, 480, 809
Aldington, Richard
  DIM 139
Aldo, G. R.
  5001 749, 803
Aldous, Lucette
  WTLGD 347
  5001 795
Aldrich, Robert
  ILIATM 303; dir., *What Ever Happened to Baby Jane?*, 8, 14, 294, 303
  KKBB 238; dir., *The Dirty Dozen*, 55; *The Big Knife*, 238
  GS 213; dir., *Attack!*, 208; *Autumn Leaves*, 208; *The Big Knife*, 75, 208; *The Dirty Dozen*, 61, 208; *The Killing of Sister George*, 206-208; *Kiss Me Deadly*, 208; *The Legend of Lylah Clare*, 208; *What Ever Happened to Baby Jane?*, 208
  DIM dir., *The Legend of Lylah Clare*, 148; *The Dirty Dozen*, 315
  R 353; dir., *The Big Knife*, 187; *The Longest Yard*, 352-355; *The Dirty Dozen*, 353, 354
  WTLGD 124-127, 276; dir., *Hustle*, 124-127; *The Dirty Dozen*, 126; *The Longest Yard*, 276
  SOTA 212
  ML 301
  5001 39, 71, 346, 417, 433, 797
Aldridge, Kitty
  H 361
  5001 471
Aleandro, Norma
  ML 96
  5001 159
Aleichem, Sholom
  DIM 330
  5001 242
Alekan, Henri
  H 473
  5001 59, 441, 465, 472, 637, 841
Alerme
  KKBB 245
  5001 121
Alex & the Gypsy
  WTLGD 183-184
  5001
Alex in Wonderland
  DIM 224-228
  R 167, 411
  WTLGD 128, 129
  TIAI 47
  ML 328
  5001

Alexander, Ben
  KKBB 231
  5001 18
Alexander, Elizabeth
  TIAI 57
Alexander, J. Grubb
  5001 489, 734
Alexander, Jane
  TIAI 23
  SOTA 115
  5001 66, 108, 304
Alexander, John
  5001 36, 578
Alexander, Karl
  5001 772
Alexander, Katharine
  5001 52, 170, 359, 703
Alexander Nevsky
  ILIATM 288
  GS 45
  5001
Alexander, Rita
  RK 32, 38
Alexander, Ross
  5001 118
Alexander the Great
  DIM 49, 221
  WTLGD 107-108, 110
Alexander's Ragtime Band
  5001
Alexandrakis, Aleko
  KKBB 351
  5001 713
Alexeieff, Alexandre
  5001 789
Alfie
  5001
Alford, Philip
  5001 777
Alfred the Great
  DIM 67-68
Alfredo Alfredo
  R 257-259
  5001
Algerian War
  WTLGD 175
Algiers (remake of Pépé le Moko)
  KKBB 244
  R 420
  WTLGD 126
  SOTA 47
  5001
Algonquin Round Table
  RK 11, 14, 18, 19, 26, 27
  WTLGD 13
Algren, Nelson
  5001 462
Ali Baba and the Forty Thieves
  5001
Ali, Muhammad
  DIM 160
  WTLGD 67, 213
Alice Adams
  KKBB 229-230:n
  GS 177
  DIM 311
  WTLGD 209

SOTA 281, 337
H 409-410
5001
Alice Doesn't Live Here Anymore
  R 408-416
  WTLGD 132, 229, 258, 415
  TIAI 109
  H 49
  5001
Alice in Wonderland
  KKBB 370
  WTLGD 27
  H 51
  5001
Alice's Adventures in Wonderland, see Alice in
      Wonderland
Alice's Restaurant
  DIM 5, 6, 197, 212, 215
  R 309
  WTLGD 411
  TIAI 284
Alien
  TIAI 10, 13, 19, 169, 192
  SOTA 188
  H 192, 194
Aliens
  H 192-194
  5001 (2nd ed)
Alison, Joan
  5001 122
All About Eve
  KKBB 189, 219, 230:n
  GS 165
  RK 83
  R 284
  WTLGD 232
  H 295
  5001
All-American Boy, The
  R 221, 260, 294
  5001
All Fall Down
  ILIATM 137-138
  H 348
  5001
All Girl Productions
  ML 72
All in the Family
  R 136, 454
"All in the Family" (TV)
  WTLGD 150, 254, 369
All My Sons (stage)
  H 351
  ML 116, 200
All My Sons
  WTLGD 37
  ML 116
  5001
All Night Long
  TIAI 155-158, 196, 224
  SOTA 217, 233
  H 73
  5001
All of Me
  SOTA 220-224, 265
  H 336
  5001 (2nd ed)

"All of Me" (music)
  SOTA 224
All Quiet on the Western Front
  KKBB 230-231:n
  DIM 16, 17, 134
  H 304
  5001
All Screwed Up (Tutto a Posto e Niente in Ordine)
  WTLGD 138
  5001
All That Heaven Allows
  WTLGD 443
  5001
All That Jazz
  TIAI 180, 345, 427
  SOTA 35, 92
  H 145
All the Boys Are Named Patrick
  WTLGD 169
All the Emperor's Horses
  DIM 151
All the Fine Young Cannibals
  ML 121
All the King's Men
  DIM 63
  ML 222
  5001
All the Loving Couples
  DIM 57-58
All the President's Men
  WTLGD 266
  TIAI 23, 74
  II 191, 278
All the Way Home
  5001
All Through the Night
  5001
Allan, Elizabeth
  KKBB 243, 266
  5001 116, 254, 466, 476, 741, 846
Allan, Richard
  5001 522
Alland, William
  RK 8, 34, 37, 39, 58
  5001 138, 161
Allegret, Catherine
  R 33
  5001 410
Allégret, Marc
  H 330
  5001 236, 617
Allégret, Yves
  KKBB 335; dir., The Proud and the Beautiful,
      335
  5001 553
Allen, Adrianne
  5001 244
Allen, Corey
  5001 130, 618
Allen, Debbie
  5001 381
Allen, Dede
  KKBB 61
  WTLGD 273, 472
  5001 22, 91, 347, 424, 685
Allen, Fred
  DIM 180

5001 796
Allen, Gracie
  H 187
  ML 300
  5001 298, 828
Allen, Hervey
  5001 31
Allen, Irwin
  R 406
  5001 785
Allen, Jay Presson
  GS 286, 288
  DIM 412
  R 460
  TIAI 326, 327
  H 245
  5001 112, 181, 260, 387, 466, 498, 596, 788
Allen, Jo Harvey
  H 215, 217
  5001 794
Allen, Joan
  5001 150, 574
Allen, Karen
  TIAI 210-211, 292
  SOTA 306, 307
  ML 41
  5001 612, 660, 676, 710
Allen, Lewis
  5001 807
Allen, Nancy
  WTLGD 210
  TIAI 37, 38, 39, 226, 227, 228-229
  H 344
  5001 84, 122, 203, 408, 530, 634
Allen, Paul
  5001 553
Allen, Penny
  5001 197
Allen, Rae
  5001 832
Allen, Robert
  5001 161
Allen, Seth
  DIM 56
Allen, Steve
  DIM 62
  TIAI 395
  5001 149
Allen, Woody
  DIM 13, 60, 62, 325, 350, 369, 370; dir.,
    Take the Money and Run, 13, 60;
    Bananas, 314, 369, 370, 426
  R 127, 131-132, 240-244; dir., Bananas,
    240-244; Everything You Always
    Wanted to Know About Sex, 240-241;
    Sleeper, 240-244; Take the Money and
    Run, 243
  WTLGD 27, 100-101, 170,171, 195, 316,
    355, 371, 437-440, 526; dir., Everything
    You Always Wanted to Know About Sex,
    101, 355; Sleeper, 188; Annie Hall, 316,
    317, 320, 412, 437, 438; Interiors, 427,
    437-440
  TIAI 86-92, 161, 345, 365-368, 394, 395,
    396, 462; dir., Stardust Memories,
    86-92, 365; Annie Hall, 87, 90, 90-92,
    462; Interiors, 90; Manhattan, 90, 91,

    92, 435, 462; Sleeper, 161, 462;
    Bananas, 345; A Midsummer Night's
    Sex Comedy, 365-368
  SOTA 23-27, 122-125, 174, 335-340, 358;
    dir., Zelig, 23-27; Broadway Danny
    Rose, 122-125; A Midsummer Night's
    Sex Comedy, 123; The Purple Rose of
    Cairo, 335-340
  H 113-116, 190, 274-278, 425-427; dir.,
    Hannah and Her Sisters, 113-116;
    Annie Hall, 113, 115, 235, 314;
    Manhattan, 113, 115; Stardust
    Memories, 115; Interiors, 116, 426; The
    Purple Rose of Cairo, 228; Radio Days,
    274-278; September, 425-427
  ML 17, 103-105; dir., Annie Hall, 202, 327;
    Another Woman, 12-16; Crimes and
    Misdemeanors, 199-203; Interiors, 13,
    15; Manhattan, 327; Oedipus Wrecks,
    103-105; September, 13; What's Up
    Tiger Lily?, 203; Zelig, 202
  5001 31, 105, 123, 162, 270, 316, 365, 479,
    521, 604, 610, 665, 666, 686, 709, 830,
    831, 864
Allende Gossens, Salvador
  WTLGD 384-388
Alley, Kirstie
  TIAI 356
  5001 707
Allgood, Sara
  KKBB 249, 341, 349
  H 336
  5001 79, 143, 342, 392, 645, 649, 701
Allied Artists
  WTLGD 111-112, 520
Allin, Michael
  TIAI 125
  5001 221
Allio, René
  KKBB 110; dir., The Shameless Old Lady,
    110-111
  5001 670
Allister, Claude
  5001 399, 586
Alloway, Laurence
  ILIATM 26
Allport, Christopher
  5001 458
Allures
  KKBB 13
Allwin, Pernilla
  TIAI 489
  5001 236
Allwyn, Astrid
  5001 254, 316, 489
Allyson, June
  5001 63, 286, 287, 296, 764, 767, 772, 848
Almeida, Joaquim de, see de Almeida, Joaquim
Almendros, Nestor
  DIM 266
  R 11
  WTLGD 59, 187, 355, 509
  TIAI 28-29, 427
  SOTA 37
  H 190
  ML 102
  5001 59, 86, 140, 177, 290, 325, 461, 467,

    571, 585, 696, 715, 717, 798
Almodóvar, Pedro
  SOTA 364-366
  H 288-290, 466-469; dir., What Have I Done
    to Deserve This! 141, 288, 467; Law of
    Desire, 288-290, 466, 467; Matador,
    466-467, 468-469; Women on the Verge
    of a Nervous Breakdown, 466; Dark
    Habits (Entre Tinieblas), 467-468
  ML dir., Law of Desire, 27; Matador, 27;
    Women on the Verge of a Nervous
    Breakdown, 23-27
  5001 172, 414, 470, 830, 848
Almond, Paul
  DIM 206; dir., The Act of the Heart,
    205-206
  5001 5, 371
"Almost Anything Goes" (TV)
  WTLGD 150
"Almost Blue" (music)
  ML 124
Along Came Jones
  KKBB 29
Alonso, Ernesto
  5001 163
Alonso, Maria Conchita
  SOTA 157, 158
  H 264-265, 463
  ML 150-151
  5001 147, 499, 783, 812
Alonzo, John
  R 296
  WTLGD 352
  TIAI 486
  5001 87, 135, 153, 164, 381, 535, 658, 697
Alpert, Hollis
  KKBB 192
Alphabet Murders, The
  5001
Alphaville
  KKBB 15, 114-115, 319
  WTLGD 314
  TIAI 329, 485
  H 107, 471
  5001
Alphen, J. P.
  5001 647
Altamont
  DIM 206-208, 210, 211, 315
Altered States
  TIAI 127-132, 169
  5001
Alterio, Hector
  SOTA 126, 127
  5001 53
Altman, Robert
  DIM 94, 148, 227, 228, 277-278, 280, 282,
    350; dir., M*A*S*H, 92-95, 147, 185,
    227, 277, 278; Brewster McCloud,
    227-228; McCabe and Mrs. Miller,
    277-280, 426
  R 79-81, 183-190, 258, 267-271, 301, 310,
    318, 331, 424, 446, 447-452; dir.,
    M*A*S*H, 55, 80, 184, 185, 241, 270,
    309, 423, 427, 446, 447; Images, 79-81;
    Brewster McCloud, 80, 267, 270,
    447-448; McCabe & Mrs. Miller, 80,

267-269, 309, 438; *The Long Goodbye*, 183, 241, 268-269; *Thieves Like Us*, 267-271; *California Split*, 350-351, 424, 447; *Nashville*, 446-452

WTLGD 147-148, 187, 202, 261, 284, 285, 324, 362, 440-445, 548-551; dir., *California Split*, 30, 202, 276, 442; *Brewster McCloud*, 82, 548; *Images*, 82, 548; *Thieves Like Us*, 86; *Nashville*, 136, 143, 202, 204, 227, 259, 267, 276, 284, 322, 400, 441, 445; *M*A*S*H*, 187, 276; *Buffalo Bill and the Indians*, 261, 274, 275, 284-285, 441-442, 550; *3 Women*, 269, 442, 548; *The Long Goodbye*, 417; *A Wedding*, 440-445; *Quintet*, 548-551

TIAI 119-124, 152, 217, 227, 264, 265, 413-418, 423; dir., *Nashville*, 33, 227, 417; *Popeye*, 119-124, 455; *M*A*S*H*, 152; *3 Women*, 157, 417; *McCabe & Mrs. Miller*, 227, 281; *Buffalo Bill and the Indians*, 264; *Come Back to the 5 and Dime Jimmy Dean, Jimmy Dean*, 413-418; *That Cold Day in the Park*, 415; *Thieves Like Us*, 423

SOTA 217, 268, 289, 318; dir., *McCabe & Mrs. Miller*, 30, 268; *Come Back to the 5 & Dime Jimmy Dean, Jimmy Dean*, 108; *M*A*S*H*, 217; *Nashville*, 268; *The Long Goodbye*, 268; *Popeye*, 284; *Brewster McCloud*, 318

H 1-4, 61, 96-100, 136, 217, 218, 233, 311; dir., *Secret Honor*, 1-4, 96; *M*A*S*H*, 1; *McCabe & Mrs. Miller*, 1, 63, 235, 424; *The Long Goodbye*, 1; *Thieves Like Us*, 1, 3; *California Split*, 1, 2; *Nashville*, 1, 2, 217, 218, 219; *Come Back to the 5 & Dime Jimmy Dean, Jimmy Dean*, 1, 96, 233; *Streamers*, 1, 97; *The Laundromat* (TV), 1, 97; *Fool for Love*, 96-100; *3 Women*, 136; *Popeye*, 421

ML dir., *Vincent & Theo*, 289-294

5001 101, 148, 254, 358, 432, 445, 468, 516, 589, 608, 609, 663, 750, 754, 757, 827

Altman, Stephen
  ML 294

Alton, Robert
  5001 30, 115, 752, 848, 857

Alvarado, Don
  5001 187

Alvarado, Trini
  5001 487

Alvin Purple
  5001

Always
  ML 245-48
  5001 (2nd ed)

Always a Bride
  5001

Always Leave Them Laughing
  TIAI 111

Alwyn, William
  5001 163, 539

Amadeus

SOTA 249-253
ML 219
5001 (2nd ed)

Amagula, Nandjiwarra
  WTLGD 535
  5001 412

Amant de cinq jours, L', see *The Five-Day Lover*
Amants de Teruel, Les, see *The Lovers of Teruel*
Amants de Vérone, Les, see *Lovers of Verona*

Amaral, Suzana
  H 267-268; dir., *The Hour of the Star*, 267-270
  5001 342

Amarcord
  WTLGD 131

Amateau, Rod
  5001 837

Amaya, Carmen
  5001 254

"Amazing Grace" (music)
  TIAI 358
  SOTA 110

Ambassadors, The (book)
  SOTA 206

Amber, Toni
  5001 453

Ambler, Eric
  KKBB 335
  5001 384, 469, 528, 601, 781

Ameche, Don
  DIM 82
  SOTA 12, 13
  H 5, 6
  ML 27-29
  5001 13, 144, 199, 253, 326, 359, 478, 692, 750, 759, 786

America, America
  DIM 50-52, 328, 331
  R 7
  TIAI 284
  5001

America at the Movies
  WTLGD 178-179
  5001

America the Beautiful
  DIM 151

American (first draft of *Citizen Kane*)
  RK 29, 35, 36, 49, 54, 57, 58, 60, 61

American Ballet Theatre
  WTLGD 343, 347

American Broadcasting Company (ABC)
  WTLGD 79
  TIAI 13

American Civil Liberties Union
  RK 8, 80

American Coalition for Traditional Values
  H 439

American Dream, An (book)
  KKBB 131, 134
  GS 10
  R 151, 351
  WTLGD 110
  H 166, 362

American Family, An (TV)
  R 223, 225, 226

American Film Institute
  DIM 165

WTLGD 178-179, 537
H 263

American Film Theatre
  R 196, 220

American Flyers
  H 70, 349

American Friend, The
  WTLGD 312-316
  TIAI 42
  5001

American Gigolo
  TIAI 33, 335, 336
  SOTA 68

American Graffiti
  R 172, 174, 193-195, 321, 413, 428
  WTLGD 106, 210, 424
  SOTA 98

American Hot Wax
  WTLGD 421-424
  5001

American in Paris, An
  KKBB 234, 273
  DIM 84
  R 34
  5001

American International Pictures (A.I.P.)
  DIM 18, 315, 342
  TIAI 3, 39, 64, 384

American Jewish Chronicle
  RK 10

American Legion
  RK 8, 41, 57
  WTLGD 172, 513-514, 517

American Madness
  5001

"American Playhouse" (TV)
  H 351

American Red Cross News Service, Paris
  RK 10

American Symphony Orchestra
  TIAI 145

American Tail, An
  H 416

American Tragedy, An
  ILIATM 67
  KKBB 331-332
  5001

American Werewolf in London, An
  H 39

Americanization of Emily, The
  KKBB 41
  TIAI 332

Ames, Adrienne
  5001 180

Ames, Leon
  KKBB 333
  DIM 147
  5001 405, 574, 592, 856

Ames, Preston
  5001 23

Amiche, Le
  DIM 113

Amici per la Pelle (also known as *Friends for Life* and *The Woman in the Painting*)
  KKBB 231:n
  5001

Amico, Gianni

5001 567
Amidei, Sergio
  KKBB 324
  TIAI 468, 470
  5001 281, 537, 551, 742
Amis, Kingsley
  ILIATM 250
Amityville Horror, The
  TIAI 16, 21, 213, 351, 352, 424
Ammons, Gene
  5001 692
Among the Living
  5001
Amore e d'Anarchia, D', see *Love and Anarchy*
Amorous Bus Driver, The
  5001 (2nd ed)
Amos, John
  WTLGD 66, 267
  5001 418
Amour de Swann, Un. see *Swann in Love*
Amour fou, L'
  5001
Amour, l'après-midi, L', see *Chloe in the*
    Afternoon
Amour redempteur, L' (book)
  KKBB 335
Amram, David
  5001 702
Amritraj, Vijay
  SOTA 5
  5001 539
Anabasis (book)
  WTLGD 555, 556, 557
analog (periodical)
  SOTA 282
Anatahan
  SOTA 374
  5001
Anatomy of a Murder
  ILIATM 306
Anatomy of Love, The
  DIM 362
Anchors Aweigh
  KKBB 184
  GS 263
  5001
Ancis, Joe
  H 280
...And Justice for All
  TIAI 153, 323
And Then There Were None
  5001
Anda, Geza
  5001 216
Anders, Glenn
  5001 413
Anders, Luana
  5001 211, 290, 408, 750
Andersen, Bibi
  5001 414
Andersen, Hans Christian
  ML 227-28
  5001 620
Anderson, Brian
  TIAI 58
Anderson, Broncho Billy
  WTLGD 9

Anderson, Daphne
  ILIATM 119
  KKBB 334
  5001 62, 596
Anderson, Donna
  5001 363, 546
Anderson, Eddie ("Rochester")
  5001 75, 106, 113, 306, 380, 679, 716, 741,
    782, 830
Anderson, Edward
  R 267-269
  5001 754, 757
Anderson, Ivie
  5001 175
Anderson, James
  5001 777
Anderson, Joseph L.
  ILIATM 121
Anderson, Judith
  SOTA 197
  5001 20, 25, 125, 189, 397, 413, 618, 700,
    708, 718, 747
Anderson, Kevin
  ML 326
Anderson, Laurie
  H 173, 232, 285
  5001 693, 737
Anderson, Lindsay
  ILIATM 18, 63, 99-100; dir., *This Sporting*
    Life, 15-18; *Every Day Except*
    Christmas, 99
  GS dir., *If...*, 279-286; *This Sporting Life*,
    281
  DIM dir., *If...*, 117
  TIAI 246
  5001 131, 355, 762, 770, 865
Anderson, Loni
  SOTA 129
  5001 431
Anderson, Mary
  5001 421, 776
Anderson, Maxwell
  KKBB 71, 231, 360, 369
  GS 175
  RK 10, 41
  DIM 95, 97
  WTLGD 256
  5001 18, 29, 391, 467, 600, 613, 776, 841,
    850
Anderson, Melody
  TIAI 124-125
  5001 250
Anderson, Michael
  KKBB 10-11; dir., *The Quiller*
    Memorandum, 10-11; *Around the World*
    in Eighty Days, 255
  GS *The Shoes of the Fisherman*, 181
  WTLGD 64-66
  5001 151, 514
Anderson, Michael Jr.
  5001 729
Anderson, Richard
  KKBB 250
  R 45
  5001 151, 196, 287, 433, 570, 572
Anderson, Robert
  DIM 169, 170

5001 351
Anderson, Sherwood
  RK 41
  ML 118
Anderson Tapes, The
  DIM 285, 314
  5001
Anderson, Warner
  5001 79, 185, 186, 705
Andersson, Bibi
  KKBB 171, 304, 346, 369
  DIM 28, 105, 348
  R 418
  WTLGD 76, 549-550
  TIAI 492
  5001 104, 451, 510, 576, 609, 669, 688, 839
Andersson, Harriet
  ILIATM 106
  KKBB 315
  R 89, 91-92
  TIAI 222, 490
  5001 161, 203, 236, 418, 514, 688
Andes, Keith
  5001 140
Andre, Annette
  5001 272
Andre, Carol
  5001 180
Andre, Jean
  5001 82
André, Marcel
  KKBB 236, 329
  5001 59, 566
André the Giant
  H 379
  5001 597
Andreas-Salomé, Lou
  DIM 250-251
Andree, Ingrid
  KKBB 251
  5001 151
Andrée, S. A.
  TIAI 476-479
Andrei, Frederic
  TIAI 328
  5001 192
Andresen, Bjorn
  5001 180
Andress, Ursula
  KKBB 69
  DIM 193
  5001 86, 123, 575, 672, 747
Andrews, Anthony
  SOTA 198, 201
  5001 806
Andrews, Dana
  ILIATM 306
  KKBB 328
  R 364
  WTLGD 218
  5001 12, 48, 65, 92, 234, 364, 411, 413,
    531, 533, 560, 711, 777, 822, 829
Andrews, Del
  KKBB 231
  5001 18
Andrews, Edward
  5001 215, 307

Andrews, Harry
　GS 235
　DIM 368
　WTLGD 337
　5001 11, 170, 181, 223, 458, 490, 523, 528,
　　529, 535, 660, 730, 784
Andrews, Julie
　KKBB 41-42, 135, 177-178
　GS 161-164
　DIM 379
　WTLGD 7, 424
　TIAI 331, 332, 333, 334, 335
　5001 322, 690, 697, 706, 763, 782, 814
Andrews, Lynn C.
　H 21
Andrews Sisters
　5001 254, 336, 611
Andrews, Tina
　R 297
　5001 153
Andrews, William C.
　5001 62
Andriot, Lucien
　5001 280
Androcles and the Lion
　5001
Andromeda Strain, The
　DIM 275-276
　R 150
　5001
Androsky, Carol
　R 221
　5001 16, 273, 424
Andrusco, Richie
　KKBB 184
Andy Hardy series
　WTLGD 210
Andy Warhol's Frankenstein
　R 311
Angel (1937)
　5001
Angel (1982, released in U.S. as *Danny Boy*)
　H 166
Angel and the Badman
　5001
"Angel Baby" (music)
　H 464
Angel Heart
　H 286-287
　5001 (2nd ed)
Angel, Heather
　5001 363, 421, 595
Angel on My Shoulder
　5001
Angeli, Pier
　R 401
Angels Over Broadway
　5001
Angels with Dirty Faces
　5001
Angelus, Muriel
　5001 302, 422
Anger, Kenneth
　ILIATM 35; dir., *Fireworks*, 35
　R 174
　WTLGD 368
　TIAI 381

Anglin, Florence
　TIAI 370
Anglo-Saxon Attitudes (book)
　ILIATM 213
Angry Silence, The
　ILIATM 119
Angst, Richard
　DIM 19
　5001 623
Anhalt, Edna
　KKBB 205
　5001 564
Anhalt, Edward
　KKBB 205
　DIM 25
　R 88
　5001 379, 450, 564, 859, 860
Animal Actors of Hollywood
　SOTA 225
Animal Crackers
　5001
Animal Farm
　GS 192
Animal House, see *National Lampoon's Animal
　House*
Anka, Paul
　DIM 109
Ankrum, Morris
　5001 296
Ann-Margret
　KKBB 41-42, 152, 331
　DIM 173, 174, 283, 284
　R 124, 444
　WTLGD 502, 510
　SOTA 332, 333
　H 75
　5001 111, 120, 127, 450, 626, 704, 796
Anna and the King of Siam
　5001
Anna Christie
　KKBB 56, 243, 285
　5001
Anna Karenina
　KKBB 56, 285
　R 453
　WTLGD 541
　SOTA 89
　H 429
　5001
Annabella
　TIAI 145
　5001 409, 481, 516, 760, 813
Annakin, Ken
　GS 181; dir., *Those Magnificent Men in
　　Their Flying Machines*, 226
　5001 4, 717
Annaud, Jean-Jacques
　TIAI 307-309; dir., *Quest for Fire*, 307-309
　ML dir., *The Bear*, 208-11; *Quest for Fire*,
　　209
　5001 57, 608
Anne of the Thousand Days
　DIM 95-97
　R 140, 387
　5001
Année dernière à Marienbad, L', see *Last Year
　at Marienbad*

Annekov, Georges
　5001 430
Annie
　TIAI 275, 343-347, 356
　5001 (2nd ed)
Annie Get Your Gun
　KKBB 185, 234
　5001
Annie Hall
　WTLGD 316, 317, 320, 412, 437, 438
　TIAI 87, 90, 91-92, 462
　H 113, 115, 235, 314
　ML 202, 327
Annie Oakley
　5001 (2nd ed)
Annis, Francesca
　DIM 400
　SOTA 285, 286
　5001 207, 444
Another Part of the Forest
　5001
Another Thin Man
　5001
Another Woman
　ML 202, 327
　5001 (2nd ed)
Anouilh, Jean
　KKBB 312
　5001 494
Ansiktet, see *The Magician*
Anspach, Susan
　WTLGD 468
　TIAI 48
　5001 70, 88, 407
Ant, Adam
　5001 478
Antheil, George
　KKBB 205
　5001 359, 700
Anthelme, Paul
　5001 349
Anthony Adverse
　KKBB 147
　DIM 117
　WTLGD 327
　5001
Anthony, Joseph
　KKBB 337; dir., *The Rainmaker*, 336-337
　5001 614, 669
Antigone
　5001
Antoinette, Marie
　WTLGD 332, 399
Antonelli, Laura
　WTLGD 540-542
　5001 364, 843
Antonio
　5001 249
Antonio and Rosario
　5001 336, 865
Antonio, Lou
　5001 22, 322
Antonioni, Michelangelo
　ILIATM 17, 21-23, 41, 149, 179-181,
　　183-185, 194-195, 296; dir., *La Notte*,
　　12, 20, 24, 179-184, 188, 192-196, 220;
　　The Eclipse, 17, 21-22, 24; *L'Avventura*,

23, 32, 41, 77, 148-149, 161, 176, 179-180, 192, 222, 282, 296
KKBB 24, 31-37, 109, 343, 368; dir., *The Red Desert*, 23-25, 93, 189; *Blow-Up*, 31-37; *L'Avventura*, 342
GS 7-8, 77; dir., *L'Avventura*, 56, 61; *Blow-Up*, 64, 121; *La Notte*, 47
DIM 113-117, 121, 211, 308, dir., *L'Avventura*, 51, 85, 113, 121, 308, 309; *Zabriskie Point*, 113-117, 131, 211; *Blow-Up*, 113, 114, 117, 197, 231; *Le Amiche*, 113; *La Notte*, 113; *Red Desert*, 116, 252
R 107, 292, 326; dir; *L'Avventura*, 34, 305; *Zabriskie Point*, 107, 305, 326; *Blow-Up*, 370, 440, 451
WTLGD 51, 87, 105, 134, 153, 201, 285, 302, 391, 421; dir., *The Passenger*, 51, 87, 201; *Blow-Up*, 201, 373; *La Notte*, 233; *The Red Desert*, 413; *Zabriskie Point*, 421
TIAI 5, 101, 227, 314, 452; dir., *The Passenger*, 5, 452; *Blow-Up*, 227
SOTA 32; dir., *Blow-Up*, 32; *L'Avventura*, 126-127
H 41, 61, 62, 176, 452; dir., *La Notte*, 41, 44, 176; *Zabriskie Point*, 452; *The Passenger*, 452
5001 41, 85, 211, 308, 536, 619, 836, 862, 863
Antonutti, Omero
WTLGD 299
TIAI 447
SOTA 126, 127
H 124, 338
5001 53, 295, 391, 527, 561
Antony, Scott
R 51
5001 655
Antrobus, John
DIM 17
5001 59
Any Wednesday
GS 38, 117
5001
Anything Goes
5001
"Anything Goes" (music)
SOTA 176
Anzell, Hy
H 421
5001 371
Aparajito (see also *The Apu Trilogy*)
ILIATM 248, 250, 290
5001
Apartment, The
ILIATM 41, 151
Ape Woman, The
TIAI 466
Apfel Ist Ab, Der (*The Original Sin*)
5001
Apicella, Tina
5001 63
Apocalypse Now
WTLGD 269, 324, 428
TIAI 18, 52, 244, 299, 346, 402
SOTA 119, 278

H 182-183, 252, 305, 462
ML 309
Apollinaire, Guillaume
ILIATM 217
Apology (TV)
ML 151
Appaloosa, The
R 40
5001
Appleton, Peter
WTLGD 261
Appointment for Love
5001 (2nd ed)
Apprenticeship of Duddy Kravitz, The
WTLGD 156, 270, 466
H 82-83
ML 98
5001 (2nd ed)
Apprenticeship of Duddy Kravitz, The (book)
R 316-317
April Fools, The
DIM 182
TIAI 21
5001
Apted, Michael
R 218-220
WTLGD 551-554; dir., *Agatha*, 551-554; *Stardust*, 553
TIAI 254-255; dir., *Coal Miner's Daughter*, 42, 135; *Agatha*, 159; *Continental Divide*, 254-255
ML dir., *Gorillas in the Mist*, 5-7
5001 10, 154, 298, 709, 790
Apu Trilogy, The (see also *Pather Panchali*, *Aparajito*, and *The World of Apu*)
ILIATM 148, 245, 248, 250-251, 255
WTLGD 70
Apur Sansar, see *The World of Apu*
Arabian Nights
5001
Arachnophobia
5001 (2nd ed)
Aragon, Art
5001 238
Aranyer din Ratri, see *Days and Nights in the Forest*
Arau, Alfonso
TIAI 97
SOTA 164
5001 638, 810
Araya, Captain
WTLGD 386
Arbatt, Alexander
SOTA 366, 367
5001 171
Arbuckle, Roscoe "Fatty"
RK 6, 69
WTLGD 9, 336
5001 831
Arbus, Alan
R 358
5001 138, 165, 414
Arbus, Diane
WTLGD 88
TIAI 5, 86, 89
SOTA 124, 340
Arcalli, Franco

R 28
5001 410
Arcand, Denys
H 237-240; dir., *The Decline of the American Empire*, 237-240, 450
5001 182
Arcand, Gabriel
H 238
5001 182
Archard, Bernard
5001 424
Archer, Anne
WTLGD 491
H 375, 376
5001 16, 116, 239, 421
Archer, John
5001 185
Archer, Peter
5001 221
Archer, Sandra
5001 273
Archibald, William
ILIATM 165, 170
5001 349, 365
Archie Savage Dancers
5001 287
Archuletta, Beulah
5001 662
Ardant, Fanny
5001 734
Arden, Eve
WTLGD 411
5001 37, 159, 322, 464, 480, 524, 550, 703, 865
Ardito, Gino
5001 12
Ardolino, Emile
H 347; dir., *Dirty Dancing*, 346-349
5001 190
Ardrey, Robert
WTLGD 115
5001 446, 754, 767, 769
"Are You Lonesome Tonight?" (music)
TIAI 201
Aren't We Wonderful? (*Wir Wunderkinder*)
KKBB 340
Argent de poche, L', see *Small Change*
Argentina, Imperia
TIAI 410
Ariane
H 33, 35
5001 854
Arista Records
TIAI 169
Arkansas Adios (book)
SOTA 219
Arkin, Alan
DIM 253, 254, 256, 330; dir., *Little Murders*, 253-257, 314, 330
R 426, 427-428
WTLGD 46, 48, 190-192
TIAI 462
ML 299
5001 125, 266, 325, 426, 611, 647, 667
Arkin, David
5001 350, 469, 516
Arledge, John

5001 718
Arlen, Alice
  SOTA 109
  5001 681
Arlen, Harold
  5001 37, 88, 157, 398, 685
Arlen, Michael
  5001 233, 845
Arlen, Richard
  KKBB 6
  RK 13
  DIM 200
  5001 15, 36, 263, 717-718, 769, 771, 815, 817
Arletty
  KKBB 247
  GS 115
  TIAI 330, 416
  5001 133, 383, 572, 817
Arliss, Dimitra
  5001 715
Arlorio, Georgio
  DIM 176
  5001 110
Armendariz, Pedro
  5001 259, 270
Armetta, Henry
  5001 358, 657
Armies of the Night, The (book)
  R 151, 157
Armored Attack, see *The North Star*
Armstrong, Bess
  H 201
  5001 535
Armstrong, Charlotte
  5001 198
Armstrong, Gillian
  TIAI 61; dir., *My Brilliant Career*, 60-61
  SOTA 290-293; dir., *Mrs. Soffel*, 290-293;
    My Brilliant Career, 292, 302;
    Starstruck, 292
  H 432-435; dir., *Mrs. Soffel*, 234, 378, 432;
    High Tide, 432-435; *My Brilliant
    Career*, 432, 433, 434; *Starstruck*, 432
  5001 333, 486, 506
Armstrong, John
  5001 756
Armstrong, Louis
  ILIATM 147
  DIM 81-83, 85, 149, 432
  R 130
  5001 36, 112, 287, 379, 574, 654
Armstrong, R. G.
  5001 48, 65, 611
Armstrong, Robert
  WTLGD 235
  5001 479, 661
Armstrong, William H.
  R 3
  5001 697
Arnaud, Georges
  5001 821
Arnaz, Desi Jr.
  WTLGD 443
Arnaz, Desi Sr.
  TIAI 354
  5001 224

Arness, James
  5001 758
Arno, Peter
  5001 36
Arnold, Edward
  RK 36, 63
  5001 30, 161, 210, 354, 357, 382, 398, 422,
    473, 489, 507, 637, 740, 760, 765, 767,
    865
Arnold, Elliott
  KKBB 242
  5001 107
Arnold, Jack
  5001 161, 361, 500
Arnold, Tichina
  H 250
  5001 427
Arnstein, Nicky
  GS 135
  R 458-459
Arosenius, Per-Axel
  DIM 80
  5001 781
Around the World in Eighty Days
  KKBB 255
  DIM 15
Around the World Under the Sea
  KKBB 183
Arquette, Rosanna
  SOTA 354, 355
  H 14, 39-40, 41, 156-157, 236
  ML 101, 103
  5001 9, 184, 213, 682
Arrangement, The
  DIM 48-53, 252
  TIAI 391
  5001
"Arrayed for the Bridal" (music)
  H 405
Arrick, Rose
  H 310
  5001 371
Arrighi, Luciana
  SOTA 333
  5001 487, 507, 626, 847
Arruzza
  5001 109
Arsenal
  ILIATM 277
  5001
Arsène Lupin
  5001
Arsenic and Old Lace
  KKBB 231-232:n
  WTLGD 29
  5001
Artaud, Antonin
  KKBB 329
  TIAI 148
  5001 516, 568
Arthur
  TIAI 230-232, 370
  SOTA 12, 153, 305
  5001
Arthur, Bea
  R 298-299
  TIAI 215

  H 59
  5001 335, 455
Arthur, Jean
  KKBB 185, 186, 347, 363, 368
  GS 134
  RK 13
  WTLGD 3, 4, 16, 47-48, 141, 142, 362
  TIAI 429
  H 378
  ML 281
  5001 116, 186, 210, 258, 307, 335, 356,
    487, 488, 497, 566, 586, 671, 721, 742,
    766, 779, 836
Artists and Models
  5001
Arzner, Dorothy
  DIM 341, 345; dir., *Christopher Strong*, 341,
    342, 346
  5001 136, 169, 566, 839
As I Lay Dying (book)
  R 271
"As Time Goes By" (music)
  DIM 432
As You Like It
  SOTA 259
  5001
Ascenseur pour l' échafaud, see *Elevator to the
    Gallows*
Ash Wednesday
  5001
Ashani Sanket, see *Distant Thunder*
Ashby, Hal
  R 274, 436-442; dir., *The Landlord*, 13, 274,
    439, 441, 436-442; *The Last Detail*,
    272-275, 441-442; *Harold and Maude*,
    274, 441; *Shampoo*, 436-442
  WTLGD 224-230, 402-405; dir., *The Last
    Detail*, 87, 403; *Bound for Glory*,
    224-230, 404; *Shampoo*, 230, 404;
    Coming Home, 402-405, 517
  TIAI 11, 429, 458; dir., *Bound for Glory*, 1;
    Shampoo, 98, 279, 302, 303, 305, 306;
    Coming Home, 163, 310; *The Last
    Detail*, 301, 302; *Being There*, 353, 458,
    459
  H 155-157; dir., *Being There*, 9; *8 Million
    Ways to Die*, 155-157, 180, 251;
    Coming Home, 243; *Shampoo*, 451
  ML dir., *Being There*, 29; *8 Million Ways to
    Die*, 262; *The Last Detail*, 29
  5001 95, 149, 213, 319, 360, 407, 408, 671,
    763
Ashcroft, Peggy
  KKBB 359
  GS 171
  DIM 290
  SOTA 300, 301, 303
  H 127
  ML 22, 324
  5001 447, 567, 573, 728, 761
Ashelbé, see La Barthe, Henri
Asher, Jane
  5001 13, 110, 202, 436
Asherson, Renee
  5001 328
Ashley, Edward
  5001 75, 595

Ashley, Elizabeth
  KKBB 213
  WTLGD 90, 395
  ML 151
  5001 121, 147, 565, 616, 675, 812
Ashley, Ted
  R 64, 65
Ashman, Howard
  H 247
  5001 426, 428
Ashmore, Jonathan
  KKBB 291
  5001 393
Ashton, John
  5001 66
Asimov, Isaac
  5001 237
Askew, Luke
  5001 839
Aslan, Gregoire
  KKBB 294, 321, 327
  5001 323, 408, 541, 556, 620
Asner, Ed
  TIAI 153
  5001 172, 214, 260
Aspegren, Chuck
  WTLGD 514-515
  5001 183
Asphalt Jungle, The
  KKBB 338
  GS 183
  WTLGD 110
  5001
Asquith, Anthony
  KKBB 265; dir., The Final Test, 265
  5001 107, 243, 358, 552, 605
Assante, Armand
  WTLGD 489, 492
  TIAI 94
  SOTA 153-154
  H 101
  5001 598, 606, 806
Assassination of Trotsky, The
  WTLGD 95
  5001
Assassins et voleurs, see Lovers and Thieves
Asta
  KKBB 241
  5001 9, 31, 104, 669, 758, 782
Astaire, Adele
  5001 50
Astaire, Fred
  ILIATM 24, 81, 145, 277-280
  KKBB 206, 208, 222, 234, 252
  GS 156, 190
  RK 17, 53
  DIM 28, 29, 84, 85, 272, 381, 409
  R 55-59, 130, 318, 406, 448
  WTLGD 5, 31, 171, 200
  TIAI 131, 208, 275-276, 345, 403
  SOTA 2, 294
  H 138, 141, 312
  5001 49, 50, 106, 106, 119, 168, 210, 244,
     253, 254, 271, 280, 546, 646, 662, 681,
     685, 717, 766, 785, 855, 856, 857, 865
Asther, Nils
  H 34

5001 75
Asti, Adriana
  R 147, 453
  5001 61, 102, 206, 237
Astin, John
  GS 224
  5001 117, 828
Astin, Patty Duke, see Duke, Patty
Astin, Sean
  5001 298
Astor, Junie
  KKBB 302
  5001 442
Astor, Lady
  RK 31
Astor, Lord
  ML 130
Astor, Mary
  KKBB 185, 305
  DIM 157
  WTLGD 123
  ML 286
  5001 4, 196, 336, 346, 391, 454, 478, 491,
     562, 597, 619, 764
Astoria Studios
  WTLGD 12, 13, 235, 470
Astruc, Alexandre
  DIM 403
At Long Last Love
  R 463-466
  TIAI 47
  5001
At the Back of the North Wind (book)
  TIAI 349
At the Circus
  5001
Atalante, L'
  KKBB 93, 140, 142
  R 33
  WTLGD 59
  5001
Ates, Roscoe
  5001 137, 266, 726
Atget, Eugene
  KKBB 142
Atherton, William
  R 300, 302, 474
  WTLGD 120, 320
  5001 176, 284, 334, 434, 725
Atkine, Féodor
  SOTA 37-38
  5001 571
Atkins, Christopher
  TIAI 28
  5001 86
Atkins, Dick
  5001 258
Atkins, Eileen
  WTLGD 337
  SOTA 115
  5001 204, 223
Atkinson, Brooks
  RK 11
Atkinson, Rowan
  ML 271
  5001 742, 842
Atlantic City

TIAI 173-178, 213, 392
  H 482
  5001
Atlantic Monthly (periodical)
  RK 63
Atlantic, The (periodical)
  TIAI 247
Atlas
  5001
Atlas, Charles
  WTLGD 525
Attack!
  GS 208
Attaway, Ruth
  R 296
  5001 153
Attenborough, Richard
  DIM 16; dir., Oh! What a Lovely War,
     14-17
  R 15-18
  WTLGD 65, 510-511; dir., Magic, 510-511
  TIAI 432-435; dir., Gandhi, 432-435
  H 399-401; dir., Gandhi, 54; Cry Freedom,
     399-401, 476
  5001 81, 104, 151, 165, 277, 357, 360, 450,
     542, 860
Attentat, L', see The French Conspiracy
Atterbury, Malcolm
  5001 726
Atwill, Lionel
  R 404
  WTLGD 547
  5001 48, 118, 187, 195, 303, 304, 341, 466,
     488, 512, 693, 694, 765, 774
Atwood, Kim
  5001 469
Au hasard, Balthazar
  5001
Au revoir les enfants (Goodbye, Children)
  H 435-438
  5001 (2nd ed)
Au-delà des grilles, see The Walls of Malapaga
Auber, Brigitte
  5001 775
Auberge rouge, L', see The Red Inn
Auberjonois, René
  R 80
  WTLGD 435
  5001 68, 230, 334, 358, 396, 422, 445, 469,
     577
Aubrey, James
  DIM 188, 420
  R 65, 217-218
Auclair, Michel
  KKBB 236
  WTLGD 144, 147
  5001 59, 268, 271, 336, 388
Auden, W. H.
  KKBB 59
  R 186
  WTLGD 38, 39, 258
Audran, Stéphane
  GS 148
  DIM 54, 404, 415
  R 42-43
  WTLGD 123, 153
  TIAI 442

5001 67, 76, 91, 95, 129, 158, 192, 241,
816, 843
Audret, Pascale
KKBB 264
5001 229
Audry, Jacqueline
5001 285, 489, 583
Auer, Gregory M.
WTLGD 212
Auer, Mischa
KKBB 20, 256
H 195, 372
5001 25, 28, 165, 185, 248, 280, 387, 404,
509, 611, 646, 668, 736, 768, 841
Auger, Claudine
5001 769
August, Joseph
5001 311, 464, 591, 739
Auld, George
5001 521
Aulin, Ewa
GS 224
5001 117
Aumont, Jean-Pierre
R 178
WTLGD 60
5001 76, 175, 422, 453
Aumont, Michel
5001 450
Aumont, Tina
5001 567
Auntie Mame
KKBB 281
R 97
Aurel, Jean
5001 590
Aurenche, Jean
TIAI 443
5001 158, 187, 263, 620, 734, 822
Auric, Georges
ILIATM 165
KKBB 236, 239, 255, 295, 315, 320, 326,
329, 330, 356
5001 1, 59, 63, 83, 114, 178, 185, 193, 225,
282, 323, 336, 365, 414, 430, 500, 511,
554, 566, 569, 637, 739, 821
Aurthur, Robert Alan
KKBB 261
5001 212
Austen, Jane
R 153
5001 595
Austin, Jerry
KKBB 345
5001 653
Austin, Karen
H 57
5001 377
Austin, Michael
SOTA 148, 151
5001 308
Austin, Ronald
5001 317
Autant-Lara, Claude
KKBB 169, 257, 267, 321; dir., *The Seven
Deadly Sins* (segment), 169; *Devil in the
Flesh*, 257, 321; *Four Bags Full*, 267;

Occupe-Toi d'Amélie, 320-321; *The
Game of Love*, 321
GS dir., *The Game of Love*, 127; *Occupe-Toi
d'Amélie*, 211
5001 186, 263, 277, 540, 619, 620, 739
Auteuil, Daniel
H 329
5001 379
Author! Author!
TIAI 368-370, 475
5001 (2nd ed)
Autobiography of Miss Jane Pittman, The
R 261-266, 324
WTLGD 184
5001 (2nd ed)
Autry, Gene
WTLGD 362-363
Autumn Leaves
GS 208
5001
Autumn Sonata (Höstsonaten)
WTLGD 476-481
H 426
5001
Avakian, Aram
DIM 111, 112; dir., *End of the Road*,
111-112, 148
R 361; dir., *Cops and Robbers*, 162, 361; *11
Harrowhouse*, 360-361
5001 215, 218, 379
Avalon
5001 (2nd ed)
Avalon Boys (group)
5001 32
Avalon, Frankie
GS 277
TIAI 115
Avco Embassy Pictures
DIM 151
"Ave Maria" (music)
TIAI 330
Avedon, Richard
5001 271
Avenging Conscience, The
5001
Averback, Hy
GS dir., *I Love You, Alice B. Toklas*, 158
DIM 9; dir., *I Love You, Alice B. Toklas*, 9
5001 301, 350
Avery, Margaret
H 83
5001 146
Avery, Val
5001 25, 154, 380, 519
Aveu, L', see *The Confession*
Avildsen, John G.
DIM 384; dir., *Joe*, 148, 152-153, 313; *Cry
Uncle*, 314, 325, 384; *Guess What We
Learned in School Today?*, 325
R 116-119, 230; dir., *Joe*, 66, 116, 161, 230,
231; *Save the Tiger*, 116-119; *Guess
What We Learned in School Today?*,
116; *Cry Uncle*, 116
WTLGD 213-216, 488-489, 493-496; dir.,
Joe, 86, 223, 369, 495; *Save the Tiger*,
124, 269; *Rocky*, 213-216, 369, 412,
488, 490, 491, 492, 493, 495; *W. W.

and the Dixie Dancekings*, 360; *Slow
Dancing in the Big City*, 488-489,
493-496; *Cry Uncle*, 495
5001 636, 655, 687, 851
Avrech, Robert J.
SOTA 264
5001 90
Avventura, L'
ILIATM 23, 32, 41, 77, 148-149, 161, 176,
179-180, 192, 222, 282, 296
KKBB 342
GS 56, 61
DIM 51, 85, 113, 121, 308, 309
R 34, 306
SOTA 126-127
5001
Awakenings
ML 318-26
Awful Truth, The
RK 48
R 408
WTLGD 3, 6, 7, 8, 16, 17, 18, 19, 26
SOTA 222
5001
Axberg, Eddie
R 181
5001 520
Axelrod, George
KKBB 18, 298-299; dir., *Lord Love a Duck*,
18, 23, 298-299
GS 95, 224
5001 99, 435, 462, 668
Axton, Hoyt
SOTA 79, 81, 187
5001 78, 307, 323
Ayars, Ann
5001 741
Aykroyd, Dan
TIAI 26-27
SOTA 12, 13-14, 19, 192, 193
ML 164, 235-37
5001 87, 205, 284, 362, 530, 786, 797
Aylmer, Felix
5001 36, 315, 328, 376, 529
Aymé, Marcel
KKBB 252, 267
GS 9
5001 161, 262
Ayres, Gerald
TIAI 248
5001 138, 627
Ayres, Lew
KKBB 231
5001 8, 18, 121, 336, 353, 381, 711
Azcona, Rafael
5001 278
Azmi, Shabana
ML 21
5001 447
Aznavour, Charles
ILIATM 211, 215
GS 224
DIM 106
WTLGD 125
5001 6, 117, 676

B

Babe, Angelus
5001 547

Babenco, Hector
TIAI 248-252; dir., *Pixote*, 248-252, 474
H 24-29, 267, 420-421; dir., *Kiss of the Spider Woman*, 24-29, 289; *Pixote*, 25, 267; *Ironweed*, 420-421
5001 370, 399, 584

Babes in Arms
5001

Babes in Toyland
KKBB 185

Babes on Broadway
5001

Babita
WTLGD 69

Baby Boom
H 377-378
5001 (2nd ed)

Baby Doll
KKBB 93, 232:n
TIAI 175
5001

Baby LeRoy
5001 15

Baby Maker, The
DIM 157-158
R 191
5001

Babylon Revisited
DIM 308

Bacall, Lauren
ILIATM 58, 300
KKBB 6, 59, 239, 249, 251, 297, 359-360
DIM 12, 247, 310, 413
R 344, 390, 392
WTLGD 330, 547
TIAI 154, 255, 256
ML 188
5001 71, 144, 152, 172, 320, 391, 503, 671, 677, 718, 776, 850

Bach, Barbara
TIAI 194, 195, 197
5001 127, 703

Bach, Johann Sebastian
WTLGD 270, 415, 416
H 115
5001 220, 236, 271, 694, 748

Bach, Steven
H 21-24

Bacharach, Burt
DIM 7
R 137
5001 9, 110, 436

Bachardy, Don
5001 627

Bachelet, Jean
5001 647

Bachelor and the Bobby-Soxer, The
WTLGD 20, 21
5001

Bachelor Mother
5001

"Back in the Saddle Again" (music)
WTLGD 363

Back Street
5001

Back to School
H 185-186
5001 (2nd ed)

Back to the Future
H 11-13, 74, 220, 300
ML 226, 227
5001 (2nd ed)

Back to the Future Part II
ML 225-27
5001 (2nd ed)

Backer, Brian
TIAI 408
5001 238

Backus, Henny
5001 303

Backus, Jim
5001 26, 198, 303, 331, 458, 569, 618

Baclanova, Olga
5001 266, 460

Bacon, Francis
R 473
WTLGD 473
H 208

Bacon, Kevin
TIAI 321, 322
SOTA 139, 140
5001 190, 250, 256

Bacon, Lloyd
KKBB 308; dir., *The 'I Don't Care' Girl*, 234; *Marked Woman*, 307-308
5001 255, 262, 359, 466, 489, 582, 686

Bacri, Jean-Pierre
SOTA 134
5001 222

Bad and the Beautiful, The
KKBB 232-233:n, 238, 363-364
R 433
WTLGD 61
5001

Bad Boys
TIAI 473-475
SOTA 315
5001 (2nd ed)

Bad Company
R 12-14, 201
WTLGD 261
5001

Bad Day at Black Rock
ILIATM 296
KKBB 233
GS 223
5001

Bad Lord Byron, The
R 111

Bad News Bear, The
WTLGD 248, 361
SOTA 16

Bad Night, see *Mala Noche*

Bad Sleep Well, The (*Warui Yatsu Hodo Yoku Nemuru*)
5001

Badal, Jean
5001 601

Badalamenti, Angelo
H 206
5001 87

Badalucco, Nicola
5001 180

Baddeley, Hermione
KKBB 330
5001 104, 229, 398, 568, 640

Badel, Alan
DIM 135
5001 6, 10, 435, 763

Badel, Sarah
SOTA 372
5001 677

Badham, John
WTLGD 367-371, 469; dir., *Saturday Night Fever*, 367-371, 422, 470, 554; *The Bingo Long Traveling All-Stars and Motor Kings*, 368; *The Law* (TV), 368
TIAI 485-486, 493-495; dir., *Saturday Night Fever*, 30, 31, 33, 227, 299; *The Bingo Long Traveling All-Stars & Motor Kings*, 221; *Blue Thunder*, 485-486, 494; *WarGames*, 493-495
SOTA 35; dir., *Saturday Night Fever*, 35, 36, 376; *Dracula* (1979), 217
H 349-351; dir., *American Flyers*, 72, 349; *Saturday Night Fever*, 169, 349; *Stakeout*, 349-351; *Blue Thunder*, 349; *WarGames*, 349; *Short Circuit*, 349; *The Bingo Long Traveling All-Stars and Motor Kings*, 349
5001 73, 87, 655, 678, 704, 712, 823

Badham, Mary
WTLGD 368
5001 777

Badlands
R 303-306, 369
5001

Baez, Joan
WTLGD 177, 397, 401

Bagneris, Vernel
TIAI 274, 275
5001 200, 574

Bagnold, Enid
KKBB 316
R 49
5001 517

Baie des anges, La, see *Bay of the Angels*

Bail, Chuck
TIAI 67
5001 724

Bailbondsman, The
WTLGD 183

Bailey, Charles W., II
GS 95

Bailey, John
TIAI 80, 335
SOTA 204
H 362
ML 70-71
5001 3, 95, 125, 165, 589, 610, 682, 784

Bailey, Pearl
5001 119, 407, 750

Bailey, Robin
KKBB 280
5001 321

Baillie, Bruce
  KKBB 13
Bain, Conrad
  5001 25
Bainbridge, Beryl
  TIAI 425
  ML 46-47
  5001 204
Baines, John
  KKBB 255
  5001 178
Bainter, Fay
  KKBB 290, 336
  DIM 310
  5001 42, 134, 344, 380, 386, 556, 607, 675,
    711, 846
Baio, Scott
  WTLGD 163-164
  5001 108
Baird, Antony
  KKBB 255
  5001 178
Baisers volés, see *Stolen Kisses*
Baker, Blanche
  SOTA 175
  5001 617, 684
Baker, Carroll
  KKBB 232, 278
  SOTA 92
  5001 43, 121, 285, 319, 343, 371, 706
Baker, Chet
  ML 121-26
  5001 418
Baker, Diane
  5001 466, 600
Baker, Elliott
  WTLGD 149-152
  5001 244
Baker, Graham
  5001 226, 335, 705, 857
Baker Hall, Philip, see Hall, Philip Baker
Baker, Ian
  TIAI 59, 371
  SOTA 161
  H 43, 314
  5001 51, 166, 227, 353, 587, 645
Baker, Joe Don
  R 206, 283, 285
  SOTA 172
  5001 131, 251, 311, 518, 822
Baker, Josephine
  SOTA 294
Baker, Kathy
  H 293, 294
  ML 205
  5001 168, 722
Baker, Kenny (Amer)
  5001 709, 772
Baker, Kenny (Brit)
  5001 37, 321, 480
Baker, Lenny
  WTLGD 127-129, 173
  5001 521
Baker, Mark Linn, see Linn-Baker, Mark
Baker, Melville
  5001 522
Baker, Phil

5001 278
Baker, Rick
  TIAI 161
  5001 361
Baker, Roy
  5001 198, 528
Baker, Ruby
  H 450
  5001 332
Baker, Russell
  TIAI 423
Baker, Stanley
  KKBB 108
  DIM 193
  5001 3, 364, 575, 628
Baker, Tom
  DIM 367
  5001 522
Baker's Wife, The (*La Femme du boulanger*)
  KKBB 233:n, 262, 279
  H 330
  5001
Bakewell, William (Billy)
  KKBB 231
  5001 18, 44, 169, 547
Bakker, Jim
  H 438
Bakker, Tammy Faye
  H 438
Bakshi, Ralph
  TIAI 202
Bakst, Léon
  WTLGD 336
Balaban, Robert (Bob)
  R 434
  TIAI 128, 130, 288, 289-290
  ML dir., *Parents*, 93-95
  5001 2, 20, 125, 142, 479, 566, 596, 624,
    721
Balalaika
  5001
Balanchine, George
  GS 70
  ML 246
  5001 720
Balchin, Nigel
  5001 235
Balcon, Jill
  5001 523
Balcon, Sir Michael
  H 119
Balcony, The
  KKBB 170
  DIM 124
Balderston, John L.
  KKBB 267
  5001 102, 201, 279, 445, 501, 815
Baldwin, Adam
  5001 271
Baldwin, Alec
  H 455
  ML 65
  5001 61, 849
Baldwin, Earl
  5001 195, 288, 686, 837
Baldwin, Faith
  TIAI 274

5001 496, 836
Baldwin, James
  H 390
Baldwin, William
  5001 250
Bale, Christian
  H 413
  ML 215
  5001 217, 329
Balin, Marty
  DIM 211
Balin, Mireille
  WTLGD 126, 233
  5001 575
Balint, Eszter
  SOTA 261
  5001 720
Balk, Fairuza
  ML 219
  5001 812
Ball, John
  5001 360
Ball, Lucille
  RK 34
  R 298, 299
  WTLGD 422
  5001 63, 169, 254, 310, 322, 393, 455, 637,
    640, 703, 764, 843, 865
Ball of Fire
  5001
Ballad of a Soldier
  ILIATM 42, 196
  KKBB 110
Ballad of Cable Hogue, The
  DIM 279
  5001
Ballard, Carroll
  KKBB 13
  TIAI 18, 347; dir., *The Black Stallion*, 8, 18,
    19, 347, 349, 353, 354, 372
  SOTA 97-100; dir., *The Black Stallion*, 63,
    97, 98, 99; *Never Cry Wolf*, 97-100;
    Beyond This Winter's Wheat, 98;
    Harvest, 98; *Pigs*, 98; *The Perils of
    Priscilla*, 98; *Rodeo*, 98
  H 240-243; dir., *Nutcracker, The Motion
    Picture*, 240-243; *The Black Stallion*,
    242
  ML dir., *The Black Stallion*, 115, 117
  5001 77, 78, 519, 537
Ballard, J. G.
  H 414, 416
  5001 217
Ballard, Lucien
  KKBB 14, 291
  R 78
  WTLGD 113
  5001 48, 161, 187, 198, 283, 394, 498, 502,
    519, 552, 629, 838
Ballet Russe de Monte Carlo
  WTLGD 346
Ballhaus, Michael
  SOTA 350
  H 40, 226
  ML 190
  5001 9, 146, 191, 232, 297, 325, 592, 849
Balliett, Whitney

14

ILIATM 74
Ballon rouge, Le, see *The Red Balloon*
Balmain, Pierre
  5001 800
Balpêtré
  5001 619
Balsam, Martin
  DIM 213
  R 224, 390
  5001 9, 25, 99, 121, 125, 424, 503, 546,
    727, 741, 795
Balthazar
  GS 80
Balzac, Honoré de
  DIM 422
  WTLGD 340, 512
  SOTA 89
Bamba, La
  H 341-343
  5001 (2nd ed)
"Bamba, La" (music)
  H 342
Bamber, David
  5001 331
Bambi
  GS 225
  R 246
  ML 209
  5001
Bambini ci Guardano, I, see *The Children Are
  Watching Us*
Bananas
  DIM 314, 369, 370, 426
  R 240-242
  TIAI 345
Bancroft, Anne
  KKBB 143-145
  R 16, 242, 318, 455
  WTLGD 120, 343-344, 346-347
  TIAI 85
  SOTA 112
  H 300, 411
  5001 197, 215, 299, 334, 483, 597, 602,
    603, 774, 794, 860
Bancroft, George
  RK 13, 20
  5001 27, 208, 487, 704, 769
Band of Outsiders (*Bande à part*)
  KKBB 17, 54, 112-115, 127
  DIM 279, 402
  5001
Band, Richard
  H 69
  5001 618
Band, The (group)
  WTLGD 434
  SOTA 69
  5001 210, 411
Band Wagon, The
  ILIATM 278
  KKBB 234:n
  GS 156
  R 46
  WTLGD 177
  SOTA 36
  5001
Bandapaddhay, B. B.

  5001 33, 569, 850
Bande à part, see *Band of Outsiders*
Banderas, Antonio
  H 289, 290, 466
  ML 24
  5001 414, 470, 848
Bandit, The, see *O Cangaceiro*
Banditi a Orgosolo, see *Bandits of Orgosolo*
Bandits of Orgosolo (*Banditi a Orgosolo*)
  ILIATM 15
  WTLGD 299
  5001
Banerjee, Victor
  SOTA 300, 301-302, 380, 381
  5001 337, 568
Bang, Joy
  5001 138
Bang the Drum Slowly
  R 172, 433
  5001
Bank Dick, The
  KKBB 184, 314
  H 314
Bankhead, Tallulah
  KKBB 265
  DIM 290, 347
  R 145
  WTLGD 6
  SOTA 338
  H 244
  5001 421, 646, 744
Banks, Jonathan
  5001 66
Banks, Leslie
  5001 328, 378, 449, 460, 499, 653
Banky, Vilma
  5001 754
Bannen, Ian
  TIAI 433
  H 278, 368-369
  5001 183, 277, 340
Bannerjee, T. S.
  5001 505
Bannerman, Margaret
  KKBB 249
  5001 143
Bantam Books
  WTLGD 111-112
Bao Dai, Emperor
  5001 360
Bara, Theda
  ILIATM 131
  GS 270
Baran, Jack
  H 358
  5001 70
Baranovskaya, Vera
  KKBB 312
  5001 499
Baranski, Christine
  H 173, 371
  5001 416, 580
Baratta, Tomasina
  5001 600
Barbarella
  GS 172-173
  R 34

  5001
Barbarosa
  TIAI 370-373
  SOTA 30
  H 10
  5001 (2nd ed)
Barbary Coast
  5001
Barbeau, Adrienne
  5001 45
Barber, Frances
  H 388, 390
  5001 652
Barber, Rowland
  5001 528
Barber, Samuel
  TIAI 84
  H 251
  5001 587
Barbier, George
  KKBB 288
  5001 71, 165, 327, 374, 459, 545, 580, 736,
    827, 837, 853
Barbieri, Gato
  R 33, 345
  5001 410
Barbour, Thomas
  5001 36
*Barbra Streisand...and Other Musical
  Instruments* (TV)
  R 459, 463
Bard, Katharine
  KKBB 283
  5001 365
Bardem, Juan
  5001 180
Bardosh, Charles K.
  5001 258
Bardot, Brigitte
  ILIATM 38-39
  KKBB 128
  GS 90
  DIM 308, 309
  WTLGD 182, 365
  5001 187, 670, 813, 818
Barefoot Contessa, The
  KKBB 143, 234-235:n
  WTLGD 393
  5001
Barefoot in the Park
  GS 38, 117
  H 173
  5001
Barfly
  H 383-385
  5001 (2nd ed)
Barhydt, Frank
  5001 609
Bari, Lynn
  5001 83, 233, 327, 551, 728
Barillet, Pierre
  5001 260
Barilli, Francesco
  5001 61
Baring, Norah
  5001 501
Barish, Keith

5001 219, 696
Barish, Leora
SOTA 354
5001 184
Barker, The
RK 13
Barker, Lex
5001 237, 744
Barker, Patricia
H 240
Barkin, Ellen
TIAI 320, 322, 480
SOTA 44, 217, 218
H 222, 358, 393
5001 7, 69, 172, 190, 200, 382, 448, 747
Barnard, Ivor
KKBB 236, 277, 350
5001 57, 302, 449, 543, 605, 710
Barnes, Alan
5001 833
Barnes, Binnie
5001 106, 193, 260, 336, 350, 599, 763, 768
Barnes, George
5001 243, 292, 531, 533, 618
Barnes, Howard
RK 43-44
Barnett, Vince
KKBB 291
5001 18, 108, 180, 394, 657, 760, 771
"Barney Miller" (TV)
WTLGD 372
Barocco
WTLGD 145
SOTA 48
Baron fantôme, Le, see *The Phantom Baron*
Baron, Sandy
SOTA 12, 124, 318
5001 74, 356, 718
Barouh, Pierre
KKBB 126
5001 456
Barr, Byron
5001 198
Barr, Jean-Marc
H 369
5001 340
Barr, Richard
RK 8, 58
Barrabas
GS 167
Barrage contre le Pacifique, see *The Sea Wall*
Barranco, Maria
ML 24
5001 848
Barrat, Robert
5001 118, 130, 253, 391, 468, 787, 837
Barrault, Jean-Louis
KKBB 247, 335, 351
WTLGD 354
TIAI 469, 470
5001 76, 130, 133, 537, 572, 603, 617
Barrault, Marie-Christine
WTLGD 204
TIAI 89
5001 158, 709, 734
Barreto, Lima
5001 117

Barrett, Edith
5001 392, 403
Barrett, Roy
TIAI 56
Barrett Sisters
TIAI 471, 472
5001 655
Barrett, Wilson
5001 680
Barrette, Yvon
WTLGD 276
5001 686
Barretts of Wimpole Street, The
RK 70
5001
Barrie, Barbara
TIAI 93
5001 598
Barrie, Elaine
5001 478
Barrie, George
WTLGD 27
5001 244
Barrie, James M.
ILIATM 106
KKBB 241, 328, 336
DIM 40
5001 36, 426, 565, 607, 828, 829
Barrie, Mona
5001 351, 440, 693
Barrie, Wendy
5001 177, 341, 373, 599
Barrier, Edgar
5001 34, 143, 251, 384, 579
Barris, Harry
5001 75, 226, 675, 679
Barron, Steve
5001 745
Barrow, Clyde
KKBB 48-58, 62
Barry, Don
5001 357
Barry, J. J.
5001 381
Barry, Jeff
TIAI 116
Barry, John
DIM 162, 250
WTLGD 160, 239
5001 270, 396, 411, 423, 495
Barry, Julian
R 371, 372, 377
5001 230, 417
Barry Lyndon
WTLGD 101-106
TIAI 1, 2, 276
5001
Barry, Philip
RK 10
DIM 261
WTLGD 21
5001 336, 580, 843
Barry, Raymond J.
5001 93, 854
Barrymore, Drew
TIAI 349, 350
5001 225

Barrymore, Ethel
KKBB 349
WTLGD 23-24
TIAI 118
5001 155, 237, 532, 565, 583, 591, 616,
617, 701, 858
Barrymore, John
KKBB 189, 195, 196, 198, 250, 251, 275,
289, 340, 355, 362
GS 67
DIM 25, 367
WTLGD 156, 240, 377
TIAI 65, 396, 457
5001 35, 71, 156, 190, 299, 303, 355, 460,
465, 472, 478, 489, 490, 616, 617, 638,
700, 733, 781, 793, 796, 850
Barrymore, Lionel
KKBB 121, 243, 275; dir., *Madame X*
(1929), 121
GS 235
DIM 367
WTLGD 23, 373
5001 11, 35, 107, 116, 118, 186, 200, 206,
266, 298, 299, 373, 392, 404, 466, 511,
616, 617, 683, 746
Barstow, Lester, see Hecht, Ben
Bart, Lionel
GS 202, 203-204
5001 543
Bart, Peter
WTLGD 271
5001 271
Bartel, Paul
TIAI 424; dir., *Death Race 2000*, 384;
Eating Raoul, 424
5001 181, 211, 324, 659
Bartels, Louis John
5001 116
Barth, John
DIM 111, 112
TIAI 376
5001 218
Barthelmess, Richard
GS 126
5001 107, 112, 218, 702, 824
Bartholomew, Freddie
5001 28, 118
Bartkowiak, Andrzej
SOTA 42, 379
5001 596, 600, 606, 813
Bartleby
DIM 417-418
5001 (2nd ed)
"Bartleby, the Scrivener" (novella)
DIM 417
Bartlett, Martine
5001 702
Bartlett, Robin
ML 274
5001 43, 592
Bartlett, Sy
5001 200, 760
Bartok, Eva
KKBB 252
5001 163
Bartolini, Elio
5001 41

Barton, James
  5001 484
Barty, Billy
  R 474
  H 474
  5001 176, 255, 291, 840
Barwood, Hal
  R 301
  TIAI 220, 222, 223
  5001 73, 155, 201, 725, 770
Baryshnikov, Mikhail
  WTLGD 344-345, 347
  SOTA 155
  H 64, 65-67
  5001 794, 835
Barzman, Ben
  5001 323
Bas-Fonds, Les, see The Lower Depths
"Baseball Boogie" (music)
  H 482
Basehart, Richard
  KKBB 351
  R 103
  5001 67, 490, 717, 774
Basic Training of Pavlo Hummel, The (stage)
  R 302
Basie, Count
  H 115
  5001 703, 704
Basileus Quartet (Quartetto Basileus)
  SOTA 125-127
  5001 (2nd ed)
Basilischi, I, see The Lizards
Basinger, Kim
  SOTA 169, 170
  H 97, 99, 352
  ML 160, 162
  5001 54, 255, 513, 517
Baskin, Elya
  SOTA 156
  5001 499
Baskin, Norton
  SOTA 56, 57
Baskin, Richard
  WTLGD 283-284
  TIAI 42, 299
  5001 340, 517, 827
Bass, Alfie
  KKBB 291, 295
  5001 14, 63, 393, 414
Bass, Ronald
  H 271, 303
  ML 81, 326
  5001 78, 279, 613
Bass, Saul
  ILIATM 39, 143, 150, 151
  KKBB 9
  5001 462
Bassani, Giorgio
  DIM 363-366
  5001 279
Basserman, Albert
  WTLGD 452
  5001 224, 258, 446, 548, 598, 621, 672, 847
Basserman, Elsa
  5001 446
Bassiak, Boris

  5001 385
Bast, William
  5001 66
Bat Whispers, The
  ML 159
Bataan
  GS 285
  SOTA 116
Bataille, Henri
  5001 599
Bataille, Sylvia
  KKBB 254
  5001 175
Batalla de Chile, La, see The Battle of Chile
Batalov, Alexei
  5001 160
Batalov, Nikolai
  KKBB 312
  5001 499
Batcheff, Pierre
  TIAI 148
  5001 132, 516
Bates, Alan
  KKBB 22
  GS 210
  DIM 139, 142
  WTLGD 50, 412-414
  SOTA 311, 330, 332
  5001 222, 237, 248, 282, 534, 535, 626,
    641, 645, 807, 833, 847, 865
Bates, Barbara
  5001 16, 386
Bates, Florence
  KKBB 225, 249
  TIAI 353
  5001 143, 326, 351, 400, 419, 469, 488,
    546, 591, 618, 654, 663, 825
Bates, H. E.
  R 218
  5001 790
Bates, Kathy
  TIAI 416-417
  H 245
  5001 148, 718
Bathing Beauty
  5001
Batman
  ML 158-64, 299
  5001 (2nd ed)
"Batman" (TV)
  KKBB 121
  WTLGD 526
Battisti, Carlo
  5001 803
"Battle Hymn of the Republic, The" (music)
  TIAI 447
  SOTA 64
Battle of Algiers, The
  GS 96
  DIM 176
  R 210-215, 315
  WTLGD 524
  SOTA 74, 278
  5001
Battle of Britain
  DIM 56
Battle of Chile, The (La Batalla de Chile)

  WTLGD 384-388
  TIAI 311
  5001
Battle of San Pietro, The
  KKBB 131
  5001 (2nd ed)
Battle of San Romano
  H 130
"Battle of San Romano" (painting)
  H 130
Battle of the Rails
  ILIATM 111
Battle of the Sexes, The
  5001
Battleship Potemkin, The, see Potemkin
Battling Butler
  5001
Bauchau, Patrick
  5001 136, 815
Bauer, David
  DIM 126
  5001 791
Bauer, Steven (pseud. Rocky Echevarria)
  SOTA 101, 103
  5001 658
Baum, L. Frank
  WTLGD 470-472
  TIAI 483
  ML 299
Baum, Thomas
  H 171, 172
  5001 121, 463
Baum, Vicki
  KKBB 275
  5001 170, 299
Baur, Harry
  KKBB 243, 244, 252, 257, 262
  DIM 367
  TIAI 146
  5001 120, 161, 187, 339, 587, 819
Bava, Mario
  TIAI 193; dir., Black Sunday, 193
  5001 78
Bavaria Studios
  WTLGD 389
Bax, Arnold
  5001 543
Baxley, Barbara
  R 450
  5001 17, 210, 516
Baxter, Alan
  5001 208, 344, 359, 384, 653, 666, 669, 787
Baxter, Anne
  KKBB 230, 266, 304
  5001 16, 27, 248, 258, 303, 349, 451, 533,
    617, 646, 747, 771
Baxter, Charles
  SOTA 199
Baxter, Keith
  KKBB 201
  5001 37, 235
Baxter, Lynsey
  TIAI 239
  5001 267
Baxter, Warner
  WTLGD 502
  5001 261, 404

Bay, Frances
  H 208
Bay of the Angels (*La Baie des anges*)
  KKBB 235:n, 307
  GS 264, 265
  R 350
  H 136
  5001
Baye, Nathalie
  TIAI 101, 102
  5001 226
Bayldon, Geoffrey
  ML 22
  5001 447
Baziga
  5001 397
Bazin, André
  ILIATM 247, 295, 307
  GS 29, 283
  DIM 360-362, 365-366
BBC
  WTLGD 382
  TIAI 274, 387
Be Yourself
  KKBB 234
  R 458
Beach, Ann
  R 115
  5001 805
Beach Party
  TIAI 407
Beach Red
  5001
Beach, Rex
  5001 702
Beach, Scott
  SOTA 63
Beacham, Stephanie
  5001 528
Beachcomber, The
  5001
Beaches
  ML 72-74
  5001 (2nd ed)
"Beacon Hill" (TV)
  WTLGD 150
Beaird, David
  H dir., *Pass the Ammo*, 452-454
  5001 567
Beal, John
  5001 99, 426, 484
Beals, Jennifer
  ML 151
  5001 250, 812
Bean, Henry
  ML 263, 264
  5001 367
Bean, Robert B.
  DIM 372; dir., *Made for Each Other*,
    369-373, 426
  5001 448
Bear, The
  ML 208-211
  5001 (2nd ed)
Beard, Charles A.
  RK 71, 72
Beard, Peter H.

5001 314
Beard, The
  WTLGD 156
Beardsley, Aubrey
  WTLGD 336
  5001 650
"Beast in the Jungle, The" (story)
  ILIATM 72
Beast Must Die, The (book)
  DIM 172
Beast with Five Fingers, The
  ILIATM 6
  H 69
Beat the Devil
  ILIATM 214, 299
  KKBB 229, 235-236:n, 248, 327
  GS 109
  R 13, 184
  WTLGD 18, 234
  SOTA 376
  5001
Beatlemania
  WTLGD 447
Beatles, The (group)
  KKBB 116, 280
  GS 149, 186-190
  DIM 208, 340, 345
  WTLGD 266, 447
  TIAI 127, 202, 294
  5001 855
Beaton, Cecil
  ILIATM 37
  KKBB 323-324
  DIM 185
  WTLGD 258
  H 467
  5001 285, 398, 454, 507, 544, 794
Beatty, Ned
  R 449
  WTLGD 222, 526
  TIAI 161
  H 359, 448, 449
  5001 45, 68, 70, 229, 361, 421, 516, 519,
    531, 682, 730, 738, 851
Beatty, Warren
  ILIATM 137-138, 140
  KKBB 56-58, 221
  DIM 115, 122, 123, 277-279, 353
  R 393, 436-440
  WTLGD 210, 274, 319, 429-430; dir.,
    Heaven Can Wait, 427, 429-430, 432
  TIAI 278-283, 305; dir., *Reds*, 278-283, 314,
    334; *Heaven Can Wait*, 280, 327
  SOTA 170, 240, 314; dir., *Reds*, 24; *Heaven
    Can Wait* (co-dir.), 170
  H 63, 235, 310, 311, 348
  5001 16, 91, 91, 197, 260, 326, 329, 371,
    422, 445, 621, 637, 670, 702
Beau Brummell
  WTLGD 191
Beau Geste
  KKBB 184
  WTLGD 516
  H 361
  5001
Beau Mariage, Le
  TIAI 400-401

SOTA 37
  5001 (2nd ed)
Beau Serge, Le
  ILIATM 132
  DIM 54
Beauman, Nick
  5001 333, 507
Beaumont, Harry
  5001 105, 169, 555
Beaumont, Hugh
  5001 86
Beauté du diable, La, see *Beauty and the Devil*
Beautiful and Damned, The
  DIM 32
Beautiful Blonde from Bashful Bend, The
  5001
"Beautiful Soup" (music)
  WTLGD 27
Beauty and the Beast (TV)
  WTLGD 503
Beauty and the Beast (*La Belle et la bête*)
  KKBB 236
  WTLGD 14
  H 473
  5001
Beauty and the Devil (*La Beauté du diable*)
  5001
Beauvoir, Simone de
  H 86
Beavan, Jenny
  5001 94
Beavers, Louise
  5001 91, 358, 448, 532, 669, 830
Becher, John C.
  WTLGD 130
  5001 521
Beck, John
  5001 68, 569, 686
Beck, Julian
  SOTA 298
  5001 156
Beck, Martha
  DIM 105-107
  5001 339
Beck, Michael
  WTLGD 557
  5001 823
Beck, Pierre-Michel
  5001 277
Beck, Robert (Iceberg Slim)
  5001 789
Beck, Stanley
  R 372
  5001 417
Becker, Desiree
  H 339
  5001 295
Becker, Jacques
  KKBB 245-246; dir., *Casque d'Or*, 245-246
  5001 95, 123, 300
Beckett, Samuel
  ILIATM 22-23
  DIM 156, 352, 356
  WTLGD 255, 294
  SOTA 15, 36, 100, 262
Beckett, Scotty
  5001 153, 326

Beckley, Tony
 5001 235
Beckmann, Max
 DIM 410
Becky Sharp
 5001
Bécourt, Alain
 5001 493
Bed and Board (Domicile Conjugal)
 DIM 243-245
 5001
Bed Sitting Room, The
 DIM 17, 148
 5001
Bedazzled
 GS 63
 DIM 10
 5001 (2nd ed)
Beddoe, Don
 5001 44, 65, 198, 220, 237, 293, 310, 526,
  763
Bedelia, Bonnie
 DIM 70
 WTLGD 467
 SOTA 79, 81-82, 83
 H 148, 149-150, 151
 ML 208
 5001 70, 239, 323, 755, 816
Bedford, Brian
 KKBB 10
Bedford Incident, The
 R 222
Bedford Lloyd, John, see Lloyd, John Bedford
Bedford, Patrick
 5001 808
Bedi, Kabir
 SOTA 5
 5001 539
Bedknobs and Broomsticks
 DIM 359-360
 5001
Bedoya, Alfonso
 KKBB 361
 WTLGD 509
 5001 788
Bedroom Window, The
 H 265-267
 5001 (2nd ed)
Bedtime Story
 KKBB 193
Bee Gees (group)
 WTLGD 368
Beecham, Sir Thomas
 KKBB 364
 SOTA 154
 5001 621, 741
Beecher, Janet
 5001 75, 466, 641, 717
Been Down So Long It Looks Like Up to Me
 DIM 350
Beer, Robert
 5001 630
Beery, Noah
 R 285
 5001 264, 391, 393, 426, 672, 822
Beery, Wallace
 KKBB 275

RK 13
R 72
WTLGD 64
5001 11, 128, 134, 174, 190, 299, 407, 634,
 831
Beethoven, Ludwig van
 DIM 198, 377
 WTLGD 53, 293, 368
 SOTA 227, 228, 229
 H 125
 5001 236, 246, 694
Beetlejuice
 H 455-457
 ML 112, 159, 161, 299, 301
 5001 (2nd ed)
"Before the Parade Passes By" (music)
 DIM 80
Before the Revolution (Prima della Rivoluzione)
 KKBB 124-125
 GS 7
 DIM 270, 272
 R 174
 WTLGD 332
 H 396
 5001
Before Winter Comes
 DIM 329
Begelman, David
 TIAI 14
Beggar's Opera, The
 ILIATM 116-119
 GS 203
 5001
"Begin the Beguine" (music)
 WTLGD 124
Beginning or the End, The
 ML 207
Begley, Ed
 5001 72, 92, 554, 734, 795
Begley, Ed Jr.
 WTLGD 321
 ML 69
 5001 3, 86, 125, 139, 290, 659
Behan, Brendan
 TIAI 211
Behm, Marc
 5001 130
Behn, Harry
 5001 328
Behold a Pale Horse
 DIM 176
Behr, Jack
 SOTA 316
 5001 74
Behrman, S. N.
 RK 10
 5001 28, 63, 153, 314, 531, 583, 659, 741,
  824
Beiderbecke, Bix
 5001 79
Beineix, Jean-Jacques
 TIAI 327-331; dir., *Diva*, 327-331
 SOTA 45-49; dir., *The Moon in the Gutter*,
  45-49; *Diva*, 45, 46
 H 136, 385; dir., *Diva*, 136; *The Moon in
  the Gutter*, 136; *Betty Blue*, 385
 5001 192, 495

Being There
 TIAI 353, 458, 459
 H 9
 ML 29
Béjart, Maurice
 WTLGD 495
"Bel Ami" (music)
 WTLGD 177
Bel Geddes, Barbara
 KKBB 296
 5001 126, 351, 564
Belack, Doris
 5001 780
Belafonte, Harry
 5001 119
Belasco, David
 GS 123
 5001 446
Belden, Charles S.
 5001 512
Beliard, Florence
 H 465
"Believe in Yourself" (music)
 WTLGD 475
Bell, Book and Candle
 R 426
Bell, Julian
 KKBB 223
Bell, Marie
 KKBB 244
 5001 120, 580
Bell, Marjorie, see Champion, Marge
Bell, Mary Hayley
 5001 832
Bell, Quentin
 R 52
Bell, Tom
 WTLGD 50
 H 322
 5001 842
Bell, Tony
 5001 573
Bell, Vanessa
 H 389
Bell' Antonio
 KKBB 236-237:n
 DIM 195
 5001
Bellah, James Warner
 5001 259, 631, 672
Bellamann, Henry
 5001 397
Bellamy, Ralph
 KKBB 281
 RK 48
 WTLGD 4, 16, 27, 235, 361
 SOTA 12
 H 449
 ML 34, 37
 5001 41, 116, 119, 169, 196, 257, 295, 316,
  335, 406, 541, 582, 643, 786
Bellaver, Harry
 WTLGD 408
 5001 86, 244, 269, 399, 439
Belle de jour
 GS 125, 254, 257
 WTLGD 126, 365

Belle et la bête, La, see *Beauty and the Beast*
Belle of the Nineties
    KKBB 314
    5001
Beller, Kathleen
    WTLGD 503
    5001 66, 260, 501
Belli, Melvin
    DIM 208, 209
Belling, Davina
    5001 365
Bellissima
    WTLGD 38
    5001
Bellocchio, Marco
    GS 7-8, 96; dir., *China Is Near,* 4-8, 211; *I Pugni in Tasca,* 6
    TIAI 418-421; dir., *Leap Into the Void,* 418-421; *Fists in the Pocket,* 418; *China Is Near,* 418; *In the Name of the Father,* 418
    SOTA 137
    H 290
    5001 134, 415
Bellocchio, Piergiorgio
    TIAI 420
    5001 415
Bellow, Saul
    GS 57
    SOTA 24
Bells of St. Mary's, The
    R 249
    WTLGD 194
Belmondo, Jean-Paul
    ILIATM 127-128, 131, 215
    KKBB 302
    DIM 31, 270, 309
    R 202, 303, 417, 420
    TIAI 102, 195
    SOTA 227
    5001 100, 123, 363, 416, 582, 712, 750, 756, 801, 122
Belmonte, Juan
    5001 109, 249
Belocchio, Marco
    5001 246
Beloin, Edmund
    5001 152, 406
Belson, Jerry
    KKBB 13; dir., *Allures,* 13
    GS 124
    R 323
    WTLGD 44, 270
    SOTA 63, 64
    5001 21, 271, 688
Belson, Jordan
    5001 630
Beltran, Richard
    TIAI 424
    5001 211
Beltran, Robert
    5001 659
Belushi, James (Jim)
    TIAI 189
    H 177, 178, 181
    5001 2, 428, 651, 756
Belushi, John

    WTLGD 509
    TIAI 26-27, 130, 254
    SOTA 122, 143
    5001 87, 154, 290, 530
Belzer, Richard
    5001 309, 528, 658
Bemelmans, Ludwig
    5001 856
Ben
    R 284, 286
Ben-Hur (1925)
    5001
Ben-Hur (1959)
    ILIATM 119, 190
    5001
Benackova, Gabriela
    ML 238
Benatar, Pat
    5001 478
Benchley, Nathaniel
    5001 647
Benchley, Peter
    5001 378
Benchley, Robert
    RK 12, 20, 72
    5001 106, 134, 251, 258, 350, 453, 594, 633, 685, 858
Bend Sinister (book)
    KKBB 269
Bendix, William
    5001 86, 152, 186, 421, 846
Benedek, Barbara
    SOTA 68
    5001 69
Benedek, Laslo
    KKBB 203-204; dir., *The Wild One,* 190, 203, 366; *Death of a Salesman,* 203
    5001 839
Benedek, Tom
    H 5
    5001 144
Benedict, Paul
    WTLGD 377
    5001 296, 462, 688, 809
Benedict, Richard
    5001 4
Beneke, Tex
    5001 551, 728
Benet, Brenda
    R 285
    5001 822
Benét, Stephen Vincent
    RK 41
    5001 667
Beniades, Ted
    5001 521
Benigni, Roberto
    H 220-221
    5001 200
Bening, Annette
    ML 219, 275, 284-86
    5001 592, 812
Benjamin
    GS 72-73
    5001
Benjamin, Richard
    DIM 347-349, 353

    R 217-218
    WTLGD 77
    TIAI 394-398; dir., *My Favorite Year,* 394-398
    SOTA 151-153; dir., *Racing with the Moon,* 151-153, 315; *City Heat,* 288
    5001 125, 438, 508, 610, 730, 829
Bennent, Heinz
    WTLGD 390
    5001 666, 700
Bennett, Alan
    SOTA 311, 341
    H 295, 297, 298
    5001 595, 598
Bennett, Alma
    5001 433
Bennett, Arnold
    KKBB 335
    5001 334, 337, 601
Bennett, Belle
    5001 713
Bennett, Bruce (Herman Brix)
    KKBB 361
    5001 457, 497, 744, 788
Bennett, Charles
    KKBB 359
    5001 258, 761, 859
Bennett, Compton
    KKBB 347; co-dir., *King Solomon's Mines,* 184; dir., *The Seventh Veil,* 346-347
    5001 397, 669
Bennett, Constance
    KKBB 59, 122, 235, 363
    WTLGD 16
    SOTA 221
    5001 373, 447, 635, 781, 782, 830
Bennett, Enid
    5001 366, 634
Bennett, Harve
    TIAI 355
    SOTA 196
    5001 708
Bennett, Hywel
    5001 110
Bennett, Jill
    GS 145
    5001 130, 257, 443, 500, 515
Bennett, Joan
    RK 20, 48
    5001 240, 428, 457, 472, 489, 659, 786, 828, 845, 846
Bennett, Leila
    5001 195
Bennett, Richard
    KKBB 304
    5001 384, 451
Bennett, Richard Rodney
    WTLGD 339
    5001 223, 237, 626
Bennett, Tony
    KKBB 142
    SOTA 123
    5001 554
Benny, Jack
    DIM 61
    WTLGD 372
    SOTA 2, 112

5001 36, 105, 310, 311, 336, 337, 774
Benson, Edward Frederick (E. F.)
  KKBB 255
  5001 178
Benson, Lucille
  5001 426, 531, 682
Benson, Robby
  TIAI 115
  SOTA 310
Benson, Sally
  5001 28
Benton, Jerome
  SOTA 215
  5001 604
Benton, Robert
  KKBB 48, 52, 54, 59-61
  DIM 229, 230
  R 12-14
  WTLGD 259-262; dir., *The Late Show*,
    259-262, 322; *Bad Company*, 261
  TIAI 426-428; dir., *Kramer vs. Kramer*, 13,
    18, 78, 427; *The Late Show*, 363, 427;
    Still of the Night, 426-428
  SOTA 246-249; dir., *Kramer vs. Kramer*,
    97, 174, 248, 249; *Places in the Heart*,
    246-249, 319; *The Late Show*, 248
  H 116, 190, 352-353; dir., *Places in the
    Heart*, 50; *Kramer vs. Kramer*, 76, 116,
    190; *Nadine*, 352-353; *The Late Show*,
    352
  5001 46, 91, 412, 513, 585, 715, 731, 752,
    831
Benton, Suzanne
  5001 750
Benvenuti, Leo
  5001 14
Bérard, Christian
  KKBB 236, 329
  5001 58, 566
Bercovici, Luca
  ML 278
  5001 561
Berenger, Tom
  WTLGD 319
  TIAI 167, 168
  SOTA 69, 70
  H 253, 386, 387
  ML 250
  5001 69, 93, 197, 434, 587, 692
Berenson, Marisa
  DIM 412
  WTLGD 103
  5001 53, 112, 180, 690
Beresford, Bruce
  TIAI 60-62, 479-481; dir., *The Getting of
    Wisdom*, 60-62; *Tender Mercies*,
    479-481
  H 233-237; dir., *Tender Mercies*, 98; *Crimes
    of the Heart*, 233-237, 378
  ML 234-38; dir., *Driving Miss Daisy*,
  5001 162, 204, 283, 747
Bergen, Candice
  KKBB 8, 71-72
  GS 268
  DIM 283-285, 312, 313
  R 70, 79, 361
  WTLGD 393

TIAI 11, 247, 248, 433
5001 6, 120, 215, 218, 277, 309, 452, 627,
  715, 785, 841
Bergen, Edgar
  5001 351
Berger, Helmut
  DIM 87, 364
  R 145-146, 345, 431
  WTLGD 35, 36, 39, 40, 93-95
  H 27
  5001 37, 154, 169, 279, 443, 581, 638
Berger, John
  WTLGD 180-182
  5001 383
Berger, Ludwig
  5001 756
Berger, Nicole
  5001 277, 323, 676
Berger, Peter E.
  5001 239
Berger, Senta
  5001 123
Berger, Thomas
  DIM 212, 213, 236
  5001 424
Bergerac, Jacques
  5001 285, 418
Bergere, Lee
  5001 89
Berggren, Thommy
  DIM 135
  5001 6, 216, 381
Berghauer, Hiroko
  5001 59
Berghof, Herbert
  WTLGD 129
  TIAI 70
  5001 247, 320, 743
Bergin, Patrick
  ML 326
Bergman, Alan and Marilyn
  SOTA 86
  5001 855
Bergman, Andrew
  TIAI 240-241; dir., *So Fine*, 240-241
  5001 81, 251, 689
Bergman, Henry
  5001 292, 491
Bergman, Ingmar
  ILIATM 12, 15, 22-23, 105-107, 245-246,
    288, 303-304; dir., trilogy, 12; *Brink of
    Life*, 15; *Smiles of a Summer Night*, 22,
    105-107, 148, 274; *The Silence*, 22, 23;
    Secrets of Women, 105, 106; *A Lesson
    in Love*, 105; *Dreams*, 105; *The Seventh
    Seal*, 107, 148, 176, 245, 288
  KKBB 14, 59, 103, 171-172, 222, 303-304,
    315, 319, 326, 342, 343, 346, 353,
    368-369; dir., *The Silence*, 128;
    Persona, 171-172; *Summer Interlude*,
    171, 353; *Smiles of a Summer Night*,
    171, 342, 353; *Prison*, 171; *Wild
    Strawberries*, 280, 368-369; *The
    Magician*, 303-304, 319; *The Naked
    Night*, 315; *The Seventh Seal*, 326, 346,
    347, 369
  GS 6; dir., *Hour of the Wolf*, 108, 157, 214,

216; *Persona*, 214, 216; *The Seventh
  Seal*, 216; *Shame*, 214-221; *The Silence*,
  214; *Smiles of a Summer Night*, 73, 211,
  216; *Summer Interlude*, 216; *Through a
  Glass Darkly*, 217; *Törst*, 216; *Torment*,
  223; *Wild Strawberries*, 216
DIM 162, 252, 348; dir., *Shame*, 17, 298;
  The Seventh Seal, 17, 18; *The Silence*,
  59; *Wild Strawberries*, 252; *Summer
  Interlude*, 252; *Dreams*, 252; *The Touch*,
  348
R 8, 89-94, 182, 226, 418, 437-438, 440;
  dir., *Through a Glass Darkly*, 44; *Cries
  and Whispers*, 89-94, 346; *The Silence*,
  89, 92, 94; *Shame*, 89, 346; *Persona*,
  90, 94; *The Naked Night*, 90; *Summer
  Interlude*, 90; *Monika*, 90; *Törst*, 91;
  Wild Strawberries, 223-225; *A Ship to
  India*, 341; *The Touch*, 418; *Smiles of a
  Summer Night*, 437-438, 440
WTLGD 54, 55, 71, 72-76, 230, 324,
  388-392, 424, 431, 437, 439, 476-481;
  dir., *Shame*, 71, 391, 478; *The Magic
  Flute*, 72-76, 111, 392; *Smiles of a
  Summer Night*, 74, 424; *The Seventh
  Seal*, 74; *Wild Strawberries*, 74, 76,
  258; *Cries and Whispers*, 74, 431;
  Scenes from a Marriage, 76, 390, 478;
  The Serpent's Egg, 388-392; *The
  Silence*, 389; *The Hour of the Wolf*, 389;
  The Magician, 389, 390; *The Passion of
  Anna*, 390, 478; *The Touch*, 390; *Face
  to Face*, 390, 478; *Autumn Sonata*,
  476-481; *Persona*, 478
TIAI 87, 88, 90, 130, 222, 291, 365, 366,
  414, 467, 486-493; dir., *Scenes from a
  Marriage*, 78, 291; *The Naked Night*,
  87; *The Seventh Seal*, 183, 484; *Smiles
  of a Summer Night*, 365; *Fanny and
  Alexander*, 486-493; *The Virgin Spring*,
  488; *Winter Light*, 488; *The Silence*,
  488; *The Passion of Anna*, 488; *The
  Serpent's Egg*, 488; *From the Life of the
  Marionettes*, 488; *The Magic Flute*, 491,
  492; *Wild Strawberries*, 491; *Shame*,
  492; *Persona*, 492
SOTA 195
H 113, 115, 137, 340, 368, 426, 430; dir.,
  Fanny and Alexander, 113, 368; *The
  Serpent's Egg*, 137; *Autumn Sonata*,
  426; *After the Rehearsal*, 430
ML 16, 200; dir., *Wild Strawberries*, 12, 14
5001 40, 104, 161, 203, 236, 418, 427, 450,
  451, 514, 576, 664, 666, 668, 670, 688,
  726, 727, 782, 813, 839
Bergman, Ingrid
  ILIATM 215
  KKBB 245, 267, 320, 345, 348
  GS 103
  R 390, 392
  WTLGD 3, 28, 32, 193-195, 476-481
  TIAI 43, 44, 135, 301
  H 66, 205
  ML 193
  5001 40, 113, 122, 214, 256, 279, 362, 366,
    382, 470, 503, 536, 653, 654, 701, 804,

820, 846
Bergmann, Martin
  ML 200-201, 202
Bergner, Elisabeth
  KKBB 260
  GS 39
  5001 36, 202, 573
Bergonzi, Carlo
  H 424
Bergren, Eric
  TIAI 85
  5001 215
Bergryd, Ulla
  5001 67
Bergson, Henri
  KKBB 287
Bergstein, Eleanor
  H 347, 348
  5001 190
Beri, Shandra
  H 313, 314
  5001 645
Berk, Howard
  5001 743
Berkeley, Busby
  ILIATM 146-147
  KKBB 234, 273, 309
  DIM 82, 380, 382-383
  R 474; dir., *For Me and My Gal*, 59
  WTLGD 371, 505, 537
  TIAI 276
  SOTA 297
  H 250
  5001 30, 42, 238, 255, 256, 262, 277, 278,
    286, 291, 292, 393, 404, 481, 637, 722,
    723, 740, 755, 865
Berkeley, Reginald
  5001 127
Berkman, Ted
  5001 123
Berkoff, Steven
  SOTA 4-5, 374
  H 160
  5001 3, 66, 539, 615
Berle, Milton
  KKBB 299
  R 16, 130, 131, 132, 377
  TIAI 111, 395
  5001 317, 440, 554, 728
Berley, André
  5001 568
Berlin, Irving
  SOTA 294
  5001 13, 29, 115, 119, 144, 210, 254, 545,
    663, 752, 762
Berlin, Jeannie
  R 68, 70, 261, 429, 430
  5001 44, 91, 324, 673, 721
Berlin Philharmonic
  WTLGD 75
Berlioz, Hector
  TIAI 150
Berman, Pandro S.
  5001 79, 119, 137, 240, 254, 376, 445, 468,
    517, 600, 607, 629, 661, 703, 739, 767,
    846, 865
Berman, Shelley

5001 65
Berman, Susan
  SOTA 354
Bernanos, Georges
  KKBB 259
  5001 189, 499
Bernard, Jacques
  KKBB 262
  5001 220
Bernard, Jason
  SOTA 222
  5001 17
Bernard, Paul
  KKBB 328
  5001 564
Bernardi, Herschel
  5001 145, 270, 339, 370, 502
Bernardi, Roberto
  5001 149
Bernhard, Sandra
  TIAI 457
  H 41
  5001 396
Bernhardt, Curtis
  5001 485, 572, 591
Bernhardt, Sarah
  DIM 383
  WTLGD 204-206, 231
  TIAI 151
Bernstein, Armyan
  TIAI 299
  5001 550
Bernstein, Carl
  H 189, 191
Bernstein, Charles
  5001 361, 438
Bernstein, Elmer
  R 435
  WTLGD 204, 446
  ML 284
  5001 295, 303, 452, 462, 624, 656, 726,
    736, 777
Bernstein, Henri
  KKBB 260
  5001 203
Bernstein, Leonard
  ILIATM 48, 143-144, 147
  TIAI 133, 216
  5001 546, 654, 828
Bernstein, Dr. Maurice
  RK 35, 65
Bernstein, Walter
  R 153
  WTLGD 170, 171, 359-361
  5001 66, 270, 327, 492, 665
Berr, Georges
  5001 793
Berri, Claude
  GS dir., *The Two of Us*, 50, 51
  SOTA 133
  H 329-331; dir., *Jean de Florette*, 329-331;
    Manon of the Spring, 329
  5001 80, 91, 379
Berridge, Elizabeth
  SOTA 252
  H 132
  5001 689

Berry Brothers
  5001 563
Berry, Chuck
  WTLGD 422, 449
  TIAI 323
  5001 23
Berry, John
  WTLGD 272
  5001 644, 757
Berry, Jules
  5001 383, 817
Berryman, Dorothée
  H 237
  5001 182
Berta, Renato
  WTLGD 286
  5001 848
Bertheau, Julien
  R 42
  5001 192, 481, 700
Berthier, Jacques
  5001 472
Bertin, Pierre
  5001 91, 214
Bertish, Jane
  5001 170
Berto, Juliet
  5001 136, 275, 488
Bertolucci, Bernardo
  KKBB 124-125; dir., *Before the Revolution*,
    124-125
  GS 7-8, 96; dir., *Before the Revolution*, 7;
    La Commare Secca, 7
  DIM 220, 270-275; dir., *La Commare Secca*,
    270; *Before the Revolution*, 270, 272;
    The Conformist, 270-275, 415, 426;
    Partner, 272-273; *The Spider's*
    Stratagem, 273
  R 27-34, 269, 447; dir., *Last Tango in Paris*,
    27-34, 345, 447; *The Conformist*, 28,
    33, 174, 258, 401; *Before the*
    Revolution, 174
  WTLGD 145, 146, 323-333, 515; dir., *Last*
    Tango in Paris, 58, 134, 333, 393, 412,
    456; *The Conformist*, 146, 326; *The*
    Spider's Stratagem, 146, 326; *1900*,
    323-333; *Before the Revolution*, 332
  TIAI 174, 309, 312-314, 335; dir., *Last*
    Tango in Paris, 172, 298; *1900*, 174,
    175; *Tragedy of a Ridiculous Man*, 309,
    312-314; *Luna*, 314; *The Conformist*,
    335
  SOTA 355; dir., *Last Tango in Paris*, 228
  H 61, 394-399, 452; dir., *The Last Emperor*,
    394-399, 452; *Tragedy of a Ridiculous*
    Man, 395; *Before the Revolution*, 396;
    The Conformist, 396, 398; *1900*, 396,
    398; *Luna*, 452
  ML dir., *The Last Emperor*, 305; *Luna*, 305;
    The Sheltering Sky, 301-306
  5001 61, 152, 408, 410, 530, 566, 567, 701,
    786, 787
Berton, Pierre
  KKBB 248
  5001 139, 864
Besch, Bibi
  TIAI 358

5001 707
Besier, Rudolf
  5001 52
Besnard, Nicole
  5001 59
Bespoke Overcoat, The
  ILIATM 65
  KKBB 263, 290
  5001
"Bess, You Is My Woman" (aria)
  WTLGD 473
Besserer, Eugénie
  5001 769
Best, Edna
  5001 284, 366, 460
Best Foot Forward
  5001
Best Friends
  TIAI 445-446, 463
  5001 (2nd ed)
Best, James
  5001 513
Best Little Whorehouse in Texas, The
  TIAI 373-375
  5001 (2nd ed)
Best Man, The
  WTLGD 278
  5001
Best of Times, The
  H 110-113, 188, 300, 421, 422, 481
  5001 (2nd ed)
"Best Things in Life Are Free, The" (music)
  DIM 70
  SOTA 81
Best, Willie
  WTLGD 67
  5001 113, 332, 391, 819
Best Years of Our Lives, The
  ILIATM 81
  KKBB 252
  R 364
  WTLGD 405
  5001
Beswick, Martine
  TIAI 77
Bête humaine, La (*The Human Beast*)
  R 33
  5001
Betjeman, John
  H 296
Betrayal
  SOTA 14-15
Betrayed
  ML 241
Betsy, The
  WTLGD 409-410, 530
  TIAI 153
  5001
Bettauer, Hugo
  5001 384
Bettelheim, Bruno
  SOTA 24
Bettger, Lyle
  5001 305, 519
Betti, Laura
  WTLGD 328-331
  TIAI 469

5001 530, 537
Betty Blue
  H 385
Beuys, Joseph
  SOTA 266
Bevan, Billy
  5001 127, 143, 741
Bevan, Donald
  5001 705
Bevans, Clem
  5001 855
"Beverly Hillbillies, The" (TV)
  DIM 58, 234
Beverly Hills Cop
  SOTA 287-288
  5001 (2nd ed)
Beverly of Graustark
  RK 5
Bey, Marki
  5001 407
Bey, Turhan
  DIM 25
  SOTA 104
  5001 14, 34, 201, 835
Beymer, Richard
  ILIATM 143
  5001 362, 723, 828
Beyond the Forest
  WTLGD 144
  5001
Beyond the Fringe (stage)
  GS 63
  SOTA 341
Beyond the Law
  GS 196
  R 30
  WTLGD 399
  H 362
Beyond the Limit
  H 167
Beyond the Valley of the Dolls
  DIM 147
Beyond Therapy
  TIAI 170
Beyond This Winter's Wheat
  SOTA 98
Bezzerides, A. I.
  5001 754
Bhowani Junction
  ILIATM 305:n
Bialik, Mayim
  ML 73
  5001 56
Bianchi, Daniele
  5001 270
Bibb, Porter
  DIM 208
Biberman, Abner
  5001 31, 311, 392, 402, 818
Biberman, Herbert J.
  5001 474, 651, 778
Bible, The
  KKBB 131-134
  H 364
  5001
Biches, Les
  GS 148

DIM 53
  5001
Bick, Jerry
  R 269
Bickford, Charles
  KKBB 205
  5001 28, 108, 206, 234, 237, 333, 381, 426,
    488, 540, 707, 832, 846
Bicycle Thief, The (*Ladri di Biciclette*)
  ILIATM 214, 231, 248, 285
  KKBB 269, 310
  DIM 361
  H 59
  5001
Bidault, Georges
  DIM 428
Biddle, Ed
  SOTA 290-293
Biddle, Jack
  SOTA 290-293
Bideau, Jean-Luc
  WTLGD 180
  5001 383
Bidone, Il (*The Swindlers*)
  5001
Biehn, Michael
  H 193
  5001 15
Bierman, Robert
  ML dir., *Apology*, 151; *Vampire's Kiss*, 150-
    52 Big, 319; *Big Chill, The* 69; *Bird*, 1-
    5; *Birdy*, 150
  5001 812
Big
  H 482-483
  5001 (2nd ed)
Big Bad Wolf, The
  TIAI 192
Big Bopper, the (J. P. Richardson)
  H 342
Big Broadcast of 1938, The
  5001
Big Brother and the Holding Company
  GS 119
Big Bus, The
  5001
Big Business
  H 483-485
  5001 (2nd ed)
Big Carnival, The, see *Ace in the Hole*
Big Chill, The
  SOTA 68-71
  H 446
  5001 (2nd ed)
Big City (1937)
  5001
Big City, The (1948), see *Mahanagar*
Big Clock, The
  H 356
Big Day, The, see *Jour de fête*
Big Deal on Madonna Street, The (*I Soliti Ignoti*)
  KKBB 238:n
  5001
Big Easy, The
  H 358-359
  5001 (2nd ed)
Big Fix, The

WTLGD 466-469
5001
Big Gamble, The
GS 167
Big Hand for the Little Lady, A
GS 18
Big Heat, The
5001
Big Knife, The
KKBB 238:n
GS 75, 208
R 118, 187
5001
Big Maybelle
5001 379
Big Pond, The
5001 (2nd ed)
Big Sky, The
ILIATM 305
Big Sleep, The
ILIATM 26, 81, 214, 300, 304
KKBB 6-7, 59, 238-239:n, 251, 279
DIM 413-415
R 184, 187
WTLGD 262
TIAI 427
5001
Big Store, The
5001
Bigagli, Claudio
H 123
Bigard, Barney
5001 62
Bigelow, Kathryn
5001 518, 519
Bignamini, Nino
5001 18
Bigney, Hugh
H 240
Bikel, Theodore
GS 38
5001 145, 220, 647
Biko, Stephen
H 399-401
Bill of Divorcement, A
5001
Bill, Tony
5001 670, 715
Billington, Francilla
5001 81
Billion Dollar Brain
5001
Billon, Pierre
KKBB 262: dir., *The Eternal Husband*, 262
5001 225
Billy Budd
ILIATM 234-239, 316
DIM 170
R 195
SOTA 273
5001
Billy Jack
DIM 341-347, 426
R 378-380
WTLGD 397
TIAI 198
5001

Billy the Kid
KKBB 50, 60
Bindon, John
GS 26
5001 589
Bing, Herman
KKBB 362
R 130-131
5001 75, 87, 106, 226, 255, 304, 309, 359, 472, 524, 736, 796
Bingo Long Traveling All-Stars and Motor Kings, The
WTLGD 368
TIAI 221
H 349
5001
Binns, Edward
5001 795, 813
Binoche, Juliette
H 428, 431
5001 803
Binyon, Claude
5001 351, 369, 780, 793
Birchall, Frederick T.
RK 11-12
Bird
ML 1-5
5001 (2nd ed)
Bird, John
5001 761
Bird Man of Alcatraz
GS 208
WTLGD 37
TIAI 173
5001
Bird of Paradise
5001
Birds, The
ILIATM 10
WTLGD 157, 371
5001
Birds in Peru (Les Oiseaux vont mourir au Pérou)
GS 193
DIM 247
5001
Birdsall, Jesse
H 332
5001 842
Birdy
SOTA 316-319
ML 150
5001 (2nd ed)
Birell, Tala
5001 161
Birinski, Leo
5001 280, 694
Birkin, Jane
5001 85, 181
Birman, Len
5001 682
Birney, Reed
TIAI 285
5001 264
Biro, Lajos
5001 248, 459, 599, 623, 756
Biroc, Joseph

5001 417
Birth of a Nation, The
ILIATM 119, 282, 287
KKBB 131
GS 20, 42-45, 60, 220
RK 69
R 5, 64
WTLGD 248, 371, 536
TIAI 58
Birth of the Blues
5001
Birthday Party, The
GS 206, 211-212
R 220
H 98
5001
"Birthmark, The" (story)
H 314
Bishop, Joey
5001 513
Bishop, Julie (Jacqueline Wells)
5001 77, 318
Bishop, Kelly
WTLGD 411
H 346
5001 190, 807
Bishop, Troy
SOTA 97
5001 749
Bishop's Wife, The
WTLGD 21
Bismarck, Otto von
WTLGD 50
Bisoglio, Val
5001 655
Bissell, Whit
5001 74, 108, 143, 161, 344, 462, 773
Bisset, Jacqueline
DIM 137
R 135-136, 178, 179, 390
WTLGD 482-484
TIAI 247-248
SOTA 198, 200
H 450
ML 213
5001 12, 109, 123, 175, 185, 332, 421, 503, 627, 659, 728, 729, 757, 799, 806, 836
Bisson, Alexandre
5001 447
Biswas, Chhabi
5001 186, 390, 505
Bitter Sweet
5001
Bitter Tea of General Yen, The
H 34
5001
Bitzer, G. W. (Billy)
5001 367, 553
Bixby, Jerome
SOTA 20
Bizarre, Bizarre (Drôle de drame)
KKBB 140
WTLGD 354
5001
Bizet, Georges
SOTA 227, 253-254, 255, 256
5001 119, 246

24

Bizet's Carmen
  SOTA 226, 253-257
  5001 (2nd ed)
Biziou, Peter
  H 478
  5001 486
Bjelvenstam, Björn
  5001 688, 839
Björk, Anita
  5001 485, 527, 664
Björk, Halvar
  WTLGD 478
  5001 40
Björnstrand, Gunnar
  ILIATM 107
  KKBB 304, 346, 369
  GS 221
  DIM 18
  WTLGD 390
  TIAI 492
  5001 203, 236, 418, 451, 510, 514, 576,
    664, 669, 670, 688, 782, 839
Black Bird, The
  WTLGD 122-123
  5001
Black Cat, The
  5001
Black-Eyed Susan
  5001 371
Black Girl
  R 60-62
  5001
Black Glossary, A
  DIM 217
Black Hole, The
  TIAI 114
Black, Jennifer
  TIAI 465
  5001 429
Black, Jeremy
  5001 97
Black, Karen
  R 358, 364-365, 448, 475
  WTLGD 140, 508
  TIAI 414, 416
  5001 12, 94, 138, 148, 176, 211, 414, 516
"Black Label Blues" (music)
  TIAI 206
Black Legion
  5001
"Black Lung" (music)
  WTLGD 253
Black Magic
  KKBB 196
Black Moon
  WTLGD 82-83, 84
  5001
Black Narcissus
  DIM 139
Black, Noel
  GS dir., *Pretty Poison*, 168-170
  5001 595
Black Orpheus
  ILIATM 135, 141, 143
Black Panthers
  WTLGD 223
Black Pirate, The

5001
Black Rose, The
  KKBB 196, 198
Black Stallion, The
  TIAI 8, 18, 19, 347, 349, 353, 354, 372
  SOTA 63, 97, 98, 99
  H 242
  ML 115, 117
  5001 (2nd ed)
Black Sunday (La Meschera del Demonio)
  WTLGD 302
  TIAI 193
  5001 (2nd ed)
Black Widow (1954)
  5001
Black Widow (1987)
  H 270-272, 303, 462
  5001 (2nd ed)
Blackboard Jungle
  ILIATM 46, 58-60
  DIM 152
  WTLGD 129, 554, 558, 559
  5001
Blackburn, Richard
  5001 211
Blackburn Twins
  5001 848
Blackmail
  5001
Blackman, Honor
  5001 528, 670
Blackmer, Sidney
  5001 157, 170, 206, 360, 425, 643, 786
Blackwell, Morton
  H 439, 442
Blade Runner
  TIAI 360-365
  SOTA 141, 358
  H 108, 344
  ML 163
  5001 (2nd ed)
Blades, Rubén
  5001 606, 799
Blain, Gérard
  ILIATM 133-135
  KKBB 310
  WTLGD 312, 314
  5001 22, 159, 489
Blaine, Vivian
  5001 311, 711
Blair, Betsy
  WTLGD 214
  5001 30, 309, 467
Blair, Janet
  5001 510, 692
Blair, Linda
  R 248, 251, 364
  5001 12, 228, 229
Blair, Lionel
  H 159
  5001 3
Blaise, Pierre
  R 336, 340
  5001 403
Blake, Amanda
  5001 287
Blake, Madge

5001 683
Blake, Michael
  ML 296
Blake, Nicholas (C. Day Lewis)
  RK 34
  DIM 172
  5001 762
Blake, Ran
  TIAI 169
Blake, Robert (Bobby)
  DIM 77
  5001 345, 746, 788, 845
Blake, William
  WTLGD 334, 348
  SOTA 84, 191
Blakeley, James
  5001 280
Blakeley, Susan
  R 434-435
  5001 624, 671, 785
Blakely, Colin
  R 390
  WTLGD 337
  TIAI 168
  5001 197, 223, 503, 582, 599, 763
Blakely, Don
  5001 679
Blakey, Art
  5001 420
Blakley, Ronee
  R 449-450
  WTLGD 397, 400, 401
  5001 204, 516
Blame it on Rio
  SOTA 132-133
  5001 (2nd ed)
Blanc, Mel
  5001 399
Blanc, Michel
  5001 476
Blanchar, Dominique
  5001 41
Blanchar, Pierre
  KKBB 244, 252, 356
  5001 120, 161, 739
Blanchard, Mari
  5001 185
Blanck, Dorothée
  5001 140
Blandick, Clara
  5001 326, 768
Blane, Ralph
  5001 296
Blane, Sally
  5001 747
Blaney, Tim
  5001 679
Blank, Les
  TIAI 404, 406-407; dir., *Burden of Dreams*,
    404, 406-407
  5001 109
Blankfield, Mark
  TIAI 161
  5001 361
Blankfort, Michael
  KKBB 242
  5001 107

Blasetti, Alessandro
   5001 24, 63, 773, 779
Blatty, William Peter
   R 247-251
   5001 228, 301
Blaue Engel, Der, see *The Blue Angel*
Blauner, Peter
   H 251
Blaze
   ML 221-25
   5001 (2nd ed)
Blaze Starr: My life as told to Huey Perry
   (book)
   ML 221
Blazing Saddles
   R 280-282, 311-312, 321, 405
   WTLGD 247, 371, 375, 448, 508
   SOTA 146
   5001
Blé en herbe, Le, see *The Game of Love*
Blessed, Brian
   TIAI 125
   ML 217
   5001 250, 329, 458
Blessed Event
   KKBB 219, 341
   RK 20
   R 425
   5001
Blessing, Bert, see Gilroy, Frank D.
Blethyn, Brenda
   5001 842
Blier, Bernard
   WTLGD 454, 457
   5001 607, 719
Blier, Bertrand
   WTLGD 362, 454-464; dir., *Going Places*,
     182, 454-457, 458, 459, 461; *Get Out*
     Your Handkerchiefs, 454, 457, 458-462;
     Calmos (Femmes Fatales), 454,
     457-458, 461
   TIAI 50; dir., *Get Out Your Handkerchiefs*,
     50, 165
   SOTA 137, 328, 350; dir., *Going Places*, 49,
     137; *Get Out Your Handkerchiefs*, 328,
     350
   5001 241, 283, 290, 476
Blind Husbands
   5001
Bliss, Arthur
   ILIATM 117
   5001 61, 759
Bliss of Mrs. Blossom
   5001
Blithe Spirit
   5001
Blithedale Romance, The (book)
   SOTA 207
Blixen, Karen (pseud. Isak Dinesen)
   H 76-80
   5001 557
Blixen-Finecke, Baron Bror von
   H 77, 78, 79-80
Block, Lawrence
   H 155
   5001 213
Block, Libby

   5001 126
Blockade
   5001
Blocker, David
   H 392
   5001 448
Blonde Bombshell, see *Bombshell*
Blonde in Love, A, see *Loves of a Blonde*
Blonde Venus
   5001
Blondell, Joan
   KKBB 185, 273, 363
   GS 116
   DIM 345
   WTLGD 44
   TIAI 370
   H 228
   ML 44
   5001 184, 255, 291, 305, 525, 529, 602,
     705, 767, 781
Blondie
   TIAI 121
Blondie of the Follies
   5001 (2nd ed)
Blood and Roses (Et mourir de plaisir)
   KKBB 365
   5001 (2nd ed)
Blood and Sand
   KKBB 118
   DIM 45
   WTLGD 303
   5001
Blood Brother (book)
   KKBB 242
Blood of a Poet, The (Le Sang d'un poète)
   ILIATM 286, 289
   KKBB 239:n, 326, 365
   GS 187
   DIM 336
   R 338
   WTLGD 113
   5001
Blood Simple
   SOTA 323-326
   H 292
   5001 (2nd ed)
Bloodbrothers
   WTLGD 445-447, 495
   SOTA 201
   5001
Bloodhounds of Broadway
   SOTA 123
Bloods (gang)
   H 460, 461, 462
Bloody Kids (TV)
   H 120
Bloom, Claire
   ILIATM 13, 305
   KKBB 10-11
   GS 151-152
   WTLGD 282
   SOTA 77
   H 384, 388, 391
   ML 199 201-202
   5001 129, 132, 162, 321, 372, 423, 433-434,
     456, 628, 652, 851
Bloom, Verna

   H 39
   5001 9
Blore, Eric
   KKBB 288, 336
   5001 123, 253, 281, 294, 374, 404, 607,
     672, 685, 726
Blossier, Patrick
   5001 811
Blossom, Roberts
   WTLGD 322
   TIAI 118
   ML 198
   5001 139, 625
Blossoms in the Dust
   5001
Blotner, Joseph
   GS 10
Blount, Roy
   ML 327
Blow Monkeys (rock group)
   H 349
Blow Out
   TIAI 226-230
   SOTA 264
   H 320
   ML 172
   5001
Blow-Up
   KKBB 31-37
   GS 64, 121
   DIM 113, 114, 117, 197, 231
   R 370, 440, 451
   WTLGD 201, 373
   TIAI 227
   SOTA 32
   5001
"Blowin' in the Wind" (music)
   WTLGD 399
Blue Angel, The (Der Blaue Engel)
   KKBB 239-240:n, 264
   GS 264
   DIM 410
   WTLGD 37
   5001
Blue, Ben
   DIM 331
   R 130
   5001 36, 106, 256, 310, 333, 563, 647, 764
Blue Bird, The
   WTLGD 424
Blue Collar
   WTLGD 406-409, 415, 546
   TIAI 335
   5001
Blue Dahlia, The
   5001
"Blue Danube Waltz" (music)
   RK 62
Blue, David
   WTLGD 397, 399
Blue Hawaii
   TIAI 28
Blue, James
   KKBB 14; dir., *The Olive Trees of Justice*,
     14
Blue Lagoon, The
   TIAI 27-30

5001
Blue Max, The
  WTLGD 238
  5001
Blue, Monte
  5001 4, 7, 392, 421, 429, 468, 469, 553,
    591, 726
Blue Movie (book)
  R 28
Blue, Robert
  SOTA 352
Blue Thunder
  TIAI 485-486, 494
  H 349
  5001 (2nd ed)
Blue Velvet
  H 202-209, 306, 307, 462
  ML 82
  5001 (2nd ed)
Bluebeard's Eighth Wife
  5001
Blues Brothers, The
  TIAI 26-27
  SOTA 12, 193
  5001
Blues in the Night
  5001
Blum, Edwin
  5001 117, 200
Blum, Len
  TIAI 225
  5001 723
Blum, Mark
  5001 184
Blume in Love
  R 167, 186, 408, 411, 415, 416
  WTLGD 128, 130, 236, 377, 411, 412, 413
  TIAI 48
  ML 328
  5001 (2nd ed)
Blumenfeld, Alan
  H 282
  5001 773
Blundell, Graeme
  5001 21
Blunt, Wilfrid
  R 147
Blye, Maggie
  5001 703
Blyth, Ann
  ML 275
  5001 30, 108, 398, 480, 488
Blythe, Betty
  5001 340
Boam, Jeffrey
  H 336
  ML 148
  5001 362, 364, 718
Boardman, Eleanor (Mrs. King Vidor)
  RK 22 (ill.), 24
Boasberg, Al
  5001 160, 524
Boat, The, see *Das Boot*
Bob & Carol & Ted & Alice
  DIM 8-14, 225
  R 184
  WTLGD 128, 411

TIAI 320
ML 328
5001
Bob and Ray
  5001 39
Bobby, Anne Marie
  H 371
  5001 581
Bobby Deerfield
  WTLGD 302-304, 305
  5001
Bobo, The
  GS 158
  WTLGD 246
Boccaccio
  5001 89
Boccaccio '70
  5001
Bochner, Hart
  WTLGD 282
  TIAI 247
  5001 372, 627
Bock, Jerry
  DIM 333
  5001 242
Bodard, Mag
  5001 161
Bode, Ralf D.
  WTLGD 368
  TIAI 40
  5001 203, 612, 655, 687, 816
Bodeen, DeWitt
  5001 72, 125, 218, 351
Boderick, Matthew
  5001 823
Body and Soul
  WTLGD 489
  TIAI 107
Body Double
  SOTA 263-265
  H 228
  ML 64, 277
  5001 (2nd ed)
Body Heat
  TIAI 255-256, 321
  SOTA 3, 40, 202
  H 272
  5001
Body Snatcher, The
  R 149
"Body Snatcher, The" (story)
  WTLGD 523
Body, The (novella)
  H 197
Boehm, Sidney
  5001 70, 627
Boetticher, Budd
  KKBB 242; dir., *The Bullfighter and the
    Lady*, 242
  5001 83, 109, 748
Boffety, Jean
  R 270
  WTLGD 153, 550
  TIAI 423
  5001 111, 128, 450, 609, 758, 816
Bofors Gun, The
  DIM 89

Bogarde, Dirk
  ILIATM 203
  KKBB 106-107, 158
  GS 19, 23, 24, 210, 221
  DIM 86, 87
  R 147, 343, 344
  WTLGD 255-258
  TIAI 129
  5001 3, 169, 173, 180, 248, 349, 527, 541,
    601, 602, 662, 694, 814
Bogart, Humphrey
  ILIATM 118, 130, 211, 214, 293, 300
  KKBB 6, 61, 190, 218, 220, 223, 229, 235,
    236, 238, 245, 279, 304-305, 307, 359,
    361
  GS 109, 114, 260, 270
  DIM 71, 271, 413, 414
  R 184-186, 253, 262, 270, 348
  WTLGD 13, 26, 110-111, 122, 272, 275,
    281, 335, 466
  TIAI 33, 255, 387
  H 136, 137, 365-366
  ML 49, 257, 269
  5001 4, 8, 19, 27, 52, 56, 57, 67, 71, 76, 77,
    122, 172, 173, 177, 179, 220, 332, 358,
    391, 393, 401, 454, 466, 577, 634, 649,
    650, 705, 718, 750, 754, 767, 776, 788,
    809, 827
Bogart, Paul
  DIM 299; dir., *Skin Game*, 299-300, 426
  5001 116-117, 466, 685
Bogdanovich, Peter
  ILIATM 297, 303, 307-308
  DIM 293-296, 299, 431, 432; dir., *The Last
    Picture Show*, 293-297, 299, 353, 426;
    What's Up Doc?, 431-433
  R 163, 464-465, 466; dir., *The Last Picture
    Show*, 13, 161, 201, 411, 465-466;
    Paper Moon, 163, 466; *What's Up,
    Doc?*, 281, 466; *At Long Last Love*,
    463-466; *Daisy Miller*, 465
  WTLGD 248, 266; dir., *Nickelodeon*, 248,
    290, *Paper Moon*, 248; *What's Up,
    Doc?*, 248
  TIAI 42, 47; dir., *Saint Jack*, 42; *At Long
    Last Love*, 47; *What's Up, Doc?*, 240
  5001 37, 104, 409, 410, 523, 743, 830, 831
Boggs, Bill
  5001 230
Bohan, Marc
  SOTA 45
Bohème, La (opera)
  H 424
Böhm, Karl
  WTLGD 75
Bohnen, Roman
  5001 65, 108, 318, 533, 689, 718-719
Bohringer, Richard
  TIAI 328
  5001 193
Bois, Curt
  KKBB 296
  GS 103
  H 470
  5001 75, 122, 126, 304, 312, 654, 751, 841
Boisset, Yves
  R 207-209, 212, 214-215

5001 267
Boland, Brian
ML 161
Boland, Bridget
5001 29, 597
Boland, Mary
KKBB 363
GS 94
RK 17
5001 322, 355, 595, 647, 847
Bolero
KKBB 246
5001
"Bolero" (music)
TIAI 141, 196
Boles, John
5001 44, 265, 624, 713, 764
Boleslawski, Richard
5001 278, 337, 475, 483, 617, 752
Boleyn, Anne
DIM 95-97
Bolger, Ray
KKBB 185, 367
R 130
WTLGD 151-152, 472, 473
5001 304, 321, 641, 704, 736, 831
Bolkan, Florinda
DIM 221
R 452
WTLGD 50, 51, 312
5001 102, 169, 369, 411, 645
Bologna, Joseph
DIM 369-372
R 361
TIAI 395
SOTA 132, 133
5001 68, 80, 448, 508
Bolognini, Mauro
KKBB 237; dir., *Il Bell'Antonio*, 236-237
5001 62
Bolster, Anita
5001 326
Bolt, Robert
KKBB 11, 136-137, 154-155
DIM 189-192
R 110-113
WTLGD 158
TIAI 434
SOTA 184
5001 96, 195, 404, 414, 456, 648
Bolton, Guy
5001 32, 286, 848
Bombay Talkie
DIM 195-196
5001
Bombeck, Erma
ML 18
Bombshell (also known as *Blonde Bombshell*)
KKBB 341
RK 20
R 425
TIAI 338, 429
5001
Bonacci, Anna
5001 399
Bonacelli, Paolo
5001 479

Bonaffé, Jacques
SOTA 227
5001 246
Bonanova, Fortunio
RK 54
5001 7, 14, 83, 138, 198, 751, 832
Bond, Derek
5001 523
Bond, Edward
DIM 369
5001 85
Bond, Gary
DIM 415
5001 557
Bond, James (character)
KKBB 8, 189, 221
WTLGD 190, 207, 246, 525
Bond, Julian
DIM 312
SOTA 370, 373
5001 677
Bond, Lilian
5001 542, 829
Bond, Peter
DIM 350
Bond, Ralph
ILIATM 343
Bond, Sudie
TIAI 417
SOTA 109
5001 148, 681, 738
Bond, Ward
KKBB 276, 305
5001 205, 233, 259, 282, 301, 327, 373,
374, 433, 455, 464, 488, 608, 653, 662,
777, 809, 837, 860
Bondarchuk, Sergei
WTLGD 324
Bondi, Beulah
5001 294, 298, 374, 489, 496, 556, 575,
613, 683, 698, 787, 818, 824
Bone
R 260-261
5001
Bonerz, Peter
DIM 350
R 265
5001 126, 272
Bonet, Lisa
H 287
5001 27
Bonfire of the Vanities, The
ML 315-317
Bonham Carter, Helena
H 126
5001 640
Bonheur, Le
KKBB 168
WTLGD 341-342
H 152
Bonnaire, Sandrine
H 151, 152
5001 811
Bonnard, Pierre
H 331
Bonne Chance, see *Lucky Partners*
Bonnes Femmes, Les

DIM 54
5001
Bonnie and Clyde
KKBB 47-63
GS 79, 82, 105, 168, 194
DIM 6, 152, 170, 173, 212
R 12-13, 154, 161, 256, 270, 283, 309, 403,
441
WTLGD 52, 261, 431
TIAI 279, 281, 282, 284, 286, 295
SOTA 225, 248, 249
ML 191, 196, 198
5001
Bonnie Parker Story, The
KKBB 49
Bono, Sonny
H 443
5001 313
"Boogie Woogie Bugle Boy" (music)
TIAI 96
Book of Daniel, The (book)
SOTA 42
Booke, Sorrell
GS 52-53
DIM 432
R 201
5001 111, 244, 354, 808, 831
Bookwalter, DeVeren
5001 221
Boom Boom (stage)
WTLGD 12
Boom!
GS 171
DIM 407
WTLGD 95
Boomerang!
5001
Boone, Pat
KKBB 184
Boone, Richard
GS 278
DIM 49, 52, 105
5001 35, 526, 677, 851
Boorman, Charley
H 18, 19
5001 216
Boorman, John
KKBB 280; dir., *Point Blank*, 63; *Having a
Wild Weekend*, 280
GS dir., *Hell in the Pacific*, 272; *Point
Blank*, 166, 272
R 166, 237, 276-280; dir., *Deliverance*, 6,
166, 238, 300; *Zardoz*, 276-280; *Point
Blank*, 279
WTLGD 429; dir., *Deliverance*, 210, 513;
Exorcist II: The Heretic, 429
TIAI 182-187, 315, 482; dir., *Excalibur*,
182-187, 482; *Zardoz*, 184; *Exorcist II:
The Heretic*, 184, 185; *Deliverance*,
257; *Point Blank*, 315
H 18-21, 367-370; dir., *The Emerald Forest*,
18-21; *Excalibur*, 18; *Hope and Glory*,
367-370
5001 216, 227, 228, 321, 327, 340, 588, 863
Boorman, Katrine
TIAI 186
Boot, Das (The Boat)

5001 (2nd ed)
Booth, James
　5001 81, 866
Booth, Shirley
　5001 148
Boothe, Powers
　TIAI 258
　H 18, 20
　5001 216, 698
Borack, Carl
　5001 70
Borchers, Cornell
　5001 193
Border, The
　TIAI 300-302
　SOTA 120
　H 182
　5001
Boretz, Allen
　5001 640, 713
Borg, Veda Ann
　5001 44, 75, 340, 393
Borgeaud, Nelly
　WTLGD 355
　5001 461
Borges, Jorge Luis
　DIM 220, 273, 417
　R 234-235, 237
　WTLGD 259
　SOTA 18
　5001 701
Borgnine, Ernest
　KKBB 233
　GS 222
　DIM 74
　R 72, 357, 358
　WTLGD 41
　5001 6, 47, 126, 155, 269, 414, 417, 467,
　　554, 591, 838
Bori, Lucrezia
　WTLGD 11
Borland, Carol
　5001 466
Born Free
　KKBB 180-182
Born Losers
　DIM 342
　5001
Born, Max
　DIM 129
　5001 240
Born on the 4th of July
　ML 249-55, 261
　5001 (2nd ed)
Born to Dance
　5001
Born to Win
　DIM 314, 351-352, 402, 426
　R 357
　5001
Born Yesterday
　KKBB 240:n
　SOTA 84
　5001
Borodin, Aleksandr
　5001 398
Borradaile, Osmond

5001 756
Borrego, Jesse
　ML 101
Borsos, Phillip
　SOTA 27-31, 334-335; dir., *The Grey Fox*,
　　27-31; *The Mean Season*, 334-335
　5001 307, 472
Bortman, Michael
　ML 34, 37
　5001 295
Borzage, Frank
　ILIATM 198; dir., *Seventh Heaven*, 197; *A
　　Man's Castle*, 198
　WTLGD 215
　SOTA 307
　5001 69, 183, 335, 464, 675, 704, 718, 765
Bosch, Hieronymus
　DIM 261, 263
　WTLGD 301
　SOTA 188, 253
Bosco, Philip
　SOTA 204
　ML 13, 65
　5001 31, 202, 589, 733, 849
Bose, Lucia
　WTLGD 233
　5001 180, 240, 443
Bosoms and Neglect (stage)
　TIAI 175
Boss' Son, The
　SOTA 351
Bost, Pierre
　5001 187, 263, 620, 822-823
Boston Strangler, The
　GS 166-167
Boston White Sox, see White Sox
Bostonians, The
　SOTA 206-211
　5001 (2nd ed)
Bostwick, Barry
　WTLGD 501-504
　5001 501
Boswell, Connee
　TIAI 273
　5001 36
Boswell Sisters
　TIAI 275
Bosworth, Hobart
　5001 165, 387, 713, 845
Botkin, Perry
　5001 502
Botley, Betty
　5001 791
Botsford, Sara
　TIAI 421, 423, 427
　H 173
　5001 111, 416, 715
Botticelli, Sandro
　WTLGD 329
Bottin, Rob
　TIAI 193, 194
　5001 344, 759
Bottle Factory Outing, The (book)
　TIAI 425
　ML 47
Bottoms, Sam
　5001 863

Bottoms, Timothy
　DIM 295, 296, 353
　R 190-191, 466
　WTLGD 199, 461
　5001 410, 564
Boucher, Francois
　H 68
Boucher, Le
　DIM 403-405
　5001
Bouchet, Barbara
　5001 734
Boudet, Jacques
　5001 734
Boudu sauvé des eaux, see *Boudu Saved from
　Drowning*
*Boudu Saved from Drowning (Boudu sauvé des
　eaux)*
　KKBB 140-142, 343
　WTLGD 180, 455
　H 103
　5001
Bouise, Jean
　R 215
　5001 151, 310, 670, 700
Boulanger, Daniel
　5001 59, 100, 382, 676, 757
Boulevard Nights
　5001
Boulez, Pierre
　5001 720
Boulle, Pierre
　GS 36
　5001 102, 586
Boulting, Ingrid
　WTLGD 216-217, 495
　5001 411
Boulting, John
　ILIATM 64-65
　5001 104, 235, 357, 769
Boulting, Roy
　ILIATM 64-65
　GS 181
　5001 104, 235, 357, 752, 769
Bound for Glory
　WTLGD 224-230
　TIAI 1
　5001
Bounty, The
　SOTA 184-186
　H 54, 121
　5001 (2nd ed)
Bouquet, Carole
　WTLGD 365-366
　5001 256, 751
Bouquet, Michel
　DIM 54
　R 216
　5001 241, 267
*Bourgeois Gentilhomme, Le (The Would-Be
　Gentleman)*
　5001
Bourgoin, Jean
　5001 175, 388
Bourguignon, Serge
　5001 729
Bourne, Whitney

5001 162, 445
Bourneuf, Philip
　5001 35, 492
Bourseiller, Antoine
　5001 140
Bourvil
　KKBB 267
　5001 482
Bouton, Jim
　R 187
　5001 432
Boutsikaris, Dennis
　ML 113
　5001 202
Bouy, Stephane
　5001 403
Bovasso, Julie
　TIAI 49
　SOTA 36, 376
　H 154, 424
　5001 172, 496, 655, 712, 813, 840, 842
Bovo, Brunella
　KKBB 310, 368
　5001 483, 835
Bow, Clara
　ILIATM 138
　KKBB 253
　GS 127
　RK 13
　H 431
　5001 170, 566, 839
Bowden, Dorris
　KKBB 276
　5001 205, 301
Bowen, Catherine Drinker
　5001 504
Bowen, Roger
　5001 469
Bowens, Malick
　H 77, 80
　5001 557
Bower, Tom
　ML 85
　5001 792
Bowers, George
　ML 86
　5001 792
Bowers, Kenny
　5001 106
Bowers, William
　R 401
　5001 290, 523
Bowery Savings Bank
　DIM 320
Bowery to Broadway
　5001 (1st ed)
Bowie, David
　WTLGD 200-201
　TIAI 332
　SOTA 314, 349
　H 159, 160
　5001 3, 459
Bowker, Judi
　SOTA 371, 372
　5001 677
Bowles, Jane
　ML 301-306

Bowles, Paul
　KKBB 264
　ML 301-306
Bowles, Peter
　5001 85
Bowman, Lee
　WTLGD 20
　5001 159, 322, 351, 688, 825
Box, John
　GS 201
　5001 195, 543, 568
Box, Muriel
　KKBB 347
　5001 669, 794
Box, Sydney
　KKBB 347
　5001 669, 794
Boxcar Bertha
　R 174
Boy Friend, The
　DIM 379-383
　WTLGD 333, 503
　5001
Boy in the Plastic Bubble, The (TV)
　WTLGD 369
Boy Named Charlie Brown, A
　DIM 91-92
　5001
Boy with Green Hair, The
　WTLGD 125
Boyar, Charles
　5001 620
Boyar, Sully
　H 172
　5001 118, 197, 396-397, 463, 564
Boyce, Christopher
　SOTA 311-315
Boyd, Guy
　H 74-75
　ML 278
　5001 90, 561, 743, 771
Boyd, James
　RK 41
Boyd, Karin
　TIAI 338
　5001 477
Boyd, Russell
　SOTA 273, 292
　H 434
　5001 276, 333, 487, 691
Boyd, Stephen
　KKBB 156
　5001 63, 67, 237, 554, 670
Boyd, Tanya
　5001 381
Boyd, William (Stage)
　5001 139
Boyden, Peter
　TIAI 230
Boyens, Phyllis
　WTLGD 252
Boyer, Charles
　ILIATM 98
　KKBB 225, 244, 248, 249, 251, 267, 285
　GS 268
　DIM 26
　R 139, 417, 419-420

WTLGD 5, 8, 126, 194, 403
　TIAI 94, 357
　SOTA 55
　5001 14, 33, 34, 44, 52, 99, 123, 128, 143,
　　144, 152, 153, 209, 251, 278, 279, 318,
　　335, 343, 436, 450, 470, 471, 575, 712,
　　741, 778, 785
Boyer, François
　5001 257
Boyer, Myriam
　WTLGD 180
Boyl, Catherine
　5001 268, 794
Boyle, Peter
　R 120, 134-135, 404, 405
　WTLGD 132, 133-134, 543, 545
　TIAI 218
　ML 113-14
　5001 202, 269, 319, 558, 687, 713, 745,
　　786, 859
Boyle, Richard
　H 180, 182
　5001 651
Boyle, W. A. (Tony)
　WTLGD 249
Boys Choir of Harlem
　ML 260
　5001 288
Boys from Brazil, The
　WTLGD 451-454, 530
　TIAI 321
　5001
Boys from Syracuse, The
　TIAI 215
　5001
Boys from Syracuse, The (play)
　H 484
Boys in Company C, The
　5001
Boys in the Band, The
　GS 199
　DIM 137-138
　SOTA 347
　5001
"Bozo Barrett" (music)
　DIM 219
Bozzufi, Marcel
　DIM 65
　R 80, 215
　TIAI 166
　5001 114, 267, 358, 862
Brabin, Charles
　5001 469
Brabourne, John
　WTLGD 463
Bracco, Lorraine
　H 386, 387
　ML 114, 266-69
　5001 202, 297, 581, 692
Brach, Gérard
　TIAI 307
　H 330, 446
　ML 209, 211
　5001 57, 266, 379, 608, 624
Bracken, Eddie
　TIAI 396
　H 112

5001 313, 483, 727
Brackett, Charles
  KKBB 318, 354-355
  RK 12
  WTLGD 12
  5001 48, 87, 248, 258, 437, 453, 478, 490,
    522, 531, 730, 774, 776, 807
Brackett, Leigh
  R 187
  5001 214, 218, 432, 630, 631
Brackman, Jacob
  5001 396
Bradbury, Lane
  5001 15
Bradbury, Ray
  KKBB 147
  R 179
  5001 233, 490, 627
Bradford, Richard
  H 93
  5001 290, 473, 790, 808
Bradford, Roark
  5001 306
Bradley, Grace
  5001 32
Bradley, Omar
  DIM 99
  5001 570
Bradley, Paul
  DIM 171
  5001 290
Bradna, Olympe
  5001 697
Brady, Alice
  TIAI 166
  5001 106, 281, 291, 359, 509, 768, 860
Brady, Matthew
  GS 45, 194, 224
Brady, Ruth
  5001 141
Brady, Scott
  5001 490
Braga, Sonia
  H 25, 28
  5001 400
Bragg, Melvyn
  DIM 239, 242
  5001 504
Brahm, John
  5001 664
Brahms, Johannes
  DIM 172, 308
  5001 25, 366
Braine, John
  ILIATM 63
  5001 640
Braithwaite, E. R.
  5001 777
Brakhage, Stan
  ILIATM 318
Bramley, Bill
  5001 828
Branagh, Kenneth
  H 451
  ML dir., *Henry V.* 212-17
  5001 328, 332
Brancati, Vitaliano

KKBB 237
5001 62, 820
Branch, Houston
  5001 771
Brand, Christianna
  5001 306
Brand, Max, see Faust, Frederick
Brand, Neville
  DIM 147
  5001 74, 705
Brandauer, Klaus Maria
  TIAI 337, 338, 339
  H 77, 80
  5001 476, 557
Brandner, Gary
  TIAI 192
  5001 344
Brando, Jocelyn
  WTLGD 503
  TIAI 236
  5001 70, 492, 501, 802
Brando, Marlon
  ILIATM 45-46, 48, 51-53, 58, 62, 68, 82,
    131
  KKBB 58, 70, 151-152, 189-195, 196, 198,
    352, 366-367
  GS 33-34, 278
  DIM 175, 177-179, 249, 322, 422-423
  R 27-34, 120, 212-213, 315, 319, 355, 397,
    399, 400, 470
  WTLGD 24, 40, 134, 169, 178, 214, 215,
    286, 319, 320, 368-369, 424, 447, 492,
    527
  TIAI 109, 110, 172, 204, 227, 229, 298,
    322, 474
  SOTA 47, 149, 335, 377
  H 132, 316, 347
  ML 75, 184-85, 257
  5001 33, 110, 117, 132, 184, 205, 289, 311,
    410, 475, 505, 526, 528, 546, 549, 621,
    661, 722, 730, 745, 802, 818, 838, 839,
    859
Brandon, Henry
  5001 662
Brandon, Michael
  5001 627
Brandt, Bill
  TIAI 84
Braschi, Nicoletta
  5001 200
Brasselle, Keefe
  5001 585
Brassens, Georges
  5001 590
Brasseur, Claude
  KKBB 112
  5001 49, 230
Brasseur, Pierre
  ILIATM 7
  KKBB 237, 247, 332
  5001 62, 74, 133, 140, 190, 230, 441, 586,
    590
Bratby, John
  KKBB 282
  5001 341
Braugher, Andre
  ML 257-62

5001 288
Brault, Michel
  5001 510, 768
Braun, Wernher von, see Von Braun, Wernher
Brautigan, Richard
  DIM 230
Brave Bulls, The
  KKBB 120, 242
  5001
Brave New World (book)
  TIAI 19
Brazil
  H 106-110, 287
  ML 107, 109, 110, 111, 163
  5001 (2nd ed)
"Brazil" (music)
  H 106
Brazzi, Rossano
  KKBB 235, 354
  DIM 190
  5001 6, 52, 304, 727
Bread, Love, and Dreams
  DIM 362
Break of Hearts
  KKBB 241
  5001
Breakfast at Tiffany's
  ILIATM 140
  WTLGD 465
  5001
Breakfast Club, The
  SOTA 346-349
  H 135, 317
  5001 (2nd ed)
Breaking Away
  TIAI 8, 12-13, 169, 196, 285
  SOTA 309
  H 70
Breaking In
  ML 191-92
  5001 (2nd ed)
Breaking Point, The
  KKBB 360
Breaking the Sound Barrier (also known as *The
  Sound Barrier*)
  KKBB 240-241:n
  5001
Breathless (*À bout de souffle*)
  ILIATM 24, 32, 127-132, 148, 187,
    210-212, 215, 222, 312
  KKBB 17, 33, 54, 127, 129, 244, 262, 302
  GS 81, 84, 142
  R 201, 269, 303, 305
  WTLGD 169, 315, 456
  TIAI 101, 279
  SOTA 227
  5001
Brecher, Irving
  5001 37, 289, 726, 856
Brecht, Bertolt
  ILIATM 116
  KKBB 110
  GS 37, 83
  DIM 159, 161, 410
  WTLGD 139, 182, 301, 331
  TIAI 113, 450
  SOTA 366

31

H 158
ML 15
5001 670, 856
Breen, Bobby
DIM 358
Breen, Richard
5001 258, 490, 522, 774
Breen, Thomas
5001 632
Bregman, Martin
WTLGD 206, 207
5001 197, 521, 658
Brejchova, Hana
5001 441
Bremer, Lucille
TIAI 131
5001 856, 865
Brendel, El
5001 58, 387
Brennan, Eileen
DIM 296
R 464
TIAI 94
5001 37, 410, 598, 715
Brennan, Stephen
H 324
5001 211
Brennan, Walter
KKBB 233, 338, 360
R 186
WTLGD 282
TIAI 387
5001 47, 51, 273, 421, 473, 496, 533, 534,
554, 596, 620, 630, 717, 753, 771, 829
Brenner, Dori
R 224
WTLGD 130
5001 43, 521
Brenon, Herbert
KKBB 253; dir., Dancing Mothers, 253
5001 170
Brent, Evelyn
ILIATM 188
Brent, George
KKBB 290, 349
5001 173, 243, 262, 380, 543, 701, 778
Brent, Romney
KKBB 260
5001 7, 202
Brenton, Guy
5001 770
Breslin, Jimmy
WTLGD 493, 495
5001 277
Breslow, Lou
5001 254, 502
Bressart, Felix
KKBB 318
WTLGD 452
5001 75, 84, 224, 531, 591, 774, 843
Bresson, Henri Cartier, see Cartier-Bresson,
Henri
Bresson, Robert
ILIATM 7, 22; dir., The Trial of Joan of
Arc, 22; Diary of a Country Priest, 133
KKBB 259, 306, 349; dir., Diary of a
Country Priest, 259; A Man Escaped,

305-306, 349
GS 205; dir., Balthazar, 80
DIM 8, 307, 308; dir., A Man Escaped, 307
R 291
WTLGD 55, 102, 545
TIAI 78, 139, 189, 403; dir., Mouchette, 403
H 152
5001 38, 189, 264, 456, 499, 789
Brest, Martin
WTLGD 536-537; dir., Hot Tomorrows,
536-537; Going in Style, 537
SOTA 287-288
5001 66
Breuer, Bessie
5001 359
Breve Vacanza, Una, see A Brief Vacation
Brewster McCloud
DIM 227-228
R 80, 267, 270, 447-448
WTLGD 82, 548
SOTA 318
5001
Brialy, Jean-Claude
ILIATM 133-134
DIM 264, 266
R 363
5001 140, 159, 237, 537
Brian, David
KKBB 286
5001 66, 169, 249, 368
Brian, Mary
RK 13
5001 81, 159, 645, 817
Brian's Song (TV)
R 324
H 317
Brice, Fanny
GS 135, 136
RK 17
DIM 84
R 38, 457-463
WTLGD 140, 191
SOTA 294
5001 304, 865
Brickman, Marshall
R 242
TIAI 461-463; dir., Lovesick, 461-463;
Simon, 462
H dir., The Manhattan Project, 171-172
5001 441, 463, 686
Brickman, Paul
WTLGD 321
SOTA 39-41; dir., Risky Business, 39-41,
122
H 274
5001 139, 632
Brickson, Carl
5001 238
Bricusse, Leslie
DIM 39, 84, 196
WTLGD 528
TIAI 331
5001 297, 659, 814, 840
Bride Came C.O.D., The
5001
Bride Comes to Yellow Sky, The
5001

Bride of Frankenstein, The
ILIATM 7
WTLGD 211
H 464
5001
Bride Wore Black, The
GS 108, 275
DIM 243
Brideshead Revisited (book)
KKBB 300
Brideshead Revisited (TV)
SOTA 201
Bridge, The (Die Brücke)
5001
Bridge at Remagen, The
WTLGD 238
Bridge of San Luis Rey, The (book)
ILIATM 101:n
Bridge on the River Kwai, The
ILIATM 8
KKBB 136
TIAI 196
5001
Bridges, Alan
SOTA 330-333, 369-373; dir., The Return of
the Soldier, 330-333, 371; The Shooting
Party, 369-373
5001 626, 677
Bridges, Beau
DIM 74
R 13, 73, 167-168, 274
WTLGD 46, 321
SOTA 57, 80, 81
ML 186-90
5001 134, 232, 275, 323, 407
Bridges, James
5001 33, 44, 103, 480, 564, 809
DIM 157, 158; dir., The Baby Maker,
157-158
R 109, 190-194; dir., The Paper Chase,
190-194; The Baby Maker, 191
TIAI 16, 30-34; dir., The China Syndrome,
11, 16, 34, 163, 310, 495; Urban
Cowboy, 30-34, 42, 212, 229, 382
H 175-176, 457-460; dir., Mike's Murder,
175-176; Urban Cowboy, 176; The
China Syndrome, 243; Bright Lights,
Big City, 457-460
Bridges, Jeff
DIM 295
R 13, 166-168, 172, 199, 200-201, 310
WTLGD 46-49, 90, 92, 95, 235-239,
450-451, 512
SOTA 145, 146, 147, 306, 307
H 56, 57, 155, 156, 157, 244, 245, 352
ML 186-90
5001 10, 46, 167, 213, 232, 238, 325, 354,
377, 396, 407, 410, 498, 513, 615, 692,
710
Bridges, Lloyd
KKBB 183, 272, 281, 337
R 13
WTLGD 46
TIAI 51
ML 98
5001 12, 159, 289, 331, 614, 822
"Bridget Loves Bernie" (TV)

TIAI 91
Bridie, James
  5001 254, 565, 804
Brief Einer Unbekannten (book)
  KKBB 296
Brief Encounter (1946)
  KKBB 354
  DIM 291
  SOTA 280
  H 130
  5001
Brief Vacation, A (*Una Breve Vacanza*)
  R 452-453
  WTLGD 312
  5001
Brière, Daniel
  H 239
  5001 182
Briers, Richard
  ML 217
  5001 329
Brigadoon
  SOTA 139
  5001
Brighouse, Harold
  KKBB 282
  5001 336
Bright, John
  5001 94, 98, 672, 768
Bright Lights, Big City
  H 457-460
  5001 (2nd ed)
Bright, Richard
  R 402
  WTLGD 93, 174
  ML 312
  5001 139, 289, 290, 564, 569, 616
Brighton Beach Memoirs
  H 258-260
  5001 (2nd ed)
Brighton Rock (also known as *Young Scarface*)
  5001
Briley, John
  TIAI 434
  H 54, 55, 400
  5001 166, 277, 465
Brimley, Wilford
  TIAI 290
  SOTA 172, 235
  H 5, 6, 7
  5001 2, 144, 157, 518, 747, 759
Brimstone and Treacle
  H 52
Bring Me the Head of Alfredo Garcia
  WTLGD 114, 116
Bringing Up Baby
  ILIATM 81, 304
  KKBB 241:n
  GS 177
  DIM 431, 432
  R 440
  WTLGD 3, 8, 16, 17, 18, 29
  TIAI 98, 429
  H 228
  5001
Brinig, Myron
  5001 683

Brink, André
  ML 185
  5001 205
Brink of Life (*Nära Livet*)
  ILIATM 15
  5001
Brisbane, Arthur
  WTLGD 373
Briskin, Mort
  R 286
  5001 822
Brissac, Virginia
  5001 494, 578, 618, 722, 726
Brisson, Carl
  5001 502
Bristow, Gwen
  5001 778
Bristowe, Tania
  SOTA 242
  5001 810
Britt, Mai
  5001 85, 859
Britton, Pamela
  5001 25, 356
Britton, Tony
  5001 10, 728
Brix, Herman, see Bennett, Bruce
Broadbent, Jim
  H 283
  5001 294
Broadcast News
  H 416-420
  5001 (2nd ed)
Broadhurst, Kent
  TIAI 463
  5001 442
Broadway Danny Rose
  SOTA 122-125
  5001 (2nd ed)
Broadway Melody (1929)
  5001
Broadway Melody of 1936
  5001 (2nd ed)
Broadway Melody of 1938
  5001
Broadway Melody of 1940
  5001
Broadway Rhythm
  5001
Broadway to Hollywood
  5001
Broccoli, Albert R.
  5001 189, 257, 496, 539, 545, 703
Brock, Louis
  5001 253
Brock, Ray
  5001 253
Brock, Stanley
  H 280
  5001 773
Brockman, John
  GS 185
Broderick, Helen
  5001 611
Broderick, James
  5001 197, 309
Broderick, Matthew

TIAI 493, 494
  SOTA 356, 358, 359
  ML 256-62
  5001 288, 406
Brodeur, Paul
  TIAI 68
  5001 724
Brodine, Norbert
  5001 92, 157, 247, 294, 399, 760
Brodney, Oscar
  5001 287
Brodsky, Jack
  5001 427
Brodsky, Joseph
  SOTA 155
Brogi, Giulio
  5001 701
Broken Arrow
  KKBB 180, 184, 241-242:n
  5001
Broken Blossoms
  ILIATM 282
  GS 45, 46
  5001
Broken Lullaby (originally called *The Man I Killed*)
  5001
Broken Noses
  ML 122, 124
Brolin, James
  R 217
  WTLGD 140-143
  5001 275, 573, 829
Brolin, Josh
  5001 298
Bromberg, J. Edward
  5001 405, 466, 579, 718
Bromley, Sydney
  5001 201
Bron, Eleanor
  DIM 10, 141
  H 131
  5001 14, 59, 60, 795, 799, 847
Bronco Billy
  SOTA 238
Bronenosets Potyomkin, see *Potemkin*
Bronson, Betty
  5001 63
Bronson, Charles
  KKBB 344
  WTLGD 40-41, 268
  TIAI 11, 25, 384
  SOTA 238, 361
  H 343
  5001 269, 318, 452, 569, 653
Bronson, Emerick
  DIM 252
  5001 604
Brontë, Emily
  5001 851
Brontë sisters, Charlotte, Emily, and Anne
  DIM 139
  WTLGD 58-59, 145
Bronze Horseman, The (book)
  SOTA 250
Brood, The
  TIAI 192

H 210
Brook, Claudio
GS 258
5001 481, 625, 682, 818
Brook, Clive
KKBB 298, 323-324; dir., *On Approval*, 30, 323-324
GS 114
5001 127, 263, 424, 544, 545, 566, 671, 744
Brook, Peter
ILIATM 119, 131; dir., *The Beggar's Opera*, 116-119
DIM 354-357; dir., *Marat/Sade*, 242, 355; *King Lear*, 354-357
R 220
SOTA 237; dir., *Marat/Sade*, 252
5001 61, 396, 734
Brooke, Eleanor
5001 750
Brooke, Hillary
5001 218
Brooke, Tyler
5001 792
Brooke, Walter
5001 407
Brookes, Jacqueline
R 349
5001 276
Brooks, Albert
WTLGD 133
TIAI 93
SOTA 19, 154, 343-346; dir., *Lost in America*, 343-346; *Real Life*, 344; *Modern Romance*, 344
H 416, 419
5001 104, 436, 598, 745, 797, 806
Brooks, Amy
ML 136
5001 656
Brooks, Donald
GS 164
5001 706
Brooks, Elisabeth
TIAI 193
5001 343
Brooks, Geraldine
5001 591
Brooks, Hadda
5001 359
Brooks, James L.
SOTA 93-97; dir., *Terms of Endearment*, 93-97, 246, 338
H 416-420; dir., *Terms of Endearment*, 76, 200, 300, 416, 418; *Broadcast News*, 416-420
5001 104, 748
Brooks, Joseph
5001 857
Brooks, Louise
RK 13
H 229
5001 116, 563
Brooks, Mel
GS 66-68
DIM 180, 226; dir., *The Twelve Chairs*, 180, 226; *The Producers*, 348
R 130-131, 280-282, 349, 404-405; dir.,

Blazing Saddles, 280-282, 311-312, 321, 405; *The Producers*, 281, 370, 404; *The Twelve Chairs*, 281, 405; *Young Frankenstein*, 403-405
WTLGD 99-100, 371-376, 505; dir., *Young Frankenstein*, 99-100, 371, 373, 375; *Silent Movie*, 246, 371, 373-375, 505; *Blazing Saddles*, 247, 371, 375, 448, 508; *High Anxiety*, 371-376, 448; *The Twelve Chairs*, 375; *The Producers*, 375
TIAI 91, 214-217, 323, 394, 396; dir., *High Anxiety*, 38, 461; *History of the World--Part I*, 214-217; *Young Frankenstein*, 215, 224
SOTA 111, 112, 287; dir., *Young Frankenstein*, 2, 287; *Blazing Saddles*, 146
H 69, 291, 302, 379; dir., *Young Frankenstein*, 69
ML 17
5001 80, 81, 330, 335, 600, 601, 774, 775, 795, 859
Brooks, Phyllis
5001 360, 672, 717
Brooks, Randy
H 156
5001 213
Brooks, Ray
5001 401
Brooks, Richard
KKBB 253, 285, 334; dir., *Elmer Gantry*, 285; *The Professionals*, 334
DIM dir., *The Happy Ending*, 148, *Blackboard Jungle*, 152; *The Professionals*, 229
WTLGD 21, 316-320; dir., *Crisis*, 21; *Blackboard Jungle*, 129, 554, 558, 559; *Looking for Mr. Goodbar*, 316-320, 446, 447; *In Cold Blood*, 318
5001 79, 108, 125, 126, 143, 164, 197, 215, 317, 391, 434, 601, 734, 835
Brooks Wilson Ltd. (book)
DIM 121
Brophy, Edward
5001 11, 101, 134, 159, 170, 226, 266, 293, 303, 445, 555, 686, 758, 836
Bror von Blixen-Finecke, Baron, see Blixen-Finecke, Baron Bror von
Brosse, Simon de la
SOTA 38
Brother Blue
TIAI 200
5001 401
"Brother, Can You Spare a Dime?" (music)
DIM 222
Brother from Another Planet, The
H 213
Brother Sun and Sister Moon (projected)
DIM 182-183
Brotherhood, The
GS 243-247
Brothers, Dr. Joyce
SOTA 129
5001 431
Brothers Karamazov, The (book)
ILIATM 237
KKBB 57

SOTA 89
Broun, Heywood
RK 10
Brower, Otto
5001 206
Brown, Ada
5001 716
Brown, Barry
R 13
Brown, Blair
TIAI 128, 131, 254, 255
5001 20, 154
Brown, Bryan
H 116, 117
ML 6-7
5001 273, 298
Brown, Carlos
TIAI 260
5001 698
Brown, Christy
ML 178-82
Brown, Clarence
KKBB 285-286, 316; dir., *Anna Christie*, 56, 243, 285; *Anna Karenina*, 56, 285; *National Velvet*, 180, 185, 285, 316; *The Yearling*, 180, 185, 285-286; *Intruder in the Dust*, 283-286; *Last of the Mohicans*, 285; *The Eagle*, 285; *The Goose Woman*, 285; *Flesh and the Devil*, 285; *A Woman of Affairs*, 285; *Inspiration*, 285; *A Free Soul*, 285, 343; *Possessed*, 285; *Emma*, 285; *Letty Lynton*, 285; *Night Flight*, 285; *Ah, Wilderness!*, 285; *Wife Versus Secretary*, 285; *Conquest*, 285; *Idiot's Delight*, 285; *The Rains Came*, 285; *Edison the Man*, 285; *The Human Comedy*, 285; *Song of Love*, 285, 353
RK 22 (ill.)
5001 11, 28, 128, 153, 251, 266, 344, 354, 368, 517, 834, 837, 845, 855
Brown, David
5001 378, 715, 726, 743, 813
Brown, Dwier
5001 242
Brown, Eleanora
5001 801
Brown, Georg Stanford
WTLGD 267
5001 109
Brown, Georgia
WTLGD 190
5001 248, 667
Brown, Harry
KKBB 331-332
5001 214, 459, 584, 821
Brown, Helen Gurley
DIM 283
R 322
Brown, Irene
5001 605
Brown, James
TIAI 26
5001 11, 88
Brown, Janet
5001 257
Brown, Jim

GS 183, 185, 223
R 62, 352
WTLGD 36, 417
TIAI 325
5001 244, 631
Brown, Joe E.
  KKBB 348
  R 129
  SOTA 171, 359
  H 249
  5001 336, 547, 679, 691
Brown, John Moulder
  DIM 162, 163
  5001 246
Brown, Johnny Mack
  5001 62, 845
Brown, Karl
  5001 367
Brown, Les
  5001 537
Brown, Lew
  5001 296, 387
Brown, Nacio Herb
  WTLGD 79
  5001 105, 683
Brown, Olivia
  5001 261
Brown, Pamela
  GS 171
  R 111
  5001 349, 443, 628, 741
Brown, Reb
  SOTA 117
  5001 804
Brown, Rowland
  5001 27, 463, 830
Brown, Ruth
  H 443
  5001 313
Brown, Steve
  5001 351
Brown, Timothy
  5001 516
Brown, Tom
  5001 360, 472
Brown, Vanessa
  5001 46, 284, 327
Browne, Coral
  GS 207, 208
  H 51, 52
  5001 202, 417, 637
Browne, Leslie
  WTLGD 343-347
  5001 794
Browne, Roscoe Lee
  DIM 80, 392
  H 173
  5001 138, 153, 160, 416, 781, 798, 809
Browne, Sam
  TIAI 276
Browning, Elizabeth Barrett
  WTLGD 159
Browning, Ricou
  5001 161
Browning, Tod
  ILIATM 6: dir., *Dracula*, 6
  KKBB 39: dir., *Freaks*, 39

5001 186, 201, 266, 367, 466, 807
Browning Version, The
  KKBB 107
  DIM 38
  5001
Brownlow, Kevin
  TIAI 143
  5001 516
Broyard, Anatole
  ML 319
Brubaker
  TIAI 20-25
  SOTA 217
  H 292
  5001
Bruce, Cheryl Lynn
  ML 241
Bruce, David
  5001 136, 406
Bruce, Lenny
  ILIATM 201
  DIM 256, 382
  R 371-376
  WTLGD 142
  TIAI 324
  SOTA 11
  H 147, 280
  ML 18
  5001 417
Bruce, Nigel
  KKBB 341
  WTLGD 191
  SOTA 373
  5001 59, 130, 155, 228, 312, 341, 423, 618,
    645, 659, 672, 732, 787
Bruce, Virginia
  RK 20
  5001 93, 278, 305, 393
Brücke, Die, see *The Bridge*
Brucker, Jane
  H 346
  5001 190
Bruckheimer, Jerry
  5001 66, 780
  H 168
Bruckman, Clyde
  5001 281, 459
Bruckner, Anton
  WTLGD 238, 513
Bruegel, Peter, see Brueghel, Pieter, the elder
Brueghel, Pieter, the elder
  DIM 248
  WTLGD 327
Bruhn, Erik
  5001 317
Bruhns, Werner
  WTLGD 330
Brulatour, Jules
  RK 67
Brundin, Bo
  R 467
  5001 304
Brundin, Lena
  5001 525
Brunel, Christopher
  ILIATM 344-345
Brunius, Jacques

5001 10, 21, 552
Bruno der Schwarze
  WTLGD 52
Bruno S.
  WTLGD 52-53, 55
  5001 512
Brunoy, Blanchette
  5001 66, 140, 465
Bruns, Philip
  5001 320, 156, 304
Brush, Katherine
  5001 464, 620
Brustein, Robert
  R 74
Brut
  WTLGD 27
Brute Force
  DIM 63
  5001
Bryan, Dora
  ILIATM 199
  KKBB 277
  5001 306
Bryan, Jane
  KKBB 307
  5001 208, 393, 466, 543, 683, 686
Bryan, John
  5001 114, 302, 543
Bryan, William Jennings
  KKBB 207
Bryant, Baird
  5001 155
Bryant, Charles
  5001 650
Bryant, Chris
  R 234
Bryant, Jim
  5001 828
Bryant, Marie
  5001 754
Bryant, Michael
  DIM 369
Bryant, Nana
  5001 474
Bryceland, Yvonne
  H 476
  5001 849
Bryne, Barbara
  SOTA 210
  5001 94
Brynner, Yul
  DIM 26
  R 217
  WTLGD 334
  TIAI 250, 382
  SOTA 38
  H 68
  5001 28, 123, 450, 452, 747, 829
Bryson, John
  ML 32
  5001 166
Brzeska, Henri Gaudier, see Gaudier-Brzeska,
    Henri
Brzeska, Sophie
  R 48, 52
Bubbles (John William Sublett)
  5001 112

Bubbles, John W.
GS 102
SOTA 296
Buchan, John
KKBB 359
5001 761
Buchanan, Edgar
KKBB 347
5001 345, 575, 661, 671, 742, 780
Buchanan, Jack
ILIATM 65
KKBB 234
WTLGD 6
5001 49, 268
Buchanan, James D.
5001 317
Buchanan, Lucianne
TIAI 389, 391
5001 746
Bücher, Georg
WTLGD 51
Buchheim, Lothar-Günther
5001 92
Buchholz, Horst
5001 151, 304, 452, 550
Buchman, Sidney
KKBB 68-81, 87-88, 91, 95-97
5001 309, 329, 336, 343, 489, 559, 680,
742, 752
Büchner, Georg
ILIATM 277
H 61
Bucholz, Horst
ILIATM 66, 151
KKBB 251
Büchse der Pandora, Die, see *Pandora's Box*
Buck and Bubbles
SOTA 294, 296
Buck and the Preacher
WTLGD 67
Buck, Pearl S.
5001 201, 293
Buckeraroo Banzai, see *The Adventures of Buckaroo Banzai*
Buckley, Betty
TIAI 480
H 446
5001 31, 265, 747
Buckley, William F. Jr.
KKBB 213
DIM 297
Buckner, Robert
5001 152, 653, 853
Bucquet, Harold S.
5001 201, 843
"Buddy Deane Show" (TV)
H 443-444
Buddy Holly Story, The
SOTA 98
Budge, Don
5001 569
Buetel, Jack
5001 558
Buffalo Bill and the Indians
WTLGD 261, 274, 275, 284, 285, 441-442,
550
TIAI 264

Bugs Bunny
WTLGD 220, 303
Bugsy Malone
WTLGD 163-165
TIAI 290
5001
Bujold, Geneviève
KKBB 164
DIM 95-97, 206, 301-302
R 386-387
WTLGD 169, 183, 184, 390, 394-395
TIAI 253
SOTA 239, 289
H 136
5001 5, 12, 28, 136, 147, 209, 310, 371,
502, 757, 771, 791
Bujones, Fernando
WTLGD 347
Bukowski, Charles
TIAI 104, 466, 467
H 383-385, 463, 465
5001 51, 439, 742
Bull Durham
H 480-482
ML 143, 222, 224
5001 (2nd ed)
Bull, Peter
5001 9, 36, 543, 649
Bullfight
5001
Bullfighter and the Lady, The
KKBB 242:n
5001
Bullitt
GS 165-166
DIM 162, 316, 402
R 161, 260, 318
5001
Bullock, Walter
5001 278
Buloff, Joseph
5001 681
Bumstead, Henry
5001 777
Bundy, Ted
H 260
Bunker, Edward
5001 718
Bunker, Robert
R 87
Bunnage, Avis
5001 229, 832
Bunny, John
WTLGD 9
Bunting, Garland
ML 224
5001 80
Buntline, Ned
TIAI 212
Buñuel, Luis
ILIATM 11, 17, 253, 287, 289, 290, 340;
dir., *The Exterminating Angel*, 11;
Viridiana, 15, 17; *Los Olvidados*, 285,
340; *Un Chien Andalou* (with Dali),
286, 290
KKBB 23, 43, 60, 118, 176, 228-229, 261,
300, 322-323; dir., *El*, 23, 261, *L'Age*

d'Or, 43; *Land Without Bread*, 118; *The
Adventures of Robinson Crusoe*,
228-229; *Los Olvidados*, 322-323
GS 7, 139, 254-262, 284; dir., *Belle de Jour*,
125, 254, 257; *Un Chien Andalou*, 257;
Diary of a Chambermaid, 258, 261; *The
Exterminating Angel*, 255; *Land Without
Bread*, 260; *Nazarin*, 255, 258 261;
Simon of the Desert, 255-262; *Viridiana*,
255, 256, 258, 260
RK 14
DIM 102-103, 128, 258, 263, 307, 336, 337,
363, 376; dir., *The Milky Way*, 102-103;
L'Age d'Or, 336; *Los Olvidados*, 376
R 41-43, 93, 362-363, 475; dir., *The
Discreet Charm of the Bourgeoisie*,
41-43, 93, 363; *The Exterminating
Angel*, 41; *The Milky Way*, 42; *Le
Fantôme de la Liberté*, 362-363
WTLGD 54, 180, 211, 293, 363-367, 431,
455; dir., *Belle de Jour*, 126, 365; *The
Discreet Charm of the Bourgeoisie*, 180,
293, 363-365; *That Obscure Object of
Desire*, 363-367; *Le Fantôme de la
Liberté*, 364; *Un Chien Andalou*, 436
TIAI 38, 104, 148, 217, 421; dir., *Un Chien
Andalou*, 148; *Los Olvidados*, 250
H 61, 63, 68, 180, 468
ML 23; dir., *The Adventures of Robinson
Crusoe*, 117
5001 8, 10, 132, 162, 187, 191, 213, 237,
440, 481, 518, 543, 682, 683, 751, 781,
851
Buono il Brutto il Cattivo, Il, see *The Good, the
Bad and the Ugly*
Buono, Victor
5001 346, 681
Burchill, Andrea
H 408
5001 342
Burden of Dreams
TIAI 404, 406-407
5001 (2nd ed)
Burdick, Eugene
5001 802
Burel, Léonce-Henry (L.-H.)
KKBB 259, 306
5001 190, 456, 789
Burge, Stuart
5001 555
Burgess, Anthony
DIM 373-376
R 347
TIAI 308
H 160
5001 141, 608
Burgess, Dorothy
5001 336
Burgess, Guy
SOTA 311
Burghers of Calais, The
TIAI 267
Burghof, Gary
5001 469
Burke, Billie
KKBB 369
DIM 341

WTLGD 473
5001 59, 72, 137, 240, 259, 370, 459, 753, 781, 782, 859
Burke, Edwin
5001 763
Burke, Johnny
5001 152
Burke, Kathleen
5001 429
Burke, Paul
5001 763
Burke, Simon
TIAI 267
Burkley, Dennis
H 454
5001 567
Burks, Robert
5001 220
Burman, Ben Lucien
5001 713
Burmese Harp, The
ILIATM 161, 226
Burmester, Leo
5001 68
Burn! (Queimada!)
DIM 175-180
R 210, 212, 214, 315
SOTA 74
5001
Burne-Jones, Edward
WTLGD 552
Burnet, Dana
5001 678
Burnett, Carol
ILIATM 26
GS 40, 58
DIM 251
R 84-87, 424, 426, 429
WTLGD 164, 409, 444, 504, 505, 506
TIAI 80, 290, 343
H 1
5001 29, 270, 577, 616, 824
Burnett, Murray
5001 122
Burnett, Russell
H 240
Burnett, W. R.
KKBB 368
5001 37, 425, 657, 761, 836
Burns, Allan
H dir., *Just Between Friends*, 150-151
5001 386
Burns, George
R 131
WTLGD 76-77, 79, 505
TIAI 471
H 187
5001 501, 541, 730, 828
Burns, Jack
5001 528
Burns, Marion
5001 472
Burns, Mark
5001 180
Burns, Michael
5001 750
Burns, Robert E.

5001 348
Burr, Raymond
5001 7, 585
Burridge, Richard
H 159
5001 3
Burroughs, Edgar Rice
WTLGD 52, 111
TIAI 208
SOTA 147-148, 149
5001 308, 744
Burroughs, Jackie
SOTA 29, 30
5001 308
Burroughs, William S.
ILIATM 238
DIM 173
TIAI 361
ML 197-98
5001 130, 205
Burrows, Abe
5001 113, 311, 691
Burstall, Tim
5001 21
Burstyn, Ellen
DIM 225, 227, 296
R 248, 251, 408, 410, 414
WTLGD 255, 258-259, 505-507
TIAI 117, 118
H 75, 76
5001 13, 15, 228, 320, 396, 410, 601, 624, 625, 651, 791, 796
Burton, Julianne
WTLGD 387
Burton, Norman
R 117
5001 655
Burton, Richard
ILIATM 69
KKBB 343-344
GS 9, 34, 40-41, 224
DIM 37, 91, 95
R 115
WTLGD 337, 339, 429
TIAI 11, 184
5001 28, 37, 117, 194, 223, 228, 433, 526, 653, 805, 845, 851
Burton, Tim
H 58-61, 455-457; dir., *Pee-wee's Big Adventure*, 58-61, 456; *Beetlejuice*, 455-457
ML dir., *Batman*, 158-64, 299; *Beetlejuice*, 112, 159, 161, 299, 301; *Edward Scissorhands*, 298-301; *Pee-wee's Big Adventure*, 159, 184, 299
5001 54, 61, 573
Burton, Wendell
DIM 33-34
5001 714
Burtt, Ben
WTLGD 523
Burum, Stephen H.
SOTA 119-120, 264
H 321
ML 172
5001 90, 124, 213, 804, 808
Bus-Fekete, L.

5001 33, 326
Bus Stop
DIM 29, 371
Busboys, The (group)
TIAI 438
5001 261
Buscemi, Steve
ML 101
Busch, Mae
5001 195, 255
Busch, Niven
5001 206, 360, 592, 829
Busey, Gary
R 166
WTLGD 242
TIAI 11, 244, 371, 372
5001 51, 121, 407, 707, 718
Busey, Jacob
5001 718
Bush, Billy Green
R 408
5001 261
Bushell, Anthony
5001 528, 659
Bushman, Francis X.
5001 63, 649
Busia, Akosua
H 82
5001 147
Bussières, Raymond
KKBB 246
WTLGD 182
5001 383, 590
Butch Cassidy and the Sundance Kid
DIM 5-7, 149, 173, 401, 402
R 98, 162, 244, 282, 318, 468
WTLGD 173, 273, 517
TIAI 437
SOTA 177
5001
Bute, Mary Ellen
5001 568
Butler, Bill
5001 12, 73, 378
Butler, David
KKBB 368; dir., *Straight, Place, and Show*, 6; *Where's Charley?* 185, 234, 367-368; *Calamity Jane*, 185, 234
5001 114, 387, 582, 596, 633, 718, 750, 819, 831
Butler, Frank
5001 633
Butler, George
5001 602
Butler, Hugo
5001 417, 698
Butler, Michael
WTLGD 380
H 15, 16, 17
5001 280, 562
Butler, Samuel
H 127
Buttercup Chain, The
5001
Butterfield 8
ILIATM 42
R 44

5001
Butterfield, Billy
5001 662
Butterfield, Paul
5001 411
Butterflies Are Free
R 434
Butterworth, Charles
5001 97, 259, 337, 452, 496, 662, 762
Buttons, Red
KKBB 278
DIM 69
R 71, 432
WTLGD 502
5001 275, 319, 501, 550, 591, 755
Buzby, Zane
WTLGD 449
5001 808
Buzzell, Edward (Eddie)
5001 37, 64, 289, 675
By Design
TIAI 421-424
5001 (2nd ed)
Bye Bye Birdie
5001
"Bye, Bye, Blackbird" (music)
TIAI 74
Bye Bye Braverman
GS 52, 53
5001
Byington, Spring
KKBB 288, 290, 341
DIM 284
5001 11, 130, 186, 196, 218, 306, 326, 356,
    374, 380, 428, 439, 443, 473, 505, 507,
    645, 752
Byrds, The (group)
5001 210
Byrne, Bobby
WTLGD 407
5001 109
Byrne, Catherine
H 334
5001 211
Byrne, David
SOTA 265-267
H 215-219, 232; dir., *True Stories*, 215-219
5001 408, 693, 716, 793, 794
Byrne, Eddie
5001 193
Byrne, Gabriel
TIAI 183
H 278
5001 183
Byrnes, Edd (Kookie)
H 461
5001 709
Byron, Arthur
5001 123, 253, 501, 542, 796, 836
Byron, George Gordon, Lord
R 112
H 451
Byrum, John
WTLGD 61, 156-157; dir., *Inserts*, 156-157
5001 365, 453, 617

C

C.I.A.
WTLGD 42, 113, 386-387
Caan, James
DIM 312, 422, 423
R 133-134, 259, 351, 457, 461-462
WTLGD 115-118, 485-488
TIAI 188, 190
H 303, 304, 305, 306
5001 137, 148, 214, 266, 272, 276, 277,
    279, 289, 290, 393, 613, 686, 755, 756,
    786
Cabaret
DIM 409-413, 426, 430
R 187, 204, 241, 277, 327, 372,459-460,
    462-463
WTLGD 151, 389, 525
ML 286
5001
Cabin in the Cotton
5001
Cabin in the Sky
KKBB 234
GS 102
5001
Cabinet of Dr. Caligari, The (*Das Kabinett des
    Dr. Caligari*)
KKBB 242-243:n, 310, 317, 367
RK 76
R 80, 367
WTLGD 550
TIAI 401
SOTA 21
ML 299
5001
Cabot, Bruce
KKBB 43, 184
WTLGD 235
5001 26, 124, 189, 234, 248, 273, 608, 851
Cabot, Sebastian
KKBB 340
5001 21, 376, 398, 639, 773
Cabot, Susan
5001 220
Cabrel, Francis
H 419
Caceres, Ernie
5001 552
Cacoyannis, Michael
KKBB 160, 270-271, 351; dir., *Zorba the
    Greek*, 160; *A Girl in Black*, 270-271,
    351; *Stella*, 271, 351
DIM 246, 300-305; dir., *Zorba the Greek*,
    35, 246; *Stella*, 246; *The Trojan
    Women*, 300-305
WTLGD 378-379
5001 214, 286, 370, 713, 791, 866
Cactus Flower
DIM 104, 233
5001
Caddie
TIAI 158-160
5001
Cadell, Jean

5001 349, 449, 605, 771
Cadillac, Rita
5001 282
Cady, Frank
5001 4
Caesar, Adolph
SOTA 271-272
H 189
5001 143, 147, 690
Caesar and Cleopatra
5001
Caesar, Arthur
5001 463
Caesar, Sid
GS 66
R 127-132, 364, 467
TIAI 216, 394, 395
5001 12, 310, 335, 508, 747
Cage, The (stage)
H 381
Cage aux folles, La
TIAI 163, 165
ML 90
Cage aux folles II, La
TIAI 164-167
5001
Cage, Nicolas
SOTA 151, 152, 153, 295, 297, 316, 318
H 219, 220, 291-292, 423
ML 150-52
5001 74, 156, 496, 573, 610, 615, 812
Caged
DIM 106
Caged Heat
WTLGD 322
H 232
Cagney, James
ILIATM 62, 150, 152, 154
KKBB 51, 190
GS 97,243
DIM 374
R 59, 187, 272
WTLGD 5, 133, 296, 537
TIAI 241 263, 265
SOTA 103
ML 114, 214
5001 27, 101, 208, 242, 255, 439, 457, 488,
    550, 582, 602, 612, 634, 692, 760, 782,
    834, 853
Cagney, Jeanne
5001 198, 458, 853
Cahan, Abraham
WTLGD 79
Cahiers du Cinema (periodical)
KKBB 360
Cahn, Sammy
5001 25, 714
Caida, La, see *The Fall*
Cain and Mabel
RK 32
Cain, James M.
KKBB 333
R 472
WTLGD 261
TIAI 178, 179, 181, 182, 412
SOTA 323
H 328, 469

5001 14, 198, 312, 480, 592
Caine, Georgia
  5001 157
Caine, Michael
  KKBB 10
  DIM 248-249, 405, 406, 408
  R 76-77
  WTLGD 93, 94, 107-111, 529-532
  TIAI 36, 38, 326, 327
  SOTA 83, 84-85, 132, 133
  H 113, 114-115, 162, 163, 165, 166, 167
  ML 74-77
  5001 13, 72, 80, 115, 181, 191, 203, 212,
      276, 282, 316, 370, 393, 411, 452, 461,
      493, 638, 686, 735, 837, 852
Caine Mutiny, The
  KKBB 203
Caine, Shakira
  5001 461
Calamity Jane
  KKBB 185, 234
  5001 (2nd ed)
Calcutta
  DIM 309
  TIAI 434
  5001
Calder-Marshall, Anna
  5001 851
Calderon, Paul
  5001 606
Caldwell, Anne
  5001 253
Caldwell, Erskine
  5001 777
Caldwell, Zoe
  SOTA 337, 338
  5001 604
Cale, John
  H 232
  5001 693
Calhern, Louis
  KKBB 320
  5001 30, 37, 79, 157, 206, 326, 536, 796
Calhoun, Rory
  ILIATM 45
  5001 771
Cali, Joseph
  5001 655
California Split
  R 350, 351, 424, 447
  WTLGD 30, 202, 276, 442
  H 1, 2
California Suite
  WTLGD 529-533
  H 243
  ML 201
  5001
Caligula
  WTLGD 498
Call, Ed
  R 285
  5001 822
Call Me Madam
  5001
"Call Me" (music)
  TIAI 336
Callaghan, Morley

WTLGD 280
Callahan, Duke
  5001 656
Callahan, Gene
  5001 22, 272
Callahan, James
  DIM 126
  5001 791
Callan, Michael
  KKBB 29-30
  5001 124
Callas, Charlie
  TIAI 215
  5001 331
Callas, Maria
  TIAI 328
  SOTA 378
Calleia, Joseph
  KKBB 314, 361
  5001 9, 14, 256, 292, 384, 386, 509, 629,
      784
Callenbach, Ernest
  ILIATM 282
Callow, Simon
  H 129, 284, 361
  5001 294, 471, 592, 640
Calloway, Cab
  TIAI 27
  SOTA 294
  5001 88, 716
Calloway, Kirk
  R 259
  5001 138
Calmos, see Femmes Fatales
Calthrop, Donald
  5001 79, 501
Calvert, E. H.
  5001 116, 307
Calvert, Phyllis
  5001 362, 398
Cambridge, Godfrey
  GS 53
  5001 111, 594
Camelot
  KKBB 35
  DIM 26, 27, 328
  R 325
  5001
Cameo Kirby
  KKBB 368
Cameron, Anne
  TIAI 263
  5001 771
Cameron, Ian
  ILIATM 306
Cameron, James
  SOTA 375
  H 192-194; dir., The Terminator, 68, 170,
      193, 344; Aliens, 192-194
  5001 15, 615
Cameron, Kate
  RK 44
Cameron, Rod
  5001 409
Camille
  KKBB 243:n
  GS 135

WTLGD 146
TIAI 345
5001
Camion, Le, see The Truck
Cammell, Donald
  R 234
Camp, Colleen
  5001 688
Camp, Shep
  5001 307
Campana, Nina
  5001 578
Campbell, Alan
  WTLGD 305
  5001 496, 706, 736, 786
Campbell, Beatrice
  KKBB 294
  5001 408, 413
Campbell, Cheryl
  TIAI 246
  SOTA 371, 372
  5001 131, 308, 677
Campbell, Delois Barrett
  TIAI 471, 472
Campbell, Douglas
  KKBB 322
  5001 539
Campbell, John
  5001 454
Campbell, John W. Jr.
  5001 758
Campbell, Joseph
  ML 295
  TIAI 385
Campbell, Mrs. Patrick
  5001 161
Campbell, Paul
  ILIATM 104
  5001 293
"Campbell Playhouse" (radio)
  RK 44
Campbell, R. Wright
  5001 458
Campbell, Stewart
  SOTA 282
  5001 361
Campbell, Tisha
  H 250
  5001 427
Campbell, William
  5001 513
"Camptown Races" (music)
  H 261
Camus, Albert
  ILIATM 22
  GS 30, 35
  DIM 68, 417
  H 317
  5001 719
Canada Terrell, John, see Terrell, John Canada
Canadian Film Development Corporation
  DIM 171
Canalejas, Lina
  DIM 264
  5001 278
Canalito, Lee
  WTLGD 489, 492

Canary Murder Case, The
RK 13
5001
Cancel My Reservation
5001
Candidate, The
R 47, 161
WTLGD 44, 45, 362
SOTA 16
Candide (music)
TIAI 216
Candy
KKBB 27, 298
GS 223-225
DIM 147
5001
Candy, John
TIAI 225
SOTA 141, 142-143
H 250
5001 428, 531, 701, 723
Cangaceiro, O (The Bandit)
5001
Cannan, Dennis
5001 61
Cannes Film Festival
DIM 305
WTLGD 294, 298, 500
SOTA 47, 260
H 25, 374
ML 124
Cannibals and Christians (book)
R 151
Canning, James
5001 98
Cannon, Dyan
DIM 11-13, 260, 383, 384
WTLGD 27, 430
TIAI 40-41, 44, 45, 326, 327, 370
SOTA 170
5001 25, 39, 89, 181, 195, 339, 724
Cannon Releasing Corporation
R 66
Can't Help Singing
5001
Can't Stop the Music
TIAI 321, 344
Canova, Judy
5001 36, 359
Cantervillle Ghost, The
5001
Cantor, Eddie
KKBB 53
RK 9
5001 288, 336, 393, 637, 750
Canutt, Yakima
5001 27, 704
Canyon, Steve (character)
WTLGD 322
ML 124
Capa, Robert
H 184
Capaldi, Peter
TIAI 464
5001 429
Cape Fear (1962)
GS 249-250

Capek, Karel
DIM 312
Capell, Peter
5001 570
Capetanos, Leon
TIAI 389
SOTA 157
H 104
5001 199, 499, 746
Capolicchio, Lino
DIM 363
5001 279
Capone, Alphonse (Al)
KKBB 50, 113
DIM 424
H 318, 320, 322, 323
Capote, Truman
ILIATM 165, 167, 170
KKBB 192, 235
GS 14
5001 57, 99, 362, 365
Capp, Al
5001 750
Capra, Frank
KKBB 232, 274; dir., *It Happened One
Night*, 48; *Mr. Smith Goes to
Washington*, 68; *It's a Wonderful Life*,
184; *Mr. Deeds Goes to Town*, 186;
Arsenic and Old Lace, 231-232; *Lost
Horizon*, 367
GS 61
DIM 5, 347, 370
R 140; dir., *Lost Horizon* (1937), 138, 140;
It Happened One Night, 176, 408-409
WTLGD 29, 108, 213, 222, 495; dir., *It
Happened One Night*, 6, 16, 29; *Arsenic
and Old Lace*, 29; *Mr. Deeds Goes to
Town*, 48; *Mr. Smith Goes to
Washington*, 48, 227; *Lost Horizon*
(1937), 107-108, 353; *It's a Wonderful
Life*, 178; *Meet John Doe*, 213
TIAI 380, 440
SOTA 187, 188, 306; dir., *Pocketful of
Miracles*, 123; *It's a Wonderful Life*,
187, 306; *It Happened One Night*, 306,
307; *Meet John Doe*, 306; *Lost Horizon*
(1937), 322
H 34, 208; dir., *The Bitter Tea of General
Yen*, 34; *It Happened One Night*, 111;
Lady for a Day, 154; *Pocketful of
Miracles*, 154
ML 42, 127; dir., *It's a Wonderful Life*, 127;
Lady for a Day, 28-29; *Pocketful of
Miracles*, 28
5001 23, 35, 75, 257, 292, 373, 403, 433,
436, 473, 478, 483, 487, 488, 489, 586,
711, 723, 724, 787
Capri, Ahna
R 124
5001 221, 572
Capri, Herson
H 26
Caprices de Marianne, Les (stage)
KKBB 343
Capshaw, Kate
SOTA 176, 178, 231, 232, 234
5001 203, 362

Captain Bligh and Mr. Christian (book)
SOTA 184
Captain Blood
KKBB 184
5001 (2nd ed)
Captain Newman, M. D.
R 209
Captain's Paradise, The
KKBB 243:n
WTLGD 286
5001
Captains Courageous
5001 (2nd ed)
Captive Mind, The (book)
DIM 203
Capucine
KKBB 69, 121
WTLGD 245
5001 240, 339, 694, 830
Car Wash
WTLGD 187-189
5001
Cara, Irene
WTLGD 166
5001 699
Carabatsos, James
H 246, 353, 355
5001 315, 325
Carabiniers, Les
GS 106, 140, 219
WTLGD 456
TIAI 450
5001 (2nd ed)
Caravaggio
SOTA 42
Carberry, Joe
WTLGD 297
5001 679, 732
Card, The, see *The Promoter*
Cardiff, Jack
ILIATM 63, 72; dir., *Sons and Lovers*, 63,
68, 72-75, 165
TIAI 168
SOTA 374
5001 9, 114, 197, 563, 615, 695, 858
Cardin, Pierre
5001 426
Cardinal, The
ILIATM 9
KKBB 134
Cardinale, Claudia
ILIATM 266
KKBB 237, 238, 334
TIAI 404
SOTA 52, 362
5001 62, 69, 122, 154, 213, 247, 417, 601,
635
Carefree
5001
Caretaker, The
R 220
H 98
Carette, Julien
KKBB 321, 343
5001 66, 300, 465, 541, 620, 647
Carewe, Arthur Edmund
KKBB 331

5001 195, 512, 579
Carewe, Edwin
    5001 624
Carey, Harry
    KKBB 338
    ML 192
    5001 11, 24, 26, 100, 206, 393, 489, 620,
        661, 697, 702, 754, 856
Carey, Harry Jr
    5001 631, 662
Carey, Joyce
    5001 102
Carey, Lynn
    5001 435
Carey, Olive
    5001 101, 662
Carey, Phil
    5001 114
Carey, Ron
    WTLGD 372
    TIAI 216
    5001 331, 335
Carey, Timothy
    KKBB 291
    5001 210, 323, 394, 549, 570
Carfagno, Edward C.
    5001 772
Cargill, Patrick
    5001 450
Cariou, Len
    WTLGD 424
    5001 405, 427
Carle, Richard
    5001 171, 787
Carlin, George
    WTLGD 188
    H 273
    5001 118, 559
Carlin, Lynn
    GS 197
    5001 233
Carlino, Lewis John
    GS 32, 244, 246
    TIAI 51-53, 117; dir., The Great Santini,
        51-53, 244
    5001 265, 303, 624, 663
Carlisle, Anne
    5001 185
Carlisle, Belinda
    5001 738
Carlisle, Kitty
    KKBB 317
    5001 502, 524
Carlisle, Mary
    5001 170, 391
Carlos, Walter
    5001 142
Carlquist, Margit
    ILIATM 106
    5001 688
Carlsen, Henning
    5001 345
Carlson, Jeff
    5001 686
Carlson, Richard
    KKBB 370
    R 150

5001 161, 343, 397, 426, 833, 859
Carlson, Sara
    5001 60
Carlson, Steve
    5001 686
Carlton, Larry
    ML 40
Carlyle Cousins, The
    TIAI 276
Carmen (music)
    DIM 158
    SOTA 253
Carmen Jones
    ILIATM 306
    SOTA 227
    5001
Carmichael, Hoagy
    KKBB 360
    TIAI 27
    SOTA 65
    5001 32, 65, 776
Carmichael, Ian
    5001 145, 357
"Carmina Burana" (music)
    TIAI 182
Carminati, Tullio
    5001 59, 636
Carnal Knowledge
    DIM 282-285, 348
    R 161
    TIAI 3
    H 176-177, 190
    5001
Carné, Marcel
    ILIATM 111, 298; dir., Port of Shadows, 48,
        135, 298; Le Jour se Lève, 298
    KKBB 140, 247, 332; dir., Bizarre, Bizarre,
        140; Children of Paradise, 247, 332; Le
        Jour se Lève, 279, 332; Port of
        Shadows, 332
    R 33; dir., Le Jour Se Lève, 290; Children of
        Paradise, 447
    5001 76, 133, 383, 465, 590, 817
Camera, Primo
    KKBB 291
    5001 393, 479
Carnet de bal, Un
    KKBB 243-244:n
    5001
Carnets du Major Thompson, Les, see The
        French They Are a Funny Race
Carney, Art
    R 376
    WTLGD 260-262, 502
    SOTA 376
    5001 310, 320, 412, 851
Carney, George
    5001 349
Carnival in Flanders (La Kermesse Héroïque)
    KKBB 244-245:n
    5001
Carnovsky, Morris
    ILIATM 173
    R 349
    5001 179, 276, 310, 785
Carny
    5001

"Carol Burnett Show, The" (TV)
    WTLGD 163, 504
    TIAI 323
    H 16
Carol, Martine
    5001 268, 430, 441, 819
Carola (play)
    ILIATM 300
Caron, Leslie
    DIM 323
    R 34
    WTLGD 336, 355
    SOTA 366
    5001 23, 168, 171, 239, 285, 287, 422, 461,
        811, 824
Carothers, A. J.
    H 299
    5001 664
Carpenter, Carleton
    5001 727, 766-767
Carpenter, David
    H 236
    5001 162
Carpenter, Don
    R 123, 124
    5001 572
Carpenter, E. C.
    5001 453
Carpenter, John
    WTLGD 547-548
    TIAI 192, 386; dir., Elvis (TV), 97;
        Halloween, 192
    SOTA 232, 306-308; dir., Escape from New
        York, 232; Halloween, 240, 307;
        Starman, 306-308
    H 192; dir., Escape from New York, 344
    5001 230, 314, 710, 759
Carpenter, Teresa
    SOTA 91
    5001 706
Carpetbaggers, The
    KKBB 134
    GS 61
    DIM 135, 420
    5001
Carpi, Fabio
    SOTA 125-127
    5001 127
Carr, Allen
    5001 127
Carr-Smith, Rodney
    5001 53
Carradine, David
    WTLGD 224, 226-228, 388-392
    TIAI 33, 260
    5001 95, 181, 473, 666
Carradine, John
    KKBB 276
    DIM 349
    WTLGD 227
    TIAI 192, 193, 287
    SOTA 298
    5001 13, 83, 118, 141, 205, 234, 278, 301,
        341, 343, 346, 409, 457, 461, 468, 484,
        574, 598, 704, 747, 841
Carradine, Keith
    R 267, 270, 449, 451

WTLGD 227, 233, 283-285, 381-383
TIAI 258
SOTA 289-290
H 137
5001 136, 206, 445, 516, 698, 757, 791, 827
Carradine, Robert
  WTLGD 404
  TIAI 425
  5001 150, 324, 473
Carras, Costa
  WTLGD 379
  5001 370
Carrel, Dany
  KKBB 333
  5001 590, 593
Carrez, Florence
  5001 789
Carrie (1952; from *Sister Carrie*)
  5001
Carrie (1976)
  WTLGD 202, 208-212, 369, 418, 419, 420,
    427, 520
  TIAI 35, 40, 229, 230, 306, 415
  SOTA 264
  H 206, 320
  ML 82, 118, 175
  5001
Carriere, Poky
  5001 75
Carrière, Jean-Claude
  WTLGD 366
  TIAI 104
  SOTA 237
  H 431
  ML 217, 218
  5001 192, 481, 734, 757, 804, 812, 818
Carrillo, Elpidia
  TIAI 301
  H 182
  5001 92, 651
Carrillo, Leo
  ML 51
  5001 82, 280, 312, 335, 356, 359, 422, 439,
    463, 579, 779
Carroll, Beeson
  5001 692
Carroll, Diahann
  5001 119
Carroll, Gordon
  5001 34
Carroll, Helena
  H 403, 405
  5001 177, 269
Carroll, John
  5001 289, 631, 732
Carroll, Leo G.
  KKBB 233, 319, 348, 352
  5001 46, 52, 118, 123, 240, 259, 533, 565,
    600, 618, 701, 720, 827, 851
Carroll, Lewis (Charles Dodgson)
  DIM 118
  WTLGD 82, 214, 537
  H 51-52, 53, 54
  5001 15, 202
Carroll, Madeleine
  KKBB 359
  WTLGD 50

5001 82, 545, 597, 663, 761
Carroll, Nancy
  RK 13, 15, 16 (ill.)
  WTLGD 6
  TIAI 392
  H 390
  5001 107, 338, 413, 566, 678
Carroll, Pat
  5001 426
Carroll, Peter
  TIAI 58
Carroll, Sidney
  5001 347
Carroll, Vinette
  5001 622
Carrosse du Saint Sacrement, Le (stage)
  ILIATM 101:n
Carruthers, Ben
  5001 457, 631
Cars, The (group)
  H 393
Carson, Jack
  KKBB 232, 256, 357
  5001 35-36, 88, 101, 119, 185, 282, 318,
    322, 443, 480, 703, 705, 707, 744, 819
Carson, John David
  R 383
  5001 655
Carson, Johnny
  R 355
  WTLGD 164, 501, 510
  TIAI 72, 355, 374, 461
  5001 116
Carson, Robert
  5001 4, 58, 706
Cartaxo, Marcelia
  H 268, 269, 270
  5001 342
Carter, Amy
  WTLGD 263
Carter, Ann
  5001 167
Carter, Arthur
  KKBB 325
  5001 551
Carter, Benny
  5001 716, 764
Carter, Helena Bonham, see Bonham Carter,
  Helena
Carter, Jack
  WTLGD 125
  TIAI 216
Carter, Janis
  5001 350
Carter, Jimmy
  WTLGD 228, 282
  TIAI 116
  5001 355
Carter, Joseph
  TIAI 107
Carter, Rubin
  WTLGD 400
Carter, T. K.
  TIAI 260
  5001 698
Cartier-Bresson, Henri
  KKBB 343

H 152
5001 647
Cartier, Caroline
  WTLGD 232
  5001 443
Cartland, Barbara
  TIAI 248
Cartouche (*The Thundering Sword*)
  5001
Cartwright, Veronica
  WTLGD 156-157, 509, 522-523
  SOTA 66
  H 324
  5001 290, 365, 368, 630, 843
Caruso, Enrico
  R 116, 326
  TIAI 404, 405
  5001 804
Caruso, Pino
  5001 729
Carvalho, Solomon S.
  RK 65
Carver, Lynne
  5001 75, 106, 472
Carver, Mary
  5001 34
Cary, Joyce
  ILIATM 10
  KKBB 282
  R 143
  5001 341
Casabianca, Camille de, see de Casabianca,
    Camille
Casablanca
  ILIATM 47, 81, 214, 324
  KKBB 194, 245:n, 360, 361
  RK 39
  DIM 65
  WTLGD 29, 116
  TIAI 452
  H 66, 446
  5001
Casanova, by Fellini, see *Fellini's Casanova*
Casanova's *Memoirs* (book)
  WTLGD 272
Casarès, Maria
  KKBB 247, 326
  5001 133, 554
Casbah, see *Pépé le Moko*
"Casey at the Bat" (poem)
  DIM 23
Casey, Bernie
  5001 141, 311, 460
Cash, Jim
  H 172, 174, 299
  5001 416, 664, 780
Cash, Johnny
  DIM 173
  R 123
  5001 426
Cash, Rosalind
  5001 7, 16
Casilio, Maria Pia
  5001 803
Casino Murder Case, The
  5001
Casino Royale

5001 (2nd ed)
Cason, Barbara
  DIM 107
  5001 339
Caspary, Vera
  5001 210, 413, 418
Casper, Robert
  5001 724
Casper, The Friendly Ghost
  SOTA 193
Casque d'or
  KKBB 245-246:n
  R 33
  WTLGD 182
  5001
Cass, Henry
  KKBB 294; dir., *Last Holiday*, 293-294
Cass, Peggy
  5001 356, 467
Cassandra Crossing, The
  WTLGD 452
Cassavetes, John
  ILIATM 91; dir., *Shadows*, 73
  KKBB 261
  GS 197; dir., *A Child Is Waiting*, 195;
    Faces, 195-199; *Shadows*, 195-196; *Too
    Late Blues*, 195
  DIM 222-224; dir., *Faces*, 36, 222;
    Husbands, 222-224; *Shadows*, 223
  R 291-300, 392-396; dir., *Husbands*, 292,
    393; *A Woman Under the Influence*,
    392-396, 411; *Faces*, 393; *Minnie and
    Moskowitz*, 394
  WTLGD 419, 421; dir., *A Child Is Waiting*,
    37
  TIAI 109, 389, 390, 391, 392, 457; dir., *A
    Child Is Waiting*, 173
  SOTA 233, 351
  5001 212, 232, 273, 346, 394, 482, 643,
    681, 746, 846
Cassavetes, Katherine
  R 393
  5001 846
Cassel, Jean-Pierre
  KKBB 265
  R 42, 390
  WTLGD 484
  ML 293-94
  5001 192, 247, 382, 438, 503, 767, 836
Cassel, Seymour
  R 394
  H 282
  5001 155, 233, 482, 773, 811
Cassidy, Claudia
  RK 44
Cassidy, Jack
  5001 130
Cassidy, Joanna
  WTLGD 261
  TIAI 363
  SOTA 72, 77-78, 167
  H 188
  5001 80, 143, 412, 413, 805
Cast a Giant Shadow
  5001
Castaneda, Carlos
  H 21

Castel, Lou
  GS 6
  H 290
  5001 247
Castellani, Renato
  ILIATM 281; dir., *Romeo and Juliet*, 281
  KKBB 339-340; dir., *Romeo and Juliet*
    (1954), 339-340
  5001 638, 798
Castellano, Richard
  DIM 371, 424
  5001 289
Castelnuovo, Nino
  5001 161
Castillo
  DIM 369
Castle, The (book)
  DIM 220
Castle, John
  5001 423
Castle, Nick
  5001 716, 727
Castle, Vernon and Irene
  5001 717
Castle, William
  5001 671
Castro, Fidel
  WTLGD 393
Casualties of War
  ML 166-77
  5001 (2nd ed)
Caswell, Robert
  ML 32
  5001 166
Cat and Mouse
  WTLGD 427
*Cat and Two Women, A (Neko to Shozo to
  Futari no Onna)*
  KKBB 246:n
  5001
Cat Ballou
  KKBB 29-30
  DIM 28
  5001
Cat on a Hot Tin Roof
  H 236
  5001
Cat People (1942)
  KKBB 246-247:n, 365
  WTLGD 522
  5001
Cat People (1982)
  TIAI 335-36
  5001 (2nd ed)
Catalani, Alfredo
  TIAI 330
Catch-22
  DIM 146, 215, 256, 282, 283
  R 293
  WTLGD 291
  TIAI 376
  ML 249
  5001
Catch Us If You Can, see *Having a Wild
  Weekend*
Catcher in the Rye, The (novel)
  TIAI 376

H 158
Catered Affair, The
  5001
Cates, Gilbert
  DIM 169, 170; dir., *I Never Sang for My
    Father*, 169-171
  R 221-226; dir., *I Never Sang for My
    Father*, 61; *Summer Wishes, Winter
    Dreams*, 221-227, 453
  5001 351, 727
Cates, Phoebe
  TIAI 408, 409
  SOTA 188, 189
  H 458
  5001 103, 238, 307, 350
Catherine Wheel, The
  SOTA 34
Catlett, Walter
  KKBB 241
  5001 44, 104, 226, 268, 464, 487, 545, 586,
    635, 806, 853
Caton-Jones, Michael
  ML dir., *Scandal*, 129-33
  5001 656
Cats (stage)
  SOTA 242
Catselli, Aleka
  5001 214
Cattle Annie and Little Britches
  TIAI 212-214
  5001
Cattrall, Kim
  ML 316
  H 445
  5001 470
Caught
  ILIATM 100, 235
  KKBB 296
  5001
Cavalcade
  DIM 16
  5001
Cavalcanti, Alberto
  ILIATM 289
  KKBB 255; dir., *Dead of Night* (segment),
    254-255, 292
  SOTA 22
  5001 178, 523
Cavalier, Alain
  H dir., *Therese*, 255-257
  5001 752, 753
Cavallo, Victor
  TIAI 313
  5001 787
Cavanagh, Paul
  5001 72, 318, 345, 391, 446, 524, 744
Cavanaugh, Hobart
  5001 118, 255, 419, 642, 768, 837
Cavani, Liliana
  R 342-345
  5001 527
Caveman
  TIAI 194-197, 307, 394
  H 273
  5001
Cavett, Dick
  DIM 222

R 30, 91, 298
TIAI 105, 106
H 456-457
5001 61
Cavett, F. M.
5001 259
Cavett, Frank
5001 155
Cawthorn, Joseph
5001 518
Cayatte, André
KKBB 264; dir., *An Eye for an Eye*, 264
DIM 419; dir., *To Die of Love*, 418-419
WTLGD 98
5001 229, 388, 441, 775
Cazale, John
R 399
WTLGD 514, 519
5001 183, 196, 289, 290
CBS, see Columbia Broadcasting System
C.C. and Company
DIM 171, 173-174
5001
Ceballos, Larry
5001 547
Cecchini, Mimi
5001 842
Cecil, Jonathan
TIAI 215
Celani, Isabella
H 126
5001 640
Celebrating Bird (TV)
ML 4
Celi, Adolfo
5001 339, 521
Céline, Louis-Ferdinand
ILIATM 227
DIM 17
Celui qui doit mourir, see *He Who Must Die*
Centennial Summer
ILIATM 306
Central Park
DIM 112, 185, 186, 254
Central Television (U.K.)
H 441
Century Magazine, The (periodical)
SOTA 206
C'Era una Volta, see *More than a Miracle*
Cerami, Vincenzo
TIAI 420
5001 415
Ceremonies in Dark Old Men (TV)
WTLGD 188
Cervantes, Miguel de
KKBB 114, 259
DIM 127
5001 197, 458
Cervi, Antonio
5001 89
Cervi, Gino
5001 362, 428
César
H 330
5001
César and Rosalie
R 95-96

WTLGD 153
TIAI 423
5001
Cet Obscur Objet du désir, see *That Obscure Object of Desire*
Chabrol, Claude
ILIATM 132-133, 135-136; dir., *Le Beau Serge*, 132; *The Cousins*, 132-136, 148
GS dir., *Les Biches*, 148
DIM 53-54, 172, 234, 243, 307, 403-405; dir., *La Femme Infidèle*, 53-54, 172, 403; *Les Biches*, 53; *Le Beau Serge*, 54; *Les Cousins*, 54; *Les Bonnes Femmes*, 54; *This Man Must Die*, 172; *Le Boucher*, 403-405
5001 67, 91, 95, 100, 128, 159, 241, 416, 438, 762
Chafed Elbows
KKBB 18
H 186
Chaikin, Joseph
5001 472
Chained
5001
Chairman Mao's Little Red Book
WTLGD 188, 331
Chakiris, George
5001 828
Chaliapin, Feodor
KKBB 259-260
GS 3
H 424-425
5001 197, 496
Challis, Christopher
DIM 187
5001 170, 281, 468, 599, 602, 799
Chalmers, Nadine
H 476
5001 850
Chamberlain, Lindy
ML 30-33
Chamberlain, Richard
GS 120
DIM 26, 239, 242
R 112, 318, 406, 452
WTLGD 140, 533-536
5001 404, 412, 450, 504, 767, 785
Chamberlin, Howland
TIAI 373
5001 51
Chamberlin, Lee
WTLGD 66
5001 418
Champ, The
TIAI 113
5001 (2nd ed)
Champagne Murders, The (*Le Scandale*)
5001
Champion
ILIATM 91
KKBB 203
WTLGD 491
Champion, Gower
5001 287, 679, 766, 848
Champion, Marge (Marjorie Bell)
5001 287, 567, 679, 717, 766
Chandlee, Harry E.

5001 586
Chandler, Chick
5001 13, 101, 623
Chandler, George
KKBB 341
5001 420, 472, 623, 645
Chandler, Helen
ILIATM 13
5001 137, 201
Chandler, Jeff
ILIATM 45
KKBB 184, 241
5001 107
Chandler, John Davis
5001 569, 860
Chandler, Raymond
KKBB 6, 238-239, 313, 352
DIM 413, 414
R 182-190
TIAI 255, 468
H 245
5001 71, 86, 198, 233, 404, 432, 466, 503, 720
Chanel, Coco
KKBB 343
5001 647
Chaney, James
ML 54
5001 486
Chaney, Lon
KKBB 39, 330-331
RK 10
5001 466, 578, 579, 807
Chaney, Lon Jr.
TIAI 194
5001 254, 143, 331, 540
Chang, Anna
WTLGD 13
"Change of Plan, A" (short story)
R 69
"Changes" (music)
SOTA 349
Channel Four (U.K.)
H 332-333, 335
Channing, Carol
5001 763
Channing, Stockard
WTLGD 205
H 189
5001 68, 260, 325
Chanslor, Roy
5001 124
Chant d'amour, Un
TIAI 250
H 252
Chant of Jimmie Blacksmith, The
WTLGD 536
TIAI 54-60, 267, 268, 269, 371
SOTA 243
5001
ML 166
Chaos, see *Kaos*
Chapeau de paille d'Italie, Un, see *The Italian Straw Hat*
"Chapel of Love" (music)
TIAI 96
Chapiteau, Marc

5001 268
Chaplin, Charles (Charlie)
   ILIATM 26, 198, 276; dir., *Limelight*, 47;
      Monsieur Verdoux, 196; *One A.M.*, 276
   KKBB 31, 141, 153, 189, 248, 273, 274,
      288, 310, 311, 317, 320, 327, 351; dir.,
      A Countess from Hong Kong, 45; *The
      Gold Rush*, 248, 273; *Modern Times*,
      311, 320; *The Kid*, 327
   GS 103, 230
   RK 14
   DIM 61, 93, 194, 360, 362; dir., *Shoulder
      Arms*, 93; *Pay Day*, 194
   R 128, 131-132, 241, 403; dir., *A Countess
      from Hong Kong*, 31
   WTLGD 9, 22, 88, 137, 231; dir., *City
      Lights*, 22, 136; *Limelight*, 231; *A
      Countess from Hong Kong*, 424
   TIAI 90, 144, 158, 217, 323, 444; dir., *City
      Lights*, 158; *Monsieur Verdoux*, 217,
      444
   SOTA 25, 125, 129, 159, 294, 340
   H 22, 145, 350, 471, 485; dir., *Monsieur
      Verdoux*, 187; *The Circus*, 471, 472
   ML 104
   5001 292, 392, 395, 422, 491, 494, 680, 831
Chaplin, Geraldine
   R 449, 451-452
   WTLGD 205, 283-284, 357, 444
   TIAI 411
   5001 195, 364, 516, 642, 767, 827
Chaplin, Michael
   5001 395
Chaplin, Sydney
   5001 423
Chapman, Ben
   5001 161
Chapman, Edward
   KKBB 265
   5001 254, 502
Chapman, Graham
   5001 450
Chapman, Lonny
   5001 43, 210
Chapman, Michael
   WTLGD 132, 523, 524
   TIAI 303
   SOTA 3, 222
   ML 41
   5001 178, 284, 368, 408, 411, 462, 521,
      576, 660, 745
Chapman Report, The
   ILIATM 305
   GS 151
   DIM 281, 408
   ML 133
   5001 (2nd ed)
Chapman, Robert H.
   5001 72
Chapman, Robin
   5001 790
Chappaqua
   5001
Charade
   ILIATM 24, 26, 82
   WTLGD 3, 5, 25, 30, 31, 32, 482
   H 173, 299

5001 (2nd ed)
Chardin, Teilhard de
   WTLGD 429
Charell, Erik
   5001 829
Charge of the Light Brigade, The (1936)
   TIAI 137
   5001
Charge of the Light Brigade, The (1968)
   KKBB 184
   GS 145-148
   DIM 15, 17, 99, 213, 215
   R 18
   5001
Chariots of Fire
   TIAI 245-247, 455
   SOTA 148, 150, 169, 278, 279
   H 75
   5001
Charisse, Cyd
   ILIATM 266
   KKBB 234, 288, 363
   GS 156
   TIAI 357
   5001 49, 50, 103, 321, 374, 681, 683, 692,
      800, 848
Charles I
   DIM 181
Charles, Jack
   TIAI 59
Charles, John
   SOTA 244
   5001 810
Charles, Josh
   ML 156
   5001 179
Charles, Ray
   KKBB 222
   DIM 85
   R 459
   TIAI 26, 284
   ML 275
   5001 88, 360
Charleson, Ian
   TIAI 245, 433
   5001 131, 277, 308
Charley Varrick
   R 205-207, 365
   5001
Charley's Aunt (stage)
   KKBB 367
   TIAI 430
Charlie Bubbles
   GS 47-48
   5001 (2nd ed)
Charlie Daniels Band (group)
   TIAI 205
"Charlie's Angels" (TV)
   SOTA 224
Charly
   GS 150-152
   DIM 59
   R 432
   ML 320
   5001
Charme discret de la bourgeoisie, Le, see *The
      Discreet Charm of the Bourgeoisie*

Charnin, Martin
   TIAI 344
   5001 29
Charon, Jacques
   GS dir., *A Flea in Her Ear*, 211
Charpin
   KKBB 233
   5001 48, 128, 236, 575
Charrier, Jacques
   5001 161
Charrière, Henri
   KKBB 124
   DIM 270
   R 237, 238
   5001 565
Charterhouse of Parma, The (book)
   DIM 270
Charteris, Leslie
   5001 405
Charters, Spencer
   5001 322
Chartoff, Robert
   5001 612, 630, 636, 793
Charulata
   WTLGD 69
Chase, The
   KKBB 21, 60, 151-153
   R 370
   5001
Chase, Anzanette
   5001 88
Chase, Barrie
   TIAI 345
   5001 681
Chase, Borden
   KKBB 338
   5001 620
Chase, Charlie
   5001 831
Chase, Chevy
   5001 251, 309
Chase, Ilka
   KKBB 238
   5001 71, 373, 536
Chase National Bank
   RK 6
Chasen, Dave
   RK 34
Chasen's
   RK 13, 31, 34, 35, 36, 37, 40
Chaskel, Pedro
   WTLGD 387
Chatterji, Soumitra
   R 141
   WTLGD 68-69
   SOTA 380
   5001 176, 186, 192, 337, 850
Chatterji, Swatilekha
   SOTA 380, 381
   5001 337
Chatterton, Ruth
   RK 13
   DIM 345
   WTLGD 16
   5001 196, 447, 566
Chautard, Emile
   5001 671

Chayefsky, Paddy
  KKBB 271-273
  GS 222
  DIM 27, 378, 379
  WTLGD 219-224, 311, 357
  TIAI 110, 127, 128, 130, 131, 132
  5001 20, 126, 289, 341, 467, 519
Chaykin, Maury
  TIAI 493
  ML 192
  5001 60, 100
Che!
  GS 167
Checker, Chubby
  H 443
Cheech and Chong, see Marin, Cheech and
    Chong, Tommy
"Cheers" (TV)
  SOTA 123
  H 273
Cheirel, Micheline
  KKBB 245
  5001 121
Chekhov, Anton
  ILIATM 149, 181-182
  GS 230-234
  DIM 163
  TIAI 174, 368
  SOTA 26, 50, 371, 373
  H 372, 373, 426
  5001 172, 660
Chekhov, Michael
  KKBB 348
  5001 700, 701
Chelsea Girls, The
  GS 196, 197
  DIM 154
Chen, Joan
  H 396
  5001 408
Chenal, Pierre
  KKBB 252; dir., *Crime and Punishment*,
    252, 262
  5001 161, 592
Cher
  TIAI 414, 416
  SOTA 108
  H 324, 393, 423, 424
  5001 148, 496, 681, 733, 843
Chéri (book)
  H 301
Cherkassky, Shura
  5001 182
Cherkassov, Nikolai
  KKBB 289
  5001 13, 375
Cherrill, Virginia
  WTLGD 22, 23
Cherry, Helen
  R 361
  5001 215, 435
Cherry Orchard, The
  ILIATM 251
Cheshire, Elizabeth
  TIAI 75
  5001 474
Chessman, Caryl

  WTLGD 506
Chesterton, G. K.
  KKBB 256
  5001 185
Chetwynd, Lionel
  5001 34
Cheung, George Kee
  5001 615
Chevalier, Maurice
  KKBB 43, 257
  DIM 430
  WTLGD 12
  5001 71, 187, 253, 285, 438, 566, 751
Cheyenne Autumn
  WTLGD 95
  TIAI 357
Chiari, Walter
  KKBB 201
  5001 63, 235
Chicago (stage)
  KKBB 341
  TIAI 232
Chicago Journal of Commerce (periodical)
  RK 44
Chicago Tribune (periodical)
  RK 10, 19, 66
Chico Hamilton Quintet (group)
  5001 736
Chien andalou, Un
  ILIATM 286, 290
  GS 257
  WTLGD 436
  TIAI 148
  5001
Chienne, La
  KKBB 142
  R 33
Chihara, Paul
  5001 596
Child Is Waiting, A
  GS 195
  WTLGD 37
  TIAI 173
Child, Julia
  WTLGD 503
Child of the Century, A (book)
  R 423
Child's Play
  R 72-73
  5001
Childhood of Maxim Gorky, The, (*Detsvo
    Gorkovo*; part of *The Donskoi Trilogy*)
  5001
Children Are Watching Us, The (*I Bambini ci
    Guardano*)
  KKBB 247:n, 269
  DIM 361
  5001
Children, films for
  KKBB 179-186
Children of Paradise (*Les Enfants du Paradis*)
  KKBB 247:n, 332
  GS 115, 239
  R 447
  TIAI 330, 492
  5001
"Children" (music)

  TIAI 123
Children's Hour, The
  ILIATM 175-176
  GS 31
  WTLGD 306, 308, 309
  5001
Chiles, Lois
  WTLGD 394-396, 463-464
  H 162, 419
  5001 105, 147, 181, 495, 656, 735, 825
Chilly Scenes of Winter
  TIAI 464
Chimes at Midnight, see *Falstaff*
China Is Near (*La Cina è Vicina*)
  GS 4-8, 211
  TIAI 418
  5001
China Seas
  H 228
  5001
China Syndrome, The
  TIAI 11, 16, 34, 163, 310, 495
  SOTA 109
  H 243
Chinatown
  R 311, 314, 352, 441-442, 473
  WTLGD 87, 118, 125, 165
  TIAI 242, 302, 364
  SOTA 145
  H 314, 364
  ML 286
  5001 (2nd ed)
Ching, William
  5001 569
Chinoise, La
  GS 76-84, 140, 141
  DIM 167, 272, 306
  WTLGD 181
  5001
Chirico, Giorgio de
  WTLGD 393
Chitty Chitty Bang Bang
  GS 225-227
Chloe in the Afternoon (*L'Amour, l'après-midi*)
  R 9-12
  5001
Chodorov, Edward
  WTLGD 13
Choice Cuts (book)
  R 330
Chong, Rae Dawn
  TIAI 307, 309
  SOTA 289
  H 82
  5001 136, 147, 608
Chong, Tommy
  WTLGD 448-450
  TIAI 196
  5001 9, 808
Choose Me
  SOTA 288-290
  H 9, 136, 137
  5001 (2nd ed)
Chopin, Frédéric
  DIM 240
  WTLGD 331, 476, 479, 515
  5001 694

Chopra, Joyce
  H 131-133; dir., *Smooth Talk*, 131-133, 206
  5001 688, 689
Chorus Line, A
  WTLGD 377, 411
  SOTA 35, 347
Chowdhry, Navin
  ML 21
  5001 447
Chris, Marilyn
  DIM 107
  5001 339
Christ Stopped at Eboli
  TIAI 60, 315, 316
Christian-Jacques
  KKBB 264; dir., *Fanfan the Tulip*, 264
  5001 236, 572
Christian, Linda
  5001 318, 492
Christian, Susanne
  5001 570
Christians, Mady
  KKBB 296
  5001 17, 419
Christiansen, Benjamin
  5001 511
Christie, Agatha
  R 318, 390-391
  WTLGD 462-465, 551-553
  TIAI 258
  5001 25, 180, 438, 503, 844
Christie, Audrey
  5001 391, 455, 702
Christie, Julie
  KKBB 148-149, 158
  GS 26, 121
  DIM 277-279
  R 233, 235-236, 436, 438
  SOTA 331, 333
  H 63
  5001 173, 195, 198, 233, 237, 445, 517,
    626, 670, 859
Christmas Carol, A (book)
  KKBB 161
  DIM 196
  ML 38-42
Christmas Holiday
  5001
Christmas in July
  5001
"Christmas Trees, The" (music)
  DIM 219
Christopher, Dennis
  TIAI 246
  5001 131
Christopher, Jordan
  5001 582
Christopher Strong
  KKBB 241
  DIM 341, 342, 346
  5001
Chronicle of a Summer (*Chronique d'un été*)
  5001
Chronique d'un été, see *Chronicle of a Summer*
Chukrai, Gigori (also spelled Grigori Chukhrai)
  KKBB 267; dir., *Ballad of a Soldier*, 110;
    The Forty-First, 266-267

GS dir., *Clear Skies*, 45
  5001 261
Chump at Oxford, A
  5001
Chung, Betty
  5001 221
Chunibala
  5001 569
Church, Sandra
  5001 802
Church, Tony
  TIAI 136
  5001 749
Churchill, Berton
  5001 112, 348, 360, 704, 713, 736
Churchill, Douglas W.
  5001 586
Churchill, Sarah
  5001 646
Churchill, Winston
  RK 5, 72
  R 15-18
  ML 130
  5001 860
Churikova, Inna
  DIM 311
  5001 181
Churubusco Studios
  TIAI 196
Chute, David
  TIAI 384
Ciannelli, Eduardo
  KKBB 278, 307-308, 369
  GS 244
  WTLGD 18
  5001 258, 311, 400, 466, 469, 718, 841
Ciel et la boue, Le, see *The Sky Above, The Mud
    Below*
Cilento, Diane
  KKBB 329
  5001 11, 514, 566, 778, 794
Cimarron
  ILIATM 25
  WTLGD 145
  5001
Cimino, Leonardo
  SOTA 284
  5001 207
Cimino, Michael
  R 254
  WTLGD 512-519; dir., *The Deer Hunter*,
    512-519; *Thunderbolt and Lightfoot*,
    512
  TIAI 112-114; dir., *Heaven's Gate*, 112-114;
    The Deer Hunter, 113, 114, 457
  H 21-24, 31-36; dir., *Heaven's Gate*, 21-24,
    31, 33; *The Deer Hunter*, 23, 32, 33, 35,
    361; *Year of the Dragon*, 31-36, 156,
    180, 183, 251
  ML 109
  5001 183, 452, 854
Cina è Vicina, La, see *China Is Near*
Cincinnati Kid, The
  KKBB 152
  GS 169
  R 441
Cinderella Liberty

R 259, 273
  WTLGD 377
  5001
Cinecittà
  SOTA 356
Cinecolor
  WTLGD 62
CinemaScope
  H 203
Ciociara, La, see *Two Women*
Cioffi, Charles
  5001 400, 486, 521, 757, 772
Ciolli, Augusta
  5001 467
Circle Jerks, The (group)
  SOTA 213
  5001 624
Circus, The
  H 471, 472
Cisco Pike
  R 415, 442
  5001 (2nd ed)
Cisyk, Kasey
  5001 857
Citadel, The
  5001
Citizen Kane
  ILIATM 24, 110, 288
  KKBB 33, 124, 197, 199, 232, 247-248:n,
    304
  GS 7, 60, 161-162, 164
  RK *passim*
  DIM 252
  R 179, 202
  WTLGD 104
  TIAI 315, 340
  SOTA 24, 179, 216
  H 295, 415
  5001
Citizens Band (also known as *Handle with Care*)
  WTLGD 320-323
  TIAI 73
  SOTA 39
  H 110, 232, 274
  5001
City Heat
  SOTA 288
City Lights
  WTLGD 22, 136
  TIAI 158
City of Gold
  KKBB 248:n
  5001
"City of the One Night Stands" (music)
  WTLGD 283
City of Women
  H 139
City Streets
  5001
Ciupka, Richard
  TIAI 177
  5001 38
Civil Rights Act
  ML 53
Clair, René
  ILIATM 278, 282-283, 290; dir., *A Nous La
    Liberté*, 282; *Le Million*, 283; *Porte des*

Lilas, 290
KKBB 235, 265, 270, 287, 311, 320, 340;
  dir., *A Nous La Liberte*, 140-141, 311,
  320; *The Ghost Goes West*, 270; *The
  Italian Straw Hat*, 287, 320; *Le Million*,
  320
GS 202; dir., *The Italian Straw Hat*, 211
RK 13
DIM 244
R 437
WTLGD 182
5001 1, 25, 59, 248, 284, 300, 350, 373,
  409, 481, 590, 697
Claire, Ina
  KKBB 318, 363
  5001 305, 531, 645
Claire's Knee (*Le Genou de Claire*)
  DIM 264-267, 275, 280
  R 10
  WTLGD 59, 186, 304
  TIAI 400
  5001
Clanton, Hampton
  5001 155
Clapton, Eric
  5001 411
Clare, Mary
  ILIATM 119
  5001 62, 406, 500, 543, 858
Clarence, O. B.
  5001 302
Clariond, Aimé
  KKBB 262, 312
  5001 225, 495
Clark, Bob
  5001 502
Clark, Bruce
  5001 685
Clark, Candy
  R 193
  WTLGD 321, 323
  TIAI 33
  5001 87, 139, 238, 460
Clark, Curtis
  H 439
  5001 770
Clark, Dane
  R 172
Clark, Dennis Lynton
  WTLGD 486-488
  5001 148
Clark, Fred
  KKBB 355
  5001 168, 249, 585, 629, 691, 730, 834
Clark, Guy
  TIAI 204, 206
  5001 326
Clark, Harry
  5001 675
Clark, Sir Kenneth
  KKBB 213
Clark, Mark
  DIM 44, 45
Clark, Matt
  TIAI 21
  SOTA 219
  5001 7, 108, 157, 360, 495, 569

Clark, Petula
  KKBB 335
  GS 159
  DIM 38, 40
  5001 244, 297, 350, 601
Clark, Ron
  WTLGD 373
  5001 331
Clark, Susan
  DIM 77, 300
  R 19
  WTLGD 140
  5001 502, 685, 746
Clark, Walter Van Tilburg
  KKBB 328
  5001 560
Clark, William A.
  5001 458
Clarke, Arthur C.
  5001 800
Clarke, Caitlin
  TIAI 221, 222
  5001 201, 574
Clarke, Grant
  5001 547
Clarke, John
  SOTA 60
  5001 431
Clarke, Kenny
  KKBB 297
  5001 420
Clarke, Mae
  R 187
  5001 265, 602, 824
Clarke, Shirley
  DIM 31
  5001 152, 155, 423, 590
Clarke, T. E. B.
  KKBB 255, 295, 330
  5001 178, 414, 451, 568, 695
Clary, Robert
  5001 334
Clash by Night
  ILIATM 235
  R 155
  5001
Clatworthy, Robert
  5001 365
Claudine
  5001
Clavell, James
  DIM 248, 249; dir., *The Last Valley*,
    248-250; *To Sir, with Love*, 343
  H 210
  5001 252, 397, 411, 777
Clay, Nicholas
  TIAI 185
  5001 227
Clayburgh, Jill
  R 135
  WTLGD 141-143, 210, 247, 359-361,
    410-414
  SOTA 108
  5001 275, 665, 682, 748, 757, 807
Clayton, Ethel
  5001 678
Clayton, Jack

ILIATM 63, 164-165; dir., *Room at the Top*,
  63, 67-68, 75, 78, 165; *The Bespoke
  Overcoat*, 65; *The Innocents*, 163-172
DIM dir., *Room at the Top*, 142; *The Pump-
  kin Eater*, 292
H 409-412; dir., *The Lonely Passion of
  Judith Hearne*, 409-412; *Room at the
  Top*, 411; *The Innocents*, 411; *The
  Pumpkin Eater*, 411
ML 167
5001 63, 364, 431, 602, 640
Clayton, John
  H 434
  5001 333
Clayton, Marion
  5001 18
Clean and Sober
  ML 112
Clean Slate, see *Coup de torchon*
Clear Skies
  GS 45
Cleary, Jon
  5001 729
Cleckley, H. M.
  5001 765
Cleese, John
  H 14
  5001 450, 682, 772
Clemenceau Case, The
  KKBB 268
  DIM 363
Clemens, Samuel, see Mark Twain
Clément, Aurore
  R 337
  5001 403
Clément, René
  ILIATM 111-112; dir., *Forbidden Games*,
    111-113; *Battle of the Rails*, 111; *Les
    Maudits*, 111; *Monsieur Ripois*, 111;
    Gervaise, 111
  KKBB 311, 346; dir., *Forbidden Games*,
    247, 342; *Monsieur Ripois*, 311-312;
    Gervaise, 333; *The Sea Wall*, 345-346
  GS 25; dir., *Purple Noon*, 242
  WTLGD 313; dir., *Les Maudits*, 147; *Purple
    Noon*, 313; *Forbidden Games*, 356
  5001 257, 282, 494, 603, 661, 822, 823
Clémenti, Pierre
  GS 72, 73
  DIM 272
  SOTA 52
  5001 63, 152, 417, 481, 567
Clements, John
  TIAI 433
  5001 277, 541, 623, 759
Clennon, David
  SOTA 280
  H 174
  5001 234, 416, 735, 759
Cléo de 5 à 7, see *Cleo from 5 to 7*
Cleo from 5 to 7 (*Cléo de 5 à 7*)
  GS 27
  WTLGD 342
  5001
Cleopatra (1934)
  5001
Cleopatra (1963)

ILIATM 8, 86, 264
GS 41
DIM 27
WTLGD 241, 325
Cleopatra Jones
R 261-262
5001
Clerval, Denys
5001 670
Clery, Corinne
5001 496
Clever, Edith
WTLGD 185-187
5001 467
Cliff, Jimmy
R 125-126
H 187, 188, 189
5001 143, 319
Clifford, Francis
5001 515
Clifford, Graeme
WTLGD 434
5001 154
Clift, Montgomery
ILIATM 46, 49
KKBB 208, 332, 338
R 452, 454
WTLGD 447
TIAI 118
H 74, 444
ML 116
5001 269, 327, 348, 362, 384, 484, 584,
585, 614, 620, 661, 725, 859
Cline, Edward F.
KKBB 314; dir., *Million Dollar Legs*, 7,
185; *The Bank Dick*, 184, 314; *Never
Give a Sucker an Even Break*, 185, 314;
My Little Chickadee, 313-314
5001 160, 481, 509, 520
Cline, Patsy
H 48-51, 234, 342
5001 734
Clinging to the Wreckage (book)
H 142
Clive, Colin
DIM 341
5001 101, 137, 265, 335, 445
Clive, E. E.
KKBB 288
5001 44, 102, 116, 118, 130, 281, 341, 369,
374, 420, 525, 545, 595, 679
Cliveden, Lord Astor's estate
ML 130
Cloak & Dagger
H 75
Cloche, Maurice
KKBB 312; dir., *Monsieur Vincent*, 312
5001 495
Clock, The
GS 102
5001
Clockwork Orange, A
DIM 373-378, 426
R 432
WTLGD 103
TIAI 2
H 108, 326, 327, 344

ML 315
5001
Clockwork Orange, A (novel)
H 160
Cloquet, Ghislain
GS 73
5001 63, 500, 749
Clork, Harry
5001 106
Close Encounters of the Third Kind
WTLGD 269, 348-354, 420
TIAI 53, 54, 98, 208, 211, 222, 347, 348,
351, 487
SOTA 182
H 6
5001
*Close Encounters of the Third Kind, Special
Edition*
TIAI 53-54
5001
Close, Glenn
TIAI 377, 378-379
SOTA 69, 71, 169, 170, 171
H 56-57, 374, 375
ML 57-62, 288, 289
5001 69, 171, 239, 377, 517, 849
Closely Watched Trains (Ostre Sledovane Vlaky)
GS 98, 105
R 120
5001
Clothier, William H.
KKBB 43
Clouds Over Europe, see *Q Planes*
Clouse, Robert
5001 221
Clouzot, Henri-Georges
ILIATM 38; dir., *La Vérité*, 37, 38
KKBB 165-166, 258, 315; dir., *The Wages
of Fear*, 165-166, 315; *Diabolique*,
258-259, 315; *Le Mystère Picasso*, 315
WTLGD 182
5001 155, 188, 482, 511, 606, 607, 719,
720, 821, 838
Clouzot, Vera
KKBB 258
5001 188, 821
Clowns, The (TV)
R 25
Club Paradise
H 186-189, 421
5001 (2nd ed)
Cluchey, Rick
H 381-382
5001 826
Clunes, Alec
5001 628
Cluny Brown
KKBB 248-249:n
5001
Cluny, Geneviève
5001 382, 438
Clute, Chester
5001 170
Cluzet, François
5001 644
Clyde, Andy
5001 30, 426, 481

Clyde, June
5001 337
Coal Miner's Daughter
TIAI 42, 135
H 51, 55
Coates, Paul
H 61-63
Cobb, Humphrey
5001 569
Cobb, Irvin S.
5001 384, 713, 728
Cobb, Lee J.
GS 247
R 248
5001 28, 92, 292, 343, 359, 546, 555, 763,
765, 795
Cobb, Randall (Tex)
SOTA 117, 119
H 292
5001 615, 804
Cobb, Tex, see Cobb, Randall
Cobbs, Bill
5001 146
Cobo, Eva
5001 470
Cobo, Roberto
KKBB 323
5001 544
Cobra Woman
5001
Coburn, Charles
5001 44, 186, 326, 354, 359, 397, 404, 448,
494, 497, 559, 565, 633, 646, 778, 818
Coburn, James
KKBB 299
GS 149, 224, 270
R 328
WTLGD 41
TIAI 253
5001 117, 130, 318, 359, 434, 440, 452,
555, 569, 594
Cobweb, The
ILIATM 58
KKBB 249:n
WTLGD 373
TIAI 461
5001
Coca, Imogene
R 128-132
TIAI 394
5001 747
Cochran, Eddie
H 342
Cochran, Steve
DIM 296
5001 65, 169, 308, 834
Cocker, Joe
DIM 198
Cockeyed World, The
DIM 93
Coco, James
DIM 269, 384
R 78
5001 218, 458, 721, 724
Cocoanuts, The
RK 83
5001

Cocoon
H 4-7
5001 (2nd ed)
Cocteau, Jean
ILIATM 7, 132, 275, 286, 290, 296,
343-344; dir., *Orpheus*, 7, 275, 286,
292; *The Blood of a Poet*, 286, 289; *Les
Parents Terribles*, 343
KKBB 16, 43, 236, 239, 256, 262, 326-327,
329, 346, 365; dir., *Orpheus*, 43, 114,
239, 326-327; *Beauty and the Beast*,
236; *The Blood of a Poet*, 239, 326,
365; *Les Parents Terribles (The Storm
Within)*, 329
GS 9, 11, 49; dir., *The Blood of a Poet*, 187;
Les Parents Terribles, 228
RK 32
DIM 278, 279, 336, 364, 365; dir., *The
Blood of a Poet*, 336
R 338, 368
WTLGD 59, 113, 146, 291, 310, 523; dir.,
The Blood of a Poet, 113; *Beauty and
the Beast* (1946), 147; *Orpheus*, 523
TIAI 335; dir., *Orpheus*, 335
SOTA 210
H 98, 288, 355, 473; dir., *Les Parents
Terribles*, 98; *Beauty and the Beast*, 473
ML 27
5001 58, 59, 83, 208, 220, 225, 554, 566,
578, 812
Cody, John
H 453
Cody, Lew
5001 192
Cody, Paul
H 453
Coe, David Allan
TIAI 204, 206
5001 326
Coe, George
ML 96
5001 159, 478
Coen, Ethan
SOTA 323, 325, 326
H 291, 292, 453
5001 83, 615
Coen, Joel
SOTA 323-326
H 290-292, 453; dir., *Raising Arizona*, 290-
292, 420, 481; *Blood Simple*, 292
5001 83, 615
Coffee, Lenore
5001 35, 67, 225, 263, 778, 858
Coffin, Frederick
5001 60
Coghill, Nevill
5001 194
Cohan, George M.
SOTA 171
5001 579, 580, 853
Cohen, Abraham
5001 329
Cohen, Alain
GS 51
Cohen, Alexander H.
SOTA 339
5001 604

Cohen, Jeff
5001 298
Cohen, Joel
H 453
5001 567
Cohen, Larry
R 260-261
5001 91
Cohen, Lawrence D.
WTLGD 208
Cohen, Lawrence J.
5001 68, 711
Cohen, Leonard
DIM 280
WTLGD 284
H 63
5001 445
Cohen, Neil
H 453
5001 567
Cohen, Ronald M.
5001 797
Cohn, Art
5001 666
Cohn, Harry
RK 30
R 322
H 53
Cohn, Nik
WTLGD 367
5001 655
Cohn, Roy
KKBB 208
DIM 316
Cokes, Curtis
5001 238
Colbert, Claudette
ILIATM 344
KKBB 48, 362, 363
GS 134
RK 15
DIM 346
WTLGD 16, 141
TIAI 429
SOTA 307
H 111
5001 71, 87, 140, 205, 349, 351, 358,
372-373, 374, 453, 478, 562, 580, 594,
623, 672, 680, 683, 778, 785, 864
Colby, Anita
5001 108
Colcord, Mabel
5001 428
"Cold-Blooded Murder" (music)
WTLGD 253
Cold, Ulrik
WTLGD 75
Cold Wind in August, A
KKBB 249-250:n
GS 127
5001
Colditz Story, The
5001 (2nd ed)
Cole, Carol
5001 490
Cole, George
KKBB 277, 294, 295

5001 306, 413, 779
Cole, Jack
KKBB 234
R 462
5001 159, 398, 418, 752, 766
Cole, Lester
5001 369
Cole, Nat King
KKBB 29-30
H 166
5001 124, 493
Cole, Olivia
WTLGD 267
Cole, Tom
H 132
5001 689
Colegate, Isabel
SOTA 370, 372-373
5001 677
Coleman, Cy
5001 734
Coleman, Dabney
TIAI 77, 162, 163, 164, 270, 271, 432, 494,
495
H 75
5001 530, 545, 656, 780, 823
Coleman, Dave
5001 578
Coleman, John
ILIATM 164, 228
Coleman, Leo
KKBB 308
5001 473
Coleman, Nancy
5001 397
Coleman, Ornette
5001 130
Coles, Honi
SOTA 296
H 348
5001 156, 190
Coles, Robert
R 4
Colesberry, Robert F.
H 41
Colette (Sidonie-Gabrielle Claudine Colette)
KKBB 165, 249-250
WTLGD 231
SOTA 91
H 301
5001 140, 277, 285, 489, 583
Colicos, John
DIM 97, 260
TIAI 180
5001 29, 196, 592
Colin, Margaret
H 231
ML 85
5001 693, 792
Collector, The
5001
College
5001
Collet, Christopher
H 171
5001 463
Colley, Kenneth

5001 504
Collier, Constance
  KKBB 225
  R 97
  SOTA 338
  5001 28, 703, 732, 832, 864
Collier, John
  KKBB 229
  R 221
  5001 9, 182, 329, 348, 691, 739
Collier, Lois
  5001 143, 524
Collier, Patience
  TIAI 239
  5001 267
Collier, William Jr.
  5001 137, 425
Collier, William Sr.
  5001 809
Collier's (periodical)
  RK 25
  WTLGD 523
Collin, John
  TIAI 136
  5001 749
Collinge, Patricia
  5001 426, 669
Collins, Cora Sue
  5001 445
Collins, Jack
  R 407
Collins, Joan
  SOTA 147
Collins, Pat
  R 453
Collins, Ray
  KKBB 304
  5001 44, 65, 138, 199, 262, 327, 344, 415,
    451, 665, 784
Collins, Richard
  5001 764
Collinson, Peter
  GS 181: dir., *Up the Junction*, 69
  5001 364
Collison, Wilson
  5001 620
Colman, Ronald
  GS 111
  R 138
  WTLGD 31, 49
  5001 57, 199, 355, 398, 422, 436, 443, 597,
    616, 741, 742
Colomby, Harry
  H 263
  5001 783
Colon, Miriam
  SOTA 102
  5001 658
Colon, Richard
  SOTA 6
  5001 250
Colonel Blimp
  DIM 16
Colonna, Jerry
  WTLGD 499
  5001 633, 641
Color of Money, The

H 223-228
5001 (2nd ed)
Color Purple, The
  H 80-83, 414
  ML 147
  5001 (2nd ed)
Colors
  H 460-463
  5001 (2nd ed)
Colosanto, Nicholas
  5001 238
Colt, Marshall
  5001 377
Colton, John
  5001 671
Coltrane, Robbie
  H 166, 167, 279
  ML 215
  5001 183, 329, 493
Columbia Broadcasting System (CBS)
  RK 39-41
Columbia Pictures
  RK 30
  DIM 176
  R 123, 445
  WTLGD 499
  TIAI 13, 14, 36, 39
  H 311
Columbia University Film School
  H 38
"Columbo" (TV)
  R 300
Columbu, Franco
  5001 602
Columbus, Chris
  SOTA 189
  H 101-102
  5001 298, 307, 860
Coma
  WTLGD 394-396, 463, 538
  TIAI 253
  5001
Comandini, Adele
  5001 768
Comanor, Jeffrey
  R 369
  5001 579
Combs, Jeffrey
  H 68
  5001 618
Comden and Green see Comden, Betty and
    Green, Adolph
Comden, Betty
  KKBB 234, 287
  GS 237
  DIM 82
  WTLGD 399
  5001 49, 296, 374, 546, 547, 683, 740
Come Back, Africa
  5001
Come Back, Little Sheba
  R 222
  WTLGD 37
  TIAI 173
  5001
*Come Back to the 5 & Dime Jimmy Dean, Jimmy
    Dean*

TIAI 413-418
SOTA 108
H 1, 96, 233
5001 (2nd ed)
Come Out of the Kitchen (stage)
  RK 18
"Come Rain or Come Shine" (music)
  TIAI 460
Comédie-Française
  WTLGD 205
  5001 96
Comedy of Errors, The (stage)
  H 484
Comencini, Luigi
  5001 729
Comer, Anjanette
  KKBB 299
  5001 33, 440
Comes a Horseman
  WTLGD 485-488
  SOTA 29
  H 243
  5001
Comfort and Joy
  SOTA 268-271
  H 408
  5001 (2nd ed)
Comic, The
  DIM 60-62
  5001
Coming Apart
  DIM 36, 59, 148
  5001
Coming Home
  WTLGD 402-405, 517
  TIAI 163, 310
  SOTA 167
  H 243
  5001
Comingore, Dorothy
  KKBB 248
  RK 46, 52, 67
  5001 138
Commare Secca, La
  GS 7
  DIM 270
Committee, The (comedy troupe)
  DIM 344
  R 265
  TIAI 195
Como, Perry
  5001 848
Companeez, Jacques
  KKBB 246
  5001 123
Companeez, Nina
  GS 72
Company of Wolves, The
  H 166
Competition, The
  TIAI 132-133
  5001
Compromising Positions
  H 36-38, 482
  5001 (2nd ed)
Compson, Betty
  KKBB 360

WTLGD 503
5001 302, 547, 776
Compton-Bennett, see Bennett, Compton
Compton, Fay
KKBB 294, 321
5001 321, 413, 539
Compton, Joyce
5001 41, 48, 464, 642, 754, 839, 856
Compton, Juliette
5001 403, 498
Compulsion
KKBB 250:n
GS 167
5001
Comstock, Howard
5001 195
Conan the Barbarian
H 180, 251
Concerto in B Flat Minor (music)
DIM 241
Condamné à mort s'est échappé, Un, see *A Man Escaped*
Conde, Eduardo
H 19
5001 216
Condemned of Altona, The
KKBB 209
Condon, Richard
GS 95
SOTA 376, 377, 378, 379
5001 462, 600
Conduct Unbecoming
WTLGD 64-66
5001
Confession, The (L'Aveu)
DIM 200-205
R 209, 212-215
WTLGD 95
TIAI 312
5001
Confessions of a Nazi Spy
RK 56
Confessions of Felix Krull, The
KKBB 251:n
WTLGD 355
5001
Confidence Man, The (book)
ILIATM 168, 206
TIAI 98
Confidential Agent
KKBB 251
R 420
5001
Confidential Report
RK 83
Conformist, The (Il Conformista)
DIM 270-275, 415, 426
R 28, 33, 174, 258, 401
WTLGD 146, 326
TIAI 335
H 396, 398
5001
Conformista, Il, see *The Conformist*
Conforti, Gino
R 78
Confucius
WTLGD 473

Congdon, James
5001 416
Congo Maisie, see *Red Dust*
Conklin, Chester
5001 58, 313, 314, 491, 726, 817
Conklin, Heinie
5001 18
Conlin, Jimmy
5001 234, 255, 302, 313, 483, 562, 662, 726, 736
Conn, Didi
5001 857
Connaughton, Shane
ML 179, 181, 182
5001 509
Connecticut Yankee in King Arthur's Court, A
TIAI 483
SOTA 357
5001
Connection, The
5001
Connell, Jane
R 298
5001 455
Connelly, Jennifer
SOTA 362
5001 548
Connelly, Marc
RK 9, 10, 18, 41, 80
5001 118, 306
Connery, Sean
KKBB 141
DIM 104, 119, 285, 329, 388, 389
R 277, 359, 390
WTLGD 107-111, 157-159, 207, 242, 538-540
TIAI 218, 219
SOTA 170
H 162, 319
ML 145-49
5001 25, 189, 244, 270, 303, 361, 461, 466, 491, 492, 503, 521, 558, 634, 669, 670, 769, 772, 807, 841, 857, 863, 864
Connolly, Bobby
5001 106
Connolly, Jon
ML 112
5001 202
Connolly, Mike
5001 356
Connolly, Myles
5001 712
Connolly, Ray
5001 709
Connolly, Walter
KKBB 320, 362
5001 75, 293, 373, 420, 464, 535, 779, 796
Connor, Edgar
5001 314
Connors, Chuck
5001 569
Connors, Mike
R 359
Conquest
KKBB 285
R 420
5001

Conrack
R 293-298, 312
WTLGD 170
5001
Conrad, Joseph
KKBB 327
RK 34
DIM 138, 415-416
WTLGD 380-383, 414, 417, 515, 518
TIAI 402
5001 101, 206, 434, 558, 617, 649, 664, 814
Conrad, Michael
R 354
Conrad, William
5001 394
Conried, Hans
5001 75, 248, 384, 548, 665, 727
Conroy, Frank
KKBB 328
5001 17, 299, 391, 405, 514, 560, 645
Conroy, Jack
ML 181
Conroy, Pat
R 294-297
TIAI 51
5001 153, 303
Conselman, William
5001 545
Conservative Digest (periodical)
H 439
"Consider Yourself" (music)
DIM 359
Considine, John
WTLGD 261, 283, 444
H 137
5001 412, 449, 791, 827
Constant Nymph, The
GS 38
DIM 34
Constantine, Eddie
5001 20
Constantine, Michael
5001 347, 356, 622
Conte, Richard
KKBB 346
DIM 424
R 172
WTLGD 415
5001 289, 341, 357, 661, 760, 822, 832
Contempt
GS 142
Conti, Albert
5001 555
Conti, Bill
WTLGD 412
TIAI 474
SOTA 63
5001 46, 139, 636, 687
Conti, Mario
5001 667
Conti, Tom
WTLGD 382
5001 206
Continental Divide, The
TIAI 254-255
5001
Contini, Alfio

5001 863
Contner, James A.
  TIAI 240
  5001 690
Conversation, The
  R 314, 318, 327
  TIAI 227-228
Conversation Piece (Gruppo di Famiglia in un Interno)
  WTLGD 35-40
  5001
Converse, Frank
  ML 308
  5001 227
"Conversing with Mother" (epilogue of *Kaos*)
  H 124
Convoy
  WTLGD 427, 428, 430, 432-434
  5001
Convy, Bert
  WTLGD 359
  5001 665
Conway, Jack
  RK 22 (ill.)
  5001 35, 201, 340, 420, 556, 620, 741, 744, 779, 807
Conway, Mrs. Jack
  RK 22 (ill.)
Conway, Kevin
  WTLGD 490
Conway, Tim
  ML 183
  WTLGD 409
Conway, Tom
  KKBB 246
  5001 125, 233, 550
Cooder, Ry
  TIAI 257
  H 142
  5001 92, 165, 698
Cooeyate, Doug
  5001 454
Coogan, Jackie
  TIAI 354
  5001 5, 224, 244, 392, 466
Coogan, Keith
  ML 97-98
  5001 159
Cook, Donald
  5001 123, 679
Cook, Elisha Jr.
  KKBB 291, 305, 347
  WTLGD 123
  TIAI 179
  SOTA 376
  5001 76, 121, 198, 301, 322, 394, 454, 531, 549, 569, 578, 643, 671
Cook, Fielder
  GS dir., *A Big Hand for the Little Lady*, 18; *How to Save a Marriage--and Ruin Your Life*, 18-24
Cook, Joe
  RK 34
Cook, Kenneth
  DIM 417
  5001 558
Cook, Peter

GS 63
SOTA 305, 341
H 379
5001 59, 170
Cook, Robin
  WTLGD 395
  5001 147
Cook, Roderick
  5001 304
Cook, Will
  5001 800
Cooke, Alan
  5001 482
Cooke, Alistair
  H 190
  5001 765
Cooke, Sam
  H 50, 337
Cool Breeze
  R 65
Cool Hand Luke
  GS 35, 60, 272
  DIM 181
  R 261, 354
  TIAI 21, 78
Cool World, The
  5001
Cooley, Denton
  5001 768
Cooley High
  WTLGD 188-189
Coolidge, Calvin
  RK 72
  DIM 46
Coolidge, Martha
  SOTA 318
  H 132; dir., *Valley Girl*, 132, 134
Coolidge, Rita
  5001 569
Coop, Denys
  GS 211
  5001 75, 763
Cooper, Ben
  5001 642
Cooper, Gary
  ILIATM 240, 242
  KKBB 184, 185, 186, 190, 223, 281, 345
  DIM 77, 347, 387
  R 87, 267
  WTLGD 15, 108, 174, 487
  TIAI 20, 33, 261
  SOTA 61, 236
  H 16, 377
  ML 48, 127, 254
  5001 15, 48, 57, 87, 139, 183, 256, 262, 268, 331, 332, 355, 421, 428, 438, 473, 487, 498, 514, 566, 577, 654, 678, 697, 777, 778, 817, 829
Cooper, Gladys
  KKBB 298
  WTLGD 64
  5001 400, 424, 446, 508, 536, 583, 618, 833
Cooper, Gordon (Gordo)
  SOTA 65, 233
Cooper, Horace
  KKBB 367
  5001 831

Cooper, Jackie
  WTLGD 433
  TIAI 223
  5001 106, 128, 730, 731, 865
Cooper, James Fenimore
  WTLGD 512, 514, 519
Cooper, Jeanne
  5001 16
Cooper, Jeff
  5001 93
Cooper, Melville
  5001 8, 174, 240, 337, 373, 595, 599, 618, 760, 780, 785
Cooper, Merian C.
  5001 194, 263, 608, 672
Cooper, Trudy
  SOTA 65
Cooper, Wyatt
  5001 129
Coote, Robert
  5001 228, 259, 284, 311, 767, 815
Copeau, Jacques
  5001 617
Copeland, Joan
  WTLGD 357
Copland, Aaron
  5001 327, 533, 540
Coppel, Alec
  KKBB 243
  5001 81, 118
Coppola, Carmine
  TIAI 145, 150
  ML 103
  5001 290, 516
Coppola, Francis Ford
  GS 170; dir., *Finian's Rainbow*, 96, 159, 227
  DIM 420, 421, 423-425; dir., *The Rain People*, 59; *The Godfather*, 420-426
  R 314, 318, 327, 330, 396-403, 441-442, 471; dir., *The Godfather*, 161, 169-170, 173-174, 228-229, 256, 269, 314, 317, 327, 396-398, 442, 469; *The Conversation*, 314, 318, 327; *The Godfather, Part II*, 396-403, 471
  WTLGD 82, 202, 324, 393, 428, 513, 515, 518; dir., *The Rain People*, 82; *The Godfather, Part II*, 133, 178, 198, 202, 204, 267, 317, 328, 416, 427, 486; *Apocalypse Now*, 269, 324, 428; *The Godfather*, 317, 320, 328, 427, 486
  TIAI 8, 18, 138, 143, 145, 185, 208, 227, 296-300, 328, 354, 399, 402, 460; dir., *Apocalypse Now*, 18, 52, 244, 299, 346, 402; *The Godfather*, 109, 190, 227, 242, 244; *The Godfather, Part II*, 109, 227, 241, 244, 457; *The Conversation*, 227-228; *One from the Heart*, 296-300, 314, 328-329, 354, 460; *The Outsiders*, 399; *Rumble Fish*, 399
  SOTA 29, 46, 47, 48, 177, 230, 293-298; dir., *One from the Heart*, 46, 47, 230, 296; *The Outsiders*, 47, 296; *The Godfather*, 53, 101, 177, 339, 362, 377; *The Godfather, Part II*, 74, 101, 103, 177, 298, 339, 362; *Rumble Fish*, 104, 120, 296, 310; *Apocalypse Now*,

119, 278; *The Cotton Club*, 293-298
H 61, 136, 219-221, 303-306, 471; dir., *The Cotton Club*, 65, 220; *Rumble Fish*, 136, 220, 462; *Apocalypse Now*, 182-183, 252, 305, 462; *Peggy Sue Got Married*, 219-221, 305; *One from the Heart*, 220, 471; *The Outsiders*, 220, 317, 348; *Gardens of Stone*, 303-306; *The Rain People*, 303; *The Godfather*, 303, 304; *The Godfather, Part II*, 303, 304
ML dir., *Apocalypse Now*, 309; *The Cotton Club*, 309; *The Godfather*, 166, 310, 311; *The Godfather Part II* 166, 309, 310, 311; *The Godfather Part III*, 309-14; *Life Without Zoe*, 103; *One from the Heart*, 309; *The Outsiders*, 309, 311; *Rumble Fish*, 198, 309; *Tucker*, 309
5001 78, 156, 244, 279, 289, 290, 516, 521, 549, 550, 570, 573, 613, 681, 770
Coppola, Sofia
ML 103, 313
5001 574
Cops and Robbers
R 162, 361
"Copulating Mermaid of Venice, California, The" (short story)
H 463
Coquelin
H 312
Coquelin, Jean
5001 572
Coquillon, John
5001 721, 790
Corbeau, Le (The Raven)
5001
Corbin, Barry
TIAI 31, 494
H 200
5001 535, 809, 823
Corbluth, J. D.
ILIATM 343
Corcoran, Donna
5001 198
Cord, Alex
GS 244, 247
Corday, Mara
5001 725
Cordy, Raymond
KKBB 320
5001 1, 59, 409
Corelli, Franco
SOTA 278
Corey, Jeff
KKBB 291, 341
DIM 213, 214
5001 75, 108, 394, 424, 508, 541, 645, 663
Corey, Professor Irwin
WTLGD 188, 271
5001 118, 757
Corey, Wendell
KKBB 238, 337
5001 71, 243, 614, 661
Corigliano, John
TIAI 130
Corkidi, Rafael
5001 781
Corkill, Danny

5001 487
Corley, Pat
5001 414
Cormack, Bartlett
5001 273, 307
Corman, Avery
TIAI 17
5001 541
Corman, Roger
ILIATM 303
TIAI 193, 194, 385; dir., *The Little Shop of Horrors* (1960), 193
SOTA 80
H 232, 247; dir., *The Little Shop of Horrors*, 247
5001 38, 181, 290, 344, 427, 629, 738, 743, 789, 837, 852
Corn Is Green, The
R 3
5001
Cornelisen, Ann
TIAI 315
Cornelius, Henry
KKBB 270, 330; dir., *Genevieve*, 270; *Passport to Pimlico*, 330
5001 281, 348, 569
Cornell, Katharine
KKBB 73, 295
5001 52, 704, 804
Cornered
ILIATM 325
DIM 63
R 262
Cornfeld, Stuart
5001 252
Cornfield, Hubert
GS dir., *The Night of the Following Day*, 277-278
DIM dir., *The Night of the Following Day*, 59
5001 526
Cornford, John
KKBB 223
Cornthwaite, Robert
5001 759
Cornu, Aurora
DIM 264
5001 140
Corot, Jean-Baptiste-Camille
WTLGD 193
SOTA 51, 255
Corporation for Public Broadcasting
H 442
Correll, Mady
5001 494
Corri, Adrienne
5001 142, 195, 632
Corsaire, Le (music)
WTLGD 345
Corson, William
5001 703
Cort, Bud
DIM 228
5001 101, 319, 469
Cortázar, Julio
5001 85
Cortese, Valentina

KKBB 235
DIM 162
R 179
5001 7, 37, 52, 175, 246, 386, 417, 664
Cortez, Ricardo
5001 409, 455, 747, 850
Cortez, Stanley
5001 451, 459, 526
Corvette Summer
TIAI 221
5001
Corwin, Norman
5001 443
Cory, Desmond
5001 221
Cosby, Bill
R 132, 281
WTLGD 66-67, 531-532
5001 115, 418
Così Fan Tutte (music)
WTLGD 73
Cosima, Renée
KKBB 262
5001 220
Cosmatos, George P.
SOTA 374-375
5001 615
Cosmological Eye, The (book)
KKBB 274
Cosmopolitan (periodical)
KKBB 192
WTLGD 223
Cosmopolitan Pictures
RK 32, 66, 68, 70
Cossart, Ernest
KKBB 249
5001 26, 143, 184, 422, 768
Costa-Gavras
DIM 63-67, 200, 202-205; dir., *Z*, 63-67, 152, 154, 200, 202, 204, 316, 317, 319; *The Sleeping Car Murder*, 64; *The Confession*, 200-205
R 163, 212-216, 391; dir., *State of Siege*, 163, 210, 213-216; *Z*, 210-215; *The Confession*, 210-215; *The Sleeping Car Murder*, 391
WTLGD 95-98; dir., *The Sleeping Car Murder*, 95; *Z*, 95, 97; *The Confession*, 95; *State of Siege*, 96; *Special Section*, 96-98
TIAI 309-312; dir., *Missing*, 309-312; *State of Siege*, 312; *The Confession*, 312
SOTA 77
H 54; dir., *Z*, 54; *State of Siege*, 182; *Missing*, 182
ML dir., *Betrayed*, 241; *Music Box*, 239-42
5001 151, 485, 486, 504, 700, 862
Costa, Mary
5001 304
Costello, Dolores
KKBB 304
5001 451, 489, 762
Costello, Elvis
ML 124
Costello, Lou
ILIATM 307
GS 186

DIM 180
WTLGD 101
TIAI 108, 467
H 155
5001 631
Coster, Nicolas
WTLGD 493
5001 70, 687, 703
Costner, Kevin
H 14, 318, 356, 357, 480, 481
ML 126-28; dir., *Dances With Wolves*, 295-97
5001 108, 242, 532, 682, 807
Cottage Productions
DIM 58
Cotten, Joseph
KKBB 10-11, 199, 248, 267, 304, 358, 361
GS 121
RK 54
DIM 415
SOTA 194
H 263
5001 66, 138, 206, 237, 279, 346, 356, 384, 451, 522, 554, 590, 669, 683, 760, 784, 798, 804
Cotton Club, The
SOTA 293-298
H 65, 220
ML 309
5001 (2nd ed)
Cotton Comes to Harlem
DIM 314
R 61
WTLGD 189
"Cotton-Eyed Joe" (music)
SOTA 247
Cotton, Oliver
H 73
5001 214
Coughlan, Mary
ML 44
Coulouris, George
KKBB 248, 251, 327
R 390
5001 138, 152, 256, 406, 503, 533, 558, 565, 824
Coulter, Clare
TIAI 422
5001 111
Coulter, Michael
5001 342
Counsellor-at-Law
KKBB 251-252:n
5001
Count Basie, see Basie, Count
Count of Monte Cristo, The (TV)
WTLGD 535
Count of Monte Cristo, The (1934)
5001 (2nd ed)
Counterfeit Traitor, The
DIM 136
Countess from Hong Kong, A
KKBB 45
GS 278
R 31
WTLGD 424
Countess Maritza (stage)

WTLGD 13
Country
SOTA 234-237, 319
5001 (2nd ed)
Country Girl, The
DIM 136
5001
Coup de foudre, see *Entre nous*
Coup de grâce
5001
Coup de torchon (*Clean Slate*)
TIAI 442-445
5001 (2nd ed)
"Couple of Swells, A" (music)
DIM 82
Couples and Robbers
H 452
Courcel, Nicole
5001 465, 685, 729
Courtenay, Tom
ILIATM 257
SOTA 113, 114-115
5001 170, 195, 203
Courtney, Inez
5001 322, 677, 733
Cousin, Cousine
ML 97
WTLGD 204
H 195
5001 (2nd ed)
Cousineau, Jean
5001 510
Cousins
ML 96-99
5001 (2nd ed)
Cousins, Les, see *The Cousins*
Cousins, The (*Les Cousins*)
ILIATM 132-136, 148
DIM 54
5001
Cousteau, Jacques-Yves
KKBB 183, 185; co-dir., *The Silent World*, 185; dir., *World Without Sun*, 185
DIM 307; co-dir., *The Silent World*, 307
Coutard, Raoul
KKBB 13, 235
GS 79
DIM 63, 202
SOTA 229, 230, 366
5001 20, 49, 135, 151, 171, 246, 385, 430, 577, 582, 676, 862
Cover Girl
5001
Cowan, Jerome
KKBB 305
5001 262, 332, 346, 386, 454, 543
Coward, Noël
KKBB 327
GS 54, 163, 164, 165
DIM 16
R 204, 347, 349
WTLGD 6, 21, 93, 311, 482, 529
5001 75, 81, 102, 127, 360, 555, 599, 706, 778, 825
Cowboys, The
DIM 390-393, 398
R 259

5001
Cowl, Darry
5001 441
Cowl, Jane
5001 572
Cowley, Graeme
SOTA 245
5001 688, 810
Cowper, Nicola
H 53, 54
5001 202
Cox, Alan
H 100
5001 860
Cox, Alex
SOTA 211-213; dir., *Repo Man*, 211-213, 262, 348
5001 623, 624
Cox, E'lon
H 145
5001 381
Cox, Paul
SOTA 59-60
5001 431
Cox, Ronny
WTLGD 229
5001 66, 95, 635
Cox, Sura
H 98
5001 255
Cox, Wally
5001 310
Coxe, Louis O.
5001 72
Coy, Walter
5001 662
Coyne, Jeanne (Jeannie)
5001 399, 727
Coyote, Peter
TIAI 350
SOTA 56, 57, 349, 351, 352, 353
H 56, 57, 273-274
5001 164, 225, 325, 377, 559, 698
Crabb, Jack
5001 424
Crabbe, Buster
TIAI 125, 126
5001 744
Crabe, James
5001 636
Crack in the Mirror
GS 167
Cracked Nuts
5001
Cracknell, Ruth
TIAI 57
Cragun, Richard
WTLGD 347
5001 795
Craig, Carolyn
5001 724
Craig, Helen
5001 754
Craig, James
5001 344, 398, 400
Craig, May
5001 608

Craig, Michael
  5001 511, 706
Craig, Stuart
  TIAI 84
Craig, Wendy
  5001 515
Craig's Wife
  WTLGD 437
  TIAI 80
Craigie, Ingrid
  H 403, 405
  5001 177
Craigie, Jill
  KKBB 307
  5001 461
Crain, Jeanne
  ILIATM 306
  5001 415, 419, 490, 583, 711
Crampton, Barbara
  H 68
  5001 618
Crandall, Edward
  5001 288
Crane, Hart
  WTLGD 297
  TIAI 435, 436
Crane, Mack
  5001 91
Crane, Norma
  DIM 332
  5001 242
Crane, Stephen
  5001 101, 619
Cranes Are Flying, The (Letyat Zhuravli)
  ILIATM 42
  5001
Cravat, Nick
  KKBB 252
  5001 163, 656
Craven, Frank
  5001 51, 391, 556, 711
Craven, Matt
  H 282
  5001 773
Crawford, Broderick
  KKBB 205, 240
  5001 19, 57-58, 67, 94, 345, 527, 554, 668
Crawford, Christina
  TIAI 234
  5001 492
Crawford, Joan
  KKBB 90, 123, 126, 189, 275, 285
  GS 125, 177, 206
  DIM 137, 406
  R 16, 429, 461
  WTLGD 27, 61
  TIAI 232, 234
  H 27, 469
  ML 193-94, 274
  5001 40, 128, 169, 249, 259, 298, 299, 336,
    337, 345, 353, 382, 439, 464, 480, 485,
    555, 556, 591, 613, 674, 705, 718, 732,
    753, 777, 782, 787, 790, 846, 847
Crawford, John
  5001 48, 221
Crawford, Martha
  H 98

5001 255
Crawford, Michael
  DIM 83
  5001 272, 343, 401
Crazy Love, see *Love Is a Dog from Hell*
Crazy Mama
  WTLGD 322
Crazy Quilt, The
  KKBB 14
  R 263, 457
  WTLGD 184
  5001
Creature from the Black Lagoon, The
  5001
Créatures, Les
  5001
Cregar, Laird
  5001 83, 326, 327, 337, 761
Cremer, Bruno
  WTLGD 97
  5001 476, 700, 719
Crenna, Richard
  DIM 86, 260
  R 359
  TIAI 256
  SOTA 308, 311
  H 348
  5001 90, 195, 249, 467, 615, 706
Crenshaw, Marshall
  5001 49
Cresson, James (pseud. is James Hicks)
  H 245
  5001 498
Crews, Laura Hope
  KKBB 243
  5001 26, 116, 248, 354, 683
Cria!
  SOTA 127
Crichton, Charles
  KKBB 255, 295; dir., *Dead of Night* (seg-
    ment), 254-255; *The Lavender Hill Mob*,
    295
  5001 55, 178, 193, 414
Crichton, Douglas
  5001 179
Crichton, Michael
  DIM 276
  R 216-217, 330
  WTLGD 394-396, 538-540; dir., *Coma*,
    394-396, 463, 538; *Westworld*, 395,
    538; *The Great Train Robbery*,
    538-540
  TIAI 252-254; dir., *Looker*, 252-254; *Coma*,
    253; *Westworld*, 254
  5001 26, 147, 179, 303, 434, 748, 829
Cries and Whispers (Viskningar och Rop)
  R 89-94, 346
  WTLGD 74, 431
  5001
*Crime and Punishment (Crime et châtiment;
    1935; directed by Pierre Chenal)*
  5001
*Crime and Punishment (1935; directed by Josef
    von Sternberg)*
  KKBB 57, 252:n, 262, 302
  DIM 161
  R 290, 351

5001
Crime et châtiment, see *Crime and Punishment*
    (Chenal)
Crime of Mr. Lange, The
  KKBB 141
Crime Without Passion
  5001
Crimean War
  WTLGD 538
Crimes and Misdemeanors
  ML 199-203
  5001 (2nd ed)
Crimes of the Heart
  H 233-237, 378
  5001 (2nd ed)
*Criminal Life of Archibaldo de la Cruz, The
    (Ensayo de un Crimen)*
  5001
Crimson Pirate, The
  ILIATM 24, 81
  KKBB 180, 252:n, 257, 297
  WTLGD 29, 37
  TIAI 173
  5001
Crin Blanc, see *White Mane*
Crippa, Maddalena
  TIAI 319
Crips (gang)
  H 460, 461, 462
Crisis
  WTLGD 21
Crisp, Donald
  KKBB 184, 290, 316, 355
  GS 46
  5001 77, 107, 130, 174, 380, 384, 409, 426,
    468, 505, 517, 518, 542, 543, 600, 620,
    660, 683, 734, 807, 830, 846, 851
Crisp, Quentin
  WTLGD 498
Crist, Judith
  ILIATM 83
Cristal, Linda
  5001 800
Cristaldi, Franco
  5001 134
Cristo Proibito, Il (Strange Deception)
  KKBB 252-253:n
  5001
Cristofer, Michael
  SOTA 279-280
  H 324
  ML 317
  5001 234, 425, 843
Criswell, Dr. W. A.
  H 440-441, 442
  5001 770
Critic, The
  R 280
Croce, Arlene
  R 55-59
Crockett, Dick
  5001 582
Crombie, Donald
  TIAI 158-160; dir., *Caddie*, 158-160
  5001 114
Cromwell
  DIM 181

R 15
5001
Cromwell, John
    KKBB 272; dir., *The Goddess*, 158,
        271-273; *Algiers*, 244
    5001 14, 28, 179, 218, 289, 359, 448, 539,
        597, 683, 689, 721, 815
Cromwell, Oliver
    DIM 181
Cromwell, Richard
    KKBB 290
    GS 126
    R 433
    5001 380, 428, 590, 860
Cronauer, Adrian
    H 422-423
Cronenberg, David
    TIAI 192; dir., *The Brood*, 192
    H 209-212; dir., *The Fly* (1986), 209-212;
        The Brood, 210
    5001 252
Cronenweth, Jordan
    SOTA 267
    H 220, 305
    5001 21, 139, 167, 275, 279, 574, 716, 863
Cronin, A. J.
    KKBB 350
    5001 138, 392, 710, 815
Cronyn, Hume
    KKBB 333
    DIM 74, 229
    R 295
    H 5, 6
    5001 35, 108, 144, 153, 276, 421, 579, 592,
        669, 752, 865
Crooke, Leland
    H 454
    5001 567
Crosby, Bing
    KKBB 7, 41
    R 286
    WTLGD 5, 25, 27, 66
    TIAI 166, 273, 274
    SOTA 5, 177
    H 187
    ML 164
    5001 32, 75, 116, 152, 157, 425, 574, 632,
        633, 828
Crosby, Bob
    5001 764
Crosby, Don
    TIAI 56
Crosby, Floyd
    KKBB 357
    5001 98, 145, 331, 740, 852
Croset, Paule
    5001 228
Crosland, Alan
    5001 547
Crosman, Henrietta
    5001 496
Cross, Ben
    TIAI 245, 246
    5001 131
Cross Creek
    SOTA 55-59
    5001 (2nd ed)

Cross, Harley
    5001 487
Cross, James
    5001 762
Cross of Iron
    WTLGD 433
Cross of Lorraine, The
    DIM 63
Crosse, Rupert
    DIM 75, 76
    5001 622
Crossfire
    ILIATM 235
    KKBB 253:n
    DIM 63
    5001
Crossing Paris (Four Bags Full)
    KKBB 267
Crossman, Henrietta
    5001 645
Crosson, Robert
    5001 480
Crossroads
    H 142-144
    5001 (2nd ed)
Crothers, Rachel
    5001 732
Crothers, Scatman
    TIAI 2
    SOTA 20
    5001 260, 396, 549, 674, 677, 682
Crouse, Lindsay
    WTLGD 277
    TIAI 441
    SOTA 43, 45, 161, 162, 247
    5001 172, 353, 585, 596, 686, 813
Crouse, Russel
    5001 32, 115, 421, 697, 711
"Crow Killer, The" (short story)
    R 87
Crowden, Graham
    R 389
Crowe, Cameron
    TIAI 409
    ML dir., *Say Anything*, 133-36
    5001 238, 656
Crowley, Mart
    DIM 137
    5001 98
Crowther, Bosley
    ILIATM 68, 71, 77, 78, 84, 85-86, 88-89,
        92, 132, 142, 146, 163-164, 206, 243,
        246, 249-250
    KKBB 8-9, 36, 157, 200, 206-207, 370
    RK 43, 44
Cruikshank, George
    GS 203
Cruikshank, Sally
    SOTA 21
Cruise, Tom
    SOTA 39, 122
    H 168, 223, 224, 225, 226, 265
    ML 78, 80-81, 249-55
    5001 93, 146, 613, 631, 780
Cruising
    SOTA 103
Crusades, The

5001
Crusoe (1989)
    ML 115-17
    5001 (2nd ed)
Crutchley, Rosalie
    5001 321, 695
Cruz, Celia
    H 232
    5001 693
Cruze, James
    5001 302, 349
Cry Freedom
    H 399-401, 476
    5001 (2nd ed)
Cry in the Dark, A
    ML 30-33
    5001 (2nd ed)
Cry Uncle
    DIM 314, 325, 384
    R 116
    WTLGD 495
Cryer, Jon
    H 133, 134
    5001 594
Crystal, Billy
    H 379
    ML 39
    5001 597
Cuban Rhythm Band
    556
Cue (periodical)
    RK 44
Cugat, Xavier
    5001 54, 174, 703
Cukor, George
    ILIATM 303-305, 312; dir., *Pat and Mike*,
        81, 304; *A Star is Born*, 207; *The
        Philadelphia Story*, 304; *Bhowani
        Junction*, 305; *Les Girls*, 305; *The
        Actress*, 305; *A Life of Her Own*, 305;
        The Model and the Marriage Broker,
        305; *Edward, My Son*, 305; *A Woman's
        Face*, 305; *Romeo and Juliet*, 305; *A
        Double Life*, 305; *The Chapman Report*,
        305
    KKBB 228, 231, 240, 243, 267, 330, 340;
        dir., *Holiday*, 68; *My Fair Lady*, 90;
        Adam's Rib, 228, 330; *Little Women*,
        229, 241; *Born Yesterday*, 240; *The
        Philadelphia Story*, 241; *Camille*, 243;
        Gaslight, 267; *A Star is Born* (1954),
        272, 283, 363; *Pat and Mike*, 330;
        Romeo and Juliet (1936), 340
    GS dir., *Camille*, 135; *The Chapman Report*,
        151; *Dinner at Eight*, 230; *Holiday*,
        176; *It Should Happen to You*, 185;
        Little Women, 177; *My Fair Lady*, 108,
        200; *The Philadelphia Story*, 177
    DIM dir., *The Women*, 137; *Pat and Mike*,
        184; *The Chapman Report*, 281, 408;
        My Fair Lady, 328
    R 97-98; dir., *Dinner at Eight*, 72, 390, 425;
        A Star is Born, 75; *Travels with My
        Aunt*, 97-98; *Let's Make Love*, 154-155;
        Justine, 343
    WTLGD 7, 240; dir., *Holiday*, 3, 18; *The
        Philadelphia Story*, 3, 18, 28; *Sylvia*

Scarlett, 7, 201; *My Fair Lady*, 8, 177; *Travels with My Aunt*, 19, 194; *Camille*, 146; *Dinner at Eight*, 155; *What Price Hollywood*, 240; *A Star Is Born* (1954), 240, 243, 244; *The Blue Bird*, 424
TIAI 237, 247-248; dir., *A Star Is Born* (1954), 45, 277; *Little Women* (1933), 61; *Rich and Famous*, 247-248; *Dinner at Eight*, 335; *Camille* (1937), 345; *Pat and Mike*, 429
5001 5, 18, 71, 94, 116, 129, 190, 199, 279, 327, 329, 336, 373, 391, 418, 428, 467, 490, 507, 569, 580, 627, 635, 638, 645, 694, 707, 732, 738, 739, 744, 788, 830, 847, 864
Cullen, Robert
5001 36
Cullum, John
R 54
5001 322, 465, 668
Culp, Robert
DIM 11-13
5001 89
Culpepper Cattle Co., The
R 428
Culver, Michael
WTLGD 65
5001 568
Culver, Roland
KKBB 255, 266, 323
5001 178, 200, 254, 544, 776, 794
Cumbuka, Ji-Tu
WTLGD 228
5001 559
Cumming, Dorothy
KKBB 253
5001 170
Cummings, Constance
5001 23, 55, 81
Cummings, Irving
5001 509, 736, 751, 829
Cummings, Jack
5001 93, 106, 106, 399, 767
Cummings, Quinn
WTLGD 376, 377
5001 296
Cummings, Robert
KKBB 259
DIM 13
WTLGD 29
H 265
5001 121, 186, 189, 251, 397, 649, 697, 856
Cummins, Peggy
KKBB 48
5001 21, 310
Cundey, Dean
SOTA 164
5001 45, 638
Cunningham, Cecil
5001 41, 82, 84, 400, 733, 856
Cunningham, George
5001 105
Cunningham, John W.
5001 331
Cunningham, Sarah
DIM 391
Cuny, Alain

KKBB 253
SOTA 126
5001 54, 163, 240, 481, 578, 817
Curie, Eve
5001 446
Curran, Homer
5001 694
Currie, Finlay
KKBB 276
R 260
WTLGD 210
5001 63, 301, 349, 376, 769
Curry, Tim
TIAI 345
H 453
5001 29, 567
Curse of the Cat People, The
WTLGD 547
5001
Curtain Up
5001 (2nd ed)
Curtin, Valerie
R 413
TIAI 323, 429, 445
SOTA 153
5001 15, 64, 682, 806
Curtis, Alan
5001 332, 464, 578, 678
Curtis, Jackie
5001 847, 850
Curtis, Jamie Lee
WTLGD 547
5001 314, 786
Curtis, Ken
5001 608, 662
Curtis, Liane
5001 684
Curtis, Lucinda
5001 535
Curtis, Richard
ML 271-72
5001 742
Curtis, Tony
ILIATM 39
KKBB 205, 298, 348, 356
GS 102, 166, 167
DIM 25, 67, 252
WTLGD 3, 29, 218-219, 396, 547
TIAI 331, 332
5001 411, 424, 691, 699, 736, 787
Curtis, Walt
ML 195
5001 454
Curtiz, Michael
KKBB 228, 245, 360; co-dir., *The Adventures of Robin Hood*, 180, 184, 228; dir., *Captain Blood*, 184; *The Charge of the Light Brigade*, 184; *The Sea Hawk*, 185; *Casablanca*, 194, 245, 360, 361; *Mildred Pierce*, 253; *The Breaking Point*, 360
DIM dir., *Casablanca*, 65
R 419
5001 8, 27, 112, 118, 122, 130, 195, 249, 263, 391, 393, 421, 480, 512, 524, 600, 653, 660, 762, 776, 796, 828, 853
Curwood, James Oliver

ML 208
5001 57
Curzi, Pierre
H 238
5001 182
Cusack, Cyril
KKBB 149, 321
R 221
TIAI 243
5001 2, 320, 338, 509, 539, 793
Cusack, Joan
H 419
ML 65, 134
5001 105, 656, 849
Cusack, John
ML 133-36, 143, 208, 284-86
5001 239, 656, 705
Cushing, Peter
5001 137, 500, 514, 815
Custer, Gen. George A.
DIM 212-216
Cuthbertson, Iain
ML 6
5001 298
Cutter's Way (also known as *Cutter and Bone*)
5001
Cyn, Mme., see Payne, Cynthia
Cyrano de Bergerac
KKBB 203
Cyrano de Bergerac (play)
H 312, 313
Cyrano et d'Artagnan
TIAI 151
Cyrus the Great
WTLGD 557
Cyrus the Younger
WTLGD 555, 557
Czapsky, Stefan
5001 812
Czerniakow, Adam
H 85
Czettell
5001 605
Czinner, Paul
KKBB 260; dir., *Dreaming Lips*, 260; *Stolen Life*, 350
5001 36, 203
Czyzewska, Elzbieta
ML 241
5001 504

D

Dabadie, Jean-Loup
WTLGD 152, 153
5001 128, 685
DaCosta, Morton
5001 504
Dad
ML 204-207
5001 (2nd ed)
Daddy Long Legs
5001
Dade, Frances

5001 201
Dafoe, Willem
  H 253
  ML 54-55, 252
  5001 93, 486, 586
Dagover, Lil
  5001 113
Dahl, Arlene
  KKBB 184
  5001 766
Dahl, Roald
  GS 226
  ML 228
  5001 840, 842, 857
Dahlbeck, Eva
  ILIATM 106-107
  5001 104, 161, 203, 418, 664, 688
Dahlen, Armin
  5001 193
Dailey, Dan
  ILIATM 223
  KKBB 222, 287-288
  5001 374, 404, 563, 752, 771, 865
Daily, Elizabeth
  TIAI 354
  H 58
  5001 224, 573
Daily Mirror (newspaper)
  KKBB 311
Dain Curse, The (TV)
  WTLGD 556
Daisy Miller
  R 465
"Daktari" (TV)
  KKBB 183
Dalban, Max
  5001 95
Dale, Esther
  5001 41, 162, 210, 448, 494, 534, 542
Dale, Grover
  5001 407
Dale, Janet
  5001 595
Daley, Robert
  H 34
  5001 596, 854
Dali, Salvador
  ILIATM 290
  KKBB 348
  TIAI 148
  5001 10, 132, 701
Dalio, Marcel
  ILIATM 108
  KKBB 245, 298, 342, 360
  5001 122, 126, 300, 318, 343, 424, 441,
    575, 647, 649, 672, 694
Dall, John
  KKBB 48
  DIM 401
  5001 30, 155, 310, 699
Dallas, Charlene
  WTLGD 93
  5001 616
Dallesandro, Joe
  DIM 155, 157
  WTLGD 82, 557
  SOTA 295, 298

5001 77, 156
Dallimore, Maurice
  5001 145-146
Dalrymple, Ian
  5001 606
Dalton, Audrey
  5001 774
Dalton, Timothy
  GS 175
  WTLGD 553
  TIAI 125, 126
  5001 10, 163, 250, 423, 468, 851
Daltrey, Roger
  WTLGD 83
  5001 424
Dalva, Robert
  5001 78
Daly, James
  5001 586
Daly, Timothy
  TIAI 322
  5001 190, 449
Daly, Tom
  5001 139
Daly, Tyne
  WTLGD 151, 254-255
  5001 221, 381
d'Amboise, Jacques
  5001 667
D'Ambrosio, Franc
  ML 312, 314
D'Amico, Masolino
  5001 37
D'Amico, Suso Cecchi
  DIM 183
  WTLGD 37
  5001 63, 69, 154, 172, 364, 637, 823
Damn Yankees
  TIAI 344
Damned, The
  DIM 86-88, 271, 272, 274
  R 145, 148, 342-343, 345
  WTLGD 330
  5001
Damned Don't Cry, The
  5001 (2nd ed)
Damone, Vic
  5001 398
D'Amore e d'Anarchia, see Love and Anarchy
Dana, Leora
  DIM 147, 391
  5001 160
Dance, Charles
  H 42, 338
  5001 294, 587
Dance Fools Dance
  5001
Dance, Girl, Dance
  5001 (2nd ed)
Dance of Death, The
  DIM 109
  TIAI 174
Dance With a Stranger
  H 29-31, 45, 283
  5001 (2nd ed)
Dances with Wolves
  ML 295-97

Dancing Mothers
  KKBB 253:n
  5001
Dandridge, Dorothy
  5001 119, 175, 728
Dandy in Aspic, A
  GS 94
  5001 (2nd ed)
Dane, Clemence
  5001 28, 71, 502
Dane, Karl
  KKBB 345
  5001 658
D'Angelo, Beverly
  H 51
  ML 44, 278
  5001 333, 561
Dangerfield, Rodney
  H 185-186, 280
  5001 44, 45
Dangerous
  R 35
  5001
Dangerous Liaisons
  ML 57-62
  5001 (2nd ed)
Dangerous Moves (La Diagonale du fou)
  SOTA 366-367
  5001 (2nd ed)
Dangler, Anita
  R 358
  5001 414, 687
Danias, Starr
  5001 794
Daniel
  SOTA 41-45, 87
  5001 (2nd ed)
Daniel, Elsa
  5001 233
Danieli, Isa
  5001 19
Daniell, Henry
  KKBB 225, 243
  5001 116, 129, 228, 245, 336, 418, 443,
    580, 600, 616, 660, 733, 824, 844
Daniels, Anthony
  5001 626, 709
Daniels, Bebe
  KKBB 252
  RK 7, 15
  WTLGD 503
  5001 156, 262, 455
Daniels, Danny
  GS 237
  DIM 83
  TIAI 276, 278
  5001 528, 574
Daniels, Jeff
  SOTA 95, 336, 338
  H 54-55, 190, 228, 230, 277
  5001 34, 325, 465, 604, 610, 693, 749
Daniels, LeRoy
  5001 50
Daniels, Stan
  SOTA 129
  5001 431
Daniels, William

DIM 10
R 53
5001 17, 299, 466, 541, 594, 668, 799, 845
Daniels, William H.
5001 300, 514
Danilova, Alexandra
WTLGD 346
5001 794
Daninos, Pierre
5001 268
Danko, Rick
5001 411
Dankworth, Johnny
5001 3, 173, 497, 576, 654
Danner, Blythe
R 53, 55, 178, 312
WTLGD 47-48, 169
TIAI 51, 52, 70
H 258, 259
ML 13, 14
5001 31, 103, 303, 325, 668, 726
D'Annunzio, Gabriele
KKBB 310
WTLGD 194, 540-541
5001 364
Danny Boy, see *Angel*
"Danny Kaye Show, The" (TV)
WTLGD 129
Dano, Royal
SOTA 62
5001 490, 619, 630
Danova, Cesare
R 170
5001 473
Danson, Ted
TIAI 256
H 150
ML 96-99, 204-207
5001 90, 159, 168, 386
Dante
H 129, 139
Dante, Joe
TIAI 191-194; dir., *The Howling*, 191-194;
    Piranha, 194
SOTA 18, 20-22, 187-192, 232; dir.,
    Twilight Zone--The Movie (co-dir.),
    18-23, 188, 232; *Gremlins*, 187-192;
    The Howling, 232
H 336-338; dir., *Gremlins*, 101; *Innerspace*,
    336-338
5001 307, 343, 364, 797
Dantine, Helmut
KKBB 245
5001 115, 122, 486, 837
Danton, Ray
5001 129, 357
D'Antoni, Philip
DIM 316
D'Arbanville, Patti
WTLGD 91
5001 772
Darby, Kim
5001 721
Darc, Mireille
GS 139
5001 45, 138, 409, 490, 594, 755
D'Arcy, Alex

5001 41, 782
D'Arcy, Roy
5001 253
Darden, Severn
5001 827
Darien, Georges
5001 757
Darin, Bobby
TIAI 323
Dark As the Grave Wherein My Friend Is Laid
    (book)
SOTA 200
Dark Crystal, The
ML 228
Dark Eyes (Otchi Tchornyia)
H 372-374
5001 (2nd ed)
Dark Habits (Entre Tinieblas) (sometimes called
    Dark Hideout or *Sisters of Darkness*)
H 467-468
5001 (2nd ed)
Dark Hideout, see *Dark Habits*
Dark Knight Returns, The
ML 159
Dark of the Sun
TIAI 111
Dark Passage
5001
"Dark Shadows" (TV)
R 108
Dark Victory
GS 116
DIM 217
R 35
5001
Darkness at Noon
DIM 201
Darling
KKBB 158-159
GS 25, 26
DIM 278
R 343, 475
SOTA 92
H 45
5001
"Darling, The" (story)
SOTA 26
Darling, Candy
5001 847
Darling Lili
R 248
TIAI 332
Darling, Scott
5001 143, 322
Darnell, Linda
ILIATM 306
KKBB 364
R 450
5001 28, 83, 234, 259, 419, 466, 806
Daroy, Jacques
5001 309
d'Arrast, Harry d'Abbadie
5001 292, 413, 781
Darrieux, Danielle
ILIATM 98
KKBB 320, 333
GS 270

5001 74, 209, 247, 436, 471, 540, 585-586,
    593, 611, 619
Darro, Frankie
5001 433, 837
Darrow, Clarence
KKBB 207, 250
Darrow, Tony
ML 268
5001 297
Dart, Iris Rainer
ML 74
5001 56
Darwell, Jane
KKBB 276, 328
5001 20, 44, 301, 409, 560, 658, 728
Darwin, Charles
WTLGD 306
da Silva, Fernando Ramos
TIAI 249
DaSilva, Howard
R 53
5001 86, 174, 391, 437, 492, 519, 668, 754
Dassin, Jules
KKBB 167, 316, 338-339; dir., *10:30 P.M.*
    Summer, 167-168; *Night and the City*,
    316; *Rififi*, 316, 338-339
GS dir., *Phaedra*, 169; *Rififi*, 183; *Topkapi*,
    23
DIM 65, 182, 246-248; dir., *Brute Force*,
    63; *Promise at Dawn*, 245-248; *Rififi*,
    248; *Never on Sunday*, 248
5001 108, 117, 323, 363, 514, 520, 524,
    578, 601, 630, 781, 809
Dasté, Jean
5001 37, 95, 300, 310
Date with Judy, A
5001
"Dating Game, The" (TV)
TIAI 72
D'Aubuisson, Roberto
H 182
Daudet, Alphonse
H 330
Daughters of the American Revolution
RK 57
Dauphin, Antonia
5001 791
Dauphin, Claude
KKBB 246, 336
DIM 26
5001 50, 123, 425, 450, 585, 608, 799
Davalos, Richard
5001 209
Dave Clark Five (group)
KKBB 280
5001 321
Davenport, Doris
5001 829
Davenport, Harry
KKBB 328
5001 44, 101, 200, 237, 345, 384, 443, 448,
    472, 560, 684, 741, 758, 765, 780
Davenport, Mary
TIAI 40
5001 684
Davenport, Nigel
DIM 249

SOTA 150
5001 131, 308, 411, 456-457, 468, 482, 662
Daves, Delmer
    KKBB 242; dir., *Broken Arrow*, 180, 184,
      241-242
    5001 74, 107, 173, 336, 578, 704
Davi, Robert
    H 170
    5001 298, 617
Daviau, Allen
    5001 40, 147, 217, 233
David and Lisa
    ILIATM 245-246
    KKBB 110
    GS 126, 150, 152
    R 444
    WTLGD 358
    5001 (2nd ed)
David, Charles
    5001 406
David Copperfield (book)
    KKBB 148
David, Eleanor
    SOTA 268
    5001 148
David, Hal
    R 137-138
    5001 110, 436
David, Keith
    5001 587, 759
David, Saul
    5001 237
David, Thayer
    5001 424
David, Zorro
    5001 622
Davidovich, Lolita
    ML 222-25
    5001 80
Davies, Jack
    5001 167, 276, 413
Davies, John Howard
    KKBB 322, 339
    5001 543, 635
Davies, John Rhys, see Rhys-Davies
Davies, Marion
    RK 5-6, 7, 8, 15, 20, 21, 22 (ill.), 24, 32,
      38, 61, 65, 68-70, 72, 79, 80, 83
    5001 337, 679, 680
Davies, Paul
    5001 721
Davies, Rachel
    SOTA 342
    5001 599
Davies, Ray
    H 159
    5001 3
Davies, Rudi
    H 411
    5001 431
Davies, Valentine
    5001 287
Davillier, Charles
    SOTA 255
Davis, Angela
    WTLGD 223
    H 147

Davis, Bette
    ILIATM 137, 313
    KKBB 110, 189, 195, 196, 225, 230, 235,
      288, 289-290, 295-296, 305, 307-308
    GS 70, 116, 176, 177
    DIM 71, 157, 281
    R 35, 220, 347, 431
    WTLGD 28, 143-144, 307, 343, 464, 504
    TIAI 247, 401, 404
    SOTA 111, 185
    ML 35, 274, 275
    5001 16, 66, 101, 112, 126, 155, 170, 173,
      181, 182, 238, 253, 336, 346, 374, 380,
      384, 386, 393, 418, 426, 455, 459, 466,
      515, 536, 539, 542, 572, 577, 599, 683,
      705, 706, 750, 754, 767, 796, 824
Davis, Brad
    WTLGD 496-500
    TIAI 246
    5001 131, 479
Davis, Carl
    TIAI 150
Davis, Carole R.
    5001 249
Davis, Donald
    5001 293
Davis, Ed
    SOTA 221
    5001 18
Davis, Frank
    5001 169, 623, 846
Davis, Geena
    H 209, 212, 455
    ML 68, 70-71
    5001 3, 61, 251, 252, 780
Davis, Ilah
    WTLGD 543
Davis, Jim
    5001 495
Davis, Joan
    WTLGD 428
    5001 728
Davis, Johanna Mankiewicz (Mrs. Peter)
    RK 11
Davis, John
    5001 545
Davis, Judy
    TIAI 61
    SOTA 300, 302-303
    H 432-433, 434-435
    5001 333, 506, 507, 567
Davis, Miles
    DIM 308
    H 294
    ML 40
    5001 215, 722
Davis, Ossie
    GS 89-90, 107
    DIM 299; dir., *Cotton Comes to Harlem*,
      314
    R 61, 262; dir., *Black Girl*, 60-62; *Cotton*
      Comes to Harlem, 61; *Gordon's War*,
      262
    WTLGD 66-67, 189; dir., *Cotton Comes to*
      Harlem, 189
    5001 77, 418, 656
Davis, Owen Sr.

5001 293, 380
Davis, Peter
    RK 11
    WTLGD 176; dir., *Hearts and Minds*, 176,
      251
Davis, Philip
    ML 89
    5001 331
Davis, Richard Harding
    RK 64
Davis, Sammi
    H 367, 369
    ML 137-40
    5001 340, 613
Davis, Sammy Jr.
    5001 734
Davis, Vicki
    TIAI 295
Davis, Viveka
    5001 676
Davis, Warwick
    H 474
    5001 840
Davison, Bruce
    WTLGD 295, 297
    5001 455, 679, 721
Davray, Dominique
    5001 140
D'Avril, Yola
    5001 18, 552
Daw, Evelyn
    5001 693
Dawn, Isabel
    5001 496
Dawn of the Dead
    TIAI 197, 198, 200
    5001
Dawn Patrol, The
    5001
Dawson, Anthony
    KKBB 259
    5001 189
Dawson, Julie
    TIAI 55
Day After the Fair, The (TV)
    ML 139
Day at the Races, A
    KKBB 184
    5001
Day, Clarence
    5001 421
Day, Doris
    ILIATM 58, 183, 233
    KKBB 184, 185
    GS 18, 22, 101, 116
    DIM 9, 12, 13, 227, 296
    WTLGD 31
    SOTA 132
    ML 98
    5001 114, 439, 441, 460, 858
Day Dreams
    KKBB 253-254:n
    WTLGD 193
    5001
Day, Ernest
    5001 568
Day for Night (*La Nuit américaine*)

R 178-180
TIAI 65
5001
Day in the Country, A (Une Partie de campagne)
ILIATM 111
KKBB 140, 254:n, 342
R 269
WTLGD 59
TIAI 368
5001
Day, Josette
KKBB 236, 329
5001 58, 566, 827
Day, Laraine
5001 258, 488, 713
Day Lewis, C.
H 119
Day-Lewis, Daniel
H 118, 119, 121, 128, 428, 430, 431
ML 178-82, 324
5001 96, 506, 509, 640, 803
Day, Marceline
5001 839
Day, Morris
SOTA 215
5001 604
Day of the Jackal, The
R 214
Day of the Dolphin, The
R 245-246
ML 211
5001
Day of the Locust, The
R 472-478
WTLGD 174, 215
SOTA 315
5001
Day of the Locust, The (book)
DIM 68
R 44, 187, 326, 472-478
TIAI 457
Day of Wrath (Vredens Dag)
ILIATM 277, 324
KKBB 254:n, 325
TIAI 403
5001
Day One (TV)
ML 207
Day, Richard
5001 314, 722
Day, Robert
KKBB 277; dir., *The Green Man*, 277
5001 306
Day the Earth Caught Fire, The
ILIATM 176-179
Day the Earth Stood Still, The
KKBB 184
Day, Vera
KKBB 291
5001 393
"Day-O" (music)
H 457
Dayan, Assaf
DIM 18, 247
5001 601, 822
Daybreak, see *Le Jour se lève*
Days and Nights in the Forest (Aranyer din

Ratri)
R 140-143
WTLGD 69
H 432
5001
Days of Glory
ILIATM 325
Days of Heaven
WTLGD 447, 509, 522
TIAI 28
H 98
5001
Days of Thrills and Laughter
KKBB 184
Déa, Marie
5001 554, 817
KKBB 326
Deacon, Brian
R 217
5001 790
Dead, The
H 402-406
5001 (2nd ed)
Dead End
KKBB 61
WTLGD 271, 489, 490
5001
Dead End Kids
KKBB 40, 71, 190, 193
5001 27, 177, 755
Dead Men Don't Wear Plaid
SOTA 2
ML 183
5001 (2nd ed)
Dead of Night
KKBB 254-255:n, 292, 368
WTLGD 432, 511
TIAI 237
SOTA 22
5001
Dead Poets Society
ML 153-57, 323
5001 (2nd ed)
Dead Reckoning
5001
*Deadly Invention, The (Vynalez Zkazy; also
known as The Fabulous World of Jules
Verne and Invention of Destruction)*
KKBB 180, 184, 255-256:n
GS 192
5001
Deadly Is the Female, see *Gun Crazy*
Deakins, Roger
H 279
5001 183, 577
Deal of the Century
SOTA 39
Dealer (book)
R 65
*Dealing: or the Berkeley-to-Boston Forty-Brick
Lost-Bag Blues*
5001
de Almeida, Joaquim
H 338
5001 294
Dean, James
ILIATM 33, 46, 55

KKBB 223
GS 194, 276
DIM 190, 298
R 304, 371
WTLGD 58, 200, 321, 334, 368, 447, 500
TIAI 66, 398, 413, 415, 474
SOTA 214
H 316
ML 121
5001 209, 284, 618
Dean, Jimmy
DIM 389
5001 189
Dean, John
WTLGD 263
Dean, Loren
ML 135-36
5001 656
Dean, Man Mountain
5001 69, 479
Deane, Hamilton
5001 201
DeAngelis, Gina
H 277
5001 159, 610
de Antonio, Emile
DIM 42-45; dir., *In the Year of the Pig*,
42-45
5001 360
Dearden, Basil
KKBB 255; dir., *Dead of Night* (segment),
254-255
GS 181
5001 178, 814
Dearden, James
H 375
5001 239
Dearly, Max
5001 409, 446
"Death and Life of Dith Pran, The" (article)
SOTA 274
"Death in Hollywood" (essay)
KKBB 300
Death in Venice
R 147-148, 204, 343
WTLGD 36, 38, 541
SOTA 126, 226
5001 (2nd ed)
Death Kiss
5001
*Death of a Cyclist (Muerte de un Ciclista; also
known as Age of Infidelity)*
5001
"Death of a Playmate" (article)
SOTA 91
Death of a Salesman (play)
R 117, 157, 224-226
H 200, 351
Death of a Salesman
ILIATM 70
KKBB 203, 361
Death on the Nile
WTLGD 462-466
5001
Death Race 2000
WTLGD 227
TIAI 384

5001
Death Takes a Holiday
  KKBB 326
Deathtrap
  TIAI 326-327
  5001 (2nd ed)
Death Wish
  R 354
  WTLGD 173
  TIAI 384
  H 344
d'Eaubonne, Jean
  5001 123, 209, 430
de Banzie, Brenda
  KKBB 282, 291, 295
  5001 222, 336, 393, 779
Debary, Jacques
  5001 848
DeBell, Kristine
  5001 840
De Bernardi, Piero
  5001 14
de Beauvoir, Simone
  ILIATM 38
  KKBB 81
  DIM 36
De Blasio, Edward
  5001 417
De Bont, Jan
  5001 251
de Bray, Yvonne
  KKBB 329
  5001 225, 285, 566, 583
de Broca, Philippe
  ILIATM 283; dir., *The Five-Day Lover*, 170,
    283
  KKBB 265; dir., *The Five-Day Lover*, 265
  5001 100, 122, 247, 382, 438, 750
de Bruijn, Lex
  5001 136
Debucourt, Jean
  KKBB 312
  5001 187, 209, 388, 495
Debussy, Claude
  WTLGD 257
  5001 591
Début, The (Naciala)
  DIM 311
  5001
Decaë, Henri
  KKBB 13
  DIM 123
  R 150
  WTLGD 304, 458
  5001 91, 215, 220, 416, 603, 729, 757, 799,
    813, 818
DeCamp, Rosemary
  5001 594, 853
De Carlo, Yvonne
  KKBB 243
  5001 108, 118, 256, 593, 747
de Carretero, Yvonne Blake
  5001 767
de Casabianca, Camille
  H 256
  5001 752
Deception

5001
de Chardin, Teilhard
  5001 228
Decima Vittima, La, see *The 10th Victim*
Decker, John
  5001 659
Declin de l'empire américain, see *The Decline of
  the American Empire*
Decline and Fall of the Roman Empire, The
  (book)
  DIM 189
*Decline of the American Empire, The (Declin de
  l'empire américain)*
  H 237-240, 450
  5001 (2nd ed)
DeClue, Denise
  H 177
  5001 2
Decoin, Henri
  KKBB 337; dir., *Razzia*, 337-338
  5001 618, 719
de Cordoba, Pedro
  5001 83, 118
de Cordova, Arturo
  KKBB 261
  5001 213, 256
de Corsia, Ted
  KKBB 291
  5001 220, 394, 514, 519, 585
de Croisset, Francis
  5001 35
DeCuir, John
  5001 178, 381
Dee, Frances
  5001 23, 59, 355, 428, 539, 572, 598, 689,
    697
Dee, Ruby
  KKBB 261
  TIAI 336
  5001 125, 212, 809
Deeley, Michael
  5001 80, 460
Deep, The
  WTLGD 429, 498
  TIAI 439
Deep Blue Sea, The
  ILIATM 140
"Deep in the Heart of Texas" (music)
  H 59
Deer Hunter, The
  WTLGD 512-519
  TIAI 113, 114, 457
  SOTA 53, 111
  H 23, 32, 33, 35, 361
  5001
Deer Park, The (stage)
  GS 11
  R 157
Deezen, Eddie
  TIAI 493
  5001 531, 823
DeFelitta, Frank
  R 383
Defense of the Realm
  H 278-279
  5001 (2nd ed)
Defiant Ones, The

ILIATM 41
KKBB 205-206
R 354, 435
TIAI 437
de Filippo, Eduardo
  5001 24, 481
de Filippo, Peppino
  KKBB 365
  5001 813
de Filippo, Titina
  5001 798
Defoe, Daniel
  KKBB 228
DeGaw, Boyce
  5001 496
Degermark, Pia
  DIM 118
  5001 216
de Givray, Claude
  5001 716
DeGovia, Jackson
  R 270
de Grasse, Sam
  5001 77, 81
de Grunwald, Anatole
  5001 845
de Gunzburg, Nicolas see West, Julian
deGuzman, Jossie
  5001 274
De Haven, Gloria
  5001 63, 106, 714, 726, 727, 732, 758, 764,
    766
de Havilland, Olivia
  KKBB 184, 189, 205, 228, 288
  WTLGD 158
  H 444
  ML 132
  5001 6, 8, 31, 118, 130, 327, 346, 374, 600,
    653, 775
Dehn, Paul
  ILIATM 164
  R 390, 391
  5001 503, 552
Dehner, John
  5001 97, 129-130, 416
Deighton, Len
  5001 72, 370
Deitch, Gene
  5001 501
Déjeuner sur l'herbe, Le, see *Picnic on the
  Grass*
Dekker, Albert
  KKBB 291
  5001 24, 57, 194, 210, 340, 394, 548, 668,
    718, 838
de Kowa, Victor
  KKBB 258
  5001 188
de la Brosse, Simon
  5001 571
de Laclos, Choderlos
  DIM 265
  5001 171
Delacorta (Daniel Odier)
  TIAI 329
  SOTA 45
  5001 193

Delahaye, Michel
  5001 20
Delair, Suzy
  5001 282, 606, 607, 635
Delaney, Pauline
  5001 535
Delaney, Shelagh
  ILIATM 196, 198, 200
  GS 47
  H 30
  5001 131, 170
Delannoy, Jean
  KKBB 356; dir., *Symphonie Pastorale*, 356
  5001 225, 739
Delany, Cathleen
  H 403, 405
  5001 177
Delany, Dana
  H 445
  ML 11
  5001 470, 571
Delany, Maureen
  KKBB 321
  5001 539
De Lacy, Philippe
  5001 264
De La Paz, Danny
  5001 51, 95
De Laurentiis, Dino
  R 230
  WTLGD 239
  TIAI 125, 265
  SOTA 184
  H 33
  5001 50, 60, 67, 87, 96, 207, 250, 396, 465,
    519, 612, 617, 661, 719, 765, 826, 854
De Laurentiis, Raffaella
  5001 207
de Lavallade, Carmen
  5001 119
de Lea, Lia
  5001 209
De Leon, Walter
  5001 580
Delerue, Georges
  ILIATM 222
  KKBB 265
  GS 50-51
  WTLGD 305, 457, 459
  TIAI 158
  H 251
  5001 176, 241, 247, 283, 382, 385, 386,
    587, 601, 603, 651, 685, 798, 818, 822,
    847
Delevanti, Cyril
  5001 526
Délibes, Clément Philibert Léo
  WTLGD 282
Delicate Balance, A
  TIAI 127
de Lint, Derek
  H 430
  5001 803
"Delirious" (music)
  SOTA 213
Delius, Frederick
  DIM 239

Deliverance
  R 6, 166, 238, 294
  WTLGD 210, 513
  TIAI 257
Dell, Dorothy
  5001 426
Dell, Gabriel
  R 386
  TIAI 354
  5001 177, 209, 224
Dell, Jeffrey
  5001 769
della Francesca, Piero
  TIAI 140
Dellesandro, Joe
  5001 326, 787
Delli Colli, Tonino
  5001 134, 549, 667
Delmar, Viña
  5001 41, 316
Del Monaco, Mario
  ML 103
Delmont
  KKBB 280
  5001 320
Delon, Alain
  GS 211
  DIM 115
  R 145
  WTLGD 334, 396
  TIAI 11
  SOTA 51, 237
  5001 37, 211, 417, 487, 488, 603, 635, 734
Delorme, Danièle
  5001 285, 482, 489
del Poggio, Carla
  KKBB 365
  5001 813
Del Prete, Duilio
  R 464, 466
  5001 37
Del Rio, Dolores
  GS 116
  RK 38
  5001 74, 253, 359, 384, 497
Del Ruth, Roy
  KKBB 341; dir., *Blessed Event*, 219, 341;
    On the Avenue, 234; *The Maltese
    Falcon* (1931), 305; *He Married His
    Wife*, 363
  5001 81, 93, 105, 106, 253, 322, 545, 781
"Delta Lady" (music)
  DIM 198
Delta Rhythm Boys (group)
  5001 254, 858
Delubac, Jacqueline
  WTLGD 233
  5001 572, 819
DeLuca, Randy
  TIAI 195
DeLuca, Rudy
  WTLGD 373
  5001 127, 331
DeLuise, Dom
  DIM 180
  WTLGD 101
  TIAI 214, 216, 374

  5001 6, 64, 81, 335, 796, 850
Demarest, William
  SOTA 12
  5001 19, 69, 186, 210, 298, 302, 305, 313,
    316, 404, 440, 483, 562, 726
de Marney, Derrick
  5001 760, 858
de Maupassant, Guy
  ILIATM 98
  KKBB 254
  5001 175, 585, 598, 643
Démazis, Orane
  KKBB 279
  WTLGD 144
  5001 127, 236, 268, 320, 465
Dembo, Richard
  SOTA 366-367
  5001 171
De Mille, Cecil B.
  ILIATM 73, 329; dir., *The Ten
    Commandments*, 329; *The Greatest
    Show on Earth*, 9, 329
  KKBB 59, 68, 132-133, 152, 205, 328, 355;
    dir., *The Sign of the Cross*, 68; *The
    Plainsman*, 185; *The Ten
    Commandments*, 205; *Male and Female*,
    328
  GS 44, 64
  RK 47
  DIM 127, 128, 130, 196, 274; dir., *The Sign
    of the Cross*, 131
  R 145, 208
  WTLGD 191, 389
  H 375, 376
  5001 140, 165, 305, 447, 565, 652, 680,
    730, 747
De Mille, Katherine
  5001 62, 165, 638
Deming, Mark R.
  WTLGD 443
Demjanjuk, John
  ML 239
Demme, Jonathan
  WTLGD 320-323, 362; dir., *Citizens Band
    (Handle With Care)*, 320-323; *Caged
    Heat*, 322; *Crazy Mama*, 322; *Fighting
    Mad*, 322
  TIAI 71-78; dir., *Melvin and Howard*, 71-78,
    292, 294; *Citizens Band (Handle with
    Care)*, 73; *Last Embrace*, 76
  SOTA 165-169, 265-267; dir., *Citizens
    Band*, 39; *Swing Shift*, 165-169; *Stop
    Making Sense*, 265-267, 327
  H 110, 217, 228-232, 274, 284-286; dir.,
    Citizens Band (Handle with Care), 110,
    232, 274; *Stop Making Sense*, 217, 218,
    232, 285; *Something Wild*, 228-232,
    285; *Caged Heat*, 232; *Melvin and
    Howard*, 232; *Swimming to Cambodia*,
    284-286
  ML dir., *Married to the Mob*, 187;
    Something Wild, 64
  5001 139, 474, 693, 716, 737
De Monaghan, Laurence
  DIM 265
  5001 140
Demongeot, Catherine

KKBB 370
5001 864
De Mornay, Rebecca
SOTA 39, 40
H 93
5001 631, 632, 790
Dempsey, Jack
RK 11
5001 69
DeMunn, Jeffrey
ML 224
5001 80
de Musset, Alfred
KKBB 343
5001 647
Demy, Jacques
KKBB 115, 235; dir., *Bay of the Angels*,
235, 307
GS dir., *Bay of the Angels*, 264, 265; *Lola*,
263-265, 266, 267; *Model Shop*,
263-267; *The Umbrellas of Cherbourg*,
194, 263, 265, 266, 267; *The Young
Girls of Rochefort*, 100, 265, 266
TIAI 47, 255
SOTA 85, 166, 288; dir., *The Umbrellas of
Cherbourg*, 85; *The Model Shop*, 166;
Lola, 288-289
H 136, 267; dir., *Lola*, 136, 267; *Bay of the
Angels*, 136
5001 55, 429, 490
De Natale, Don
WTLGD 357
5001 642
Dench, Judi
H 46, 129
ML 217
5001 329, 640, 829
De Negri, Giuliani G.
TIAI 446
5001 527
Deneuve, Catherine
GS 73, 270
DIM 244
R 20, 179
WTLGD 58, 124-127
5001 34, 63, 161, 346, 471, 624
Denham, Maurice
5001 20, 386, 436, 515, 728
Denham, Reginald
5001 403
De Niro, Robert
R 167, 170, 172, 397-400
WTLGD 131-135, 154, 169, 199, 210, 211,
216-217, 319, 320, 325-326, 328-332,
447, 506, 512-519
TIAI 35, 67, 106-107, 109, 110-111, 190,
241, 242, 457, 458
SOTA 103, 279, 280, 281, 298, 315, 360,
361, 362
H 14-15, 32, 108, 129, 225, 286, 287, 320,
396, 397
ML 150, 266-70, 321-26
5001 27, 50, 98, 183, 234, 277, 290, 297,
307, 329, 396, 411, 473, 520, 521, 530,
548, 612, 744, 793, 807
Denis, Jacques
WTLGD 181

Denishawn troupe
H 339
Denison, Michael
5001 358, 794
Deniz, Hernanos
5001 556
Dennehy, Brian
SOTA 98
H 5, 14, 117-118, 173
ML 207
5001 144, 239, 273, 416, 519, 682, 796
Denner, Charles
DIM 65
R 214
WTLGD 354-356
5001 363, 450, 461, 757, 862
Denning, Richard
5001 161
Dennis, Nick
5001 210
Dennis, Patrick
5001 455
Dennis, Sandy
GS 30, 34, 38-41
DIM 59
R 328, 433
WTLGD 263-264
TIAI 414, 415, 416
ML 13, 14, 94, 95
5001 31, 148, 265, 517, 566, 702, 750, 808
Dennis, Winston
ML 108
5001 7
Denny, Reginald
5001 33, 124, 407, 447, 540, 599, 618, 628,
638, 663
Denslow, W. W.
WTLGD 470
Dent, Alan
5001 315, 628
Denton, Crahan
5001 777
Denver, John
WTLGD 359
TIAI 11
5001 541
De Palma, Brian
GS dir., *Greetings*, 206, 212-213, 237
DIM 350; dir., *Greetings*, 314
R 195, 330, 366-371; dir., *Sisters*, 189,
194-195, 368; *Greetings*, 194, 329,
368-369; *Phantom of the Paradise*,
366-371; *Get to Know Your Rabbit*,
368; *Woton's Wake*, 368
WTLGD 202, 203, 208-212, 362, 418-421,
547; dir., *Obsession*, 184, 209, 210, 211,
212, 420; *Carrie*, 202, 208-212, 369,
418, 427, 520; *Phantom of the Paradise*,
209; *The Wedding Party*, 210;
Greetings, 211-212; *The Fury*, 418-421,
427, 431, 432, 523
TIAI 35-40, 67, 192, 201, 217, 226-230,
306, 424; *Dressed to Kill*, 35-40, 228,
230; *Sisters*, 35, 424; *Carrie*, 35, 40,
229, 230, 306, 415; *The Fury*, 38, 39,
40, 228, 230; *Home Movies*, 38, 39, 40;
Greetings, 39, 227; *Hi, Mom!* 67, 217,

457; *Phantom of the Paradise*, 99, 201,
212; *Blow Out*, 226-230; *Obsession*,
228; *Get to Know Your Rabbit*, 228
SOTA 100-106, 233, 263-265; dir., *Scarface*
(1983), 100-106; *The Fury*, 233; *Body
Double*, 263-265; *Obsession*, 263; *Hi,
Mom!* 264; *Phantom of the Paradise*,
264; *Carrie*, 264; *Dressed to Kill*, 264;
Blow Out, 264
H 32, 117, 153-155, 206, 318-323, 356, 467;
dir., *Scarface* (1983), 33, 34, 117, 156,
180, 183, 251; *Wise Guys*, 153-155;
Carrie (1976), 206, 320; *Body Double*,
228; *The Untouchables*, 318-323;
Dressed to Kill, 320, 356; *The Fury*,
320; *Blow Out*, 320
ML dir., *Blow Out*, 172; *Body Double*, 64;
The Bonfire of the Vanities, 315-17;
Carrie, 82, 118, 175; *Casualties of War*,
166-77; *Dressed to Kill*, 175; *Hi Mom!*,
317; *Phantom of the Paradise*, 317;
The Untouchables,145, 167
5001 84, 89, 122, 124, 203, 273, 307, 329,
579, 657, 658, 684, 716, 807, 841
De Palma, Rossy
ML 24
5001 848
Depardieu, Elisabeth
H 329
5001 379
Depardieu, Gérard
WTLGD 153, 154-155, 169, 285-286, 292,
325-326, 328-329, 332, 454-456,
459-462
SOTA 45, 47, 48-49
H 329, 331
5001 283, 291, 379, 476, 495, 530, 712,
792, 815-816, 848
dePaul, Gene
5001 667
De Pauw, Josse
H 464, 465
5001 439
de Poligny, Serge
5001 140, 578
Depp, Johnny
ML 298-300
de Putti, Lya
5001 812
Derby
DIM 426
Derek, Bo
TIAI 185
5001 744
Derek, John
5001 19, 401, 747
Deren, Maya
ILIATM 20
Dermithe, Édouard
KKBB 262, 326
GS 6
DIM 364
5001 220, 554
Dern, Bruce
DIM 323, 391, 392
R 260
WTLGD 43, 402, 405

TIAI 51, 163
SOTA 81
5001 149, 159, 204, 346, 396, 413, 466,
    688, 755, 790, 837, 839
Dern, Laura
    H 131, 132-133, 204, 206, 331
    ML 208
    5001 87, 239, 688
Dernier Milliardaire, Le, see *The Last
    Millionaire*
Dernier Tango à Paris, see *Last Tango in Paris*
de Rochemont, Louis
    5001 91, 760
De Roy, Richard
    R 149
    5001 800
Derricks, Cleavant
    SOTA 157
    5001 499
Dershowitz, Alan
    ML 287-89
Dershowitz, Elon
    ML 289
Deruddere, Dominique
    H dir., *Love Is a Dog from Hell*, 463-466
    5001 439
De Sade
    DIM 18-19
Desailly, Jean
    KKBB 321, 356
    5001 541, 739
deSaint Exupery, Antoine, see Saint Exupery de
deSainte-Beuve, Charles Augustin, see
    Sainte-Beuvede
DeSalvo, Albert
    GS 166, 167
DeSalvo, Anne
    TIAI 88, 231, 395, 463
    H 37
    5001 36, 150, 442, 508, 710
De Santis, Joe
    KKBB 250
    5001 145, 447
De Santis, Pasqualino
    WTLGD 311
    TIAI 317, 318
    SOTA 226, 254
    5001 37, 76, 180, 364, 497, 673, 700, 764
Deschamps, Bernard
    5001 643
Deschanel, Caleb
    TIAI 303, 353-355; dir., *The Escape Artist*,
    349, 353-355; *Trains*, 353
    SOTA 63, 170
    ML dir., *Crusoe*, 115-17; *The Escape Artist*,
    116
    5001 78, 165, 224, 518, 576, 630
Deschanel, Mary Jo
    SOTA 64
    5001 630
De Seta, Vittorio
    WTLGD 299
    5001 50
Des Forets, Guillaume
    5001 264
Des Longchamps, Ines
    5001 709

Desert Song, The
    TIAI 70
Deserto Rosso, Il, see *Red Desert*
De Sica, Vittorio
    ILIATM 68, 98, 110, 115, 231, 247, 248,
    255, 284, 285, 341; dir., *Shoeshine*, 110,
    114-116, 149, 290; *Umberto D*, 149,
    247, 284-285, 290; *The Bicycle Thief*,
    214, 231, 248, 285; *Two Women*, 283;
    Miracle in Milan, 284, 341; *The Roof*,
    285
    KKBB 198, 247, 268-269, 283, 310, 364,
    366, 368; dir., *Shoeshine*, 198, 269, 366;
    The Condemned of Altona, 209; *The
    Children Are Watching Us*, 247, 269;
    Umberto D., 247, 269, 283-284, 310,
    364; *The Gates of Heaven*, 269; *The
    Bicycle Thief*, 269, 310; *Miracle in
    Milan*, 269, 310, 368
    DIM 360-366; dir., *The Children Are
    Watching Us*, 361; *Shoeshine*, 361, 362;
    The Bicycle Thief, 361; *Miracle in
    Milan*, 361, 362; *Umberto D.*, 361; *The
    Roof*, 361; *The Gold of Naples*, 362;
    Marriage--Italian Style, 362; *Yesterday,
    Today, and Tomorrow*, 362; *The Garden
    of the Finzi-Continis*, 363-366, 426
    R 6, 452-453; dir., *After the Fox*, 69; *A Brief
    Vacation*, 452-453
    WTLGD 301, 312, 330; dir., *Two Women*,
    311; *A Brief Vacation*, 312; *The Garden
    of the Finzi-Continis*, 330
    TIAI 151, 319; dir., *Shoeshine*, 250
    SOTA 26
    H 267, 268; dir., *The Bicycle Thief*, 59;
    Umberto D., 267, 268, 269; *Miracle in
    Milan*, 267
    5001 9, 24, 67, 89, 102, 133, 209, 279, 281,
    292, 362, 482, 483, 676, 773, 779, 801,
    803
Design for Living
    WTLGD 361
    TIAI 49
Desire
    DIM 193
    5001
Désirée
    KKBB 193
    5001
Desk Set
    5001
Desmouceaux, Geory
    WTLGD 168
Desny, Ivan
    5001 430, 449, 472, 694
De Sota, Rosana
    5001 48
de Souza, Steven E.
    TIAI 438
    5001 261
Desperate Characters
    DIM 348
    WTLGD 546
Desperate Hours, The
    KKBB 252
Desperately Seeking Susan
    SOTA 354-355

    H 40
    5001 (2nd ed)
Despotovich, Nada
    H 425
    5001 496
Destination Moon
    5001
Destination Tokyo
    WTLGD 24
Destruction of the European Jews, The (book)
    H 85
Destry Rides Again
    KKBB 29, 45, 185, 256:n
    WTLGD 17, 175
    5001
DeSylva, B. G.
    5001 93, 296, 387
Det Sjunde Inseglet, see *The Seventh Seal*
Det stora äventyret, see *The Great Adventure*
Detective, The (1954; in England known as
    Father Brown)
    KKBB 256-257:n
    5001
Detective, The (1968)
    GS 88
    5001
Detective Story
    5001
Detmers, Maruschka
    SOTA 226
    5001 246
de Toulouse-Lautrec, Henri, see
    Toulouse-Lautrec
Detsvo Gorkovo, see *The Childhood of Maxim
    Gorky*
Deutch, Howard
    H dir., *Pretty in Pink*, 133-135
    5001 594
Deutsch, Adolph
    5001 4, 30, 455
Deutsch, Helen
    5001 287, 357, 397, 422, 517
Deux Anglaises et le continent, Les, see *Two
    English Girls*
Deval, Jacques
    5001 48, 329, 785
Devan, Donald
    KKBB 349
Devane, William
    WTLGD 174
    5001 445, 464
De Vargas, Valentin
    5001 784
Devi
    ILIATM 245, 251, 253-255
    WTLGD 69
    5001
Devigny, André
    KKBB 306
    5001 456
Devil and Daniel Webster, The
    R 198, 367
Devil and Miss Jones, The
    5001 (2nd ed)
Devil Doll, The
    5001
Devil in the Flesh (*Le Diable au corps*)

KKBB 124, 249, 257:n, 321
DIM 419
5001

Devil Is a Woman, The
WTLGD 365
5001 (2nd ed)

Devil Strikes at Night, The (Nachts, Wenn der Teufel Kam)
KKBB 257-258:n
5001

Devil's Disciple, The
WTLGD 37
TIAI 173
5001

Devil's Envoys, The, see *Les Visiteurs du soir*

Devil's General, The (Des Teufels General)
KKBB 258:n
WTLGD 177
5001

Devil's Playground, The
TIAI 59, 266-269, 371
5001

de Villalonga, José-Luis
5001 99, 386

Deville, Michel
GS dir., *Benjamin,* 72-73
5001 63

de Vilmorin, Louise
ILIATM 97, 98
SOTA 55
5001 209

Devils, The
DIM 315
R 49
WTLGD 83

Devine, Andy
TIAI 44
5001 14, 248, 360, 461, 619, 704, 707, 782, 800

Devine, George
ILIATM 119
5001 62, 434, 778

De Vinna, Clyde
5001 74

DeVito, Danny
SOTA 164-165
H 153, 154, 179, 281, 282
5001 290, 549, 638, 647, 773, 841

Devlin, Alan
H 410

Devlin, Bernadette
R 21, 24

Devlin, Don
DIM 121
5001 442

DeVore, Christopher
TIAI 85
5001 215

DeVore, Gary M.
TIAI 169
H 169
5001 197, 617

De Vorzon, Barry
WTLGD 559

De Vries, Peter
R 85
5001 577

Dewaere, Patrick
WTLGD 454-456, 459-462
5001 283, 291, 751

Dewey, Thomas E.
KKBB 307

Dewhurst, Colleen
DIM 390
R 276
5001 160, 244, 410, 445

deWilde, Brandon
ILIATM 79, 83, 137
KKBB 309, 347
DIM 25, 163
5001 16, 344, 474, 671

DeWitt, Jack
DIM 358
5001 457, 625

De Wolfe, Billy
5001 115

Dexter, Anthony
WTLGD 140

Dexter, Brad
5001 671

Dexter, John
5001 582

Dey, Susan
TIAI 253
5001 434

DeYoung, Cliff
5001 86, 274, 361

Dhiegh, Khigh
5001 462

Diable au corps, Le, see *Devil in the Flesh*

Diabolique
KKBB 258-259:n, 315
TIAI 326
SOTA 323
5001

Diaghilev, Sergei Pavlovich
WTLGD 344

Diagonale du fou, La, see *Dangerous Moves*

Dial M for Murder
ILIATM 297
KKBB 259:n
5001

Diamond, I.A.L.
ILIATM 151-153
KKBB 348
DIM 187
R 422-423, 425
5001 113, 260, 270, 370, 399, 438, 494, 551, 599, 692, 750

Diamond, Neil
5001 411

Diamond, Selma
TIAI 397, 462
SOTA 20
5001 50, 441, 508

Diamonds Are Forever
DIM 388-389
5001

Diary of a Mad Housewife
DIM 314, 348, 383, 384
R 45

Diary of a Chambermaid
GS 258, 261
5001

Diary of a Country Priest (Le Journal d'un curé de campagne)
ILIATM 133
KKBB 259:n
5001

Diary of Anne Frank, The
GS 210
5001 659

Diaz, Edith
5001 659

Di Benedetto, Tony
5001 508, 702

Di Cicco, Bobby
SOTA 140
5001 528, 531, 702

DiCillo, Tom
SOTA 262
5001 720

Dick, Charlie
H 49, 50

Dick, Douglas
5001 619

Dick, Philip K.
TIAI 361
5001 80

Dick, R. A.
5001 284

Dickens, Charles
KKBB 276, 322, 331
GS 43, 201, 202, 203, 204
DIM 196, 420
WTLGD 191, 210, 264, 270, 428, 489
TIAI 134, 221, 238
SOTA 82, 89, 125, 284
H 61, 127, 412
ML 38-42
5001 301, 523, 543, 581, 660, 741

Dickens, Hazel
WTLGD 253

Dickerson, Ernest
H 213
5001 674

Dickerson, George
H 207

Dickey, James
R 166

Dickinson, Angie
R 278
TIAI 35, 36, 416
ML 197
5001 123, 132, 203, 394, 588, 630

Dickinson, Emily
TIAI 435, 436

Dickinson, Thorold
KKBB 267
5001 280, 664

Dickson, Gloria
5001 405, 755, 763

"Did You Ever See a Dream Walking?" (music)
TIAI 273

Didden, Marc
H 465
5001 439

Didion, Joan
DIM 250-252
R 44-45
WTLGD 114, 241
TIAI 242, 414

5001 564, 587, 707, 793
Diem, Ngo Dinh, see Ngo Dinh Diem
Dien Bien Phu
    DIM 43, 306
Dierkes, John
    5001 416, 619, 759, 852
Dieskau, Dietrich Fischer, see Fischer-Dieskau
Diessl, Gustav
    5001 563, 834
Dieterle, William
    KKBB 367; dir., *Satan Met a Lady*, 305;
        co-dir., *A Midsummer Night's Dream*,
        348
    5001 82, 206, 238, 253, 345, 356, 384, 398,
        590, 824
Dietrich, Marlene
    ILIATM 188
    KKBB 59, 185, 208, 239-240, 256, 360-361
    GS 114, 263-264
    DIM 74, 86, 87, 193, 207, 347
    R 152, 405
    WTLGD 6, 17, 35, 282, 294, 365, 403, 536
    TIAI 363
    SOTA 219
    ML 48
    5001 26, 82, 85, 183, 185, 187, 192, 248,
        254, 258, 278, 384, 398, 405, 464, 498,
        616, 658, 668, 671, 694, 702, 776, 783,
        844
Dietz, Howard
    KKBB 234
    5001 50, 337, 765
Dieudonné, Albert
    TIAI 142, 148
    5001 515
Diffring, Anton
    KKBB 149
    5001 145, 348
Digges, Dudley
    KKBB 262
    5001 134, 217, 369, 422, 505, 830
Digges, Richard H.
    5001 307
Dighton, John
    KKBB 278, 292, 306
    5001 254, 317, 395, 457, 523, 637
di Giacomo, Franco
    5001 527
Dignam, Arthur
    TIAI 267, 268
    5001 188
Dignam, Mark
    5001 316
di Lampedusa, Giuseppe Tomasi
    5001 417
DiLello, Richard
    TIAI 473
    H 462
    5001 46, 147
Diller, Phyllis
    5001 702
Dillinger
    WTLGD 116
Dillinger, John
    KKBB 50
    RK 35, 82, 83
Dillman, Bradford

KKBB 250
R 200, 359-360
5001 151, 221, 291, 354, 725, 825
Dillon, Carmen
    5001 628
Dillon, Denny
    H 132
Dillon, Kevin
    5001 587
Dillon, Matt
    TIAI 398-399
    SOTA 308, 310
    H 73, 74
    ML 196-98
    5001 205, 249, 743, 749
Dillon, Melinda
    WTLGD 224, 229, 275, 348-349, 351, 492
    TIAI 289, 290
    H 8, 9
    5001 2, 95, 142, 686, 695
Dillon, Robert
    H 94
    5001 627, 852
Di Lorenzo, Edward
    TIAI 115
    5001 354
DiMaggio, Joe
    R 155
Dimanches de Ville d'Avray, Les, see *Sundays and Cybèle*
Din, Ayub Khan, see Khan Din, Ayub
Dinehart, Alan
    5001 829
Diner
    TIAI 320-323, 354
    SOTA 202, 309
    H 280, 281, 287
    ML 278, 281
    5001 (2nd ed)
Dinesen Blixen, Karen, see Blixen, Karen
Dinesen, Isak, see Blixen, Karen
Dinesen, Karen, see Blixen, Karen
Dingle, Charles
    5001 382, 426, 711, 742
Dinner at Eight
    GS 230
    RK 18
    R 72, 390, 425
    WTLGD 155
    TIAI 335
    5001
Diop, Abdoulaye
    5001 158
Diop, Omar
    5001 136
Dior, Christian
    SOTA 45
Di Palma, Carlo
    TIAI 314
    H 299
    5001 85, 316, 611, 664, 787
Dirty Dancing
    H 346-349
    5001 (2nd ed)
Dirty Dozen, The
    KKBB 55
    GS 61, 208

DIM 315
R 353, 354
WTLGD 126
Dirty Hands (Les Mains sales)
    5001
Dirty Harry
    DIM 385-388, 392, 398
    R 100, 205-207, 253-256, 260, 283, 288,
        310
    WTLGD 125, 126, 253-254
    TIAI 437, 444
    SOTA 240
    5001
Dirty Harry series
    WTLGD 253-255, 380
    H 17
Dirty Pictures from the Prom (book)
    SOTA 218-219
Dirty Rotten Scoundrels
    ML 74-77
    5001 (2nd ed)
Discreet Charm of the Bourgeoisie, The (Le Charme discret de la bourgeoisie)
    R 41-43, 93, 363
    WTLGD 180, 293, 363, 364, 365
    5001
Disenchanted, The
    RK 19
Dishonored
    5001
Dishy, Bob
    WTLGD 264
    TIAI 369
    H 258, 259-260
    5001 39, 68, 103
Disney Studios (also Disney-Touchstone)
    TIAI 28
    H 58, 81, 273, 319, 422, 456, 479
Disney, Walt
    KKBB 91, 178, 179-181, 184
    GS 116, 189-190, 191-192
    DIM 76, 315, 345, 359
    R 38, 145
    WTLGD 165, 204, 257, 282, 299
    ML 107-108
    5001 49, 236, 337, 426
"Distant Episode, A" (short story)
    ML 303, 305
Distant Thunder (Ashani Sanket)
    WTLGD 68-72
    5001
Distel, Sacha
    DIM 415
    5001 843
Ditchburn, Anne
    WTLGD 493-495
    5001 687
Diva
    TIAI 327-331
    SOTA 45, 46
    H 136
    ML 58
    5001 (2nd ed)
Di Venanzo, Gianni
    KKBB 13, 119
    5001 213, 339, 386, 429, 492, 651, 749
Diversion

H 375
Divided Heart, The
 5001
Divine
 H 137, 442, 443, 444
 5001 313, 791
Divine Madness
 TIAI 95-97
 ML 73
 5001
Divorce American Style
 GS 21-22
Divorce of Lady X, The
 5001
Divorce--Italian Style
 R 258
 WTLGD 137
Divorcée, The
 5001
Dix, Richard
 RK 13
 R 466
 5001 137, 787
Dix, William
 5001 515
Dixon, Ivan
 WTLGD 188
 5001 118
Dixon, Jean
 5001 336, 509, 857
Dixon, Lee
 5001 26
Dixon, Leslie
 H 273
 5001 559
Dixon, Malcolm
 5001 772
Dmytryk, Edward
 KKBB 203, 253, 313; dir., *The Carpetbaggers*, 134; *The Caine Mutiny*, 203; *Crossfire*, 253; *Murder, My Sweet*, 313
 GS dir., *The Carpetbaggers*, 61
 DIM 65, 135; dir., *Crossfire*, 63; *The Carpetbaggers*, 135; *The Young Lions*, 249
 5001 85, 121, 164, 503, 614, 670, 859
Do Androids Dream of Electric Sheep? (book)
 TIAI 361
"Do It Again" (music)
 WTLGD 194
"Do You Love Me?" (music)
 H 346
"Do You Want to Dance?" (music)
 TIAI 96
Dobai, Péter
 TIAI 340
 5001 477
Dobson, Kevin
 TIAI 157
 5001 17
Dobson, Tamara
 R 261
 5001 141
Doc
 DIM 349
Docks of New York

KKBB 360
Dr. Cyclops
 5001
Doctor Dolittle
 GS 159, 167, 227
 DIM 26, 120, 328
 WTLGD 325
Doctor Faustus
 GS 41
 5001 (2nd ed)
Dr. Jekyll and Mr. Hyde
 5001
Dr. John
 5001 411
Dr. Knock (*Knock*)
 KKBB 140
 5001
Dr. Seuss
 5001 248
 ML 317
Dr. Strangelove, Or: How I Learned to Stop Worrying and Love the Bomb
 KKBB 33, 62-63, 310
 GS 122, 123
 DIM 99, 375
 WTLGD 182, 421
 TIAI 276, 487
 H 327
 ML 317
Dr. X
 5001
Doctor Zhivago
 KKBB 11, 135-137
 GS 29, 75, 94
 DIM 188-192, 279
 5001
 H 82
Doctorow, E. L.
 WTLGD 121, 164, 248
 TIAI 263, 264, 265
 SOTA 42, 43
 5001 171, 612
Doctors' Wives
 DIM 259-260, 262
 TIAI 41
 5001
Dodd, Claire
 5001 255, 555
Dodds, Steve
 TIAI 57, 59
Dodge, David
 5001 775
Dodgson, Reverend Charles, see Carroll, Lewis
Dodson, Jack
 R 79
Dodsworth
 TIAI 74
 5001
Does a Tiger Wear a Necktie? (stage)
 WTLGD 188
Dog Day Afternoon
 WTLGD 198-199, 303, 470
 TIAI 153, 368
 SOTA 203
 5001
Dogs of War, The
 TIAI 167-169, 275

SOTA 119
 H 169, 353
 5001
Dohrn, Bernardine
 DIM 166
Dolby Sound
 WTLGD 434, 514, 520
Dolce Vita, La
 ILIATM 44, 119, 149, 181-184, 190-196, 262, 264-266, 283
 KKBB 133, 152, 159, 342, 363, 365, 366, 370
 RK 70, 73
 DIM 127-131, 308
 R 26, 171
 SOTA 105, 161
Dole, Emily
 TIAI 304
$
 DIM 369
 5001
Dollmaker, The (TV)
 H 243
Dolman, Bob
 H 474
Dombasle, Arielle
 SOTA 37
 5001 571
Domicile conjugal, see *Bed and Board*
Domingo, Plácido
 SOTA 254, 256
 5001 76
Dominguín
 5001 109
Domino, Fats
 TIAI 323
Dommartin, Solveig
 H 471
 5001 841
Don Giovanni (music)
 WTLGD 73
 TIAI 469
 SOTA 253
D'Onofrio, Vincent
 H 326
 5001 271
Don Quixote
 KKBB 259-260:n
 GS 260
 DIM 127
 TIAI 249
 5001
"Don't Blame Me" (music)
 TIAI 292
Don't Bother to Knock
 R 154
 5001
Don't Look Back
 GS 14, 15
 WTLGD 399-400
Don't Look Now
 R 233-237
 WTLGD 200, 434, 533
 5001
 5001 (2nd ed)
"Don't Nobody Bring Me No Bad News" (music)

WTLGD 473
"Don't Rain on My Parade" (music)
  SOTA 89
Dona Flor and Her Two Husbands
  WTLGD 427
Donaggio, Pino
  WTLGD 212
  TIAI 40
  SOTA 264
  5001 90, 203
Donahue, Jack
  WTLGD 12
Donahue, Phil
  TIAI 37, 346, 379
Donahue, Troy
  R 401
  5001 290
Donald, James
  KKBB 331
  WTLGD 65
  ML 291
  5001 102, 123, 443, 581
Donaldson, Roger
  TIAI 341-343; dir., *Smash Palace*, 341-343;
    Sleeping Dogs, 341, 342
  SOTA 184-186; dir., *The Bounty*, 184-186;
    Smash Palace, 184, 242
  H 54-56, 355-358; dir., *Marie*, 54-56, 356;
    Smash Palace, 54, 165; *The Bounty*, 54,
    121; *No Way Out*, 355-358
  5001 96, 465, 532, 687, 688
Donaldson, Walter
  5001 563
Donat, Peter
  5001 334
Donat, Richard
  5001 506
Donat, Robert
  KKBB 270, 275, 359
  DIM 38
  5001 138, 157, 284, 296, 599, 761
Donatello
  SOTA 124
Donath, Ludwig
  5001 782
Donati, Danilo
  DIM 129
  R 26
  TIAI 125
  5001 240, 241, 250
Donati, Sergio
  H 169
  5001 617
Donen, Stanley
  KKBB 287; dir., *Seven Brides for Seven
    Brothers*, 29; *Funny Face*, 53; co-dir.,
    Singin' in the Rain, 185, 232, 234; *It's
    Always Fair Weather*, 222, 234,
    287-288; *On the Town*, 287-288
  GS dir., *Bedazzled*, 63; *Funny Face*, 23;
    co-dir., *On the Town*, 263
  DIM dir., *Bedazzled*, 10; *Two for the Road*,
    10; *Seven Brides for Seven Brothers*, 29;
    co-dir., *Singin' in the Rain*, 209, 322
  R 387-389; dir., *The Little Prince*, 387-389,
    462
  WTLGD 25, 106-107, 482, 501-505; dir.,

Charade, 3, 5, 25, 30, 31, 32, 482; *Kiss
    Them for Me*, 23; *Funny Face*, 61;
    Singin' in the Rain (co-dir.), 79; *Lucky
    Lady*, 106-107; *The Little Prince*, 200;
    Movie Movie, 501-505
  SOTA 132-133; dir., *Blame It on Rio*,
    132-133; *Seven Brides for Seven
    Brothers*, 320; *Singin' in the Rain*
    (co-dir.), 338
  5001 25, 59, 80, 130, 159, 271, 287, 362,
    374, 427, 443, 500, 546, 646, 667, 683,
    740, 798
Donizetti, Gaetano
  SOTA 379
  5001 600
Donlevy, Brian
  KKBB 256
  5001 51, 57, 75, 185, 287, 302, 360, 399,
    483
Donlon, Yolande
  KKBB 263
  5001 229
Donna della Domenica, La, see *Sunday Woman*
"Donna" (music)
  H 343
Donnell, Jeff
  5001 359, 559
Donnelly, Donal
  H 402, 405
  ML 313
  5001 177, 401, 482
Donnelly, Dorothy
  5001 589
Donnelly, Patrice
  TIAI 303, 305
  5001 576
Donnelly, Ruth
  5001 81, 255, 316, 487, 489, 686, 762
Donner, Clive
  GS 181; dir., *Here We Go Round the
    Mulberry Bush*, 64-65
  DIM 67-68; dir., *Alfred the Great*, 67-68
  H 98
  5001 535, 830
Donner, Richard
  WTLGD 524-528; dir., *Superman*, 524-528,
    540
  SOTA 356-359; dir., *Superman*, 8, 10, 225,
    357; *Ladyhawke*, 356-359; *The Omen*,
    357; *Inside Moves*, 357; *The Toy*, 357
  ML dir., *Scrooged*, 38-42
  5001 297, 406, 660, 730
Donoghue, Mary Agnes
  ML 74
  5001 56
Donohoe, Amanda
  ML 139-40
  5001 614
Donovan
  GS 15, 25
  5001 588
Donovan, Arlene
  5001 715
Donovan, King
  5001 220
Donskoi, Mark
  5001 132-133

Donskoi Trilogy, The, see *The Childhood of
    Maxim Gorky, My Apprenticeship*, and
    My Universities
Doody, Alison
  SOTA 368
  ML 147
  5001 361, 815
Dooley, Paul
  WTLGD 444
  TIAI 122
  5001 589, 684, 686, 809
Doqui, Robert
  R 450
  5001 516, 635
Dor, Karin
  5001 781
Doran, Ann
  5001 11, 35, 318, 473, 575, 618
Doran, Mary
  5001 105
Doré, Edna
  ML 88
  5001 331
Doré, Gustave
  WTLGD 234
  SOTA 255
Dorfman, Robert
  5001 151
Dorfman, Ron
  5001 309
Dorléac, Françoise
  R 20, 179
  WTLGD 58
  5001 72, 750
Dorn, Philip
  5001 224, 351, 616
Dornacker, Jane
  SOTA 63
  5001 630
Dornisch, William P.
  TIAI 357
Doroff, Sarah Rowland
  ML 90
  5001 766
Dörrie, Doris
  H dir., *Men...*, 194-197
  5001 475
Dors, Diana
  KKBB 291
  5001 393, 543
Dorsey Brothers Orchestra
  TIAI 275
Dorsey, Jimmy
  5001 336, 349, 404
Dorsey, Thomas A.
  TIAI 470-471, 472
  5001 655
Dorsey, Tommy
  5001 106, 286, 675
Dorville
  5001 197
Dorziat, Gabrielle
  KKBB 312, 329
  5001 425, 489, 495, 566, 578
Dos Passos, John
  RK 65, 72, 73, 81
  SOTA 295

5001 187
Dostoyevsky, Fyodor
  ILIATM 10, 158, 225, 237-239, 256, 262,
    294-295, 324
  KKBB 262, 310, 324
  DIM 142, 272, 417
  WTLGD 132, 186, 222, 296, 328, 333, 389,
    414, 415, 428
  H 66
  ML 101
  5001 225, 264, 354, 567
Dotrice, Roy
  5001 110
Dotson, Rhonda
  H 9
  5001 695
Doty, Douglas
  5001 413
Double, The (book)
  DIM 272
Double Indemnity
  ILIATM 81, 129, 131, 160
  KKBB 219, 352
  R 135-136, 184, 186, 412
  WTLGD 207, 262
  TIAI 256
  5001
Double Life, A
  ILIATM 305
  5001
Doucet, Catherine
  5001 590, 753
Douchet, Jean
  ILIATM 306
Douglas, Gordon
  KKBB 41, 279; dir., *Harlow*, 28, 134,
    278-279; *Stagecoach* (1966), 41
  5001 185, 319, 359, 704, 858
Douglas, Helen Gahagan, See Gahagan, Helen
Douglas, John
  5001 480
Douglas, Kirk
  ILIATM 123
  KKBB 40, 42-46, 190, 232-233, 298,
    363-364
  GS 243, 246, 247
  DIM 48-50, 52, 173, 229, 353
  WTLGD 21, 31, 419
  TIAI 38, 39
  ML 291
  5001 4, 35, 46, 123, 186, 187-188, 273, 419,
    423, 443, 500, 548, 557, 570, 699, 718,
    752, 800, 801
Douglas, Lawrence
  5001 393
Douglas, Lloyd C.
  5001 306, 451
Douglas, Melvyn
  ILIATM 79, 83, 85
  KKBB 252, 318
  DIM 170, 347
  WTLGD 8
  5001 26, 30, 72, 118, 156, 298, 341, 344,
    351, 531, 542, 660, 672, 674, 752, 753,
    763, 779, 798, 825, 846
Douglas, Michael
  DIM 42

WTLGD 86, 395
TIAI 11
SOTA 164
H 374
5001 147, 239, 549, 638
Douglas, Mike
  WTLGD 510
  TIAI 161
Douglas, Paul
  5001 140, 330, 419, 564, 691
Douglas, Robert
  5001 7, 262, 376
Douglas, Sarah
  TIAI 224
  5001 731
Douglass, Kent, see Montgomery, Douglass
Douglass, Robyn
  5001 431
Dourif, Brad
  WTLGD 86-87, 435-436
  TIAI 266
  SOTA 286
  ML 53
  5001 87, 207, 230, 486, 549, 612
Dove, Billie
  5001 77
Dovzhenko, Alexander
  ILIATM 248, 277, 281; dir., *Earth*, 248,
    274; *Arsenal*, 277
  KKBB 60, 260; dir., *Earth*, 260
  DIM 274
  R 209
  WTLGD 324, 326, 330, 434; dir., *Earth*, 326
  TIAI 113, 448
  5001 35, 209
Dowd, Nancy
  WTLGD 273, 276-277, 404
  SOTA 167
  5001 150, 686, 738
Dowd, Ned
  WTLGD 276
Dowell, Anthony
  WTLGD 335
  5001 811
Dowling, Allan
  5001 346
Dowling, Doris
  5001 86, 437
Dowling, Kathryn
  TIAI 322
Down All the Days (book)
  ML 181
Down and Out in Beverly Hills
  H 102-106, 272, 350
  ML 73, 328
  5001 (2nd ed)
Down Argentine Way
  5001
Down by Law
  H 221-223
  5001 (2nd ed)
Down, Lesley-Anne
  WTLGD 246, 424, 539
  5001 66, 303-304, 427, 582
Down There (book)
  ILIATM 210
Down to Earth

5001
Down to the Sea in Ships
  5001
Downey, Robert
  KKBB 18; dir., *Chafed Elbows*, 18
  DIM dir., *Putney Swope*, 154
  5001 Jr., 45, 580, 792
Downey, Robert Jr.
  H 186, 370, 371
  ML 83-86
Downhill Racer
  DIM 45-47, 173
  R 167
  WTLGD 44
  SOTA 16
Downs, Johnny
  DIM 262
  5001 14, 582
Doyle, Conan
  WTLGD 191, 192
  5001 341
Doyle, Laird
  5001 171, 542
Doyle-Murray, Brian
  H 187, 189
  5001 143, 684
D'Oyly Carte players
  5001 480
Dozier, William
  KKBB 121
Drach, David
  R 420
Drach, Michel
  R 420-422
  5001 816
Dracula (1931)
  ILIATM 6
  KKBB 319
  5001
Dracula (1979)
  SOTA 217
Drago, Billy
  H 320
  5001 808
Dragon Seed
  KKBB 353
  5001
Dragonslayer
  TIAI 220-223
  5001
Dragoti, Stan
  5001 437
Drake, Betsy
  WTLGD 14, 21
Drake, Charles
  5001 11, 19, 35, 287, 524, 536
Drake, Dona
  5001 30, 67, 690
Drake, Fabia
  ML 219
  5001 812
Drake, Frances
  5001 259, 445, 484
Drake, Herbert
  RK 34
Drake, Judith
  5001 742

Drake, Paul
     5001 725
Drake, Tom
     5001 614, 834, 848
Drake, William A.
     5001 300
Drama of Jealousy, A, see *The Pizza Triangle*
Dramma della Gelosia, see *The Pizza Triangle*
Draper, Peter
     5001 110
Dratler, Jay
     5001 413
Draughtsman's Contract, The
     SOTA 31-34
     5001 (2nd ed)
Dravic, Milena
     5001 850
Drayton, Alfred
     5001 523
Dream King, The (book)
     R 147
Dream Play, A (stage)
     R 90
     TIAI 491
Dream Team, The
     ML 122-14
     5001 (2nd ed)
Dream Wife
     WTLGD 21, 23
Dreamchild
     H 51-54
     ML 82
     5001 (2nd ed)
Dreaming Lips
     KKBB 260:n
     5001
Dreams (*Kvinno dröm*)
     ILIATM 105
     DIM 252
     5001 (2nd ed)
Dreamscape
     SOTA 231-234
     H 261, 263
     ML 83, 327
     5001 (2nd ed)
Dreier, Hans
     5001 107, 187, 198, 671
Dreiser, Theodore
     ILIATM 67, 296
     KKBB 331
     5001 23, 121, 584
Drescher, Fran
     WTLGD 422
     5001 22, 655
Dresdel, Sonia
     5001 234
Dresner, Hal
     TIAI 233
     5001 34, 866
Dressed to Kill
     TIAI 35-40, 228, 230
     SOTA 264
     H 320
     ML 175
     5001
Dresser, The
     SOTA 113-116, 200

     5001 (2nd ed)
Dresser, Louise
     5001 658, 711
Dresser, Paul
     5001 508
Dressler, Marie
     KKBB 285
     5001 28, 190, 337
Dressmaker, The
     ML 45-47
     5001 (2nd ed)
Drew, Ellen
     5001 136, 298, 355, 372
Drew, Lowell
     5001 307
Dreyer, Carl
     ILIATM 6, 275, 277, 302, 318, 324, 344;
          dir., *Vampyr*, 6, 275; *The Passion of
          Jeanne d'Arc*, 277; *Day of Wrath*, 277,
          324
     KKBB 254, 259, 325-326, 329, 365, 368;
          dir., *Day of Wrath*, 254, 325; *The
          Passion of Joan of Arc*, 254, 259, 325,
          329; *Ordet*, 325-326; *Vampyr*, 325, 365,
          368
     GS 205
     DIM 419; dir., *The Passion of Joan of Arc*,
          419
     WTLGD 102, 324, 545; dir., *The Passion of
          Joan of Arc*, 519
     TIAI 2, 148, 403; dir., *The Passion of Joan
          of Arc*, 148; *Ordet*, 403; *Day of Wrath*,
          403
     SOTA 381
     ML 182
     5001 176, 552, 568, 812
Dreyfuss, Richard
     R 172
     WTLGD 156, 195, 348, 351-354, 376-378,
          466-468
     TIAI 53, 132, 133
     H 103, 104-105, 197, 281, 282, 349, 350,
          351
     ML 246-47, 274
     5001 21, 33, 70, 142, 150, 199, 296, 365,
          378, 592, 704, 705, 773
Drier, Moosie
     WTLGD 423
     5001 23, 809
Drimmer, John
     SOTA 162
     5001 353
Driscoll, Bobby
     5001 318
Driscoll, Peter
     5001 837
Drive, He Said
     DIM 294, 323, 350
     WTLGD 508
Driver, The
     WTLGD 558
     TIAI 190
     5001
Driving Miss Daisy
     ML 234-38
     5001 (2nd ed)
Drôle de drame, see *Bizarre, Bizarre*

Drowning Pool, The
     TIAI 21
Dru, Joanne
     ILIATM 318
     KKBB 338
     5001 19, 620, 672
Drugstore Cowboy
     ML 195-98
     5001 (2nd ed)
Drum
     WTLGD 369
Drums Along the Mohawk
     WTLGD 178
     5001
Druon, Maurice
     WTLGD 193
     5001 470
Drury, Allen
     5001 8
Drury, David
     H dir., *Defense of the Realm*, 278-279
     5001 183
Drury, Norma
     5001 366
Drutman, Irving
     KKBB 153
Dry White Season, A
     ML 184-85
     5001 (2nd ed)
Dryden, Wheeler
     5001 494
Dubarry (opera)
     TIAI 337
Du Barry Was a Lady
     GS 102
Du Rififi chez les hommes, see *Rififi*
Dubĉek, Alexander
     DIM 201
Dubin, Al
     KKBB 273
     5001 255, 262, 288, 291, 292, 637
Dubois, Marie
     ILIATM 211
     KKBB 356
     WTLGD 153, 155, 541
     5001 364, 385, 676, 757, 816
Du Bois, Marta
     5001 95
Dubost, Paulette
     KKBB 343
     5001 647, 818
Duceppe, Jean
     5001 510
Duchaussoy, Michel
     5001 241, 762
     DIM 172
Duchess and the Dirtwater Fox, The
     SOTA 166
Duck Soup
     KKBB 7, 184
     RK 15, 24, 83
     DIM 16
     R 229
     WTLGD 17
     TIAI 217
     H 114, 485
     5001

Dudgeon, Elspeth (John)
    5001 542
Dudley, Doris
    5001 846
Due Soldi di Speranza, see *Two Cents Worth of
    Hope*
Duel (TV)
    WTLGD 349
"Duel, The" (book)
    WTLGD 380-383
Duel at Diablo
    KKBB 39
Duel in the Sun
    ILIATM 55, 329
    KKBB 143
    WTLGD 373
    TIAI 364
    SOTA 361
    H 468
    5001
Duellists, The
    WTLGD 380-383
    SOTA 30
    5001
Duet for Cannibals
    DIM 35-36
    5001
Dufaux, Guy
    5001 182
Duff, Howard
    WTLGD 260, 262, 444
    5001 17, 108, 412, 514, 532
Duff, Warren
    5001 27
Duffell, Peter
    R 202-205
    5001 221
Duffy
    GS 149-150
    DIM 148
Duffy, Jack
    ML 114
    5001 202
Duffy, Sherman Reilly
    R 423
Dufy, Raoul
    WTLGD 32
Dugan, Dennis
    5001 343
Dugan, Tom
    5001 195, 296, 546, 740, 774, 837
Duggan, Andrew
    R 260
    5001 91, 129, 359
Dugger, Florrie
    WTLGD 163
    5001 108
Duhamel, Antoine
    GS 141
    5001 716, 827
Duhour, Clément
    5001 441
Dukakis, Olympia
    H 424
    ML 204, 205
    5001 168, 496, 849
Duke, Bill

5001 118
Duke, Daryl
    R 122-125, 312, 329
    5001 572
"Duke in His Own Domain, The" (article)
    KKBB 192
Duke, Patty (Patty Duke Astin)
    KKBB 272
    WTLGD 209
    TIAI 421, 423
    5001 111, 289, 483
Duke Power (company)
    WTLGD 251
Duke, Robin
    H 188
    5001 143
Duke, Vernon
    5001 113
Dulces Horas, see *Sweet Hours*
Dullea, Keir
    GS 30
    DIM 18-19, 119
    WTLGD 140
    SOTA 64
    5001 174, 265, 447, 564, 565, 800
Dulles, John Foster
    DIM 43, 44
Dullin, Charles
    5001 607, 819
Dumarcay, Philippe
    WTLGD 458
    5001 241, 291
Dumas, Alexandre
    RK 35
    5001 116, 157, 767
du Maurier, Daphne
    R 80, 234
    5001 198, 377-378, 618
Du Maurier, George
    KKBB 355
    5001 577, 733, 734
Dumbo
    GS 225
    SOTA 180
Dumbrille, Douglass
    5001 71, 161, 175, 245, 253, 312, 429, 439,
        487, 518, 577, 747
Dummar, Melvin
    TIAI 72, 76
    5001 474
Dummont, Denise
    H 27, 277
    5001 610
Dummy, The
    RK 13
Dumont, José
    H 268
    5001 342
Dumont, Margaret
    KKBB 314, 317
    R 241
    5001 28, 37, 71, 144, 175, 206, 391, 520,
        524, 847
Dun, Dennis
    5001 854
Duna, Steffi
    5001 302, 824

Dunaway, Faye
    KKBB 56-58
    DIM 49, 50, 52, 213, 214, 250-253
    R 178, 311, 407
    WTLGD 42, 207, 219-224, 435
    TIAI 113, 234, 235, 236, 237, 427
    H 383, 384, 385
    5001 35, 51, 91, 135, 230, 317, 424, 492,
        519, 604, 763, 765, 767, 785, 799, 819
Dunbar, Dixie
    5001 13, 582
Duncalf, Bill
    5001 222
Duncan, Andrew
    5001 442
Duncan, Isadora
    RK 11, 29, 83
    WTLGD 307
    TIAI 284
    H 482
Duncan, Lindsay
    H 297
    5001 595
Duncan, Sandy
    TIAI 332
    5001 707
Dundas, Jennie
    SOTA 290
    5001 416, 487
Dune
    SOTA 282-287
    H 206, 207
    5001 (2nd ed)
Dunham, Katherine
    5001 716
Dunn, Andrew
    ML 328
Dunn, Conrad
    TIAI 225
Dunn, Emma
    5001 81, 107, 170, 421, 487, 693, 742
Dunn, James
    5001 554
Dunn, Josephine
    5001 556
Dunn, Liam
    DIM 432
    R 404
    5001 81, 831, 859
Dunn, Michael
    5001 2, 675
Dunn, Nell
    GS 25, 68
    5001 588, 589
Dunn, Nora
    ML 65
    5001 849
Dunne, Dominick
    R 45
    5001 37, 564
Dunne, Griffin
    H 38, 39, 41
    5001 9
Dunne, Irene
    GS 40, 120
    DIM 312
    R 85

WTLGD 3, 7, 16, 17, 19, 20, 144
TIAI 332
SOTA 93, 222
ML 246
5001 28, 41, 44, 137, 333, 351, 369, 421,
    451, 508, 559, 575, 679, 751, 778, 806,
    833, 834
Dunne, John Gregory
R 45
WTLGD 241
TIAI 242
5001 564, 707, 793
Dunne, Philip
5001 11, 157, 259, 284, 583
Dunning, Decla
5001 719
Dunning, George
GS dir., *Yellow Submarine*, 189
5001 855
Dunnock, Mildred
KKBB 367
H 371
5001 43, 155, 399, 580-581, 734, 818
Duperey, Anny
WTLGD 302-303
5001 712
Dupont, E. A.
5001 812
Dupree, Minnie
KKBB 370
5001 859
Duprez, June
WTLGD 23
5001 25, 533, 756
Duran, Duran
5001 815
Duran, Jorge
TIAI 249
5001 584
Durang, Christopher
TIAI 170
H 299
5001 574, 664
Durante, Jimmy
KKBB 184
5001 106, 337, 459, 580, 865
Duras, Marguerite
ILIATM 33
KKBB 167, 345
WTLGD 291-295
TIAI 21; dir., *The Truck*, 21
H 221
5001 334, 661, 792
Durbin, Deanna
KKBB 283
RK 17
TIAI 31, 375
5001 117, 136, 245, 373, 405, 768, 808
Durham, Clive
5001 471
Durning, Charles
WTLGD 120
TIAI 241, 374, 432
SOTA 112
5001 64, 196, 270, 273, 334, 684, 715, 775,
    780, 793, 797
Duruisseau, Alan

TIAI 423
5001 111
Duryea, Dan
5001 30, 48, 406, 426, 482, 533, 659, 845
Duse, Elèonora
KKBB 310
GS 234
WTLGD 194, 335
TIAI 383
H 123
Dusenberry, Ann
5001 167
Dusenberry, Phil
SOTA 170
5001 518
Dutronc, Jacques
TIAI 101, 102, 156
5001 226, 450
Dutton, Charles S.
5001 606
Duvall, Robert
DIM 423
R 402
WTLGD 115, 190-191, 220-222, 524
TIAI 51, 52, 241, 244-245, 479, 480-481
SOTA 64, 171-172
H 460, 463
ML 312
5001 66, 109, 132, 147, 185, 289, 290, 303,
    368, 394, 469, 518, 519, 613, 667, 747,
    770, 777, 793
Duvall, Shelley
R 267-270, 450
WTLGD 188, 442
TIAI 2, 4, 6, 119, 120, 157
H 314
5001 445, 516, 589, 645, 674, 757, 772
Duvivier, Julien
ILIATM 111; dir., *Flesh and Fantasy*, 188
KKBB 142, 243-244, 328, 333; dir.,
    Panique, 142, 328; *La Fin du Jour*, 142;
    Un Carnet de Bal, 243-244; *Poil de
    Carotte*, 243-244; *Pépé Le Moko*, 244;
    Pot Bouille (*Lovers of Paris*), 333
WTLGD 365; dir., *Pépé le Moko*, 126-127,
    233; *A Woman Like Satan*, 365
5001 120, 187, 251, 304, 336, 428, 564,
    575, 587, 588, 592, 593, 741
Dux, Pierre
DIM 65
5001 700, 862
Dvorak, Ann
5001 309, 598, 657, 767
Dvorák, Anton
TIAI 284
Dwaj Ludzie z Szafa, see *Two Men and a
    Wardrobe*
Dwan, Allan
5001 337, 634
Dwan, Dorothy
WTLGD 471
Dwyer, Ruth
5001 667
Dyall, Valentine
KKBB 265
5001 102, 243, 321, 349, 376
Dyer, George

5001 253
Dyer, Peter John
ILIATM 86-91
Dylan, Bob
GS 14-15
WTLGD 226, 397-401; dir., *Renaldo &
    Clara*, 397-401
H 99
5001 411, 569, 623
Dylan, Sara
WTLGD 397, 400-401
"Dynasty" (TV)
H 99, 485
Dysart, Richard
5001 176, 334, 341, 562, 703, 748, 759
Dzundza, George
WTLGD 513-515, 519
5001 183, 532

E

E. T. The Extra Terrestrial
TIAI 347-351, 358, 380, 493
SOTA 57, 163, 182, 188
H 45, 74, 83, 464
ML 108
5001 (2nd ed)
Each Dawn I Die
5001
Eagels, Jeanne
KKBB 295
WTLGD 157
5001 182, 485
Eagle, The
KKBB 285
Eagle, S. P., see Spiegel, Sam
Eagle with Two Heads, The (*L'Aigle à deux
    têtes*)
5001
Ealing Studios
SOTA 60, 340, 342
H 119
Eames, David
TIAI 422
5001 111
Earhart, Amelia
RK 48
DIM 341
Earl, Kenneth
5001 101
Earl of Louisiana, The (articles)
ML 222
Earles, Daisy
5001 266
Earles, Harry
5001 266, 807
Early Frost, An (TV)
H 351
ML 116
Earp, Wyatt
WTLGD 328
Earrings of Madame De..., The (*Madame De...*)
ILIATM 97-101, 298
DIM 279, 362

R 420, 440
WTLGD 541
SOTA 55
ML 166
5001

Earth (Zemlya; also known as *Soil)*
ILIATM 248, 274
KKBB 260:n
WTLGD 326
5001

Earthquake
R 364, 384-387
WTLGD 121
5001

Easdale, Brian
5001 621

Eason, B. Reeves
5001 206

East, Jeff
WTLGD 527
5001 730

East Lynne
DIM 138

East of Eden
ILIATM 33, 46, 55-57
KKBB 223
DIM 252
WTLGD 447, 500
5001

East Side, West Side (TV)
R 264

East, Sister Carol
H 232, 285
5001 693

East West Players
SOTA 161

Easter Parade
DIM 82
5001

Eastman, Carol (pseudonyms: Adrien Joyce,
    Adrian Joyce)
DIM 251-252
5001 260, 490, 604, 676-677

Eastman, Charles
R 221
5001 16, 426

Eastman Color
WTLGD 458

Eastman, Kevin
5001 745

Easton, Richard
ML 216
5001 329

Eastover Mining (company)
WTLGD 251

Eastwood, Alison
SOTA 239
5001 771

Eastwood, Clint
GS 104
DIM 27-29, 350, 385-387
R 251-254, 275-286, 310, 319, 322
WTLGD 125, 197, 200, 253-255, 268,
    379-380, 430, 487, 512-513; dir., *The
    Outlaw Josey Wales*, 254; *The Eiger
    Sanction*, 255; *The Gauntlet*, 379-380
TIAI 11, 25, 33, 261, 384

SOTA 120-121, 238, 239, 240, 288; dir.,
    Sudden Impact, 120-121, 240; *Bronco
    Billy*, 238; *Honkytonk Man*, 238
H 14-17, 246-247, 343; dir., *Pale Rider*, 14-
    17; *Heartbreak Ridge*, 246-247, 353
ML dir., *Bird*, 1-5
5001 73, 191, 220, 280, 296, 324, 445, 452,
    562, 724, 725, 771

Easy Living
ILIATM 24
KKBB 363
GS 103
RK 26
TIAI 429
5001

Easy Rider
DIM 3, 4, 78, 84, 117, 147, 152, 173, 297,
    298
R 161, 174, 194, 272, 309, 378, 445
WTLGD 84, 86, 455, 554
SOTA 308, 343
H 97, 232, 462
5001 (2nd ed)

Eat the Peach
H 324-326
5001 (2nd ed)

Eating Raoul
TIAI 424
5001 (2nd ed)

Eaton, Mary
5001 144, 287

Eaton, Shirley
KKBB 183, 294
5001 861

Eatwell, Brian
5001 767

Ebb, Fred
DIM 411
R 460
5001 112, 272, 521

Eberle, Bob
5001 349

Eberle, Ray
5001 728

Ebersberg, Horst
5001 89

Ebinger, R. F.
5001 618

Ebsen, Buddy
R 130
SOTA 140
5001 93, 99, 105, 105, 527

Eburne, Maude
KKBB 225
5001 309, 590, 596, 647, 774, 819

Eccentricities of a Nightingale, The (TV)
WTLGD 169
TIAI 70

Eccles, Aimee
WTLGD 490

Eccles, Amy
5001 424

Ecclesiastes
H 251

Echevarria, Rocky, see Bauer, Steven

Eck, Johnny
5001 266

Eckstine, Billy
H 146
5001 381

Eclipse, The (L'Eclisse)
ILIATM 17, 21-22, 24
5001

Eclisse, L', see *The Eclipse*

Ecstasy (Extase)
KKBB 260-261:n
GS 207
DIM 189
TIAI 467
5001

Eda-Young, Barbara
R 230

Eddy, Helen Jerome
5001 400, 446

Eddy, Nelson
GS 159
RK 17
DIM 28
WTLGD 13, 345
5001 48, 75, 107, 350, 472, 518, 579, 641,
    736

Ede, H. S.
R 49, 52

Edelman, Herbert
R 426
WTLGD 48, 531
5001 52, 270, 325, 350

Edelmann, Heinz
GS 189, 190
5001 855

Eden, Anthony
DIM 428, 429

Edens, Roger
5001 30, 141, 271, 296, 404, 683, 723, 740

Edeson, Arthur
KKBB 231
5001 4, 18, 505

Edge, The
DIM 164, 165

Edge of Darkness
ILIATM 324
GS 219
DIM 63

Edge of the City (also known as *A Man Is Ten
    Feet Tall)*
ILIATM 91
KKBB 261:n
5001

Edison, the Man
KKBB 285

Edison, Thomas Alva
WTLGD 191

"Édition Spéciale, L'" (music)
H 419

Edmonds, Mike
5001 772

Edmonds, Walter D.
5001 205

Edson, Richard
SOTA 261
5001 185, 295, 720

Educating Rita
SOTA 83-85
5001 (2nd ed)

Edwall, Allan
  TIAI 487
  5001 236
Edward, My Son
  ILIATM 305:n
Edward Scissorhands
  ML 298-301
Edwards, Annie Jo
  SOTA 337
  5001 604
Edwards, Anthony
  SOTA 80
  5001 323, 780
Edwards, Antoinette
  DIM 107-110
Edwards, Billy
  DIM 107-110
Edwards, Blake
  KKBB 18, 325; dir., *What Did You Do in
    the War, Daddy?* 18; *The Great Race*,
    28
  WTLGD 245-246, 362; dir., *Operation
    Petticoat*, 21,26; *The Pink Panther
    Strikes Again*, 245-246; *The Return of
    the Pink Panther*, 245; *The Pink
    Panther*, 245; *A Shot in the Dark*, 246;
    Breakfast at Tiffany's, 465
  TIAI 331-335; dir., *10*, 196, 331, 332, 333;
    Victor/Victoria, 331-335; *The Great
    Race*, 331; *S.O.B.*, 331, 332, 333;
    Darling Lili, 332; *The Tamarind Seed*,
    332
  SOTA 304-306; dir., *Pink Panther* pictures,
    154, 305; *Micki & Maude*, 304-306; *The
    Man Who Loved Women*, 305; *The
    Party*, 305
  5001 99, 461, 478, 551, 567, 582, 690, 814
Edwards, Cliff
  KKBB 281
  5001 169, 335
Edwards, Harry
  5001 787
Edwards, Hilton
  5001 814
Edwards, James
  5001 462
Edwards, Jennifer
  5001 690
Edwards, Michael
  5001 492
Edwards, Robert Gordon
  5001 527
Edwards, Sebastian Rice, see Rice Edwards,
    Sebastian
Edwards, Sherman
  R 54
  5001 668
Edwards, Snitz
  KKBB 331
  5001 55, 511, 579, 667, 756
Edwards, Vince
  5001 394, 502
*Effect of Gamma Rays on Man-in-the-Moon
    Marigolds, The*
  R 74-76
  5001
Efron, Marshall

DIM 325
5001 50, 273, 371, 770
Egan, Michael
  WTLGD 129
  5001 521
Egan, Richard
  5001 169, 626, 627
Eggar, Samantha
  DIM 104
  WTLGD 190
  5001 145, 491, 492, 667
Eggerth, Marta
  5001 256
Eglevsky, André
  5001 423
Egoist, The (book)
  SOTA 373
Egyptian, The
  ILIATM 55
Ehlers, Alice
  5001 851
Ehrlich, Max
  R 383
  5001 514
Ehrlichman, John
  WTLGD 263
Eichhorn, Lisa
  5001 167
Eiger Sanction, The
  WTLGD 255
8½
  ILIATM 262-266
  KKBB 16, 36, 365
  GS 100, 121, 194
  DIM 129, 130, 225, 227
  R 171
  WTLGD 136
  TIAI 65, 87, 89
  H 372
  5001
8 Million Ways to Die
  H 155-157, 180, 251
  ML 262
  5001 (2nd ed)
Eikenberry, Jill
  TIAI 231
  H 171
  5001 36, 463
Eilbacher, Lisa
  TIAI 383
  5001 66, 540
Eilers, Sally
  5001 711
Einstein, Albert
  WTLGD 306
Eisenhower, Dwight D.
  DIM 44, 100
  WTLGD 376
Eisenhower, Mamie
  DIM 107
Eisenstein, Sergei
  ILIATM 32, 109-110, 248, 255, 271, 273,
    281-282, 284, 287, 341; dir., *Potemkin*,
    32, 109-110, 276; *Ten Days That Shook
    the World* (*October*), 32, 285; *Alexander
    Nevsky*, 288
  KKBB 16, 55, 60, 132, 202, 288-289, 312,

333-334, 357-358, 367; dir., *Potemkin*,
    55, 273, 333-334, 357-358; *Ivan the
    Terrible* (Part II, *The Boyars' Plot*),
    288-289, 367; *Ten Days That Shook the
    World*, 357-358; *Strike*, 358
  GS 45, 98, 210; dir., *Alexander Nevsky*, 45;
    Ivan the Terrible, 157
  DIM 175, 258
  R 209, 210
  WTLGD 195, 203, 302, 324, 331, 431, 434,
    550; dir., *Ivan the Terrible*, 324, 331,
    550
  TIAI 147; dir., *Ten Days That Shook the
    World*, 279
  SOTA 217
  5001 13, 375, 538, 593, 768, 769, 773, 824
Eisholz, Lutz
  WTLGD 52
Eisinger, Jo
  KKBB 316
  5001 524
Eisler, Hanns
  5001 533, 846
Ek, Anders
  5001 161, 348, 514
Ekberg, Anita
  ILIATM 36
  5001 20, 89
Ekborg, Lars
  5001 206
Ekerot, Bengt
  KKBB 304, 346
  5001 451, 669
Ekland, Britt
  GS 237, 239
  WTLGD 50
  5001 9, 283, 462, 528, 645, 657
Ekman, Gösta
  TIAI 43
  5001 206
Ekman, Hasse
  KKBB 315
  5001 514
Ekmanner, Agneta
  5001 206
El (also known as *This Strange Passion*)
  KKBB 23, 261:n
  5001
El Cordobes
  KKBB 119
El Dorado
  KKBB 42, 45
  5001
El-Kadi, Nameer
  TIAI 307, 309
  5001 607
Elam, Jack
  SOTA 362
  5001 380, 569, 616, 631
Elcar, Dana
  SOTA 223
  5001 17, 715
El Cojo, Enrique
  SOTA 256
Elder, Lonne, III
  R 3
  5001 697

Eldredge, John
  5001 171, 542
Eldridge, Florence
  5001 30, 194, 307, 363, 468, 484
Eleanor and Franklin (TV)
  TIAI 153
Electra
  5001
Electric Horseman, The
  TIAI 42
  SOTA 157
  H 243
"Elegance" (music)
  DIM 82
Eléna et les hommes (first released in U.S. as
        Paris Does Strange Things)
  5001
Eleni
  H 69-73
  5001 (2nd ed)
Elephant Man, The
  TIAI 82-86
  SOTA 100, 282
  H 207, 251
  5001
Elevator to the Gallows (*Ascenseur pour
        l'échafaud*; also known as *Frantic* and
        Lift to the Scaffold)
  DIM 308
  5001
11 Harrowhouse
  R 360-361
  5001
Elfand, Martin
  5001 197
Elfman, Danny
  WTLGD 536
  ML 161, 299
  5001 54
Elfman, Marie
  WTLGD 536
Elg, Taina
  5001 418
Elgar, Edward
  DIM 377
Elias, Alix
  WTLGD 322-323
  H 215
  5001 139, 794
Elias, Jeannie
  TIAI 423
  5001 111
Eliot Feld Dance Company
  H 348
Eliot, George
  R 153
  WTLGD 428
Eliot, T. S.
  GS 43, 259
  TIAI 247
  H 110
Elisa, Vida Mia
  TIAI 411
Eliscu, Edward
  5001 253
Elisofon, Eliot
  5001 500

Elizabeth I
  DIM 96, 97
Elizabeth of Toro
  SOTA 224
  5001 673
Elizabeth R
  R 219-220
  SOTA 332
Elizondo, Hector
  SOTA 308, 309
  H 200, 202
  5001 94, 249, 535, 624
Elkin, Stanley
  WTLGD 183
  5001 12
Elli, Frank
  5001 631
Ellin, Stanley
  5001 535
Ellington, Duke
  R 39
  SOTA 294
  5001 62, 113, 502
Elliot, Shawn
  5001 679
Elliott, Bob
  TIAI 369
Elliott, Denholm
  GS 235
  WTLGD 160
  SOTA 12-13, 341
  H 82-83, 127, 272, 278, 361, 426
  ML 148
  5001 14, 34, 97, 100, 183, 361, 471, 528,
        534, 535, 598, 613, 640, 660, 666, 786,
        819
Elliott, George P.
  KKBB 207
Elliott, Jack
  WTLGD 226, 397
Elliott, Janice
  5001 110
Elliott, Laura
  KKBB 352
  5001 720
Elliott, Lorraine
  5001 728
Elliott, Patricia
  5001 692
Elliott, Sam
  5001 421
Elliott, Shawn
  WTLGD 297
Elliott, Stephen
  SOTA 288
  5001 36, 66, 167, 334
Ellis, Anita
  ML 190
  5001 200, 285, 767
Ellis, Antonia
  DIM 382
  5001 96
Ellis, Diane
  RK 16 (ill.)
  5001 413
Ellis, Don
  5001 267

Ellis, Edward
  KKBB 283, 369
  5001 273, 348, 453, 758, 841
Ellis, Patricia
  5001 582, 767
Ellis, Ruth
  H 29-31
Ellison, Harlan
  KKBB 135
  WTLGD 125
  5001 554
Ellison, James
  5001 278, 819
Ellison, Ralph
  WTLGD 68
Ellsberg, Daniel
  DIM 318
  WTLGD 176
Elmer Gantry
  KKBB 285
  R 432
  5001
Elmer the Great
  SOTA 171
Elmes, Frederick
  H 207
  5001 87, 632
Elmes, Guy
  5001 4
Elross, Bob
  5001 680-681
Elsom, Isobel
  5001 184, 403, 443, 494, 565
Elstree Studios
  WTLGD 263
Elvey, Maurice
  5001 787
Elvira Madigan
  GS 80, 270
  DIM 7, 41, 154, 365
  TIAI 29
  5001
Elvis (TV)
  TIAI 97
Elwes, Cary
  H 379, 380
  5001 288, 597
Ely, David
  5001 663
Emerald Forest Diary, The (book)
  H 18, 20
Emerald Forest, The
  H 18-21
  5001 (2nd ed)
Emerson, Faye
  5001 11, 318, 464, 469
Emerson, George
  5001 121
Emerson, Hope
  KKBB 228
  5001 6
Emerson, Ralph Waldo
  KKBB 195
  H 127
Emery, Gilbert
  5001 407, 837
Emery, John

KKBB 348
5001 329, 675, 701
Emery, Katherine
5001 372, 598
Emge, David
5001 174
Emhardt, Robert
5001 12, 309
EMI-Elstree Studios
TIAI 2
Emigrants, The (Utvandrarna)
R 6-9, 181-182, 346
WTLGD 478
TIAI 477
5001
Emilfork, Daniel
WTLGD 485
5001 836
Emitai
5001
Emma
KKBB 285
Emmanuel, Takis
TIAI 159
5001 114
Emmanuelle
SOTA 232
Emmich, Cliff
R 123
5001 572
Emperor Jones, The
KKBB 262:n
5001
Empire of the Sun
H 413-416
ML 147
5001 (2nd ed)
Empire Strikes Back, The
TIAI 8, 18, 39, 208, 349, 482, 483, 484
5001 (2nd ed)
Emshwiller, Ed
R 323
5001 314
Enchanted Cottage, The
RK 82
DIM 34
5001
End, The
TIAI 214
End as a Man, see *The Strange One*
End of the Road
DIM 111-112, 148
5001
End of the World in Our Usual Bed in a Night Full of Rain, The
WTLGD 392-394
5001
End to Innocence, An (book)
SOTA 41
Enders, Robert
WTLGD 263, 265
5001 517
Endgame
ILIATM 23
DIM 356
Endless Love
5001

Endless Summer, The
DIM 154
Endore, Guy
5001 445, 832
Enemies, A Love Story
ML 229-34, 283
5001 (2nd ed)
Enemy Below, The
5001
Enemy of the People, An
ML 308
Enfants du Paradis, Les, see *Children of Paradise*
Enfants terribles, Les (also known as *The Strange Ones*)
ILIATM 132
KKBB 114, 231, 262:n
GS 6
DIM 364-365
R 337
5001
Enfield, Norman
5001 731
Enforcer, The (1950)
5001
Enforcer, The (1976)
WTLGD 253-255, 380
SOTA 240
5001
Engels, Friedrich
WTLGD 306, 474
England, Barry
WTLGD 64
5001 151
England Made Me
R 203-205
5001
Englishman Abroad, An (TV)
SOTA 311, 313
Englund, George
GS 182
5001 802, 863
Englund, Ken
5001 26, 663, 763
Englund, Robert
5001 84
Engstrand, Stuart
5001 67
Enjo
ILIATM 161, 226
Eno, Brian
SOTA 285
Enoch Arden (book)
WTLGD 19
Enright, Ray
5001 702
Enriquez, René
SOTA 74
5001 805
Ensayo de un Crimen, see *The Criminal Life of Archibaldo de la Cruz*
Ensor, James
KKBB 114
DIM 410
R 473
Enter Laughing
GS 102

DIM 10, 61
Enter Madam
WTLGD 6
Enter the Dragon
R 311
SOTA 232
5001
Entertainer, The (1960)
ILIATM 63, 68, 70-71, 74, 197
KKBB 142, 174
GS 136
WTLGD 148-151
5001
Entertainer, The (1976, TV)
WTLGD 149-152, 254
Entertaining Mr. Sloane (stage)
H 297
Entertainment of the Senses, The (stage)
WTLGD 38
Entre nous (also known as *Coup de foudre*)
SOTA 133-139
5001 (2nd ed)
Entre Tinieblas, see *Dark Habits*
Ephron, Henry
5001 184, 752
Ephron, Nora
SOTA 109
H 189, 190, 191
5001 162, 325, 681
Ephron, Phoebe
5001 184, 752
Epic That Never Was, The
5001
Epps, Jack, Jr.
H 172, 174, 299
5001 416, 664, 780
Epstein, Jacob
R 50
Epstein, Julius J.
KKBB 245
R 85-86
5001 32, 36, 101, 122, 263, 359, 459, 531, 548, 577, 858
Epstein, Philip G.
KKBB 245
5001 36, 101, 122, 445, 459, 531
Equus
WTLGD 337-339
SOTA 250, 252
5001
Eraserhead
TIAI 82, 83, 84, 86
SOTA 100, 282
H 207, 332, 392
5001 (2nd ed)
Erbe, Mickey
5001 768
Erections, Ejaculations, Exhibitions and General Tales of Ordinary Madness (book)
TIAI 466
Eréndira
SOTA 182-183
5001 (2nd ed)
Erhard, Werner
WTLGD 359, 522
Ericksen, Leon
R 259

WTLGD 445, 550
5001 445, 469, 750
Erickson, Leif
  5001 34, 121, 153, 546
Ericson, Eric
  WTLGD 75
Ericson, John
  KKBB 233
  5001 47
Eriksen, Dan
  KKBB 94-95
  GS dir., *A Midsummer Night's Dream*, 70-71

Ermey, Lee
  H 325
  5001 98, 271
Ernst, Max
  TIAI 258
  5001 10
Eroica
  ILIATM 148, 153
Eroticism in the Cinema (book)
  ILIATM 35
Errol, Leon
  KKBB 314
  5001 305, 520, 828
Erskine, Chester
  5001 17, 26
Erskine, Eileen
  5001 302
Erté
  WTLGD 336
Erwin, Stuart
  RK 20
  5001 101, 128, 336, 582
Erwin, Trudy
  5001 562
Esalen
  DIM 13
Escape
  KKBB 364
  5001
Escape Artist, The
  TIAI 349, 353-355
  ML 116
  5001 (2nd ed)
Escape from Alcatraz
  TIAI 413
Escape from Fort Bravo
  ILIATM 296
  GS 223
Escape from New York
  SOTA 232
  H 344
Escape Me Never
  DIM 34
Escoffier, Marcel
  5001 83, 472
Esham, Faith
  SOTA 254, 256
  5001 76
Esmond, Carl
  5001 174, 563, 688, 843
Esmond, Jill
  5001 527, 616, 834
Espoir, L'
  KKBB 367

Esquire (periodical)
  KKBB 57, 207
  RK 44, 49
  TIAI 30
Essen, Viola
  5001 700, 701
Essene
  TIAI 205
Essex, David
  5001 709
Essex, Harry
  5001 161
est
  WTLGD 303, 359
Estabrook, Howard
  5001 137, 264, 328
Esterman, Laura
  5001 371
Estevez, Emilio
  SOTA 212, 347, 348
  H 349, 350
  5001 99, 624, 704
Estienne, Marie-Hélène
  SOTA 237
  5001 734
Eszterhas, Joe
  H 56
  ML 241, 242
  5001 250, 377, 504
Et mourir de plaisir, see *Blood and Roses*
Eternal Husband, The (*L'Homme au chapeau rond*)
  KKBB 262:n
  5001
Eternal Return, The
  5001 (2nd ed)
Eternal Road, The (stage)
  KKBB 71
Eternel Retour L', see *The Eternal Return*
Étranger, L'
  ILIATM 130
Etting, Ruth
  5001 637
Eunson, Dale
  5001 706
Euripides
  DIM 300-301, 303, 304
  WTLGD 378-379
  5001 214, 370, 578, 790
Euro International Productions
  DIM 183
Europeans, The
  TIAI 159-160
Eurythmics, The
  H 94
Eustache, Jean
  R 289-293
  WTLGD 315
  5001 499
Evans, Art
  SOTA 273
  5001 381, 691
Evans, Barry
  GS 64
Evans, Bruce A.
  SOTA 307
  H 198, 392

5001 448, 705, 710
Evans, Edith
  DIM 25, 323
  R 97
  WTLGD 263
  5001 358, 434, 450, 517, 778, 832, 845, 859
Evans, Evans
  5001 91
Evans, Gene
  R 283
  5001 48, 519, 752, 822
Evans, Gil
  H 159
  5001 3
Evans, Herbert
  5001 26
Evans, Madge
  KKBB 363
  5001 106, 305, 314, 574, 787
Evans, Maurice
  5001 25, 586, 643
Evans, Max
  5001 48
Evans, Peter
  5001 36
Evans, Ray
  H 166
Evans, Robert
  DIM 183, 216
  WTLGD 174, 175
  5001 135, 458
Evans, Walker
  KKBB 52
  R 4
  TIAI 274
Eve, Trevor
  5001 657
Evelyn, Judith
  5001 285
Evelyn Prentice
  5001
Everest, Barbara
  5001 807
Everett, Chad
  5001 130
Everett, Rupert
  H 29
  5001 170
Evergreen
  5001
Everton, Deborah
  5001 85
"Every Day a Little Death" (music)
  WTLGD 424
Every Day Except Christmas
  ILIATM 99
Every Girl Should Be Married
  WTLGD 21
Every Man for Himself (*Sauve qui peut/La Vie*)
  TIAI 101-106
  SOTA 230
  5001
Every Man for Himself and God Against All, see *The Mystery of Kaspar Hauser*
Every Night at Eight
  ILIATM 292-293
  5001

Every Secret Thing (book)
  ML 8
Every Which Way but Loose
  TIAI 200
Everybody Wins
  ML 306-308
  5001 (2nd ed)
*Everything You Always Wanted to Know About
  Sex*
  R 240-241
  WTLGD 101, 355
Evil Angels (book)
  ML 32
Ewell, Tom
  KKBB 228
  5001 5, 668
Excalibur
  TIAI 182-187, 482
  SOTA 114
  H 18
  5001
Execution of Private Slovik, The (TV)
  R 324
Executioner's Song, The (TV)
  H 39-40, 157
Executive Action
  R 209
  5001
Executive Suite
  ILIATM 143, 323
  R 149
Exile, The
  5001
"Exiles" (story)
  SOTA 380
Exiles, The
  KKBB 263:n
  5001
Exorcist, The
  R 247-251, 310, 320-321, 411
  WTLGD 173
  TIAI 128, 351
  H 286
  5001
Exorcist II: The Heretic
  WTLGD 429
  TIAI 184, 185
  5001 (2nd ed)
Experiment, The (TV)
  GS 276
Exposed
  H 370
Expresso Bongo
  ILIATM 65, 77
  KKBB 263:n, 290
  SOTA 125
  5001
Extase, see *Ecstasy*
Exterminating Angel, The
  ILIATM 11
  GS 255
  R 41
  SOTA 347
Exxon (company)
  WTLGD 386
Eye for an Eye, An (*Oeil pour oeil*)
  KKBB 264:n

  5001
Eye of the Needle
  TIAI 481
  H 69
Eyer, Richard
  5001 268
Eyes of Laura Mars
  WTLGD 427, 431, 434-436
  5001
Eyes Without a Face (*Les Yeux sans visage*; *The
  Horror Chamber of Dr. Faustus*)
  ILIATM 7, 18
  5001
Eyewitness
  TIAI 169-172, 327
  H 70
  5001
Eyre, David
  TIAI 213
  5001 126
Eyre, Peter
  TIAI 221, 222
  H 361
  5001 201, 471
Eythe, William
  KKBB 328
  5001 560, 646

F

F/X
  H 116-118, 263
  5001 (2nd ed)
F.B.I., see Federal Bureau of Investigation
F.C.C., see Federal Communications Commission
F.I.S.T.
  WTLGD 490, 492
  TIAI 289
Fabbri, Diego
  5001 281
Faber, Juliette
  5001 720
Fabergé
  WTLGD 27
Fabian
  TIAI 115
Fabian, Françoise
  5001 651, 757
Fabray, Nanette
  KKBB 234
  TIAI 394
  5001 49, 317
Fabre, Saturnin
  5001 309, 482, 575
Fabrizi, Aldo
  KKBB 324
  5001 551
Fabrizi, Franco
  KKBB 366
  5001 67, 180, 286, 817
"Fabulas Panicas" (comic strip)
  DIM 334
Fabulous Baker Boys, The
  ML 186-90

  5001 (2nd ed)
Fabulous Invalid, The (stage)
  RK 37, 84
Fabulous World of Jules Verne, The, see *The
  Deadly Invention*
Face in the Crowd, A
  KKBB 152
  R 127
  5001
Face to Face, see also *The Bride Comes to
  Yellow Sky* and *The Secret Sharer*
  WTLGD 390, 478
Faces
  GS 195-196
  DIM 36, 222
  R 393
  5001
Facing the Flag (book)
  KKBB 256
Fagen, Donald
  H 460
  5001 103
Fahrenheit 451
  KKBB 146-150
  GS 141
  R 179, 236
  H 471
  5001
Fail-Safe
  KKBB 70
Fain, Sammy
  5001 114, 238, 255, 765
Fair Coed, The
  RK 69
Fairbanks, Douglas Jr.
  KKBB 184, 278, 369-370
  DIM 364
  WTLGD 18, 32, 49
  H 380
  5001 27, 228, 311, 322, 425, 482, 498, 556,
    597, 611, 845, 859
Fairbanks, Douglas Sr.
  ILIATM 118, 241, 325
  KKBB 252
  RK 15
  WTLGD 11, 18
  SOTA 179, 215
  H 22
  5001 77, 466, 599, 634, 680, 756
Fairchild, June
  WTLGD 449
  5001 808
Fairchild, Morgan
  5001 573
Fairchild, William
  KKBB 328
  GS 161, 165
  5001 558, 706
Faith, Adam
  5001 709
Faithfull, Marianne
  GS 210
  5001 316, 791
Falcon and the Snowman, The
  SOTA 311-315
  5001 (2nd ed)
Falcon Takes Over, The

5001
Falconetti, Maria
  KKBB 329
  WTLGD 519
  H 325
  5001 568
Falk, Peter
  DIM 222, 224
  R 393
  WTLGD 188
  H 380, 472
  5001 346, 597, 841, 846
Falk, Rossella
  5001 213, 417
Falkenburg, Jinx
  5001 159
Fall, The (La Caida)
  5001
Fallen Angel
  5001
Fallen Idol, The
  ILIATM 297
  KKBB 321
  GS 202
  5001
Fallet, René
  5001 590
Falling Angel (novel)
  H 286
Falling in Love
  SOTA 279-281
  5001 (2nd ed)
Fallon, William
  RK 48
Falstaff (also known as *Chimes at Midnight*)
  KKBB 197, 200-202
  RK 51
  TIAI 187
  ML 163, 215
  5001
Falwell, Jerry
  H 438, 454
Fame
  TIAI 30, 290
  SOTA 35, 139
Fame is the Spur
  5001
Family Circle (periodical)
  TIAI 188
Family Game, The
  H 308
Family Life, see *Wednesday's Child*
"Family Ties" (TV)
  H 12
  ML 204
Fancher, Hampton
  TIAI 361
  5001 80
Fanck, Arnold
  5001 696, 834
Fanfan la tulipe (Fanfan the Tulip)
  KKBB 264:n
  R 436
  5001
Fanfan the Tulip, see *Fanfan la tulipe*
Fanfan the Tulip (character)
  GS 73

Fanny
  H 330
  5001
Fanny and Alexander
  TIAI 486-493
  H 113, 368
  5001 (2nd ed)
Fanny Hill (book)
  KKBB 27
Fanon, Frantz
  DIM 175, 258
Fantasia
  GS 192
  DIM 131
  R 38
  TIAI 299
  5001
Fantastic Voyage
  KKBB 156-157
  GS 167
  DIM 216
  H 336
  5001
"Fantasy Island" (TV)
  TIAI 357, 358
Fantasy Records
  R 123
  WTLGD 86
Fantôme de la liberté
  R 362-363
  WTLGD 364
  5001
Fapp, Daniel L.
  5001 828, 546
Far From the Madding Crowd
  GS 233-234
  DIM 141
  R 236
  5001 (2nd ed)
Farago, L.
  5001 570
Faragoh, Francis
  5001 425
Faraldo, Claude
  5001 751
Farber, Hagit
  5001 681
Farceur, Le, see *The Joker*
Faress, Souad
  H 120
  5001 506
Farewell, My Lovely (book)
  KKBB 313
  R 182
Farewell, My Lovely, see *Murder, My Sweet*
Farewell to Arms, A
  KKBB 257
  DIM 217
Farewell Uncle Tom
  R 60, 66-67
  5001 (2nd ed)
Fargas, Antonio
  R 296
  WTLGD 130
  5001 118, 138, 141, 154, 521
Fargo, James
  WTLGD 253-255; dir., *The Enforcer*,

    253-255, 380
  5001 221
Farina (Hoskins)
  WTLGD 67
Farley, Walter
  5001 78
Farmer, Frances
  5001 24, 850
Farmer's Daughter, The
  5001
Farnham, Johnny
  DIM 59
  5001 589
Farnsworth, Richard
  WTLGD 486
  TIAI 117
  SOTA 27, 29, 172
  5001 148, 307, 361, 518, 625, 799
Farnum, William
  5001 157, 165, 355, 702
Farr, Derek
  5001 794
Farr, Felicia
  5001 131, 399, 402
Farrar, Geraldine
  WTLGD 364
  5001 187
Farrebique
  GS 49
Farrell, Charles
  ILIATM 197
  GS 126
Farrell, Glenda
  KKBB 283
  WTLGD 16
  5001 288, 292, 348, 359, 382, 425, 464,
    512, 742, 767
Farrell, Henry
  5001 346
Farrell, James T.
  GS 11
  R 173
  5001 724
Farrell, Nicholas
  5001 131
Farrell, Sharon
  DIM 76
  5001 466, 622, 724
Farrell, Suzanne
  GS 70
  WTLGD 344
  5001 720, 794
Farris, John
  WTLGD 419
  5001 273
Farrow, Mia
  GS 171
  DIM 72-73
  R 178, 221, 443
  WTLGD 444, 464
  TIAI 240, 365, 366-367
  SOTA 24, 26-27, 123-124, 217, 335-336,
    337, 340
  H 113, 114, 177, 276, 277, 425, 426
  ML 13, 14, 104, 202
  5001 31, 105, 162, 170, 181, 316, 381, 479,
    521, 602, 604, 610, 643, 665, 864

Farrow, Stephanie
SOTA 337
5001 604, 864
Farrow, Tisa
R 222
WTLGD 416
5001 244, 691
Fashions of 1934
5001
Fassbinder, R. W.
SOTA 350
H 63
Fassbinder, Rainer Werner
5001 477
Fast, Howard
KKBB 75
5001 699
Fast Times at Ridgemont High
TIAI 407-409, 473
SOTA 315
H 131-132
ML 134
5001 (2nd ed)
Fat City
R 6, 13, 124, 201, 432
5001 (2nd ed)
Fat Man and Little Boy
ML 207-208
5001 (2nd ed)
Fatal Attraction
ML 203
H 374-377
5001 (2nd ed)
Fatal Glass of Beer, The
5001
Father Brown, see *The Detective* (1954)
Father Goose
5001 (2nd ed)
Father of the Bride
DIM 296
5001
Fattori, Giovanni
WTLGD 327
Fauchois, René
H 103
5001 199
Faulk, John Henry
WTLGD 172
Faulkner, James
WTLGD 65
5001 151
Faulkner, William
ILIATM 90-91
KKBB 6, 153, 238, 278, 284-286, 357, 360
GS 10, 114
RK 10
DIM 75, 76, 237, 318
R 269, 271
WTLGD 18
5001 7, 11, 71, 310, 367, 432, 622, 698,
743, 776, 777
Faure, Edgar
WTLGD 177
Faust (theme)
KKBB 357
TIAI 339
SOTA 36

ML 227-28
Faust, Frederick (Max Brand)
5001 7, 185
Fawcett, George
5001 264
Fawcett-Majors, Farrah
WTLGD 369, 450-451
5001 692
Fay, Frank
5001 535, 754
Fay, W. G.
KKBB 321
5001 539
Faye, Alice
ILIATM 292
DIM 82
R 48, 413-415
5001 13, 226, 234, 253, 278, 327, 359, 422,
545, 642, 750, 773, 827
Faye, Herbie
TIAI 77
Faylen, Frank
5001 86, 186, 301, 437, 532, 779
Faylen, Frank
KKBB 276
Fazenda, Louise
DIM 200
5001 15, 123, 543, 547
Fear and Desire
KKBB 291
WTLGD 129
Fear on Trial (TV)
WTLGD 172
Fearing, Kenneth
5001 532
Feather, Leonard
ML 3
Fechner, Ellen
KKBB 264
5001 243
Federal Bureau of Investigation (F.B.I.)
DIM 203
WTLGD 404-405, 466
Federal Communications Commission (F.C.C.)
WTLGD 321
Federal Theatre Project
RK 56
Feelies, The (rock group)
H 232
5001 693
Feher, Friedrich
5001 113
Fehmiu, Bekim
DIM 136
5001 6
Fehr, Rudi
5001 591
Feidman, Gloria
ML 233-34
Feiffer, Jules
DIM 253-257, 282, 283
TIAI 119, 122
H 176
5001 120, 426, 501, 589
Feinberg, Nina
5001 463
Feinstein, Alan

WTLGD 318
5001 434
Feinstein, Barry
GS 148
Fejtö, Raphaël
H 436
5001 38
Feld, Eliot
5001 828
Feld, Fritz
TIAI 216
5001 37, 51, 52, 104, 354, 663, 785, 793,
850
Feldman, Charles K.
KKBB 67-72
RK 30
5001 123, 254, 339, 722
Feldman, Corey
H 197
5001 298, 705, 772
Feldman, Marty
R 404
WTLGD 99-100, 371
5001 6, 59, 859
Feldman, Phil
R 401
5001 290, 838
Feldon, Barbara
WTLGD 44-45
5001 688
Feldshuh, Tovah
TIAI 115
5001 172, 355
Felix, Otto
WTLGD 449
5001 808
Felix, Seymour
5001 13, 159, 305, 387, 545, 642
Fell, Norman
5001 109, 131, 356, 363
Fellini Satyricon
DIM 127-132
H 139
5001
Fellini, Federico
ILIATM 180, 183, 185, 190-192, 194,
264-266; dir., *La Dolce Vita*, 44, 119,
149, 181-184, 190-196, 262, 264-266,
283; *Nights of Cabiria*, 149, 265; *La
Strada*, 192; *8½*, 262-266
KKBB 14, 16, 59, 103, 109, 153, 222, 298,
318, 351, 365, 366, 368; dir., *8½*, 16,
36, 365; *Juliet of the Spirits*, 16, 189,
365; *La Dolce Vita*, 133, 152, 159, 342,
363, 365, 366, 370; *Nights of Cabiria*,
298, 318, 368; *La Strada*, 318, 351;
Variety Lights (with Alberto Lattuada),
365; *I Vitelloni*, 366; *The White Sheik*,
366, 368
GS 7-8; dir., *8½*, 100, 121, 194; *La Strada*,
46
RK 47
DIM 13, 127-132, 189, 225, 247, 274; dir.,
Fellini Satyricon, 127-132; *La Dolce
Vita*, 127-131, 308; *8½*, 129, 130, 225,
227; *Juliet of the Spirits*, 129, 130
R 26-27, 94, 149, 171-172; dir., *The Clowns*,

25; *Fellini's Roma*, 25-27, 172; *La Dolce Vita*, 26, 171; *I Vitelloni*, 169, 171-172; *8½*, 171

WTLGD 103, 131, 136, 272, 324, 497; dir., *Amarcord*, 131; *8½*, 136; *I Vitelloni*, 136; *Fellini's Casanova*, 272

TIAI 65, 87, 88, 125, 296, 299, 450; dir., *8½*, 65, 87, 89; *Nights of Cabiria*, 251; *I Vitelloni*, 252, 320; *Fellini's Roma*, 364

SOTA 161, 298; dir., *La Dolce Vita*, 105, 161

H 54, 63, 138-142, 267, 373; dir., *Nights of Cabiria*, 63; *Orchestra Rehearsal*, 63; *Ginger and Fred*, 138-142; *Fellini Satyricon*, 139; *Fellini's Roma*, 139; *Fellini's Casanova*, 139; *City of Women*, 139; *Juliet of the Spirits*, 140; *La Strada*, 268-269; *8½*, 372

5001 13, 67, 89, 212, 240, 241, 285, 286, 386, 482, 529, 551, 562, 717, 734, 813, 817, 818, 835, 836, 850

Fellini's Casanova
WTLGD 272
H 139
5001

Fellini's Roma
R 25-27, 172
TIAI 364
H 139
5001

Fellows, Edith
5001 574, 672

Felton, Earl
5001 318, 516

Femme du boulanger, La, see *The Baker's Wife*
Femme et le pantin, La (book)
WTLGD 364

Femme infidèle, La
DIM 53-54, 172, 403
5001

Femme mariée, Une, see *A Married Woman*
Femmes fatales (also known as *Calmos*)
WTLGD 454, 457-458, 461
5001

Fender, Freddie
5001 92

Fennell, Michael
WTLGD 188

Fenton, Frank
5001 233, 405, 685

Fenton, Leslie
5001 123

Fenwick, Peg
5001 19

Ferber, Edna
KKBB 345
RK 18
WTLGD 144
5001 137, 190, 284, 645, 653, 679, 703

Ferdin, Pamelyn
5001 317

Ferguson, Elsie
5001 694

Ferguson, Otis
RK 51, 52, 63

Ferguson, Perry

5001 139
Ferko, Milan
R 121

Fermaud, Michel
WTLGD 355

Fernandel
KKBB 142, 244, 279
5001 120, 320, 428, 620, 643, 644, 781, 827

Fernandes, Miguel
ML 86
5001 792

Fernández, Angel Luis
5001 414, 470

Fernandez, Emilio
5001 569, 806, 838

Fernandez, James
KKBB 229
5001 8

Fernandez, Raymond
DIM 106, 107
5001 339

Fernandez, Wilhelmenia
TIAI 328, 329
5001 192

Ferren, Bran
5001 463

Ferreol, Andrea
TIAI 469
5001 537

Ferrer, José
KKBB 173, 277; dir., *The Great Man*, 277; *The High Cost of Loving*, 277
GS 102
WTLGD 21, 553
TIAI 365
SOTA 111, 284
H 3
5001 68, 207, 302, 331, 415, 479, 485, 500, 675, 775, 819, 832

Ferrer, Mel
5001 82, 98, 214, 422, 616

Ferrer, Miguel
5001 635

Ferreri, Marco
WTLGD 362
TIAI 466-469; dir., *Tales of Ordinary Madness*, 466-469; *The Ape Woman*, 466; *La Grande Bouffe*, 466; *The Last Woman*, 466, 467
H 385; dir., *Tales of Ordinary Madness*, 385, 463
5001 742

Ferrero, Jesús
5001 470

Ferrero, Martin
ML 44
5001 333

Ferretti, Dante
ML 110
5001 6

Ferreux, Benoit
DIM 306, 310
5001 503

Ferrier, Noel
TIAI 453
5001 854

Ferrigno, Louis

5001 602
Ferriol, Caroline
TIAI 67

Ferris, Barbara
KKBB 280
TIAI 43
5001 321

Ferro, Pablo
GS 114, 115
5001 109, 139, 763

Ferry, Jean
5001 607

Fertis, Yannis
5001 214

Ferzetti, Gabriele
GS 56
DIM 85-86, 204
SOTA 126-127
5001 41, 53, 151, 527, 545, 825

Fessier, Michael
5001 857

Fetchit, Stepin
WTLGD 411
5001 384, 679, 713, 728

Fête à Henriette, La, see *Holiday for Henrietta*
Feu follet, Le, see *The Fire Within*
Feuer, Cy
DIM 413
5001 112

Feuillère, Edwige
KKBB 262
GS 127
DIM 419
TIAI 150
5001 208, 277, 354, 583

Feydeau, Georges
KKBB 321
R 433
TIAI 174, 176
5001 540

Feyder, Jacques
ILIATM 111
KKBB 244; dir., *Carnival in Flanders*, 244-245
5001 121

Fiddler on the Roof
DIM 327-333, 426
SOTA 44
5001

Fiedler, John
5001 795

Fiedler, Leslie
WTLGD 85
SOTA 41

Field, Betty
GS 22
5001 73, 88, 251, 397, 540, 698, 814

Field, Connie
SOTA 167

Field, Fritz
KKBB 241

Field of Dreams
ML 126-28, 295
5001 (2nd ed)

Field, Ron
WTLGD 151

Field, Sally

WTLGD 267, 430
TIAI 288, 289
SOTA 246, 247-248
H 256
ML 17-20
5001 2, 585, 603
Field, Shirley Anne
H 119, 120
5001 14, 222, 506, 654
Field, Virginia
5001 169, 488, 824
Fielding, Henry
5001 778
Fielding, Jerry
R 349
5001 276, 838
Fields, Dorothy
5001 30, 226, 734, 808
Fields, Gracie
5001 334, 337
Fields, Herbert
5001 30, 316
Fields, Joseph
5001 30, 252, 524
Fields, Lew
5001 422, 717
Fields, Robert
DIM 262
5001 703
Fields, Stanley
5001 139, 160, 280, 393, 425
Fields, Verna
5001 378, 724
Fields, W. C.
KKBB 7, 93, 163, 184, 185, 198, 201, 299, 313-314
GS 94, 230
RK 15, 17
DIM 28, 85, 183, 269, 329, 431
R 113, 128, 243, 425
WTLGD 178, 414, 542
TIAI 99, 157, 197, 221, 344, 420
SOTA 364
H 9, 312, 384, 444, 457
ML 118
5001 15, 68, 239, 254, 355, 459, 481, 509, 520, 589, 590
Fiesta
TIAI 357
Fiestas, The (group)
WTLGD 448
Fifty Year Decline and Fall of Hollywood, The
RK 33
R 155
55 Days at Peking
ILIATM 8, 10
H 308
Figgis, Mike
ML dir., *Internal Affairs*, 262-64; *Stormy*
5001 367
Fighting 69th, The
5001
Fighting Mad
WTLGD 322
Figueroa, Gabriel
KKBB 323
SOTA 199

5001 544, 806
Figures in a Landscape
WTLGD 95
Filardi, Peter
5001 250
File on Thelma Jordan, The
5001
Fille du puisatier, La, see *The Well-Digger's Daughter*
Film Acting (book)
KKBB 312
Film Comment (periodical)
TIAI 111, 335, 385
SOTA 46, 47, 295
Film Culture (periodical)
ILIATM 293, 311, 314, 316-318
KKBB 28
Film Daily (periodical)
RK 44
Film of Memory (book)
WTLGD 193
Film ohne Titel, see *Film Without a Name*
Film Quarterly (periodical)
ILIATM 316
Film Society of Lincoln Center
DIM 146
Film Without a Name (*Film ohne Titel*)
KKBB 264:n
5001
Films and Filming (periodical)
ILIATM 64
Films in My Life, The (book)
WTLGD 428
Films in Review (periodical)
KKBB 241
Fimberg, Hal
5001 71, 359, 555
Fin du jour, La
KKBB 142
Final Cut: Dreams and Disaster in the Making of "Heaven's Gate" (book)
H 21-24
Final Test, The
KKBB 265:n
5001
Finch, Flora
WTLGD 9
Finch Hatton, Denys
H 77, 78, 79
Finch, Jon
DIM 399, 401
R 112
WTLGD 465
5001 181, 404, 444
Finch, Peter
KKBB 167, 257
DIM 289-290
R 138-139, 203-204, 345-346
WTLGD 220-222
5001 1, 185, 221, 237, 416, 436, 519, 602, 717, 728
Fine Madness, A
KKBB 14
DIM 105, 119
WTLGD 150
5001 (2nd ed)
Fine, Sylvia

5001 402, 663
Fine Young Cannibals (group)
H 389
Fingers
WTLGD 414-418
H 370
5001
Fini, Leonor
KKBB 339-340
5001 638, 822
Finian's Rainbow
GS 96, 159, 227
5001
Fink, Harry
DIM 386
5001 191
Fink, Margaret
TIAI 61
5001 506
Fink, R. M.
DIM 386
5001 191
Finkel, Abem
KKBB 308
5001 380, 466
Finkel, Fyvush
5001 606
Finklehoffe, Fred
5001 42, 256, 286, 722, 848
Finlay, Frank
KKBB 173
GS 183
DIM 104
SOTA 332
5001 163, 492, 502, 555, 626, 767
Finlayson, James
5001 137, 825
Finlayson, Jon
SOTA 60
5001 431
Finley, Bill
5001 684
Finley, William
R 367-368
5001 579
Finnegan, John
SOTA 172
5001 518
Finnerty, Warren
5001 153, 211, 564
Finney, Albert
ILIATM 75
GS dir., *Charlie Bubbles*, 47-48
DIM 196, 197
R 390-392
WTLGD 382-383
TIAI 253, 254, 291, 293, 295, 338, 345
SOTA 113-114, 115, 198, 200
H 120
5001 29, 131, 203, 206, 222, 434, 503, 525, 654, 659, 676, 778, 798, 799, 805
Finney, Jack
WTLGD 523
5001 368
Fiore, Elena
WTLGD 137
5001 437, 667

Fiore, Maria
    5001 24, 798
Fiore, Robert
    5001 307, 602
Fiorentino, Linda
    H 39, 40
    5001 9
Firbank, Ronald
    H 296
Fire Over England
    5001
Fire Within, The (Le Feu follet)
    DIM 308, 309
    R 336
Firefly, The
    5001 (2nd ed)
Fires on the Plain (Nobi)
    ILIATM 225-228
    GS 138
    SOTA 327
    5001
Firesign Theatre
    5001 863
Fireworks
    ILIATM 35
First a Girl
    TIAI 332
First Baptist Church of Dallas
    H 440-441, 442
First Blood
    SOTA 116
First Blood (book)
    SOTA 375
First Circle, The
    R 101-106
    5001
First Love (1939)
    5001
First Love (1970)
    DIM 162-163
    5001
First Name: Carmen (Prenom: Carmen)
    SOTA 226-230
    5001 (2nd ed)
First, Ruth
    H 475
First You Cry (TV)
    TIAI 80
Firth, Colin
    ML 217-18
    5001 812
Firth, Peter
    WTLGD 337, 339
    TIAI 136
    5001 223, 749
Fischer, Corey
    5001 445, 469
Fischer-Dieskau, Dietrich
    WTLGD 75
Fischer, Gunnar
    KKBB 304, 353
    5001 451, 688, 727, 839
Fish, Billy
    5001 461
Fishburne, Larry
    5001 156
Fishburne, Laurence III

    5001 840
Fisher, Carrie
    R 439
    TIAI 211, 481
    H 116
    ML 274
    5001 88, 218, 316, 592, 626, 670, 709
Fisher, Eddie
    DIM 27
    ML 274
    5001 110
Fisher, Gerry
    DIM 357
    R 348
    5001 3, 316, 457, 488, 638, 660, 662
Fisher, Jasen
    5001 842
Fisher, Marion
    RK 35
Fisher, Robert
    5001 117
Fisher, Tricia Leigh
    5001 715
Fisher, Vardis
    R 87
Fishman, Kenneth Harris
    5001 414
Fisk, Jack
    R 369
    WTLGD 212, 502
    TIAI 354; dir., *Raggedy Man*, 350, 354, 372
    SOTA 91; dir., *Raggedy Man*, 91, 204
    H 148-150; dir., *Violets Are Blue*, 148-150, 151; *Raggedy Man*, 149, 234
    5001 47, 224, 579, 611, 816
Fiskin, Jeffrey Alan
    5001 167
Fistful of Dollars, A
    R 253
Fists in the Pocket (I Pugni in Tasca)
    GS 6
    TIAI 418
    H 290
    5001
Fitch, Robert
    TIAI 275
    5001 574
Fitz-Richard, Arthur
    5001 646
Fitzcarraldo
    TIAI 401-407
    5001 (2nd ed)
Fitzgerald, Barry
    KKBB 241
    R 272-273
    WTLGD 23
    SOTA 190
    H 172
    5001 25, 104, 126, 174, 342, 433, 514, 533, 608
Fitzgerald, F. Scott
    ILIATM 221
    KKBB 115, 153
    GS 10, 82
    RK 10, 30, 43
    DIM 308, 310
    R 44

    WTLGD 91, 92, 216-219
    TIAI 269
    5001 411, 764, 765, 793
Fitzgerald, Geraldine
    R 166
    WTLGD 266
    TIAI 232
    5001 36, 173, 320, 407, 571, 824, 851
Fitzgerald, Zelda
    ILIATM 221
    H 30
Fitzmaurice, George
    RK 23 (ill.)
    5001 733
Fitzmaurice, George, Mrs.
    RK 23 (ill.)
Fitzpatrick, Colleen
    H 443
    5001 313
Fitzsimmons, Margot
    5001 349
Five Corners
    ML 143
Five-Day Lover, The (L'Amant de cinq jours)
    ILIATM 170, 283
    KKBB 265:n
    5001
Five Easy Pieces
    DIM 152, 153, 231, 251, 252
    R 46, 162, 221, 224, 303, 309, 413
    WTLGD 554
Five Fingers
    5001
Five Graves to Cairo
    5001
Five Star Final
    RK 20
Five Thousand Fingers of Dr. T., The
    KKBB 203
    5001
Fixer, The
    GS 206, 208-210
    DIM 199, 200
    R 237
    5001
Flack, Roberta
    5001 692
Flagstad, Kirsten
    5001 68
Flaherty, Joseph P. (Joe)
    TIAI 225
    H 187, 337
    5001 143, 531, 723
Flaherty, Robert
    ILIATM 22, 248; dir., *Man of Aran*, 22, 248; *Nanook of the North*, 248; *Louisiana Story*, 276
    KKBB 180, 185, 306-307, 316, 324, 356-357; dir., *Nanook of the North*, 180, 185, 316, 324, 357; *Man of Aran*, 185, 306-307, 324, 357; *Tabu* (with F. W. Murnau), 356-357; *Moana*, 357; *Louisiana Story*, 357
    GS 3
    5001 458, 515, 740
Flaiano, Ennio
    KKBB 368

5001 67, 213, 386, 637, 818, 836
Flame of New Orleans, The
5001
Flamenco
5001
Flaming Creatures
ILIATM 19
Flamingo Kid, The
SOTA 308-311, 345
H 200, 348
5001 (2nd ed)
Flamingo Road
5001
Flanders, Ed
TIAI 244
5001 793
Flanders, Michael
DIM 324
Flanner, Janet, see Genêt
Flannery, Susan
R 406
Flash Gordon
TIAI 124-127, 184
SOTA 225
5001
Flashdance
SOTA 6-7, 35, 169, 171, 374
H 134, 375
5001 (2nd ed)
"Flat Foot Floogie with the Floy Floy" (music)
TIAI 175
Flatliners
5001 (2nd ed)
Flaubert, Gustave
DIM 191
TIAI 183
5001 446
Flea in Her Ear, A
GS 206, 211
TIAI 174
Fledermaus, Die (music)
WTLGD 13, 300
Fleeman, Gregory
H 116, 117
5001 273
Fleischer family
TIAI 123
Fleischer, Richard
KKBB 156, 203, 250; dir., *Fantastic
Voyage*, 156-157; *The Happy Time*, 203;
Compulsion, 250
GS dir., *Barrabas*, 167; *The Big Gamble*,
167; *The Boston Strangler*, 167; *Che*,
167; *Compulsion*, 167; *Crack in the
Mirror*, 167; *Doctor Dolittle*, 167;
Fantastic Voyage, 167; *The Girl in the
Red Velvet Swing*, 167; *The Happy
Time*, 167; *20,000 Leagues Under the
Sea*, 167; *The Vikings*, 167
DIM 147; dir., *Doctor Dolittle*, 26, 120, 328;
Tora! Tora! Tora! 147-148; *Fantastic
Voyage*, 216; *The Last Run*, 294, 353
R 318; dir., *Tora! Tora! Tora!* 209; *The New
Centurions*, 441
WTLGD 204-206; dir., *The Incredible
Sarah*, 204-206; *The New Centurions*,
206; *Mandingo*, 206, 223, 369, 453;

Doctor Dolittle, 325
5001 151, 237, 318, 360, 410, 516, 690
Fleming, Ian
GS 226
5001 270
Fleming, Rhonda
KKBB 349
5001 152, 338, 557, 701
Fleming, Victor
DIM dir., *Gone with the Wind*, 28, 74
5001 91, 118, 620, 783, 817
Flemyng, Gordon
GS dir., *The Split*, 181, 183-185
Flemyng, Robert
5001 271, 784, 788
Flesh
DIM 153, 157
Flesh & Blood
H 345
Flesh and Fantasy
ILIATM 188
5001
Flesh and the Devil
KKBB 285
5001
Fletch
5001 (2nd ed)
Fletcher, Bramwell
KKBB 355
5001 501, 616, 659, 734, 833
Fletcher, Dexter
5001 627
Fletcher, Jay
5001 94
Fletcher, Louise
R 271
WTLGD 86
5001 229, 549, 758
Fletcher, Lucille
5001 696
Fletcher-Cook, Graham
H 159
5001 3
Fleugel, Darlanne
SOTA 362
5001 548
Flicker, Theodore
DIM dir., *The President's Analyst*, 10
5001 594
Flight of the Eagle, The (*Ingenjör Andrées
Luftfärd*)
TIAI 475-479
5001 (2nd ed)
Flight of the Seventh Moon (book)
H 21
Flim Flam Man, The
GS 75
"Flintstones, The" (comic strip)
TIAI 197
Flippen, Jay C.
KKBB 291
5001 124, 200, 394, 490, 724, 754, 839
"Flipper" (TV)
KKBB 183
Flon, Suzanne
5001 500, 789
Flores, Stefano Satta, see Satta Flores, Stefano

Florey, Robert
KKBB 219; dir., *The Murders in the Rue
Morgue*, 219
5001 144, 494
Flournoy, Richard
5001 497
Flower Drum Song
5001
Floyd, Joey
TIAI 41
5001 340
Fluegel, Darlanne
5001 230
Fly, The (1958)
WTLGD 443, 523
H 210
5001 (2nd ed)
Fly, The (1986)
H 209-212
5001 (2nd ed)
Flying Down to Rio
DIM 382
TIAI 299
5001 (2nd ed)
"Flying Nun, The" (TV)
WTLGD 505, 507
Flynn, Errol
KKBB 180, 184, 185, 228
DIM 177
WTLGD 49
TIAI 396
H 162
5001 7, 117, 130, 174, 282, 306, 600, 634,
653, 660, 683, 717, 750
Flynn, John
GS dir., *The Sergeant*, 240-242
Focal Point
TIAI 156
Foch, Nina
WTLGD 60
5001 23, 453, 627, 699, 724, 747
Fog Over Frisco
5001
Fogle, James
ML 195-96
5001 205
Folies-Bergère
5001
Follow the Boys
5001
Follow the Fleet
R 56, 57
TIAI 275
5001
Folly to Be Wise
KKBB 265:n
5001
Folsey, George Jr.
5001 91
Folsey, George
5001 476
Fonda, Bridget
ML 130-33, 313
5001 657
Fonda, Henry
ILIATM 40, 242
KKBB 42, 49, 276, 290, 328, 363

GS 166
RK 17
DIM 229, 349
R 206, 267, 431
WTLGD 4, 5, 8, 328
TIAI 269, 270, 272, 456
SOTA 12, 291, 361
5001 8, 37, 64, 81, 82, 205, 259, 301, 343,
    380, 383, 404, 422, 445, 488, 496, 545,
    559, 699, 741, 752, 787, 795, 850, 857,
    860
Fonda, Jane
    ILIATM 305
    KKBB 29
    GS 171-172, 173
    DIM 71, 280-282, 352, 426
    R 34, 120, 178
    WTLGD 167, 269-271, 304-310, 390,
        402-405, 485-488, 529-530, 532
    TIAI 162-163, 270, 271, 293, 310
    SOTA 77, 167, 234, 247
    H 46, 243-244, 245
    ML 133
    5001 32, 50, 52, 115, 124, 129, 132, 148,
        149, 271, 385, 400, 419, 497, 498, 530,
        545, 713, 755, 784
Fonda, Peter
    DIM 78, 115, 349; dir., *The Hired Hand*,
        323, 353
    R 149-150, 378
    5001 210, 409, 422, 789, 799, 837
Foner, Naomi
    H 149
    5001 816
Fong, Benson
    5001 182, 252, 380, 392, 690
Fontaine, Frank
    5001 490
Fontaine, Joan
    KKBB 184, 278, 296
    SOTA 357
    5001 311, 375, 419, 607, 618, 847
Fontaine, Lillian
    5001 437
Fontanne, Lynn
    5001 309
Fontelieu, Stocker
    5001 27
Fonvielle, Lloyd
    H 340
    5001 295
Fool for Love
    H 96-100
    5001 (2nd ed)
Fool There Was, A
    ILIATM 131
Foolin' Around
    TIAI 11
Foolish Wives
    5001 (2nd ed)
Foote, Horton
    KKBB 151
    TIAI 480
    H 92, 93, 233
    5001 132, 747, 776, 790
Footlight Parade
    5001

Footloose
    SOTA 139-141, 169, 220
    5001 (2nd ed)
"For I Am a Pirate King" (music)
    SOTA 353
For Me and My Gal
    R 59
    5001
For Pete's Sake
    R 318, 328, 459
    WTLGD 242, 270
"For the Union Dead" (poem)
    ML 256
For Whom The Bell Tolls
    5001
For Your Eyes Only
    SOTA 4
    5001
Foran, Dick
    KKBB 314
    5001 77, 171, 243, 263, 509, 578, 684, 724
Forbes, Brenda
    5001 815, 834
Forbes, Bryan
    DIM 25, 321, 323-324; dir., *The Madwoman
        of Chaillot*, 25-26; *Long Ago,
        Tomorrow*, 321-324; *The L-Shaped
        Room*, 323; *The Whisperers*, 323
    R 442-446; dir., *Seance on a Wet Afternoon*,
        237; *The Stepford Wives*, 442-446
    5001 145, 431, 450, 461, 714, 832, 833
Forbes, J. Scott
    5001 576
Forbes, Kathryn
    5001 351
Forbes, Mary
    5001 91, 703
Forbes, Ralph
    5001 52, 137, 341, 355, 600, 638, 703, 796
Forbidden
    5001
Forbidden Games (Jeux interdits)
    ILIATM 111-113
    KKBB 247, 342
    WTLGD 356
    H 317
    5001
Forbidden Planet
    KKBB 266:n
    GS 36
    R 216
    WTLGD 350
    5001
Forced March
    5001 (2nd ed)
Ford, Alexander
    R 101-106
    5001 245
Ford Foundation
    WTLGD 387
Ford, Francis
    KKBB 328
    5001 560, 608, 672, 704, 713
Ford, Gerald R.
    WTLGD 265
Ford, Glenn
    GS 176

WTLGD 527
5001 66, 70, 79, 137, 285, 345, 689, 730,
    745
Ford, Grace
    5001 186
Ford, Harrison
    WTLGD 468
    TIAI 208, 209, 361, 362, 364, 482
    SOTA 164, 176, 319, 322
    H 446, 447
    ML 64, 145-49
    5001 79, 80, 217, 265, 361, 362, 612, 626,
        709, 844, 849
Ford, John
    ILIATM 242-243, 312; dir., *The Long Gray
        Line*, 44; *The Informer*, 119; *My
        Darling Clementine*, 242; *She Wore a
        Yellow Ribbon*, 242; *Fort Apache*, 242;
        The Grapes of Wrath, 289
    KKBB 41-43, 45, 61, 143, 202, 266, 276,
        368; dir., *Stagecoach*, 41; *The Man Who
        Shot Liberty Valance*, 42; *Young Mr.
        Lincoln*, 61; *Seven Women*, 143; *The
        Grapes of Wrath*, 275-276, 350-351;
        How Green Was My Valley, 350; *The
        Whole Town's Talking*, 368; *Cameo
        Kirby*, 368
    GS dir., *The Informer*, 9; *Stagecoach*, 62;
        The Whole Town's Talking, 62
    RK 75, 76
    DIM 296; dir., *Tobacco Road*, 155;
        Wagonmaster, 296; *The Grapes of
        Wrath*, 349
    R 98; dir., *The Long Voyage Home*,
        272-273; *Stagecoach*, 282; *Mogambo*,
        385
    WTLGD 225, 226, 324, 328, 430, 544; dir.,
        Cheyenne Autumn, 95; *Drums Along the
        Mohawk*, 178; *The Grapes of Wrath*,
        225, 226, 227; *My Darling Clementine*,
        328; *The Searchers*, 544
    TIAI 137, 141; dir., *Fort Apache*, 137;
        Cheyenne Autumn, 357
    SOTA 62, 241; dir., *The Grapes of Wrath*,
        234
    H 18, 308, 322; dir., *The Searchers*, 18; *The
        Grapes of Wrath*, 252
    ML 156
    5001 205, 259, 301, 342, 343, 346, 362,
        384, 408, 433, 461, 467, 488, 491, 510,
        608, 630, 662, 672, 704, 712, 713, 728,
        777, 800, 808, 836, 858, 859, 860
Ford, Paul
    5001 8, 505, 647, 745
Ford, Ruth
    R 45
    5001 392, 587
Ford, Wallace
    KKBB 337
    5001 20, 88, 179, 266, 362, 476, 614, 666,
        836
Foree, Ken
    5001 174
Foreign Affair, A
    5001
Foreign Correspondent
    KKBB 352

5001
Foreman, Carl
  KKBB 281
  GS 209
  R 15-17
  5001 102, 331, 475, 690, 860
Foreman, George
  WTLGD 66
Forest, Michael
  5001 38
Forester, C. S.
  KKBB 205, 229
  5001 9
Forever Amber
  ILIATM 306
  5001
Forman, Milos
  DIM 351; dir., *Taking Off*, 351
  WTLGD 84-90; dir., *Loves of a Blonde*, 79,
    88; *One Flew Over the Cuckoo's Nest*,
    84-90, 200; *Taking Off*, 89
  TIAI 175, 263-266; dir., *One Flew Over the
    Cuckoo's Nest*, 77, 179, 292; *Taking
    Off*, 175; *Ragtime*, 263-266; *Hair*, 264,
    265, 266
  SOTA 249-253; dir., *Ragtime*, 87; *Amadeus*,
    249-253
  H 190, 429-430
  ML dir., *Amadeus*, 219; *One Flew Over the
    Cuckoo's Nest*, 113, 320; *Valmont*, 217-
    20
  5001 21, 325, 441, 549, 612, 812
Foronjy, Richard
  H 245
Forqué, Verónica
  SOTA 365
  5001 830
Forrest, Christine
  TIAI 199
  5001 401
Forrest, Frederic
  TIAI 297, 298, 329
  ML 241
  5001 504, 550, 641, 799
Forrest, George
  5001 694
Forrest, Helen
  5001 54
Forrest, Irene
  5001 770
Forrest, Steve
  5001 327, 492
Forristal, Susan
  ML 328
Forsaking All Others
  5001
Forslund, Bengt
  5001 520
Forslund, Constance
  5001 43
Forst, Willi
  5001 470
Forster, E. M.
  SOTA 299, 300-301, 302, 303
  H 125-126, 127, 128, 129, 359-360, 361
  5001 470, 567, 640
Forster, Margaret

5001 282
Forster, Robert
  GS 249, 252
  5001 622
Forsyth, Bill
  TIAI 463-466; dir., *Local Hero*, 463-466;
    Gregory's Girl, 466
  SOTA 268-271; dir., *Comfort and Joy*,
    268-261; *Local Hero*, 268, 269, 270;
    Gregory's Girl, 269; *That Sinking
    Feeling*, 269
  H 406-409; dir., *Housekeeping*, 406-409;
    That Sinking Feeling, 408; *Gregory's
    Girl*, 408; *Local Hero*, 408, 476;
    Comfort and Joy, 408
  ML dir., *Breaking In*, 191-92
  5001 100, 148, 342, 429
Forsyth, Frederick
  TIAI 168
  5001 197
Forsythe, Drew
  TIAI 159
  5001 114
Forsythe, John
  DIM 80, 190
  R 359
  ML 40
  5001 317, 447, 660, 781
Forsythe, William
  H 291, 381, 382-383
  ML 10, 11
  5001 548, 571, 615, 826
Fort Apache
  ILIATM 242
  TIAI 137
  5001
Fort Apache, the Bronx
  TIAI 151-155, 288, 289, 412, 441
  5001
Fort, Garrett
  5001 201
Forte, Fabrizio
  WTLGD 299
Forte, Nick Apollo
  SOTA 123
  5001 105
Fortescue, Kenneth
  WTLGD 485
  5001 836
Forth, Jane
  DIM 156
  5001 788, 848
Fortier, Robert
  5001 445
Fortune (periodical)
  RK 63
Fortune, The
  WTLGD 87
  TIAI 3
  5001
Fortune Cookie, The
  GS 242
  R 425
  5001
Fortunes of War (TV)
  ML 214
40 Carats

R 434
  5001
48 Hrs.
  TIAI 437-440
  SOTA 72, 78, 287
  H 143
  5001 (2nd ed)
Forty-First, The (*Sorok Pervyi*)
  KKBB 266-267:n
  5001
42nd Street
  DIM 380
  WTLGD 502, 503
  5001
"42nd Street" (music)
  WTLGD 537
"Forza del Destina, La" (music)
  GS 99
  H 330
Fosse, Bob
  DIM 410, 411; dir., *Sweet Charity*, 26, 409;
    Cabaret, 409-413, y26, 430
  R 371-377, 389, 460, 462, 463; dir.,
    Cabaret, 187, 204, 241, 277, 327, 372,
    459, 460, 462, 463; *Lenny*, 371-377;
    Sweet Charity, 372; *Pippin*, 462
  WTLGD 334, 389; dir., *Cabaret*, 151, 389,
    525
  TIAI 427; dir., *All That Jazz*, 180, 345, 427
  SOTA 91-92; dir., *All That Jazz*, 35, 92;
    Star 80, 91-92, 204
  H 145
  5001 112, 287, 398, 417, 427, 510, 645,
    706, 734
Fossey, Brigitte
  ILIATM 112
  WTLGD 356, 454, 457-458, 549
  5001 242, 257, 291, 461, 609
Fossey, Dian
  ML 5-7
Foster, David
  5001 664
Foster, Gloria
  5001 155
Foster, Jodie
  WTLGD 132-133, 163
  TIAI 29
  5001 15, 108, 121, 745
Foster, Julia
  5001 13
Foster, Lewis R.
  5001 489, 497
Foster, Meg
  5001 121, 216, 771
Foster, Norman
  5001 384, 488, 711
Foster, Phil
  5001 50
Foster, Preston
  KKBB 185
  5001 30, 195, 321, 348, 363, 508
Foster, Susanna
  5001 579
Fouché, Joseph
  WTLGD 383
Foul Play
  TIAI 163, 412

SOTA 192
Foundas, Georges
  KKBB 271, 351
  5001 286, 713
Fountainhead, The
  KKBB 143
  GS 111, 151
  DIM 48, 386
  H 20
  5001 (2nd ed)
*Four Bags Full (La Traversée de Paris; Pig
    Across Paris; Crossing Paris)*
  KKBB 267:n
  WTLGD 210, 367-371
  TIAI 31, 32, 33, 226, 227, 228-229, 230
  SOTA 35, 36, 263, 376
  5001
Four Covans, the (dance group)
  5001 547
Four Daughters
  5001 (2nd ed)
Four Feathers, The
  SOTA 67
  5001
Four Friends
  TIAI 283-286
  H 70
  5001
400 Blows, The
  ILIATM 132
  KKBB 81, 129, 310
  GS 273
  DIM 244, 245, 307
  R 291
  WTLGD 57, 168, 169
Four Musketeers, The, see *The Three Musketeers
    (The Queen's Diamonds)*
*Four Nights of a Dreamer (Quatre Nuits d'un
    rêveur)*
  R 291
  5001
Four Seasons, The
  TIAI 207, 208, 415
  ML 201
Four Tops, The (group)
  H 249
Fourcade, Christian
  5001 425
4th Man, The
  SOTA 194-196
  H 343, 344
  5001 (2nd ed)
Foutz, Anthony
  TIAI 468
  5001 742
Fowle, Susannah
  TIAI 61
  5001 283
Fowler, Gene
  RK 10
  WTLGD 240
  5001 830
Fowler, Harry
  KKBB 331
  500121 581
Fowles, John
  TIAI 237, 238, 239

5001 145, 267, 452
Fowley, Douglas
  KKBB 225
  5001 13, 270, 480, 653, 683
Fox, The
  GS 30-35
  DIM 59
  5001
Fox, Edward
  WTLGD 308, 382
  TIAI 433
  SOTA 113, 370, 372, 373
  5001 96, 204, 206, 277, 541, 677
Fox, George
  5001 209
Fox, Huckleberry
  SOTA 97
  5001 749
Fox, James (William)
  SOTA 151, 300, 303
  H 159, 450
  5001 3, 132, 308, 332, 451, 568, 763
Fox, John
  5001 Jr., 787
Fox, Michael J.
  H 11, 12, 298, 299-300, 458
  ML 168-77, 225-27
  5001 45, 103, 124, 664
Fox, Paula
  DIM 348
Fox, Sidney
  5001 547
Foxwell, Ivan
  5001 784
Foy, Eddie Jr.
  5001 422, 761, 853
Fragonard, Jean-Honoré
  H 68
Fraker, William A.
  DIM 162; dir., *Monte Walsh*, 162
  WTLGD 90, 319, 352, 423
  TIAI 96; dir., *The Legend of the Lone
    Ranger*, 231
  5001 23, 43, 109, 176, 193, 229, 277, 434,
    495, 531, 643
Framing of Roger Rabbit, The
  ML 146
France, Pierre Mendes, see Mendes-France,
    Pierre
Francen, Victor
  KKBB 251
  5001 152, 446, 469, 523, 741
Frances
  TIAI 432
  SOTA 234
  H 51
Franchi, Franco
  H 124
Franchi, Rudi
  ILIATM 308
Franciosa, Anthony
  5001 232, 433
Francis, Anne
  KKBB 233, 266
  5001 47, 79, 257, 272, 726
Francis, Arlene
  ILIATM 150, 152, 154

KKBB 71
  5001 550
Francis, Carole
  WTLGD 417
Francis, Connie
  5001 286
Francis, Freddie
  ILIATM 63, 72, 75, 165
  TIAI 84, 238
  SOTA 285
  ML 257
  5001 57, 207, 215, 267, 288, 364, 640, 654,
    695, 790
Francis, Jon
  5001 839
Francis, Kay
  R 419
  WTLGD 20
  5001 144, 359, 566, 721, 792
Francis, Noel
  5001 358, 809
Franciscus, James
  WTLGD 140
  5001 467
Francke, Caroline
  5001 91
Francks, Don
  GS 159
Franco, Generalissimo Francisco
  H 289
  ML 23
Franju, Georges
  ILIATM 7; dir., *Eyes Without a Face*, 7, 18
  TIAI 193, 442; dir., *Thérèse Desqueyroux*,
    442
  5001 230, 753
Frank, Bruno
  5001 345
Frank, Gerold
  5001 356
Frank, Harriet Jr. (also see Ravetch, Irving)
  ILIATM 90-91
  DIM 76, 390
  R 294, 296, 297
  5001 153, 160, 344, 433, 622
Frank, Melvin
  KKBB 292; co-dir., *Knock on Wood*, 292
  R 454; dir., *A Touch of Class*, 180, 204,
    219, 312, 432; *The Prisoner of Second
    Avenue*, 453-457
  WTLGD 21, 147; dir., *A Touch of Class*, 27,
    147; *The Prisoner of Second Avenue*,
    150
  5001 272, 402, 597, 633, 750
Frank, Robert
  5001 130, 472
Frank, Tony
  5001 93
Frankau, Gilbert
  5001 137
Frankel, Art
  SOTA 345
  5001 437
Franken, Steve
  5001 567
Frankenheimer, John
  KKBB 9, 70, 83; dir., *Grand Prix*, 9-10, 59;

The Manchurian Candidate, 47, 49, 62,
83; *Seven Days in May*, 83
GS 94; dir., *Bird Man of Alcatraz*, 208; *The
Fixer*, 208-210; *The Manchurian
Candidate*, 95, 208; *Seven Days in May*,
95, 208
DIM 199-200; dir., *The Gypsy Moths*, 52,
200; *I Walk the Line*, 199-200; *The
Manchurian Candidate*, 199, 261; *Seven
Days in May*, 199; *The Fixer*, 199, 200
R 195-201; dir., *The Iceman Cometh*,
195-201; *The Fixer*, 237
TIAI 431; dir., *The Young Savages*, 173
5001 16, 73, 248, 351, 354, 462, 663, 860
Frankenstein
ILIATM 13
KKBB 38, 146, 148
SOTA 161
H 344
5001
Frankenstein, by Andy Warhol, see *Andy
Warhol's Frankenstein*
Frankeur, Paul
R 42
5001 192, 481
Franklin, Aretha
DIM 85
R 39
WTLGD 165
TIAI 26, 27
SOTA 69
H 294
5001 88, 722
Franklin, Dean
5001 243
Franklin, Howard
H 387
5001 692
Franklin, J. E.
R 60
5001 77
Franklin, Miles
5001 506
Franklin, Pamela
5001 365, 515, 526, 596
Franklin, Richard
H 74
Franklin, Sidney
5001 52, 294, 309, 393, 407, 599, 824, 834,
855
Frankovich, Mike
DIM 260
5001 89, 195
Frantic (1957) see *Elevator to the Gallows*
Frantic (1988)
H 446-447
5001 (2nd ed)
Frantz, Chris
SOTA 266
Franz, Dennis
TIAI 37, 227
SOTA 263
5001 85, 90, 203, 273
Franz, Eduard
5001 446, 759, 832
Franz, Elizabeth
H 300

5001 664
Fraser, Bill
KKBB 243
5001 118
Fraser, Elizabeth
5001 858
Fraser, George MacDonald
WTLGD 49
SOTA 4
5001 538-539, 645, 767
Fraser, John
5001 624, 794
Fraser, Liz
5001 357
Fraser, Ronald
5001 662, 729, 832
Frawley, James
5001 68
Frawley, William
5001 90, 101, 184, 282, 333, 494, 616, 642,
645, 693
Frazer, Dan
5001 141
Frazer, Rupert
SOTA 372
5001 677
Frazier, Sheila
WTLGD 532
Freaks
KKBB 39
WTLGD 480
TIAI 419
5001
Frears, Stephen
H 118-122, 295-298, 387-391; dir., *My
Beautiful Laundrette*, 118-122, 128, 387,
389, 391; *Bloody Kids* (TV), 120;
Gumshoe, 120; *The Hit*, 120, 121; *Prick
Up Your Ears*, 295-298; *Sammy and
Rosie Get Laid*, 387-391
ML dir., *Dangerous Liaisons*, 57-62, 218;
The Grifters, 283-87
5001 171, 506, 595, 652
Frechette, Mark
DIM 115
5001 862
Fred Astaire & Ginger Rogers Book, The (book)
R 55-59
Frederick, Lynn
5001 819
Frederick, Pauline
KKBB 121
GS 127
Fredericks, Ellsworth
5001 268, 368, 723
Free Soul, A
KKBB 285, 343
WTLGD 142
5001
Free to Be...You and Me (TV)
R 373
Freebie and the Bean
R 427
TIAI 64
5001
Freed, Alan
WTLGD 421-424

Freed, Arthur
WTLGD 79
5001 23, 30, 42, 103, 105, 105, 113, 141,
256, 285, 296, 370, 374, 398, 404, 546,
563, 679, 683, 723, 856, 865
Freed, Bert
DIM 345
5001 92, 186, 519, 570, 752
Freed, Donald
R 209
H 2, 3-4
5001 228, 663
Freed, Josh
TIAI 262, 263
5001 771
Freed, Ralph
5001 42
Freeland, Thornton
5001 253
Freeman, Al Jr.
GS 159
5001 185, 244
Freeman, Damita Jo
TIAI 94
5001 598
Freeman, David
TIAI 301
H 293
5001 92, 721
Freeman, Denis
5001 4
Freeman, Everett
5001 663
Freeman, Fred
5001 68, 711
Freeman, Gillian
5001 750
Freeman, Helen
5001 694
Freeman, Howard
5001 86
Freeman, Joel
5001 438
Freeman, Kathleen
5001 48, 65, 252, 537
Freeman, Mona
5001 327, 778
Freeman, Morgan
TIAI 22, 172
H 292-293, 294
ML 193, 235-38, 257-62, 316
5001 108, 204, 231, 288, 382, 465, 721
Freeman, Paul
TIAI 167, 209, 210
5001 197, 612
Frégis, Lucien
5001 493
Fregonese, Hugo
KKBB 203; dir., *My Six Convicts*, 203
Freidhofer, Hugo
5001 549
French Connection, The
DIM 315-319, 385, 387, 426
R 42, 64, 161, 208, 214, 223, 248, 260, 310,
435
WTLGD 95, 173
TIAI 188, 437, 486

5001
French Conspiracy. The (L'Attentat)
  R 207-209, 212, 214-215
  5001
French, Harold
  5001 379
French, Leslie
  SOTA 53
  5001 417, 497, 552
French Lieutenant's Woman, The
  TIAI 237-241
  H 49, 162
  5001
French Provincial (Souvenirs d'en France)
  WTLGD 143-147
  TIAI 21
  SOTA 48
  5001
French, They Are a Funny Race, The (released in
  France as *Les Carnets du Major
  Thompson*)
  5001
French, Victor
  5001 631, 670
Frend, Charles
  5001 451
Frenzy
  R 47
Fresholt, Myrna
  5001 257
Fresnay, Pierre
  ILIATM 108, 110
  KKBB 312, 335
  5001 127, 155, 236, 300, 460, 465, 494,
    603, 617, 720
Fresson, Bernard
  5001 310, 450
Freud
  ILIATM 11
Freud, Sigmund; Freudianism
  KKBB 5, 261, 266, 322, 346
  DIM 77, 108, 149, 220, 245, 247, 254, 337,
    370, 371
  WTLGD 24, 85, 127, 154, 187, 190-192,
    224, 256, 259, 306, 310, 333, 338, 355,
    390
  TIAI 6
  H 62
Freudlose Gasse, Die, see *The Joyless Street*
Freund, Karl
  KKBB 219; dir., *The Mummy*, 219
  RK 76, 79
  5001 44, 153, 201, 293, 294, 392, 409, 445,
    477, 501, 642, 758, 812-813, 843
Frey, Leonard
  DIM 331
  5001 98, 242, 450
Frey, Sami
  KKBB 112
  R 95-96
  SOTA 259
  H 271
  5001 49, 78, 128, 425, 753
Fricker, Brenda
  ML 179
  5001 509
"Fridays" (TV)

TIAI 161
Fridell, Åke
  5001 451, 514, 688, 839
Fridh, Gertrude
  5001 451, 839
Fried, Yakov
  5001 795
Friedan, Betty
  KKBB 344
Frieder, Sol
  ML 241
  5001 504
Friedhofer, Hugo
  5001 859
Friedkin, William
  GS dir., *The Birthday Party*, 206, 211-212;
    The Night They Raided Minsky's, 238
  DIM 137, 138, 315, 317; dir., *The Night
    They Raided Minsky's*, 83; *The Boys in
    the Band*, 137-138; *The French
    Connection*, 315-319, 385, 387, 426
  R 248-251, 322, 331; dir., *The French
    Connection*, 42, 64, 161, 208, 214, 223,
    248, 260, 310, 435; *The Exorcist*,
    247-251, 310, 320-321, 411
  WTLGD 173; dir., *The French Connection*,
    95, 173; *The Exorcist*, 173
  H 98; dir., *The Birthday Party*, 98; *The
    Exorcist*, 286
  ML dir., *To Live and Die in L.A.*, 262
  5001 75, 98, 228, 267, 528
Friedman, Anthony
  DIM 318; dir., *Bartleby*, 417-418
  5001 53
Friedman, Bruce Jay
  R 69
  SOTA 129, 142
  ML 13
  5001 31, 324, 431, 702
Friedman, Ken
  SOTA 79, 80, 83z
  5001 323, 382
Friedman, Stephen
  WTLGD 446
  5001 686
Friedrich, Caspar David
  ML 210
Friedrich, Lawrence W., S. J.
  KKBB 152-153
Friels, Colin
  H 433, 434, 435
  5001 333
Friendly Fire (TV movie)
  TIAI 80
Friendly, Fred
  5001 654
Friendly Persuasion
  KKBB 194
  5001
Friends for Life, see *Amici per la Pelle*
Friends of Eddie Coyle, The
  R 173, 318, 470
  5001
Friml, Rudolf
  ILIATM 143
  TIAI 70
  5001 245

Frings, Ketti
  5001 148, 243
Frisby, Terence
  5001 752
Fritsch, Willy
  KKBB 264
  5001 243
Fröbe, Gert
  KKBB 340
  GS 227
  WTLGD 388
  5001 197, 323, 643
Froeschel, George
  5001 824, 834
Frogs
  WTLGD 443
Fröhlich, Gustav
  5001 477
Frohman, Clayton
  SOTA 73
  5001 805
Fröling, Ewa
  TIAI 487, 489
  5001 236
From Caligari to Hitler
  ILIATM 270
  KKBB 242
From Here to Eternity (book)
  WTLGD 462
From Here to Eternity
  ILIATM 25, 47, 49, 54, 93, 305
  DIM 421
  WTLGD 41, 305
  TIAI 173
  H 303, 304
  5001
From Noon Till Three
  WTLGD 546
  5001
From Russia with Love
  5001 (2nd ed)
From the Life of the Marionettes
  TIAI 488
Front, The
  WTLGD 170-172
  5001
Front Page, The (1931; see also *His Girl Friday*)
  RK 21
  WTLGD 19
  TIAI 209
Front Page, The (1974)
  R 422-426
  WTLGD 150
  5001
Front Page, The (stage)
  KKBB 281
  RK 4, 17, 19, 20, 21, 48, 57, 63
  WTLGD 18
  SOTA 73
  H 447
Frontiere, Dominic
  TIAI 63
  5001 724
"Frontline" (TV)
  H 441
Frost, David
  DIM 200

Frost, Robert
  H 222
Fry, Christopher
  ILIATM 117
  5001 61, 63
Fry, Roger
  R 49
Frye, Dwight
  ILIATM 6, 13
  H 68
  5001 102, 201, 265
Frye, E. Max
  H 229, 230
  5001 693
Frye, William
  R 364
Fuchs, Daniel
  5001 318, 439, 564
Fudge, Alan
  5001 800
Fuest, Robert
  5001 851
Fugard, Athol
  TIAI 433
  SOTA 277
  5001 277, 395
Fugate, Caril Ann
  R 302
Fugitive Kind, The
  KKBB 70, 191
  GS 121
Fugs (group)
  5001 130
Fujimoto, Tak
  TIAI 76
  H 230
  5001 474, 594, 693, 738
Full Metal Jacket
  H 325-329, 353
  5001 (2nd ed)
Fuller, Charles
  SOTA 271, 272, 273
  5001 690
Fuller, Dale
  5001 255
Fuller, Samuel
  ILIATM 316
  DIM 78, 297
  R 471
  WTLGD 315
  SOTA 181, 230
  5001 22, 409, 581, 582
Fulton, John P.
  5001 369
Fun with Dick and Jane
  WTLGD 269-271, 484
  5001
Funeral, The
  H 307
Funeral in Berlin
  KKBB 10-11
Fung, Willie
  5001 303, 419, 542, 647, 779
Funicello, Annette
  GS 277
  5001 323
Funk, Terry

WTLGD 491
Funkquist, George
  KKBB 353
  5001 727
Funny Face
  KKBB 53
  GS 23
  WTLGD 61
  5001
Funny Girl
  KKBB 23
  GS 133-137
  DIM 328
  R 38, 177, 457, 459, 460, 462
  WTLGD 346
  TIAI 95
  SOTA 89
  5001
Funny Lady
  R 457-463
  WTLGD 242, 487
  TIAI 190
  5001
*Funny Thing Happened on the Way to the
    Forum, A*
  KKBB 138-139
  R 236
  TIAI 215
  5001
Funnyman
  DIM 350
  R 263, 265
  WTLGD 184
  5001
Furie, Sidney J.
  GS dir., *The Naked Runner*, 94
  DIM 173; dir., *Little Fauss and Big Halsy*,
    171, 173-174
  R 35-40, 429, 430; dir., *Lady Sings the
    Blues*, 35-40; *The Leather Boys*, 40; *The
    Ipcress File*, 40; *The Appaloosa*, 40;
    The Naked Runner, 40; *The Lawyer*, 40;
    Little Fauss and Big Halsy, 40; *Sheila
    Levine Is Dead and Living in New York*,
    429-432
  WTLGD 141-143; dir., *Lady Sings the
    Blues*, 61; *Gable and Lombard*,
    140-143, 191
  5001 33, 97, 275, 370, 406, 426, 514, 673
Furlong, Kirby
  R 298
  5001 455
Furneaux, Yvonne
  ILIATM 119
  5001 62, 129, 624
Furness, Betty
  5001 253
Furse, Margaret
  5001 423
Furse, Roger
  5001 628
Furst, Anton
  ML 163
  5001 54
Furst, Stephen
  ML 144
  5001 202

Furth, George
  5001 81, 277, 462, 541, 671
Furthman, Jules
  KKBB 6, 59, 360
  GS 114
  RK 13
  5001 82, 91, 134, 498, 505, 529, 558, 630,
    671, 699, 700, 770, 776
Fury (1936)
  5001
Fury, The (1978)
  WTLDG 418-421, 427, 431, 432, 523
  TIAI 38, 39, 40, 228, 230
  SOTA 233
  H 320
  5001
Fusco, John
  H 144
  5001 165
Fussell, Paul
  ML 170
Fussgänger, Der, see *The Pedestrian*
Futz
  DIM 54-57, 59, 112, 148, 241
Fyodorova, Victoria
  H 74
  5001 743

G

Gabel, Martin
  DIM 229
  5001 435, 466, 752
Gabin, Jean
  ILIATM 108, 110
  KKBB 244, 267, 302, 332, 337-338
  DIM 329
  R 238
  WTLGD 126, 223
  SOTA 47, 48, 78
  5001 66, 263, 300, 383, 442, 465, 575, 585,
    590, 618, 822, 823
Gable and Lombard
  WTLGD 140-143, 191
  5001
Gable, Christopher
  DIM 242, 381
  ML 140
  5001 96, 504, 614, 847
Gable, Clark
  KKBB 44, 48, 192, 285
  GS 34, 270
  RK 20, 32, 59
  DIM 110, 329, 353
  R 153, 176, 208, 456
  WTLGD 4, 5, 27, 28, 110, 140-143, 191
  TIAI 334
  SOTA 307
  H 138
  5001 128, 134, 169, 259, 266, 336, 340,
    354, 373, 439, 463, 475, 484, 491, 505,
    525, 619, 620, 718, 732, 779, 836
Gabor, Eva
  5001 285, 794

Gabor, Zsa Zsa
   KKBB 361
   5001 422, 500, 784
Gabriel, Peter
   SOTA 317
   ML 134
   5001 74
Gabriello
   KKBB 254
   5001 175
Gabrio, Gabriel
   KKBB 279-280
   5001 320, 575, 817
Gaddis, Thomas E.
   5001 74
Gades, Antonio
   SOTA 256
Gaffney, Marjorie
   5001 226
Gage, Nicholas (Nicholas Gatzoyianni)
   H 70, 72
   5001 214
Gagnon, Jacques
   5001 510
Gago, Jenny
   SOTA 74
Gahagan, Helen
   R 277
   5001 672
Gai Savoir, Le
   5001
Gail, Max
   SOTA 350
   5001 325
Gaillard, Slim
   5001 3
Gaily, Gaily
   DIM 73-74
   R 13
   5001
Gaines, Boyd
   5001 325
Gaines, Ernest J.
   R 265, 266
   5001 39
Gaines, Leonard
   5001 86, 521
Gaines, Richard
   5001 198, 343, 439, 497
Gaiser, Gerald
   WTLGD 270
   5001 271
Gaisseau, Pierre-Dominique
   KKBB 348; dir., *The Sky Above, The Mud
      Below*, 347-348
   5001 685
Galabru, Michel
   5001 700
Galati, Frank
   ML 69
   5001 3
Gale, Bob
   TIAI 98, 99, 100
   SOTA 164, 212
   H 12, 13, 280
   ML 226, 227
   5001 45, 530, 810

Gale, David
   H 68
   5001 618
Gale, Edra
   5001 213, 350, 721
Galeen, Henrik
   KKBB 319
   5001 534
Galento, Tony
   5001 546
Galindo, Nacho
   5001 662
Gallagher, Helen
   WTLGD 357
   5001 642
Gallagher, Peter
   TIAI 115, 116
   H 53, 54
   ML 44
   5001 202, 333, 354
Gallagher, Skeets
   5001 338, 354, 566
Gallant, Mavis
   DIM 418, 419
   5001 775
Gallico, Paul
   RK 48
   5001 141, 422, 591
Gallico, Pauline
   5001 141
Galligan, Zach
   SOTA 187, 189
   5001 307
Gallipoli
   TIAI 454, 455, 456
   ML 157
   5001 (2nd ed)
Gallo, George
   H 153
   5001 842
Gallo, Guy
   SOTA 198, 199
   5001 806
Gam, Rita
   5001 400, 527, 724
Gambit
   KKBB 364
   5001 (2nd ed)
Gambler, The
   R 349-351
   WTLGD 417
   H 49
   5001
Gambon, Michael
   H 130
   ML 185
   5001 205, 795
Game of Love, The (*Le Blé en herbe*)
   KKBB 250, 321
   GS 127
   TIAI 303-304
   5001
Games
   5001
Gammon, James
   H 392
   5001 448

Gance, Abel
   ILIATM 277; dir., *Napoléon*, 277
   KKBB 132
   R 149, 180
   WTLGD 324
   TIAI 142-151; dir., *Napoléon*, 142-151;
      J'Accuse, 145, 147; *La Roue*, 147; *Un
      Grand Amour de Beethoven*, 146;
      Lucrezia Borgia, 150; *Cyrano et
      D'Artagnan*, 151
   5001 515, 526, 865
Gandhi
   TIAI 432-435
   H 54
   5001 (2nd ed)
Gandhi, Mahatma
   DIM 67, 226
Gang That Couldn't Shoot Straight, The
   DIM 369
   R 167
   TIAI 457
   H 154
   5001
Gang's All Here, The
   5001
Gangelin, Victor
   5001 828
Gangster as Tragic Hero, The (book)
   SOTA 105
Ganguly, Sunil
   R 142
Ganios, Tony
   5001 154
Ganz, Bruno
   WTLGD 185-187, 233, 312-316, 452
   H 470, 472
   5001 22, 97, 443, 467, 841
Ganz, Lowell
   TIAI 393
   SOTA 142
   5001 528, 702
Garbo, Greta
   ILIATM 193
   KKBB 35, 56-57, 191, 236, 243, 275, 285,
      318
   GS 45, 135, 234
   DIM 302, 313, 353, 364, 365
   R 82, 152, 344, 346
   WTLGD 28, 142, 146, 223, 307, 330, 334
   TIAI 345, 403, 436
   SOTA 111, 289, 322
   H 46, 66-67
   ML 99, 283
   5001 28, 116, 153, 251, 299, 384, 531, 649,
      681, 732, 845
Garbuglai, Mario
   5001 364
Garcés, Delia
   KKBB 261
   5001 213
Garcia, Andy
   H 156, 319
   ML 262, 263, 313, 314
   5001 213, 366, 473, 807
García Márquez, Gabriel
   TIAI 249
   SOTA 131, 182-183

H 221
5001 224
Garden, Mary
RK 66
Garden Murder Case, The
5001
Garden of Allah, The
5001
Garden of Delights, The (El Jardín de las Delicias)
DIM 263-264
5001
"Garden of Earthly Delights, The" (Bosch)
DIM 261
Garden of Evil
ILIATM 55
Garden of the Finzi-Continis, The (Il Giardino dei Finzi-Contini)
DIM 363-366, 426
WTLGD 330
5001
Gardenia, Vincent
DIM 255
R 426
H 248, 424
5001 50, 270, 347, 427-428, 496, 832
Gardens of Stone
H 303-306
5001 (2nd ed)
Gardiner, Reginald
KKBB 249
5001 25, 78, 93, 143, 459, 736
Gardner, Ava
ILIATM 177
KKBB 206, 234-235, 291
GS 95, 271
DIM 28
R 99, 385, 386
WTLGD 166, 281
TIAI 183
H 200, 469
5001 51, 67, 209, 394, 421, 471, 472, 491, 526, 546, 550, 563, 619, 679, 825
Gardner, Cyril
5001 645
Gardner, Fred
5001 863
Gardner, Herb
R 373
WTLGD 271-272
5001 371
Gardner, Joan
5001 459, 599, 659
Gardner, Leonard
5001 238
Garett, Betty
5001 740
Garfein, Jack
5001 719
Garfield, Allen (Allen Goorwitz)
DIM 325, 384
R 134, 449
WTLGD 211
TIAI 67
5001 270, 275, 307, 330, 516, 559, 687, 724
Garfield, Brian
5001 714

Garfield, John
ILIATM 57
KKBB 190, 238, 333
R 172, 250
TIAI 180
5001 11, 263, 336, 345, 384, 592, 750, 755, 782, 783, 858
Garfield, John Jr.
5001 750
Garfinkle, Louis
WTLGD 518
Garfunkel, Arthur
DIM 283, 284, 348
5001 120, 125
Gargan, Edward
KKBB 362
5001 316, 796
Gargan, William
KKBB 54
5001 117, 613, 754, 857
Garland, Beverly
R 364
5001 595
Garland, Judy
KKBB 185, 208, 283
DIM 407, 420
R 59, 75
WTLGD 240, 243, 244, 471, 472
5001 29, 42, 106, 141, 210, 256, 286, 320, 349, 384, 438, 582, 583, 677, 707, 722, 727, 764, 772, 848, 865
Garland, Robert
TIAI 429
H 356
5001 532
Garmes, Lee
GS 19
5001 23, 27, 126, 140, 162, 186, 192, 206, 498, 529, 565, 657, 671, 701, 865
Garner, Eroll
WTLGD 415
Garner, Herb
5001 757
Garner, James
KKBB 9
DIM 299-300
R 100, 359
TIAI 332, 333, 334, 335
5001 134, 466, 487, 685, 814
Garner, Jay
TIAI 276
5001 574
Garner, Peggy Ann
KKBB 185
WTLGD 444
H 477
5001 78, 359, 392
Garnett, Tay
KKBB 333; dir., *One Way Passage*, 213; *The Postman Always Rings Twice*, 332-333
R 328
5001 134, 152, 592, 668, 696, 705, 786
Garr, Teri
R 405
WTLGD 351
TIAI 297, 298, 354, 429, 432

H 9, 39
ML 91-93
5001 9, 78, 142, 224, 541, 780
Garrett, Betty
5001 546, 848
Garrett, Oliver H. P.
5001 346, 463, 525
Garrick, John
5001 387
Garrison, Ellen
SOTA 24
5001 864
Garry, Marshall
5001 437
Garson, Greer
ILIATM 339, 344
KKBB 135, 178, 275, 304
DIM 38, 419
WTLGD 344
SOTA 94
5001 84, 297, 446, 486, 595, 616
Garstin, Crosbie
5001 134
Garve, Andrew
5001 784
Garvey, Stanley
5001 226
Garwood, Norman
5001 98
Gary, Coleen
5001 394
Gary, Lorraine
WTLGD 189
5001 118, 378, 531
Gary, Romain
GS dir., *Birds in Peru*, 193
DIM 245-247; dir., *Birds in Peru*, 247
5001 74, 601, 684
Gaslight
KKBB 267:n
5001
Gassman, Vittorio
KKBB 238
WTLGD 443, 444, 549, 551
TIAI 357, 390
5001 69, 609, 746
Gaster, Nicolas
H 478
Gate of Hell (Jigokumon)
KKBB 266, 267-268:n
5001
Gates, Larry
5001 360, 368, 719
Gates of Heaven, The
KKBB 269
Gates of Paris, see *Porte des lilas*
Gateson, Marjorie
5001 128, 685, 837
Gatti, Marcello
DIM 176
5001 55, 110
Gattopardo, Il, see *The Leopard*
Gatzoyianni, Eleni
H 70-73
Gatzoyianni, Nicholas, see Gage, Nicholas
Gaudí, Antonio
H 155

Gaudier-Brzeska, Henri
   R 47-52
   TIAI 128
Gauguin, Paul
   SOTA 245
   ML 292, 294
Gauntlet, The
   WTLGD 379-380
   5001
Gavin, John
   DIM 26
   TIAI 216
   5001 450, 699, 763
Gaxton, William
   5001 64, 692
Gay Desperado, The
   ML 51
   5001 (2nd ed)
Gay Divorcée, The
   R 57
   5001
Gay, John
   ILIATM 116-117
   WTLGD 193
   5001 61
Gayle, Crystal
   TIAI 296
   5001 550
Gayle, Jackie
   SOTA 123
   H 281, 282
   5001 746, 773
Gaynes, George
   TIAI 432
   5001 478, 775, 780
Gaynor, Janet
   ILIATM 197
   KKBB 167, 369-370
   GS 105
   R 285
   WTLGD 240, 244, 377
   TIAI 273
   SOTA 337
   5001 706, 711, 729, 859
Gaynor, Mitzi
   5001 418, 752
Gayton, Joe
   SOTA 118
   5001 804
Gazelle, Wendy
   H 389
   5001 652
Gazzara, Ben
   DIM 222
   TIAI 466, 467, 468, 469
   H 385
   5001 346, 719, 742, 819
Gazzo, Michael V.
   R 402
   WTLGD 415-416
   5001 244, 290, 546, 725
Gear, Luella
   5001 119
Geary, Anthony
   H 454
   5001 567
Gee, Prunella

5001 837
Geer, Ellen
   5001 320
Geer, Will
   R 209
   5001 8, 228, 368, 379, 622, 663
Geeson, Judy
   5001 777
Geffen Company
   H 41
Gehman, Martha
   5001 274
Gehret, Jean
   5001 95
Geisel, Theodore, see Dr. Seuss
Gelbart, Larry
   KKBB 138
   R 131
   WTLGD 501-505
   TIAI 394, 429
   SOTA 133
   5001 80, 272, 500, 541, 780
Gelber, Jack
   5001 152
Gélin, Daniel
   DIM 306
   TIAI 469
   5001 190, 503, 537, 585
Geller, Stephen
   5001 594
Gellhorn, Martha
   WTLGD 282
Gelsey, Erwin
   5001 291
General, The
   KKBB 184
   5001 (2nd ed)
General della Rovere (Il Generale della Rovere)
   KKBB 268-270:n
   5001
Generale della Rovere, Il, see General della
   Rovere
Generals Without Buttons, see La Guerre des
   boutons
Genet, Jean
   ILIATM 101
   KKBB 167
   DIM 124
   WTLGD 39
   TIAI 250; dir., *Un Chant D'Amour*, 250
   H 252
   ML dir., *Un Chant d'Amour*, 195
Genêt (pseud. of Janet Flanner)
   DIM 308
Genevieve
   KKBB 270:n
   5001
Genn, Leo
   5001 114, 306, 328, 490, 500
Gennari, Lina
   5001 803
Genou de Claire, Le, see Claire's Knee
Genovese, Kitty
   KKBB 34
Genthe, Arnold
   WTLGD 307
Gentleman Jim

5001
Gentleman's Agreement
   ILIATM 81
   WTLGD 396
Gentlemen Prefer Blondes
   RK 13
   R 154
Gentlemen's Quarterly (periodical)
   TIAI 94
Geoffrey, Paul
   TIAI 185
   5001 227, 308
Geordie, see Wee Geordie
George III
   WTLGD 102
George, Chief Dan
   DIM 213, 215
   5001 116, 320, 424
George, Gladys
   KKBB 121, 305
   WTLGD 501
   5001 65, 136, 249, 318, 447, 454, 465, 634
George, Maude
   5001 255
George, Nathan
   5001 679
George, Susan
   DIM 394, 395
   5001 721
"Georgia on My Mind" (music)
   TIAI 284, 285
Georgy Girl
   KKBB 20, 22-23, 31, 142
   GS 124, 125
   R 344
   5001 (2nd ed)
Geraghty, Carmelita
   5001 587
Gérard, François Pascal Simon
   WTLGD 381
Gérard, Henriette
   KKBB 365
   5001 812
Geray, Steven
   5001 115, 359, 402, 469
Gere, Richard
   WTLGD 319, 446-447
   TIAI 33, 381, 382
   SOTA 294, 295, 296, 297
   H 224
   ML 262-64
   5001 84, 156, 177, 366, 434, 540
Geret, Georges
   DIM 65
   5001 862
Géricault, Jean Louis Andre Théodore
   WTLGD 59, 381
Gering, Marion
   5001 446, 647, 760
Germaine, Mary
   KKBB 367
   5001 831
Germi, Pietro
   KKBB 303; dir., *Mademoiselle Gobette*, 303
   GS dir., *Mademoiselle Gobette*, 211
   R 257-258; dir., *Alfredo Alfredo*, 257-259;
      Divorce--Italian Style, 258; *Seduced and*

Abandoned, 258
WTLGD 137
5001 14, 449
Gerolmo, Chris
ML 55
5001 486
Gerroll, Daniel
5001 68
Gershe, Leonard
5001 260, 271
Gershwin, George
ILIATM 143-144
GS 163
DIM 333
WTLGD 194, 217, 368, 370, 412
5001 23, 271, 286, 404, 641, 692, 706, 722,
865
Gershwin, Ira
GS 163
RK 80
DIM 333
5001 157, 159, 271, 286, 287, 404, 692,
706, 722, 865
Gershwin, Jerry
GS 40
Gershwin, Lee (Leonore)
RK 80
Gert, Valeska
5001 158, 384, 386
Gertz, Jami
H 143
5001 165
Gervaise
ILIATM 111
KKBB 333
5001
Gerzso, Gunther
SOTA 199
Get Carter
TIAI 125, 126
5001
Get Out Your Handkerchiefs (Préparez vos
mouchoirs)
WTLGD 454, 457, 458-462
TIAI 50, 165
SOTA 328, 350
5001
Get to Know Your Rabbit
R 368
TIAI 228
Getaway, The
R 78-79, 135, 310
WTLGD 112, 557
5001
Getchell, Robert
R 408, 413
WTLGD 229
TIAI 236
H 49
5001 15, 96, 492, 735
Getino, Octavio
DIM 257, 258
Getting of Wisdom, The
TIAI 60-62
5001
Getting Straight
DIM 149-151, 236

TIAI 64
Getz, John
SOTA 323
H 210
5001 83, 252
Ghare-Baire, see The Home and the World
Gherardi, Piero
5001 110
Ghetto Lites (group)
H 389
5001 652
Ghostley, Alice
5001 777
Ghost and Mrs. Muir, The
5001 (2nd ed)
Ghost Breakers, The
ILIATM 11
Ghost Goes West, The
KKBB 270:n
5001
Ghostbusters
SOTA 192-194
H 174
ML 42, 164
5001 (2nd ed)
Ghostbusters II
ML 164-65
5001 (2nd ed)
Ghosts (1936)
WTLGD 335
Giallelis, Stathis
5001 22, 123
Giannini, Giancarlo
WTLGD 99, 136-137, 393-394, 540-542
5001 218, 364, 437, 584, 666, 736
Giant
TIAI 415, 480
5001
Giardino dei Finzi-Contini, Il, see The Garden of
the Finzi-Continis
Gibb, Barry, Robin, and Maurice
5001 655
Gibb, Cynthia
5001 651
Gibbon, Edward
DIM 128
Gibbons, Ayllene
KKBB 299
5001 440
Gibbons, Cedric
5001 23, 46, 153, 300, 511, 744, 845
Gibbs, Anthony
GS 120
Gibbs, Wolcott
RK 56
Gibney, Sheridan
5001 31, 548
Gibran, Kahlil
KKBB 32
DIM 163
Gibson, Henry
R 187, 447
TIAI 26
H 448
ML 183
5001 88, 361, 399, 432, 516, 537, 738
Gibson, Mel

TIAI 385, 386, 452, 453, 454, 456
SOTA 184, 185-186, 290, 291
ML 48-52
5001 96, 276, 486, 633, 748, 854
Gibson, William
KKBB 60, 249
5001 144, 483
Gibson, Wynne
5001 139, 355
Gidding, Nelson
WTLGD 120
5001 321, 334
Giddins, Gary
ML 2, 4
Gide, André
KKBB 356
GS 9
5001 739
Gideon, Raynold
SOTA 307
H 198, 392
5001 448, 705, 710
Gidget Goes Hawaiian
H 293
Giehse, Thérèse
R 338
WTLGD 82
5001 77, 403
Gielgud, John
KKBB 201, 299, 340
GS 19, 22, 23, 145, 183
DIM 15, 37
R 139, 359-360, 390, 391
WTLGD 77, 255-258
TIAI 85, 230-231, 232, 246, 433, 470
SOTA 12, 305, 371, 372, 373
H 44, 128
5001 36, 52, 130, 131, 215, 235, 277, 291,
436, 440, 502, 503, 541, 587, 601, 602,
628, 639, 662, 663, 677
Gierasch, Stefan
5001 347, 682
Gifford, G. Adam
WTLGD 494
Gifford, Gloria
WTLGD 531
Gifle, La, see The Slap
Gift, Donn
5001 854
Gift, Roland
H 389
5001 652, 657
Gigi (1950)
5001
Gigi (1958)
5001
Gilbert & Sullivan
5001 480
Gilbert and Sullivan
DIM 16
Gilbert, Billy
KKBB 256, 281
5001 25, 34, 106, 185, 245, 335, 472, 545,
641, 774
Gilbert, Bruce
TIAI 163
5001 530, 545

Gilbert, Craig
  R 225
Gilbert, Edwin
  5001 19
Gilbert, Joanne
  KKBB 277
  5001 303, 331
Gilbert, John
  KKBB 285, 368
  RK 23 (ill.), 24
  DIM 196
  TIAI 436
  5001 251, 337, 680, 845
Gilbert, Lewis
  KKBB 328; dir., *Paradise Lagoon*, 328-329
  GS 181; dir., *You Only Live Twice*, 122
  DIM 133, 135; dir., *The Adventurers*, 132-136, 148, 420
  SOTA 83-85; dir., *Moonraker*, 4; *Educating Rita*, 83-85
  5001 6, 13, 212, 436, 495, 565, 703, 857
Gilbert, Lou
  KKBB 367
  5001 304, 386, 818
Gilchrist, Connie
  5001 296, 373, 382, 419, 771, 783, 847
Gilda
  TIAI 33
  ML 190
  5001
Giler, David
  WTLGD 122-123, 270; dir., *The Black Bird*, 122-123
  TIAI 260
  5001 76, 271, 698
Gilford, Jack
  KKBB 138
  R 117
  WTLGD 264
  TIAI 196, 197
  H 7
  5001 126, 127, 144, 248, 272, 487, 655
Gill, Brendan
  ILIATM 70, 90, 92, 152-153, 169
  GS 29
  DIM 308
Gillespie, Arnold
  5001 294
Gillespie, Dizzy
  ML 1, 2
  5001 155
Gillette, Anita
  H 425
  5001 496
Gilliam, Terry
  H 106-110; dir., *Brazil*, 106-110, 287; co-dir., *Monty Python and the Holy Grail*, 106; dir., *Jabberwocky*, 106; *Time Bandits*, 106, 108
  ML dir., *The Adventures of Baron Munchausen*, 106-11; *Brazil*, 107, 109, 110, 111, 163; co-dir., *Monty Python and the Holy Grail*, 109
  5001 6, 98, 772
Gilliat, Sidney
  KKBB 277, 293
  5001 254, 306, 351, 378, 398, 406, 826

Gilliatt, Penelope
  ILIATM 17, 23, 85, 90, 164
  DIM 292, 293
  5001 728
Gillingwater, Claude
  5001 741
Gillis, Ann
  5001 8
Gillis, Richard
  5001 48
Gillmor, Noelle
  DIM 195
  5001 32
Gilmore, Lowell
  5001 397, 581
Gilmore, Virginia
  5001 552
Gilpin, Jack
  H 231
  5001 693
Gilroy, Frank D. (pseud. is Bert Blessing)
  DIM 122, 348; dir., *Desperate Characters*, 348
  WTLGD 546-547; dir., *Once in Paris*, 546-547; *Desperate Characters*, 546; *From Noon Till Three*, 546
  TIAI 412
  5001 269-270, 380, 547
Gimme Shelter
  DIM 206-211
  WTLGD 251
Gindes, Mark
  5001 438
Gindorff, Bryan
  WTLGD 41
  5001 318
Ginger and Fred (Ginger e Fred)
  H 138-142
  5001 (2nd ed)
Gingold, Hermione
  KKBB 331
  5001 285, 505, 514, 581
Ginnes, Abram S.
  DIM 74
  5001 275
Ginsberg, Allen
  WTLGD 397, 398, 399-400
  TIAI 193
  5001 130, 472
Ginsberg, Milton Moses
  DIM 36; dir., *Coming Apart*, 36, 59, 148
  5001 149
Giono, Jean
  KKBB 140, 233, 279
  H 330
  5001 47, 320
Giornata Particolare, Una, see *A Special Day*
Giotto
  H 129
Gipe, George
  5001 178, 462
Giradot, Etienne
  KKBB 362
Girard, Rémy
  H 237
  5001 182
Girardot, Annie

DIM 419
R 145
TIAI 156, 157
5001 635, 685, 775
Girardot, Etienne
  5001 278, 345, 391, 717, 796, 836
Giraud, Bernadette
  ML 294
Giraudoux, Jean
  GS 9
  DIM 25
  5001 450
Girl Can't Help It, The
  H 159
Girl Crazy
  RK 80
  5001 (2nd ed)
Girl in Black, A (Koritsi me ta Mavra)
  KKBB 270-271:n, 351
  5001
Girl in the Mist, A (Kiri no Naka no Shojo)
  KKBB 271:n
  5001
Girl in the Red Velvet Swing, The
  GS 167
Girl on a Motorcycle, The
  GS 206, 210-211
Girl Was Young, The, see *Young and Innocent*
Girl Who Had Everything, The
  KKBB 343
Girotti, Massimo
  R 32, 33
  5001 364, 410
Gish, Dorothy
  R 179
  5001 553
Gish, Lillian
  ILIATM 206
  KKBB 191, 249, 317, 345, 352
  GS 45-46
  R 179
  WTLGD 144, 443
  TIAI 134
  H 92, 440
  5001 107, 144, 206, 305, 334, 367, 385, 526, 552, 553, 591, 658, 659, 735, 790, 793, 824
Gisondi, Toni Ann
  TIAI 345
  5001 29
Giulietta degli Spiriti, see *Juliet of the Spirits*
Give a Girl a Break
  5001
Givenchy, Hubert de
  5001 99, 130, 230, 271
Glamour (periodical)
  KKBB 129
Glaser, Paul Michael
  DIM 332
  5001 242
Glasmon, Kubec
  5001 768
Glass Key, The
  5001
Glass Menagerie, The (stage)
  R 75
  WTLGD 114

H 233
Glass Menagerie. The
 R 246-247
Glass, Ned
 5001 16, 130, 260, 533, 828
Glass Slipper. The
 5001 (2nd ed)
Glass, Sydney A.
 5001 86
Glasser, Leonard
 ML 93
 5001 557
Glazer, Benjamin
 5001 783
Glazer, Mitch
 ML 38
 5001 660
Glazer, Tom
 5001 232
Glazier, Sidney
 5001 601
Gleason, Jackie
 TIAI 395
 SOTA 376
 H 199, 201
 5001 19, 346, 535, 552
Gleason, James
 KKBB 232, 317
 5001 35, 42, 141, 200, 233, 266, 329, 392,
  409, 473, 508, 526, 741
Gleason, Joanna
 ML 201
 5001 162
Gleason, Lucille
 5001 141
Gleason, Paul
 SOTA 347, 348
 5001 99, 786
Gleason, Ralph J.
 R 123
 5001 572
Gleason, Russell
 KKBB 231
 5001 18
Gleiberman, Owen
 H 109
Glen and Randa
 WTLGD 82
Glen, John
 SOTA 3-5, 368; dir., *Octopussy*, 3-5; *For
  Your Eyes Only*, 4; *A View to a Kill*,
  368
 5001 257, 538, 545, 815
Glenarvon (book)
 R 112
Glengarry Glen Ross
 H 179, 280
Glenn, Annie
 SOTA 64-65
Glenn, John
 SOTA 64-65
Glenn Miller Story. The
 5001
Glenn, Roy
 5001 120, 244
Glenn, Scott
 TIAI 32, 33, 212, 303, 306

SOTA 65-66
H 14
5001 44, 126, 485, 516, 576, 630, 682, 809
Glennon, Bert
 5001 704
Glenville, Peter
 ILIATM 138, 313; dir., *Summer and Smoke*,
  137-139
 KKBB 141, 321; dir., *Hotel Paradiso*, 321
 GS 181; dir., *Hotel Paradiso*, 211
 5001 597, 726
Gliese, Rochus
 5001 729
"Glittering Prizes, The" (TV)
 SOTA 371
Glogauer, Herman
 5001 547
Glorifying the American Girl
 5001
Glory
 ML 256-62
 5001 (2nd ed)
"Glory, Glory, Hallelujah" (music)
 TIAI 447
Glover, Crispin
 H 11, 13, 315, 316
 5001 45, 632
Glover, Danny
 SOTA 246, 247
 H 14, 83
 5001 146, 585, 682, 844
Glover, John
 WTLGD 308
 TIAI 77
 H 66, 445
 ML 40
 5001 361, 386, 469, 660, 692, 835
Glover, Julian
 5001 256-257, 362
Gluck, Christoph Willibald von
 WTLGD 541
 5001 209
Glyn, Elinor
 KKBB 213
 GS 194
 5001 680
Glynn, Carlin
 H 93
 5001 154, 684, 790
Go Ask Alice
 R 263, 266
Go Into Your Dance
 5001
Go West (1925)
 5001
Go West (1941)
 KKBB 184
 WTLGD 192
 5001
Go-Between, The
 DIM 292, 363
 R 235
 WTLGD 95
 SOTA 33
 H 45
God's Little Acre
 ILIATM 235

Godard, Jean-Luc
 ILIATM 15, 24, 128, 130, 132, 187,
  210-212, 215; dir., *My Life to Live*
  (*Vivre Sa Vie*), 15; *Breathless*, 24, 32,
  127-132, 148, 187, 210-212, 215, 222,
  312
 KKBB 14-17, 54, 112-115, 127-130, 319;
  dir., *Alphaville*, 15, 114-115, 319; *The
  Married Woman*, 15, 17, 130, 164;
  Breathless, 17, 33, 54, 127, 129, 244,
  262, 302; *Band of Outsiders*, 17, 54,
  112-115, 127; *Masculine Feminine*,
  127-130; *My Life to Live*, 128-129;
  Pierrot le Fou, 130
 GS 4, 8, 16, 61, 76, 100, 194, 205, 273,
  284; dir., *Breathless*, 81, 84, 142; *Les
  Carabiniers*, 106, 140, 219; *La
  Chinoise*, 76-84, 140, 141; *Contempt*,
  142; *The Married Woman*, 138;
  Masculine Feminine, 4, 76, 81; *Pierrot
  le Fou*, 277; *My Life to Live*, 27;
  Weekend, 138-144, 220
 RK 17
 DIM 63, 168, 209, 220, 243, 253, 259, 272,
  273, 279, 306, 372, 402, 404; dir., *La
  Chinoise*, 167, 272, 306; *One Plus One*,
  168, 209; *Weekend*, 253, 298, 404; *Band
  of Outsiders*, 279, 402; *Masculine
  Feminine*, 306
 R 33, 120, 168, 269, 303, 424, 450; dir.,
  Masculine Feminine, 168; *Breathless*,
  201, 269, 303, 305; *Weekend*, 269
 WTLGD 145, 146, 147, 169, 181, 182, 301,
  315, 420, 442, 456, 523, 525; dir.,
  Breathless, 169, 315, 456; *All the Boys
  Are Named Patrick*, 169; *La Chinoise*,
  181; *Alphaville*, 314; *Weekend*, 456; *Les
  Carabiniers*, 456
 TIAI 35, 48, 101-106, 279, 330, 450, 485;
  dir., *Breathless*, 101, 279; *Every Man
  for Himself*, 101-106; *Pierrot le Fou*,
  102; *My Life to Live*, 104; *Two or Three
  Things I Know About Her*, 105;
  Alphaville, 329, 485; *Masculine
  Feminine*, 330; *Les Carabiniers*, 454
 SOTA 212, 226-230, 267; dir., *Weekend*,
  212, 227; *First Name: Carmen*,
  226-230; *Breathless*, 227; *Pierrot le
  Fou*, 229, 230; *Numéro Deux*, 230;
  Every Man for Himself, 230
 H 61, 62, 107, 308, 311, 389; dir., *Two or
  Three Things I Know About Her*, 9;
  Alphaville, 107, 471
 ML 23, 174
 5001 20, 49, 100, 118, 135, 226, 246, 275,
  419, 438, 467, 468, 577, 582, 784, 826,
  827, 865
Goddard, Paulette
 KKBB 370
 5001 189, 393, 491, 637, 662, 847, 859
Godden, Rumer
 5001 435, 632
Goddess. The
 KKBB 158, 271-273:n
 R 13
 WTLGD 209, 219, 223, 224

5001
Godey, John
  R 365
  5001 382, 741
Godfather, The
  DIM 420-426
  R 161, 169-170, 173, 174, 228, 229, 256,
    269, 314, 318, 327, 396-398, 442, 469
  WTLGD 317, 320, 328, 427, 486
  TIAI 109, 190, 227, 242, 244
  SOTA 53, 101, 177, 339, 362, 376, 377
  H 303, 304
  ML 166, 310, 311
  5001
Godfather, Part II, The
  R 396-403, 471
  WTLGD 133, 178, 198, 202, 204, 267, 317,
    328, 416, 427, 486
  TIAI 109, 227, 241, 244, 457
  SOTA 74, 101, 103, 177, 298, 339, 362
  H 303, 304
  ML 166, 309, 310, 311
  5001
Godfather, Part III, The
  ML 309-14
Godfrey, Arthur
  H 50
Godreau, Miguel
  TIAI 130
Godunov, Alexander
  SOTA 322
  5001 844
Goebbels, Joseph
  ILIATM 108
Goethe, Johann Wolfgang von
  H 61
Goetz, Augustus
  5001 122, 327
Goetz, Ruth
  5001 122, 327
Goff, Ivan
  5001 458, 834
Gogol, Nikolai
  5001 63, 78
Goin' Down the Road
  DIM 171-172
  TIAI 425
  5001
Goin' South
  WTLGD 507-510
  TIAI 3, 75
  5001
Going Home
  DIM 353-354
Going in Style
  WTLGD 537
Going My Way
  ILIATM 9
  R 249
  WTLGD 25
Going Places (Les Valseuses)
  WTLGD 182, 454-457, 458, 459, 461
  SOTA 49, 137
  5001 (2nd ed)
Gold
  R 359-360
  5001

Gold Diggers of 1933
  ILIATM 147
  KKBB 234, 273:n
  R 474
  5001
Gold Diggers of 1935
  5001
Gold Diggers of 1937
  WTLGD 16
Gold, Ernest
  DIM 35
  5001 546
"Gold Fever" (music)
  DIM 28
Gold, Jack
  DIM 89; dir., The Bofors Gun, 89; The
    Reckoning, 89
Gold of Naples, The (L'Oro di Napoli)
  DIM 362
  5001
Gold Rush, The
  KKBB 248, 273:n
  5001
Gold, Tracey
  TIAI 295
  5001 676
Goldberg, Dan
  TIAI 225
  5001 723
Goldberg, Doc
  5001 552
Goldberg, Gary David
  ML dir., Dad,
  ML 204-207
  5001 168
Goldberg, Rube
  5001 36
Goldberg, Whoopi
  H 82, 83
  5001 146
Goldblatt, Mark
  TIAI 194
  5001 344
Goldblatt, Stephen
  H 100
  5001 156, 558, 626, 860
Goldblum, Jeff
  WTLGD 130, 522-523
  SOTA 63, 69-70, 217, 218, 219-220
  H 14, 209, 211, 212
  ML 270-72
  5001 7, 69, 252, 368, 516, 521, 630, 682,
    742, 768
Golden Age of Comedy, The
  KKBB 184, 273-274:n
  5001
Golden Bowl, The (book)
  SOTA 206
Golden Boy
  ILIATM 143
  KKBB 349
  WTLGD 175, 489
  TIAI 107
  5001
Golden Coach, The
  ILIATM 101-104
  KKBB 55

GS 239
5001 (2nd ed)
Golden Dawn (stage)
  WTLGD 12, 13
Golden Earrings, The
  KKBB 360
Golden, Ray
  5001 71
Goldfinger
  KKBB 183
  SOTA 146
Goldin, Marilyn
  WTLGD 145, 147
  5001 268
Golding, Louis
  R 173
Goldman, Albert
  R 375
  TIAI 26
  H 185
Goldman, Bo
  WTLGD 85
  TIAI 72, 73, 77, 291, 292, 294
  SOTA 167-168, 310
  5001 249, 474, 549, 641, 676, 738
Goldman, James
  GS 174, 175
  DIM 369
  WTLGD 158-160
  H 65
  5001 423, 523, 634, 835
Goldman, William
  KKBB 279
  DIM 6, 7, 327-328, 401-402
  R 443-468
  WTLGD 172-175, 510-511
  H 378
  5001 110, 304, 320, 341, 450, 464, 597, 714
Goldmann, Philippe
  WTLGD 168
Goldner, Charles
  KKBB 243
  5001 21, 118, 664
Goldoni, Lelia
  R 411-412
  5001 15, 84, 176, 368
Goldsmith, Jerry
  WTLGD 282, 540
  TIAI 220
  SOTA 76
  5001 48, 86, 135, 185, 565, 612, 724, 805
Goldstein, Jenette
  H 193
  5001 15, 518
Goldstone, James
  5001 277
Goldthwait, Bobcat
  ML 40
Goldwyn Girls
  TIAI 215
  5001 311, 393, 637
Goldwyn, Samuel
  KKBB 152
  RK 23 (ill.), 24
  R 316
  WTLGD 21
  5001 48, 51, 65, 66, 178, 196, 305, 311,

317, 346, 393, 426, 533, 596, 637, 663, 713, 753, 829, 851
Goldwyn, Samuel, Mrs.
RK 22 (ill.), 24
Golem, The
H 344
Golino, Valeria
ML 81
5001 613
Golissano, Francesco
KKBB 310
5001 483
Golitzen, Alexander
5001 419, 777
Gollomb, Joseph
5001 502
Gombell, Minna
5001 65, 304, 332, 345, 758, 837
Gomberg, Sy
5001 727, 777
Gomez, Thomas
ILIATM 139
5001 34, 392, 578, 629, 726, 835
Gomez, Vicente
5001 83
Gone with the Wind
ILIATM 283, 329
KKBB 135, 163, 290
GS 45
DIM 28, 74
R 265
WTLGD 118, 146, 327, 329, 504
SOTA 50
Gonzales, Peter
R 26
5001 241
Gonzalez, Cordelia
5001 93
Good Earth, The
ILIATM 85
5001
Good Fairy, The
5001
Good Father, The
H 283-284
5001 (2nd ed)
Good Fellow, The (stage)
RK 10
Good Housekeeping (periodical)
KKBB 26
Good Morning, Babylon
H 338-341
5001 (2nd ed)
Good Morning, Vietnam
H 421-423
ML 282, 323
5001 (2nd ed)
Good Mother, The
ML 33-37
5001 (2nd ed)
Good News
5001
Good Night, Sweet Prince (book)
WTLGD 240
Good, the Bad, and the Ugly, The (Il Buono il Brutto il Cattivo)
GS 53-54

5001 (2nd ed)
Goodbye, Children, see *Au revoir les enfants*
Goodbye, Columbus
DIM 4, 32, 218, 260, 364, 384
SOTA 310
Goodbye Girl, The
WTLGD 376-378, 466, 532
TIAI 276
H 350
5001
Goodbye, Mr. Chips (1939)
KKBB 275:n
5001
Goodbye, Mr. Chips (1969)
DIM 38-41
TIAI 65
5001
Goodbye, My Lady
KKBB 180
WTLGD 190
Goodbye Pork Pie
SOTA 244
"Goodbye to Berlin" (book)
DIM 410
GoodFellas
ML 265-70, 286-87
5001 (2nd ed)
Goodhart, William
5001 229
Goodis, David
ILIATM 210
SOTA 45
5001 173, 495, 676
Goodman, Andrew
ML 54
5001 486
Goodman, Benny
R 39, 116, 118
TIAI 27
5001 278, 703, 704
Goodman, David Zelag
DIM 394
5001 230, 458, 495, 503, 721
Goodman, Dody
5001 702
Goodman, Ezra
RK 33
R 155
Goodman, John
H 215, 216, 218, 291, 359
ML 19, 247
5001 21, 34, 70, 603, 615, 793
Goodrich, Frances
KKBB 358
5001 9, 11, 30, 240, 245, 287, 518, 667, 758
Goodrow, Garry
5001 89, 153, 211, 396
Goodwin, Bill
5001 690, 776
Goodwin, Richard
WTLGD 463
Goodyear Television Playhouse, The (TV)
H 92
Goonies, The
H 13, 101
5001 (2nd ed)
Goorwitz, Allen, see Garfield, Allen

Goose Woman, The
KKBB 285
Gora, Claudio
5001 729
Gorcey, Leo
5001 177, 464, 690
Gordon, C. Henry
5001 130, 153, 165, 657
Gordon, Colin
KKBB 266
5001 254
Gordon, Dexter
ML 323
5001 644
Gordon, Don
5001 109
Gordon, Gavin
5001 23, 75, 102, 402, 512, 658
Gordon, Hannah
TIAI 85
5001 215
Gordon, Harold
KKBB 367
5001 210, 818
Gordon, Huntley
5001 703
Gordon, Keith
TIAI 37, 38-39, 40
H 186
5001 45, 203
Gordon, Leon
5001 48, 106, 733, 744, 833
Gordon, Mack
5001 727, 736, 827, 828
Gordon, Michael
KKBB 203; dir., *Cyrano de Bergerac*, 203
5001 30
Gordon, Ruth
KKBB 228, 283, 299, 330
DIM 186
5001 5, 68, 199, 319, 365, 435, 467, 559, 569, 643, 831
Gordon, Steve
TIAI 230-232; dir., *Arthur*, 230-232, 370
5001 36
Gordon, Stuart
H dir., *Re-Animator*, 67-69
5001 618
Gordon's War
R 261
Gordy, Berry
WTLGD 60-61
5001 453
Goretta, Claude
WTLGD 285-287; dir., *The Wonderful Crook (Pas Si Méchant Que Ça)*, 285-287; *The Invitation*, 286
5001 848
Gorgeous Hussy, The
5001
Gorillas in the Mist
ML 5-7
5001 (2nd ed)
Gorin, Igor
5001 106
Gorin, Jean-Pierre
TIAI 104

5001 419, 784
Goring, Marius
  KKBB 235
  DIM 162
  5001 52, 246, 563, 621, 623, 794
Gorky, Maxim
  KKBB 302, 312
  5001 442, 499
Gorman, Cliff
  R 371, 373
  WTLGD 411
  5001 98, 807
Gorman, Herbert
  5001 733
Gorman, Robert
  ML 70
  5001 3
Gorney, Karen Lynn
  WTLGD 368-370
  5001 655
Gorsen, Norah
  5001 826
Gorshin, Frank
  5001 724
Gortner, Marjoe
  R 386
  5001 209
*Gospel According to St. Matthew, The (Il
  Vangelo Secondo Matteo)*
  KKBB 133
  5001
Gossett, Louis Jr.
  DIM 299
  WTLGD 267
  TIAI 382, 383
  5001 407, 413, 540, 685, 788
Gothard, Michael
  5001 767
Götterdämmerung (music)
  TIAI 278
Gottlieb, Carl
  TIAI 194-197, 307; dir., *Caveman*, 194-197,
    307, 394
  5001 127, 378, 469, 809
Gottlieb, Linda
  R 109
Gottlieb, Lou
  5001 350
Gottlieb, Stan
  5001 25
Gottschalk, Ferdinand
  KKBB 275
  5001 141, 291, 299, 484, 680
Goudge, Elizabeth
  5001 306
Gough, Lloyd
  KKBB 355
  5001 616, 730
Gough, Michael
  KKBB 282
  5001 97, 341, 628, 790, 822, 847
Gould, Dave
  DIM 382
  5001 97, 253, 254
Gould, Elliott
  DIM 11, 12, 93, 94, 254, 256, 348
  R 183-189, 351, 418

WTLGD 147-148, 346
H 265
5001 89, 352, 406, 427, 432, 469, 517, 528
Gould, Glenn
  WTLGD 415
  5001 748
Gould, Harold
  5001 35, 68, 365, 715
Gould, Heywood
  TIAI 152
  5001 97, 259
Gould, Jason
  ML 136
  5001 656
Gould, Joe
  DIM 125
Gould, John
  5001 246
Gould, Lois
  5001 724
Goulding, Alfred
  5001 137
Goulding, Edmund
  KKBB 253, 275; dir., *Grand Hotel*, 210,
    249, 275
  5001 170, 173, 174, 300, 472, 529, 540,
    543, 617
Goulding, Ray
  TIAI 369
Goulet, Robert
  TIAI 177
  H 456-457
  5001 38, 61
Governor, Jimmy
  TIAI 54
Gowland, Gibson
  KKBB 331
  5001 81, 511, 579, 696
Goya, Chantal
  KKBB 127-128
  5001 468
Goya, Francisco
  KKBB 119
  WTLGD 431
  SOTA 255
Goya, Tito
  WTLGD 298
  5001 679
Goya y Lucientes, Francisco José de, see Goya,
  Francisco
Goz, Harry
  5001 492
Gozzi, Patricia
  5001 729
Grable, Betty
  KKBB 186
  R 152
  TIAI 373
  H 331, 333
  5001 58, 199, 254, 281, 393, 582, 736, 765,
    766, 773, 780
Gracie Allen Murder Case, The
  5001
Graczyk, Ed
  TIAI 413, 414, 415, 416, 417, 418
  5001 148
Grade, Lew

WTLGD 452
5001 819
Graduate, The
  GS 14, 97, 124-127, 153, 198, 274, 276
  DIM 9, 10, 152, 283, 395
  R 309, 444-445
  WTLGD 165, 173, 554
  TIAI 166
  H 300
  5001 (2nd ed)
Grady, James
  5001 765
Graham, Barbara
  KKBB 50
Graham, Bill
  H 305
  5001 279
Graham, Billy
  GS 216
  R 107
Graham, Gerrit
  R 369-370
  TIAI 99
  5001 307, 330, 579, 810
Graham, Heather
  ML 196-97, 198
  5001 205, 350
Graham, Martha
  WTLGD 336
  5001 804
Graham, Ronny
  TIAI 216
  SOTA 111
  5001 775
Graham, Sheilah
  WTLGD 217
Graham, Winston
  5001 466
Grahame, Gloria
  ILIATM 58
  KKBB 205, 233, 249, 253
  GS 212
  DIM 296
  TIAI 77, 108
  H 271
  5001 46, 66, 70, 144, 164, 305, 345, 359,
    374, 843
Grahame, Margot
  ILIATM 119
  KKBB 252
  5001 62, 163, 363
Gramatica, Emma
  ILIATM 284-285
  KKBB 310
  DIM 362
  5001 483
Granach, Alexander
  KKBB 221, 290, 318
  5001 256, 390, 531, 689
Granahan, Kathryn
  ILIATM 43-44
*Grand Amour de Beethoven, Un (The Life and
  Loves of Beethoven)*
  TIAI 146
Grand Ballet Classique de France
  5001 472
Grandval, Charles

5001 95
Grand Hotel
  KKBB 210, 249, 275:n
  R 71, 390, 447, 451
  WTLGD 344, 532
  5001
Grand Illusion, see *La Grande Illusion*
Grand Maneuver, The (*Les Grandes Manoeuvres*)
  5001
Grand Prix
  KKBB 9-10, 59
Grande Bouffe, La
  TIAI 466
Grande Illusion, La (*Grand Illusion*)
  ILIATM 22, 108-111, 226, 283
  KKBB 140, 206, 254, 279, 342, 349
  DIM 430
  R 237
  TIAI 449
  ML 166
  5001
Grande Marade, La (book)
  WTLGD 154
Grandes Manoeuvres, Les, see *The Grand Maneuver*
Grandview, U.S.A.
  H 348
Grandville
  WTLGD 471
Granger, Farley
  ILIATM 135
  KKBB 48, 352
  DIM 401
  R 268
  5001 317, 533, 720, 754
Granger, Michael
  5001 502
Granger, Stewart
  KKBB 184
  R 51
  H 332
  5001 114, 397, 597
Grant, Barra
  WTLGD 495
  5001 687
Grant, Cary
  KKBB 184, 190, 205, 232, 241, 278, 281, 318-319, 320, 348, 363
  RK 20, 48
  DIM 351, 431
  R 85, 186
  WTLGD 3-31, 68, 351, 360, 450, 482, 493, 506
  TIAI 37, 429
  SOTA 93, 221, 222, 223, 304
  H 352, 449
  5001 15, 35, 41, 44, 62, 82, 104, 130, 239, 311, 335, 336, 343, 352, 357, 359, 362, 446, 488, 494, 497, 508, 523, 532, 533, 536, 548, 575, 580, 672, 733, 738, 739, 742, 760, 775, 781, 782, 830
Grant, Douglas
  5001 407
Grant, Helena
  KKBB 336
  5001 607

Grant, Hugh
  H 360, 361
  5001 471
Grant, James Edward
  5001 26, 109, 382, 405
Grant, Kathryn
  KKBB 325
  5001 551
Grant, Lawrence
  5001 116, 671
Grant, Lee
  R 436, 439
  5001 186, 360, 407, 670, 752, 819
Grant, Richard E.
  ML 328
Grant, Dr. Toni
  H 102
Granville, Bonita
  KKBB 288, 336
  5001 11, 224, 374, 453, 536, 607, 753
Granville, Sydney
  5001 480
Grapes of Wrath, The
  ILIATM 289
  KKBB 275-276:n, 350-351
  RK 76
  DIM 349
  WTLGD 84, 225, 226, 227
  SOTA 234
  H 252
  5001
Grapewin, Charley
  KKBB 276
  5001 11, 106, 118, 293, 301, 420, 577, 765, 777
Grappelli, Stephane
  5001 291
Grass, Günter
  TIAI 376
Grateful Dead, The
  GS 149
Grateful Dead, The (group)
  GS 119
Grave, Louis
  DIM 430
Graves, Peter
  TIAI 51
  5001 12, 526, 705
Graves, Ralph
  5001 403
Graves, Robert
  5001 223
Graves, Rupert
  H 128, 360, 361
  5001 471
Gravet, Fernand
  DIM 26
  5001 304, 343, 450, 489, 592
Gravina, Carla
  DIM 413
  R 258
  5001 14, 69, 363, 651, 843
Gravina, Cesare
  5001 255
Gravity's Rainbow
  TIAI 66
  SOTA 232

Gray, Charles
  WTLGD 190
  5001 163, 189, 667
Gray, Coleen
  KKBB 291
  5001 399, 529, 620
Gray, Dolores
  KKBB 288
  5001 374, 398
Gray, Dorian
  5001 309
Gray, Gilda
  5001 305
Gray, Sally
  5001 306
Gray, Simon
  WTLGD 266
Gray, Spalding
  H 215, 217, 284-286
  5001 395, 737, 794
Gray, Virginia
  5001 690
Grayson, Kathryn
  KKBB 234
  TIAI 357
  5001 25, 355, 398, 631, 679, 764, 777, 865
Grazer, Brian
  5001 528, 702
Grease
  WTLGD 429, 431, 470
Great Adventure, The (*Det stora äventyret*)
  KKBB 180, 184, 276:n
  5001
"Great Balls of Fire" (music)
  H 10
Great Bank Robbery, The
  R 248
  5001
Great Escape, The
  GS 223
Great Expectations
  ILIATM 214
  KKBB 276-277:n, 322
  R 260
  WTLGD 210
  5001
Great Gabbo, The
  5001
Great Gatsby, The
  R 313-314, 329
  WTLGD 3, 92, 121, 463
  TIAI 240
Great Lie, The
  DIM 157
Great Man, The
  KKBB 277:n
  5001
Great McGinty, The
  5001
Great Northfield Minnesota Raid, The
  R 428
  WTLGD 424
  SOTA 63
Great Profile, The
  5001 (2nd ed)
Great Race, The
  KKBB 28

TIAI 331
Great Santini, The (also known as *The Ace*)
    TIAI 51-53, 244
    5001
Great Train Robbery, The (1903)
    SOTA 28, 29-30
Great Train Robbery, The (1979)
    KKBB 44
    GS 183
    WTLGD 538-540
    5001
Great Waldo Pepper, The
    R 464, 467-469
    WTLGD 174, 273
    5001
Great Waltz, The (1938)
    5001
Great Waltz, The (1972)
    5001
Great White Hope, The
    DIM 158-161
    5001
Great Ziegfeld, The
    5001
Greatest Question, The
    5001
Greatest Show on Earth, The
    ILIATM 9, 329
    5001
Greco, Jose
    5001 675
Greco, Juliette
    KKBB 326
    WTLGD 153
    5001 214, 554
Gredy, J. C.
    5001 260
Greed
    KKBB 131
    WTLGD 324
Greeg, Jane
    5001 387
Greeks Had a Word for Them, The (also known
    as *Three Broadway Girls*)
    KKBB 363
    5001
Green, Adolph
    KKBB 234, 287
    GS 237
    DIM 82
    WTLGD 399
    TIAI 396
    5001 49-50, 296, 374, 508, 546, 547, 683,
    740
Green, Alfred E.
    5001 171, 298
Green Berets, The
    KKBB 45
    GS 251
    DIM 316
Green, Danny
    KKBB 293
    5001 407
Green Dolphin Street
    5001
Green, F. L.
    KKBB 321

5001 539
Green for Danger
    5001
Green, Guy
    ILIATM 119, 159; dir., *The Angry Silence*,
    119; *The Mark*, 119, 155-159, 201, 203
    KKBB 277, 322; dir., *The Mark*, 68, 78-79
    GS 181; dir., *A Matter of Innocence*, 54; *The
    Monk*, 75; *A Patch of Blue*, 54
    5001 62, 302, 452, 543, 548, 717
Green, Harry
    5001 338, 395
Green Hat, The
    DIM 364, 365
Green, Howard J.
    5001 81, 356
Green, Janet
    5001 814
Green, Johnny
    5001 54, 614
Green, Kerri
    5001 298
Green Light, The
    5001 (2nd ed)
Green, Lil
    TIAI 323
Green Man, The
    KKBB 277:n
    5001
Green, Martyn
    R 201
    ML 132
    5001 354, 480
Green, Mitzi
    5001 338
Green, Nigel
    DIM 105
    5001 370
Green Pastures, The
    5001
Green, Paul
    RK 41
    5001 112, 711
Green, Seth
    H 275
    5001 610
Green, Walon
    TIAI 301
    ML 117
    5001 92, 165, 838
Greenaway, Peter
    SOTA 31-34
    5001 201
Greenbaum, Mutz
    5001 769
Greenberg, Adam
    5001 519
Greenberg, Jerry
    TIAI 39
    5001 203
Greene, Clarence
    5001 554
Greene, David
    GS 181; dir., *Sebastian*, 19-20
    5001 662
Greene, Ellen
    WTLGD 128-130

H 248-249
5001 427, 521
Greene, Graham
    KKBB 11, 251, 252, 327, 336, 358-359
    R 97, 173-174, 180, 203-204
    TIAI 283
    H 167, 180, 279
    5001 4, 104, 152, 221, 234, 482, 556, 608,
    760, 761, 788
Greene, Leon
    KKBB 138
    5001 272
Greene, Lorne
    R 386
    5001 40, 209
Greene, Max
    5001 524
Greene, Michael
    5001 437
Greene Murder Case, The
    5001
Greene, Richard
    5001 259, 341
Greene, Shecky
    TIAI 216
    5001 702
Greenfield, Josh
    5001 320
Greenfield, Ruth and Kate
    H 474
Greengage Summer, The, see *Loss of Innocence*
Greenquist, Brad
    H 266
    5001 60
Greenstreet, Sydney
    KKBB 245, 305
    H 446
    5001 4, 122, 249, 336, 454, 469
Greenwood, Charlotte
    5001 199, 278
Greenwood, Joan
    KKBB 257, 292, 306, 312
    GS 173
    R 111
    TIAI 246
    SOTA 372
    5001 185, 358, 395, 457, 494, 771, 778
Greer, Germaine
    R 207
Greer, Jane
    SOTA 145, 146
    5001 10, 458, 557
Greer, Jo Ann
    5001 562
Greetings
    GS 206, 212-213, 237
    DIM 314
    R 194, 329, 368, 369
    WTLGD 211-212
    TIAI 39, 227
    5001
Gregg, Everley
    5001 605
Gregg, Virginia
    5001 357
Greggory, Pascal
    SOTA 38

5001 571
Gregor, Manfred
   5001 102
Gregor, Nora
   KKBB 343
   5001 647
Gregorio, Rose
   TIAI 244
   5001 230, 793
Gregory, André
   TIAI 286, 288, 369
   H 293, 294
   ML 317
   5001 39, 507, 722
Gregory, Celia
   WTLGD 553
   5001 10
Gregory, James
   KKBB 364
   5001 462, 801
Gregory, Paul
   5001 514, 526
Gregory's Girl
   TIAI 466
   SOTA 269
   H 408
Gregson, John
   KKBB 270
   5001 281, 771
Greig, Robert
   5001 341, 726, 792
Greist, Kim
   H 107
   ML 20
   5001 98, 603
Gremlins
   SOTA 187-192
   H 101
   5001 (2nd ed)
Grenada TV (U.K.)
   H 476
Grenfell, Joyce
   KKBB 278, 294, 331
   DIM 269
   TIAI 378
Gresham, William
   5001 529
Greuze, Jean-Baptiste
   SOTA 54
Greville-Bell, Anthony
   5001 576
Grey, Denise
   5001 187
Grey Fox, The
   SOTA 27-31
   5001 (2nd ed)
Grey, Harry
   5001 548
Grey, Jennifer
   H 346, 347, 348
   5001 190
Grey, Joel
   DIM 409-412
   R 187
   WTLGD 151, 190
   TIAI 174
   H 347

5001 112, 458, 667
Grey, Lita
   5001 392
Grey, Nadia
   5001 799
Grey, Nan
   5001 369, 768
Grey, Virginia
   5001 19, 31, 109, 354, 447, 641, 642, 736,
      847
Grey, Zane
   WTLGD 46, 48
*Greystoke: The Legend of Tarzan, Lord of the
   Apes*
   SOTA 147-151
   H 19
   5001 (2nd ed)
Gribbon, Harry
   5001 511, 680
Grido, Il
   5001
Grieg, Edvard
   DIM 187
   5001 366, 444, 693, 694
Griem, Helmut
   DIM 412
   5001 112, 169, 819
Grier, David Alan
   SOTA 273
Grier, Pam
   TIAI 152
   5001 260
Grierson, John
   DIM 251
Gries, Tom
   5001 839
Grifasi, Joe
   H 117
   5001 274, 715
Griffies, Ethel
   5001 654, 815
Griffin, Merv
   SOTA 129
   5001 431
Griffith, Andy
   WTLGD 46, 48
   5001 232, 325
Griffith, Charles B.
   H 247
   5001 181, 427, 837
Griffith, D. W.
   ILIATM 25, 188, 222, 262, 273, 281-282,
      287, 302, 341; dir., *The Birth of a
      Nation*, 119, 282, 287; *Way Down East*,
      199; *Intolerance*, 222, 277, 282, 341;
      Broken Blossoms, 282
   KKBB 16, 132, 153, 199, 202, 313, 345;
      dir., *The Birth of a Nation*, 131;
      Intolerance, 131-132, 309
   GS 3; dir., *The Birth of a Nation*, 20, 42-45,
      60, 220; *Broken Blossoms*, 45, 46;
      Intolerance, 42-47; *Way Down East*, 45,
      46
   RK 14, 46, 69
   DIM 149, 275, 362; dir., *Intolerance*, 319,
      320; *Orphans of the Storm*, 319
   R 149, 269, 286; dir., *The Birth of a Nation*,

5, 64; *An Unseen Enemy*, 179; *True
   Heart Susie*, 269
WTLGD 324, 331, 404, 557; dir., *The Birth
   of a Nation*, 248, 371, 536; *Intolerance*,
   324, 557
TIAI 134, 145, 147; dir., *The Birth of a
   Nation*, 58; *Way Down East*, 134;
   Intolerance, 146; *Orphans of the Storm*,
   146
H 22, 35, 338-339, 340, 341; dir.,
   Intolerance, 338, 339, 340
5001 40, 107, 305, 367, 384, 508, 553, 589,
   793, 824
Griffith, Edward H.
   5001 522, 685
Griffith, Hugh
   ILIATM 119
   KKBB 294
   DIM 123
   5001 62, 63, 248, 343, 413, 711, 778, 845
Griffith, Jane
   KKBB 307
   5001 461
Griffith, Kenneth
   5001 229, 423, 597, 832
Griffith, Kristin
   WTLGD 439-440
   5001 366
Griffith, Melanie
   SOTA 263, 264
   H 228, 229-230
   ML 63-65, 276, 277, 316
   5001 89, 561, 688, 693, 848, 849
Griffith, Raymond
   KKBB 231
   5001 18
Griffith, Richard
   ILIATM 271, 282-283
Griffith, Simone
   5001 181
Griffith, Tracy
   ML 34
   5001 295
Griffiths, Richard
   SOTA 341
   5001 277, 598
Griffiths, Trevor
   WTLGD 266
   TIAI 278, 280
   5001 621
Grifters, The
   ML 283-87
Griggs, Loyal
   KKBB 347
   5001 671
Grillet, Alain Robbe, see Robbe-Grillet, Alain
Grimaldi, Alberto
   WTLGD 325
   5001 110, 286, 410
Grimes, Tammy
   R 45
   WTLGD 205, 451
   TIAI 214
   5001 587, 692
Grimm, Jacob and Wilhelm
   H 473
Gris, Juan

DIM 299
Grismer, Joseph R.
5001 824
Grissom, Betty
SOTA 66-67
Grissom, Gus
SOTA 66-67
Grizzard, George
TIAI 490
5001 8, 148, 317
Grizzly King, The (book)
ML 208
Grodin, Charles
R 68, 70, 360-361
WTLGD 235, 239, 271-272, 430, 506
TIAI 160, 163
SOTA 128, 129, 140
H 310-311
5001 126, 215, 324, 361, 371, 396, 431,
643, 757
Groenberg, Åke
KKBB 315
5001 514
Grogan, Claire
SOTA 269
5001 149
Gromo, Mario
KKBB 366
Groom, Sam
DIM 157
5001 44
Grooms, Red
WTLGD 474-475
H 457
Groove Tube, The
R 384
WTLGD 448
H 141
5001
Gros, Antoine Jean
WTLGD 381
Grosbard, Ulu
TIAI 241-245; dir., *True Confessions*,
241-245, 457; *The Subject Was Roses*,
244; *Straight Time*, 244; *Who Is Harry
Kellerman and Why Is He Saying Those
Terrible Things About Me?* 244
SOTA 279-281
5001 234, 718, 793
Gross, Ayre
5001 748
Gross, Larry
TIAI 438
5001 261
Gross, Mary
H 188
5001 43, 68, 143
Gross, Michael
5001 68
Grossman, Ladislav
5001 678
Grossmith, Lawrence
5001 532
Grosz, George
DIM 410
Grot, Anton
5001 591

Grotowski, Jerzy
TIAI 287
Groundlings (group)
H 60
Group, The
KKBB 67-100, 241
5001
Group Theatre
RK 56
WTLGD 489
Groupies
DIM 197-199
5001
Groves, General Leslie R.
ML 207-208
Groves of Academe, The (book)
KKBB 79
Gruault, Jean
5001 119, 385, 798
Grubb, Davis
KKBB 317
5001 526
Grubel, Ilona
H 74
5001 743
Gruber, Frank
5001 469
Gründgens, Gustav
TIAI 337, 339, 340
5001 444, 476
Grünenwald, Jean-Jacques
KKBB 259
5001 189
Gruning, Ilka
5001 122
Gruppo di Famiglia in un Interno, see
Conversation Piece
Grusin, Dave
WTLGD 304
SOTA 281
ML 51, 188, 189, 317
5001 234, 748
Gruskoff, Michael
WTLGD 106
Gruzdev, I.
5001 133
Grzimek, Dr. Bernhard
KKBB 182; dir., *Serengeti Shall Not Die*,
182-183, 185
Grzimek, Michael
KKBB 182
Guaraldi, Vince
5001 97
Guardino, Harry
5001 191, 221
Guardsman, The
5001
Guare, John
TIAI 173, 174, 175, 176
5001 38
Guareschi, Giovanni
5001 428
Guarnieri, Ennio
5001 102
Guber, Peter
WTLGD 498
Guérin, François

5001 230, 489
Guerney, Claude
5001 306
Guernica (painting)
TIAI 141
Guerra, Castulo
5001 715
Guerra, Ruy
SOTA 182-183
5001 224
Guerra, Tonino
TIAI 319
SOTA 256
H 140, 340
5001 41, 76, 85, 286, 295, 391, 497, 527,
764, 863
Guerre des boutons, La (*Generals Without
Buttons*)
5001
Guerre est finie, La
KKBB 162-166
DIM 64
R 212, 215
5001
Guess What We Learned in School Today?
DIM 325
R 116
Guess Who's Coming to Dinner
GS 61, 176, 178
H 29
Guest, Christopher
H 250, 379
5001 428, 597
Guest, Edgar
WTLGD 228, 284
Guest, Judith
TIAI 81
5001 553
Guest, Val
KKBB 263; dir., *Expresso Bongo*, 263, 290
GS 181
5001 123, 229
Guétary, Georges
5001 23
Guevara, Che
GS 76, 285
DIM 257, 258
Guffey, Burnett
DIM 159
5001 19, 74, 91, 269, 359, 450, 719
Guffey, Cary
WTLGD 348, 351, 352
5001 142, 164
Guide for the Married Man, A
GS 117
5001
Guidelli, Micol
TIAI 446
Guido, Beatriz
5001 234
Guilaroff, Sydney
KKBB 10
5001 84
Guild, Nancy
5001 724
Guiles, Fred Lawrence
R 152

Guilfoyle, Paul
    KKBB 369
    5001 534, 834, 835, 841
Guillén, Fernando
    ML 24
    5001 848
Guillermin, John
    R 405-407
    WTLGD 234-239, 462-466; dir., *The*
        Towering Inferno, 106, 121, 238, 325;
        King Kong (1976), 234-239, 419;
        Tarzan's Greatest Adventure, 238;
        Never Let Go, 238; *Waltz of the*
        Toreadors, 238; *Guns at Batasi*, 238;
        The Blue Max, 238; *The Bridge at*
        Remagen, 238; *Skyjacked*, 238; *Death*
        on the Nile, 462-466
    SOTA 224-226; dir., *Sheena*, 224-226; *King*
        Kong (1976), 225, 234
    5001 86, 180-181, 395, 673, 785
Guinan, Texas
    5001 288
Guinness, Alec
    KKBB 10, 141, 243, 256, 274, 276, 282,
        292, 293, 295, 306, 322, 327, 335
    DIM 37, 181, 185, 197, 203
    R 77, 97, 360-361
    WTLGD 171, 286, 295, 353
    TIAI 462, 484
    SOTA 300, 301
    H 8, 108, 464
    ML 92, 183
    5001 102, 118, 163, 185, 195, 218, 301,
        341, 395, 406, 408, 414, 415, 441, 457,
        543, 555, 568, 597, 601, 709, 794
Guiol, Fred
    5001 285, 310
Guiomar, Julien
    5001 268, 450, 700, 757
Guitry, Sacha
    ILIATM 210, 289; dir., *Lovers and Thieves*
        (*Assassins et Voleurs*), 214
    KKBB 301-302; dir., *Lovers and Thieves*,
        301-302; *The Story of a Cheat*, 301; *The*
        Pearls of the Crown, 301
    GS dir., *Lovers and Thieves*, 275
    DIM 194
    R 42
    WTLGD 167, 233, 355, 459; dir., *Lovers*
        and Thieves, 459
    TIAI 165; dir., *Lovers and Thieves*, 165
    H 308
    5001 87, 440, 443, 572
Guittard, Laurence
    5001 692
Gulliver's Travels (book)
    H 473
Gulpilil
    WTLGD 535
    TIAI 455
    5001 412
Gumshoe
    H 120
Gun, The (book)
    KKBB 205
Gun Crazy (originally called *Deadly Is the*
    Female)

KKBB 48
    5001
Gun Runners, The
    KKBB 360
Gunfighter, The
    ILIATM 242
    KKBB 40
Gunga Din
    ILIATM 24, 241
    KKBB 180, 184, 278:n
    WTLGD 17, 18, 19, 23, 29, 107
    TIAI 209
    SOTA 176, 177, 179
    5001
Gunn, Moses
    R 201
    5001 325, 354, 612, 851
Gunn, William
    R 274
    5001 407
Guns at Batasi
    WTLGD 238
Guns of the Magnificent Seven
    5001 (2nd ed)
Guns of the Trees
    ILIATM 189
"Gunsmoke" (TV)
    DIM 191
    WTLGD 114
Gunther, John
    RK 82
Gunton, Bob
    H 371
    5001 580
Gunty, Morty
    SOTA 123
Gurian, Paul R.
    5001 167
Gurie, Sigrid
    5001 14
Gurry, Eric
    TIAI 370, 475
    5001 39, 46
Guru, The
    DIM 195
Guss, Louis
    H 424
    5001 496
Guthrie, A. B. Jr.
    KKBB 347
Guthrie, A. B.
    5001 Jr., 671
Guthrie, Arlo
    DIM 7, 197, 215
    WTLGD 226, 397
Guthrie, Tyrone
    KKBB 321-322; co-dir., *Oedipus Rex*,
        321-322
    5001 539
Guthrie, Woody
    WTLGD 224-230
    5001 96
Gutierrez, Zaide Silvia
    5001 533
Guttenberg, Steve
    TIAI 321
    H 6, 265-266, 267

ML 43, 44
    5001 60, 97, 144, 190, 333, 678, 679
Guve, Bertil
    TIAI 487
    5001 236
Guy Named Joe, A
    ML 245-46
Guyana Tragedy, The (TV)
    TIAI 258
Guys and Dolls
    DIM 409
    SOTA 123
    5001
Guzman, Luis
    5001 606, 792
Guzman, Pato
    5001 88
Guzmán, Patricio
    WTLGD 384-388
    5001 55
Gwenn, Edmund
    5001 186, 258, 306, 392, 421, 595, 738, 739
Gwynne, Fred
    SOTA 298
    5001 156, 371, 546, 690
Gwynne, Michael C.
    R 123
    5001 572, 748
Gycklarnas Afton, see *The Naked Night*
Gyenes, Magda
    SOTA 154
    5001 806
"Gymnopédie No. 3" (music)
    ML 12
Gypsy
    DIM 409
    5001
Gypsy Moths, The
    DIM 52, 200
Gypsy Wildcat
    5001

H

Haake, James
    SOTA 112
    5001 775
Haas, Charlie
    TIAI 399
    5001 750
Haas, Dolly
    5001 349
Haas, Hugo
    5001 397, 596, 598
Haas, Lukas
    SOTA 319, 321
    H 479
    5001 405, 504, 844
Haas, Willy
    5001 384
"Habañera" (music)
    SOTA 227
Habich, Matthias
    5001 158

Hack, Shelley
 TIAI 459
 H 261
 5001 396, 714
Hackes, Peter
 5001 105
Hackett, Albert
 KKBB 358
 5001 9, 11, 30, 240, 245, 287, 518, 667, 758
Hackett, Bobby
 5001 552, 662
Hackett, Buddy
 SOTA 123
 H 280
 ML 39
 5001 505
Hackett, Joan
 KKBB 93
 WTLGD 171
 TIAI 354
 SOTA 59
 5001 224, 309, 748, 839
Hackett, Raymond
 5001 555
Hackford, Taylor
 TIAI 114-117, 381-383; dir., *The Idolmaker*,
  114-117, 381; *An Officer and a
  Gentleman*, 381-383
 SOTA 145-147; dir., *An Officer and a
  Gentleman*, 6, 95, 146, 169; *Against All
  Odds*, 145-147, 158
 H 64-67; dir., *White Knights*, 64-67; *An
  Officer and a Gentleman*, 134
 5001 10, 354, 540, 835
Hackman, Gene
 KKBB 61
 DIM 47, 170, 316, 318
 R 71, 259, 314, 351, 405
 WTLGD 45-46, 106-107, 199, 526
 TIAI 155, 156-157, 158, 196, 224, 282, 486
 SOTA 72, 73, 76-77, 116, 117-118, 119
 H 73, 74, 75, 76, 356, 357
 ML 13, 14, 53-56, 274
 5001 17, 31, 91, 138, 196, 267, 322, 351,
  422, 442, 486, 532, 591, 592, 621, 631,
  730, 731, 743, 796, 804, 805, 859, 863
Hackney, Alan
 5001 357
Haddon, Dayle
 5001 564
Haden, Sara
 5001 445, 451, 677
Hadjidakis, Manos
 5001 22, 520, 781
Hadley, Reed
 5001 415
Hagegård, Håken
 WTLGD 75
Hagen, Jean
 KKBB 228, 238
 GS 59, 158
 5001 5, 37, 71, 683
Hagen, Uta
 WTLGD 452
 5001 97
Hagerty, Julie
 TIAI 51, 366-367

SOTA 343, 344, 346
 5001 12, 436, 479
Haggard, H. Rider
 R 277
 5001 397, 672
Haggerty, H. B.
 5001 478
Hagman, Larry
 5001 68, 309, 320, 690, 709
Hagmann, Stuart
 DIM 150; dir., *The Strawberry Statement*,
  149-151
 5001 721
Hahn, Archie
 R 369
 5001 579
Hahn, Jess
 5001 122, 526, 789
Haid, Charles
 TIAI 128, 130
 5001 20
"Hail, Fredonia" (music)
 H 114
Hail, Hero!
 DIM 42
 R 209
Hail the Conquering Hero
 R 301
 WTLGD 213
 H 110
 5001
Hailey, Arthur
 DIM 136
 5001 12, 341
Haines, Fred
 5001 803
Haines, William
 5001 680
Hainia, Marcelle
 5001 95
Hair
 DIM 31, 130
 R 371
 TIAI 264, 265, 266
Hairspray
 H 442-444
 5001 (2nd ed)
Hairston, Jester
 5001 244
Haitkin, Jacques
 WTLGD 537
Hajos, Karl
 5001 498
Hakim, Robert
 5001 698
Hakuchi, see *The Idiot*
Halberstam, David
 DIM 44
Haldeman, H. R.
 WTLGD 263
Hale, Alan
 KKBB 180, 228
 5001 7, 8, 14, 165, 243, 253, 282, 294, 333,
  358, 373, 457, 464, 524, 540, 634, 653,
  660, 684, 713, 732, 752, 754, 858
Hale, Barbara
 5001 12

Hale, Georgia
 KKBB 273
 5001 292
Hale, Georgina
 DIM 382
 5001 96
Hale, John
 5001 29, 468
Hale, Louise Closser
 5001 586, 671, 778
Hale, Richard
 5001 777
Hale, Scott
 5001 677
Hale, Sonnie
 ILIATM 65
 5001 226
Halévy, Geneviève
 SOTA 254
Halévy, Ludovic
 SOTA 254
 5001 119
Haley, Bill
 5001 79
Haley, Jack
 WTLGD 473
 5001 13, 582
Half a Sixpence
 GS 94, 159
Hall, Alexander
 5001 200, 329, 426, 510, 753, 763
Hall, Anthony Michael
 SOTA 173, 174, 347, 348
 ML 299
 5001 99, 684
Hall, Carol
 TIAI 374
 5001 64
Hall, Conrad
 GS 272
 DIM 7
 R 472
 ML 49
 5001 79, 110, 176, 238, 317, 320, 327, 464,
  601, 688, 746, 748
Hall, Grayson
 5001 218, 526
Hall, Huntz
 5001 177, 811, 822
Hall, James
 RK 13
 5001 116, 328
Hall, James Norman
 5001 346, 505
Hall, Jerry
 5001 54
Hall Johnson Choir
 5001 113, 741
Hall, Jon
 SOTA 104
 5001 14, 34, 143, 311, 346, 404, 835
Hall, Juanita
 5001 252
Hall, Peter
 DIM 193; dir., *Perfect Friday*, 193
 R 220-221
 H 98

5001 338, 573, 575
Hall, Philip Baker
  H 1, 2, 3, 4
  5001 656, 663
Hall, Porter
  KKBB 225, 281, 286
  5001 4, 58, 198, 335, 368, 483, 489, 502,
    578, 697, 726, 793
Hall, Ruth
  5001 393
Hall, Thurston
  5001 302, 349
Hall, Willis
  GS 54
  5001 832
Hallam, John
  TIAI 221
  5001 201, 822
Hallelujah Chorus, The (music)
  SOTA 63
Hallelujah, I'm a Bum
  KKBB 234
  5001
Hallelujah the Hills
  5001
Haller, Ernest
  5001 380, 619
Halley, Marian
  5001 732
Halliday, John
  5001 82, 184, 366, 577, 580
Halliwell, Kenneth
  H 295-298
Halloween
  WTLGD 547-548
  TIAI 192
  SOTA 240, 307
  5001
Halop, Billy
  5001 177
Halprin, Daria
  DIM 115, 117
  5001 862
Halsey, Richard
  R 124
Halston
  R 361
Halton, Charles
  5001 4
Hambling, Gerry
  TIAI 295
  5001 676
Hamburger Hill
  H 353-355
  5001 (2nd ed)
Hamer, Robert
  KKBB 255, 256-257, 292; dir., *Dead of
    Night* (segment), 254-255; *The
    Detective*, 256-257; *Kind Hearts and
    Coronets*, 256-257, 292, 294, 302
  5001 178, 185, 395
Hamill, Mark
  TIAI 222, 481
  5001 155, 218, 626, 709
Hamill, Pete
  H 14
Hamilton, Chico

TIAI 423
5001 111, 379, 624, 858
Hamilton, Cosmo
  5001 228
Hamilton, Edith
  DIM 305
Hamilton, Gay
  WTLGD 102
  5001 53
Hamilton, George
  KKBB 364
  TIAI 232
  ML 313
  5001 437, 548, 593, 801, 818, 866
Hamilton, Guy
  KKBB 10-11; dir., *Funeral in Berlin*, 10-11;
    Goldfinger, 183
  GS 181
  DIM 389; dir., *Diamonds Are Forever*,
    388-389
  5001 145, 187, 189, 462, 784
Hamilton, Hale
  5001 733
Hamilton Latzen, Ellen, see Latzen, Ellen
    Hamilton
Hamilton, Margaret
  KKBB 314
  DIM 227-228
  WTLGD 210
  TIAI 292
  SOTA 190
  5001 25, 42, 58, 496, 509, 535, 753, 857
Hamilton, Murray
  TIAI 22, 23
  5001 108, 299, 347, 356, 378, 531, 663
Hamilton, Neil
  5001 683, 744, 830
Hamilton, Patrick
  KKBB 267
  5001 279
Hamilton Phelan, Anna, see Phelan, Anna
    Hamilton
Hamilton, Suzanna
  H 46, 80
  5001 557, 829
Hamlet (1948)
  ILIATM 280-281
  KKBB 174
  5001
Hamlet (1969)
  DIM 89-91
  5001
Hamlet (stage)
  ILIATM 115, 258
  RK 35
  DIM 127
  TIAI 489
Hamlin, Harry
  WTLGD 501-502
  TIAI 319
  5001 501
Hamlisch, Marvin
  WTLGD 149, 151, 505
  H 13
  5001 703, 715
Hamm, Sam
  ML 159

5001 54
Hamme, Jean Van, see Van Hamme, Jean
Hammer Films
  WTLGD 331
  H 67
Hammerstein, Arthur
  WTLGD 12, 15
Hammerstein, Oscar II
  WTLGD 12
  5001 106, 119, 333, 404, 679, 697, 711, 717
Hammerstein, Reggie
  WTLGD 12
Hammett, Dashiell
  KKBB 305, 313, 358
  DIM 69, 414
  R 64, 186, 188
  WTLGD 123, 305, 306, 308, 309
  ML 91
  5001 140, 287, 454, 758, 823
Hammid, Alexander
  5001 473
Hammond, John
  SOTA 58
  5001 164
Hammond, Kay
  5001 81, 379
Hamnett, Olivia
  WTLGD 534, 535
  5001 412
Hampden, Walter
  5001 16, 247, 345, 649
Hampshire, Susan
  5001 229
Hampton, Christopher
  H 283
  ML 57, 62
  5001 171, 294
Hampton, Hope
  RK 67
Hampton, Lionel
  5001 574
Hampton, Paul
  R 37
Hamsun, Knut
  5001 345
Han, Maggie
  5001 408
Hancock, Herbie
  5001 147, 644
Hancock, John
  H dir., *Weeds*, 380-383
  ML 316
  5001 50, 826
Hand, The
  H 183
Handel, George Frideric
  5001 454, 694
Handke, Peter
  H 470
  5001 841
Handl, Irene
  5001 102, 357, 497
Handle with Care, see *Citizens Band*
Händler der Vier Jahreszeiten, Der, see *The
    Merchant of Four Seasons*
HandMade Films
  H 411

Hands Across the City
KKBB 118
Hands Across the Table
5001
Handy, W. C.
5001 650
Haney, Carol
5001 369, 399, 727
Hanft, Helen
TIAI 87
5001 840
Hanin, Roger
5001 323, 635
Hankin, Larry
5001 273
Hanks, Tom
SOTA 141, 142, 143
H 199, 200, 482, 483
ML 16-20, 193, 316
5001 67, 68, 535, 603, 701
Hanley, Gerald
TIAI 434
Hanline, Maurice
5001 374
Hannah and Her Sisters
H 113-116
ML 72
5001 (2nd ed)
Hannah, Daryl
TIAI 363
SOTA 141-142, 144, 202, 205
H 173, 174, 194, 313, 314
ML 43, 44
5001 80, 162, 273, 333, 416, 589, 644, 701
Hannan, Peter
5001 170, 795
Hannant, Brian
TIAI 387
5001 634
Hannen, Nicholas
5001 628
Hans Christian Andersen
5001
Hansard, Peter
TIAI 342
5001 688
Hansen, Gale
ML 156
5001 179
Hansen, William
R 119
5001 655
Hanson, Curtis
H 265-267; dir., *The Bedroom Window*, 265-267; *Losin' It*, 265, 266, 273
5001 60
Hanson, David
5001 686
Hanson, Einar
5001 384
Hanson, Lars
KKBB 345
5001 251, 649, 658, 659
Hansson, Maud
KKBB 346
5001 669, 839
Happening, The

KKBB 295
H 179
5001 (2nd ed)
Happiest Days of Your Life, The
KKBB 278:n
5001
Happy Birthday, Wanda June
DIM 369
R 81, 106
5001
"Happy Days" (TV)
SOTA 309
Happy Ending, The
DIM 148
5001
Happy Time, The
KKBB 203
GS 167
5001
Hara, Setsuko
5001 354
Harada, Mieko
H 91
5001 615
Harareet, Haya
5001 63
Harari, Clément
TIAI 478
5001 252
Harari, Robert
5001 258
Harbach, Otto
WTLGD 12
Harburg, E. Y.
5001 117, 398, 563
Hard Day's Night, A
KKBB 116
GS 14, 118, 120
SOTA 216
Hard Times (1975)
WTLGD 40-42, 558
SOTA 72
5001
Hard Times (TV)
H 169
Hard Way, The
WTLGD 503
5001
"Hard Workin' Man" (music)
WTLGD 406
Hardcore
WTLGD 543-546
TIAI 335
5001
Harder They Come, The
R 125-127
5001
Hardie, Kate
5001 166
Hardie, Russell
5001 107
Hardin, Jerry
ML 224
5001 80, 746
Hardin, Ty
5001 129
Harding, Ann

WTLGD 16
5001 336, 438, 533, 577
Harding, Gilbert
5001 229
Hardwick, Elizabeth
KKBB 107
DIM 291
Hardwick, Michael
WTLGD 111
Hardwicke, Cedric
5001 59, 152, 306, 343, 345, 351, 369, 392, 484, 523, 529, 602, 628, 747, 759, 814
Hardy, Francoise
KKBB 9
Hardy, Jonathan
SOTA 60
5001 431
Hardy, Oliver
KKBB 185, 274, 366
GS 77
WTLGD 471, 536, 537
TIAI 119, 121, 139
H 153
ML 143
5001 137, 292
Hardy, Robert
SOTA 372, 373
5001 677
Hardy, Sam
KKBB 325
5001 478, 483, 547, 552
Hardy, Thomas
ILIATM 169
KKBB 349-350
DIM 141
WTLGD 47
TIAI 134, 238
ML 139
5001 237, 749, 824
Hare, David
H 41, 42, 43, 44, 45-48; dir., *Wetherby*, 43, 45-48
5001 587, 829
Hare, Lumsden
KKBB 355
5001 130, 165, 311, 734
Harewood, Dorian
WTLGD 165-166
TIAI 253
SOTA 147, 315
ML 278
5001 10, 233, 271, 434, 561, 699
Hargreaves, Alice Liddell
H 51-52, 53, 54
Hargrove, Marion
5001 505
Harkins, John
TIAI 290
5001 2, 74
Harkrider, John
5001 305
Harlan County, U.S.A.
WTLGD 249-253
5001
Harlan, Russell
KKBB 338
5001 79, 443, 620, 646, 759, 777

Harlettes, The (group)
TIAI 96
5001 193
Harlow
KKBB 28, 134, 278-279:n
5001
Harlow, Jean
KKBB 27, 59, 274, 278, 341
RK 20
DIM 227
R 72, 151, 328
WTLGD 15, 422
TIAI 108, 335, 429
SOTA 110
H 228
5001 91, 134, 190, 292, 328, 336, 420, 491,
    586, 602, 619, 620, 629, 733, 836, 837
Harmon, Deborah
TIAI 99
5001 810
Harmony Four Quartette (group)
5001 547
Harnick, Sheldon
DIM 333
5001 242
Harold and Maude
R 274, 441
5001
Harolde, Ralf
KKBB 313
5001 357, 503, 525, 582
Harper
KKBB 279:n
GS 57
5001
Harper, James
ML 224
Harper, Jessica
R 367, 370
WTLGD 156
TIAI 89, 277, 396
5001 365, 508, 574, 579, 709
Harper, Tess
TIAI 479, 480
H 236
5001 162, 371, 747
Harper, Valerie
WTLGD 359
5001 80, 267
Harper's (periodical)
ILIATM 48, 54, 59
Harper's Bazaar (periodical)
KKBB 32
H 247
Harrigan, William
5001 369
Harriman, Averell
ML 130
Harrington, Curtis
5001 277
Harris, Barbara
R 451
WTLGD 504
SOTA 84
H 219
5001 191, 516, 574
Harris, Bill and Emily

ML 10, 11
Harris, Cassandra
5001 257
Harris, David
WTLGD 557
SOTA 273
5001 108, 691, 823
Harris, Ed
TIAI 198
SOTA 64, 72, 165, 247
H 49, 50, 51
5001 401, 585, 630, 735, 738, 805
Harris, Elmer
5001 382
Harris, Emmylou
TIAI 45
5001 340, 411
Harris, Fox
5001 624
Harris, Frank
R 49
Harris, Glenn Walker Jr.
5001 656
Harris, James B.
R 221
5001 394, 570, 691
Harris, Jed
KKBB 325
5001 551
Harris, Julie
ILIATM 13, 139
KKBB 279, 309
DIM 311
R 75
TIAI 455
5001 210, 298, 320, 321, 348, 474, 621,
    794, 819
Harris, Julius
5001 372, 396, 418
WTLGD 66, 282
Harris, Leonard
WTLGD 133
5001 745
Harris, Lewis
5001 679
Harris, Mark
5001 50
Harris, Richard
KKBB 135
DIM 104, 181, 357-359
R 348
WTLGD 158, 197
5001 67, 116, 163, 322, 385, 457, 491, 492,
    619, 625, 634, 762
Harris, Richard A.
ML 328
Harris, Rosalind
DIM 331
5001 242
Harris, Rosemary
GS 177, 211
WTLGD 453
ML 214
5001 97, 851
Harris, Sam
5001 547
Harris, Timothy

SOTA 12
5001 786
Harris, Vernon
5001 543
Harrison, Cathryn
R 80
WTLGD 82
SOTA 113
5001 77, 204, 358
Harrison, George
H 411
5001 772
Harrison, Jerry
SOTA 266
Harrison, Joan
5001 258, 378, 578, 618, 629
Harrison, Kathleen
5001 525, 543
Harrison, Linda
H 6
5001 586
Harrison, Philip
TIAI 219
5001 558
Harrison, Rex
KKBB 82, 364
DIM 37
TIAI 333
SOTA 153, 154
5001 11, 28, 81, 138, 283, 339, 453, 508,
    806
Harrison, Susan
KKBB 356
5001 736
Harrold, Kathryn
SOTA 350
H 170
5001 325, 617
Harron, Robert
GS 126
5001 305, 367, 385, 793
Harry & Tonto
R 376, 409, 411
WTLGD 128, 129, 411
TIAI 49
SOTA 158
5001 (2nd ed)
Harry and Walter Go to New York
WTLGD 490
Harry, Debbie
TIAI 336
H 443
5001 313
Hart, Henry
KKBB 241
Hart, Lorenz
KKBB 234
H 115
5001 42, 97, 226, 314, 350, 463, 562, 580,
    848
Hart, Moss
KKBB 273
GS 68, 238
RK 10, 18, 20, 28, 37, 84
R 322
WTLGD 13, 22
5001 317, 404, 459, 547, 707

Hart, Richard
  5001 305
Hart, William S.
  DIM 344
Hartford, Huntington
  5001 101, 664
Hartley, Mariette
  5001 629
Hartman, Don
  5001 200, 633
Hartman, Elizabeth
  R 284-285
  WTLGD 210
  5001 248, 309, 822
Hartman, Phil
  H 60
  5001 573
Hartmann, Sadakichi
  5001 756
Hartnell, William
  KKBB 321
  5001 104, 500, 539, 763
Harvest (Regain)
  KKBB 140, 279-280:n
  WTLGD 144
  SOTA 98
  H 330
  5001
Harvey
  ML 127
Harvey Allen, Jo, see Allen, Jo Harvey
Harvey, Anthony
  GS 181; dir., *The Lion in Winter*, 174-178
  DIM dir.,*The Lion in Winter*, 37
  R 245-246, 345-347; dir., *The Glass Menagerie*, 246-247; *The Lion in Winter*, 246; *The Abdication*, 345-347
  5001 1, 114, 423
Harvey, Don
  ML 170-171, 173, 176
  5001 124
Harvey, Forester
  5001 744
Harvey, Frank
  5001 357
Harvey Girls, The
  5001
Harvey, Laurence
  KKBB 263, 339
  DIM 142, 182
  WTLGD 553
  SOTA 125
  5001 110, 170, 173, 229, 348, 450, 462, 540, 639, 640, 726, 794, 851
Harvey, Paul
  5001 114, 578, 766, 767
Harwood, Joanna
  5001 270
Harwood, Ronald
  SOTA 113, 114
  5001 203
Hasegawa, Kazuo
  KKBB 268
  5001 280
Hasegawa, Kiyoshi
  5001 454
Hasford, Gustav

H 325, 327, 328
  5001 270, 271
Haskell, David
  5001 90
Haskell, Molly
  WTLGD 138
Haskell, Peter
  5001 568
Haskin, Byron
  5001 593
Haskins, Bob
  5001 365
Hasse, O. E.
  5001 349
Hasso, Signe
  WTLGD 123
  5001 76, 199, 326
Hastings, Michael
  5001 6, 529
Hatari!
  ILIATM 294, 297, 300, 318
Hatch, Eric
  5001 509
Hatch, Robert
  ILIATM 133
Hatfield, Hurd
  KKBB 146
  H 236
  5001 162, 189, 201, 416, 581
Hathaway, Henry
  ILIATM 297; dir., *Garden of Evil*, 55; *North to Alaska*, 297
  5001 200, 343, 399, 428, 519, 522, 540, 577, 696, 697, 699, 760, 787
Hattangady, Rohini
  5001 277
Hatton, Denys Finch, see Finch Hatton, Denys
Hatton, Raymond
  5001 438, 713
Hauben, Lawrence
  WTLGD 85
  5001 549
Haudepin, Didier
  5001 364
Hauer, Rutger
  TIAI 363-364, 404
  SOTA 356, 358
  ML 287
  5001 80, 406
Haunting, The
  ILIATM 10-13
  R 150
  5001
Haupt, Ullrich
  H 74
  5001 307, 498
Hauser, Fay
  5001 381
Hauser, Kaspar
  WTLGD 51
Hauser, Thomas
  TIAI 311
  5001 486
Hauser, Wings
  H 146, 362, 363
  5001 381, 784
Hausmanis, Andris

ML 94
  5001 566
"Hava Nagilah" (music)
  TIAI 389
Haver, June
  DIM 159
Haver, Phyllis
  5001 645
Havers, Nigel
  SOTA 300
  5001 131, 217, 568
Having a Wild Weekend (also known as *Catch Us If Your Can*)
  KKBB 280:n
  5001
"Having It All" (music)
  H 158
Having Wonderful Time
  WTLGD 370
  5001
Havoc, June
  5001 327, 510
Havrilla, Jo Ann
  H 443
  5001 313
Hawaii
  KKBB 135-136
  GS 235
  R 182
  TIAI 332
  5001 (2nd ed)
Hawke, Ethan
  ML 156, 206
  5001 168, 179
Hawkins, Jack
  5001 63, 102, 415, 434, 523, 541, 597, 670, 860
Hawkins, Ronnie
  5001 411
Hawkins, Screamin' Jay
  SOTA 262
Hawks, Howard
  ILIATM 300, 304, 312, 318-319; dir., *His Girl Friday*, 24, 304; *To Have and Have Not*, 24, 81, 214, 300, 304, 324; *The Big Sleep*, 26, 81, 214, 300, 304; *Bringing Up Baby*, 81, 304; *Hatari!* 294, 297, 300, 318; *Twentieth Century*, 304; *Only Angels Have Wings*, 305; *The Big Sky*, 305; *I Was a Male War Bride*, 307; *Red River*, 318; *Rio Bravo*, 318
  KKBB 6, 45, 59, 113, 239, 241, 281, 338, 359-360, 362; dir., *The Big Sleep*, 6-7, 59, 238-239, 251, 279; *El Dorado*, 42, 45; *Only Angels Have Wings*, 59; *To Have and Have Not*, 59, 194, 251, 359-360; *Rio Bravo*, 59; *Scarface*, 113, 338; *His Girl Friday*, 219, 281; *Bringing Up Baby*, 241; *Red River*, 338; *Twentieth Century*, 362
  GS dir., *Bringing Up Baby*, 177; *His Girl Friday*, 228; *Scarface*, 243, 246; *Twentieth Century*, 67
  RK 48, 75
  DIM 296-297; dir., *To Have and Have Not*, 235, 237, 413; *Red River*, 297; *The Big Sleep*, 413-415; *Bringing Up Baby*, 431,

432
R 300; dir., *Gentlemen Prefer Blondes*, 154;
  The Big Sleep, 184, 187; *Scarface*, 208;
  Bringing Up Baby, 440
WTLGD 17, 18; dir., *Bringing Up Baby*, 3,
  8, 16, 17, 18, 29; *Only Angels Have
  Wings*, 3, 4, 18, 30; *His Girl Friday*, 4,
  16, 18, 19, 23; *Twentieth Century*, 6, 16,
  141; *I Was a Male War Bride*, 30; *The
  Big Sleep*, 262; *To Have and Have Not*,
  281, 282
SOTA 62, 102; dir., *Only Angels Have
  Wings*, 62; *Scarface*, 100-101, 102, 103,
  104
ML dir., *His Girl Friday*, 315; *Scarface*,
  268; *To Have and Have Not*, 48
5001 11, 48, 51, 71, 104, 214, 310, 335,
  352, 421, 494, 620, 630, 631, 657, 758,
  771, 776, 778, 796
Hawley, Cameron
  ILIATM 323
Hawn, Goldie
  R 300, 301, 436, 438-439
  TIAI 92-94, 163, 305, 412, 445
  SOTA 165, 166-167, 168
  5001 64, 113, 197, 598, 670, 725, 738, 752
Hawthorne, Christopher
  ML 94
  5001 566
Hawthorne, Nathaniel
  KKBB 254, 345
  SOTA 207, 208
  H 61, 314
  5001 658-659
Hay, Alexandra
  5001 490
Hay, Ian
  KKBB 359
  5001 761
Hayakawa, Sessue
  5001 102
Haycox, Ernest
  5001 704
Haydée, Marcia
  WTLGD 347
  5001 795
Hayden, James
  5001 548
Hayden, Melissa
  5001 423
Hayden, Sterling
  KKBB 291
  R 187, 352
  WTLGD 325, 326, 328, 330
  5001 37, 289, 394, 432, 442, 530, 705
Haydn, Richard
  KKBB 249
  5001 25, 48, 143, 259, 684, 697, 859
Haye, Helen
  5001 398, 628
Hayer, Nicholas
  KKBB 326
  5001 554
Hayes, Alfred
  5001 140, 381
Hayes, Bernadene
  5001 354, 856

Hayes, Billy
  WTLGD 496-501
Hayes, Gabby
  WTLGD 508
  TIAI 371
Hayes, Helen
  GS 177
  DIM 137, 311, 345
  R 352, 432
  WTLGD 16
  TIAI 118
  5001 12, 162, 829
Hayes, John Michael
  KKBB 14
  5001 110, 121, 519, 775
Hayes, Margaret
  5001 79, 726
Hayes, Patricia
  5001 840
Hayes, Peter Lind
  5001 248, 665
Hayes, Steve
  5001 772
Hayes, Terry
  TIAI 387
  5001 634
Hayman, David
  H 368
  5001 340
Haymes, Dick
  5001 550, 711, 808
Haynes, Stanley
  KKBB 322
  5001 449, 543
Hays, Robert
  TIAI 51
  5001 12
Hayter, James
  KKBB 252, 331
  5001 21, 163, 581, 694, 717
Hayward, Brooke
  WTLGD 481
Hayward, David
  5001 516
Hayward, Leland
  RK 65
  5001 488
Hayward, Louis
  WTLGD 49
  TIAI 321
  H 361
  5001 25, 31, 169, 403
Hayward, Susan
  ILIATM 34-35
  DIM 407
  R 36, 111, 429
  WTLGD 166
  TIAI 185
  SOTA 216
  H 431
  5001 57, 339, 350, 356, 688
Haywire (book)
  WTLGD 481
Hayworth, Rita
  ILIATM 266
  DIM 324
  WTLGD 3, 261, 464

TIAI 33, 195
H 469
ML 190
5001 27, 83, 159, 200, 232, 285, 474, 485,
  508, 562, 732, 741, 857, 858
Hazard, Lawrence
  5001 702, 718
Haze, Jonathan
  5001 210, 427
HBO, see Home Box Office
He, see *Le Rosier de Madame Husson*
He Married His Wife
  KKBB 363
  RK 17
  5001 (2nd ed)
"He Needs Me" (music)
  TIAI 123
He Who Must Die (Celue qui doit mourir)
  ILIATM 141
  5001
"He's Me Pal" (music)
  H 421
Head
  GS 185-186
  5001
Head, Edith
  R 86
  WTLGD 109
  5001 16, 178, 554, 585
Head, Murray
  DIM 289
  5001 728
Headly, Glenne
  ML 76
  5001 191, 513
Healy, Mary
  5001 248, 322, 662
Healy, Ted
  DIM 318
  5001 91, 123, 337, 445
Heard, John
  TIAI 336
  H 40, 93
  ML 72, 325
  5001 9, 56, 68, 125, 167, 790
Hearst, Lord of San Simeon (book)
  RK 71
Hearst, Millicent (Mrs. William Randolph)
  RK 6, 60
Hearst, Patty
  WTLGD 223
  ML 8-11
Hearst, William Randolph
  KKBB 52, 247
  RK 3, 5-6, 7, 8, 19, 20, 21, 24, 32, 34-36,
    38, 41-42, 43, 45, 47, 50, 52, 55-61, 63-
    67, 68-73, 74, 79-81, 82
  WTLGD 373
  5001 463, 679, 680, 699
"Heart and Soul" (music)
  H 483
Heart Like a Wheel
  SOTA 79-83
  H 149
  5001 (2nd ed)
Heart of Darkness (book)
  RK 34

TIAI 144, 402
Heart, Pearl
5001 641
Heartaches
TIAI 424-426
ML 47
5001 (2nd ed)
"Heartbreak Hotel" (music)
H 335
Heartbreak Kid, The
R 68-71, 261, 361, 430, 465
5001
Heartbreak Ridge
H 246-247, 353
5001 (2nd ed)
Heartbreakers
SOTA 349-353
5001 (2nd ed)
Heartburn
H 189-192
ML 275
5001 (2nd ed)
Heartland
SOTA 236
Hearts and Minds
WTLGD 176, 251
Hearts of the West
WTLGD 45-49
5001
Heartworn Highways
TIAI 204-207
5001
Heat
5001
Heath, Gordon
ILIATM 66
DIM 26
Heather, Jean
5001 198, 503
Heathers
ML 118-20
5001 (2nd ed)
Heaven Can Wait (1943)
5001
Heaven Can Wait (1978)
WTLGD 427, 429-430, 432
TIAI 280, 327
SOTA 170
Heaven Has No Favorites
WTLGD 302
Heaven Knows, Mr. Allison
ILIATM 299
Heaven's Gate
TIAI 112-114
H 21-24, 31, 33
Hebuterne, Jeanne
DIM 54
Hecht, Ben (pseud. Lester Barstow)
KKBB 33, 59, 113, 234, 278, 281, 319-320,
341, 348, 362; co-dir., *Specter of the
Rose*, 143, 234
GS dir., *Specter of the Rose*, 157
RK 4, 9, 16, 18, 19, 20, 21, 29, 39, 48, 49,
50, 61
DIM 73, 74
R 422, 423
WTLGD 18

TIAI 240; dir., *Specter of the Rose*, 132
SOTA 102
5001 27, 51, 123, 162, 270, 275, 302, 310,
314, 335, 374, 399, 494, 535, 536, 629,
637, 657, 700, 701, 704, 741, 758, 781,
796, 832, 851
Hecht, Gina
5001 528
Hecht, Harold
KKBB 29, 252
Heckart, Eileen
GS 74
5001 325, 327, 808, 863
Heckerling, Amy
TIAI 407-409; dir., *Fast Times at Ridgemont
High*, 407-409, 473
H 131
5001 238
Hedaya, Dan
SOTA 323, 325
H 153
5001 83, 561, 842
Hedin, June
5001 351
Hedison, David (Al)
5001 252
Hedley, Tom
5001 250
Hedren, Tippi
DIM 192
ML 278
5001 74, 466, 561
"Hee Haw" (TV)
DIM 234
Heerman, Victor
5001 28, 428, 713
Heffer, Richard
5001 847
Heffernan, John
5001 715
Heffernan, Terence
TIAI 425
5001 324
Heflin, Frances
5001 492
Heflin, Marta
5001 148
TIAI 414, 416, 417
Heflin, Van
KKBB 347
5001 78, 305, 382, 446, 591, 653, 671, 718,
767, 846
Hefner, Hugh
GS 195
DIM 110
TIAI 215
SOTA 91
Hegel, Georg Wilhelm Friedrich
ILIATM 272-273
WTLGD 306
Heggen, Thomas
5001 488
Heggie, O. P.
5001 102, 157, 865
Heifetz, Jascha
SOTA 2
5001 804

"Heigh-Ho" (music)
SOTA 191
Heilveil, Elayne
R 123
5001 572
Heineman, Laurie
R 118
5001 655
Heiress, The
TIAI 221
H 444
5001 (2nd ed)
Heisler, Stuart
5001 24, 287, 332, 688, 706
Held, John, Jr.
DIM 379
TIAI 159
Helen Keller in Her Story, see *The Unconquered*
Helgenberger, Marg
5001 21
Hell in the Pacific
GS 271-272
5001
Hell, Richard
5001 185
Hell to Eternity
KKBB 233
R 284
Hell's Angels
DIM 174, 208-211
Hell's Angels (1930)
5001
Hell's Angels on Wheels
TIAI 64
Heller in Pink Tights
5001
Heller, Joseph
5001 125
Heller, Lukas
5001 495
Heller, Otto
5001 163, 193, 628, 794, 845
Heller, Paul M.
5001 174, 221
Hellinger, Mark
5001 108, 514, 634
Hellman, Jerome
5001 150, 244, 479
Hellman, Lillian
ILIATM 82, 175-176
KKBB 107, 151, 153
RK 19
R 219
WTLGD 304-310
5001 30, 132, 133, 178, 385, 426, 533, 753,
758, 785, 823
Hellman, Monte
R 304
5001 629, 676, 677, 837
Hellman, Sam
5001 322, 502, 760
Hello, Dolly!
DIM 80-85, 185, 328, 432
R 460
5001
"Hello, Dolly!" (music)
DIM 83

Hello, Frisco, Hello
  5001 (2nd ed)
Hellzapoppin
  ILIATM 153
  GS 186
  R 281
Helm, Brigitte
  KKBB 309
  GS 45
  5001 477
Helm, Fay
  5001 578
Helm, Levon
  SOTA 65
  H 132
  5001 411, 630, 689
Helmond, Katherine
  H 108
  5001 98, 334, 405, 772
Help!
  KKBB 8, 116-117, 139
  GS 120, 189
Helpmann, Robert
  GS 225
  5001 328, 621, 741
Helter Skelter (TV)
  TIAI 66
Helvick, James (Claud Cockburn)
  5001 57
Hembrow, Mark
  H 433
  5001 333
Hemdale (group of backers)
  5001 651, 812
Hemingway, Ernest
  ILIATM 91, 223-224
  KKBB 223, 291, 360
  DIM 46
  R 151, 186
  WTLGD 91, 278-283, 308, 516
  TIAI 179, 333, 453
  H 364
  5001 256, 372, 394, 776
Hemingway, Margaux
  WTLGD 236
Hemingway, Mariel
  TIAI 92, 302, 304, 305
  SOTA 91, 92, 334, 335
  5001 472, 576, 706
Hemingway, Mary
  WTLGD 282
Hemingway's Adventures of a Young Man
  ILIATM 91, 222-225
  TIAI 357
Hemmings, David
  KKBB 34
  GS 146, 173
  DIM 67
  R 348
  WTLGD 282
  ML 140
  5001 50, 85, 116, 131, 372, 385, 502, 614
Henderson, Dell
  5001 680
Henderson, Florence
  5001 694
Henderson, Ray

  5001 296, 387
Hendrix, Jimi
  DIM 198
  SOTA 213
  5001 210
Hendrix, Wanda
  KKBB 251
  5001 152, 629
Hendry, Ian
  5001 283, 624
Henie, Sonja
  5001 663, 728
Henley, Beth
  H 218, 233, 235, 236
  ML 141-44
  5001 162, 484, 485, 738, 794
Henley, Hobart
  5001 71
Henn, Carrie
  H 193
  5001 15
Hennequin, Maurice
  KKBB 303
  5001 449
Henner, Marilu
  WTLGD 446
  ML 328
  5001 84
Henning, Paul
  ML 75
  5001 191, 441
Henreid, Paul
  KKBB 245
  DIM 26
  WTLGD 116
  5001 122, 182, 229, 450, 536, 540
Henrey, Bobby
  5001 234
Henriksen, Lance
  5001 15, 519
Henry, Buck
  DIM 184, 324-325
  R 246
  WTLGD 498
  ML 211
  5001 117, 125, 175, 211, 299, 371, 460, 559, 831
Henry, Charlotte V.
  5001 15, 257
Henry, David Lee
  H 156
  5001 213
Henry, Gloria
  5001 616
Henry, Gregg
  5001 90
Henry II, King
  GS 174, 175
Henry IV (stage)
  KKBB 201
Henry, Justin
  SOTA 174
  5001 684
Henry, Mike
  5001 631, 744
Henry, O. (Wiliam Sidney Porter)
  GS 50

  DIM 267
  H 179
  5001 648
Henry V (1944)
  ILIATM 120, 283
  KKBB 174, 200, 201
  ML 212
  5001
Henry V (1989)
  ML 212-217
  5001 (2nd ed)
Henson, Jim
  H 53, 54
  ML 209
  5001 202, 842
Henstell, Bruce
  WTLGD 41
  5001 318
Henze, Hans-Werner
  5001 734
Henzell, Perry
  R 125-127
  5001 319
Hepburn, Audrey
  ILIATM 199
  KKBB 185, 294, 295
  DIM 71, 381
  R 60
  WTLGD 3, 5, 32, 61, 157-159, 214, 345, 482
  TIAI 65
  H 273
  ML 247
  5001 21, 99, 130, 133, 271, 343, 413, 414, 438, 507, 634, 636, 649, 664, 753, 798, 799
Hepburn, Katharine
  ILIATM 4
  KKBB 89, 228, 229-230, 241, 285, 298, 330, 336, 353-354
  GS 175, 176-177, 178, 234
  DIM 25, 184, 218, 290, 301, 302, 311, 313, 341, 346, 353, 431
  R 97, 246-247
  WTLGD 3, 7, 16, 17, 18, 19, 20, 28, 29, 61, 62-64, 157, 201, 209, 233
  TIAI 61, 65, 214, 254, 269, 270, 271, 272, 379, 429
  SOTA 29, 86, 110, 281
  H 83, 228, 306, 364-367, 409, 411
  ML 304
  5001 5, 8, 14, 56, 71, 99, 104, 136, 184, 201, 336, 391, 423, 426, 428, 432, 450, 467, 498, 545, 569, 580, 607, 614, 640, 660, 703, 704, 711, 725, 727, 738, 739, 790, 830, 843, 845, 846
Herbert, F. Hugh
  5001 238, 356, 684
Herbert, Frank
  SOTA 282, 283, 284, 286
  5001 206
Herbert, Holmes
  5001 118, 157
Herbert, Hugh
  5001 58, 238, 253, 255, 291, 304, 690
Herbert, Victor
  ILIATM 143

TIAI 70
5001 518, 736
Her Cardboard Lover
5001
Here Comes Mr. Jordan
KKBB 68
5001
Here We Go Round the Mulberry Bush
GS 63-65
Heritage USA
H 439
Héritier, L', see *The Inheritor*
Herlie, Eileen
GS 235
5001 315, 660
Herlihy, James Leo
TIAI 284, 285
5001 16, 264, 479
Herman, Jerry
DIM 84
5001 455
Herman, Pee-Wee (pseud. of Paul Reubens)
H 58-61
5001 573
Hermann, Irm
5001 477
Hernández, Juano
KKBB 161, 285-286
DIM 75, 76
5001 368, 571, 622
Hero with a Thousand Faces, The (book)
TIAI 385
Heroes
WTLGD 467-468
SOTA 322
H 353
Heroux, Denis
5001 38
Herr, Michael
H 252, 327
5001 271
Herrand, Marcel
KKBB 247, 264
5001 133, 235, 817
Herrmann, Bernard
RK 8, 66, 67
R 195
WTLGD 134, 352
TIAI 36
H 69
5001 28, 139, 284, 466, 514, 533, 684, 851
Herrmann, Edward
R 467
TIAI 280
SOTA 291, 337, 338
H 36, 37
5001 29, 66, 68, 150, 304, 487, 604, 621
Hersey, John
KKBB 75
Hershewe, Michael
WTLGD 446
5001 70, 84
Hershey, Barbara
DIM 157
TIAI 67-68
SOTA 62, 172
H 113, 114, 281, 282, 475, 477

ML 72-73
5001 44, 56, 179, 316, 518, 630, 724, 773, 849
Hersholt, Jean
KKBB 275
5001 13, 299, 469, 476, 599, 733
Hertzberg, Michael
5001 796
Hervey, Harry
5001 671
Hervey, Irene
KKBB 256
5001 97, 113, 157, 185, 488
Herzig, Sig
5001 349, 755
Herzog, Werner
GS dir., *Signs of Life*, 215
WTLGD 51-55; dir., *The Mystery of Kaspar Hauser* (*Every Man for Himself and God Against All*), 51-55; *Signs of Life*, 54
TIAI 401-407; dir., *Fitzcarraldo*, 401-407; *Aguirre, the Wrath of God*, 401, 402, 405, 406
SOTA 199
H 61
ML 116
5001 109, 247, 511, 512, 534
Hesketh-Harvey, Kit
H 361
5001 471
Hesse, Hermann
DIM 230, 348
WTLGD 258
Hester Street
WTLGD 79-82
5001
Heston, Charlton
KKBB 361
GS 37
DIM 351
R 348, 364-365, 385-386, 456
WTLGD 178, 179, 198
TIAI 387
SOTA 149
H 392
5001 11, 12, 63, 209, 305, 586, 646, 747, 767, 784, 839, 851
Hets, see *Torment*
Hewitt, Martin
5001 219
Hewitt, Mary
WTLGD 368
"Hey Now" (music)
H 216
Heyes, Douglas
GS 222
Heyl, John
5001 665
Heyman, Edward
5001 32
Heyward, Dubose
5001 217
Heywood, Anne
GS 30
5001 265
Heywood, Pat

GS 154
R 17
H 333
5001 639, 842, 860
"Hi-Lili, Hi-Lo" (music)
WTLGD 163
Hi, Mom!
TIAI 67, 217, 457
SOTA 264
ML 317
5001
Hi, Nellie
RK 20
Hichens, Robert
5001 278, 565
Hickey, William
SOTA 377
ML 75
5001 103, 317, 600
Hickman, Darryl
KKBB 276
5001 301, 344, 434, 718
Hickman, Dwayne
KKBB 29-30
5001 124
Hickman, G. M.
5001 221
Hickok, Wild Bill
DIM 213
Hicks, Catherine
5001 574, 708
Hicks, Edward
WTLGD 471
Hicks, Granville
KKBB 78
Hicks, James, see Cresson, James
Hicks, Tommy Redmond
H 213
5001 674
Hidaka, Shinya
5001 454
Hidalgo, David
H 341
5001 48
Higby, Mary Jane
DIM 107
5001 339
Higgins, Anthony
SOTA 31
H 101
5001 201, 860
Higgins, Colin
WTLGD 247
TIAI 162-164, 373-375; dir., *Nine to Five*, 162-164, 373; *Foul Play*, 163, 412; *The Best Little Whorehouse in Texas*, 373-375
5001 64, 319, 530, 681
Higgins, George V.
5001 269
Higgins, Ken
5001 173
Higgins, Michael
DIM 267
5001 27, 35, 823
High and Dry (also known as *The Maggie*)
5001

High and the Mighty, The
  ILIATM 55
High Anxiety
  WTLGD 371-376, 448
  TIAI 38, 461
  5001
High Cost of Loving, The
  KKBB 277
  5001
High Hopes
  ML 87-89
  5001 (2nd ed)
High Noon
  ILIATM 242
  KKBB 40, 151-152, 194, 203, 219,
    280-281:n
  GS 53
  DIM 387
  TIAI 218, 219
  H 16
  5001
High School
  DIM 20-24
  R 163
  WTLGD 43
  5001
High Season
  H 449-452, 476
  ML 88
  5001 (2nd ed)
High Sierra
  ILIATM 293-294
  H 464
  5001
High Spirits
  ML 42-45
  5001 (2nd ed)
High Stakes (book)
  TIAI 72
High Tide
  H 432-435
  5001 (2nd ed)
High, Wide, and Handsome
  5001
Highsmith, Patricia
  KKBB 352
  WTLGD 312-314
  5001 22, 603, 720
Hightower, Harold
  5001 264
Hiken, Barbara
  5001 273
Hiken, Gerald
  5001 239, 273
Hilberg, Raul
  H 85
Hilboldt, Lise
  H 162
  5001 735
Hildyard, Jack
  KKBB 282, 354
  5001 100, 114, 254, 328, 336, 727-728, 729
Hill, The
  KKBB 82
  R 61
Hill, Arthur
  KKBB 279

DIM 276
  WTLGD 115, 117
  5001 26, 320, 394, 802
Hill, Dana
  TIAI 291, 295
  SOTA 57, 58
  5001 164, 676
Hill, Debra
  WTLGD 547
  5001 314
Hill, Derek
  ILIATM 16
Hill, Elizabeth
  5001 555
Hill, George
  5001 294
Hill, George Roy
  KKBB 136; dir., *Hawaii*, 135-136;
    Thoroughly Modern Millie, 172
  DIM 6; dir., *Butch Cassidy and the
    Sundance Kid*, 5-7, 149, 173, 401, 402;
    Period of Adjustment, 281
  R 245, 317, 331, 466-469; dir., *Butch
    Cassidy and the Sundance Kid*, 98, 162,
    244, 283, 317, 468; *Hawaii*, 182; *The
    Sting*, 244-245, 303, 314, 315, 317, 321,
    322, 422, 468; *Slaughterhouse-Five*,
    317; *The Great Waldo Pepper*, 464,
    466-469
  WTLGD 273-278; dir., *The Sting*, 67, 106,
    273, 275; *Butch Cassidy and the
    Sundance Kid*, 173, 273, 517; *The Great
    Waldo Pepper*, 174, 273; *Slap Shot*,
    273-278
  TIAI 332, 376-381; *Slap Shot*, 151, 288,
    289, 441; *A Little Romance*, 213;
    Hawaii, 337; *The World According to
    Garp*, 376-381; *Slaughterhouse-Five*,
    380; *The Sting*, 390; *Butch Cassidy and
    the Sundance Kid*, 437
  SOTA 257-260; dir., *The World According
    to Garp*, 22; *Butch Cassidy and the
    Sundance Kid*, 177;
    Slaughterhouse-Five, 253; *The Little
    Drummer Girl*, 257-260
  5001 110, 304, 322, 425, 685, 715, 763,
    785, 849, 850
Hill, Gladys
  WTLGD 108, 111
  5001 461, 622
Hill, Henry
  ML 265-270
Hill, Roger
  WTLGD 555
  5001 823
Hill, Steven
  KKBB 272
  TIAI 172
  SOTA 90
  H 170, 173, 190
  5001 231, 289, 325, 416, 617, 627, 855
"Hill Street Blues" (TV)
  SOTA 74
Hill, Walter
  R 135-137
  WTLGD 40-42, 554-559; dir., *Hard Times*,
    40-42, 558; *The Warriors*, 554-559; *The*

Driver, 558
  TIAI 18, 190, 257-261, 437-440; dir., *The
    Long Riders*, 18, 75, 259, 260, 438; *The
    Driver*, 190; *Southern Comfort*,
    257-261, 438; *The Warriors*, 259; *48
    Hrs.*, 437-440
  SOTA 72; dir., *Hard Times*, 72; *48 Hrs.*, 72,
    78, 287; *The Long Riders*, 120; *The
    Warriors*, 233
  H 142-144; dir., *Crossroads*, 142-144; *The
    Warriors*, 143; *The Long Riders*, 143;
    Southern Comfort, 143; *48 Hrs.*, 143;
    Streets of Fire, 344
  ML dir., *Johnny Handsome*, 193-94
  5001 165, 204, 261, 283, 318, 382, 698,
    757, 823
Hiller, Arthur
  DIM 219, 378; dir., *Love Story*, 216-220,
    237, 321, 322, 432-433; *The Hospital*,
    378-379, 426
  R 77-78; dir., *Man of La Mancha*, 77-78;
    Love Story, 176; *Promise Her Anything*,
    248; *Plaza Suite*, 260
  WTLGD 246-248; dir., *The Hospital*, 220;
    Silver Streak, 246-248, 269; *The
    Out-of-Towners*, 264; *Love Story*, 302,
    458
  TIAI 332, 368-370; dir., *Silver Streak*, 163;
    The Americanization of Emily, 332;
    Author! Author!, 368-370, 475; *The
    Out-of-Towners*, 415
  SOTA 128-130; dir., *The Lonely Guy*,
    128-130, 140; *Romantic Comedy*, 129,
    168; *Making Love*, 129
  H 272-274; dir., *Outrageous Fortune*, 272-
    274, 484
  5001 39, 341, 431, 458, 559, 682
Hiller, Wendy
  ILIATM 73
  KKBB 327
  DIM 142
  R 390-391
  TIAI 85
  H 306, 412
  5001 215, 349, 431, 453, 456, 503, 558,
    605, 695, 785, 819
Hillerman, John
  R 464
  TIAI 216
  5001 37, 81, 135, 831
Hilliard, Harriet
  5001 254
Hillier, Erwin
  5001 349
Hilsman, Roger
  DIM 44
Hilton, Daisy and Violet
  5001 266
Hilton, James
  KKBB 275
  DIM 38, 39
  R 137-140
  5001 116, 296, 297, 436, 446, 616
Hilyard, Jack
  5001 102
Himmel über Berlin, Der, see *Wings of Desire*
Hinchley, Pippa

ML 46
5001 204
Hindenburg, The
R 318
WTLGD 119-122
5001
Hindle, Art
WTLGD 521-522
5001 368
Hinds, Samuel S.
KKBB 256
5001 143, 185, 374, 428, 647, 702, 703
Hine, Al
5001 435
Hine, Lewis H.
WTLGD 250
Hines, Gregory
TIAI 216, 217
SOTA 295, 296, 297-298
H 64, 65-66
5001 156, 335, 835
Hines, Johnny
5001 779
Hines, Maurice
SOTA 295, 296, 298
5001 156
Hingle, Pat
ILIATM 137
DIM 182
TIAI 439
SOTA 315
ML 286
5001 19, 43, 233, 280, 519, 546, 702, 719,
    725, 802, 851
Hinton, S. E. (Susan E. Hinton)
TIAI 399, 400
H 317
5001 749, 750
Hird, Thora
5001 222, 451, 529
Hired Hand, The
DIM 323, 353
Hiroshima
DIM 112
Hiroshima, mon amour
ILIATM 24, 31-35, 42
WTLGD 292
5001 (2nd ed)
Hirsch, Charles
GS 212
5001 307, 329
Hirsch, Judd
TIAI 79, 81, 383
5001 553
Hirsch, Paul
WTLGD 212
TIAI 39, 228
SOTA 140
H 299
5001 218, 256, 330, 664
Hirschmuller, Hans
5001 477
His Double Life
5001
His Girl Friday
ILIATM 24, 304
KKBB 219, 281:n

GS 228
RK 20, 21, 48, 75
WTLGD 4, 16, 18, 19, 23
H 151, 352, 447, 448, 449
ML 315
5001
Hiss, Alger
ILIATM 327
Histoire d'Adèle H., L', see *The Story of Adèle
    H.*
History Is Made at Night
5001
History of the World--Part I
TIAI 214-217
5001
Hit, The
H 120, 121
"Hit the Road, Jack" (music)
ML 113
Hitchcock, Alfred
ILIATM 9, 131-132, 135, 294, 297-299; dir.,
    The Birds, 10; *Strangers on a Train*, 24,
    81, 135; *Saboteur*, 294; *The Thirty-Nine
    Steps*, 294; *North by Northwest*, 294;
    Dial M for Murder, 297; *Rear Window*,
    297; *Vertigo*, 297
KKBB 48, 59, 75-76, 150, 259, 293, 318,
    320, 348, 352, 359; dir., *Rope*, 48; *The
    39 Steps*, 206, 319, 352, 359; *Dial M
    for Murder*, 259; *The Lady Vanishes*,
    293, 350; *North by Northwest*, 318-319;
    Notorious, 320, 348; *Spellbound*, 348,
    Strangers on a Train, 352; *Foreign
    Correspondent*, 352
GS 113, 181, 275; dir., *Notorious*, 113;
    Psycho, 88, 168; *Strangers on Train*,
    242; *To Catch a Thief*, 23
DIM 79-80, 192, 317, 404; dir., *Marnie*, 79;
    Topaz, 79-80; *Torn Curtain*, 79; *The
    Birds*, 192; *Strangers on a Train*,
    261-262; *Psycho*, 316; *Rope*, 401
R 79, 179, 180, 236; dir., *Frenzy*, 47; *Rear
    Window*, 195; *Psycho*, 248, 367
WTLGD 25, 82, 138, 146, 208, 212, 351,
    366, 371-375, 418, 421, 436, 547; dir.,
    Notorious, 3, 25, 26, 29, 30, 31; *To
    Catch a Thief*, 3, 25, 30, 31, 304; *North
    by Northwest*, 3, 25, 30, 31, 352, 373;
    Suspicion, 25; *Lifeboat*, 138; *The Birds*,
    157, 371; *Psycho*, 209, 373, 436;
    Strangers on a Train, 313; *Spellbound*,
    372; *Vertigo*, 372, 373; *Rebecca*, 373
TIAI 35, 37, 38, 39, 40, 192; dir., *Psycho*,
    37, 40; *Suspicion*, 37; *Spellbound*, 461
SOTA 36, 264, 326; dir., *Rebecca*, 111;
    Rear Window, 188, 264; *Vertigo*, 264
H 117, 263; dir., *The 39 Steps* (1935), 117;
    North by Northwest, 117; *Shadow of a
    Doubt*, 263; *Juno and the Paycock*, 336;
    Strangers on a Train, 446
5001 74, 79, 189, 258, 349, 377, 406, 421,
    460, 466, 501, 502, 533, 536, 565, 587,
    618, 649, 663, 669, 701, 720, 761, 775,
    780, 782, 804, 850, 858
Hitchcock, Jane
WTLGD 248

5001 523
Hitchcock, Patricia
KKBB 352
5001 720
Hitchens, Dolores
5001 49
Hitler, Adolf
KKBB 5, 147, 210-212, 257-258, 294, 309,
    323
RK 58
DIM 87, 427, 429
WTLGD 120, 224, 281, 306, 390, 453-454,
    515
Hixon, Ken
TIAI 200
5001 401
Hjelm, Keve
5001 525
Hjortsberg, William
H 286
5001 27
Ho Chi Minh
DIM 42, 45
Hoag, Judith
5001 745
Hoagland, John
H 182
Hoban, Russell
H 130
5001 795
Hobart, Alice Tisdale
5001 542
Hobart, Rose
5001 194, 237, 732
Hobbes, Halliwell
5001 118, 329, 586, 774
Hobel, Mara
TIAI 235
5001 492
Hobson, Valerie
KKBB 276, 292, 312, 335, 339
5001 102, 301, 395, 494, 601, 606, 635, 779
Hobson's Choice
KKBB 282:n
5001
Hockney, David
WTLGD 529
Hoctor, Harriet
5001 305
Hodges, Johnny
5001 62
Hodges, Mike
TIAI 124-127; dir., *Flash Gordon*, 124-127,
    184; *Get Carter*, 125, 126; *Pulp*, 125;
    Terminal Man, 125
5001 250, 283, 748
Hodiak, John
5001 321, 421, 438
Hoellering, G. M.
ILIATM 344
Hoey, Iris
5001 605
Hoffe, Monckton
5001 404
Hoffenberg, Mason
GS 223
5001 117

Hoffenstein, Samuel
  5001 23, 143, 153, 184, 304, 413, 579, 694
Hoffer, William
  WTLGD 496
Hoffman, Abbie
  WTLGD 468
  5001 93
Hoffman, Alice
  SOTA 281
  5001 361
Hoffman, Basil
  5001 508
Hoffman, Dustin
  GS 125, 276
  DIM 72-73, 213, 215, 349, 352, 394, 395
  R 172, 229, 238-240, 257-258, 371, 373,
    375, 377
  WTLGD 172-173, 175, 378, 526, 552-553
  TIAI 19, 244, 428-429, 430, 431
  H 177, 310, 311, 351
  ML 78-82, 324
  5001 10, 14, 299, 371, 381, 417, 424, 464,
    478, 479, 565, 613, 718, 720, 780
Hoffman, Gaby
  ML 126
  5001 242
Hoffmann, E. T. A.
  H 62, 241
  5001 537
Hoffmann, Kurt
  KKBB 251; dir., The Confessions of Felix
    Krull, 251; Aren't We Wonderful?, 340
  WTLGD 355
  5001 151
Hofstra, Jack
  TIAI 67
Hogan, Michael
  5001 34
Hogarth, William
  SOTA 32
Hogg, Michael Lindsay, see Lindsay-Hogg,
  Michael
Hohl, Arthur
  5001 141, 186, 391, 464, 680, 837
Holbrook, Hal
  GS 91, 107
  R 255
  WTLGD 305
  5001 309, 386, 452, 838
Holby, Kristin
  5001 786
Hold Your Man
  5001
Holden, Anne
  H 265
  5001 60
Holden, David
  WTLGD 558-559
Holden, Fay
  5001 75, 438
Holden, Gloria
  5001 763
Holden, Lansing C.
  5001 672
Holden, William
  KKBB 240, 349, 354-355
  R 318, 407

WTLGD 117, 220-223
  5001 94, 102, 123, 157, 292, 519, 556, 649,
    690, 705, 729, 730, 785, 838
Holder, Geoffrey
  R 164
  5001 29
Holender, Adam
  5001 479, 564, 605, 722
Holgate, Diane
  5001 833
Holgate, Ron
  R 54
  5001 668
Holiday
  KKBB 68
  GS 176
  WTLGD 3, 18
  5001
Holiday, Billie
  ILIATM 116
  R 35-40
  WTLGD 140, 191
  H 146
Holiday for Henrietta (La Fête à Henriette)
  5001
Holinshed's Chronicles
  KKBB 201
  5001 235
Holland, Anthony
  5001 25, 111, 400, 445, 479, 842
Holland, Betty Lou
  KKBB 272
  5001 289
Holland, Erik
  5001 470
Holland, Marty
  5001 234, 243
Holland, Tony
  5001 746
Hollander, Frederick
  5001 85, 126, 184, 185, 248, 258
Holliday, Jason
  5001 590
Holliday, Judy
  KKBB 228, 240
  GS 185
  SOTA 84
  5001 5, 94, 373, 467, 691
Holliday, Polly
  SOTA 187, 190-191
  5001 307
Holliman, Earl
  KKBB 337
  5001 285, 593, 614, 726
Hollis, Carey Jr.
  5001 611
Holloway, Jean
  5001 726, 848
Holloway, Stanley
  ILIATM 118
  KKBB 295, 330
  5001 62, 102, 114, 315, 414, 453-454, 508,
    523, 568, 599, 779
Holloway, Sterling
  5001 15, 58, 82, 291, 635, 822, 837
Holly, Buddy
  WTLGD 423

H 342
Hollywood Babylon (book)
  ILIATM 35
  TIAI 381
Hollywood Canteen
  5001
Hollywood Party
  5001
Hollywood Reporter (periodical
  RK 25, 38, 44
Hollywood Revue of 1929, see The Hollywood
  Revue
Hollywood Revue, The (also known as
  Hollywood Revue of 1929)
  WTLGD 79
  5001
Holm, Celeste
  KKBB 230
  5001 16, 419
Holm, Claus
  KKBB 258
  5001 187
Holm, Ian
  GS 210
  R 220, 452
  WTLGD 158
  SOTA 15, 150, 333
  H 30, 47, 52
  ML 13, 214, 217
  5001 31, 98, 131, 170, 202, 248, 308, 329,
    338, 468, 541, 626, 772, 829, 860
Holman, Bill
  5001 79
Holmes, Christopher
  5001 118
Holmes, Milton
  5001 488
Holmes, Phillips
  KKBB 221
  WTLGD 357
  5001 23, 107
Holmes, Taylor
  5001 92, 399, 529
Holt, Charlene
  TIAI 77
  5001 214
Holt, Jack
  RK 13
  5001 125, 815
Holt, Jany
  KKBB 302
  H 74
  5001 442, 578
Holt, Seth
  5001 515
Holt, Tim
  KKBB 304, 361
  5001 451, 704, 713, 788
Holton, Mark
  H 58
  5001 573
Holy Matrimony
  5001
Hombre
  KKBB 39
Home
  WTLGD 77

Home and the World, The (Ghare-Baire)
    SOTA 380-382
    H 432
    5001 (2nd ed)
Home Before Dark
    ILIATM 313
    KKBB 282:n
    5001
Home Box Office (HBO)
    WTLGD 321, 454, 464, 491
    TIAI 51
    SOTA 16, 281
    H 1, 20, 175
    ML 151
Home for Life
    DIM 207
Home Movies
    TIAI 38-39, 40
Home of the Brave
    KKBB 203, 284
"Home on the Range" (music)
    WTLGD 27
Homecoming, The
    KKBB 107-108
    R 220-221
    H 98
    5001
Homeier, Skip
    5001 78
Homes, Geoffrey (Daniel Mainwaring)
    5001 368, 557
Homme au chapeau rond, L', see *The Eternal Husband*
Homme de Rio, L', see *That Man from Rio*
Homme et une femme, Un, see *A Man and a Woman*
Homme qui aimait les femmes, L', see *The Man Who Loved Women*
Homolka, Oscar
    5001 48, 72, 317, 351, 450, 649, 668, 694
Honegger, Arthur
    KKBB 280
    TIAI 150
    5001 320, 605
Honey
    RK 18
    5001
Honey Pot, The
    5001
Honeymoon Killers, The
    DIM 105-107
    5001
"Honeymooners, The" (TV)
    SOTA 376
Honeysuckle Rose
    TIAI 40-45, 372
    H 10
    5001
Hong, James
    H 272
    5001 78
Honky Tonk
    5001
Honkytonk Man
    SOTA 238
Honorary Consul, The (book)
    H 167

Hood, Don
    TIAI 290
    5001 2
Hoodlum Priest, The
    ILIATM 134
    KKBB 14
    DIM 119
Hooker, Brian
    H 314
Hooker, Richard
    5001 469
Hooks, Jan
    H 59
    5001 573
Hooks, Kevin
    R 3
    5001 697
Hooper
    WTLGD 430
    TIAI 200
Hooper, Tobe
    TIAI 351-353; dir., *Poltergeist*, 351-353
    5001 588
"Hooray for Hollywood" (music)
    DIM 227
Hoover, Herbert
    RK 5
Hopcraft, Arthur
    5001 10
Hope and Glory
    H 367-370
    ML 58, 139
    5001 (2nd ed)
Hope, Bob
    ILIATM 11
    KKBB 7
    DIM 61
    R 131, 281
    WTLGD 66
    TIAI 90, 166
    SOTA 5, 177, 358
    ML 164
    5001 68, 116, 554, 596, 632, 633, 646, 750
Hope, Edward
    5001 766
Hopkins, Anthony
    GS 175
    DIM 91, 118
    R 347
    WTLGD 186, 510-511
    TIAI 83, 85, 261
    SOTA 184, 185, 186
    H 283
    5001 96, 215, 294, 315, 385, 423, 450, 860
Hopkins, Arthur
    5001 334
Hopkins, Bo
    5001 176, 394, 479, 495, 838
Hopkins, G. J.
    5001 722
Hopkins, John
    5001 502, 769
Hopkins, Kenyon
    5001 43, 347, 422, 719
Hopkins, Miriam
    KKBB 363
    WTLGD 343, 344

    TIAI 247
    5001 51, 59, 122, 132, 134, 194, 327, 542, 628, 753, 792
Hoppe, Rolf
    TIAI 337
    5001 477
Hopper, Dennis
    DIM 148, 297-299; dir., *Easy Rider*, 3, 4, 78, 84, 117, 147, 152, 173, 297, 298; *The Last Movie*, 297-299
    WTLGD 312-316; dir., *Easy Rider*, 84, 86, 455, 554
    H 204, 206, 271, 315, 317-318, 371, 460-463; dir., *Easy Rider*, 97, 232, 462; *Colors*, 460-463; *The Last Movie*, 461
    5001 22, 78, 87, 147, 210, 285, 409, 581, 618, 632, 790
Hopper, Edward
    TIAI 273
    SOTA 288
Hopper, Hedda
    KKBB 230, 355
    RK 23 (ill.), 24, 31, 40, 41
    R 151
    5001 15, 478, 535, 552, 554, 555, 730, 781, 847
Hopper, William
    5001 618
Hopton, Russell
    5001 483, 547
Hopwood, Avery
    5001 291
Hora da Estrela, A, see *The Hour of the Star*
Hora de los Hornos, La, see *The Hour of the Furnaces*
Hordern, Michael
    KKBB 138
    DIM 97
    R 203
    WTLGD 50, 104
    TIAI 433
    5001 29, 53, 59, 123, 221, 272, 277, 343, 717
Horgan, Patrick
    5001 864
Horman, Charles
    TIAI 310-312
Horman, Ed
    TIAI 310-312
Horn, Dimitri
    KKBB 271
    5001 286
Hornbeck, William
    5001 585
Hornblow, Arthur Jr.
    RK 33
Horne, Collin Wilcox, see Wilcox-Horne, Collin
Horne, Geoffrey
    5001 102, 719, 800
Horne, James
    5001 825
Horne, Lena
    WTLGD 475
    SOTA 294
    5001 106, 112, 349, 562, 716, 764, 772, 844, 848, 865
Horne, Marilyn

5001 119
Horner, Harry
    5001 327, 347
Horner, Jackie
    5001 563
Horner, James
    ML 260
    5001 288
Horniman, Roy
    KKBB 292
    5001 395
Horovitz, Israel
    DIM 150, 151
    TIAI 369, 370
    5001 39, 721
Horrocks, Jane
    ML 45-46, 47
    5001 204, 842
Horror Chamber of Dr. Faustus, The, see *Eyes Without a Face*
Horse Feathers
    KKBB 184
    RK 15, 83
    5001
Horse's Mouth, The
    KKBB 282:n
    H 8
    5001
Horseman, Pass By (book)
    DIM 294
Horton, Edward Everett
    KKBB 232
    SOTA 338
    5001 26, 35, 87, 187, 200, 278, 281, 329,
        336, 350, 359, 406, 436, 646, 792, 865
Horton, Louisa
    5001 17
Horwin, Jerry
    5001 642
Hoskins, Bob
    SOTA 298
    H 162-163, 164, 165, 166, 167, 409, 411-
        412
    5001 156, 431, 493, 735
Hoskins, see Farina
Hospital
    DIM 101-102
Hospital, The
    DIM 378-379, 426
    WTLGD 220
    5001
Hossein, Robert
    KKBB 339
    5001 630
Höstsonaten, see *Autumn Sonata*
Hot Millions
    GS 106
Hot Rock, The
    DIM 401-403
    R 318
    5001
Hot Tomorrows
    WTLGD 536-537
Hotchner, Tracy
    TIAI 236
    5001 492
Hotel

DIM 136
    5001 (2nd ed)
Hotel Paradiso
    KKBB 321
    GS 211
Hotz, Sandra
    5001 568
Hough, Richard
    SOTA 184
    5001 96
Hound of the Baskervilles, The
    5001
Hour of the Furnaces, The (*La Hora de los Hornos*)
    DIM 257-259
    5001
Hour of the Star, The (*A Hora da Estrela*)
    H 267-270
    5001 (2nd ed)
Hour of the Wolf
    GS 108, 157, 214, 216
    WTLGD 389
House & Garden (periodical)
    WTLGD 441
House Beautiful (periodical)
    WTLGD 377
House, Billy
    5001 719
House, Jane
    5001 273
House of Blue Leaves, The (stage)
    R 302
    TIAI 174
House of Games
    ML 28
House of Lovers, The, see *Pot-Bouille*
House of Strangers
    DIM 424
    R 173
House Un-American Activities Committee (HUAC)
    RK 28
    WTLGD 170
Houseboat
    WTLGD 21, 23
Household, Geoffrey
    5001 457
Housekeeping
    H 406-409
    5001 (2nd ed)
Houseman, John
    KKBB 49, 198, 363
    RK 8, 29, 31-32, 33, 34, 36-37, 38, 39, 50,
        52, 55, 56, 82, 84
    R 190, 268
    H 458-459
    ML 13, 40, 154
    5001 17, 31, 46, 86, 103, 144, 419, 443,
        564, 754, 765, 800
Houser, Jerry
    5001 686
Houser, Lionel
    5001 245
Houston, Donald
    5001 640, 819
Houston, George
    5001 343

Houston, Penelope
    ILIATM 64-65
Houston, Renée
    KKBB 282
    5001 341, 624
Houtem, Micheline Van, see Van Houtem, Micheline
"How Big Am I" (music)
    H 311
"How Do I Love Thee?" (poem)
    DIM 162
How Green Was My Valley
    KKBB 350
    5001
How I Won the War
    GS 118, 145-146
    DIM 15, 17
    TIAI 448
    SOTA 9
    5001
How the West Was Won
    5001
How to Beat the High Cost of Living
    TIAI 180
How to Marry a Millionaire
    ILIATM 322
How to Save a Marriage--and Ruin Your Life
    GS 18-24
How to Steal a Million
    DIM 37
    5001
How to Succeed in Business Without Really Trying
    H 300
Howard, Arliss
    5001 271, 748
Howard, Esther
    KKBB 313
    5001 58, 302, 313, 400, 483, 503, 726
Howard, Frankie
    KKBB 293
Howard, Gertrude
    5001 357
Howard, James Newton
    5001 250
Howard, John
    5001 436, 580
Howard, Kathleen
    5001 459
Howard, Ken
    R 53, 55
    5001 668, 724
Howard, Leslie
    KKBB 180, 288, 340
    TIAI 43
    H 136-137
    5001 266, 366, 374, 539, 577, 605, 638,
        659, 705
Howard, Mel
    WTLGD 80-82
    5001 329
Howard, Ron (Ronny)
    R 193
    TIAI 392-394; dir., *Night Shift*, 392-394
    SOTA 141-145; dir., *Splash*, 141-145, 157,
        163, 265; *Night Shift*, 142, 143
    H 4-7, 142, 473-475; dir., *Cocoon*, 4-7;

Splash, 6; *Night Shift*, 263, 273; *Willow*,
    473-475
  5001 144, 505, 514, 528, 677, 701, 840
Howard, Shemp
  5001 34
Howard, Sidney
  RK 10
  DIM 74
  TIAI 179
  5001 196, 305, 754
Howard, Trevor
  ILIATM 72
  KKBB 193, 327, 358
  GS 145, 147
  DIM 142, 190, 192
  R 147, 361
  WTLGD 65
  TIAI 426, 433
  H 306
  5001 102, 130, 151, 215, 239, 277, 306,
    351, 393, 443, 468, 505, 558, 648, 695,
    730, 760
Howard, William K.
  5001 244, 225, 593
Howard, Willie
  5001 106
Howards of Virginia, The
  WTLGD 4, 26
  5001
Howe, Irving
  SOTA 24
Howe, James Wong
  ILIATM 91
  KKBB 356
  RK 75
  DIM 103, 159
  5001 14, 98, 152, 244, 318, 344, 397, 463,
    466, 491, 533, 594, 597, 642, 663, 694,
    736, 755, 758, 782, 853
Howell, Dorothy
  5001 586
Howerd, Frankie
  5001 407
Howes, Sally Ann
  KKBB 255, 329
  GS 226-227
  5001 178, 523, 566
Howey, Walter
  RK 19-20, 41, 69
Howl (book)
  TIAI 193
Howland, Jobyna
  5001 338, 407, 635
Howling, The
  TIAI 191-194
  SOTA 232
  5001
Hoyningen-Huené, George
  5001 129, 327, 418, 707
Hoyt, Arthur
  5001 302, 313, 373, 726, 856
Hoyt, John
  5001 25-26, 79, 108, 184, 699, 852
Hrabal, Bohumil
  5001 142
HUAC, see House Un-American Activities
    Committee

Hubbard, John
  5001 109, 858
Hubbard, Lucien
  5001 511, 768
Huber, Harold
  5001 169, 280, 293, 400, 445, 686, 758
Hubert, Roger
  5001 225, 817
Hubley, Season
  WTLGD 544
  5001 319
Huckleberry Finn (Mark Twain)
  ILIATM 201
  TIAI 6
Hud
  ILIATM 24, 79-94
  DIM 173, 294-295
  WTLGD 170
  H 348
  5001
Huddleston, David
  R 14
  5001 46, 81, 266, 631
Huddleston, Michael
  TIAI 284
  5001 264
Hudson, Ernie
  SOTA 193
  H 381, 382
  ML 165
  5001 284, 826
Hudson, Garth
  5001 411
Hudson, Hugh
  TIAI 245-247; dir., *Chariots of Fire*,
    245-247, 455
  SOTA 147-151; dir., *Greystoke: The Legend
    of Tarzan, Lord of the Apes*, 147-151;
    Chariots of Fire, 148, 150, 169, 278,
    279
  H 94-96; dir., *Greystoke: The Legend of
    Tarzan, Lord of the Apes*, 19; *Chariots
    of Fire*, 75; *Revolution*, 94-96
  5001 131, 308, 627
Hudson, Rochelle
  5001 358, 384, 484, 589, 618, 672, 837
Hudson, Rock
  ILIATM 41
  KKBB 357
  GS 101, 222, 223, 226
  DIM 47, 225, 353
  R 51
  WTLGD 31, 147
  SOTA 132
  5001 19, 285, 441, 451, 663, 743, 850
Hudson, Toni
  SOTA 58
  5001 164
Huebsch, Edward
  5001 797
Huffhines, Kathy
  TIAI 190
Hugh Kelly, Daniel, see Kelly, Daniel Hugh
Hughes, Barnard
  5001 64, 341, 479, 541, 684, 832
Hughes, David
  5001 525

Hughes, Dorothy B.
  5001 359, 629
Hughes, Eric
  SOTA 146
  H 65
  5001 10, 835
Hughes, Finola
  SOTA 35
  5001 712
Hughes, Gerald Vaughan, see Vaughan-Hughes,
    Gerald
Hughes, Howard
  KKBB 296
  RK 81
  DIM 389, 420
  TIAI 72
  5001 328, 558, 616, 657
Hughes, John
  SOTA 173-175, 346-349; dir., *Sixteen
    Candles*, 173-175, 347, 348; *The
    Breakfast Club*, 346-349
  H 133, 135, 142, 317, 371; dir., *Sixteen
    Candles*, 133, 135, 371; *The Breakfast
    Club*, 135, 317; *Planes, Trains and
    Automobiles*, 421
  ML 118
  5001 99, 594, 684
Hughes, Ken
  GS dir., *Chitty Chitty Bang Bang*, 226
  DIM 181; dir., *Cromwell*, 181
  5001 123, 163, 540
Hughes, Lloyd
  5001 489, 511
Hughes, Mary Beth
  DIM 25
  5001 303, 552
Hughes, Wendy
  SOTA 59-60
  5001 431, 507
Hugo, Adèle
  WTLGD 55-60
  5001 717
Hugo, Léopoldine
  WTLGD 58
Hugo, Michel
  5001 490
Hugo, Victor
  WTLGD 55, 57, 59-60
  5001 345, 460, 483
Huie, William Bradford
  5001 626
Hulce, Thomas (Tom)
  TIAI 69, 70
  SOTA 249, 251, 253
  5001 21, 763
Hull, Dianne
  5001 458
Hull, Henry
  5001 132, 262, 304, 332, 421, 591, 765
Hull, Josephine
  KKBB 232
  5001 35
Humain, trop humain
  5001
Human Beast, The, see *La Bête humaine*
Human Comedy, The
  KKBB 285

5001

Human Desire
5001

Human Voice. The (stage)
WTLGD 310
H 288
ML 27

Humanité. L' (periodical)
DIM 203
WTLGD 97

Humberstone, H. Bruce
5001 327, 728

Hume, Alan
5001 815

Hume, Benita
5001 278, 599, 733

Humes, Mary-Margaret
TIAI 216

Humoresque (1946)
WTLGD 175
5001

Humperdinck, Engelbert
TIAI 116

Humphrey, Hubert H.
DIM 43

Humphries, Barry
5001 60

Hunaerts, Geert
H 464
5001 439

Hunchback of Notre Dame, The
KKBB 330
R 367
TIAI 82
ML 161
5001

Hunger (Sult)
5001

Hungry Men (book)
R 268

Hunnicutt, Arthur
5001 214, 619

Hunnicutt, Gayle
WTLGD 546
H 73, 74, 75
5001 466, 547, 743, 837

Hunt, H. L.
WTLGD 359
H 440

Hunt, Linda
TIAI 451, 455
SOTA 210, 286-287
H 14, 71
5001 94, 207, 214, 682, 854

Hunt, Marsha
5001 84, 318, 344, 563, 595, 688

Hunt, Martita
KKBB 265, 276, 329
5001 254, 301, 566, 649, 694, 717, 778-779

Hunt, Peter
DIM 85, 389; dir., *On Her Majesty's Secret
Service*, 85-86, 389
R 360; dir., *Gold*, 359-360; *On Her
Majesty's Secret Service*, 360
5001 291, 545

Hunt, Peter H.
R dir., *1776*, 53-55

5001 668

Hunt, Ruth
H 440

Hunter, Evan
5001 74, 79, 487, 860

Hunter, Holly
H 290, 417, 419-420
ML 141-44, 246-47
5001 21, 104, 484, 614, 738

Hunter, Ian
KKBB 228
5001 8, 75, 106, 683-684, 718, 865

Hunter, Ian McLellan
5001 637

Hunter, Jeffrey
ILIATM 66
WTLGD 398
5001 409, 661

Hunter, John
SOTA 28
5001 308

Hunter, Kaki
TIAI 49
5001 840

Hunter, Kim
KKBB 353
GS 38
5001 422, 586, 722

Hunter, Kristin
R 274
5001 407

Hunter, Ross
KKBB 121
GS 108
DIM 136, 173, 285
R 137-138, 140, 316
5001 12, 19, 436, 447, 451, 763

Hunter, Tab
KKBB 299
H 445
5001 421, 440

Hunter, Tim
TIAI 398-400; dir., *Tex*, 398-400
H 315-318; dir., *River's Edge*, 315-318; *Tex*,
316, 317, 445
5001 632, 749

Hunters of the Deep
KKBB 183, 184
5001

Huntley, Raymond
KKBB 277
5001 306, 351, 357, 569, 597, 623, 640, 826

Huntsberry, Howard
H 342
5001 48

Huppert, Isabelle
TIAI 101, 102, 104, 113, 114, 442, 444
SOTA 133, 135, 137
H 265, 266
5001 60, 128, 158, 222, 226, 291

Hurd, Gale Anne
5001 16

Hurd, Peter
WTLGD 527

Hurlbut, William
5001 102

Hurricane (1979)

TIAI 73

Hurricane. The (1937)
5001

Hurry Sundown
GS 208
DIM 59

Hurst, Brandon
5001 307, 756

Hurst, David
5001 97

Hurst, Fannie
5001 44, 263, 345, 358, 858

Hurst, Paul
5001 27, 280, 360, 685, 829

Hurst, Ralph
5001 285

Hurt, John
WTLGD 497-498
TIAI 83, 85, 113, 216
H 120
ML 129-32
5001 215, 335, 457, 479, 656, 759

Hurt, Mary Beth
WTLGD 439-440
TIAI 378
H 37
ML 88, 93-95
5001 150, 366, 566, 849

Hurt, Wesley Ivan
TIAI 123
5001 589

Hurt, William
TIAI 128, 129, 130, 170, 171, 256
SOTA 69, 70, 71
H 24, 25, 26, 416, 419
ML 67-71
5001 3, 20, 69, 90, 104, 230, 350, 400

Husák, Gustav
DIM 203

Husbands
DIM 222-224, 284
R 291, 393
5001

Hush...Hush, Sweet Charlotte
5001

Hussey, Olivia
GS 154
R 138
WTLGD 466
5001 181, 436, 639

Hussey, Ruth
5001 31, 534, 580, 732, 807, 847

Hustle
WTLGD 124-127
5001

Hustler, The
ILIATM 24, 159
DIM 47
R 165, 167
WTLGD 210
SOTA 152
H 223, 226
5001

Hustling (TV)
WTLGD 141

Huston, Anjelica
DIM 18

WTLGD 508
TIAI 181
SOTA 378
H 277, 304, 306, 403, 404, 406
ML 199, 203, 230-34, 283-87
5001 162, 177, 219, 279, 592, 600, 822, 842
Huston, John
ILIATM 11, 25, 298-304; dir., *The List of Adrian Messenger*, 10-11; *Freud*, 11; *The African Queen*, 24, 299; *The Maltese Falcon*, 25, 214, 299-300; *The Treasure of Sierra Madre*, 25, 299-300; *The Misfits*, 37-38, 40, 299; *Moulin Rouge*, 47, 298-299; *Beat the Devil*, 214, 299; *Moby Dick*, 298-299, 303; *Key Largo*, 299; *Across the Pacific*, 299; *In This Our Life*, 299; *The Roots of Heaven*, 299; *Heaven Knows, Mr. Allison*, 299
KKBB 131-134, 229, 235-236, 290, 291, 297-298, 305, 360, 361; dir., *The Bible*, 131-134; *The Maltese Falcon*, 131, 304-305; *The Battle of San Pietro*, 131; *The Treasure of Sierra Madre*, 131, 134, 305, 361-362; *The Red Badge of Courage*, 131; *The African Queen*, 131, 180, 229 *Moby Dick*, 131, 134, 198; *The Roots of Heaven*, 131, 198; *The Night of the Iguana*, 221, 343; *Beat the Devil*, 229, 235-236, 248, 327; *The List of Adrian Messenger*, 297-298; *The Asphalt Jungle*, 338; *Key Largo*, 360
GS dir., *The Asphalt Jungle*, 183; *Beat the Devil*, 109; *Reflections in a Golden Eye*, 30, 31, 33-34
RK 52
DIM 17-18, 104, 105, 358; dir., *A Walk With Love and Death*, 17-18; *Reflections in a Golden Eye*, 17, 422; *The Kremlin Letter*, 104-105; *The Treasure of Sierra Madre*, 298
R 98-100, 316, 352; dir., *Fat City*, 6, 13, 124, 200, 432; *Beat the Devil*, 13, 184; *The Life and Times of Judge Roy Bean*, 98-100, 255, 283; *The Maltese Falcon*, 135; *The Misfits*, 153, 155; *The Treasure of Sierra Madre*, 270; *The African Queen*, 316
WTLGD 107-112, 122, 324; dir., *Beat the Devil*, 18, 234; *The African Queen*, 62-63, 275, 281, 508; *The Man Who Would Be King*, 107-112; *The Maltese Falcon*, 26, 110, 122-123; *The Asphalt Jungle*, 110; *The Treasure of Sierra Madre*, 26, 110, 178, 509
TIAI 65, 253, 343-347, 462; dir., *Annie*, 275, 343-347, 356; *The Treasure of Sierra Madre*, 387, 388, 479
SOTA 198-201, 375-379; dir., *Under the Volcano*, 198-201; *Prizzi's Honor*, 375-379; *Beat the Devil*, 376; *The Maltese Falcon*, 376; *The Man Who Would Be King*, 376
H 364-367, 402-406, 411; dir., *The Man Who Would Be King*, 119, 319; *The African Queen*, 364-366; *The Bible*, 364;

The Dead, 402-406
ML dir., *Chinatown*, 286; *The Dead*, 286, 313; *The Maltese Falcon*, 286; *The Man Who Would Be King*, 145; *Prizzi's Honor*, 75, 265, 283; *The Treasure of Sierra Madre*, 287
5001 4, 9, 29, 37, 55, 57, 67, 76, 117, 123, 135, 177, 238, 380, 384, 391, 394, 421, 424, 441, 454, 457, 461, 484, 490, 500, 526, 600, 619, 621, 719, 776, 788, 805, 822, 841
Huston, Tony
H 404, 405
5001 177
Huston, Walter
KKBB 134, 361-362
TIAI 74, 388
5001 23, 25, 196, 201, 206, 422, 455, 533, 558, 613, 672, 726, 788, 817, 853
Hutchings, Geoffrey
H 332
5001 842
Hutchins, Robert
ILIATM 211
Hutchins, Will
5001 677
Hutchinson, Josephine
5001 519, 533, 542, 646, 693
Hutchinson, Ken
5001 406
Hutton, Barbara
WTLGD 11, 23
Hutton, Betty
KKBB 185
R 134
TIAI 95
SOTA 178
5001 29, 305, 483
Hutton, Brian G.
5001 852
DIM 405, 407; dir., *X, Y and Zee*, 405-409
Hutton, Jim
TIAI 81
Hutton, Lauren
DIM 173
R 349
WTLGD 283, 444
5001 276, 426, 827, 866
Hutton, Robert
5001 459
Hutton, Timothy
TIAI 78, 81
SOTA 37, 42, 43, 162-163, 314
H 392, 393
5001 171, 233, 353, 448, 553, 606
Huxley, Aldous
TIAI 19
5001 595
Huyck, Willard
WTLGD 106
SOTA 177
5001 362, 443
Hyams, Joe
TIAI 21
Hyams, Leila
KKBB 253
5001 170, 266, 620, 647

Hyams, Peter
TIAI 217-220; dir., *Outland*, 213, 217-220
5001 516, 558, 786
Hyde-White, Wilfred
KKBB 294, 327
5001 408, 450, 459, 461, 508, 558, 794
Hyer, Martha
WTLGD 63
5001 121, 317, 640-641, 649
Hylan, Mayor
RK 68
Hylton, Jane
5001 569
Hyman, Bernard
5001 744
Hyman, Dick
H 424
5001 496, 604
Hymer, Warren
KKBB 256
5001 87, 185, 473, 487, 796, 809, 856, 857
Hynek, J. Allen
WTLGD 348
Hypatia
DIM 36

I

I Am a Camera
DIM 412
5001
I Am a Fugitive from a Chain Gang
KKBB 273, 283:n
GS 45
R 163, 208
5001
I Am Curious--Yellow (*Jag Ar Nyfiken*)
DIM 18
5001
"I Can't Get No Satisfaction" (music)
TIAI 26
I Ching (book)
DIM 230
WTLGD 90
I, Claudius (TV)
WTLGD 498
I Confess
5001
I Could Go On Singing
5001
I Cover the Waterfront
TIAI 300
5001
"I Don't Care" Girl, The
KKBB 234
I Dood It
5001
"I Feel the Earth Move Under My Feet" (music)
WTLGD 493
"I Guess I'll Have to Change My Plan" (music)
WTLGD 177
"I Hate People" (music)
DIM 197
I Heard the Owl Call My Name (TV)

R 324
"I Idolize You" (music)
   H 482
I Know Where I'm Going
   5001 (2nd ed)
"I Like Life, Life Likes Me"
   DIM 197
"I Love How You Love Me" (music)
   H 464
I Love My Wife
   DIM 231, 232
I Love You, Alice B. Toklas!
   GS 158, 237
   DIM 9
   ML 327-28
   5001
I Love You to Death
   5001 (2nd ed)
I Loved a Woman
   RK 36
I Married a Witch
   5001
I Married an Angel
   5001
I Met Him in Paris
   5001
I Never Promised You a Rose Garden
   WTLGD 316
I Never Sang for My Father
   DIM 169-171
   R 61
   5001
"I Only Have Eyes for You" (music)
   H 53
I Pagliacci, see *Pagliacci*
"I Put a Spell on You" (music)
   SOTA 262
I Remember Mama
   5001
I See a Dark Stranger (originally released in
      U.S. as *The Adventuress*)
   5001
I Walk Alone
   DIM 133
   TIAI 111
"I Shall Be Released" (music)
   TIAI 97
"I Talk to the Trees" (music)
   DIM 28
I Walk the Line
   DIM 199-200
   5001 (2nd ed)
I Walked with a Zombie
   WTLGD 534
I Wanna Hold Your Hand
   TIAI 98
   SOTA 164
   ML 226
I Want to Live!
   ILIATM 35, 143
   KKBB 50
   RK 10
   R 111, 149
   SOTA 216
   H 31
"I Want to Be Bad" (music)
   TIAI 274

I Was a Teen-Age Werewolf
   GS 91
I Was a Male War Bride
   ILIATM 307
   WTLGD 30
   5001
"I Went to the Animal Fair" (music)
   WTLGD 467
I Will, I Will...For Now
   WTLGD 147-148, 316, 317
   5001
"I Yam What I Yam" (music)
   TIAI 120, 123
Iannacci, Enzo
   5001 667
Ibañez, Vicente Blasco
   5001 83
Ibbetson, Arthur
   DIM 97
   WTLGD 424
   5001 96
Ibert, Jacques
   KKBB 260
   5001 197, 369
Ibsen, Henrik
   DIM 50, 52
   SOTA 140, 373
Ice
   DIM 163-168
   5001
Ice Follies of 1939
   TIAI 235
   5001
Ice Station Zebra
   GS 222-223
Iceberg Slim, see Robert Beck
Iceman
   SOTA 160-163
   H 34
   5001 (2nd ed)
Iceman Cometh, The
   KKBB 85-86
   R 196-201
   TIAI 413
   SOTA 331
   5001
Ichikawa, Kon
   ILIATM 161-162, 225-228; dir., *Kagi*, 148,
      160-163, 226; *The Burmese Harp*, 161,
      226; *Enjo*, 161, 226; *Fires on the Plain*
      (*Nobi*), 225-228
   KKBB 246
   SOTA 326-330; dir., *The Makioka Sisters*,
      326-330; *The Key* (*Odd Obsession*),
      327; *Fires on the Plain*, 327; *An Actor's
      Revenge*, 327; *Tokyo Olympiad*,   327
   H 307, 308, 432; dir., *The Makioka Sisters*,
      307, 432
   5001 245, 390, 454
Ide, Masato
   5001 389
Idiot, The (book)
   ILIATM 238
   KKBB 310
Idiot, The (1946)
   KKBB 262
   5001

Idiot, The (*Hakuchi*; 1951)
   5001
Idiot, The (*Nastasia Filipovna*; 1958)
   5001
Idiot's Delight
   KKBB 285
   5001
Idle, Eric
   ML 108
   5001 7
Idolmaker, The
   TIAI 114-117, 381
   5001
If...
   GS 279-286
   DIM 117
   5001
If Five Years Pass (stage)
   R 93
"If I Fell" (music)
   TIAI 294
If I Had a Million
   KKBB 68
   5001
If I Had a Gun
   R 120-122
"If I Only Had a Brain" (music)
   ML 64
If I Were King
   5001
If It's Tuesday, This Must Be Belgium
   5001
"If You Could See Her" (music)
   DIM 412
If You Could Only Cook
   5001
Ikawa, Hisashi
   5001 615
Ike (TV)
   TIAI 52, 245
Ikiru
   ILIATM 170, 244
   TIAI 301
   5001
Ilf and Petrov
   DIM 180
   5001 796
Iliad
   KKBB 280
   DIM 430
I'll Be Seeing You
   5001
I'll Cry Tomorrow
   R 36
   SOTA 216
   5001
"I'll Give My Heart" (music)
   TIAI 337
"I'll Never Have to Dream Again" (music)
   TIAI 273
"I'll String Along with You" (music)
   DIM 284
"Ill Wind" (music)
   SOTA 296
Illicit Interlude, see *Summer Interlude*
Illustrated London News (periodical)
   KKBB 208

Illustrious Corpses
   TIAI 315, 316
Ilou, Edward L.
   5001 120
"I'm a Mean Ole Lion" (music)
   WTLDG 473
I'm All Right, Jack
   ILIATM 64-65, 77
   WTLGD 245
   5001
"I'm Confessing That I Love You" (music)
   H 53
I'm No Angel
   ILIATM 81
   KKBB 314
   GS 223
   WTLGD 6, 17
   5001
"I'm Still Here" (music)
   ML 274
Images
   R 79-81
   WTLGD 82, 548
   5001
"Imagination [Is Funny]" (music)
   ML 124
Iman
   5001 532
Imhof, Roger
   5001 713
Imitation of Life
   DIM 131, 217
   R 137
   WTLGD 145
   5001
Immediate Experience, The
   SOTA 41
Immoral Mr. Teas, The
   ILIATM 8
   DIM 58
Imperial Hearst (book)
   RK 71, 81, 82
Importance of Being Earnest, The
   5001
Impossible Camera, The
   DIM 309
"Impossible Dream, The" (music)
   H 382
In a Lonely Place
   5001
In and Out Book, The (book)
   SOTA 249
In Caliente
   5001
In Cold Blood
   GS 32, 102, 167, 272
   WTLGD 318
"In Dreams" (music)
   H 206
In Like Flint
   5001 (2nd ed)
In Name Only
   WTLGD 20
   5001
In Old Chicago
   5001
In Search of Noah's Ark

WTLGD 269
In the Heat of the Night
   GS 34, 75, 109-112, 242
   DIM 330
   R 441
   TIAI 437
   SOTA 271
   5001
In the Heat of the Summer (book)
   SOTA 334
In the Name of the Father
   TIAI 418
"In the Region of Ice" (story)
   DIM 32
In the Year of the Pig
   DIM 42-45
   5001 (2nd ed)
In This Our Life
   ILIATM 299
In Which We Serve
   5001
"In Your Eyes" (music)
   ML 134
Inadmissable Evidence
   DIM 89
   WTLGD 149
Inconnus dans la maison, Les, see *Strangers in the House*
Incredible Sarah, The
   WTLGD 204-206
   5001
Incredible Shrinking Man, The
   KKBB 184
   TIAI 160
   5001 (2nd ed)
Incredible Shrinking Woman, The
   TIAI 160-162
   5001
Inda, Estela
   KKBB 323
   5001 544
Indagine su un Cittadino al di sopra di Ogni Sospetto, see *Investigation of a Citizen Above Suspicion*
Independence Day
   SOTA 281-282
   H 263
   5001 (2nd ed)
Indiana Jones and the Last Crusade
   ML 145-49
   5001 (2nd ed)
Indiana Jones and the Temple of Doom
   SOTA 175-182, 234
   H 101
   ML 148, 149
   5001 (2nd ed)
Indiscreet
   5001
Indiscretion of an American Wife
   5001
Industrial Light & Magic
   SOTA 179-180
   H 6, 474
Inescort, Frieda
   KKBB 296
   5001 278, 356, 419, 468, 595, 623, 858
Infancia dos Mortos (book)

TIAI 249
Informer, The
   ILIATM 119
   GS 9
   5001
Ingalls, Joyce
   WTLGD 491-492
Inge, William
   ILIATM 137-138
   R 74, 76, 222, 393
   TIAI 284, 413
   H 233
   5001 16, 148, 702, 723
Ingels, Marty
   5001 356
Ingenjör Andrées Luftfärd, see *The Flight of the Eagle*
Ingersoll, Amy
   TIAI 198
   5001 401
Inglis, Sarah
   H 131
   5001 689
Ingram, Rex
   KKBB 185
   5001 113, 215, 306, 650, 742, 756
Ingrassia, Ciccio
   H 124
Inherit the Wind
   KKBB 207
   5001
Inheritor, The (L'Héritier)
   R 202, 214
   DIM 151
   5001
Inn of the Sixth Happiness, The
   R 391
Innerspace
   H 336-338
   5001 (2nd ed)
Innocent, The (L'Innocente)
   WTLGD 540-542
   5001
Innocent Bystanders
   5001
Innocente, L', see *The Innocent*
Innocents, The
   ILIATM 163-172
   H 411
   5001 (2nd ed)
Inserts
   WTLGD 156-157
   5001
Inside Daisy Clover
   KKBB 283:n
   GS 73
   5001
Inside Moves
   SOTA 357
Inside the Third Reich (TV)
   TIAI 363
   SOTA 195
"Inside the Whale" (essay)
   DIM 125
Inspiration
   KKBB 285
Insull, Gladys Wallis

RK 10-11, 66, 67
Insull, Samuel
　RK 11, 66-67, 81
Interiors
　WTLGD 427, 437-440
　TIAI 90
　ML 13, 15
　H 116, 426
　5001
Interlenghi, Franco
　ILIATM 115
　KKBB 366
　R 171
　5001 52, 817
Interlude
　TIAI 43
Intermezzo: A Love Story
　WTLGD 477
　TIAI 43, 44
　5001
Internal Affairs
　ML 262-64
　5001 (2nd ed)
International Chrysis
　5001 606
International Settlement
　GS 116
International Velvet
　5001 479
"Internationale" (music)
　WTLGD 331
Intimate Lighting (Intimní osvetlení)
　R 357
　WTLGD 79
　5001
Intimní osvetlení, see *Intimate Lighting*
Intolerance
　ILIATM 222, 277, 282, 341
　KKBB 131-132, 309
　GS 42-47
　RK 69
　DIM 319, 320
　WTLGD 324, 557
　TIAI 146
　H 338, 339, 340
　5001
Intruder in the Dust
　KKBB 283-286:n
　DIM 75
　5001
Invasion of the Body Snatchers, The (1956)
　KKBB 286:n
　DIM 275
　R 109, 305, 442
　WTLGD 520, 524
　SOTA 187
　H 211
　5001
Invasion of the Body Snatchers (1978)
　WTLGD 520-524
　SOTA 63, 70, 217
　H 211, 432
　5001
Invention of Destruction, see *The Deadly Invention*
Investigation of a Citizen Above Suspicion (Indagine su un Cittadino al di sopra de

Ogni Sospetto)
　DIM 221-222
　R 208, 215
　5001
Invisible Man, The
　5001
Invisible Man Returns, The
　5001
Invitation, The
　WTLGD 286
Invitation to Happiness
　5001
Invitation to the Dance
　5001
Ionesco, Eugène
　KKBB 20
　GS 150
　WTLGD 520
Ipalé, Aharon
　SOTA 373
　5001 371, 677
Ipcress File, The
　KKBB 10
　R 40
　5001
Iphigenia
　WTLGD 378-379
　5001
Iphigenia in Aulis (stage)
　WTLGD 378-379
Ireland, Jill
　WTLGD 42
　5001 269, 318
Ireland, John
　KKBB 338
　5001 6, 19, 620, 699, 822
Irene
　WTLGD 13
　5001
Irish, William
　5001 578
Irma la Douce
　ILIATM 10, 14
　5001
Irons, Jeremy
　TIAI 238, 239
　SOTA 237
　ML 287-89
　5001 267, 734
Ironweed
　H 420-421
　5001 (2nd ed)
Irreconcilable Differences
　H 273
Irvin, John
　TIAI 167-169; dir., *The Dogs of War*, 167-169, 275; *Tinker, Tailor, Soldier, Spy* (TV), 168
　H 130-131, 169-171, 353-355; dir., *Turtle Diary*, 130-131, 353; *Raw Deal*, 169-171, 353; *Hard Times* (TV), 169; *Tinker, Tailor, Soldier, Spy* (TV), 169, 353; *The Dogs of War*, 169, 353; *Hamburger Hill*, 353-355
　5001 197, 315, 617, 795
Irving, Amy
　WTLGD 210, 419

TIAI 38, 43, 44, 45, 132, 133
　SOTA 88, 90, 304, 305
　5001 122, 150, 273, 340, 478, 855
Irving, John
　TIAI 376, 378, 379-380, 381
　5001 849
Irving, Robert
　5001 III, 722
Irwin, Mark
　5001 567
Is There Sex After Death?
　DIM 324-326
　5001
Isaacs, Susan
　H 36, 37
　ML 40
　5001 150
Isabel
　5001
Isadora
　WTLGD 307
　TIAI 212
　H 49
Isakssom, Ulla
　5001 104
Isham, Mark
　5001 791
Isherwood, Christopher
　KKBB 300
　DIM 410-412
　5001 99, 112, 348, 440, 627, 720
Ishtar
　H 309-312
　5001 (2nd ed)
Island, The
　KKBB 286-287:n
　5001
Island of Lost Souls
　WTLGD 451
Islands in the Stream
　WTLGD 278-283, 452, 453
　5001
Isle of the Dead
　5001
Israel Rank (book)
　KKBB 292
It Can't Happen Here
　GS 90
It Happened One Night
　KKBB 48
　RK 20, 48
　R 176, 408-409
　WTLGD 6, 16, 29
　SOTA 306, 307
　H 111
　5001
"It Hurts to Face Reality" (music)
　TIAI 481
It Should Happen to You
　GS 185
　5001
It Started with Eve
　5001
It's a Gift
　TIAI 157
"It's a Good Life"
　SOTA 20

126

It's a Mad, Mad, Mad, Mad World
  KKBB 209
It's a Wonderful Life
  KKBB 184
  WTLGD 178
  SOTA 187, 306
  ML 127
  5001
It's a Wonderful World
  5001
It's Always Fair Weather
  KKBB 222, 234, 287-288:n
  WTLGD 45
  5001
It's in the Bag
  DIM 180
It's Love I'm After
  KKBB 288
  5001
"It's Never Too Late to Fall in Love" (music)
  DIM 382
"It's Not Easy Being Me" (music)
  TIAI 123
"It's the Girl" (music)
  TIAI 275
Italian Straw Hat, The (Un Chapeau de paille d'Italie)
  KKBB 287:n, 320
  GS 211
  5001
Itami, Juzo
  H 306-309; dir., *Tampopo*, 306-309; *The Funeral*, 307
  5001 454, 743
"Itsy Bitsy Spider, The" (music)
  H 191
Ittimangnaq, Zachary
  5001 519
Iturbi, José
  WTLGD 335
  5001 25, 764, 765
Ivan, Rosalind
  5001 155, 382, 533, 659, 733
Ivan the Terrible, Parts I and II (Ivan Grosny)
  KKBB 288-289:n, 367
  GS 157
  DIM 242
  WTLGD 324, 331, 550
  5001
Ivanhoe
  KKBB 180, 184
  TIAI 198
  SOTA 357
  5001
Ivano, Paul
  5001 672
Ivanoff, Alexandra
  5001 600
"I've Got a Gal in Kalamazoo" (music)
  SOTA 296
Ivens, Joris
  ILIATM 289
Ives, Burl
  KKBB 327
  5001 125, 210, 556
Ivey, Dana
  5001 147, 191, 592

Ivey, Judith
  SOTA 128
  H 36, 37, 258, 259, 260
  ML 308
  5001 103, 150, 227, 431
Ivory, James
  DIM 195, 196; dir., *Shakespeare Wallah*, 195; *The Guru*, 195; *Bombay Talkie*, 195-196
  WTLGD 356-358
  TIAI 159; dir., *The Europeans*, 159-160
  SOTA 206-211
  H 125-130, 359-362; dir., *A Room with a View*, 125-130, 359, 361; *Maurice*, 359-362
  5001 90, 94, 470, 640, 642

J

J'Accuse
  WTLGD 500
  TIAI 145, 147
Jabara, Paul
  5001 479
Jabberwocky
  H 106
Jackson, Anne
  WTLGD 263-264
  TIAI 174
  5001 517, 674
Jackson, Charles
  5001 437
Jackson, Desreta
  H 82, 83
  5001 146
Jackson, Felix
  5001 33, 44, 185
Jackson Five (group)
  WTLGD 472
Jackson, Freda
  KKBB 277
  5001 302
Jackson, Frederick
  5001 716
Jackson, Glenda
  DIM 139, 141, 239, 242, 289-291, 380, 382
  R 51, 217-219, 346, 432
  WTLGD 93-95, 205-206, 262-266, 503
  TIAI 214
  SOTA 331-332
  H 130, 131
  ML 140
  5001 96, 360, 468, 504, 517, 600, 614, 626, 638, 728, 790, 795, 847
Jackson, Gordon
  SOTA 371, 373
  5001 123, 316, 596, 677, 771, 794
Jackson, Kate
  R 107-108
Jackson, Mahalia
  WTLGD 475
  TIAI 472
  5001 65, 379

Jackson, Michael
  WTLGD 472, 473
  5001 844
Jackson, Mick
  ML dir., *L.A. Story*, 327-28; *A Very British Coup*, 328
Jackson, Philip
  ML 88
  5001 331
Jackson, Ray
  KKBB 265
  5001 243
Jackson, Shirley
  R 320
  5001 321
Jackson, Shoeless Joe
  ML 126, 127, 128
Jackson, Victoria
  H 371
  5001 43, 350, 580
"Jacob's Ladder" (hymn)
  SOTA 57
Jacobi, Derek
  ML 216
  5001 329, 555
Jacobi, Lou
  DIM 255
  WTLGD 130, 357
  ML 282
  5001 36, 40, 370, 427, 508, 521, 642
Jacobson, Harlan
  ML 244
Jacobsson, Ulla
  ILIATM 106
  5001 688
Jacoby, Michael
  5001 130
Jacopetti, Gualtiero
  R 66; dir., *Farewell Uncle Tom*, 60, 66-67; *Mondo Cane*, 66; *Women of the World*, 66; *Africa Addio*, 66
  5001 237, 493
Jacques, Yves
  H 238
  5001 182
Jade, Claude
  GS 275
  DIM 244-245
  5001 59, 716, 781
Jaeckel, Richard
  5001 148, 513, 569, 710, 798
Jaffe, Sam
  KKBB 180, 278
  WTLGD 18
  5001 37, 60, 63, 301, 311, 436, 658, 760
Jaffrey, Saeed
  WTLGD 108
  TIAI 433
  H 119, 389
  5001 277, 461, 506, 568, 837
Jag Ar Nyfiken, see I Am Curious--Yellow
Jagged Edge
  H 56-58
  5001 (2nd ed)
Jagger, Dean
  KKBB 233, 277
  5001 47, 215, 303, 322, 534

Jagger, Mick
    DIM 112, 156, 206-211
    WTLGD 449
    TIAI 26, 95, 203
    SOTA 214, 215
    ML 301
Jaglom, Henry
    5001 409
Jaguar Woman (book)
    H 21
Jahan, Marine
    5001 250
Jailhouse Rock
    5001
Jakoby, Don
    TIAI 485
    5001 34, 87
Jalsaghar, see *The Music Room*
Jamaica Inn
    5001
James, Brion
    5001 80, 261
James Brothers
    KKBB 48, 50
James, Clifton
    R 347
    WTLGD 90
    5001 174, 408, 462, 546, 616, 622, 682,
      719, 839
James, Clive
    WTLGD 509
James, Elizabeth
    5001 93
James, Emrys
    TIAI 221
James, Geraldine
    ML 272
    5001 277, 742
James, Harry
    H 115
    5001 64
James, Henry
    ILIATM 131, 149, 164, 166-171
    KKBB 112, 354
    GS 171
    WTLGD 111
    SOTA 206-209, 210, 211
    H 61, 125
    5001 94, 327, 364, 528, 677
James, Olga
    5001 119
James P. Johnson's Orchestra
    5001 650
James, Peter
    5001 205
James, Rian
    5001 262
James, Sidney
    KKBB 291, 294, 295
    5001 185, 393, 408, 414, 779
Jamies, The
    WTLGD 415
Jandl, Ivan
    5001 661
Jane Eyre (1943)
    H 447
Janis, Conrad

5001 535
Janis, Elsie
    5001 566
Janney, Leon
    5001 132
Janney, William
    5001 478
Jannings, Emil
    KKBB 240, 243, 315, 367
    GS 265
    WTLGD 37, 316
    5001 85, 409, 812, 824
Janowitz, Hans
    KKBB 243
    5001 113
Jansen, Pierre
    GS 148
Janssen, David
    DIM 86
    R 359
    WTLGD 140
    5001 467, 548
Janssen, Werner
    5001 698
Japanese Film, The (book)
    ILIATM 121
"Jar, The" (story)
    H 124
Jardín de las Delicias, El, see *The Garden of
    Delights*
Jarman, Claude
    5001 Jr., 368, 631, 854
Jarman, Claude Jr.
    KKBB 185, 286
Jarmin, Gary
    H 439
Jarmusch, Jim
    SOTA 260-263
    H 221-223; dir., *Down by Law*, 221-223;
      Stranger Than Paradise, 221, 222
    ML 198
    5001 200, 720
Jarre, Kevin
    ML 257
    5001 288, 615
Jarre, Maurice
    ILIATM 7
    DIM 189
    WTLGD 109
    TIAI 117, 453
    ML 7
    5001 146, 230, 298, 415, 461, 568, 601,
      625, 648, 854
Järrel, Stig
    5001 782
Jarrell, Randall
    WTLGD 421
Jarrico, Paul
    5001 764, 778
Jarrott, Charles
    DIM 96-97; dir., *Anne of the Thousand
      Days*, 95-97
    R 137, 140; dir., *Lost Horizon* (1973),
      137-140; *Anne of a Thousand Days*,
      140; *Mary, Queen of Scots*, 140
    5001 29, 436, 468
Jarvis, Howard

5001 12
Jason, Leigh
    5001 445
Jaubert, Maurice
    WTLGD 58
    5001 37, 120, 383, 409, 461
Javal, Bertrand
    5001 151
Jaws
    WTLGD 40, 123, 156, 195, 203, 208, 349,
      350, 352, 427, 520
    TIAI 195, 427
    SOTA 22, 182
    5001
Jaws II
    TIAI 195
Jayston, Michael
    DIM 368
    R 219, 220
    5001 163, 338, 522, 602
Jazz (book)
    ML 2
"Jazz Hot, Le" (music)
    TIAI 332
Jazz Messengers (group)
    KKBB 297
    5001 420
Jazz on a Summer's Day
    5001
Jazz Singer, The
    RK 8
    H 342
Jeakins, Dorothy
    5001 322
Jean de Florette
    H 329-331
    5001 (2nd ed)
Jean, Gloria
    KKBB 314
    5001 520
Jean Le Bleu (book)
    KKBB 233
Jeanmaire, Zizi
    R 339
    5001 317
Jeannie
    5001
Jeans, Isabel
    5001 285, 785
Jeans, Ursula
    5001 127
Jeanson, Francis
    5001 136
Jeanson, Henri
    5001 120, 336, 575
Jeder für Sich und Gott Gegen Alle, see *The
    Mystery of Kaspar Hauser*
Jefferson Airplane (group)
    DIM 211
Jefford, Barbara
    5001 803
Jeffreys, Anne
    5001 714
Jeffries, Lionel
    WTLGD 50
    5001 116, 145, 443, 552, 645
Jellicoe, Ann

5001 401
Jemison, Anna
  TIAI 341
  5001 687
Jendly, Roger
  WTLGD 180
Jenkins, Albin
  WTLGD 164
Jenkins, Allen
  KKBB 256, 307
  5001 48, 177, 185, 233, 262, 348, 406, 466,
    665, 686, 753, 768, 783
Jenkins, Dan
  WTLGD 358-359, 361
  5001 665
Jenkins, Jackie "Butch"
  KKBB 316
  R 389
  5001 344, 507, 517, 726
Jenkins, Larry Flash
  5001 251
Jenkins, Megs
  5001 365, 664
Jenkins, Paul
  WTLGD 412
Jenks, Frank
  KKBB 281
  5001 248, 254, 293, 335
Jennings, Talbot
  5001 28, 293, 505, 638, 689, 700
Jennings, William Dale
  DIM 390
  5001 160
Jenny Lamour, see *Quai des Orfèvres*
Jens, Salome
  5001 387, 663
Jensen, Wiers
  5001 176
Jeremiah Johnson
  R 87-88, 98-99, 283
  5001
Jergens, Adele
  5001 144
Jericho Mile, The (TV)
  TIAI 188
Jerk, The
  TIAI 195
  SOTA 2, 3
Jerome, Helen
  5001 153, 595
Jersey, William C.
  GS dir., *A Time for Burning*, 13
  DIM 207; dir., *A Time for Burning*, 207
Jessel, Patricia
  5001 272
Jessop, Clytie
  5001 365
Jessua, Alain
  DIM 418; dir., *Life Upside Down*, 418
  WTLGD 354
Jesus Christ Superstar
  R 321, 371
Jetée, La
  KKBB 292
Jeune homme et la mort, Le (dance)
  H 65
Jeux de l'amour, Les, see *The Love Game*

Jeux interdits, see *Forbidden Games*
Jewel in the Crown, The (TV)
  H 369
  ML 46
Jewell, Isabel
  KKBB 252, 308
  DIM 69
  5001 81, 91, 123, 156, 226, 332, 436, 463,
    466, 741
Jewison, Norman
  GS dir., *The Cincinnati Kid*, 169; *In the
    Heat of the Night*, 34, 75, 109-112, 242;
    The Thomas Crown Affair*, 92, 111-115,
    117, 166
  DIM 74, 327, 330-332; dir., *Gaily, Gaily*,
    73-74; *Fiddler on the Roof*, 327-333,
    426; *In the Heat of the Night*, 330; *The
    Russians Are Coming*, 330
  R 441; dir., *Gaily, Gaily*, 13; *The Thomas
    Crown Affair*, 135, 441; *The Cincinnati
    Kid*, 441; *The Russians Are Coming*,
    302, 427, 441; *In the Heat of the Night*,
    441
  TIAI 445-446; dir., *...And Justice for All*,
    153, 329; *F.I.S.T.*, 289; *In the Heat of
    the Night*, 437; *Best Friends*, 445-446,
    463
  SOTA 271-274; dir., *Fiddler on the Roof*,
    44; *A Soldier's Story*, 271-274; *In the
    Heat of the Night*, 271
  H 423-425; dir., *Agnes of God*, 243;
    Moonstruck, 423-425
  5001 64, 197, 242, 275, 353, 360, 407, 496,
    647, 691, 763
Jezebel
  KKBB 289-290:n
  R 431
  5001
Jhabvala, Ruth Prawer
  WTLGD 356-357
  SOTA 209
  H 126, 129
  ML 21
  5001 90, 94, 447, 640, 642
Jigokumon, see *Gate of Hell*
Jillian, Ann
  5001 311
Jim Henson's Creature Shop
  H 53
  5001 745
Jiminez, Neal
  H 316, 317
  5001 632
Jinx, The
  5001
Jinxed!
  TIAI 411-413
  ML 73
  5001 (2nd ed)
Jo Jo Dancer, Your Life Is Calling
  H 144-148
  5001 (2nd ed)
Joan of Arc
  DIM 311
Joanna
  GS 193-195, 199
  DIM 151

Joano, Clotilde
  5001 91
Job, Enrico
  SOTA 254
  5001 76, 667
Jobert, Marlène
  WTLGD 286
  5001 757, 848
Jobim
  5001 6
Jodorowsky, Alexandro
  DIM 334, 337-340; dir., *El Topo*, 334-340
  R 98-99
  WTLGD 82
  TIAI 127
  5001 781
Joe
  DIM 148, 152-153, 313
  R 66, 116, 161, 229-230, 309
  WTLGD 86, 223, 369, 495
  H 169, 482
Joe Hill
  5001 (2nd ed)
Joffé, Roland
  SOTA 274-279; dir., *The Killing Fields*, 270,
    274-279
  ML dir., *Fat Man and Little Boy*, 207-208
  5001 239, 395
Johann, Zita
  5001 501, 771
Johansen, David (Buster Poindexter)
  ML 40
  5001 660
Johar, I. S.
  WTLGD 465
  5001 181
John and Mary
  DIM 72-73
  R 318
  H 177
  5001
"John Brown's Body" (song)
  TIAI 447
John-Frederics
  5001 82, 405
John Goldfarb, Please Come Home
  R 248
John Meade's Woman
  RK 36
John Paul, Pope
  ML 310-11
John, Rosamund
  5001 235, 306
Johnny Belinda
  5001
Johnny Eager
  5001
Johnny Got His Gun (book)
  ML 251
Johnny Guitar
  DIM 335
  H 474
Johnny Handsome
  ML 193-94
  5001 (2nd ed)
Johns, Glynis
  ILIATM 305

KKBB 335
GS 195
R 115
5001 56, 129, 601, 729, 805
Johns, Mervyn
KKBB 255, 339
5001 178, 490, 639, 729
Johns, Tracy Camila
H 212
5001 673
Johnson, Alan
WTLGD 100
SOTA 111-112
5001 775
Johnson, Albert
KKBB 363
Johnson, Arnold
SOTA 152
5001 610
Johnson, Arte
5001 438
Johnson, Ben
DIM 295, 296
R 301-302
WTLGD 125
TIAI 399
5001 283, 410, 480, 549, 631, 671, 672,
   725, 749, 838, 839
Johnson, Brad
ML 246, 247
5001 21
Johnson, Brian
TIAI 222
Johnson, Celia
KKBB 243, 291
GS 288
5001 102, 118, 360, 393, 595
Johnson, Chubby
5001 114
Johnson, Diane
TIAI 3
5001 674
Johnson, Dots M.
5001 562
Johnson, George Clayton
SOTA 20
Johnson, J. J.
5001 826
Johnson, Jack
DIM 160
Johnson, James P.
5001 650
Johnson, Julia Migenes, see Migenes-Johnson,
   Julia
Johnson, Katie
KKBB 293
5001 407
Johnson, Kay
5001 23, 447, 488, 540
Johnson, Kelly
SOTA 242
5001 810
Johnson, Lamont
R 164-168, 330
WTLGD 450-451; dir., *Fear on Trial* (TV),
   172; *Somebody Killed Her Husband*,
   450-451

TIAI 212-214; dir., *Cattle Annie and Little
   Britches*, 212-214
SOTA 173
5001 126, 407, 692
Johnson, Larry H.
5001 435
Johnson, Lyndon B.
DIM 43, 112, 165
SOTA 63, 65
ML 95
Johnson, Lynn-Holly
5001 256
Johnson, Malcolm
5001 546
Johnson, Michelle
SOTA 132-133
5001 80
Johnson, Monica
SOTA 344
5001 437
Johnson, Noble
5001 264, 429, 501, 518, 672, 756
Johnson, Nora
5001 850
Johnson, Nunnally
ILIATM 320, 322; dir., *Night People*,
   319-331
KKBB 276
RK 10, 12, 18, 49-50
5001 78, 301, 337, 392, 488, 527, 642, 645,
   665, 765, 777, 845, 850
Johnson, Richard
5001 321, 602, 795
Johnson, Rita
KKBB 185
5001 33, 329, 453, 508
Johnson, Robert
H 142-143, 144
Johnson, Scott
ML 11
5001 571
Johnson, Van
SOTA 337, 338
ML 246
5001 103, 344, 446, 604, 677-678, 711, 772,
   834
Johnsrud, Harold
KKBB 98
Johnston, Alva
RK 47, 84
Johnston, Julanne
5001 756
Johnston, Margaret
KKBB 312
5001 494
Johnstone, Anna Hill
GS 237
Johnstone, Will B.
5001 341, 493
Johnstown Jets (team)
WTLGD 276
Joiner, Pat
5001 220
Joker, The (Le Farceur)
5001
Joli Mai, Le
5001

Jolson, Al
5001 288, 314, 642
Jolson Sings Again
KKBB 68
*Jonah Who Will Be 25 in the Year 2000 (Jonas
   qui aura 25 ans en l'an 2000)*
WTLGD 179-183
SOTA 137
5001
Jonas qui aura 25 ans en l'an 2000, see *Jonah
   Who Will Be 25 in the Year 2000*
Jones, Allan
KKBB 317
5001 97, 175, 244, 305, 524, 642, 679
Jones, Amy
H 131
Jones, B. J.
5001 90
Jones, Barry
5001 103, 287
Jones, Carolyn
KKBB 286
5001 70, 184, 368, 668
Jones, Christopher
GS 91, 276
DIM 117, 118, 189, 190, 191
5001 648, 766, 838
Jones, Chuck
5001 307
Jones, Constance
5001 488
Jones, Dean
5001 32, 377
Jones, Duane
5001 526
Jones, Edward Burne, see Burne-Jones, Edward
Jones, Elvin
5001 863
Jones, Evan
DIM 417
5001 558
Jones, Freddie
R 347
TIAI 84
5001 207, 215
Jones, Grace
SOTA 368
5001 815
Jones, Griffith
5001 794
Jones, Grover
5001 787
Jones, Guy
5001 488
Jones, Henry
5001 34, 181
Jones, James
5001 269
Jones, James Earl
DIM 112, 158-159
H 304, 305-306
ML 126, 128
5001 73, 218, 229, 242, 279, 304, 766
Jones, Janet
SOTA 309
5001 249
Jones, Jeffrey

130

SOTA 253
ML 219
5001 21, 61, 812
Jones, Jennifer
    KKBB 236, 248
    GS 39
    R 135, 318, 406
    WTLGD 57, 178
    SOTA 361
    H 392
    5001 52, 57, 122, 143, 206, 362, 446, 590,
        646, 683, 785
Jones, Jo
    5001 399
Jones, L. Q.
    5001 48, 513, 569, 838
Jones, Laura
    H 432, 435
    5001 333
Jones, Lauren
    WTLGD 188
    5001 118
Jones, Lawrence
    WTLGD 251-252
Jones, LeRoi
    KKBB 128
    GS 257
Jones, Madison
    5001 352
Jones, Marcia Mae
    5001 525, 753
Jones, Mervyn
    5001 381
Jones, Mickey
    5001 513
Jones, Peter
    5001 21
Jones, Quincy
    GS 184-185
    WTLGD 472
    H 82
    5001 147, 283, 341, 360, 381, 571, 844
Jones, Robert C.
    WTLGD 404
    5001 96, 150
Jones, Robertearl
    5001 715
Jones, Sam J.
    TIAI 124
    5001 250
Jones, Shirley
    R 432
    5001 215, 317, 504, 800
Jones, Spike
    5001 750
Jones, Susan
    5001 386
Jones, Terry
    H 301-302; dir., *Personal Services*, 301-302,
        331; *Life of Brian*, 301, 302
    5001 577
Jones, Tommy Lee
    WTLGD 435-436
    TIAI 66
    5001 66, 230
Jones, Trevor
    TIAI 187

5001 27, 34, 227, 486
"Jonny" (music)
    WTLGD 536
Jonson, Ben
    WTLGD 455
    SOTA 34
    5001 339, 819
Joplin, Janis
    DIM 85
Joplin, Scott
    R 245
    H 13
    5001 62, 715
Joppolo, Benjamino
    5001 119
Jorah, Samson
    5001 520
Jordan, Bobby
    5001 177, 686
Jordan, Dorothy
    5001 112, 662, 728
Jordan, Louis
    5001 254
Jordan, Neil
    H 164-168; dir., *Mona Lisa*, 164-168, 301,
        331, 369, 411; *Angel (Danny Boy)*
        (1982), 166; *The Company of Wolves*,
        166
    ML dir., *High Spirits*, 42-45; *Mona Lisa*, 42,
        139
    5001 332, 493
Jordan, Richard
    R 470
    WTLGD 62, 63
    SOTA 334-335
    H 298, 300
    5001 207, 268, 366, 473, 664, 853
Jordan, Will
    SOTA 123
Jory, Victor
    GS 121
    DIM 162
    5001 208, 474, 483, 711
Joseph, Edmund
    5001 853
Joseph II, Emperor
    SOTA 252, 253
Josephson, Erland
    WTLGD 390
    TIAI 487, 492
    H 431
    5001 104, 161, 236, 451, 804
Joslyn, Allyn
    5001 302, 326, 510, 531, 675, 736, 763, 774
Jour de fête (The Big Day)
    KKBB 290:n
    R 73
    5001
Jour se lève, Le (Daybreak)
    ILIATM 298
    KKBB 279, 332
    R 290
    5001
Jourdan, Louis
    KKBB 296
    SOTA 4
    5001 74, 285, 318, 419, 446, 531, 539, 565

Jourdan, Pierre
    5001 580
Journal d'un curé de campagne, see *The Diary
        of a Country Priest*
Journey into Fear
    5001
Journey to Jerusalem
    KKBB 71
Journey to the Center of the Earth
    KKBB 184
Journey to the Lost City
    ILIATM 300
Jouvet, Louis
    KKBB 140, 244, 245, 302
    5001 76, 120, 121, 194, 339, 442, 482, 606,
        781, 819
Joy of Sex, The (book)
    WTLGD 147
Joy, Robert
    TIAI 176
    5001 38, 184, 612, 768, 771
"Joy to the World" (music)
    SOTA 69
Joyce, Adrien/Adrian, see Eastman, Carol
Joyce, Alice
    KKBB 253
    GS 127
    5001 170
Joyce, James
    KKBB 169-170, 315
    GS 11, 43, 142
    DIM 124
    R 115, 449, 450
    SOTA 380
    H 402, 404, 405, 406
    5001 177, 568, 803
Joyce, Peggy Hopkins
    KKBB 313
Joyce, Yootha
    KKBB 280
    5001 321, 602
Joyeux, Odette
    5001 739
Joyless Street, The (Die Freudlose Gasse; also
        known as *The Street of Sorrow*)
    WTLGD 389
    5001
Joyride
    SOTA 232
Juarez
    WTLGD 206
    5001
    H 374
    5001
Juárez, Benito
    WTLGD 206
Judd, Robert
    5001 165
Judge and the Assassin, The
    TIAI 443, 445
Judge, Arline
    5001 405
Judge Dee (TV)
    WTLGD 467
Judge Priest
    5001
Judgment at Nuremberg

KKBB 207-209
TIAI 173
5001
Judith of Bethulia
5001
Jugert, Rudolf
KKBB 264; dir., *Film Without a Name*, 264
5001 243
Juggernaut
R 347-349, 407
WTLGD 50
5001
Jules and Jim (*Jules et Jim*)
ILIATM 211-212, 216-222
KKBB 33, 54, 61, 81, 125, 150
GS 20, 100
DIM 243
R 19, 21
WTLGD 56
TIAI 46, 48, 49, 50, 280
SOTA 183
5001
Jules et Jim, see *Jules and Jim*
Julia
WTLGD 304-310
H 243
5001
Julia, Raul
TIAI 297, 299, 354, 355, 389
H 24, 28, 37, 245
ML 51
5001 150, 224, 230, 400, 498, 550, 564, 746, 748
Julian, Rupert
KKBB 331; dir., *The Phantom of the Opera*, 330-331
5001 579
Juliâo, Jorge
TIAI 251
5001 584
Julien, Martin (pseud.)
5001 641
Julien, Max
5001 141
Juliet of the Spirits (*Giulietta degli Spiriti*)
KKBB 16, 189, 365
GS 100-101
DIM 129, 130
H 140
5001
Julius Caesar
KKBB 197-198
Julius Caesar (stage)
RK 62
Jumbo
KKBB 184, 234
June Bride
5001
Jung, C. G.
DIM 128
WTLGD 548
Junge, Alfred
5001 349, 376
Jungle Book
KKBB 184
5001
Junior Bonner

R 285
TIAI 333
Juno and the Paycock
H 336
Jurado, Katy
KKBB 242, 281
5001 109, 331, 549, 569, 806
Jurgens, Adele
5001 326
Jurgens, Curt
KKBB 258, 264
5001 85, 188, 219, 229, 434, 703
Just Between Friends
H 150-151
5001 (2nd ed)
Just Imagine
5001
Just Tell Me What You Want
5001
Justice est faite, see *Justice Is Done*
Justice Is Done (*Justice est faite*)
5001
Justice, James Robertson
5001 472, 490, 552, 717, 771
Justice, Katherine
R 107
Justin, John
KKBB 241
R 50
5001 100, 756
Justine
R 343
Jutra, Claude
R 6, 172; dir., *My Uncle Antoine*, 6; *A Tout Prendre*, 172
TIAI 421-424; dir., *By Design*, 421-424; *Mon Oncle Antoine*, 421, 423
5001 110, 510
Juvenile Court
5001

K

Kaa, Wi Kuki
SOTA 243
5001 96, 810
Kabinett des Dr. Caligari, Das, see *The Cabinet of Dr. Caligari*
Kaczmarek, Jane
SOTA 280
5001 234
Kadár, Ján
5001 678
Kafka, Franz
KKBB 112, 254, 306
GS 55, 78
DIM 220-222, 256, 417
WTLGD 389, 414, 479-480
SOTA 26, 70, 158
H 61, 109, 138, 211
ML 110
5001 368
Kagan, Jeremy Paul
WTLGD 466-469; dir., *The Big Fix*,

466-469; *Heroes*, 467-468; *Unwed Father* (TV), 467; *Judge Dee* (TV), 467; *Katherine* (TV), 467
5001 70
Kagawa, Kyoko
KKBB 246
5001 124
Kagemusha (*The Shadow Warrior*)
TIAI 137-142
H 92
5001
Kagi (*The Key*; also known as *Odd Obsession*)
ILIATM 148, 160-163, 226
SOTA 327, 329
5001
Kahal, Irving
5001 238, 255
Kahn, Gus
5001 253
Kahn, Herman
GS 122
Kahn, Madeline
DIM 432
R 280, 281, 404-405, 464-466
WTLGD 99-101, 373, 375
TIAI 216
H 379
5001 6, 37, 80, 331, 335, 831, 859
Kahn, Michael
WTLGD 435
TIAI 100
SOTA 179, 279
5001 147, 230, 234, 239, 531, 810
Kahn, Otto
5001 288
Kalatozov, Mikhail
5001 160
Kalem, Toni
TIAI 94
5001 598
Kalfon, Jean-Pierre
5001 74, 24
Kalitta, Connie
SOTA 80, 81
Kallay, Sandor
5001 446
Kallen, Lucille
R 131
TIAI 394
Kallman, Chester
WTLGD 38
Kalmar, Bert
5001 28, 206, 341, 391, 393, 766
Kamen, Michael
5001 493
Kamen, Milt
R 130
Kameradschaft
KKBB 290:n
5001
Kaminska, Ida
5001 678
Kaminsky, Stuart
5001 549
Kamp, Irene and Louis
KKBB 344
Kampmann, Steven

H 187-188
5001 45, 143
Kanawa, Kiri Te
H 129
Kanchenjungha
5001
Kandel, Aben
5001 790
Kander, John
DIM 411
R 460
5001 112, 272, 521
Kandy-Kolored Tangerine-Flake Streamline Baby
(book)
R 164
Kane, Bob
ML 159, 161
5001 54
Kane, Byron
5001 582
Kane, Carol
R 275
WTLGD 79-82
SOTA 152
H 379
ML 39-40
5001 120, 197, 329, 371, 408, 597, 610,
660, 811, 850
Kane, Helen
TIAI 274
5001 566, 766
Kane, J. D.
WTLGD 433
5001 154
Kane, Michael
TIAI 260
5001 698
Kane, Whitford
RK 65
"Kangaroo Hop, The" (music)
WTLGD 100-101
Kanin, Fay
5001 199, 627
Kanin, Garson
KKBB 228, 240, 330
R 322
5001 5, 44, 94, 199, 373, 467, 508, 569,
754, 778
Kanin, Michael
5001 845
Kantor, MacKinlay
5001 65, 310
Kaos (*Chaos*)
H 122-125, 340
5001 (2nd ed)
Kapelos, John
SOTA 347
5001 99
Kaper, Bronislau
KKBB 43
5001 422, 435, 619, 847
Kaplan, Jonathan
SOTA 79-83
5001 323
Kapoor, Shashi
GS 54
DIM 195, 196

H 388, 389, 391
5001 90, 652
Kaputt (book)
KKBB 252
Karas, Anton
KKBB 359
5001 760
Karate Kid, The
H 143
Karate Kid: Part II, The
H 143
Karin, Rita
5001 70
Karina, Anna
KKBB 112
DIM 281
TIAI 104
SOTA 227
H 390
5001 20, 49, 452, 577, 582, 719
Karlen, John
SOTA 153
5001 610
Karloff, Boris
KKBB 38, 232
GS 211
H 35, 68
5001 76, 101, 160, 265, 372, 469, 501, 542,
657, 663, 693, 743
Karlson, Phil
ILIATM 313
KKBB 233; dir., *The Silencers*, 8; *Hell to
Eternity*, 233
R 284, 285, 288; dir., *The Silencers*, 63,
284; *Walking Tall*, 282-288, 310, 313,
314; *Tight Spot*, 284; *The Phenix City
Story*, 284; *Hell to Eternity*, 284; *The
Young Doctors*, 284; *Rampage*, 284, *The
Wrecking Crew*, 284; *Ben*, 284, 286
5001 46, 681, 822
Karlweis, Oscar
5001 247
Karno, Fred
KKBB 274
Karns, Roscoe
KKBB 281, 362
5001 335, 373, 542, 754, 778, 796, 856
Karoubi, Jimmy
5001 582
Karras, Alex
TIAI 335
SOTA 146
5001 10, 81, 814
Karsh, Yousuf
WTLGD 281
Karski, Jan
H 84, 86
Karvan, Claudia
H 433, 434
5001 333
Kasdan, Lawrence
TIAI 208, 254, 255-256, 438; dir., *Body
Heat*, 255-256, 321
SOTA 68-71; dir., *Body Heat*, 3, 40, 202;
The Big Chill, 68-71
H 13-14; dir., *Silverado*, 13-14; *Body Heat*,
272; *The Big Chill*, 446

ML dir., *The Accidental Tourist*, 67-71; *The
Big Chill*, 69
5001 3, 69, 90, 154, 218, 350, 613, 626, 682
Kasdan, Mark
H 13
5001 682
Kastle, Leonard
DIM 106; dir., *The Honeymoon Killers*,
105-107
5001 339
Kastner, Elliott
GS 40
5001 223
Kasznar, Kurt
5001 287, 318, 399, 422
Kath, Katherine
5001 500
Katherine (TV)
WTLGD 467
Katisha
5001 480
Katrakis, Manos
5001 31, 214
Katselas, Milton
R 434-435; dir., *Report to the
Commissioner*, 432-435; *Butterflies Are
Free*, 434; *Forty Carats*, 434
5001 260, 624
Katsulas, Andreas
H 386
5001 692
Katt, William
WTLGD 209
5001 122
Katz, Alex
TIAI 36
Katz, Gloria
WTLGD 106
SOTA 177
5001 362, 443
Katz, Jonathan
5001 759
Katz, Mike
5001 602
Katzenbach, John
SOTA 334
5001 473
Kauffmann, Stanley
ILIATM 65, 89, 144-145, 154, 168-169,
174, 204-205, 212, 218, 221
Kaufman, Andy
TIAI 72
H 379
Kaufman, Bel
5001 808
Kaufman, Boris
KKBB 93, 298
5001 19, 37, 43, 111, 309, 432, 546, 571,
702, 795, 809
Kaufman, George S.
KKBB 273, 317
GS 68, 238
RK 9, 10, 11, 17-18, 24, 28, 37, 65, 66, 83-
84
R 242
ML 165
5001 28, 144, 190, 459, 524, 547, 637, 645,

665, 691, 703
Kaufman, Millard
   5001 47, 310, 614
Kaufman, Philip
   WTLGD 520-524; dir., *The White Dawn*,
      199, 523; *Invasion of the Body
      Snatchers* (1978), 520-524; *The Great
      Northfield Minnesota Raid*, 524
   TIAI 208
   SOTA 61-68; dir., *The Right Stuff*, 61-68,
      233; *The Great Northfield Minnesota
      Raid*, 63; *The White Dawn*, 63; *Invasion
      of the Body Snatchers* (1978), 63, 70,
      217; *The Wanderers*, 63
   H 427-432; dir., *The Right Stuff*, 98, 337,
      432; *Invasion of the Body Snatchers*
      (1978), 211, 432; *The Unbearable
      Lightness of Being*, 427-432
   5001 368, 613, 630, 803, 804
Kaufman, Robert
   DIM 150-151
   TIAI 428
   5001 266, 437
Käutner, Helmut
   KKBB 258, 264; dir., *The Devil's General*,
      258
   5001 33, 188, 243
Kava, Caroline
   5001 93, 854
Kavanaugh, Dorrie
   WTLGD 79-80
   5001 329
Kavner, Julie
   H 275
   ML 105, 324
   5001 316, 521, 610
Kay, Bernard
   5001 790
Kay, Dianne
   5001 531
Kaye, Claudelle
   5001 123
Kaye, Danny
   KKBB 234, 292
   DIM 25, 93
   R 131
   5001 253, 317, 401, 450, 663, 751
Kaye, John
   R 428
   WTLGD 422-423
   5001 22, 611
Kaye, Judy
   5001 387
Kaye, Nora
   WTLGD 346-347
   5001 795
Kaye, Norman
   SOTA 59-60
   5001 431
Kaye, Stubby
   KKBB 30
   5001 124, 311, 734
Kaylin, Samuel
   5001 713
Kaylor, Robert
   5001 121
Kaynkov, Stepan

5001 510
Kazakos, Costa
   WTLGD 378
   5001 370
Kazan, Elia
   ILIATM 48, 50-51, 55; dir., *East of Eden*,
      33, 46, 55-57; *On the Waterfront*, 47-55,
      57, 60, 93; *A Streetcar Named Desire*,
      47, 82; *Gentleman's Agreement*, 81;
      Splendor in the Grass, 137-138
   KKBB 93, 152, 232, 350, 352, 367; dir., *On
      the Waterfront*, 93, 191, 223, 350; *Baby
      Doll*, 93, 232; *Splendor in the Grass*,
      93; *A Face in the Crowd*, 152; *A Tree
      Grows in Brooklyn*, 185; *East of Eden*,
      223; *A Streetcar Named Desire*, 309,
      352-353; *Viva Zapata!*, 366-367
   GS 61; dir., *A Streetcar Named Desire*, 229
   DIM 48-53, 328; dir., *The Arrangement*,
      48-53, 252; *America America*, 50-52,
      328, 331; *On the Waterfront*, 152, 338,
      421, 426; *Viva Zapata!*, 175; *East of
      Eden*, 252
   R 126, 321, 330, 393; dir., *America
      America*, 7; *Splendor in the Grass*, 76,
      393; *A Face in the Crowd*, 127
   WTLGD 216-219; dir., *A Streetcar Named
      Desire*, 178; *Splendor in the Grass*, 210;
      On the Waterfront, 213, 447; *The Last
      Tycoon*, 216-219, 495; *Gentleman's
      Agreement*, 396; *East of Eden*, 447, 500
   TIAI 175, 284, 297, 391; dir., *On the
      Waterfront*, 110, 229, 322; *Baby Doll*,
      175; *The Last Tycoon*, 238, 241, 457;
      Splendor in the Grass, 284; *America
      America*, 284
   ML dir., *The Visitors*, 167
   5001 22, 35, 43, 88, 91, 209, 232, 411, 546,
      564, 583, 660, 702, 722, 818
Kazan, Joe
   5001 92
Kazan, Lainie
   TIAI 397
   5001 508, 550
Kazan, Nicholas
   ML 8, 11, 288
   5001 571
Kazantzakis, Nikos
   5001 322-323, 866
Kazin, Alfred
   TIAI 274
Kazurinsky, Tim
   H 177
   5001 2
Keach, Stacy
   DIM 112, 228, 349
   R 99, 432
   WTLGD 65, 140, 449
   5001 151, 218, 238, 421, 808
Kean, Marie
   H 403, 405, 412
   5001 53, 177, 431
Keane, Walter
   SOTA 189
Kearney, Gene
   5001 277
Kearney, Michael

5001 19
Keating, Larry
   5001 168, 287, 494
Keaton, Buster
   ILIATM 277
   KKBB 184, 325, 354; dir., *The General*, 184
   RK 14
   DIM 61, 244, 372, 431
   R 128, 131, 240
   WTLGD 47, 49, 160; co-dir., *The Navigator*,
      136
   TIAI 6, 115, 120
   SOTA 179, 222, 337, 340; dir., *Sherlock Jr.*,
      337, 340
   H 312, 313
   ML 75
   5001 55, 146, 272, 281, 288, 349, 423, 518,
      667, 673, 712, 730, 831
Keaton, Diane
   DIM 424
   R 241, 401
   WTLGD 147, 148, 316-320, 439-440
   TIAI 91, 279, 280, 282, 291, 293, 294, 295
   SOTA 27, 200, 257, 258, 259, 260, 290,
      291-292
   H 46, 233, 234, 235-236, 277, 377-378
   ML 33-37, 240, 310, 312
   5001 42, 162, 289, 290, 295, 352, 366, 425,
      434, 486, 610, 621, 676, 686
Keaton, Joe
   5001 673
Keaton, Michael
   TIAI 392-393, 394
   SOTA 143
   H 263-264, 265, 455, 456, 457
   ML 112-14, 158-64, 276, 277
   5001 54, 61, 202, 527, 528, 561, 783
Keats, John
   KKBB 223
Keats, Steven
   WTLGD 79-81
   5001 269, 329
Kedrova, Lila
   KKBB 160, 338
   5001 618, 782, 865
Keel, Howard
   KKBB 43, 185
   5001 30, 114, 398, 667, 679
Keeler, Christine
   ML 129-32
Keeler, Ruby
   KKBB 273
   R 474
   WTLGD 502, 504
   5001 255, 262, 288, 291
Keen, Geoffrey
   5001 193, 195, 281
Keene, Tom
   5001 555
Keeper of the Flame
   5001
Kehoe, Jack
   TIAI 77
   SOTA 204
   5001 118, 269, 414, 474, 589, 715, 808
Keighley, William
   KKBB 228; co-dir., *The Adventures of Robin*

Hood, 180, 184, 228
5001 8, 101, 208, 243, 306, 459, 532, 782
Keiko, Kishi, see Kishi, Keiko
Keitel, Harvey
R 170, 172, 414-415
WTLGD 132-133, 283-285, 381-383,
  406-408, 415-417
TIAI 301, 469
H 152, 371
ML 268
5001 15, 85, 92, 206, 234, 244, 473, 537,
  581, 745, 799, 827, 842
Keith, Brian
GS 33-34, 98
DIM 74
R 469
WTLGD 322
5001 275, 519, 523, 621, 622, 647, 719,
  841, 853
Keith, David
TIAI 22, 25, 52, 383
5001 108, 303, 361, 540, 641, 799
Keith, Ian
5001 141, 165, 248, 529, 680, 733, 767
Keith, Robert
5001 92, 399, 439, 475, 839, 850, 858
Kelber, Michael
KKBB 329
5001 566
Kelland, Clarence Budington
ILIATM 294-295
5001 487, 705, 760
Kellaway, Cecil
KKBB 296, 333
5001 200, 311, 346, 350, 366, 369, 419,
  591, 592, 594, 851
Kelleher, John
H 335
5001 211
Keller, Harry
5001 784
Keller, Helen
KKBB 55
5001 804
Keller, Hiram
DIM 130
5001 240
Keller, Marthe
WTLGD 174, 302-304
H 372
5001 89, 172, 464
Keller, Sheldon
WTLGD 501-505
5001 141, 500
Kellerman, Sally
DIM 93, 228
R 55, 133-134, 138, 426, 427
WTLGD 283
H 186
5001 34, 45, 68, 101, 436, 469, 611, 687,
  827
Kellerman, Susan
H 300
5001 664
Kelley, DeForest
TIAI 358
SOTA 197

5001 614, 707, 708
Kelley, Martin J.
5001 568
Kelley, Sheila
ML 192
5001 100
Kelley, William
SOTA 320
5001 844
Kellin, Mike
WTLGD 128, 500
5001 267, 479, 521, 690
Kellino, Pamela, see Mason, Pamela
Kellogg, John
5001 220, 816
Kellogg, Virginia
5001 834
Kelly (costume designer), see Orry-Kelly
Kelly, Brian
KKBB 183
Kelly, Daniel Hugh
H 387
5001 692
Kelly, David Patrick
WTLGD 558
SOTA 231, 233
5001 203, 261, 823
Kelly, Emmett
5001 305
Kelly, Gene
ILIATM 145; co-dir., *Singin' in the Rain*,
  24, 81, 142, 145, 278; *On the Town*,
  278
KKBB 184, 185, 207, 222, 234, 287; co-dir.,
  Singin' in the Rain, 185, 232, 234; *It's
  Always Fair Weather*, 222, 234,
  287-288; *On the Town*, 287-288
GS 102, 263
DIM 82, 83; dir., *Hello, Dolly!*, 80-85, 185,
  328, 423; co-dir., *Singin' in the Rain*,
  209, 322
R 58-59, 130; co-dir., *Singin' in the Rain*,
  240; dir., *Hello, Dolly!*, 460
WTLGD 178; dir., *It's Always Fair Weather*,
  45; co-dir., *Singin' in the Rain*, 79;
  That's Entertainment, Part 2, 178
SOTA 338
H 174
ML 18
5001 23, 25, 103, 136, 159, 256, 260, 310,
  327, 363, 369, 374, 418, 546, 583, 683,
  727, 740, 764, 767, 848, 865
Kelly, George
RK 18
DIM 170
Kelly, Grace
KKBB 259, 281
GS 270
WTLGD 3, 126
5001 157, 189, 331, 491, 619, 775
Kelly, Jim
5001 221
Kelly, Nancy
KKBB 363
RK 17
5001 322
Kelly, Patsy

ILIATM 292
5001 226, 288, 582, 643
Kelly, Paul
5001 164, 243, 634
Kelly, Paula
H 145
5001 26, 381, 734
Kelly, Peter
ML 272
5001 742
Kelly, Tommy
5001 8
Kelton, Pert
DIM 62
5001 30, 149, 505
Kemble-Cooper, Violet
5001 638
Kemp, Jeremy
WTLGD 190
5001 123, 626, 667
Kemper, Charles
5001 368
Kemper, Victor J.
WTLGD 511
TIAI 369
SOTA 129
5001 39, 431, 541, 686
Kempson, Rachel
KKBB 10
5001 282, 778
Ken, Shih
5001 221
Ken, Takakura
R 469-470
Kendal, Felicity
5001 811
Kendal, Jennifer
DIM 195
5001 90
Kendall, Kay
KKBB 270
H 355
5001 167, 281, 418
Kendall, Suzy
GS 69
5001 761, 777
Keneally, Thomas
WTLGD 536
TIAI 54, 56, 59, 60, 268
5001 129, 188
Kennaway, James
5001 794
Kennedy, Arthur
TIAI 179
5001 11, 92, 215, 237, 332, 415, 519, 616
Kennedy, Burt
KKBB 43; dir., *The War Wagon*, 42-45
DIM 149
Kennedy, Edgar
KKBB 362, 364
DIM 123
SOTA 154
5001 25, 206, 374, 707, 793, 796, 806, 831
Kennedy, George
R 138, 364
WTLGD 466
TIAI 153

5001 12, 130, 181, 209, 311, 346, 417, 436
Kennedy, Jay Richard
    5001 357
Kennedy, Jihmi
    ML 258
    5001 288
Kennedy, Jo
    SOTA 292
Kennedy, John F.
    KKBB 151
    DIM 64, 112, 207
    WTLGD 5
Kennedy, Joseph P.
    DIM 43
Kennedy, Kristina and Michelle
    5001 43
Kennedy, Madge
    5001 126, 443, 467
Kennedy, Margaret
    GS 38
Kennedy, Merna
    H 471, 472
Kennedy, Phyllis
    5001 703
Kennedy, Robert
    RK 11
    DIM 31, 112
Kennedy, Tom
    5001 692
Kennedy, William
    SOTA 295
    H 420, 421
    5001 156, 370
Kennel Murder Case, The
    5001
Kenny, Catherine
    H 96
Kenny, William
    WTLGD 212
Kensit, Patsy
    H 158-159
    5001 3
Kent, Barbara
    5001 251
Kent, Christopher, see Kjellin, Alf
Kent, Jean
    5001 107
Kenton, Erle
    5001 478
Kenton, Stan
    5001 79
Kentucky Kernels
    5001
Kentucky Moonshine
    R 404
    H 483
Kenyatta, Caro
    5001 141
Kenyon, Charles
    5001 525, 578
Kenyon, Doris
    KKBB 252
    5001 156
Kerby, William
    R 166
    5001 407, 641
Kerensky, Alexander

KKBB 357
Kerima
    KKBB 327
    5001 558, 608
Kerkorian, Kirk
    DIM 188
    R 217
    TIAI 163
    H 21
Kermesse Héroïque, La, see *Carnival in Flanders*
Kern, James V.
    5001 750
Kern, Jerome
    GS 19
    5001 106, 117, 159, 333, 404, 679, 772
Kerouac, Jack
    WTLGD 398
Kerr, Anita
    R 110
Kerr, Bill
    TIAI 454
    5001 276, 854
Kerr, Deborah
    ILIATM 164-165, 172
    KKBB 184
    DIM 49, 52, 269, 347
    H 411
    5001 28, 35, 123, 269, 351, 365, 397, 453, 514, 526, 597, 729
Kerr, E. Katherine
    SOTA 109
    5001 681, 733
Kerr, Jean
    5001 750
Kerr, John
    KKBB 249
    5001 144, 824
Kerr, Laura
    5001 238
Kerr, Walter
    RK 4, 19, 84
Kerr-McGee (company)
    SOTA 106, 107, 109, 110
Kerrigan, J. M.
    5001 363, 532
Kerry, Norman
    KKBB 331
    5001 579
Kersh, Gerald
    KKBB 316
    5001 524
Kershner, Irvin
    KKBB 14; dir., *The Hoodlum Priest*, 14; *The Luck of Ginger Coffey*, 14; *A Fine Madness*, 14
    GS dir., *The Flim-Flam Man*, 75; *The Luck of Ginger Coffey*, 61
    DIM 119-122, 350; dir., *A Fine Madness*, 105, 119; *Loving*, 119-122, 351; *The Hoodlum Priest*, 119; *The Luck of Ginger Coffey*, 119-120, 122
    R 84, 318, 330; dir., *Up the Sandbox*, 82-84, 463; *Loving*, 83, 310; *Stakeout on Dope Street*, 329
    WTLGD 197-198, 435; dir., *The Return of a Man Called Horse*, 197-198; *Eyes of*

Laura Mars, 427, 431, 434-436
    TIAI 18, 294, 482; dir., *The Empire Strikes Back*, 8, 18, 39, 208, 349, 482, 483, 484; *Loving*, 294
    H 411, 432; dir., *Loving*, 432; *The Empire Strikes Back*, 473
    5001 217, 230, 244, 442, 625, 635, 809
Kerwin, Maureen
    R 202
Kesey, Ken
    WTLGD 84-90
    5001 549
Kessel, Barney
    5001 692
Kesselring, Joseph
    KKBB 232
    5001 35
Kestelman, Sara
    R 277
    WTLGD 83
    5001 424, 864
Kesting, Hans
    ML 292
Key, The (Odd Obsession), see *Kagi*
Key Largo
    ILIATM 299
    KKBB 360
    5001
Keyes, Daniel
    5001 132
Keyes, Evelyn
    5001 329, 668
Keyloun, Mark
    H 175, 176
    5001 480
Keys of the Kingdom, The
    5001
Keystone Cops
    KKBB 54, 273
    WTLGD 9, 17, 246, 456
    H 314
    5001 292, 831
Khambatta, Persis
    5001 837
Khan Din, Ayub
    H 388
    5001 652
Khmara, Edward
    SOTA 357
    5001 406
Khmer Rouge
    H 284
Khrushchev, Nikita
    DIM 201
Kibbee, Guy
    KKBB 273
    5001 42, 118, 139, 255, 262, 286, 291, 374, 489, 556, 613, 765
Kibbee, Roland
    KKBB 252
    5001 33, 163, 524, 656
Kid, The
    KKBB 327
    5001
Kid for Two Farthings, A
    KKBB 263, 290-291:n
    GS 202

5001
Kid from Spain, The
  5001
Kid from Texas, The
  DIM 296
Kid Galahad
  5001
Kidd, Michael
  KKBB 234, 287, 292
  GS 164
  DIM 82
  WTLGD 45, 503, 504
  5001 50, 311, 374, 402, 501, 667, 688, 706
Kidder, Margot
  R 195, 468
  WTLGD 526, 528
  TIAI 46, 47, 224, 424-425, 426
  SOTA 289
  ML 47
  5001 304, 324, 684, 730, 731, 840
Kidnapped
  5001
Kiefer, Anselm
  TIAI 450
Kiel, Richard
  TIAI 240
  H 16
  5001 495, 562, 682, 690, 703
Kienholz, Edward
  WTLGD 490
Kierkegaard, Søren
  KKBB 325
Kiesser, Jan
  SOTA 288
  5001 136
Kihn, Albert
  5001 770
Kilbourne, Fannie
  5001 453
Kilbride, Percy
  5001 234, 391, 698
Kilburn, Terry
  KKBB 275
  5001 297, 517, 736
Kiley, Richard
  R 388
  WTLGD 318
  5001 79, 219, 427, 434, 581
Kilian, Victor
  5001 83, 194
Kill Me If You Can (TV)
  WTLGD 506
  ML 201
"Killer Blow" (song)
  H 159
Killer Elite, The
  WTLGD 112-119, 557
  5001
Killers, The
  ILIATM 224
  KKBB 257, 291:n
  TIAI 173
  5001
Killer's Kiss
  KKBB 291
  5001
Killing, The

ILIATM 209
KKBB 291:n
GS 183, 277
WTLGD 105
5001
Killing Fields, The
  SOTA 270, 274-279
  H 183, 284, 475
  ML 203
  5001 (2nd ed)
Killing Joke, The (book)
  ML 159, 161
Killing of Sister George, The
  GS 206-208
Kilmer, Val
  H 474
  5001 780, 840
Kilpatrick, Tom
  5001 194
Kimmins, Anthony
  KKBB 243; dir., *The Captain's Paradise*, 243
  5001 118
Kimursi
  5001 397
Kind Hearts and Coronets
  ILIATM 289
  KKBB 256-257, 292:n, 294, 302
  5001
Kind of Alaska, A (stage)
  ML 319
King, Alan
  GS 52
  TIAI 369, 462
  ML 232, 317
  5001 25, 39, 111, 219, 387, 441
King, Allan
  DIM 107-109; dir., *A Married Couple*, 107-111
King and Country
  KKBB 105
King and I, The
  ILIATM 279
  WTLGD 334
King, Andrea
  5001 457, 629
King, Andrew
  5001 488
King, Betty R.
  SOTA 94
King, Carole
  WTLGD 493
  5001 687
King, Charles
  5001 105
King, Dennis
  5001 355, 566
King, Erik
  ML 168-69, 174, 176
  5001 124
King, Frank
  5001 310
King, Henry
  5001 13, 359, 623, 711
King in New York, A
  5001
King Kong (theme)

ML 7
KKBB 20, 38, 43, 249
GS 248
King Kong (1933)
  KKBB 184
  GS 36
  WTLGD 136, 234, 235, 237
  TIAI 483
King Kong (1976)
  WTLGD 234-239, 419, 475
  TIAI 180
  SOTA 225, 234
  5001
King, Larry L.
  TIAI 374, 375
  5001 64
King Lear
  ILIATM 251
  KKBB 161, 201-202
  DIM 354-357
  WTLGD 436
  ML 309, 313
  5001
King Lear (stage)
  H 89, 90-91
King, Mabel
  WTLGD 473
  ML 40
  5001 844
King, Martin Luther
  DIM 112, 226
  R 63, 295
  5001 348
King, Maurice
  5001 310
King, Morgana
  R 400
  5001 290
King of Comedy, The
  TIAI 456-461
  SOTA 123
  H 38, 41, 227
  5001 (2nd ed)
King of Kings
  WTLGD 398
King of Marvin Gardens, The
  R 272
  TIAI 175
  5001
King of the Gypsies
  SOTA 204
King, Philip
  5001 167
King, Rick
  5001 258
King Solomon's Mines
  KKBB 184
  5001
King, Stephen
  WTLGD 208
  TIAI 1, 5, 199
  H 197, 198
  5001 401, 674, 705
King Steps Out, The
  5001
King, Tony
  R 434

WTLGD 166
5001 624
King, Walter Woolf
KKBB 317
R 241
5001 48, 289, 524
King, Zalman
R 221
5001 685, 691
Kings Row
DIM 294
5001
Kingsford, Walter
5001 119
Kingsley, Ben
TIAI 432-433
H 130-131, 361
5001 277, 471, 795
Kingsley, Dorothy
5001 106, 399, 562
Kingsley, Sidney
WTLGD 271
5001 177, 186, 475
Kinison, Sam
H 186
5001 45
Kinks, The (group)
H 159
Kinnear, Roy
R 347
WTLGD 50, 100, 526
TIAI 233
5001 6, 343, 385, 767, 840
Kinsella, W. P.
ML 126
5001 242
Kinskey, Leonid
5001 48, 117, 122, 429, 462, 463, 472, 484,
577, 689, 717, 751, 792, 827
Kinski, Klaus
TIAI 363, 401, 404, 405
SOTA 217, 258, 259
H 253
5001 195, 247, 425
Kinski, Nastassja (Nastassia)
TIAI 135, 136, 296, 299, 336
SOTA 45, 46, 47, 155
H 94, 471
5001 125, 495, 550, 627, 749, 806
Kinsky, Leonid
KKBB 245
Kinugasa, Teinosuke
KKBB 268; dir., *Gate of Hell*, 266, 267-268
5001 280
Kipling, Rudyard
KKBB 278
WTLGD 18, 107-112
5001 118, 310, 386, 422, 461
Kipps
5001
Kirby, Bruno
H 282, 422
5001 290, 295, 773
Kirby, George
5001 791
Kirgo, George
5001 65

Kiri no Naka no Shojo, see *A Girl in the Mist*
Kirk, Lisa
5001 311
Kirkland, Alexander
5001 744, 760
Kirkland, Geoffrey
TIAI 295
5001 676
Kirkland, Jack
5001 777
Kirkland, Sally
DIM 55
5001 149, 715
Kirkop, Oreste
5001 355
Kirkwood, Gene
5001 355
Kirkwood, James
5001 728
Kirov, Ivan
5001 700, 701
Kirsanov, Dmitri
5001 476
Kirschstein, Rudiger
5001 158
Kishi, Keiko
R 471
SOTA 327
5001 454
Kismet (1944)
5001
Kismet (1955)
5001 (2nd ed)
Kiss (rock group)
WTLGD 556
Kiss and Make Up
WTLGD 27
Kiss Me Deadly
GS 208
SOTA 212
Kiss Me Kate
KKBB 234
GS 153
TIAI 275
5001
Kiss Me, Stupid
5001
Kiss of Death
SOTA 233
5001
Kiss of the Spider Woman
H 24-29, 289
5001 (2nd ed)
Kiss Them for Me
WTLGD 23
Kissing Bandit, The
TIAI 357
Kissinger, Henry
WTLGD 265, 284
H 2, 3
Kitchen, Michael
H 78, 80
5001 557
Kitt, Eartha
R 261
"Kitten on the Keys" (music)
TIAI 253

Kitty Foyle
RK 7
5001
Kitzmiller, John
KKBB 365
5001 813
Kjellin, Alf (Christopher Kent)
KKBB 353
GS 223
5001 446, 675, 727, 782
Klane, Robert
DIM 186
SOTA 153
5001 806, 832
Klauber, Gertan
5001 667
Klein, Adelaide
5001 220
Klein, Calvin
ML 122
Klein, Robert
DIM 184
5001 407, 559
Klein-Rogge, Rudolf
5001 477
Kleiner, Harry
5001 109, 120, 234, 237, 485
Kleiser, Randal
TIAI 27-30; dir., *The Blue Lagoon*, 27-30
5001 86
Kleist, Heinrich von, see von Kleist, Heinrich
Klemperer, Werner
5001 331, 384, 675
Klempner, John
5001 419
Klimt, Gustav
ML 14
Kline, Kevin
TIAI 435, 436, 494
SOTA 69, 70
H 14, 148, 149, 399, 400
5001 69, 166, 350, 682, 695, 816
Kline, Richard H.
WTLGD 419
SOTA 222
H 264
5001 90, 116, 396, 783
Klos, Elmar
5001 678
Kloves, Steven
SOTA 152
ML dir., *The Fabulous Baker Boys*, 186-90
5001 232, 610
Klugman, Jack
5001 185, 349, 795
Klute
DIM 281-282, 285, 314, 352, 426
WTLGD 486
TIAI 293
H 243
5001
Knack...and How to Get It, The
KKBB 22, 23, 29, 116-117, 139
GS 14, 120, 145
5001
Knapp Commission
R 228, 232

Knave of Hearts, see *Monsieur Ripois*
Kneale, Nigel
   5001 222, 434
Knebel, Fletcher
   GS 95
Knebel, Levi L.
   SOTA 236
   5001 157
Knef, Hildegarde
   KKBB 264
   5001 243, 336, 456
Knickerbocker, Paine
   ILIATM 164
Knife in the Water
   ILIATM 15
Knight, Arthur
   ILIATM 84, 144
   KKBB 206
Knight, Christopher
   5001 724
Knight, David
   5001 4
Knight, Esmond
   5001 315, 328, 621, 628, 632
Knight, Fuzzy
   5001 200, 616, 700, 787
Knight, June
   5001 105
Knight, Shirley
   KKBB 89-90, 93
   GS 121
   R 348
   5001 219, 309, 385, 613, 734
Knight, Ted
   5001 800
Knightriders
   TIAI 197-201
   5001
Knights of the Round Table
   TIAI 182
Knoblock, Edward
   5001 398
Knock, see *Dr. Knock*
Knock on Any Door
   5001
Knock on Wood
   KKBB 292:n
   5001
"Knockin' on Heaven's Door"
   WTLGD 398
Knoll, H. H.
   5001 112
Knopfler, Mark
   5001 429
Knott, Frederick
   KKBB 259
   5001 189, 339
Knowles, John
   5001 665
Knowles, Patric
   KKBB 288
   5001 8, 130, 374, 684
Knox, Alexander
   5001 3, 193, 343, 523, 559, 670, 857
Knute Rockne--All American
   R 355
Kober, Arthur

RK 10, 18
   5001 322, 337, 472
Koch, C. J.
   TIAI 454
   5001 854
Koch, Carl
   5001 647
Koch, Howard
   KKBB 245, 295, 296
   GS 32
   RK 39-40, 55
   5001 122, 265, 419, 436, 548, 660
Koch, Howard W. Jr.
   5001 355
Koch, Ilse
   WTLGD 138
Koch, Marianne
   KKBB 258
   5001 188
Koehler, Ted
   5001 716
Koenekamp, Fred J.
   SOTA 219
   5001 7, 565, 570, 785
Koenig, Walter
   5001 708
Koenig, Wolf
   KKBB 248; co-dir., *City of Gold*, 248
   5001 139
Koerner, Diana
   WTLGD 105
   5001 53
Kohl, Herbert
   R 378
   5001 72
Kohler, Fred
   5001 769-770
Kohner, Susan
   DIM 131
Kojak (TV)
   R 423
   WTLGD 254
Kokoschka, Oskar
   TIAI 140
Kolb, Clarence
   5001 6, 119, 531, 685
Kolb, Ken
   DIM 236
Koline, Nicolas
   TIAI 145
   5001 516
Kolker, Henry
   5001 336, 358, 445, 779
Komai, Tetsu
   5001 419
Komroff, Manual
   5001 658
Kon Tiki
   KKBB 184
Kongi's Harvest (stage)
   WTLGD 188
Koningsberger, Hans
   DIM 17
   5001 822
Konstam, Phyllis
   5001 502
Konstantin, Madame

KKBB 320
   5001 536
Kooper, Al
   5001 407
Kopple, Barbara
   WTLGD 249-253
   5001 319
Korda, Alexander
   KKBB 359
   SOTA 98
   H 330, 368; dir., *Marius*, 330
   5001 193, 222-223, 244, 386, 459, 465, 599,
     606, 623, 628, 652, 659, 756, 760, 774,
     845
Korda, Vincent
   KKBB 354
   5001 459, 623, 756, 759
Korda, Zoltán
   5001 386, 650, 652, 756
Korea
   WTLGD 125
   DIM 93
Koritsi me ta Mavra, see *A Girl in Black*
Korjus, Miliza
   5001 304
Korkes, Jon
   5001 427
Korman, Harvey
   DIM 182
   R 130
   WTLGD 373, 375
   TIAI 216
   H 16
   5001 34, 81, 331, 335, 435, 616, 824
Korngold, Erich Wolfgang
   KKBB 228
   5001 8, 182, 306, 600, 660
Kortner, Fritz
   KKBB 221
   WTLGD 177
   5001 563
Korty, John
   KKBB 14; dir., *The Crazy Quilt*, 14
   DIM 350; dir., *Funnyman*, 350
   R 262-266, 330; dir., *The Autobiography of*
     Miss Jane Pittman, 261-266, 324; *The*
     Crazy Quilt, 263, 457; *Funnyman*, 263,
     265; *Go Ask Alice*, 263, 266
   WTLGD 183-184; dir., *Alex & the Gypsy*,
     183-184; *The Crazy Quilt*, 184;
     Funnyman, 184; *The Autobiography of*
     Miss Jane Pittman (TV movie), 184
   5001 12, 39, 160, 272
Korvin, Charles
   5001 675
Koscina, Sylva
   5001 386
Kosinski, Jerzy
   R 121
   WTLGD 301, 354
   TIAI 281, 282, 458
   ML 29
   5001 621
Kosleck, Martin
   DIM 97
   R 207
   5001 20, 258, 534

Koslow, Ron
  5001 422
Kosma, Joseph
  KKBB 254
  5001 175, 214, 300, 465, 581, 817, 819
Kossoff, David
  KKBB 291
  5001 63, 393, 500
Kostal, Irwin
  5001 697
Koster, Henry
  KKBB 178; dir., *The Singing Nun*, 176, 178;
    Désirée, 193; *The Robe*, 220
  5001 184, 245, 252, 373, 611, 768
Köstlinger, Josef
  WTLGD 74
Kostmayer, John
  5001 350
Kotch
  DIM 345
  5001 (2nd ed)
Kotcheff, Ted
  DIM 417; dir., *Outback*, 415-417
  WTLGD 269-271, 482-485; dir., *The
    Apprenticeship of Duddy Kravitz*, 156,
    270, 466, *Fun with Dick and Jane*,
    269-271, 484; *Who is Killing the Great
    Chefs of Europe?*, 482-485
  SOTA 116-120; dir., *Uncommon Valor*,
    116-120; *First Blood*, 116; *North Dallas
    Forty*, 145
  H 447-449; dir., *The Apprenticeship of
    Duddy Kravitz*, 82-83; *Who Is Killing
    the Great Chefs of Europe?* 299;
    Uncommon Valor, 348; *Switching
    Channels*, 447-449
  5001 33, 271, 557, 640, 738, 804, 836
Koteas, Elias
  5001 745
Kotegawa, Yuko
  SOTA 327
  5001 454
Kotero, Patty Apollonia
  SOTA 213
  5001 604
Kott, Jan
  DIM 356, 400
Kotto, Yaphet
  R 260-261, 434
  WTLGD 406, 408
  TIAI 24
  5001 85, 91, 108, 624, 763
Kouf, Jim
  H 349
  5001 704
Koumiko Mystery, The (Le Mystère Koumiko)
  KKBB 129, 292-293:n
  5001
Kovacs, Ernie
  KKBB 325, 327
  R 132
  WTLGD 465
  ML 201
  5001 551, 556
Kovacs, Laszlo
  DIM 298
  R 134

WTLGD 248, 352, 490
TIAI 48, 64
SOTA 193
5001 13, 37, 211, 284, 397, 409, 411, 416,
  521, 523, 656, 671, 750, 831
Kove, Martin
  5001 615
Kovic, Ron
  WTLGD 402
  ML 249-55
  5001 93
Kozak, Harley Jane
  5001 34
Kozlowski, Linda
  H 452
  5001 567
Krabbé, Jeroen
  SOTA 194-195, 196
  H 475
  ML 132
  5001 264, 657, 795, 849
Kracauer, Siegfried
  ILIATM 269-292
  KKBB 242
Kramer, Larry
  DIM 140
  R 137
  5001 436, 847
Kramer, Robert
  DIM 164, 165, 168; dir., *Ice*, 163-168; *The
    Edge*, 164, 165
  5001 352, 480
Kramer, Stanley
  ILIATM 141, 177; dir., *The Defiant Ones*,
    41; *Not as a Stranger*, 45; *On the
    Beach*, 177
  KKBB 203-214; dir., *Not as a Stranger*,
    204-205; *The Pride and the Passion*,
    205; *The Defiant Ones*, 205-206; *On the
    Beach*, 206-207; *Inherit the Wind*, 207;
    Judgment at Nuremberg, 207-209; *It's a
    Mad, Mad, Mad, Mad World*, 209; *Ship
    of Fools*, 209-213
  GS 109; dir., *Guess Who's Coming to
    Dinner*, 61, 176, 178
  DIM 34, 150, 216, 383; dir., *The Secret of
    Santa Vittoria*, 34-35; *R.P.M.*, 150
  WTLGD 98, 177; dir., *The Pride and the
    Passion*, 25; *Ship of Fools*, 120
  TIAI 494; dir., *Judgment at Nuremberg*,
    173; *The Defiant Ones*, 437; *On the
    Beach*, 495
  5001 248, 318, 332, 363, 384, 475, 545,
    546, 664, 675, 690, 839
Kramer vs. Kramer
  TIAI 13, 18, 78, 427
  SOTA 97, 174, 248, 249
  H 76, 116, 190
Krasker, Robert
  ILIATM 235
  KKBB 321, 336, 339, 359
  5001 72, 102, 114, 146, 328, 539, 608, 623,
    756, 760, 787
Krasna, Norman
  5001 44, 186, 248, 273, 316, 362, 373, 594,
    628, 836, 856
Krasner, Milton

5001 666, 801, 845
Krause, Willi
  KKBB 294
  5001 410
Krauss, Werner
  KKBB 242, 367
  5001 113, 384, 824
Kreisler, Fritz
  5001 397
Kremlin Letter, The
  DIM 104-105
Kreuger, Kurt
  KKBB 364
  5001 220, 806
Kriemhild's Revenge, see *Nibelungen Saga*
Kriener, Ulrike
  H 195
  5001 475
Krige, Alice
  TIAI 246
  SOTA 150
  H 384
  5001 51, 131
Krikes, Peter
  5001 708
Krim, Seymour
  H 391
Krims, Milton
  5001 306, 683
Kristofferson, Kris
  R 413-415
  WTLGD 240-244, 358-361, 402, 433
  TIAI 41, 48, 112, 113, 114
  H 8, 10, 31, 105, 136
  5001 15, 88, 138, 154, 238, 339, 409, 569,
    665, 695, 707, 791
Kroeger, Berry
  5001 310
Kroeger, Wolf
  5001 854
Kroiter, Roman
  5001 139
Kroner, Josef
  5001 678
Kroopf, Sandy
  SOTA 316
  5001 74
Kruger, Alma
  KKBB 281
  5001 48, 335, 753
Krüger, Hardy
  DIM 35
  WTLGD 104
  5001 53, 729
Kruger, Otto
  KKBB 281, 313
  5001 31, 78, 128, 159, 206, 331, 476, 503,
    572, 649
Krupa, Gene
  TIAI 27
  5001 48, 287
Kruschen, Jack
  5001 267, 317, 441, 724
Kuay, Uikey
  H 422
  5001 295
Kubrick, Stanley

ILIATM 206, 209: dir., *Lolita*, 24, 203-209,
246; *The Killing*, 209; *Paths of Glory*,
209
KKBB 231, 291; dir., *Dr. Strangelove*, 33,
62-63, 310; *Paths of Glory*, 231; *The
Killing*, 291; *Fear and Desire*, 291;
Killer's Kiss, 291
GS dir., *Dr. Strangelove*, 122; *The Killing*,
183, 277; *2001*, 121-124
RK 62
DIM 131, 373, 374-377; dir., *Dr.
Strangelove*, 99, 375; *2001*, 131; *A
Clockwork Orange*, 373-378, 426
R 38; dir., *2001*, 216, 277; *Lolita*, 361; *A
Clockwork Orange*, 432
WTLGD 101-106, 129, 160, 350-351; dir.,
Barry Lyndon, 101-106; *A Clockwork
Orange*, 103; *2001*, 103, 104, 140,
350-351, 353; *The Killing*, 105; *Lolita*,
128, 236, 246; *Fear and Desire*, 129;
Dr. Strangelove, 182, 421
TIAI 1-7, 127, 144, 308; dir., *The Shining*,
1-7, 179; *2001: A Space Odyssey*, 1, 7,
125; *Barry Lyndon*, 1, 2, 276; *A
Clockwork Orange*, 2; *Paths of Glory*,
2; *Dr. Strangelove*, 276, 494
SOTA 195; dir., *2001: A Space Odyssey*, 65;
Lolita, 195, 196; *The Shining*, 322
H 325-329; dir., *A Clockwork Orange*, 108,
326, 327, 344; *Full Metal Jacket*, 325-
329, 353; *Dr. Strangelove*, 327; *2001:
A Space Odyssey*, 328
5001 52, 53, 141, 270, 394, 430, 569, 570,
674, 699, 800
Kuby, Erich
KKBB 340
5001 643
"Kugelmass Episode, The" (story)
SOTA 336, 338
Kulik, Buzz
5001 631
Kulle, Jarl
TIAI 487
5001 236, 510, 664, 688
Kuller, Sid
5001 71
Kullers, John
DIM 222, 224
Kumonosu-jo, see *The Throne of Blood*
Kundera, Milan
H 427-428, 429-430, 431
5001 803
Kunen, James
5001 721
"Kung Fu" (TV)
WTLGD 227
Kunstler, William
ML 84
Kupferberg, Tuli
5001 850
Kurant, Willy
5001 526
Kureishi, Hanif
H 119-120, 121, 122, 387, 388, 390, 391
5001 506, 652
Kurita, Toyomichi
5001 791

Kurnitz, Harry
5001 7, 343, 456, 550, 669, 844
Kuroda, Fukumi
H 307
5001 743
Kurosawa, Akira
ILIATM 119-122, 124, 239-246, 281; dir.,
The Seven Samurai, 119-124, 244;
Rashomon, 120, 122, 244; *Ikiru*, 170,
244; *Yojimbo*, 239-245, 316; *Throne of
Blood*, 244
KKBB 41, 200, 202, 246, 337; dir., *Throne
of Blood*, 200; *Rashomon*, 246, 337
GS 53, 138, 210; dir., *Throne of Blood*, 157
DIM 139, 248; dir., *Throne of Blood*, 139,
336; *The Seven Samurai*, 248
R 98
WTLGD 113, 324, 431; dir., *The Seven
Samurai*, 113; *Yojimbo*, 523, 556
TIAI 137-142, 301; dir., *Kagemusha* (*The
Shadow Warrior*), 137-142; *The Seven
Samurai*, 139; *Rashomon*, 141; *Throne
of Blood*, 140; *Ikuru*, 301
SOTA 244; dir., *Rashomon*, 161, 204;
Throne of Blood, 244
H 89-92, 308; dir., *Ran*, 89-92, 473; *The
Seven Samurai*, 90; *Throne of Blood*,
91; *Rashomon*, 91; *Kagemusha*, 92;
Yojimbo, 308
5001 47, 311, 354, 356, 389, 452, 615, 616,
668, 768, 769, 856
Kurtz, Swoosie
TIAI 380
SOTA 145, 147
H 215, 217-218, 460
ML 59
5001 10, 103, 171, 686, 794
Kurys, Diane
SOTA 133-139
5001 222
Kvinnodröm, see *Dreams*
Kvinnors Väntan, see *Secrets of Women*
Kwan, Nancy
5001 252
Kwarian, Kola
KKBB 291
5001 394
Kwouk, Burt
5001 582, 587
Kyo, Machiko
ILIATM 160, 162-163
KKBB 268, 337
H 91
5001 280, 389, 616, 745, 802
Kyser, Kay
5001 703, 764

L

L.A. Story
ML 327-28
L-Shaped Room, The
DIM 323
La Bamba, see *Bamba, La*

La Dolce Vita, see *Dolce Vita, La*
La Mama
DIM 55-57
Laage, Barbara
5001 59
La Barthe, Henri (Ashelbé)
5001 575
LaBelle, Patti
SOTA 273
Labiche, Eugène
KKBB 287
5001 373
Labourdette, Elina
5001 214, 430, 794
Labourier, Dominique
WTLGD 180, 286
5001 848
Labro, Philippe
DIM 413-415; dir., *Without Apparent
Motive*, 413-415
R 201; dir., *The Inheritor*, 201-202, 214;
Without Apparent Motive, 201, 258
5001 363, 843
Lacan, Jacques
H 389
La Cava, Gregory
5001 509, 672, 703, 806-807, 829
Lacey, Catherine
KKBB 293
5001 349, 406, 599, 771
Lacey, Franklin
5001 504
Lacey, Ronald
TIAI 211
SOTA 219
5001 7, 613
Lachman, Edward (Ed)
SOTA 354
H 216
5001 184, 793
Laclos, Choderlos de
KKBB 296
ML 57-62, 217
5001 420, 812
Lacombe, Lucien
R 335-341
H 437
5001
Lacouture, Jean
DIM 44
Ladd, Alan
ILIATM 240
KKBB 347
RK 58
R 161
WTLGD 41
TIAI 20, 385
5001 86, 121, 287, 671, 761
Ladd, Alan Jr.
TIAI 10, 220
Ladd, Diane
R 411
TIAI 156
5001 15, 17, 78, 135, 622, 837
Ladies and Gentlemen Lenny Bruce!! (book)
R 375
Ladies in Retirement

5001
Ladies of Leisure
 5001
Ladies' Home Journal (periodical)
 WTLGD 9
Ladmiral, Nicole
 5001 189
Ladri di Biciclette, see *The Bicycle Thief*
Lady Be Good
 5001 (2nd ed)
Lady Caroline Lamb
 R 110-113
 5001
Lady Eve. The
 ILIATM 24, 81
 KKBB 363
 RK 52
 WTLGD 8
 TIAI 456
 SOTA 12, 222
 5001
Lady for a Day
 H 154
 ML 28-29
Lady from the Sea (stage)
 WTLGD 307
Lady in the Dark
 DIM 346
 5001
Lady in the Lake
 5001
Lady in White
 H 478-479
 5001 (2nd ed)
Lady Is Willing. The
 5001
Lady of Burlesque
 5001
Lady on a Train
 5001
Lady Sings the Blues
 R 35-40
 WTLGD 61
 SOTA 216
 5001
 H 146
Lady Surrenders. A (Love Story)
 H 332
Lady Vanishes. The
 KKBB 293:n, 350
 5001
Lady's Morals. A
 5001
Ladyhawke
 SOTA 356-359
 5001 (2nd ed)
Ladykillers. The
 KKBB 293:n
 5001
Lafont, Bernadette
 KKBB 310
 R 289
 5001 91, 416, 489, 499, 757
Laforêt, Marie
 5001 603
La Garde, Jocelyne
 KKBB 135-136

5001 322
Lagerlöf, Selma
 5001 649
LaHaye, Tim
 H 439
Lahr, Anthea
 H 297
Lahr, Bert
 R 389
 WTLGD 23, 472, 473
 SOTA 359
 H 249, 424
 5001 528, 675, 864
Lahr, John
 H 295, 297
 5001 595
Lahti, Christine
 SOTA 166, 167
 H 150, 151, 408-409
 5001 342, 386, 738
Lahti, Gary
 TIAI 199
 5001 401
Lai, Francis
 5001 456, 465
Laine, Frankie
 R 280
Laing, Hugh
 5001 103
Laing, R. D.
 R 392, 394-396
 WTLGD 87
Lair of the White Worm, The
 ML 139
Laird, Peter
 5001 745
Lake, Arthur
 5001 547, 781
Lake, Florence
 KKBB 336
 5001 607, 704
Lake, Ricki
 H 442
 5001 313
Lake, Stuart N.
 5001 829
Lake, Veronica
 TIAI 426
 SOTA 40
 5001 86, 287, 350, 726, 761
LaLoggia, Frank
 H dir., *Lady in White,* 478-479
 5001 405
Lamarr, Hedy
 KKBB 244, 260
 R 145, 152
 WTLGD 126
 TIAI 467
 SOTA 47
 5001 14, 211, 575, 652, 783, 833, 865
Lamb, Gil
 5001 99, 594
Lambert, Anne Louise
 SOTA 33
 5001 202
Lambert, Christopher
 SOTA 149, 150

5001 308
Lambert, Gavin
 ILIATM 72, 140
 KKBB 208, 283
 5001 365, 627, 637, 695
Lambert, Jack
 5001 220
Lambert, Paul
 R 45
Lambetti, Ellie
 KKBB 270
 5001 286
Lambrakis, Gregorios
 DIM 63-64
Lament of the Path. The, see *Pather Panchale*
Lamont, Duncan
 ILIATM 104
 5001 293, 784
Lamorisse, Albert
 KKBB 180, 185, 291; dir., *White Mane,* 180,
  185, 291; *The Red Balloon,* 180
 5001 619, 835
Lamorisse, Pascal
 5001 619
Lamorisse, Sabine
 5001 619
Lamour, Dorothy
 5001 68, 305, 333, 346, 633, 699
L'Amour, Louis
 5001 117, 327, 670
La Motta, Jake
 TIAI 106
 ML 266
Lampedusa, Giuseppe Tomasi di
 SOTA 50, 51
Lampell, Millard
 5001 822
Lampert, Zohra
 GS 52
 5001 111, 244, 702
Lampin, Georges
 5001 354
Lampkin, Charles
 H 7
Lampreave, Chus
 SOTA 365
 H 467
 5001 470, 830
LaMure, Pierre
 5001 500
Lancaster, Bill
 5001 759
Lancaster, Burt
 ILIATM 49
 KKBB 42, 44, 208, 252, 291, 297, 334, 336,
  356
 GS 89-90, 107, 270
 DIM 137, 299, 353
 R 209
 WTLGD 29, 35-38, 325, 326, 328, 330, 335
 TIAI 173-174, 175, 212, 213, 250, 261, 464,
  465
 SOTA 50, 51, 53
 H 304
 ML 126, 128
 5001 12, 17, 38, 73, 108, 126, 148, 154,
  163, 188, 215, 228, 242, 269, 384, 394,

417, 424, 429, 530, 601, 614, 642, 656, 696, 736, 787, 797, 860
Lanchester, Elsa
ILIATM 7
KKBB 253, 270, 349
WTLGD 198
5001 25, 56, 101, 175, 284, 287, 403, 518, 599, 623, 701, 741, 844
Lanci, Giuseppe
5001 295, 391
Lanctôt, Micheline
5001 34
Land, Paul
TIAI 115, 116
5001 354
Land Without Bread
KKBB 118
GS 260
Landau, David
KKBB 283
5001 112, 341, 672
Landau, Ely
5001 338, 354, 432, 450
Landau, Martin
KKBB 319
ML 199-203
5001 162, 519, 533
Lander, David L.
TIAI 99
5001 810
Landham, Sonny
TIAI 439
5001 261
Landi, Elissa
5001 9, 157, 680
Landi, Marla
5001 4
Landis, Carole
5001 508, 552, 782
Landis, Jessie Royce
KKBB 318-319
5001 12, 533, 775, 779
Landis, John
TIAI 26-27; dir., The Blues Brothers, 26-27; National Lampoon's Animal House, 26, 69
SOTA 12-14, 18, 19-20; dir., Trading Places, 12-14, 192; National Lampoon's Animal House, 12; The Blues Brothers, 12, 193; Twilight Zone--The Movie (co-dir.), 18-23, 344
5001 88, 786, 797
Landlord, The
DIM 314
R 13, 274, 439, 441
5001
Landon, Margaret
5001 28
Landovsky, Pavel
H 430
5001 804
Lane, Burton
5001 42, 287, 646
Lane, Charles
5001 116
Lane, Diane
TIAI 29, 212, 213

SOTA 295, 297
5001 126, 156
Lane, Jackie
5001 794
Lane, Lola
KKBB 308
5001 263, 466
Lane, Mark
DIM 64
R 209
5001 228
Lane, Priscilla
KKBB 232
WTLGD 29
5001 35, 88, 634, 649
Lane, Rosemary
5001 97
Lanfield, Sidney
5001 341, 663, 858
Lang, Charles
5001 184, 429, 700
Lang, Charles, Jr.
5001 70, 130, 549
Lang, Daniel
ML 167, 168, 172, 174-75
5001 124
Lang, Fritz
ILIATM 146, 299-300; dir., M, 57, 157, 299; Metropolis, 146, 284-285, 299; Clash by Night, 235; You Only Live Once, 299; Journey to the Lost City, 300
KKBB 49, 132, 302-303, 309-310, 339; dir., You Only Live Once, 49-52, 54; M, 302-303; Metropolis, 309-310
RK 76
DIM 87
R 148, 356; dir., Siegfried, 148; Kriemhild's Revenge, 148; Clash by Night, 155
WTLGD 296, 324, 392, 429, 557; dir., M, 296, 392; Metropolis, 429
TIAI 186, 187, 339, 364; dir., Siegfried, 186; Kriemhild's Revenge, 186; M, 339; Metropolis, 364
ML 111; dir., Metropolis, 163
5001 66, 70, 140, 273, 344, 444, 457, 477, 482, 522, 616, 659, 845, 856, 857
Lang, Jennings
R 363-364, 385, 387, 423
Lang, Robert
WTLGD 539
5001 304, 555, 822
Lang, Stephen
5001 796
Lang, Walter
5001 115, 184, 303, 684, 752, 827
Langan, Glenn
5001 259
Langdon, Harry
KKBB 141, 273, 351
WTLGD 17
H 58, 140
ML 299
5001 137, 292, 314, 433, 723, 768, 787, 831
Langdon, Sue Ane
5001 244, 310
Lange, Dorothea

KKBB 52
DIM 342
R 4, 5
WTLGD 40
Lange, Hope
H 208
5001 87, 859
Lange, Jessica
WTLGD 234-238
TIAI 180, 431, 432
SOTA 234, 235, 236
H 48, 49, 51, 137, 233, 234-235, 342
ML 239-42
5001 157, 162, 395, 504, 592, 734, 735, 780
Langelaan, George
H 210
5001 252
Langella, Frank
DIM 180, 348
TIAI 69, 70
5001 763, 796
Langford, Frances
ILIATM 292
5001 93, 105, 226, 287, 762, 853
Langlet, Amanda
SOTA 38
5001 571
Langley, Noel
KKBB 331; dir., The Pickwick Papers, 331
5001 376, 472, 581
Langrick, Margaret
5001 505
Langtry, Lily
5001 829
Lanham, Edwin
5001 665
Lannom, Les
5001 698
Lanoux, Victor
5001 159, 670
Lansbury, Angela
ILIATM 137
KKBB 267, 279, 316
GS 103, 227
DIM 359, 360
WTLGD 150, 465
TIAI 343
5001 16, 60, 181, 279, 319, 321, 406, 433, 462, 487, 517, 581, 598, 652, 711, 767, 850
Lansing, Sherry
5001 442, 631
Lanteau, William
5001 545
Lanyer, Charles
H 262
5001 714
Lanza, Mario
WTLGD 216
5001 777
Lanzmann, Claude
H 83-88; dir., Shoah, 83-88; Why Israel? 86
5001 675
Lao-tse
DIM 399
La Plante, Laura
5001 679

Lara, Claude Autant, see Autant-Lara, Claude
Lardner, Ring
  RK 10, 18
  SOTA 171
  5001 288, 690
Lardner, Ring Jr.
  DIM 94
  5001 259, 469, 845
Larionov, Vsevolod
  H 372
  5001 172
Larkin, John
  5001 642
Larner, Steve
  DIM 30
Laroche, Pierre
  5001 817
La Rocque, Rod
  5001 473, 556, 696
Larriva, Tito
  H 215, 217
  5001 794
Larroquette, John
  TIAI 226
  5001 136
Larson, Darrell
  5001 480, 796
Larson, Gary
  H 393
  5001 449
La Rue, Jack
  WTLGD 6, 261
  5001 118, 137, 391, 768
Lary, Pierre
  R 363
Lasker, Lawrence
  TIAI 495
  5001 823
Laski, Marghanita
  5001 425
Lasky Jedne Plavovlasky, see Loves of a Blonde
Lasky, Jesse L.
  WTLGD 336
  5001 593
Laslo, Nikolaus
  5001 677
"Lass of Aughrim, The" (music)
  H 404, 406
Lassally, Walter
  ILIATM 17, 343
  KKBB 271
  5001 94, 214, 286, 770, 866
Lasser, Louise
  R 134-135
  WTLGD 355
  SOTA 124
  5001 687, 724
Lassick, Sydney
  WTLGD 89
  5001 549
Lassie
  KKBB 177
Lassie Come Home
  KKBB 180, 184
Lasswell, Mary
  KKBB 209
Last American Hero, The

  R 164-168, 172, 200, 310
  5001
Last Command, The
  KKBB 240
Last Days of Dolwyn, The, see Woman of
  Dolwyn
Last Detail, The
  R 272-275, 441-442
  WTLGD 87, 403
  TIAI 301, 302
  ML 29
  5001
Last Embrace
  TIAI 76
Last Emperor, The
  ML 306
  H 394-399, 452
  5001 (2nd ed)
Last Holiday
  KKBB 293-294:n
  5001
Last Hurrah, The
  5001
Last Laugh, The (Letxte Mann)
  KKBB 357
  GS 265
  RK 76
  5001 (2nd ed)
Last Millionaire, The (Le Dernier Milliardaire)
  5001
Last Movie, The
  DIM 297-299
  H 461
  5001
Last of Chéri, The
  H 301
Last of Sheila, The
  R 163
Last of the Mohicans, The
  KKBB 285
Last Outpost, The
  WTLGD 6
Last Picture Show, The
  DIM 293-297, 299, 353, 426
  R 13, 161, 200, 411, 465, 466
  5001
Last Run, The
  DIM 294, 353
  5001
Last Supper, The (art)
  H 184
Last Tango in Paris (Ultimo Tango a Paragi;
  Dernier Tango à Paris)
  R 27-34, 345, 447
  WTLGD 58, 134, 333, 393, 412, 456
  TIAI 172, 298
  SOTA 228
  5001
Last Temptation of Christ, The
  H 226
  ML 102
Last Ten Days, The (Der Letzte Akt)
  KKBB 294:n
  5001
Last Tycoon, The
  WTLGD 216-219, 495
  TIAI 238, 241, 457

  5001
Last Valley, The
  DIM 248-250
  5001
Last Waltz, The
  WTLGD 427, 434, 523
  H 227
  5001
Last Wave, The
  WTLGD 533-536
  TIAI 455
  H 20
  5001
Last Woman, The
  TIAI 466, 467
Last Year at Marienbad (L'Année dernière à
  Marienbad
  ILIATM 11, 17, 20-21, 24, 179, 181-183,
    186-190, 192-196, 220, 265
  KKBB 31, 35, 94, 109, 119, 164, 189, 342,
    363
  DIM 244
  R 419
  WTLGD 201, 257, 258
  SOTA 32
  5001 (2nd ed)
Laszlo, Aladar
  5001 792
Laszlo, Andrew
  WTLGD 556
  TIAI 257
  5001 528, 698, 823
Late Show, The
  WTLGD 259-262, 322
  TIAI 363, 395, 427
  SOTA 248
  H 352
  5001
Latham, Aaron
  TIAI 30, 31, 32, 34
  5001 809
Latham, Louise
  5001 466, 725
Lathrop, Philip
  WTLGD 113
  5001 204, 588
Latimer, Jonathan
  5001 287
Latimore, Frank
  5001 760
Latin Lovers
  TIAI 357
Latouche, John
  TIAI 216
  5001 113
Lattanzi, Matt
  5001 627
Lattuada, Alberto
  KKBB 365; co-dir., Variety Lights, 365
  5001 813
Latzen, Ellen Hamilton
  H 375
  5001 239
Lau, Alice
  SOTA 119
  5001 804
Lauder, Sir Harry

144

TIAI 463
"Laugh-In" (TV)
   TIAI 94, 162
Laughing Policeman, The
   R 232, 253, 260, 365
   TIAI 21
   5001
Laughlin, Frank
   R 378
   5001 789
Laughlin, Teresa
   R 378, 380
Laughlin, Tom
   DIM 342-345, 350; dir., *Billy Jack*, 341-347,
      426; *Born Losers*, 342
   R 378-382, 384
   TIAI 198; dir., *Billy Jack*, 198
   5001 72, 73, 93, 789
Laughter
   RK 15, 16 (ill.)
   5001
Laughter in Paradise
   KKBB 294:n
   5001
Laughter in the Dark
   DIM 41, 89
Laughton, Charles
   KKBB 142, 196, 198, 253, 282, 294, 317;
      dir., *The Night of the Hunter*, 317
   DIM 95
   R 433
   WTLGD 337, 451
   TIAI 113
   SOTA 43
   H 356
   5001 8, 52, 56, 117, 175, 223, 335, 345,
      355, 373, 378, 459, 483, 484, 505, 526,
      532, 542, 565, 599, 623, 646, 680, 699,
      733, 741, 742, 754, 844
Launder, Frank
   KKBB 266, 277, 278, 293; dir., *Folly To Be
      Wise*, 265-266; *The Happiest Days of
      Your Life*, 278
   5001 254, 306, 317, 351, 398, 406, 826
Laundromat, The (TV)
   H 1, 97
Launer, Dale
   H 179
   ML 75-76
   5001 191, 648
Laura
   ILIATM 298
   5001
Laure, Carole
   WTLGD 459-462
   SOTA 328, 350-351
   5001 283, 325
Laurel & Hardy
   DIM 431
   WTLGD 17, 18, 87, 536, 537
   TIAI 119, 121, 139, 417
   H 153, 281
   5001 137, 337, 819, 824, 831
Laurel, Stan
   KKBB 185, 273-274, 351
   GS 77
   DIM 61

   WTLGD 18, 171, 536, 537
   SOTA 24
   H 153, 154
   ML 143, 183
   5001 137, 292
Lauren, S. K.
   5001 82
Laurenson, James
   SOTA 353
   5001 325
Laurent, Jacqueline
   5001 383
Laurent, Yves Saint
   WTLGD 94
Laurents, Arthur
   ILIATM 143
   KKBB 354
   R 175
   WTLGD 343-347
   5001 126, 311, 727, 794, 825, 828
Lauria, Dan
   5001 704
Laurie, John
   KKBB 294, 359
   5001 36, 315, 349, 413, 563, 628, 761
Laurie, Piper
   WTLGD 210-211
   TIAI 415
   5001 122, 347
Lauter, Ed
   R 165, 354
   WTLGD 237, 510
   H 170
   5001 396, 407, 433, 450, 617
Lauterbach, Heiner
   H 194
   5001 475
Laval, Pierre
   DIM 428
Lavender Hill Mob, The
   KKBB 295:n
   R 360
   5001
"Laverne and Shirley" (TV)
   SOTA 309
LaVerne, Lucille
   5001 391, 741
Lavi, Daliah
   KKBB 363
   5001 123, 435, 681, 800
Lavine, Charles
   5001 396
Lavrenyov, Boris
   5001 261
Law, The (TV)
   WTLGD 368
Law and Disorder
   R 356-359
   5001
Law and Order (TV)
   DIM 20, 23, 207
Law, John Phillip
   GS 173, 240, 242
   5001 50, 409, 647
Law of Desire (*La Ley del Deseo*)
   H 288-290, 466, 467
   ML 27

   5001 (2nd ed)
Lawes, Lewis E.
   5001 796
Lawford, Peter
   KKBB 249, 279
   5001 8, 34, 117, 143, 210, 296, 319, 373,
      486, 507, 554, 581, 616, 646, 834
Lawrence, Barbara
   KKBB 364
   5001 419, 705, 806
Lawrence, Bruno
   TIAI 341, 342, 343
   SOTA 242, 243-244
   H 165
   5001 687, 688, 810
Lawrence, Carol
   5001 815
Lawrence, D. H.
   ILIATM 17, 72-74, 140, 149, 224
   KKBB 260, 339
   GS 30-35, 259
   DIM 57, 138-142, 191
   WTLGD 183, 186, 301, 512
   TIAI 247
   SOTA 88
   H 61, 125-126, 306, 361
   ML 137-40
   5001 265, 613, 635, 695, 847
Lawrence, Frieda
   DIM 141
Lawrence, Gertrude
   GS 161, 163-164, 165
   DIM 41
   5001 482, 623, 732
Lawrence, Jerome
   5001 363
Lawrence, Marc
   WTLGD 174
   5001 37, 184, 392, 462, 596, 761
Lawrence of Arabia
   KKBB 132, 136
   GS 269
   DIM 192
   R 236
   WTLGD 496
   TIAI 23, 405
   5001
Lawrence, Steve
   SOTA 129
   5001 431
Lawrence, T. E.
   KKBB 132, 136
   DIM 178
   5001 414
Lawrence, Vicki
   WTLGD 163
Lawrence, Vincent
   5001 141, 316, 661
Lawson, Denis
   TIAI 464, 465, 484
   5001 429
Lawson, Elsie
   KKBB 253
   5001 170
Lawson, John Howard
   5001 14, 82, 555, 650, 688
Lawson, Leigh

TIAI 136
5001 447, 749
Lawson, Richard
5001 715
Lawson, Tony
TIAI 222
5001 721
Lawson, Wilfrid
KKBB 263
5001 229, 379, 433, 514, 597, 605, 778
Lawton, Frank
5001 127, 186, 528
Lawton, Harry
5001 746
Lawyer, The
R 40
"Lay Your Money Down for Jesus" (music)
H 453
Laydu, Claude
KKBB 259
5001 189
Layton, Joe
TIAI dir., Richard Pryor Live on the Sunset
Strip, 323-326
5001 29, 628
Lazarus, Erna
5001 322
Lazarus, Milton
5001 694
Lazenby, George
DIM 85
R 360
5001 545
Lazurus, Paul N. III
5001 51
Le, Thuy Thu
ML 170-77
5001 124
Lea, Tom
5001 98
Leach, Britt
H 378
5001 43
Leach, Elias James
WTLGD 9, 10, 22
Leach, Elsie Kingdom
WTLGD 9, 22, 32
Leach, Rosemary
H 129
5001 640, 795
Leachman, Cloris
DIM 182, 296
R 404
WTLGD 373, 375
TIAI 11, 216
SOTA 29, 287
5001 129, 331, 335, 410, 851, 859
Leacock, Richard
5001 720
Leadership Institute
H 439
Lean, David
KKBB 132, 136-137, 240, 276, 282, 322,
350, 354; dir., Dr. Zhivago, 11,
135-137; Lawrence of Arabia, 132, 136;
The Bridge on the River Kwai, 136;
Breaking the Sound Barrier, 240-241;

Great Expectations, 276-277, 322;
Hobson's Choice, 282; Oliver Twist,
322, 350; Summertime, 353-354; Brief
Encounter, 354
GS dir., Doctor Zhivago, 75; Lawrence of
Arabia, 269; Oliver Twist, 204;
Summertime, 23
DIM 188-192, 270, 368; dir., Doctor
Zhivago, 188-192, 279; Ryan's
Daughter, 188-193, 218; Lawrence of
Arabia, 192
R 110-112, 379; dir., Ryan's Daughter, 110,
113, 432; Lawrence of Arabia, 236;
Great Expectations, 260
WTLGD 278, 305; dir., Great Expectations,
210; Summertime, 487; Lawrence of
Arabia, 496
TIAI 65; dir., Lawrence of Arabia, 23, 405;
The Bridge on the River Kwai, 196
SOTA 184, 299-304; dir., Brief Encounter,
280; A Passage to India, 299-304, 380
H 82, 433; dir., Doctor Zhivago, 82; A
Passage to India, 127, 433; Brief
Encounter (1946), 130
5001 81, 100, 102, 102, 195, 301, 336, 360,
414, 449, 543, 567, 605, 648, 727
Leap into the Void (Salto net Vuoto)
TIAI 418-421
5001 (2nd ed)
Lear, Norman
GS 238
WTLGD 150
5001 528
Leary, Timothy
GS 14
DIM 13
TIAI 130
Leather Boys, The
R 40
Leatherstocking Tales (book)
WTLGD 512, 514, 519
Léaud, Jean-Pierre
KKBB 127, 129
GS 273, 275
DIM 244, 245
R 19-20, 28, 33, 178-179, 289-291
WTLGD 57
TIAI 330
SOTA 227-228
5001 59, 136, 175, 275, 410, 468, 499, 582,
716, 798
Leave Her to Heaven
5001
"Leave It to Beaver" (TV)
H 12
Leaves of Grass (book)
DIM 124
TIAI 436
SOTA 299
Leaving Cheyenne (book)
WTLGD 47
Leavitt, Sam
5001 462
LeBeau, Madeleine
KKBB 245
5001 122, 213, 282
Lebedeff, Ivan

5001 26, 91, 335, 440, 472, 672
Le Blanc, Maurice
5001 35
Lebrun, Françoise
R 290-291
5001 268, 499
le Carré, John
KKBB 75
DIM 117
SOTA 258
5001 425
Leclerc, Georges
5001 581
Leclerc, Ginette
KKBB 233
5001 47, 155, 586, 791
Léda (also known as Web of Passion and À
double tour)
5001
Ledda, Gavino
WTLGD 299-302
5001 561
Ledebur, Friedrich
5001 286, 386, 490
Lederer, Charles
KKBB 281
RK 20-21, 45, 64, 83
WTLGD 19
5001 335, 352, 399, 494, 629, 758
Lederer, Francis
GS 157
5001 189, 478, 563
Lederer, William J.
5001 802
Ledoux, Fernand
5001 66, 323, 789, 817
Lee, Andrew Daulton
SOTA 311-315
Lee, Anna
5001 259, 284, 359, 409, 668, 697, 800
Lee, Bernard
5001 57, 185, 270, 408, 462, 769, 833
Lee, Bill
H 213
5001 674
Lee, Bruce
WTLGD 369
5001 221, 466
Lee, Canada
5001 421
Lee, Carl
5001 153, 155, 730
Lee, Christopher
5001 450, 462, 500, 531, 599, 767, 794
Lee, Dorothy
5001 160
Lee, Gwen
KKBB 325
5001 552
Lee, Gypsy Rose
5001 311, 405, 723
Lee, Harper
5001 776
Lee, Lila
5001 446, 807
Lee, Mark
5001 276

146

Lee, Michele
DIM 61
5001 149
Lee, Peggy
5001 704
Lee, Pinky
5001 405
Lee, Robert E.
5001 363
Lee, Robert N.
5001 253
Lee, Rowland V.
5001 157, 438, 566, 693, 865
Lee, Ruta
5001 271
Lee, Spike
H dir., *She's Gotta Have It*, 212-215
5001 674
Lee, Stephen
H 342
5001 48
Leeds, Andrea
KKBB 88
5001 703
Leeds, Marcie
5001 519
Leeds, Phil
ML 233
5001 219
Leegant, Dan
5001 680
Leenhardt, Roger
5001 467
Leeson, Michael
SOTA 16
5001 732
Le Fanu, Sheridan
KKBB 365
5001 82, 812
Lefcourt, Carolyn
5001 714
Lefèvre, Louis
5001 38
Lefèvre, René
5001 481
Left Handed Gun, The
KKBB 55, 60
5001
Legal Eagles
H 172-175, 176, 299
5001 (2nd ed)
Le Gallienne, Eva
TIAI 118
5001 188, 625
Le Gault, Lance
WTLGD 395
5001 148
Legend of Lylah Clare, The
GS 88, 208
DIM 148
5001
Legend of the Lone Ranger, The
TIAI 231
Legion of Decency
KKBB 96, 232
Legrand, Michel
KKBB 235

GS 19, 40, 54, 266
R 40
SOTA 85, 86
H 449
5001 49, 56, 140, 317, 430, 738, 763, 767, 855
Le Gros, James
ML 196
5001 205
Leguizamo, John
5001 124
Le Henry, Alain
SOTA 134
5001 222
Lehman, Ernest
ILIATM 143
KKBB 319, 356
DIM 83
5001 533, 600, 697, 736, 828
Lehmann, Beatrix
5001 272
Lehmann, Carla
5001 235
Lehmann, Michael
ML dir., *Heathers*, 118-20
5001 326
Lehne, John
WTLGD 422
Leiber, Fritz
5001 345, 494, 741
Leibman, Ron
DIM 186, 401-403
TIAI 233
SOTA 57
5001 341, 831, 866
Leichtling, Jerry
H 220
5001 574
Leigh, Janet
KKBB 361
WTLGD 547
TIAI 37
5001 111, 320, 462, 784, 848
Leigh, Jennifer Jason
TIAI 408, 409
5001 238
Leigh, Mike
ML dir., *High Hopes*, 87-89
5001 331
Leigh, Rowland
5001 130
Leigh, Vivien
ILIATM 51, 82, 140, 283
KKBB 213, 352-353
GS 235
5001 114, 244, 637, 675, 722, 824
Leighton, Margaret
KKBB 299
DIM 25
R 112
5001 65, 404, 440, 450, 804, 852
Leisen, Mitchell
5001 68, 210, 316, 404, 405, 478, 502, 594, 775
Leiterman, Richard
5001 506
Leith, Virginia

5001 78
Lektion i Kärlek, En, see *A Lesson in Love*
Leland, David
H 165, 301, 302, 331-333; dir., *Wish You Were Here*, 331-333
5001 493, 577, 842
Lelouch, Claude
KKBB 126; dir., *A Man and a Woman*, 126
GS 59, 62, 195; dir., *A Man and a Woman*, 158
DIM dir., *A Man and a Woman*, 72, 322
WTLGD 125, 204, 304; dir., *A Man and a Woman*, 125; *Cat and Mouse*, 427
ML dir., *A Man and a Woman*, 71
5001 456
Le Maire, Charles
5001 16
Le Mat, Paul
WTLGD 321-322
TIAI 73, 77
5001 139, 474
LeMay, Alan
5001 662
LeMay, Curtis
DIM 44, 45
Lembeck, Harvey
5001 705
Lembeck, Michael
5001 98
LeMesurier, John
WTLGD 485
5001 836
Lemmon, Jack
KKBB 325, 348
GS 242
DIM 350; dir., *Kotch*, 345
R 116, 118, 422, 425-426, 453-454, 456
WTLGD 29, 124, 149-152, 183, 184, 254
TIAI 34, 309-310, 312
ML 204-207
5001 12, 34, 168, 222, 260, 270, 370, 373, 402, 485, 488, 551, 597, 655, 691, 766
Lemmons, Kasi
ML 151, 152
5001 812
Le Nain, Antoine, Louis, and Mathieu
WTLGD 381
Lengyel, Melchior
5001 26, 531, 774
Leni, Paul
KKBB 289, 367; dir., *Waxworks*, 289, 367
5001 460, 824
Lenin, Vladimir Ilyich
DIM 203, 369
WTLGD 387
Lennart, Isobel
5001 272, 439, 729
Lennon, John
TIAI 379
5001 343
Lennox, Annie
H 94
5001 627
Lenny
R 371-377
5001
Leno, Jay

WTLGD 422-423
5001 23
Lenoir, Jack
WTLGD 546-547
5001 547
Lenya, Lotte
WTLGD 362
5001 270, 637
Lenz, Richard
5001 677
"Lenz" (short story)
WTLGD 51
Leo, Malcolm
TIAI 201-204; co-dir., *This is Elvis*, 201-204
5001 761, 762
Leonard, Elmore
SOTA 368
5001 714
Leonard, Herbert B.
DIM 354; dir., *Going Home*, 353-354
Leonard, Lu
5001 478, 710
Leonard, Queenie
5001 25, 143, 516
Leonard, Robert Sean
ML 155, 156, 157
5001 179
Leonard, Robert Z.
RK 22 (ill.)
5001 194, 245, 305, 472, 595, 733, 825, 865
Leonard, Robert Z., Mrs.
RK 22 (ill.)
Leonard, Sheldon
5001 31, 311, 783
Leonardo da Vinci
H 340
Leone, Sergio
GS dir., *The Good, the Bad, and the Ugly*, 53-54
R 470; dir., *A Fistful of Dollars*, 253
WTLGD 331
TIAI 371, 384
SOTA 240, 244, 326, 359-364; dir., *Once Upon a Time in the West*, 244, 361; *Once Upon a Time in America*, 359-364
H 14-15, 17, 169, 291, 308, 320; dir., *Once Upon a Time in America*, 14-15, 320
5001 50, 296, 548, 856
Leone, Vincenzo
SOTA 360
Leonetti, Matthew F.
H 10
5001 231, 695
Leonhardt, Gustav
H 115
Leopard, The (*Il Gattopardo*)
ILIATM 264
WTLGD 37, 104, 330
TIAI 174, 465
SOTA 50-55
5001 (2nd ed)
Leopold, Nathan
KKBB 48, 250
Leopold of Belgium
5001 435
Léotard, Philippe
WTLGD 286

5001 798, 848
Le Person, Paul
5001 757
Lepine, Jean
ML 294
Lerner, Alan Jay
DIM 27, 29
R 388
5001 23, 102-103, 115, 285, 427, 507, 646
Lerner, Carl
5001 401
Lerner, Irving
KKBB 322; co-dir., *Oedipus Rex*, 321-322
DIM 25; dir., *The Royal Hunt of the Sun*, 24-25
5001 502, 521, 539, 646, 724
Lerner, Ken
WTLGD 536-537
Lerner, Michael
TIAI 181
5001 592, 768
Leroux, Gaston
KKBB 331
5001 578, 579
Leroy, Philippe
5001 467, 527
LeRoy, Mervyn
ILIATM 313; dir., *Quo Vadis?*, 25, 322; *Gold Diggers of 1933*, 147; *Home Before Dark*, 313; *Rose-Marie*, 321
KKBB 273, 282, 283, 325; dir., *Quo Vadis?*, 232; *Gold Diggers of 1933*, 234, 273; *I Am a Fugitive from a Chain Gang*, 273, 283; *Home Before Dark*, 282
5001 31, 37, 84, 224, 291, 311, 338, 348, 382, 425, 446, 481, 488, 542, 552, 616, 767, 824
Les Girls
ILIATM 305
5001
Leskin, Boris
SOTA 315
5001 233
Leslie, Bethel
5001 492
Leslie, Joan
H 464
5001 318, 332, 627, 685, 762, 853
Lesotho, Albee
H 475
5001 849
Lesser, Sol
5001 556
Lessing, Doris
H 407
Lesson in Love, A (*En Lektion i Kärlek*)
ILIATM 105
5001 (2nd ed)
Lester, Bruce
KKBB 296
5001 355, 419, 595
Lester, Buddy
5001 567
Lester, Mark
GS 201, 202
5001 543
Lester, Richard

KKBB 8, 58, 94, 116-117, 138-139, 298, 370; dir., *Help!*, 8, 116-117, 139; *The Knack*, 22, 23, 29, 116-117, 139; *A Hard Day's Night*, 117; *A Funny Thing Happened on the Way to the Forum*, 138-139
GS 118-121, 186; dir., *A Hard Day's Night*, 118, 120; *Help!*, 120; *How I Won the War*, 118, 145-146; *The Knack*, 14, 120, 145; *Petulia*, 92, 117-121
DIM 4, 15, 17, 308; dir., *Petulia*, 4; *How I Won the War*, 15, 17; *The Bed Sitting Room*, 17; *The Running, Jumping and Standing Still Film*, 17
R 120, 347-348; dir., *Petulia*, 236, 348, 451; *A Funny Thing Happened on the Way to the Forum*, 236; *The Three Musketeers*, 311-312, 348, 352; *Juggernaut*, 347-349, 407
WTLGD 49-51, 157-160, 526; dir., *Royal Flash*, 49-51; *Juggernaut*, 50; *The Three Musketeers* (1973), 49, 535; *The Four Musketeers*, 49; *Robin and Marian*, 157-160
TIAI 215, 223-224, 448, 481; dir., *Petulia*, 64; *A Funny Thing Happened on the Way to the Forum*, 215; *The Three Musketeers* (1973), 215; *Superman II*, 223-224; *How I Won the War*, 448
SOTA 7-12; dir., *Superman III*, 7-12, 225; *Superman II*, 8, 225; *How I Won the War*, 9; *Petulia*, 9; *The Three Musketeers*, 9; *The Four Musketeers*, 9; *A Hard Day's Night*, 216
5001 59, 272, 342, 385, 401, 634, 645, 730, 731, 767, 864
Let It Be
WTLGD 266
Let Us Now Praise Famous Men (book)
KKBB 52
R 4
Let's Do It Again
WTLGD 66-68
5001
"Let's Face the Music and Dance" (music)
TIAI 275
Let's Get Lost
ML 121-26
5001 (2nd ed)
"Let's Go All the Way" (music)
TIAI 206
"Let's Make a Deal" (TV)
TIAI 72, 77
Let's Make Love
R 154-155
"Let's Twist Again" (music)
H 476
Leterrier, François
KKBB 306
5001 456
Letter, The
KKBB 295-296:n
GS 62
RK 39
5001
Letter for Queen Victoria, A (stage)
ML 79

Letter from an Unknown Woman
  ILIATM 100
  KKBB 296:n
  5001
Letter to Jane. A
  5001
Letter to Three Wives. A
  KKBB 219
  RK 83
  5001
Letterman, David
  H 264
Lettieri, Al
  DIM 424
  R 79
  5001 283, 289
Letty Lynton
  KKBB 285
Letyat Zuravli, see *The Cranes Are Flying*
Letzte Akt. Der, see *The Last Ten Days*
Letzte Mann, see *The Last Laugh*
Lev, Martin
  WTLGD 163
  5001 108
Levans, Daniel
  5001 794
Levant, Oscar
  KKBB 234, 249
  GS 53
  DIM 424
  WTLGD 239
  5001 23, 49, 144, 345
Leven, Boris
  5001 13, 146, 285, 672, 828
Levene, Sam
  KKBB 253, 291, 356
  5001 9, 92, 108, 164, 292, 349, 394, 445,
    669, 678, 724, 736
Levi, Carlo
  TIAI 60, 315
Levien, Sonya
  5001 205, 345, 360, 711, 865
Le Vigan, Robert
  KKBB 280, 302
  5001 320, 442, 446
Levin, Bernard
  5001 535
Levin, Charles
  TIAI 44
  5001 340
Levin, Ira
  R 442-443
  WTLGD 451
  TIAI 326
  5001 97, 97, 181, 643, 714
Levin, Meyer
  5001 151
Levine, Floyd
  5001 84
Levine, Joseph E.
  KKBB 134-135, 278
  DIM 132, 136, 151, 345
  R 316
  WTLGD 511
  5001 121, 319, 450, 519, 554
LeVino, Albert S.
  5001 116

Levinson, Barry
  WTLGD 373
  TIAI 320-323, 354, 429, 445; dir., *Diner*,
    320-323, 354
  SOTA 153, 169-173; dir., *The Natural*,
    169-173; *Diner*, 202, 309
  H 100-102, 279-282, 421-423; dir., *Young
    Sherlock Holmes*, 100-102; *The Natural*,
    173; *Tin Men*, 279-282, 350; *Diner*,
    280, 281, 287; *Good Morning, Vietnam*,
    421-423
  ML dir., *Avalon*, 278-82; *Diner*, 278-282;
    Good Morning Vietnam, 282, 323; *The
    Natural*, 72, 280; *Rain Man*, 78-82, 282,
    320, 324; *Tin Men*, 278
  5001 40, 64, 190, 295, 331, 517, 613, 773,
    806, 860
Levinson, Richard
  5001 334
Levison, Charles
  KKBB 362
  5001 796
Levitt, Helen
  R 4
Levy, Benn W.
  5001 226, 542, 781
Levy, Eugene
  SOTA 143, 144
  H 188
  5001 143, 702
Lewin, Albert
  KKBB 146; dir., *The Picture of Dorian
    Gray*, 146, 148
  GS dir., *Pandora and the Flying Dutchman*,
    171; *Saadia*, 171
  WTLGD 147
  TIAI 392; dir., *Pandora and the Flying
    Dutchman*, 392
  5001 293, 505, 563, 581, 598, 689, 700,
    746, 864
Lewin, Albert Elmar
  5001 352
Lewis, Al
  TIAI 97
  5001 810
Lewis, Andy
  DIM 281
  5001 400
Lewis, C. Day, see Blake, Nicholas (pseud)
Lewis, Daniel Day, see Day-Lewis, Daniel
Lewis, Dave
  DIM 281
  5001 400
Lewis, Diana
  5001 75, 382
Lewis, Edward
  5001 486
Lewis, Fiona
  WTLGD 421
Lewis, Gene
  5001 143
Lewis, Geoffrey
  5001 304, 625, 688
Lewis, Harry
  5001 392
Lewis, Jerry
  ILIATM 26; dir., *The Nutty Professor*, 26

  R 319
  WTLGD 375
  TIAI 457, 459
  H 134, 154
  ML 75
  5001 396, 453, 536, 537
Lewis, Jerry Lee
  WTLGD 423
  TIAI 323, 452
  5001 23
Lewis, Joseph H.
  5001 310
Lewis, Mildred
  5001 486
Lewis, Mitchell
  5001 157
Lewis, Richard
  5001 582
Lewis, Robert
  5001 494
Lewis, Ronald
  5001 72
Lewis, Sinclair
  KKBB 223
  DIM 44
  5001 196, 215
Lewis, Ted
  5001 254, 283
Lewis, Therese
  5001 829
Lewis, Tommy
  TIAI 55, 58
  5001 129
Lewis, Wyndham
  R 49
Lewton, Val
  KKBB 246, 365
  WTLGD 547
  5001 125, 166, 372, 741
Ley del Deseo, La, see *Law of Desire*
Lhevinne, Rosina
  TIAI 132
Lhomme, Pierre
  5001 471
Liaisons dangereuses, Les (1959)
  ILIATM 43
  KKBB 296-297:n
  TIAI 36
  5001
Liaisons Dangereuses, Les (book)
  ML 57-58, 217
Libeled Lady
  RK 20
  5001
Liberace
  KKBB 299
  R 137
  WTLGD 147, 526
  TIAI 201
  SOTA 214
  5001 440
Libertini, Richard
  SOTA 154, 221, 222, 224
  ML 317
  5001 17, 64, 251, 806
Liberty (periodical)
  KKBB 220

Libido
  TIAI 59
Licht, Jeremy
  SOTA 21
  5001 797
Lichtenstein, Roy
  TIAI 125
Liddell, Alice, see Hargreaves, Alice Liddell
Liebelei
  ILIATM 100
Lieberson, Sanford
  5001 709
Liebling, A. J.
  ML 222
Liebling at Home (Liebling)
  ML 222
Liebman, Max
  R 128, 131
  TIAI 394
  5001 747
Lieven, Albert
  5001 379
Life and Loves of Beethoven, The, see *Un Grand amour de Beethoven*
Life and Times of Rosie the Riveter, The
  SOTA 167
Life and Times of Judge Roy Bean, The
  R 98-100, 255, 283
  5001
"Life Is Just a Bowl of Cherries" (music)
  TIAI 277
Life Lessons
  ML 100-103, 270
Life magazine (old)
  ILIATM 37, 74, 115, 323
  KKBB 119, 144, 232, 269
  RK 12
  DIM 36, 50, 111
  WTLGD 142, 280
  TIAI 108, 450
  SOTA 61, 64, 166
  H 13, 281
Life magazine (present-day)
  RK 43, 64
Life of Brian
  H 301, 302
Life of Emile Zola, The
  GS 209
  WTLGD 206
  SOTA 250
  H 374
Life of Her Own, A
  ILIATM 305
Life Upside Down
  DIM 418
  WTLGD 354
Life with Father
  WTLGD 178
  5001
Life Without Zoe
  ML 103
Lifeboat
  WTLGD 138
  5001
Lifeguard
  TIAI 153
  5001

"Lifestyle of a Pimp, The" (article)
  H 293
Lift to the Scaffold, see *Elevator to the Gallows*
Lifton, Robert Jay
  WTLGD 176
Light of Day
  H 300
Light Snowfall, A (1950)
  SOTA 327
Light Snowfall, A (1959)
  SOTA 327
Light That Failed, The
  5001
Lightfoot, Gordon
  WTLGD 485
Ligon, Tom
  5001 50
Lili
  5001
Lilienthal, Peter
  WTLGD 315
Lilith
  KKBB 57
  TIAI 282
  5001
Lillian Russell
  5001
Lillie, Beatrice
  KKBB 323-324
  GS 161
  WTLGD 264
  5001 544, 763
Lilly, Dr. John
  TIAI 129
Lim, Kwan Hi
  SOTA 119
  5001 804
Limbo
  R 106-110
Limelight
  ILIATM 47
  WTLGD 231
  5001
Linares, Aida
  5001 325
Lincoln, Abraham
  KKBB 61
  DIM 161
Lincoln Center
  DIM 188
Lincoln, Elmo
  5001 367
Lindberg, Andy
  H 199
  5001 705
Lindbergh, Charles
  RK 5
Lindblom, Gunnel
  5001 345, 839
Linden, Eric
  WTLGD 87
  5001 11
Linden, Jennie
  DIM 141
  5001 847
Linder, Max
  H 485

Lindfors, Viveca
  DIM 252
  WTLGD 444
  5001 7, 149, 604, 825
Lindley, Audra
  R 70
  5001 64, 324
Lindley, John W.
  H 263
  ML 85
  5001 714, 792
Lindon, Lionel
  5001 17, 860
Lindsay-Hogg, Michael
  WTLGD 262-266; dir., *Nasty Habits*, 262-266; *Let It Be*, 266
  5001 517
Lindsay, Howard
  5001 32, 115, 421, 686, 697, 711
Lindsay, John V.
  DIM 313
  WTLGD 219
Lindsay, Margaret
  KKBB 290
  5001 127, 171, 253, 380, 702
Lindsay, Vachel
  GS 42
Lindsey, Robert
  SOTA 313, 315
  5001 233
Lindstedt, Pierre
  R 181
Lindström, Jörgen
  5001 576
Lindway, Margaret
  5001 306
Linhart, Buzzy
  5001 309
Link, William
  5001 334
Linley, Betty
  5001 327
Linn-Baker, Mark
  TIAI 396, 397
  5001 508
Linow, Ivan
  5001 807
Linson, Art
  WTLGD 422
  5001 22, 118
Lint, Derek de, see de Lint, Derek
Lion in Winter, The
  KKBB 107
  GS 174-178
  DIM 37
  R 246
  WTLGD 158, 159
  5001
Lions Love
  DIM 30-31
  5001
Liotard, Thérèse
  WTLGD 339-342
  5001 550
Liotta, Ray
  H 230
  ML 126, 127, 128, 265-270

5001 242, 297, 693
Lippin, Renee
  H 275
  5001 610
Lipscomb, Dennis
  SOTA 273
  5001 165, 691
Lipscomb, W. P.
  5001 278, 484, 741
Lipsky, Eleazar
  5001 399
Lispector, Clarice
  H 268
  5001 342
List, John
  H 260
List of Adrian Messenger, The
  ILIATM 10-11
  KKBB 297-298:n
  5001
Lister, Francis
  5001 505
Liszt, Franz
  WTLGD 83-84
  TIAI 128
  5001 366, 694
Lisztomania
  WTLGD 83-84
  5001
Litel, John
  KKBB 290
  5001 243, 380, 519, 686
Lithgow, John
  WTLGD 468
  TIAI 228, 377-378
  SOTA 22-23, 96-97, 139, 140, 217, 220
  H 171, 172
  ML 25, 92
  5001 7, 70, 85, 179-180, 256, 463, 556, 749, 797, 849
Little Big Horn
  DIM 214
Little Big Man
  DIM 212-216, 236, 252
  R 162, 309
  WTLGD 554
  TIAI 284
  5001
Little Boy Lost
  DIM 136
  5001
Little Caesar
  GS 243
  SOTA 101, 103
  5001
Little, Cleavon
  R 280-281
  5001 80
Little Darlings
  TIAI 399
Little Drummer Girl, The
  SOTA 257-260
  H 378
  5001 (2nd ed)
Little Fauss and Big Halsy
  DIM 171, 173-174
  R 40

5001
Little Flower of Jesus, The, see Theresa of
  Lisieux, St.
Little Foxes, The
  KKBB 107, 252
  GS 174
  WTLGD 478
  5001
Little Friendship Missionary Baptist Church
  Choir
  ML 238
Little Fugitive, The
  KKBB 184
"Little House on the Prairie" (TV)
  SOTA 171
  H 197
Little Mermaid, The
  ML 227-28
  5001 (2nd ed)
Little Minister, The
  KKBB 241
  5001
Little Miss Marker
  SOTA 123
  H 154
  5001
Little Murders
  DIM 253-257, 314, 330
  5001
Little Night Music, A
  WTLGD 424
  5001
Little Old New York
  RK 68
Little Orphan Annie (comic)
  TIAI 344
Little Prince, The
  R 387-389, 462
  WTLGD 200
  TIAI 287, 311
  SOTA 316
  5001
Little Red Book, see Chairman Mao's Little Red
  Book
"Little Red Corvette" (music)
  SOTA 213
Little Richard
  TIAI 453
  SOTA 214
  H 104
  5001 199, 854
Little Romance, A
  TIAI 213
Little Shop of Horrors (1986)
  H 247-250
  5001 (2nd ed)
Little Shop of Horrors (stage)
  H 247
Little Shop of Horrors, The (1960)
  TIAI 193
  H 247
  5001
Little Women
  KKBB 229, 241
  GS 177
  DIM 198
  TIAI 61

5001
*Little World of Don Camillo, The (Le Retour de
  Don Camillo)*
  5001
Littlefield, Lucien
  5001 75, 107, 333, 496, 647, 760
Littlewood, Joan
  5001 541
Littman, Lynne
  SOTA 146
Litto, George
  5001 85
Litvak, Anatole
  5001 88, 383, 471, 683, 696, 785
Live and Let Die
  R 164, 359
Lives of a Bengal Lancer, The
  KKBB 184
  WTLGD 18, 108, 174, 512
  H 361
  5001 (2nd ed)
Livesey, Roger
  DIM 91
  5001 222, 315, 349, 623
"Living Newspaper, The"
  RK 56
Livingston, Jay
  H 166
Livingston, Margaret
  5001 729
Lizards, The (I Basilischi)
  WTLGD 136
  5001
Lizzani, Carlo
  GS dir., *The Violent Four*, 96
Llewellyn, Richard
  WTLGD 23
  5001 532
Llewelyn, Desmond
  5001 270, 462, 496
Lloyd, Alma
  5001 355
Lloyd, Christopher
  SOTA 111, 197, 218
  H 11, 13
  5001 7, 45, 202, 290, 549, 708, 775
Lloyd, Danny
  TIAI 1
  5001 674
Lloyd, Doris
  KKBB 296
  5001 419, 578, 815
Lloyd, Emily
  H 331-332
  5001 842
Lloyd, Frank
  5001 127, 343, 355, 453, 505, 702
Lloyd, Gabrielle
  WTLGD 539
  5001 304
Lloyd, Harold
  GS 158
  DIM 61
  R 243
  WTLGD 48
Lloyd, John Bedford
  H 362

5001 784
Lloyd, Norman
    ML 155
    5001 179, 423, 531, 698
Lloyd Webber, Andrew
    ML 271, 272
    5001 742
Lloyd, Christopher
    ML 114, 225-27
Lloyds of London
    WTLGD 191
Lo, foreign titles beginning with, see under
    following word
Loach, Kenneth
    GS 181; dir., *Poor Cow*, 25-28
    R 394
    5001 588, 589, 825
Lobell, Mike
    5001 690
LoBianco, Tony
    DIM 106
    WTLGD 446-447
    5001 84, 267, 339
Lobos, Los (group)
    H 341, 342
    5001 48
Local Hero
    TIAI 463-466, 484
    SOTA 268, 269, 270
    H 408, 476
    5001 (2nd ed)
Locke, Sondra
    WTLGD 379-380
    SOTA 121
    5001 280, 725
Lockhart, Calvin
    WTLGD 66
    5001 418
Lockhart, Gene
    KKBB 281
    RK 40
    5001 14, 26, 161, 200, 335, 415, 446, 473,
        693, 736
Lockhart, June
    5001 834, 855
Lockhart, Kathleen
    5001 736
Lockridge, Ross
    5001 614
Lockwood, Gary
    GS 123, 264
    5001 490, 702, 800
Lockwood, Margaret
    KKBB 293, 350
    H 332
    5001 406, 710
"Loco De Amor" (music)
    H 232
Loden, Barbara
    DIM 267-269; dir., *Wanda*, 267-269
    5001 702, 823
Loder, John
    5001 282, 536, 542, 599, 649
Lodge, Henry Cabot, Senator
    RK 57
Lodge, John
    5001 428, 658

Loeb, Philip
    5001 199
Loeb, Richard
    KKBB 48
Loesser, Frank
    5001 185, 311, 317, 831
Loew, David L.
    5001 525, 689, 698
Loesser, Frank
    KKBB 368
Loew's International
    RK 5, 7
Loewe, Frederick
    R 388
    DIM 27, 29
    5001 102-103, 115, 285, 427, 507
Loftus, Cecilia
    5001 443
Logan, Janice
    5001 194
Logan, Joshua
    KKBB 192; dir., *Camelot*, 35; *Sayonara*,
        194
    DIM 27, 29; dir., *Paint Your Wagon*, 26-30,
        31, 328; *Camelot*, 26, 27, 328; *Bus
        Stop*, 29, 371; *South Pacific*, 409
    5001 116, 488
Loggia, Robert
    TIAI 383
    SOTA 101, 102, 377
    H 56, 58, 483
    5001 68, 377, 540, 600, 658, 690
Logue, Christopher
    GS 25
    R 49, 50
    5001 588
Lohmann, Paul
    5001 517, 772
Lohr, Marie
    5001 21, 605
Lola
    GS 263-265, 266, 267
    SOTA 288-289
    H 136, 267
    5001
Lola Montès
    5001
Lolita
    ILIATM 24, 203-209, 217, 246
    R 361
    WTLGD 128, 236, 246
    SOTA 195, 196
    H 168
    5001
Lollobrigida, Gina
    KKBB 198, 236, 264
    DIM 362
    5001 57, 235, 773, 787
Lom, Herbert
    KKBB 293, 316, 346
    WTLGD 246
    5001 276, 407, 524, 579, 582, 669, 699
Lombard, Carole
    KKBB 274, 320, 362
    GS 120, 134
    R 37
    WTLGD 6, 16, 141-143, 191, 236, 356

TIAI 240, 274
SOTA 112
H 187
ML 188
5001 90, 292, 316, 359, 448, 509, 535, 647,
    753, 754, 774, 792, 796, 815, 828
Lombardo, Guy
    5001 704
Lombardo, Lou
    WTLGD 261, 444, 449; dir., *Russian
        Roulette*, 123
    H 424
    5001 445, 496, 838
London, Artur
    DIM 202-204
    5001 151
London, Jack
    TIAI 295
London, Julie
    KKBB 277
    5001 303
London, Lise
    5001 151
London *Sunday Times* (periodical)
    ILIATM 37
    SOTA 275
Lone, John
    SOTA 161, 162-163
    H 34-35, 395, 396, 397
    5001 353, 408, 854
"Lone Star Man" (music)
    TIAI 466
Loneliness of the Long Distance Runner, The
    ILIATM 16, 256-261
    KKBB 244
    GS 120
Lonely Are the Brave
    KKBB 7, 40
    R 209
Lonely Boy
    DIM 109
Lonely Guy, The
    SOTA 128-130, 140
    5001 (2nd ed)
Lonely Guy's Book of Life, The (book)
    SOTA 129
Lonely Hearts
    SOTA 59-60
    5001 (2nd ed)
Lonely Passion of Judith Hearne, The
    H 409-412
    5001 (2nd ed)
Lonesome Cowboys
    DIM 153
Long Ago, Tomorrow
    DIM 321-324
    5001
Long, Avon
    5001 244, 715
Long Day's Journey Into Night
    ILIATM 25
    KKBB 53, 70, 85-86, 229, 298:n
    GS 178, 232
    DIM 169
    R 195, 197, 199, 200
    WTLGD 480
    TIAI 53, 221-222, 294

H 306
5001
Long, Earl K.
  ML 221-25
Long Goodbye, The
  R 182-190, 241, 268, 269
  WTLGD 417
  SOTA 268
  H 1
  5001
Long Gray Line, The
  ILIATM 44
Long, Hal
  5001 254
Long Hot Summer, The
  ILIATM 91
  DIM 76
  WTLGD 170
  5001
Long, Huey
  ML 222
Long, Jean
  TIAI 158
Long, Joan
  5001 114
Long, Jodi
  ML 10
  5001 571
Long, Louise
  5001 307, 865
Long Pants
  5001 (2nd ed)
Long, Richard
  5001 719, 778
Long Riders, The
  TIAI 18, 75, 259, 260, 438
  SOTA 120
  H 143
Long, Shelley
  TIAI 196, 197, 394
  H 265, 272-273
  5001 127, 528, 559
Long Voyage Home, The
  RK 76
  R 272-273
  5001
Longden, John
  5001 79
Longest Yard, The
  R 352-355
  WTLGD 276
  5001
Longet, Claudine
  5001 567
Lonsdale, Frederick
  KKBB 323
  WTLGD 21
  5001 544, 599
Lonsdale, Michel
  GS 275
  DIM 309
  WTLGD 96
  5001 224, 488, 495, 503, 700, 712, 716, 789
Loo, Richard
  5001 4, 75, 392, 462, 608
Look After Amelia, see *Oh, Amelia!*
Look Back in Anger

ILIATM 63, 67-71, 74, 197
KKBB 263, 276, 311
GS 150
DIM 90
WTLGD 149
H 42-43
5001
Look Homeward, Angel (book)
  TIAI 436
Look (periodical)
  H 327
Looker
  TIAI 252-254
  5001
Looking for Mr. Goodbar
  WTLGD 316-320, 446, 447
  H 224
  5001
Looking Glass War, The
  DIM 117-119, 148
  WTLGD 242
Loomis, Nancy
  5001 314
Loos, Anita
  RK 13
  5001 84, 336, 620, 629, 732, 847
Loos, Mary
  5001 771
Looters, The (book)
  R 206
Loper, Don
  5001 404
Lopez, Perry
  5001 135
Lopez, Pilar
  5001 249
López Vásquez, J. L.
  5001 278
Loquasto, Santo
  SOTA 354
Lorca, Federico Garcia
  R 93
Lord, Jack
  R 359
Lord Jim
  H 308
  5001 (2nd ed)
Lord Love a Duck
  KKBB 18, 23, 298-299:n
  GS 169, 224
  WTLGD 43, 210
  ML 118
  5001
Lord Mountdrago
  5001
Lord of the Flies (book)
  ILIATM 10
Lord of the Rings (book)
  H 473
Lord, Robert
  5001 292, 547
Lord, Walter
  5001 528
Lords of the Forest (also known as *Masters of the Congo Jungle*)
  KKBB 181
  5001

Loren, Sophia
  KKBB 198, 205
  GS 103, 112
  DIM 361
  R 78, 257
  WTLGD 310-312
  TIAI 11, 452
  SOTA 158
  H 264
  5001 89, 292, 327, 458, 496, 497, 700, 779, 801
Lorimer, Graeme
  5001 386
Loring, Eugene
  TIAI 131
  5001 248, 271, 777, 782, 856
Lorne, Marion
  KKBB 352
  5001 720
Lorre, Peter
  ILIATM 57, 157
  KKBB 221, 232, 236, 245, 251, 262, 302-303, 305
  GS 224
  RK 76, 77 (ill.), 78 (ill.), 79
  SOTA 259
  H 297
  5001 20, 35, 57, 122, 152, 161, 336, 444, 445, 454, 460, 469, 488, 663, 681, 718
Lorring, Joan
  5001 155
Los Angeles *Daily News*
  ILIATM 331
Los Angeles Examiner
  RK 61
Los Angeles Herald Examiner
  WTLGD 500
Los Angeles Times
  RK 61
  TIAI 10
Los Lobos, see Lobos, Los
Losch, Tilly
  5001 206, 278, 293
Losey, Joseph
  ILIATM 303
  KKBB 105-109; dir., *Accident*, 105-109; *King and Country*, 105; *The Servant*, 107-108; *Modesty Blaise*, 367
  GS dir., *Boom!*, 171; *Secret Ceremony*, 171
  DIM 307; dir., *The Go-Between*, 292, 363; *Boom!*, 407; *Secret Ceremony*, 407
  R 148, 235; dir., *The Servant*, 220, 343; *Accident*, 220, 235, 343; *The Go-Between*, 235; *Secret Ceremony*, 235; *Modesty Blaise*, 343
  WTLGD 93-95, 315, 396; dir., *The Romantic Englishwoman*, 93-95; *Modesty Blaise*, 94; *Boom!*, 95, *Figures in a Landscape*, 95; *The Go-Between*, 95; *The Assassination of Trotsky*, 95; *The Boy with Green Hair*, 125; *Mr. Klein*, 396
  SOTA 32, 33; dir., *The Go-Between*, 33; *The Servant*, 303
  H 45; dir., *The Servant*, 45; *Accident*, 45; *The Go-Between*, 45
  5001 3, 37, 198, 487, 638

Losin' It
　　H 265, 266, 273
Loss of Innocence (The Greengage Summer)
　　5001
Loss of Roses, A (stage)
　　R 76
Lost Boundaries
　　KKBB 284
Lost Horizon (1937)
　　KKBB 367
　　GS 182
　　DIM 39
　　R 138, 140
　　WTLGD 107-108, 353
　　SOTA 322
　　5001
Lost Horizon (1973)
　　R 137-140, 298, 346, 361
　　5001
"Lost in a Dream" (music)
　　H 333
Lost in America
　　SOTA 343-346
　　5001 (2nd ed)
Lost Patrol, The
　　TIAI 257
Lost Squadron, The
　　R 467
Lost Weekend, The
　　5001
Lot in Sodom
　　DIM 55, 242
　　5001
Lothar, Rudolph
　　5001 254, 751
Loucka, David
　　ML 112
　　5001 202
Loud family
　　R 223, 225, 226
Loughery, David
　　SOTA 232
　　5001 203
Louis, Joe
　　5001 762
Louis, Morris
　　WTLGD 412
　　SOTA 98
Louis XVI
　　DIM 123
　　WTLGD 399, 483
Louise, Anita
　　DIM 157
　　5001 31, 306, 384, 465, 683, 785
"Louise" (music)
　　DIM 185
Louisiana Story
　　ILIATM 276
　　KKBB 357
Louÿs, Pierre
　　WTLGD 364-365, 366
　　5001 187, 751
Louzeiro, Jose
　　TIAI 249
　　5001 584
Love and Anarchy (D'Amore e d'Anarchia)
　　WTLGD 136

5001
Love and Bullets
　　TIAI 21
Love at First Bite
　　TIAI 193
　　5001
Love at Twenty
　　GS 273
Love Before Breakfast
　　TIAI 274
Love, Bessie
　　5001 52, 105, 367
"Love Boat, The" (TV)
　　SOTA 132
Love Finds Andy Hardy
　　5001
Love from a Stranger
　　5001
Love Game, The (Les Jeux de l'amour)
　　5001
Love Happy
　　R 209
"Love Hurts" (music)
　　H 464
Love in the Afternoon
　　5001
Love Is a Dog from Hell (European title: Crazy
　　　　Love)
　　H 463-466
　　5001 (2nd ed)
"Love Is Good for Anything That Ails You"
　　　　(music)
　　TIAI 276
Love Is News
　　RK 20
　　H 53
Love Letters
　　H 131
Love Machine, The
　　DIM 198
"Love Man" (music)
　　H 349
Love Me Forever
　　5001
Love Me or Leave Me
　　R 36
　　5001
Love, Montagu
　　5001 8, 165, 311, 355, 466, 511, 785
Love on the Run
　　5001
Love Parade, The
　　WTLGD 12
Love, Phyllis
　　5001 268
"Love Song of J. Alfred Prufrock, The" (poem)
　　H 334
Love Story
　　DIM 216-220, 237, 321, 322, 432-433
　　R 176
　　WTLGD 302, 458
　　ML 74
Love Story (1944), see A Lady Surrenders
Love with the Proper Stranger
　　R 429
Lovecraft, H. P.
　　H 67

5001 618
Loved One, The
　　KKBB 299-301:n
　　DIM 4
　　R 326, 370, 476
　　5001
Lovejoy, Frank
　　5001 359
Lovell, Dyson
　　DIM 183
　　5001 219
Lovelock, Raymond
　　DIM 332
　　5001 242
"Lover Come Back to Me" (music)
　　ML 210
Lover Come Back
　　ILIATM 233
　　GS 18
　　5001 (2nd ed)
Loverboy
　　5001 477-478
Lovers, The
　　KKBB 260-261, 370
　　DIM 306, 308, 309
　　R 278, 341
　　WTLGD 94, 143
Lovers and Other Strangers
　　DIM 370-371
　　WTLGD 316
　　SOTA 81
　　H 149
Lovers and Thieves (Assassins et voleurs)
　　ILIATM 214
　　KKBB 301-302:n
　　GS 275
　　R 42
　　WTLGD 459
　　TIAI 165
　　5001
Lovers of Paris, see Pot-Bouille
Lovers of Teruel, The (Les Amants de Teruel)
　　5001
Lovers of Verona (Les Amants de Vérone)
　　5001 (2nd ed)
Loves of a Blonde (Lasky Jedne Plavovlasky,
　　　　also known as A Blonde in Love)
　　GS 98, 207
　　R 120
　　WTLGD 79, 88
　　5001
Loves of Isadora, The
　　RK 29
　　DIM 239, 302
Lovesick
　　TIAI 461-463
　　5001 (2nd ed)
Lovin' Molly
　　R 312
　　WTLGD 47
Loving
　　DIM 119-122, 351
　　R 83, 310
　　TIAI 294
　　H 432
　　5001
"Loving Her Was Easier" (music)

154

TIAI 41
Lovitz, Jon
 5001 68
Lovsky, Celia
 5001 458
Low, Colin
 KKBB 248; co-dir., *City of Gold*, 248
 5001 139
Lowe, Arthur
 5001 59, 763
Lowe, Edmund
 DIM 93, 94
 H 304
 5001 116, 190, 278, 327, 409
Lowe, Rob
 H 177, 178, 200, 444, 445, 466
 5001 2, 469
Lowell, Robert
 R 157
 ML 301
Löwenadler, Holger
 R 337, 340
 5001 348, 403
Lower Depths, The (Les Bas-fonds)
 KKBB 302:n
 WTLGD 181
 500121
 H 74
Lowe, Frederick
Lowery, Robert
 5001 January 26, 1992205, 860
Lowry, Malcolm
 SOTA 198-199, 200, 201
 5001 805
Loy, Myrna
 KKBB 285, 358
 GS 134
 R 364
 WTLGD 16, 20, 28
 5001 9, 12, 30, 34, 44, 65, 225, 304, 387,
  420, 463, 469, 475, 665, 669, 758, 779,
  781, 836
Lozano, Margarita
 H 123
 5001 295, 390
Lualdi, Antonella
 WTLGD 153
 5001 416, 619, 816
Lubin, Arthur
 5001 14, 579, 835
Lubitsch, Ernst
 KKBB 248-249, 318, 363; dir., *Ninotchka*,
  243, 318; *Cluny Brown*, 248-249;
  Trouble in Paradise, 363
 GS 114-115, 211; dir., *Trouble in Paradise*,
  115
 RK 13, 75
 DIM 427
 R 417, 437
 WTLGD 12, 27, 177, 324, 482; dir., *The
  Love Parade*, 12; *The Merry Widow*
  (1934), 99; *Design for Living*, 361; *The
  Shop Around the Corner*, 370
 TIAI 70, 150, 156, 424, 463; dir., *So This Is
  Paris*, 150; *Ninotchka*, 403
 SOTA 89, 111; dir., *To Be or Not To Be*
  (1942), 111; *The Shop Around the

 Corner*, 281
 H 298, 372, 430; dir., *The Shop Around the
  Corner*, 372
 5001 26, 87, 107, 143, 183, 316, 326, 355,
  531, 566, 677, 774, 792
Lucas, George
 R 193; dir., *American Graffiti*, 172, 174,
  192-194, 321, 413, 428
 WTLGD 291; dir., *American Graffiti*, 106,
  210, 424; *Star Wars*, 291, 295, 350,
  353, 527
 TIAI 8, 138, 208, 209, 212, 213, 308, 358,
  481, 482, 483, 485; dir., *Star Wars*, 8,
  182, 208, 211, 212, 308, 389, 481, 482,
  485
 SOTA 177, 179, 180; dir., *American
  Graffiti*, 98; *Star Wars*, 217
 H 473, 474-475; dir., *Star Wars*, 473
 ML 148
 5001 217, 362, 612, 613, 626, 709, 770, 840
Lucas, Lisa
 WTLGD 410
 5001 794, 807
Lucas, Marcia
 R 413
 5001 521
Luce, Claire
 5001 809
Luce, Clare Boothe
 RK 72
 5001 847
Luce, Henry
 RK 43, 56-57, 58-59
 SOTA 61, 62
Lucero, Enrique
 5001 625
Luchaire, Corinne
 5001 592
Luchko, Klara
 5001 795
Luci del Varietà, see *Variety Lights*
Luciano, Lucky
 KKBB 307-308
 WTLGD 5
Lucien, Marcel
 5001 95
Luck of Ginger Coffey, The
 KKBB 14
 GS 61
 DIM 119-120, 122
Luckinbill, Laurence
 DIM 383
 5001 98, 724
Lucky Lady
 WTLGD 106-107
 5001
Lucky Luciano
 TIAI 316
Lucky Partners (adapted from *Bonne Chance*)
 5001
Lucrezia Borgia
 TIAI 150
Ludivig, William
 5001 438
Ludlam, Charles
 WTLGD 504, 505
 H 67, 359

 5001 70, 143
Ludwig
 R 144-149
 WTLGD 35
 5001
Ludwig, Pamela
 TIAI 399
 5001 750
Ludwig, Salem
 5001 22, 350
Luedke, Bruno
 KKBB 257-258
Luedtke, Kurt
 TIAI 289
 H 77
 5001 2, 557
Lugosi, Bela
 KKBB 318
 5001 76, 180, 201, 466, 531, 693
Lui, Roland
 5001 293
Lukacs, George
 ILIATM 269
Lukas, Paul
 KKBB 293
 5001 116, 122, 139, 196, 406, 428, 434-435,
  635, 718, 824
Luke, Benny
 TIAI 166
Luke, Keye
 SOTA 187, 191
 5001 4, 293, 307, 445, 542
Lulli, Folco
 KKBB 165, 264, 365
 5001 229, 813, 821
Lully, Jean-Baptiste
 5001 96
Lumbly, Carl
 SOTA 219
 ML 278
 5001 7, 60, 561
Lumet, Baruch
 KKBB 71
Lumet, Jenny
 5001 606
Lumet, Sidney
 ILIATM 174-175; dir., *Long Day's Journey
  into Night*, 25; *Twelve Angry Men*,
  40-41; *A View from the Bridge*, 172-175
 KKBB 69-100, 141, 161, 298; dir., *The
  Group*, 67-100; *Twelve Angry Men*, 70;
  Stage Struck, 70; *The Fugitive Kind*, 70,
  191; *A View from the Bridge*, 70; *Long
  Day's Journey into Night*, 70, 85-86,
  229, 298; *Fail-Safe*, 70; *The
  Pawnbroker*, 82, 88, 146, 160-161, 163;
  The Hill, 82; *The Iceman Cometh* (TV),
  85-86
 GS dir., *Bye Bye Braverman*, 52; *Long
  Day's Journey into Night*, 178, 232; *The
  Pawnbroker*, 75; *The Sea Gull*, 232-233,
  234
 DIM dir., *The Anderson Tapes*, 285, 314
 R 196, 229, 231, 390-392; dir., *The Hill*, 61;
  Child's Play, 72-73; *Serpico*, 227-233,
  435; *Lovin' Molly*, 312; *Murder on the
  Orient Express*, 390-392

WTLGD 199, 213, 219-224, 337-339, 378, 469-476; dir., *Lovin' Molly*, 47; *Murder on the Orient Express*, 192, 194, 463; *Dog Day Afternoon*, 198-199, 303, 470; *Serpico*, 206, 223, 369; *Network*, 219-224; *Equus*, 337-339; *The Wiz*, 469-476, 556

TIAI 153, 326-327, 440-441; dir., *Dog Day Afternoon*, 153, 368; *Long Day's Journey Into Night*, 221-222; *Network*, 244; *Deathtrap*, 326-327; *Serpico*, 368; *The Verdict*, 440-441

SOTA 41-45; dir., *Daniel*, 41-45, 87; *Prince of the City*, 42; *The Verdict*, 42; *Dog Day Afternoon*, 202; *The Wiz*, 217; *Equus*, 250, 252

H 243-246, 321; dir., *Serpico*, 169; *The Verdict*, 226, 321; *The Morning After*, 243-246; *Long Day's Journey Into Night*, 306

5001 25, 111, 134, 171, 181, 196, 223, 309, 387, 432, 498, 503, 519, 571, 596, 606, 660, 666, 795, 813, 815, 844

Lumière
WTLGD 230-233
5001

Lumière, August
KKBB 255

Lumière, Louis
ILIATM 273
KKBB 255
WTLGD 231

Luna
TIAI 314
H 452
ML 305

Lunceford, Jimmy
5001 88

Lund, Art
R 166
5001 407, 492

Lund, John
5001 258, 775

Lundberg, Ferdinand
RK 71, 81-82

Lundigan, William
5001 243, 543, 583

Lune dans le caniveau, La, see *The Moon in the Gutter*

Lunghi, Cherie
TIAI 185
5001 227

Lunt, Alfred
5001 309

Lupino, Ida
ILIATM 293
KKBB 238
ML 4
5001 32, 36, 71, 280, 318, 332, 336, 403, 422, 457, 577, 750, 754

LuPone, Patti
SOTA 321
H 154
ML 236
5001 205, 531, 842, 844

Lurie, John
SOTA 261

H 221, 222
5001 185, 200, 720

Lust for Life
ML 290-91
5001

Lustig, Jan
5001 834

Lutter, Alfred
R 413
5001 15

Lutz, Adelle
5001 61

Luu, Thuy An
TIAI 328, 330
5001 193

Luv
DIM 10

Luxemburg, Rosa
DIM 182, 203

Luz, Maria
5001 249

Lyarsky, Alexei
5001 133, 506

Lydia Bailey
DIM 177

Lydon, Jimmy
5001 421

Lynch, David
TIAI 82-86; dir., *The Elephant Man*, 82-86; *Eraserhead*, 82, 83, 84, 86
SOTA 100, 282-287; dir., *Eraserhead*, 100, 282; *The Elephant Man*, 100, 282; *Dune*, 282-287
H 202-209; dir., *Blue Velvet*, 202-209, 306, 307, 462; *Dune*, 206, 207; *Eraserhead*, 207, 332, 392; *The Elephant Man*, 207, 251
ML 94; dir., *Blue Velvet*, 82
5001 87, 206, 215, 223

Lynch, Kelly
ML 196, 197, 198
5001 205

Lynde, Paul
TIAI 163
5001 111

Lyne, Adrian
H 374-377; dir., *Flashdance*, 134, 375; *Fatal Attraction*, 374-377
5001 239, 250

Lynen, Robert
KKBB 243
5001 588

Lynley, Carol
R 71
5001 591, 723

Lynn, Betty
5001 386

Lynn, Diana
5001 453, 483

Lynn, Hilary
5001 303

Lynn, Jeffrey
5001 243, 263, 419, 634

Lynn, Loretta
SOTA 33

Lynne, Sharon
5001 288, 809, 825

Lyon, Ben
5001 328, 349, 525

Lyon, Sue
ILIATM 208
5001 430, 526

Lyons, Nan and Ivan
WTLGD 482
5001 836

Lyons, Robert F.
5001 179

Lys, Lya
5001 10

M

M
ILIATM 57, 157, 299
KKBB 302-303:n
WTLGD 296, 392
TIAI 339
H 297
5001

M-G-M, see Metro-Goldwyn-Mayer

M*A*S*H
DIM 92-95, 147, 185, 227, 277, 278
R 55, 184-185, 241, 270, 309, 423, 427, 446-447
WTLGD 187, 276, 346
TIAI 152
SOTA 217
H 1
5001

"M*A*S*H" (TV)
WTLGD 505, 506
ML 201

Maas, Peter
R 228, 230-231
H 54
5001 465, 666

McAllister, Lon
5001 282

McAlpine, Don
TIAI 61, 392
SOTA 159
H 102
5001 199, 283, 499, 507, 746

McAnally, Ray
ML 43-44, 179, 182, 328
5001 509

McAndrew, Marianne
DIM 83

Macardle, Dorothy
5001 807

MacArthur
TIAI 221

MacArthur, Charles
KKBB 33, 278, 281, 362
RK 4, 20, 21, 29, 48, 61
R 422-423
WTLGD 18
TIAI 240
5001 51, 162, 270, 310, 335, 617, 665, 796, 851

MacArthur, Gen, Douglas A.

156

ILIATM 161
DIM 204
WTLGD 235
Macaulay, Richard
5001 4, 464, 634, 782
McAvoy, May
5001 63
McBain, Ed
DIM 415
5001 843
Macbeth (1948)
KKBB 198, 200, 338
Macbeth (1971)
DIM 399-401
5001
Macbeth (stage)
ILIATM 282
KKBB 56, 200
RK 62
DIM 139
SOTA 242, 244
MacBird (stage)
KKBB 63
MacBride, Donald
KKBB 291
5001 296, 298, 329, 332, 394, 640, 717, 782, 858
McBride, Jim
WTLGD 82
H dir., *The Big Easy*, 358-359
5001 70
McCabe & Mrs. Miller
DIM 277-280, 426
R 80, 270-271, 309, 438
TIAI 227, 281
SOTA 30, 270
H 1, 63, 235, 424
5001
McCabe, Ruth
5001 509
McCain, Frances Lee
SOTA 190
5001 45, 307
McCall, C. W.
5001 155
McCallister, Lon
WTLGD 87, 500
5001 704
McCallum, David
KKBB 183, 294
5001 72, 408, 528
McCambridge, Mercedes
KKBB 361
DIM 335
WTLGD 271
5001 19, 285, 757, 784
McCann, Donal
H 403, 406
ML 44
5001 177, 333
McCarey, Leo
ILIATM 307; dir., *Going My Way*, 9
KKBB 274; dir., *Duck Soup*, 7, 184; *Belle of the Nineties*, 314
WTLGD 17; dir., *The Awful Truth*, 3, 6, 7, 8, 16, 17, 18, 19, 26; *My Favorite Wife*, 3, 18, 19; *Duck Soup*, 17; *Once Upon a*

Honeymoon, 20; *Going My Way*, 25; *The Bells of St. Mary's*, 194
5001 41, 62, 206, 292, 306, 393, 508, 548, 646, 831
McCarten, John
ILIATM 69
McCarthy, Abigail
R 225
McCarthy, Andrew
H 133
5001 594
McCarthy, Eugene
DIM 168
McCarthy, Frank
5001 570
McCarthy, Joseph
5001 370
McCarthy, Sen. Joseph
ILIATM 326-328, 345
KKBB 147
GS 95
RK 3, 26, 28
DIM 43, 63
WTLGD 170, 173, 174, 335, 336
McCarthy, Justin
5001 355
McCarthy, Kevin
KKBB 286
WTLGD 524
TIAI 71, 193
SOTA 21
5001 65, 341, 343, 368, 484, 600, 764
McCarthy, Mary
KKBB 67-71, 76-81, 87-92, 96-98, 241
5001 309
McCartney, Paul
KKBB 34
WTLGD 214
McCarty, Mary
5001 692
Macchio, Ralph
H 143, 144
5001 164
McClanathan, Michael
5001 564
McCleery, Albert
5001 405
McClory, Sean
5001 608
McClure, Marc
5001 45, 730, 731
McClure, Michael
WTLGD 156
Maccone, Ron
5001 596
McConnico, Hilton
5001 193, 495
McCord, Ted
KKBB 361
5001 210, 244, 250, 382, 788
MacCorkindale, Simon
WTLGD 464
5001 181
McCormick, Edith Rockefeller
RK 66
McCormick, F. J.
KKBB 321

5001 539
McCormick, Harold
RK 66
McCormick, John
5001 814
McCormick, Myron
5001 347, 766, 841
McCormick, Pat
WTLGD 444
TIAI 216
McCourt, Malachy
5001 492
McCowan, Alec
R 97
H 301
ML 217
McCoy, Horace
DIM 68-70, 72
5001 282, 755, 787
McCracken, Joan
5001 296
McCrea, Joel
KKBB 363
RK 17, 20
DIM 353
R 466
WTLGD 17, 117, 260
SOTA 330
5001 51, 74, 177, 185, 258, 322, 332, 497, 499, 562, 628, 629, 635, 726, 753
McCullers, Carson
KKBB 308-309
GS 30, 34, 35
DIM 32
5001 474, 621, 622
McDaniel, Hattie
KKBB 230
SOTA 337
5001 15, 82, 119, 358, 384, 445, 535, 675, 678, 679, 683, 750
McDaniel, Sam
5001 20
McDermott, Dylan
H 354
5001 315
McDiarmid, Ian
5001 191
Macdonald, Dwight
ILIATM 20, 24, 31-32, 37, 92-93, 154, 172, 184, 214, 218, 243-244, 246, 250
KKBB 163, 192
MacDonald, George
TIAI 349
McDonald, Grace
5001 254
McDonald, Gregory
5001 251
MacDonald, J. Farrell
5001 58, 472, 483, 726
MacDonald, Jeanette
GS 159
RK 17
R 55
WTLGD 12, 13, 99, 345
5001 75, 244, 254, 350, 355, 472, 518, 641, 736, 765
MacDonald, Joe

5001 200, 424, 564, 583, 818, 859
MacDonald, Peter
5001 315
MacDonald, Philip
KKBB 298
5001 424
McDonald, Ray
5001 42, 296
MacDonald, Richard
R 472
H 43
5001 176, 229, 237, 587
Macdonald, Ross
5001 320
McDonough, Tom
H 221
McDormand, Frances
SOTA 323
ML 53, 56
5001 83, 329, 486, 528, 577, 615, 788
MacDougall, Ranald
5001 386, 591
MacDougall, Roger
KKBB 306
5001 457, 500, 784
McDowall, Roddy
KKBB 181, 184, 185, 283, 299
R 71, 459, 461-462
5001 60, 342, 365, 392, 421, 435, 440, 457,
    508, 586, 833-834
MacDowell, Andie
SOTA 150
5001 308
McDowell, Claire
5001 63
McDowell, Malcolm
DIM 322, 374, 376
WTLGD 49-51, 103
TIAI 336, 359, 485, 486
SOTA 57
5001 87, 125, 142, 164, 355, 431, 645, 772,
    819
McDowell, Michael
H 456-457
5001 61
McEnery, John
GS 153
DIM 417
WTLGD 382
5001 53, 639
McEnery, Peter
5001 814
McEnroe, Annie
H 215
5001 732, 794
McEwan, Geraldine
ML 216
5001 329
McFarland, Spanky
5001 391, 787
McGann, Paul
ML 137-40
5001 614
McGavin, Darren
KKBB 354
H 170
5001 462, 518, 617, 727

McGee, Vonetta
5001 624
McGhee, Brownie
5001 27
McGill, Bruce
WTLGD 321
ML 91-92
5001 139, 557, 766
McGill, Everett
TIAI 21, 307, 309
SOTA 286
5001 108, 207, 325, 607
MacGill, Moyna
5001 141, 765
GS 102
McGillis, Kelly
SOTA 319, 321
H 168, 392, 393
5001 448, 780, 844
McGinley, John C.
5001 239
MacGinnis, Niall
5001 72, 328, 443
McGiver, John
5001 99, 455, 462, 479
McGivern, William P.
5001 70
McGoohan, Patrick
GS 223
5001 468, 682
McGovern, Elizabeth
TIAI 79, 266, 462, 463
SOTA 152, 153, 362
H 266-267
5001 60, 382, 442, 548, 553, 610, 612
McGovern, George
WTLGD 265, 411
McGovern, Maureen
5001 12
McGowan, Jack
5001 42, 93, 106, 106, 286
MacGowan, Kenneth
5001 457
MacGowran, Jack
5001 195, 343, 608, 711
McGrath, Doug
DIM 171
5001 290, 562
McGrath, John
ML 46
5001 72, 204
McGrath, Joseph
GS 181; dir., *30 Is a Dangerous Age,
    Cynthia*, 63
DIM 123; dir., *The Magic Christian*, 123,
    148
5001 81, 123, 450, 761
MacGrath, Leueen
5001 605
MacGraw, Ali
DIM 216-219, 313
R 70, 78, 79, 135
WTLGD 366, 433-434
H 6, 33, 355
5001 154, 283, 387
McGraw, Charles
5001 394, 516, 699, 746

McGuane, Thomas
DIM 261
WTLGD 90-93, 95
5001 615, 616, 703
McGuinness, James Kevin
5001 134, 524, 631, 744
McGuire, Dennis
DIM 111
5001 218
McGuire, Don
TIAI 428
5001 780
McGuire, Dorothy
KKBB 185, 349
5001 218, 268, 701
McGuire, John
5001 713
McGuire, Kathryn
5001 518, 673
McGuire, William Anthony
5001 305, 641, 865
Machaty, Gustav
KKBB 260; dir., *Ecstasy*, 260-261
5001 211
McHugh, Frank
5001 19, 238, 243, 255, 263, 292, 329, 464,
    480, 512, 634
McHugh, Jimmy
5001 226
McInerney, Jay
H 457, 458
5001 103
McInnerny, Tim
H 46
5001 829
MacInnes, Colin
H 157, 159, 160, 161
5001 2
McIntire, John
5001 37, 215, 726
McIntire, Tim
WTLGD 422
TIAI 21
5001 22, 108
McIntyre, Peggy
5001 351
Mack, Helen
KKBB 281
5001 335, 672
Mack, Marion
5001 281
Mack, Russell
5001 547
Mack, Wilbur
5001 809
Mack, Willard
5001 107
McKay, Brian
5001 445
Mackay, Fulton
H 279
5001 183, 429
McKay, Gardner
5001 614
McKay, Louis
R 36, 37
McKayle, Donald

DIM 359
5001 60
McKean, Michael
TIAI 99
5001 810
McKee, Lonette
WTLGD 165-166
SOTA 295, 296, 298
H 304, 306
5001 156, 279, 644, 698
McKellen, Ian
H 44
ML 131-32
5001 587, 657
Mackendrick, Alexander
KKBB 293, 306, 356; dir., *Sweet Smell of Success*, 33, 263, 348, 356; *The Ladykillers*, 293; *The Man in the White Suit*, 306
5001 330, 407, 457, 736, 771
McKenna, Siobhan
5001 195
McKenna, T. P.
5001 803
McKenney, Ruth
5001 509, 510
Mackenzie, Compton
5001 738, 771
Mackenzie, Kent
KKBB 236; dir., *The Exiles*, 263
5001 228
McKeon, Doug
TIAI 270, 271
5001 545
McKeown, Charles
H 107
ML 107, 108
5001 7, 98
McKern, Leo
DIM 190
WTLGD 101
SOTA 356
5001 6, 267, 406, 456, 500, 648
Mackie, Bob
R 460
TIAI 277, 278
SOTA 36
5001 574
McKinley, William
RK 57, 60
McKinney, Bill
TIAI 400
5001 141, 750
McKinney, Nina Mae
5001 583, 653
McKuen, Rod
GS 194
DIM 91
5001 97
MacLachlan, Janet
R 3
SOTA 239
5001 697, 771
MacLachlan, Kyle
SOTA 285
H 203, 206
5001 87, 207

McLaglen, Andrew V.
KKBB 43; dir., *The Way West*, 39, 42-43, 45
McLaglen, Victor
KKBB 184, 278
GS 9
DIM 93, 94
WTLGD 18
SOTA 339
H 304
5001 192, 259, 311, 362, 400, 502, 596, 608, 631, 672
MacLaine, Shirley
GS 172
DIM 200, 346, 385
R 178
WTLGD 343-344, 346-347
TIAI 117, 436
SOTA 84, 94, 95, 96
H 228, 229, 374
ML 20-22, 273-276
5001 81, 133, 276, 370, 447, 591, 734, 748, 749, 753, 794
MacLane, Barton
KKBB 305, 361
5001 20, 288, 332, 455, 464, 788, 856, 857
McLaren, Hollis
TIAI 176
5001 38
McLaughlin, Lee
WTLGD 228
5001 95
McLean, Nick
5001 298
MacLeod, Gavin
5001 567
McLeod, Norman Z.
5001 15, 341, 404, 493, 563, 574, 663, 781, 782
MacLeod, Robert
5001 33
McLerie, Allyn Ann
KKBB 367
5001 114, 138, 379, 495, 622-623, 755, 831, 848
McLiam, John
R 201
5001 354, 495, 622
McLuhan, Marshall
KKBB 4-5
GS 186
DIM 24, 236
MacMahon, Aline
KKBB 273
5001 11, 19, 201, 291, 349, 405, 547, 661
McMahon, Ed
5001 271
McMahon, Horace
5001 79, 186, 298
McManus, Sharon
5001 25
McMartin, John
TIAI 23, 227
5001 108, 416, 734
Macmillan, Harold
ML 129
MacMillan, Kenneth (Kenneth McMillan)

WTLGD 345, 446-447
TIAI 172, 245, 266
SOTA 204-205, 284
5001 84, 121, 207, 229, 231, 589, 612, 766, 793
MacMurray, Fred
KKBB 230
R 184
WTLGD 29
TIAI 256
H 291
5001 15, 198, 316, 369, 405, 453, 502, 594, 779, 787, 793
McMurray, Sam
5001 615
McMurtry, Larry
ILIATM 88
DIM 293-296, 299
WTLGD 47
SOTA 94, 97
5001 344, 410, 748
McNally, Stephen (Horace)
5001 256, 381, 391
McNally, Terrence
5001 434
McNamara, Brian
5001 34, 679
Macnaughton, Robert
TIAI 350
5001 225
Macnee, Patrick
TIAI 192, 193
5001 343, 418, 815
McNeice, Ian
H 412
5001 431
McNeil, Claudia
R 61
5001 77
MacNicol, Peter
TIAI 221, 222, 435, 436
ML 165
5001 201, 284, 695
Macomber Affair, The
TIAI 333
McOmie, Maggie
5001 770
Macon County Line
WTLGD 200
MacPhail, Angus
KKBB 255
5001 178, 771, 851
McPhail, Douglas
5001 106
McPherson, Aimee Semple
RK 35, 82, 83
Macpherson, Jeanie
5001 447
MacPherson, Don
H 159
5001 3
McQ
R 275-276, 314
WTLGD 197
5001
McQueen, Butterfly
ML 144

159

5001 206, 349
McQueen, Steve
  GS 114, 115, 166, 270
  R 78-79, 135, 208, 238-239, 275, 318-319,
    406
  TIAI 11, 333, 388, 438, 439
  5001 109, 283, 452, 519, 565, 622, 763, 785
McRae, Carmen
  H 145
  5001 341, 381
Macrae, Duncan
  5001 556, 761, 794
McRae, Frank
  WTLGD 490, 491
  TIAI 99, 440
  5001 261, 531, 810
MacRae, Heather
  5001 50
McRae, Hilton
  TIAI 238
  5001 267
Macready, George
  DIM 147, 262
  WTLGD 254
  5001 186, 200, 254, 285, 570, 801
McShane, Ian
  5001 355-356
McVey, Patrick
  5001 50
McWade, Robert
  5001 44, 262, 299, 391, 522, 760
Macy, Bill
  WTLGD 261
  TIAI 395
  5001 412, 508
Macy, Dora
  5001 525
Macy, W. H.
  5001 759
Mad (periodical)
  KKBB 300
  DIM 15, 186, 325
  TIAI 51
  SOTA 63
Mad Love
  RK 76, 77 (ill.), 78 (ill.), 79
  5001
Mad Max
  TIAI 384, 386
  H 324, 344
Mad Max 2, see *The Road Warrior*
Mad Miss Manton, The
  5001
Madama Butterfly (music)
  TIAI 334
  H 376
Madame Bovary (1934)
  5001
Madame Bovary (1949)
  5001
Madame Bovary (book)
  SOTA 336
Madame Butterfly (1932)
  5001
Madame Curie
  5001
Madame De..., see *The Earrings of Madame*

De...
Madame Satan
  5001
Madame Sousatzka
  ML 20-22
  5001 (2nd ed)
Madame X (1966)
  KKBB 121-123
  DIM 217
  R 137
  TIAI 357
  SOTA 173
  5001
"Madame's Song, The" (music)
  WTLGD 190
Mädchen in Uniform
  KKBB 303:n
  GS 45, 207
  5001
Mädchen Rosemarie, Das, see *Rosemary*
Madden, Donald
  R 54
  5001 668
Maddock, Brent
  5001 679
Maddow, Ben
  KKBB 286
  5001 37, 368
Made for Each Other (1939)
  5001
Made for Each Other (1971)
  DIM 369-373, 426
  R 162
  5001
Made in Heaven
  H 392-393
  5001 (2nd ed)
Madeleine
  5001
Mademoiselle
  KKBB 167
Mademoiselle (periodical)
  KKBB 27
Mademoiselle Gobette
  KKBB 303:n
  GS 211
  5001
Madigan
  R 207
Madigan, Amy
  SOTA 247
  H 1, 50, 76
  ML 126, 127
  5001 242, 585, 796
Madison, Guy
  5001 683
Madison Square Garden
  DIM 208
Mado
  5001
Madonna
  SOTA 354, 355
  5001 184
Madorsky, Bryan
  ML 93-95
  5001 566
Madsden, Virginia

SOTA 284
5001 207
Madsen, Michael
  5001 518
Madwoman of Chaillot, The
  DIM 25-26
  5001
Maedchen in Uniform, see *Mädchen in Uniform*
Magee, Patrick
  GS 211
  DIM 375
  R 432
  WTLGD 102, 103
  5001 53, 75, 131, 142, 163, 860
Maggie, The, see *High and Dry*
Magic
  WTLGD 510-511
  5001
Magic Box, The
  DIM 16
Magic Christian, The
  DIM 123, 148
  5001
Magic Flute, The (*Trollflöjten*)
  R 343
  WTLGD 72-76, 111, 392
  TIAI 491, 492
  SOTA 252
  5001
Magic Mountain, The (book)
  R 148, 452
Magician, The (*Ansiktet*)
  KKBB 303-304:n, 319
  WTLGD 389, 390
  5001
Magnani, Anna
  ILIATM 101-104, 290
  KKBB 55, 70, 324, 342
  DIM 35, 329
  WTLGD 193, 301
  TIAI 174, 252
  SOTA 111
  H 48, 288
  5001 63, 293, 482, 551, 642, 664
Magnet, The
  5001
Magnificent Ambersons, The
  ILIATM 251
  KKBB 197, 199, 219, 304:n
  RK 8, 47, 63
  5001
Magnificent Obsession (1935)
  KKBB 147
  DIM 217
  5001
Magnificent Obsession (1954)
  R 137
  WTLGD 443
Magnificent Seven, The (1954), see *The Seven
  Samurai*
Magnificent Seven, The (1960)
  5001
Magnoli, Albert
  SOTA 213-217
  5001 604
Magnum Force
  R 251-256, 310

WTLGD 253, 255, 512
H 35
5001
Magnuson, Ann
ML 50
5001 185, 748
Magritte, René
DIM 307
Maguire, Kathleen
5001 840
Magus, The
GS 206, 211
DIM 148
5001
Mahal, Taj
R 3, 4, 5
5001 697
Mahanagar (The Big City)
5001
Maharis, George
5001 317
Maher, Joseph
TIAI 71
5001 387, 764, 772
Mahin, John Lee
5001 91, 118, 128, 200, 382, 440, 491, 518,
620, 657, 679, 779, 783, 836
Mahler, Gustav
DIM 106
R 349
WTLGD 513
5001 180, 276, 339
Mahogany
WTLGD 60-61
SOTA 217
5001
Mahoney, Jock
ML 135
5001 744
Mahoney, John
H 281, 282, 425
5001 463, 496, 656, 733, 773
Maibaum, Richard
DIM 389
SOTA 4, 368
5001 257, 270, 462, 539, 545, 703, 769, 815
Maid of Salem
5001
Maidstone
R 30
WTLGD 399
H 362
5001
Mailer, Norman
KKBB 131-132, 195
GS 31; dir., *Wild 90*, 9-17, 196
DIM 17, 50, 124, 222, 398
R 30-32, 151-158, 172, 349, 447; dir., *Wild
90*, 30; *Beyond the Law*, 30; *Maidstone*,
30
WTLGD 85, 110, 134, 399, 401, 414; dir.,
Wild 90, 399; *Beyond the Law*, 399;
Maidstone, 399
TIAI 265, 467
H 166, 362-364; dir., *Tough Guys Don't
Dance*, 362-364; *Wild 90*, 362; *Beyond
the Law*, 362; *Maidstone*, 362

5001 453, 513, 612, 784
Mailer, Stephen
ML 289
Main, Marjorie
KKBB 61
H 291
5001 31, 177, 268, 321, 326, 340, 502, 713,
727, 732, 779, 825, 847
Main sales, Les, see *Dirty Hands*
Mainwaring, Daniel, see Geoffrey Homes
Mairesse, Valérie
WTLGD 339-342
5001 550
Maitland, Marne
5001 185, 357, 435, 462, 582
"Mairzy Doats" (music)
WTLGD 163
Major and the Minor, The
5001
Major Barbara
5001
Major Dundee
KKBB 14
DIM 358, 393
Majors, Farrah Fawcett, see Fawcett-Majors,
Farrah
Majors, Lee
5001 839
Makavejev, Dusan
5001 850
"Make 'Em Laugh" (music)
WTLGD 79
"Makin' Whoopee" (music)
ML 189
Making Love
TIAI 319
SOTA 129
*Making of "The African Queen," The; Or, How I
Went to Africa with Bogart, Bacall and
Huston and Almost Lost My Mind*
(book)
H 364-367
Makioka Sisters, The (Sasame Yuki)
SOTA 326-330
H 307, 432
5001 (2nd ed)
Mako
ML 278
Mala Noche (Bad Night)
ML 195, 198
5001 (2nd ed)
Malahide, Patrick
5001 149
Malamud, Bernard
GS 209, 210
SOTA 171
5001 248, 517
Malaparte, Curzio
KKBB 252-253; dir., *Il Cristo Proibito*,
252-253
5001 163
Malcolm, Janet
H 431
Malcolm X
DIM 161
Malden, Karl
ILIATM 51

KKBB 232, 353
DIM 99
5001 17, 43, 72, 73, 92, 311, 341, 343, 349,
399, 519, 546, 549, 570, 646, 722, 760
Male and Female
KKBB 328
Malet, Pierre
SOTA 126
5001 53
Malick, Terrence
R 302-305, 369
WTLGD 509; dir., *Days of Heaven*, 447,
509, 522
5001 47, 176
Malik, Art
5001 568
Malina, Judith
ML 231, 323
5001 197, 219
Malko, George
TIAI 169
ML 93
5001 197, 557
Malkovich, John
SOTA 247, 276, 277
H 70, 72, 414
ML 57-62, 301-305
5001 171, 214, 217, 395, 585
Malle, Louis
KKBB 370; co-dir., *The Silent World*, 185;
dir., *The Lovers*, 260-261, 370; *Zazie
dans le Métro*, 370
DIM 306-310; dir., *Murmur of the Heart*,
305-310, 426; *The Lovers*, 306, 308,
309; *Lift to the Scaffold (Frantic)*, 308;
Zazie dans le Métro, 308, 309; *Vie
Privée*, 308; *Le Feu Follet (The Fire
Within)*, 308, 309; *Viva Maria!*, 309;
The Thief of Paris, 309; *Calcutta*, 309;
The Impossible Camera, 309; *Phantom
India*, 309; co-dir., *The Silent World*,
307
R 335-341; dir., *The Lovers*, 278, 341;
Lacombe, Lucien, 335-341; *The Fire
Within*, 336; *Murmur of the Heart*, 339;
Phantom India, 339; *Viva Maria!*, 341;
Zazie dans le Métro, 341
WTLGD 82-83, 84; dir., *Black Moon*, 82-83,
84; *The Lovers*, 94, 143; *Pretty Baby*,
427
TIAI 173-178, 286-288, 392, 415, 434, 435;
dir., *Atlantic City*, 173-178, 213, 392;
Pretty Baby, 176, 177, 392; *My Dinner
with André*, 286-288, 415; *Zazie dans le
Métro*, 327; *Calcutta*, 434; *Phantom
India*, 434
H 435-438; dir., *Alamo Bay*, 50; *My Dinner
with André*, 364; *Au Revoir les Enfants
(Goodbye, Children)*, 435-438; *Murmur
of the Heart*, 437; *Lacombe, Lucien*,
437; *Atlantic City*, 482
5001 38, 77, 115, 215, 344, 403, 503, 507,
756, 813, 818, 864
Malleson, Miles
KKBB 243, 255, 265, 292, 294-295
5001 118, 178, 254, 357, 358, 395, 529,
756, 826, 861

Mallowan, Max
  WTLGD 551
Malm, Mona
  TIAI 487
  5001 236
Malmsjö, Jan
  TIAI 490
  5001 236
Malmsten, Birger
  KKBB 353
  5001 664, 726
Malneck, Matty
  5001 692
Malone, Dorothy
  KKBB 239, 357
  DIM 296
  5001 71, 458, 523, 744, 850, 858
Malory, Sir Thomas
  TIAI 184
Malraux, André
  KKBB 367
  GS 9, 78
  WTLGD 256
Malraux, Florence
  WTLGD 256
Maltby, Richard Jr.
  WTLGD 368
Maltese Falcon, The (book)
  R 188
Maltese Falcon, The
  ILIATM 25, 214, 299-300
  KKBB 131, 304-305:n
  RK 52
  DIM 69
  R 135
  WTLGD 26, 110, 122-123
  SOTA 376
  ML 286
  5001
Maltz, Albert
  5001 514, 761
Malzacher, Gunther
  R 103
  5001 245
Mamakos, Peter
  5001 662
Maman et la putain, La, see *The Mother and the Whore*
Mame
  R 298-299, 313
  WTLGD 19, 20, 297, 302
  5001
Mamet, David
  TIAI 178-179, 180, 181, 182, 440, 441
  H 176, 177, 178, 179, 280, 318, 319, 321, 323
  ML dir., *House of Games*, 28; *Things Change*, 27-29
  5001 2, 79, 592, 759, 807, 813
Mamo
  5001 505
Mamoulian, Rouben
  RK 13
  5001 59, 83, 139, 194, 280, 292, 333, 466, 681, 694, 726
Mamzelle Champagne (stage)
  TIAI 265

Man and a Woman, A (*Un Homme et une femme*)
  KKBB 126
  GS 158
  DIM 72, 322
  WTLGD 125
  ML 71
  5001
Man Between, The
  ILIATM 303
  KKBB 10-11
  GS 202
  5001
Man Called Peter, A
  ILIATM 45
Man Escaped, A (*Un Condamné à mort s'est échappé*)
  KKBB 305-306:n, 349
  DIM 307
  5001
Man for All Seasons, A
  KKBB 50, 154-155
  GS 108, 174
  DIM 95
  R 110
  WTLGD 305, 309
  ML 156
  5001
"Man from U.N.C.L.E., The" (TV)
  KKBB 183
Man Hunt
  5001
Man I Killed, The, see *Broken Lullaby*
Man I Love, The
  RK 13
  5001
"Man in the Brooks Brothers Shirt, The" (short story)
  KKBB 68, 77-78
Man in the White Suit, The
  KKBB 306:n
  5001
Man in the Iron Mask, The
  WTLGD 49
Man in the Wilderness
  DIM 357-359
  5001
Man Is Ten Feet Tall, A, see *Edge of the City*
Man of a Thousand Faces
  5001
Man of Aran
  ILIATM 22, 248
  KKBB 185, 306-307:n, 324, 357
  RK 4
  5001
Man of La Mancha
  R 77-78
  5001
Man on a Swing
  5001
Man on the Eiffel Tower, The
  5001
Man on the Flying Trapeze
  ILIATM 215
  5001
Man Who Came to Dinner, The
  5001

Man Who Could Work Miracles, The
  5001
Man Who Fell to Earth, The
  WTLGD 200-201
  5001
Man Who Knew Too Much, The (1934)
  5001
Man Who Laughs, The
  ML 161
  5001
Man Who Loved Women, The (*L'Homme qui aimait les femmes*)
  WTLGD 354-356
  SOTA 305
  5001
Man Who Mistook His Wife for a Hat, The (book)
  H 376
  ML 319
Man Who Shot Liberty Valance, The
  KKBB 42
  5001
Man Who Would Be King, The
  WTLGD 107-112
  SOTA 376
  H 119, 319
  ML 145
  5001
Man with a Million (English title: *The Million Pound Note*)
  KKBB 185, 307:n
  5001
Man with the Golden Arm, The
  TIAI 108
  5001
Man with the Golden Gun
  5001
Man with Two Brains, The
  SOTA 1-3, 222
  5001 (2nd ed)
Man's Blessing, A
  GS 55
  DIM 221
Man's Castle, A
  ILIATM 198
  DIM 73
  WTLGD 215
  5001
Manahan, Anna
  5001 803
Manchurian Candidate, The
  ILIATM 24, 81, 214, 244, 316
  KKBB 47, 49, 62, 83
  GS 95, 208
  DIM 99, 261
  WTLGD 521
  SOTA 231
Mancini, Henry
  DIM 104
  R 135
  WTLGD 484
  TIAI 331
  5001 99, 130, 492, 757, 814
Mancuso, Nick
  TIAI 261, 262
  SOTA 349, 351, 352

5001 325, 770
Mandel, Babaloo
   TIAI 393
   SOTA 142
   5001 528, 702
Mandel, Johnny
   R 275
   5001 750
Mandel, Loring
   SOTA 258
   5001 425
Mandel, Rena
   KKBB 365
   5001 812
Mandel, Robert
   SOTA 281-282
   H 116-118, 263-265; dir., *F/X*, 116-118,
      263; *Touch and Go*, 263-265;
      Independence Day, 263
   5001 273, 361, 783
Mandela (TV)
   H 476
Mander, Jerry
   5001 273
Mander, Miles
   KKBB 251, 313
   5001 152, 248, 445, 501, 503, 587, 774, 851
Mandingo
   WTLGD 206, 223, 369, 453
   H 169
Mandrell Sisters
   TIAI 211
Mane, Samba
   5001 158
Manès, Gina
   TIAI 149
   5001 516
Manesse, Gaspard
   H 435
   5001 38
Mangano, Silvana
   KKBB 346
   R 147
   WTLGD 35
   SOTA 378
   H 372, 374
   5001 154, 172, 180, 207, 292, 443, 661, 748
Manhattan
   TIAI 90, 91, 92, 435, 462
   H 113, 115
   ML 327
Manhattan Dance Company
   5001 687
Manhattan Melodrama
   5001
Manhattan Project, The
   H 171-172
   5001 (2nd ed)
"Manhattan Skyline" (music)
   WTLGD 368
Manhoff, Bill
   DIM 184
   5001 559
Manilow, Barry
   TIAI 115
Mankiewicz, Don M.
   RK 10

5001 129
Mankiewicz, Frank
   RK 10-11
Mankiewicz, Herman J.
   KKBB 248
   RK 8, 9, 10-12, 13, 15, 16 (ill.), 17, 18, 20,
      21, 23 (ill.), 24-25, 27, 28, 29-33, 34-
      37, 38-39, 45, 46, 49-51, 53, 55-59, 60,
      62, 63-68, 70-73, 79-83, 84
   5001 116, 136, 138, 190, 218, 338, 341,
      374, 413, 481, 645, 770
Mankiewicz, Joseph L.
   ILIATM 303; dir., *Cleopatra*, 8, 86, 264;
      Suddenly, Last Summer, 139
   KKBB 82, 197-198, 219, 230, 234-235, 336,
      364; dir., *The Barefoot Contessa*, 143,
      234-235; *All About Eve*, 189, 219, 230;
      Julius Caesar, 197-198; *A Letter to*
      Three Wives, 219; *The Quiet American*,
      336; *Escape*, 364
   RK 10, 33, 59, 83
   DIM 229; dir., *Cleopatra*, 27; *There Was a*
      Crooked Man..., 229-230; *Guys and*
      Dolls, 409; *House of Strangers*, 424
   R 14, 76-77; dir., *There Was a Crooked*
      Man..., 12, 14; *Sleuth*, 76-77; *House of*
      Strangers, 173; *All About Eve*, 284
   5001 15, 16, 46, 51, 52, 247, 259, 273, 283,
      311, 339, 392, 419, 439-440, 463, 481,
      555, 580, 608, 678, 686, 718, 725, 752,
      765
Mankiewicz, Sara Aaronson (Mrs. Herman)
   RK 9, 10, 11, 21, 23 (ill.), 24, 29, 31, 32,
      36, 56, 80, 82
Mankiewicz, Tom
   DIM 389
   SOTA 357
   5001 406, 462, 731
Mankiewicz, Tony
   TIAI 223
Mankowitz, Wolf
   ILIATM 63, 65
   KKBB 263, 290-291
   5001 63, 123, 229, 392
Mann, Abby
   KKBB 208-213
   R 433
   5001 185, 384, 675
Mann, Anthony
   5001 170, 287, 475
Mann, Claude
   KKBB 235
   WTLGD 145
   5001 56, 268, 364
Mann, Daniel
   5001 110, 148, 357, 555, 642, 745
Mann, Delbert
   5001 18, 393, 441, 467, 487
Mann, Erika
   KKBB 251
   5001 152
Mann, Hank
   5001 187, 458, 491
Mann, Heinrich
   KKBB 239
   5001 85
Mann, Klaus

5001 476
Mann, Michael
   TIAI 187-191; dir., *Thief*, 187-191; *The*
      Jericho Mile (TV), 188
   SOTA 146
   5001 755, 756
Mann, Paul
   DIM 52, 331
   5001 22, 242
Mann, Stanley
   5001 145, 500, 514
Mann, Thomas
   KKBB 251
   R 145
   5001 151, 180
Manne, Shelly
   5001 462, 692
Mannequin
   5001
Männer..., see *Men*
Manners, David
   GS 120
   R 150
   SOTA 338
   5001 72, 77, 180, 201, 305, 483, 501, 637,
      846
Mannheimer, Albert
   5001 94
Manning, Bruce
   5001 33, 245, 572
Manning, Irene
   5001 853
Manning, Mary
   5001 568
"Mannington" (music)
   WTLGD 253
Manoff, Arnold
   5001 531
Manoff, Dinah
   TIAI 81
Manolete
   5001 109
Manon of the Spring
   H 329
Manpower
   5001
Mansfield, David
   5001 854
Mansfield, Jayne
   ILIATM 35
   H 159
   5001 310
Mansfield, Katherine
   DIM 141
   R 49, 51-52
Manson, Charles
   DIM 375, 399
Mantee, Paul
   5001 303
Mantegna, Andrea
   SOTA 161
Mantegna, Joe
   H 36, 37, 382
   ML 28, 29, 311
   5001 150, 733, 759, 826
Mantell, Joe
   5001 135, 467, 799

Mantle, Burns
　RK 38
Manuel, Richard
　5001 411
Manuel, Robert
　KKBB 339
　5001 630
Manver, Kiti
　ML 24
　5001 848
Manville, Lesley
　H 451
　ML 88
　5001 331, 332
Manz, Linda
　5001 177
Manzi, Warren
　H 172
　5001 463
Mao Tse-tung
　DIM 418
　WTLGD 188, 293, 331
Marais, Jean
　KKBB 236, 326, 329
　5001 58, 208, 214, 225, 554, 566
Marangosoff, Janna
　H 196
Marasco, Robert
　R 72
　5001 134
Marat/Sade
　DIM 242, 355
　TIAI 67
　SOTA 252
Marathon Man
　WTLGD 172-175, 191, 204
　SOTA 315
　5001
Marceau, Marcel
　KKBB 31, 351
　DIM 334
　H 60
　5001 50
March, Fredric
　KKBB 207, 320, 326
　RK 13, 15, 16 (ill.), 19-20
　DIM 348
　R 199-200
　WTLGD 17, 141, 240
　5001 28, 30, 31, 52, 65, 182, 194, 350, 354,
　　　363, 413, 467, 484, 535, 566, 645, 680,
　　　689, 706, 732, 786, 814, 839
March, Joseph Moncure
　5001 328, 666
March of the Wooden Soldiers
　KKBB 185
March of Time, The
　RK 55-59
　TIAI 205
Marchand, Colette
　5001 500
Marchand, Corinne
　5001 140
Marchand, Guy
　SOTA 134, 136
　5001 158, 222
Marchand, Henri

5001 1
Marchand, Nancy
　SOTA 210
　5001 94, 341
Marchant, William
　5001 184
"Marching Through Georgia" (music)
　SOTA 244
Marco Polo Sings a Solo (stage)
　TIAI 174
Marconi, Saverio
　WTLGD 300
　5001 561
Marcorelles, Louis
　ILIATM 128
Marcovicci, Andrea
　WTLGD 171
　5001 270
Marcucci, Bob
　TIAI 115
Marcus, Frank
　GS 206
Marcus, Lawrence B.
　DIM 353
　WTLGD 184
　TIAI 64, 65, 66, 68
　5001 12, 724
"Marcus Welby, M.D." (TV)
　RK 10
Mare, Il
　ILIATM 12, 20-21
Margo
　KKBB 367, 369
　5001 162, 357, 436, 647, 818, 841
Margolin, Janet
　5001 174, 519
Margolin, Stuart
　5001 690
Margolis, Jeff
　5001 628
Margolyes, Miriam
　H 284
　5001 294, 350
Margulies, David
　5001 284
Maricle, Leona
　5001 318
Marie
　H 54-56, 356
　5001 (2nd ed)
Marie Antoinette
　WTLGD 105, 483
　5001
Marie du port, La
　5001
Marie: A True Story (book)
　H 54
Marielle, Jean-Pierre
　WTLGD 457-458, 461
　5001 158, 241, 843
Marilyn (Norman Mailer)
　R 151-158
Marilyn Monroe (Zolotow)
　R 153
Marin, Cheech
　WTLGD 448-450
　TIAI 196

ML 165
　5001 9, 284, 808
Marin, Edwin L.
　5001 123, 180, 278
Marion, Frances
　KKBB 345
　5001 116, 128, 659
Marion, George F.
　5001 28, 407
Maris, Mona
　RK 22 (ill.)
　5001 180, 350, 547
Marius
　H 330
　5001
Mark, The
　ILIATM 119, 155-159, 201, 203
　KKBB 68, 78-79
　GS 75
　WITLGD 296
Mark Goodson Productions
　TIAI 413
Mark of the Vampire
　5001
Mark of Zorro, The (1940)
　WTLGD 49, 50
　ML 159
　5001
Marked Woman
　KKBB 307-308:n
　5001
Marken, Jeanne (Jane)
　KKBB 254, 333
　5001 175, 593
Marker, Chris
　KKBB 129, 292; dir., *The Koumiko Mystery*,
　　　129, 292-293; *La Jetée*, 292
　GS 4
　WTLGD 386
　5001 383, 402
Markey, Gene
　5001 545
Markfield, Wallace
　GS 51-52
　5001 111
Markham, Kika
　R 20
　TIAI 219
　5001 558, 798
Markham, Monte
　5001 311
Markowitz, Mitch
　H 422
　5001 295
Marks, Richard
　ML 135
Markson, Ben
　5001 830
Marley, John
　GS 197
　5001 22, 124, 233, 289, 768
Marley, Peverell J.
　5001 157
Marlowe
　5001 (2nd ed)
Marlowe, Christopher
　GS 41

5001 194
Marlowe, Derek
  5001 170
Marlowe, Hugh
  KKBB 230, 316
  5001 16, 74, 215, 494, 524
Marlowe, Scott
  KKBB 250
  5001 145
Marly, Florence
  5001 277
Marmont, Percy
  5001 858
Marnie
  DIM 79
  5001
Marooned
  DIM 86
  5001
Marquand, Christian
  GS dir., *Candy*, 224-225
  DIM dir., *Candy*, 147
  5001 117, 435
Marquand, John P.
  5001 488
Marquand, Richard
  TIAI 481-485; dir., *Return of the Jedi*,
    481-485; *Eye of the Needle*, 481; *The
    Search for the Nile* (TV), 481
  H 56-58; dir., *Jagged Edge*, 56-58; *Eye of
    the Needle*, 69; *Return of the Jedi*, 450,
    473
  5001 377, 625
Marquand, Tina
  KKBB 367
Marquet, Henri
  5001 383
Marquez, Evaristo
  DIM 178
  5001 110
Márquez, Gabriel García, see García Márquez,
    Gabriel
Marquis, Rosalind
  KKBB 308
  5001 466
Marquise of O..... The (Die Marquise von O....)
  WTLGD 184-187
  5001
Marquise von O..... Die, see *The Marquise of
    O....*
Marr, Sally
  R 376
  5001 320
Marrama, Alberto
  5001 247
Marriage of Figaro. The (music)
  WTLGD 460
Marriage--Italian Style
  DIM 362
Married Couple. A
  DIM 107-111
Married to the Mob
  ML 187
Married Woman. A (Une Femme mariée)
  KKBB 15, 17, 130, 164
  GS 138
  5001 (2nd ed)

Marriott, Sylvia
  5001 798
Marrying Kind, The
  5001
Mars, Kenneth
  R 404
  H 277
  5001 251, 601, 831, 859
Marsani, Claudia
  5001 154
Marsh, Carol
  5001 104
Marsh, Jean
  H 473
  5001 840
Marsh, Joan
  5001 354
Marsh, Linda
  DIM 52
  5001 22, 267
Marsh, Mae
  GS 42, 45, 46
  5001 41, 205, 259, 367, 385, 608, 662, 728
Marsh, Marian
  KKBB 355
  5001 161, 733
Marsh, Michele
  DIM 332
  5001 242
Marsh, Reginald
  TIAI 273
  SOTA 288
Marshal, Alan
  5001 9, 153, 345, 370, 525, 778, 833
Marshall, Alan
  TIAI 295
Marshall, Brenda
  KKBB 185
  5001 660
Marshall, E. G.
  KKBB 250
  DIM 147
  WTLGD 438
  5001 132, 151, 366, 795
Marshall, Frank
  5001 34
Marshall, Garry
  SOTA 308-311, 345; dir., *The Flamingo
    Kid*, 308-311, 345; *Young Doctors in
    Love*, 310
  H 199-202; dir., *Nothing in Common*, 199-
    202; *The Flamingo Kid*, 200, 348
  ML dir., *Beeches*, 72-74
  5001 56, 249, 535
Marshall, Gen. George C.
  DIM 100
Marshall, George
  KKBB 256; dir., *Destry Rides Again*, 29, 45,
    185, 256; *Murder, He Says*, 232
  5001 86, 185, 343, 502
Marshall, Herbert
  KKBB 295-296, 298
  DIM 190
  WTLGD 478
  5001 26, 82, 206, 218, 252, 258, 294, 356,
    419, 424, 426, 501, 617, 792, 846, 864
Marshall, Neal

SOTA 309-310
  5001 249
Marshall, Patricia
  5001 296
Marshall, Penny
  H dir., *Big*, 482-483
  ML dir., *Awakenings*, 318-27; *Big*, 319
  5001 67, 531
Marshall, Peter
  DIM 321
Marshall, Sarah
  KKBB 299
  5001 435
Marshall, Tully
  5001 35, 48, 112, 299, 367, 620, 657, 741,
    761, 769
Marshall, William
  5001 798
Marshall, Zena
  5001 435
Marshman, D. M. Jr.
  KKBB 355
  5001 730
Martelli, Otello
  5001 562, 661
Martha and the Vandellas (group)
  WTLGD 559
Martí, José
  DIM 257
Martian Chronicles, The (book)
  KKBB 147
Martin, Andrea
  H 187-189, 337
  ML 17, 88
  5001 143
Martin, Barney
  TIAI 232
  5001 36, 132
Martin, Charles
  5001 356
Martin, Chris-Pin
  5001 58, 280, 704
Martin, Dean
  GS 18, 22, 24
  DIM 82, 137, 431
  R 63, 136, 352, 465
  H 307, 424
  5001 12, 399, 453, 630, 681, 785, 859
Martin, Dean Paul
  5001 324
Martin, Dewey
  5001 759
Martin, Dick
  GS 58
Martin, Freddy
  5001 703-704
Martin, George
  5001 234
Martin, Harry, Dr.
  RK 22 (ill.)
Martin, Hugh
  5001 296
Martin, Jean
  R 210, 213-214
  5001 54
Martin, Kiel
  R 114

165

5001 564, 789
Martin, Mardik
  R 173
  TIAI 107
  5001 473, 521, 812
Martin, Marion
  5001 405, 711
Martin, Mary
  DIM 40
  5001 74, 75, 523, 678
Martin, Millicent
  5001 14, 535
Martin, Pamela Sue
  R 71
Martin, Rosemary
  ML 46
  5001 204
Martin, Sallie
  TIAI 472
Martin, Steve
  TIAI 273, 275, 276, 278
  SOTA 1-2, 3, 122, 128-130, 174, 220,
    222-223, 224, 304, 337
  H 58, 248, 249, 250, 310, 311, 312-314, 421
  ML 74-77, 183, 327-328
  5001 17, 178, 191, 427, 431, 462, 574, 644
Martin, Strother
  WTLGD 41, 63
  TIAI 78
  5001 48, 318, 320, 461, 686, 808, 838
Martin, Tony
  5001 14, 254, 772, 865
Martinelli, Elsa
  GS 224
  5001 82, 117, 789
Martinelli, Jean
  5001 619
Martínez, Juan
  SOTA 365
Martínez, Nacho
  H 468
  5001 470
Martini, Nino
  5001 280, 566
Martino, Al
  5001 289
Martins, Peter
  WTLGD 347
  5001 795
Marton, Andrew
  5001 397
Marty
  ILIATM 54, 63
  GS 151
  WTLGD 213, 214, 215, 311, 494
  5001
Marvin, Lee
  ILIATM 58
  KKBB 29-30, 205, 233, 334
  GS 271-272
  DIM 27-30, 162
  R 197-198, 279
  ML 170
  5001 47, 70, 124, 327, 353, 394, 461, 495,
    588, 601, 614, 675, 839
Marx, Arthur
  5001 117

Marx Brothers
  ILIATM 215
  KKBB 7, 184, 185, 317
  GS 230
  RK 15, 17, 24, 26, 29, 54, 66, 83
  DIM 15, 84, 369
  R 241
  WTLGD 17, 192
  TIAI 27, 99, 217
  SOTA 112
  H 114, 128, 456
  5001 28, 37, 71, 144, 174, 205, 289, 340,
    493, 524, 640, 713
Marx, Chico
  5001 524
Marx, Groucho
  KKBB 314, 317
  RK 15, 26, 29, 83
  DIM 122
  R 128, 131, 229, 243, 281, 404
  WTLGD 120, 390, 439
  TIAI 87, 216, 217
  H 456
  ML 165
  5001 28, 37, 174, 524
Marx, Harpo
  KKBB 31
  DIM 254, 402
  R 403
  WTLGD 151, 374
  TIAI 240
  SOTA 3, 124, 158, 251
  5001 144, 524
Marx, Karl
  DIM 163
  R 210, 362
  WTLGD 180, 294, 387
  H 62
Marxism
  DIM 16, 77, 175, 176
"Mary Hartman, Mary Hartman" (TV)
  WTLGD 450
  TIAI 424
  SOTA 94
Mary of Scotland (1936)
  5001
Mary Poppins
  WTLGD 470
Mary, Queen of Scots (1971)
  R 140
  5001
"Mary Tyler Moore Show, The" (TV)
  R 429
  SOTA 93
  H 150, 417, 418
Masada (TV)
  TIAI 396
Mascagni, Pietro
  TIAI 108
Maschwitz, Eric
  5001 48
Masculin-féminin, see *Masculine Feminine*
Masculine Feminine (*Masculin-féminin*)
  KKBB 127-130
  GS 4, 76, 81
  DIM 306
  R 168

TIAI 330
  5001
"Mashed Potato" (music)
  H 443
Masina, Giulietta
  KKBB 318, 351, 365, 368
  GS 46
  DIM 25
  H 138, 140, 141
  5001 67, 107, 285, 386, 450, 529, 717, 813,
    836
Mask
  H 206
Mask of Dimitrios, The
  5001
Mask of Fu Manchu, The
  5001
Masked Ball, A (music)
  WTLGD 101
Maskerade, see *Masquerade in Vienna*
Masoch, Leopold van Sacher, see van
    Sacher-Masoch, Leopold
Mason, A. E. W.
  5001 263
Mason, Hilary
  R 234
Mason, Jackie
  TIAI 216
Mason, James
  ILIATM 98, 206-207
  KKBB 22, 184, 283, 296, 319, 321, 346
  GS 235, 271
  DIM 412
  R 73, 75, 361
  WTLGD 25, 240, 243, 453
  TIAI 440
  SOTA 195, 370-371
  5001 86, 97, 126, 134, 215, 247, 282, 430,
    434, 446, 456, 471, 502, 533, 539, 563,
    602, 603, 660, 664, 669, 677, 707, 769,
    784, 813, 819
Mason, Margery
  H 379
  5001 597
Mason, Marsha
  R 259
  WTLGD 376-378, 466
  H 247
  5001 88, 138, 296, 325
Mason, Pamela (Kellino)
  5001 563
Mason, Sarah Y.
  5001 428, 713
Masquerade
  H 444-446
  5001 (2nd ed)
Masquerade in Vienna (*Maskerade*)
  5001
Mass in C minor (music)
  KKBB 306
Massacre at Central High
  ML 118
Massalitinova, Varvara
  5001 133
Massari, Léa
  DIM 305-306, 309-310
  H 437

5001 41, 503
Massen, Osa
　5001 847, 858
Massenet, Jules
　RK 67
Massey, Anna
　ML 272
　5001 425, 742
Massey, Daniel
　GS 164, 165
　5001 222, 360, 468, 657, 706
Massey, Ilona
　5001 48, 641
Massey, Raymond
　KKBB 232, 260
　GS 165
　5001 35, 203, 209, 244, 262, 343, 346, 500,
　　513, 542, 591, 597, 653, 659, 759, 845
Massie, Paul
　5001 552
Massie, Robert K.
　DIM 369
　5001 523
Massine, Léonide
　5001 621, 741
Massot, Joe
　5001 863
Master Builder, The (stage)
　DIM 50
"Masterpiece Theatre" (TV)
　WTLGD 383, 441, 538, 554
　TIAI 60, 478
　SOTA 333, 370, 371
　H 190, 330
Masters, Anthony
　5001 207
Masters of the Congo Jungle, see *Lords of the
　Forest*
Masterson, Mary Stuart
　H 305
　5001 279
Masterson, Peter
　TIAI 375
　H dir., *The Trip to Bountiful*, 92-93
　5001 64, 360, 458, 714, 790
Masterson, Whit
　5001 784
Mastrantonio, Mary Elizabeth
　SOTA 102
　H 224, 226
　5001 146, 658
Mastroianni, Marcello
　ILIATM 181-182
　KKBB 237, 238
　DIM 193-195, 220-221
　R 171, 207, 257
　WTLGD 4, 137, 153, 274, 310-312
　TIAI 469, 470
　H 44, 138, 140, 141, 142, 372, 374
　5001 62, 69, 172, 212, 285, 536, 584, 651,
　　700, 719, 728, 747, 779, 813
Masur, Richard
　SOTA 73, 334
　H 189
　5001 325, 473, 759, 805
Mat', see *Mother*
Mata Hari

KKBB 56
Matador
　H 466-467, 468-469
　ML 27
　5001 (2nd ed)
Matania, Clelia
　R 233
Maté, Rudolph
　KKBB 329, 365
　5001 196, 248, 409, 568, 650, 713, 774,
　　786, 812
Mather, Aubrey
　5001 36, 48, 327
Matheson, Richard
　TIAI 160
　SOTA 20, 21, 22
　5001 361, 797
Matheson, Tim
　SOTA 112
　5001 251, 452, 531, 775
Mathis, Johnny
　R 283
　TIAI 265
Mathison, Melissa
　TIAI 348, 349, 353
　5001 78, 225
Matisse, Henri
　WTLGD 363, 366
Matlovsky, Samuel
　5001 277
Matofsky, Harvey
　5001 863
Matras, Christian
　KKBB 264
　DIM 103
　5001 74, 209, 229, 236, 300, 430, 481, 753
Matshikiza, John
　5001 166
Mattei Affair, The
　R 202, 208-210
　TIAI 315, 316, 317
Matter of Innocence, A
　GS 54
Matter of Time, A
　WTLGD 192-195, 477
　5001
Matthau, Walter
　KKBB 40
　GS 224
　DIM 81, 83, 269
　R 85-86, 205-206, 260, 355, 365-366, 422,
　　424-425
　WTLGD 77-78, 531
　SOTA 15, 16, 18
　5001 113, 115, 117, 130, 131, 209, 232,
　　260, 270, 310, 402, 413, 577, 730, 732,
　　741
Matthews, A. E.
　KKBB 294, 307
　5001 413, 461, 771
Matthews, Carmen
　SOTA 44
　5001 172
Matthews, Jessie
　ILIATM 65
　TIAI 332
　5001 226

Matthews, Sheila
　R 407
Matthius, Gail
　H 132
Mattox, Matt
　5001 667
Mature, Victor
　WTLGD 13, 130, 214
　5001 9, 26, 399, 481, 508, 652, 671
Matuszak, John
　TIAI 194, 195-196
　5001 127, 298
"Maude" (TV)
　R 136
　WTLGD 261
Maudits, Les
　ILIATM 111
　WTLGD 147
Maugham, Somerset
　KKBB 295, 343
　5001 56, 136, 418, 435, 485, 539, 613, 617,
　　663, 766, 780
Mauldin, Bill
　5001 619
Maura, Carmen
　SOTA 364, 365
　H 288, 290, 467, 468
　ML 24-27
　5001 172, 414, 470, 830, 848
Maurey, Nicole
　5001 189, 425
Mauri, Glauco
　GS 5
　5001 134
Mauriac, Claude
　5001 753
Mauriac, François
　GS 80
　TIAI 442
　5001 753
Maurice
　H 359-362
　5001 (2nd ed)
Maurice Williams & the Zodiacs (group)
　H 349
Maurstad, T.
　5001 694
Maury, Jean-Louis
　5001 438
Max, Peter
　DIM 222
Maxwell, Edwin
　5001 18, 187, 299, 512, 531, 657, 677
Maxwell, Lois
　5001 270, 321, 462, 769
Maxwell, Marilyn
　5001 726
May, Elaine
　KKBB 300
　DIM 10, 73, 269, 369, 384; dir., *A New
　　Leaf*, 269
　R 69-70; dir., *The Heartbreak Kid*, 68-71,
　　261, 361, 430, 465; *A New Leaf*, 71
　WTLGD 272, 429, 531
　TIAI 429
　H dir., *Ishtar*, 309-312
　5001 115, 324, 371, 440, 520, 660, 724, 780

May, Jodhi
  H 475, 477
  5001 849
May, Joe
  5001 369
"Maybe" (music)
  TIAI 344
Mayer, Carl
  KKBB 243, 260
  5001 113, 203, 409, 729
Mayer, Edwin Justus
  RK 10
  5001 184, 478, 646, 760, 774
Mayer, Irene
  RK 31
Mayer, Louis B.
  KKBB 56, 207
  RK 5-6, 7, 26, 31, 45, 60, 70
  DIM 151
  WTLGD 216, 218, 431, 517
  SOTA 171
  H 53, 278
  5001 438, 641, 680
Mayerling (1936)
  ILIATM 98
  GS 80, 268
  R 420
  5001
Mayerling (1969)
  GS 268-271
  5001
Mayersberg, Paul
  ILIATM 306
  WTLGD 201
  5001 460
Mayes, Wendell
  R 72
  5001 8, 220, 341, 591
Mayfield, Curtis
  WTLGD 66, 165, 295
  5001 699
Mayfield, Julian
  5001 809
Mayhew, Peter
  5001 626, 709
Mayne, Ferdy
  5001 6
Mayniel, Juliette
  ILIATM 133, 135
  5001 159, 230
Mayo, Archie
  KKBB 288, 355; dir., *It's Love I'm After*,
    288; *Svengali*, 355
  5001 27, 77, 288, 374, 524, 551, 578, 733,
    734
Mayo, Virginia
  5001 65, 596, 663, 834
Mayron, Melanie
  TIAI 310, 311
  5001 118, 275, 320, 486, 857
Maysles, Albert and David
  DIM 206-209, 211
Maytime
  5001
Mayuzumi, Toshiro
  5001 622
Mazur, Richard

  5001 632
Mazurki, Mike
  KKBB 143, 313, 316
  5001 117, 503, 524, 529, 672, 691
Mazursky, Betsy
  5001 746
Mazursky, Meg
  DIM 227
  5001 13
Mazursky, Paul
  GS 158
  DIM 9-11, 14, 148, 225-227, 350; dir., *Bob
    & Carol & Ted & Alice*, 8-14, 225; *Alex
    in Wonderland*, 224-228
  R 167, 241, 330, 409-410; dir., *Alex in
    Wonderland*, 167, 411; *Blume in Love*,
    167, 186, 408, 411, 415-416; *Bob &
    Carol & Ted & Alice*, 184; *Harry &
    Tonto*, 376, 409, 411
  WTLGD 127-131, 147, 242, 377, 410-414;
    dir., *Next Stop, Greenwich Village*,
    127-131, 173, 411, 412, 413; *Bob &
    Carol & Ted & Alice*, 128, 411; *Alex in
    Wonderland*, 128, 129; *Blume in Love*,
    128, 130, 236, 377, 411, 412, 413;
    Harry & Tonto, 128, 129, 411; *An
    Unmarried Woman*, 410-414
  TIAI 46-50, 216, 320, 323, 389-392; dir.,
    Willie and Phil, 46-50, 392; *An
    Unmarried Woman*, 47, 49, 135; *Alex in
    Wonderland*, 47; *Blume in Love*, 48;
    Harry & Tonto, 49; *Next Stop,
    Greenwich Village*, 320; *Bob & Carol &
    Ted & Alice*, 320; *Tempest*, 389-392
  SOTA 135, 155-160, 173; dir., *An
    Unmarried Woman*, 108, 135; *Moscow
    on the Hudson*, 155-160; *Harry &
    Tonto*, 158; *Tempest*, 173
  H 102-106, 139, 248-249; dir., *Down and
    Out in Beverly Hills*, 102-106, 272, 350;
    Moscow on the Hudson, 103, 105, 188,
    264, 421; *An Unmarried Woman*, 105;
    Next Stop, Greenwich Village, 248-249;
    Tempest, 371, 482
  ML dir., *Alex in Wonderland*, 328; *Blume in
    Love*, 328; *Bob & Carol & Ted & Alice*,
    328; *Down and Out in Beverly Hills*, 73,
    328; *Enemies, A Love Story*, 229-34,
    283
  5001 12, 79, 88, 89, 199, 219, 320, 335,
    350, 499, 521, 659, 707, 746, 807, 839,
    840
Me and My Brother
  5001
Me and My Gal
  5001
Me Two (book)
  SOTA 221
Meacham, Anne
  5001 422
Mead, Margaret
  ILIATM 12
  TIAI 472
Mead, Taylor
  5001 479
Meadows, Jayne

  5001 405
Mean Season, The
  SOTA 334-335
  H 156
  5001 (2nd ed)
Mean Streets
  R 168-175, 256, 268, 302, 310, 315, 320,
    329, 399, 414-415
  WTLGD 132, 202, 420, 434, 446, 447
  TIAI 109, 153, 457, 460
  SOTA 201, 204
  H 227
  ML 268
  5001
Meara, Anne
  R 130
  WTLGD 265
  TIAI 225
  ML 323
  5001 97, 517
Meatballs
  TIAI 225
  SOTA 192
Meck, Mme. von, see von Meck
Medak, Peter
  TIAI 232-233; dir., *Zorro, the Gay Blade*,
    232-233
  5001 866
Meddings Magic Camera Company
  ML 44
  5001 333
Medea (stage)
  KKBB 56
Medford, Harold
  5001 169
Medford, Kay
  5001 244, 272
Medicine Woman (book)
  H 21
Medina, Ofelia
  5001 70
Medina, Patricia
  5001 767
Medioli, Enrico
  WTLGD 37
  5001 154, 364
Medium, The
  ILIATM 286
  KKBB 308:n
  5001
Medium Cool
  DIM 117
Medivin, Michael
  5001 167
Meehan, John
  5001 266, 327, 483
Meehan, Thomas
  SOTA 111
  5001 775
Meek, Donald
  5001 42, 51, 118, 134, 322, 391, 577, 704,
    783, 836, 847, 860
Meeker, George
  5001 332, 628
Meeker, Ralph
  DIM 199
  5001 25, 185, 352, 570

Meerson, Lazare
KKBB 245, 287
5001 1, 121, 373, 481
Meerson, Steve
5001 708
Meet John Doe
WTLGD 213
SOTA 306
5001
Meet Me in St. Louis
KKBB 185
WTLGD 547
TIAI 348
Meet Nero Wolfe
5001
Megginson, Robert T.
H 116, 117
5001 273
Megna, John
5001 777
Meighan, Thomas
RK 13
Meilhac, Henri
SOTA 254
5001 119
Meillon, John
5001 729
"Mein Herr" (music)
DIM 410
Meinardi, Helen
5001 351
Meiselas, Susan
SOTA 73
Mekas, Adolfas
5001 314
Mekas, Jonas
ILIATM 19, 189, 303, 314-318; dir., *Guns of the Trees*, 189
Mela, Ina
5001 160
Melato, Mariangela
WTLGD 138
TIAI 126, 240
5001 250, 437, 689, 736
Melendez, William
5001 97
Méliès, Georges
ILIATM 275
KKBB 255-256; dir., *A Trip to the Moon*, 255
GS 3
TIAI 124, 125
ML 111
Melinda
R 65
Mell, Joseph
5001 435, 502
Mell, Marisa
5001 453
Mello-Men, The (group)
5001 287
Mellor, William C.
KKBB 233, 332
5001 47, 151, 285, 585
Melnick, Daniel
TIAI 14
5001 721

Melnick, Mark
SOTA 120
Melnick, Peter
ML 328
Melo (stage)
KKBB 260
Melton, James
5001 865
Meltzer, Lewis
5001 462
Melville, Herman
ILIATM 206, 234-239, 296
KKBB 134
DIM 417, 418
TIAI 98
SOTA 26, 163
5001 53, 72, 489
Melville, Jean-Pierre
ILIATM 132; dir., *Les Enfants Terribles*, 132
KKBB 262; dir., *Les Enfants Terribles*, 114, 231, 262
R 339; dir., *Les Enfants Terribles*, 337
5001 100, 220
Melvin and Howard
TIAI 71-78, 292, 294
H 232
5001
Melvin, Murray
ILIATM 197
5001 14, 53, 248
Melvin Simon Productions
TIAI 69
Member of the Wedding, The (1952)
ILIATM 47
KKBB 203, 308-309:n
5001
Member of the Wedding, The (1983, TV)
SOTA 58
Memmoli, George
R 370
WTLGD 408
5001 86, 473, 521
Memories of a Catholic Girlhood (book)
KKBB 77
Memories of Underdevelopment
WTLGD 280
Memory of Justice, The
WTLGD 175-177
5001
Men, The
ILIATM 47
KKBB 203
DIM 322
5001
Men... (Männer...)
H 194-197
5001 (2nd ed)
Men in War
5001
Men in White
5001
Ménage (Tenue de soirée)
5001 (2nd ed)
Mencken, H. L.
KKBB 207
R 424

Mendelssohn, Felix
TIAI 365
5001 479, 658, 694
Mendes, Lothar
5001 263-264, 459
Mendès-France, Pierre
DIM 428
Mengele, Dr. Josef
WTLGD 451, 453
Menges, Chris
SOTA 270, 274, 278
H 54, 449, 475-478; dir., *A World Apart*, 475-478
5001 149, 332, 395, 465, 849
Menilmontant
ILIATM 291
KKBB 352
5001
Menjou, Adolphe
KKBB 341
RK 20, 22 (ill.)
5001 257, 292, 293, 426, 498, 570, 645, 703, 707, 711, 714, 736
Menken, Alan
H 247
5001 426, 428
Menotti, Gian-Carlo
ILIATM 286; dir., *The Medium*, 286
KKBB 308; dir., *The Medium*, 308
5001 473
Menuhin, Yehudi
WTLGD 176
Menzel, Jiri
5001 142
Menzies, William Cameron
5001 15, 127, 186, 397, 689, 756, 759
Mephisto
TIAI 337-340
5001 (2nd ed)
Mephisto Waltz
WTLGD 523
Merande, Doro
R 426
5001 399, 462, 647, 668
Mercado, Hector Jaime
WTLGD 494, 495
5001 687
Mercer, Beryl
5001 18, 127, 341, 426, 483, 628
Mercer, David
R 394
WTLGD 256-259
5001 497, 602, 825
Mercer, Frances
5001 717
Mercer, Johnny
5001 19, 88, 99, 168, 321, 667, 685
Merchant, Ismail
SOTA 209
H 126, 359
5001 90, 94, 640, 642-643
Merchant of Four Seasons, The (Der Händler der Vier Jahreszeiten)
5001
Merchant of Venice, The (stage)
ILIATM 201
Merchant, Vivien

KKBB 107, 109
DIM 68
R 115, 220
5001 3, 14, 338, 805
Mercier, Michèle
5001 676
Mercouri, Melina
KKBB 167, 351
GS 169
DIM 74, 182, 245-248
WTLGD 265
5001 276, 323, 517, 520, 548, 578, 601,
713, 781
Mercure, Jean
5001 619
Mercure, Monique
WTLGD 550
5001 609
Mercury Theatre
RK 4, 8, 31-32, 33, 34, 36, 38, 39-40, 45,
46, 55, 65, 84
Meredith, Burgess
KKBB 369
DIM 76, 229, 384
R 473-474
WTLGD 120, 214-215, 510
TIAI 243, 346
5001 8, 160, 176, 189, 334, 354, 447, 450,
459, 540, 622, 636, 662, 724, 752, 778,
793, 841
Meredith, George
SOTA 373
Meredyth, Bess
5001 254, 555, 845
Méril, Macha
5001 467, 811
Mérimée, Prosper
ILIATM 101-102
SOTA 227, 254
5001 119, 246, 293
Merivale, John
KKBB 298
5001 424
Merivale, Philip
5001 719
Merkel, Una
ILIATM 137
KKBB 256, 314
5001 91, 93, 105, 107, 185, 225, 262, 599,
620, 726, 762, 793
Merle, Robert
R 246
5001 176
Merman, Ethel
KKBB 6
R 299, 388
TIAI 344
H 187
5001 12, 13, 32, 115, 717, 752, 828
Merrick, David
R 72, 319
5001 134, 665
Merrill, Bob
5001 272
Merrill, Dina
5001 110, 184, 387, 729, 860
Merrill, Gary

KKBB 230
WTLGD 271
5001 16, 123, 593, 757
Merrill, Robert
WTLGD 61
Merritt, Abraham
5001 186
Merritt, Theresa
WTLGD 470
5001 64, 296, 303
Merrow, Jane
5001 423
Merry Maidens
RK 60
Merry Widow, The
ILIATM 105, 322
WTLGD 99
Merry Wives of Windsor, The (stage)
KKBB 201
"Merv Griffin Show, The" (TV)
TIAI 248
Meschera del Demonio, La, see Black Sunday
Messel, Oliver
5001 114, 756
Messemer, Hannes
KKBB 258, 270
5001 187, 281
Metamorphosis, The (book)
GS 78
H 211
Metcalf, Laurie
ML 262, 263, 278
5001 184, 367, 561
Metcalfe, Stephen
ML 97
5001 159
Methot, Mayo
KKBB 252, 308
5001 156, 466, 487, 684
Metrano, Art
5001 16
Metro-Goldwyn-Mayer (M-G-M)
RK 5, 17, 24, 26, 31, 36, 69, 70, 74, 80
DIM 51, 67, 105, 155, 188, 211, 225, 226,
406
R 65-66, 111, 217, 327
WTLGD 15, 142, 216, 471, 474, 475
TIAI 14, 99, 198, 234, 278, 297, 353, 357
SOTA 110
H 21, 158, 306, 356, 456
ML 121
Metropolis
ILIATM 146, 284-285, 299
KKBB 309-310:n
GS 45
RK 76
WTLGD 429
TIAI 364
ML 163
5001
Metter, Alan
H dir., Back to School, 185-186
5001 45
Metty, Russell
5001 33, 484, 598, 699, 719, 763, 784
Metzler, Jim
TIAI 284, 399

5001 264, 632, 749
Metzman, Irving
TIAI 240, 494
5001 604, 690, 715
Meurisse, Paul
KKBB 259
5001 188, 581
Mexicali Rose
5001
Meyer, David and Tony
SOTA 5
5001 539
Meyer, Emile
5001 79, 462, 570, 671, 736
Meyer, Greta
5001 75
Meyer, Jean
5001 96
Meyer, Nicholas
WTLGD 190-192
TIAI 355-360; dir., Time After Time, 75,
355; Star Trek II: The Wrath of Khan,
355-360
SOTA 197-198
5001 667, 707, 772
Meyer, Russ
DIM dir., The Immoral Mr. Teas, 58
WTLGD 208
TIAI 198
Meyer, Tony, see Meyer, David and Tony
Meyers, Nancy
TIAI 94
H 377
5001 42, 598
Meyjes, Menno
H 82, 414
ML 148
5001 147, 217, 362
Meynier, Geronimo
KKBB 231
5001 24
Mezière, Myriam
WTLGD 181
Mezzogiorno, Vittorio
TIAI 316, 319
SOTA 46
5001 495, 764
MGM-UA Classics
H 122
Miami and the Siege of Chicago (book)
R 151
"Miami Vice" (TV)
H 14
Michael Dunn Memorial Repertory Theatre
Company
TIAI 353
Michael, Gertrude
5001 141, 249, 357, 502
Michael, Ralph
KKBB 255
5001 178, 528
Michaels, Sidney
GS 238
5001 528
Michel, Dominique
H 239
5001 182

Michel, Marc
  KKBB 287
  5001 373, 430
Michelangeli, Marcella
  WTLGD 299, 301
Michelangeli, Margella
  5001 561
Michelangelo
  H 14, 340
Michell, Helena
  H 361
  5001 471
Michell, Keith
  5001 851
Michener, James A.
  KKBB 161
  5001 322
Michi, Maria
  KKBB 324
  R 33
  5001 410, 551, 562
Mickey One
  KKBB 60
  GS 157
Micki & Maude
  SOTA 304-306
  5001 (2nd ed)
Middle of the World, The
  WTLGD 180
Middlemarch (book)
  ILIATM 282, 324
  SOTA 89
Middlemass, Frank
  WTLGD 102
Middleton, Charles
  TIAI 126
Middleton, Guy
  KKBB 294
  5001 413
Middleton, Malcolm
  5001 558
Middleton, Ray
  5001 668
Middleton, Robert
  5001 268
Midgette, Allen
  5001 61
Midler, Bette
  TIAI 42, 43, 95, 97, 229, 411, 412
  SOTA 178
  H 103, 104, 179, 180, 272-273, 274, 288,
    421, 483-484, 485
  ML 72-74
  5001 56, 68, 193, 199, 380, 559, 641, 647,
    713, 779
Midnight
  KKBB 362
  RK 26
  TIAI 429
  5001
Midnight Cowboy
  DIM 4, 76, 147, 152, 314
  R 161, 172, 185, 239, 293, 309, 326, 475
  WTLGD 175
  H 24
  5001
Midnight Express

WTLGD 496-501
  TIAI 20, 122, 188, 290
  SOTA 284
  H 35, 157, 180, 251
  ML 53
  5001
Midnight Run
  ML 81
Midsummer Night's Dream, A
  ILIATM 287
  KKBB 331, 348
  GS 70-71
  WTLGD 75, 264
  ML 42-43
Midsummer Night's Dream, A (stage)
  GS 159
Midsummer Night's Sex Comedy, A
  TIAI 365-368
  SOTA 123
  5001 (2nd ed)
Miéville, Anne-Marie
  TIAI 104
  SOTA 227
  5001 246
Mifune, Toshiro
  ILIATM 123, 239-240, 242
  KKBB 9, 337
  GS 271-272
  DIM 336
  SOTA 161, 244
  5001 47, 327, 354, 531, 616, 668, 769, 856
Migenes-Johnson, Julia
  SOTA 254, 255
  5001 76
Mighty Joe Young
  5001
Mignot, Pierre
  TIAI 415
  H 1, 99
  5001 148, 255, 663
Miguelin
  KKBB 119
  5001 492
Mikado, The
  TIAI 124
  5001
Mikael, Ludmilla
  WTLGD 153
Mike's Murder
  H 175-176
  5001 (2nd ed)
Mikhalkov, Nikita
  H dir., *Dark Eyes*, 372-374
  5001 172
Milan, Lita
  5001 416
Mildred Pierce
  KKBB 253
  GS 127
  WTLGD 145
  TIAI 236, 237
  ML 275
  5001
Miles, Bernard
  KKBB 276
  5001 235, 302, 490, 523, 769
Miles, Joanna

R 246
  5001 164
Miles, Lillian
  5001 281
Miles, Richard
  5001 750
Miles, Sarah
  DIM 189, 190
  R 110-111, 113
  H 367, 370
  5001 85, 340, 404, 648
Miles, Sylvia
  5001 326, 409, 479
Miles, Vera
  5001 40, 461, 662, 784, 850
Milestone, Lewis
  KKBB 230-231; dir., *Mutiny on the Bounty*,
    193; *All Quiet on the Western Front*,
    230-231; *Hallelujah, I'm a Bum*, 234
  RK 24
  DIM dir., *All Quiet on the Western Front*,
    16, 17, 134; *Edge of Darkness*, 63;
    Mutiny on the Bounty, 177
  5001 18, 32, 314, 443, 531, 534, 540, 613,
    718, 821
Milestones
  5001
Milford, Kim
  5001 156
Milford, Penelope
  WTLGD 403
  5001 150, 219
Milhaud, Darius
  5001 598
Milian, Tomas
  KKBB 237
  5001 62, 89, 409
Military, Frank
  ML 308
  5001 227
Milius, John
  R 88, 98-100, 254-255, 469
  WTLGD 42, 196, 203, 512; dir., *The Wind
    and the Lion*, 42, 196; *Dillinger*, 116,
    196
  TIAI 98, 127
  SOTA 119
  H 35, 185; dir., *Conan the Barbarian*, 180,
    251; *Red Dawn*, 348
  5001 191, 379, 421, 452, 531, 840
Miljan, John
  5001 35, 62, 393, 555, 579, 732, 807
Milky Way, The (*La Voie lactée*)
  DIM 102-103
  R 42
  5001
Millais, Hugh
  R 80
  TIAI 168
  5001 358, 445
Millais, John Everett
  H 53
Milland, Ray
  KKBB 184, 259
  R 359
  WTLGD 8, 30, 218, 443
  TIAI 429

5001 57, 90, 189, 210, 291, 370, 404, 411,
    437, 453, 482, 522, 768, 807, 828, 852
Millar, Gavin
    H dir., *Dreamchild*, 51-54
    5001 202
Millar, Stuart
    WTLGD 62-64; dir., *Rooster Cogburn*,
        62-64, 197
    5001 424, 640
Miller, Alice Duer
    RK 10, 18
    5001 338, 370, 834, 836
Miller, Allen C.
    5001 195
Miller, Ann
    TIAI 275, 357
    5001 210, 322, 398, 546, 640, 703
Miller, Arnold R.
    WTLGD 249-250
Miller, Arthur
    ILIATM 173-175
    GS 209
    RK 19
    DIM 50, 208
    R 116-117, 153, 156-158
    H 179, 351
    ML 200, 306-308
    5001 17, 226, 484, 815
Miller, Barry
    5001 574, 655
Miller, David
    KKBB 40; dir., *Lonely Are the Brave*, 7, 40
    R 209; dir., *Executive Action*, 208-209; *Love
        Happy*, 209; *Captain Newman, M.D.*,
        209; *Hail, Hero!*, 209; *Lonely Are the
        Brave*, 209
    5001 228
Miller, Denny
    5001 567, 744
Miller, Dick
    TIAI 193
    SOTA 190
    5001 9, 307, 324, 343
Miller, Frank
    ML 159
Miller, George
    TIAI 384-389; dir., *The Road Warrior*,
        384-389, 456; *Mad Max*, 384, 386
    SOTA 18, 22-23; dir., *Twilight Zone--The
        Movie*, (co-dir.), 18-23; *The Road
        Warrior*, 22
    H 323-325; dir., *The Witches of Eastwick*,
        323-325, 482; *Mad Max*, 344
    5001 633, 634, 797, 843
Miller, Glenn
    5001 287, 551, 552, 728
Miller, Harvey
    TIAI 94
    5001 598
Miller, Henry
    ILIATM 210
    KKBB 260, 274
    DIM 123-127, 219
    WTLGD 182, 455
    5001 621, 791
Miller, J. P.
    5001 860

Miller, Jason
    R 248-250
    5001 228
Miller, Jonathan
    SOTA 341
    H 100
Miller, Joshua
    H 315
    5001 519, 632
Miller, Lara Jill
    5001 783
Miller, Linda
    WTLGD 411
    5001 807
Miller, Marilyn
    WTLGD 12
Miller, Max
    5001 349
Miller, Penelope Ann
    ML 322,
Miller, Robert Ellis
    GS dir., *Sweet November*, 40
    5001 32, 110
Miller, Seton I.
    5001 8, 329, 547, 657, 660
Miller, Sue
    ML 34
    5001 295
Miller, Warren
    5001 155
Miller's Beautiful Wife, The
    DIM 362
Millhauser, Bertram
    5001 733
Millholland, Bruce
    KKBB 362
    TIAI 240
    5001 690, 796
Milligan, Spike
    DIM 17
    TIAI 216
    5001 59, 335, 450, 767
Million, Le
    ILIATM 283
    KKBB 320
    5001
Million Dollar Legs
    KKBB 7, 185
    RK 15, 26
    ML 118
    5001
Million Dollar Mermaid
    5001
Million Pound Note, The, see *Man with a Million*
Millionaires of Naples (*Napoli Milionaria*; also
        known as *Side Street Story*)
    5001
Millöcker, Karl
    TIAI 337
Mills-Cockell, Juno
    5001 566
Mills, Hayley
    ILIATM 66
    GS 54
    5001 833
Mills, James
    R 433

5001 564, 624
Mills, John
    KKBB 276, 282, 339
    DIM 190
    R 17, 432
    TIAI 433
    5001 145, 277, 301, 336, 360, 529, 541,
        635, 648, 794, 860
Mills-Cockell, Juno
    ML 94-95
Milne, Peter
    5001 292
Milner, Martin
    KKBB 250, 356
    5001 151, 421, 736
Milo, Sandra
    KKBB 270
    5001 213, 281, 386
Milosz, Czeslaw
    DIM 203
Milton, David Scott
    DIM 351
    5001 94
Milton, Joyce
    SOTA 41, 44
Miluwi, John Omirah
    ML 7
    5001 298
Mimei, Wu Jun
    H 397
    5001 408
Mimi
    5001
Mimieux, Yvette
    KKBB 185
    5001 766, 773, 785
Minciotti, Esther
    5001 467, 850
Mind Benders, The
    TIAI 129
Mind of Mr. Soames, The
    5001
Mindszenty, Cardinal Joseph
    DIM 201, 202
Mineo, Sal
    5001 285, 618
Miner, Bill
    SOTA 27-31
Miner, Jan
    R 372
    TIAI 49
    5001 417, 840
Miner, Michael
    H 344
    5001 635
Minh, Ho Chi, see Ho Chi Minh
Minion, Joseph
    H 38
    ML 151
    5001 9, 812
Ministry of Fear
    5001
Minnelli, Liza
    DIM 32-34, 409-412, 432
    R 178, 204, 460, 462
    WTLGD 61, 106-107, 167, 193-194
    TIAI 109, 231, 232, 391

5001 36, 112, 131, 442, 470, 520, 521, 714
Minnelli, Vincente
 ILIATM 299, 301, 307, 317; dir., *The Cob-*
  web, 58; *The Band Wagon*, 278
 KKBB 233, 234, 249, 344, 363-364; dir.,
  The Sandpiper, 28, 143, 221, 343-344;
  Meet Me in St. Louis, 185; *Ziegfield*
  Follies, 222; *The Bad and the Beautiful*,
  232-233, 238, 363-364; *The Band*
  Wagon, 234; *An American in Paris*, 234,
  273; *Cabin in the Sky*, 234; *The*
  Cobweb, 249; *Undercurrent*, 353; *Two*
  Weeks in Another Town, 363-364
 GS 163; dir., *The Band Wagon*, 156; *Cabin*
  in the Sky, 102; *The Clock*, 102
 DIM 275; dir., *An American in Paris*, 84;
  On a Clear Day You Can See Forever,
  185; *Father of the Bride*, 296
 WTLGD 192-195, 513, 547; dir., *The Bad*
  and the Beautiful, 61; *The Band Wagon*,
  177; *A Matter of Time*, 192-195, 477;
  On a Clear Day You Can See Forever,
  193; *The Cobweb*, 373; *Meet Me in St.*
  Louis, 547
 TIAI 348; dir., *Meet Me in St. Louis*, 348
 H 158; dir., *Some Came Running*, 307
 ML dir., *Lust for Life*, 290-291
 5001 23, 42, 46, 50, 103, 112, 141, 144,
  240, 285, 349, 398, 443, 446, 470, 583,
  653, 772, 800, 856, 865
Minnesota Fats
 H 223
Minnie and Moskowitz
 R 394
 5001
"Minnie the Moocher" (music)
 TIAI 27
 SOTA 295
Minotis, Alexis
 5001 564
Minsker, Andy
 ML 122, 123
Minsky, Louis
 GS 239
Minty, Emil
 TIAI 385
"Minute Waltz" (music)
 DIM 137
Miou-Miou
 WTLGD 181, 182, 455-456
 SOTA 134, 137
 5001 222, 291, 383, 476, 751
Miquette et sa mère
 5001
Miracle, The (Il Miracolo)
 5001
Miracle in Milan (Miracolo a Milano)
 ILIATM 284, 341
 KKBB 269, 310:n, 368
 DIM 361, 362
 SOTA 26
 H 267
 5001
Miracle, Irene
 WTLGD 497
Miracle of Morgan's Creek, The
 R 301

H 110
5001
Miracle of Our Lady of Fatima, The
 WTLGD 354
Miracle on 34th Street
 DIM 136
Miracle Woman, The
 5001
Miracle Worker, The
 KKBB 55, 60, 143
 5001
Miracolo a Milano, see *Miracle in Milan*
Miracolo, Il, see *The Miracle*
Miranda
 R 115
Miranda, Carmen
 WTLGD 473
 H 275
 5001 174, 199, 278, 751, 827
Miranda case
 DIM 386, 388
Miranda, Isa
 KKBB 354
 5001 727, 822
Mirbeau, Octave
 5001 189
Mirisch, Walter
 5001 322
Miró, Joan
 DIM 299
Miroslava
 5001 98
Mirren, Helen
 TIAI 185
 H 66
 5001 227, 835
Mischief-Makers, The, see *Les Mistons*
Misérables, Les
 KKBB 276
 WTLGD 489
 5001 (2nd ed)
Misfits, The
 ILIATM 37-38, 40, 299
 R 153, 155
 5001
Mishima, Yukio
 ILIATM 161
Misraki, Paul
 5001 20
Miss Dupont
 5001 255
Miss Firecracker
 ML 141-44
 5001 (2nd ed)
Miss Firecracker Contest, The (book)
 ML 141
Miss Hargreaves
 H 366-367
Miss Julie
 5001
Miss Lonelyhearts (book)
 R 44, 476
 TIAI 87
Miss Sadie Thompson
 5001
Missa Luba (music)
 DIM 175

Missing
 TIAI 309-312
 SOTA 77
 H 182
 5001
Mission, The
 H 476
 ML 191
Mississippi
 RK 26
Mississippi Burning
 ML 53-56
 5001 (2nd ed)
Missouri Breaks, The
 WTLGD 427
 TIAI 283
Mrs. Miniver
 KKBB 221, 304
 DIM 359
 5001
Mrs. Soffel
 SOTA 290-293
 H 234, 378, 432
 5001 (2nd ed)
Mr. Blandings Builds His Dream House
 WTLGD 21
Mr. Buddwing
 5001 (2nd ed)
Mr. Deeds Goes to Town
 KKBB 186
 RK 20
 WTLGD 48
 5001
Mr. Hulot's Holiday (Les Vacances de Monsieur
  Hulot)
 KKBB 185, 312-313:n
 DIM 194
 R 73
 ML 134
 5001
Mr. Klein
 WTLGD 396
 5001
Mr. Lucky
 5001
Mr. Mom
 SOTA 174
 H 264
Mr. Moto Takes a Vacation
 5001 (2nd ed)
Mr. Peabody and the Mermaid
 5001
Mister Roberts
 5001
Mr. Skeffington
 ML 275
Mr. Smith Goes to Washington
 KKBB 68
 WTLGD 48, 227
 5001
Mr. T.
 TIAI 346
 5001 636
Mistons, Les (The Mischief-Makers)
 KKBB 310-311:n
 R 291
 5001

Mitchell, Aleta
  5001 812
Mitchell, Arthur
  GS 70
Mitchell, Cameron
  TIAI 397
  5001 439, 508, 629
Mitchell, Charlotte
  5001 267
Mitchell, Eddy
  5001 158
Mitchell, Elvis
  H 32
Mitchell, Grant
  KKBB 276
  5001 36, 292, 301, 459, 522, 768, 777
Mitchell, James
  5001 50, 364, 777, 794
Mitchell, Joni
  R 309
  5001 411
Mitchell, Julian
  ML 290, 293
Mitchell, Millard
  WTLGD 13
  5001 199, 258, 399, 683
Mitchell, Thomas
  KKBB 281
  5001 27, 251, 331, 345, 346, 374, 392, 433,
    436, 489, 556, 558, 704, 741, 752, 786
Mitchell, Yvonne
  KKBB 369
  5001 193, 304, 360, 844
Mitchlll, Scoey
  H 145
  5001 381
Mitchum, Chris
  5001 631
Mitchum, John
  5001 221
Mitchum, Robert
  KKBB 42-46, 205, 253, 297, 317
  GS 171, 250
  DIM 189, 190, 353, 354
  R 469-470
  WTLGD 218
  ML 40
  5001 71, 164, 214, 220, 268, 411, 424, 503,
    526, 557, 648, 660, 729, 853
Mitra, Subrata
  5001 90, 569
Mitrione, Dan
  R 213
Mitsou
  5001
Mix, Tom
  KKBB 256
Miyamoto, Nobuko
  H 306, 307
  5001 743
Mizoguchi, Kenji
  5001 802
Mme. Cyn, see Payne, Cynthia
Moana
  KKBB 357
Moberg, Vilhelm
  R 8

  5001 216, 520
Mobil Oil
  WTLGD 150, 386
Moby Dick (1930)
  5001
Moby Dick (1956)
  ILIATM 298-299, 303
  KKBB 131, 134, 198
  5001
Model and the Marriage Broker, The
  ILIATM 305
  5001
Model Shop
  GS 263-267
  SOTA 166
  5001
Modern Romance
  SOTA 344
Modern Times
  KKBB 311, 320
  5001
Modernaires (group)
  5001 287, 551, 728
Modest Proposal, A (book)
  KKBB 120
Modesty Blaise
  KKBB 367
  GS 19, 172
  R 343
  WTLGD 94
Modiano, Patrick
  R 336
  5001 403
Modigliani, Amedeo
  H 371
Modine, Matthew
  SOTA 290, 316, 318, 319
  H 325
  ML 276, 277
  5001 74, 271, 486, 561
Modot, Gaston
  KKBB 246, 343
  5001 10, 59, 123, 300, 575, 647
Modugno, Enrica Maria
  H 123
Moeller, Philip
  5001 99
Moffat, Donald
  SOTA 63
  H 111
  5001 65, 504, 630, 759, 804
Moffat, Ivan
  5001 285
Moffitt, Jack
  5001 502
Moffo, Anna
  DIM 135
  5001 6
Mogambo
  R 385
  5001
Mohner, Carl
  KKBB 339
  5001 630
Moholy-Nagy, László
  5001 759
Mohr, Gerald

  5001 186
Mohr, Hal
  5001 118, 839
Moi Universiteti, see *My Universities*
Moissi, Bettina
  5001 33
Mokae, Zakes
  ML 185, 205
  5001 168, 205
Mokri, Amir
  5001 561
Molander, Gustaf
  5001 366
Molière
  WTLGD 530
  5001 96
Molina, Alfred
  H 295, 297
  5001 595
Molina, Angela
  WTLGD 365-366
  5001 751
Molina, Miguel
  H 289, 290
  5001 414
Molinaro, Edouard
  TIAI 164-167; dir., *La Cage aux Folles II*,
    164-167; *La Cage aux Folles*, 164, 165
  5001 114
Moll, Georgia
  KKBB 336
  5001 608
Molly Maguires, The
  DIM 103-104, 159
  WTLGD 170
  5001
Molnár, Ferenc
  ILIATM 154
  5001 294, 309, 551, 741
Moment by Moment
  TIAI 32
Moment of Truth, The (Il Momento della Verità)
  KKBB 118-120
  GS 96
  DIM 171
  R 125
  5001
Momento della Verità, Il, see *The Moment of Truth*
Mommie Dearest
  TIAI 233-237
  5001
Mon Oncle
  KKBB 311:n
  DIM 245
  R 73
  5001
Mon Oncle Antoine, see *My Uncle Antoine*
Mona Lisa
  H 164-168, 301, 331, 369, 411
  ML 42, 139
  5001 (2nd ed)
"Mona Lisa" (painting)
  H 166
"Mona Lisa" (music)
  H 166
Monash, Paul

R 423
5001 269
Mondo Cane
  ILIATM 10
  KKBB 63
  GS 119
  R 66
  5001
Mondo Trasho
  DIM 130
"Money" (music)
  DIM 412
Monica, Corbett
  SOTA 123
Monicelli, Mario
  KKBB 238; dir., *Big Deal on Madonna Street*, 238
  5001 69
Monika
  R 91
Monk, Meredith
  H 173
Monk, Thelonious
  KKBB 297
  GS 173
  ML 1
  5001 338, 379, 420
Monkees, The (rock group)
  GS 186
  SOTA 212
"Monkees, The" (TV)
  GS 63
Monkey Business (1931)
  KKBB 185
  RK 15, 83
  5001
Monkey Business (1952)
  5001
Monks, John Jr.
  5001 722, 760, 831
Monnet, Gabriel
  SOTA 46
Monnoyer, Jean-Maurice
  5001 264
Monogram Pictures
  WTLGD 291, 379
Monroe, Marilyn
  ILIATM 37-39
  KKBB 58, 191, 230, 272, 334, 348
  GS 194, 224
  DIM 156, 209, 371
  R 151-158
  WTLGD 3, 39, 219, 316
  TIAI 32, 157, 330, 373
  H 30
  ML 307-308
  5001 16, 37, 140, 197, 484, 494, 522, 596, 668, 691, 752, 771, 839
Monsieur Beaucaire
  WTLGD 336
Monsieur Ripois (also known as *Knave of Hearts*; U.S. titles: *Lovers. Happy Lovers* and *Lover Boy*)
  ILIATM 111
  KKBB 311-312:n
  5001
Monsieur Verdoux

ILIATM 196
TIAI 217, 444
H 187
5001
Monsieur Vincent
  KKBB 312:n
  5001
Montagu, Ivor
  KKBB 253; dir., *Day Dreams*, 253-254
  5001 175
Montalban, Ricardo
  ILIATM 223
  KKBB 178
  TIAI 356, 357, 358
  5001 447, 707, 734
Montana, Lenny
  5001 289
Montand, Yves
  KKBB 9, 163, 165
  DIM 64, 184, 202, 204
  R 95-96, 158, 210, 211
  WTLGD 153-155, 223
  H 329, 330-331
  5001 128, 151, 309, 379, 784, 815, 821, 862
Montanelli, Indro
  5001 281
Monte Walsh
  DIM 162
  5001
Montenegro, Conchita
  WTLGD 364-365
  5001 187
Montenegro, Fernanda
  H 269
  5001 342
Monterey Pop
  DIM 208
Montevecci, Liliane
  5001 287
Montez, Lola
  R 146
  WTLGD 50
Montez, Maria
  ILIATM 314
  KKBB 28
  DIM 25
  TIAI 125
  SOTA 104
  5001 14, 34, 143, 228, 254, 311, 751, 835
Montgomery, Gen. Bernard
  DIM 99, 100
Montgomery, David
  WTLGD 471
Montgomery, Douglass (Kent Douglass)
  5001 428, 824
Montgomery, George
  KKBB 341
  R 186
  5001 551, 645
Montgomery, James H.
  5001 370
Montgomery, Lee H.
  R 383
Montgomery, Robert
  DIM 347
  R 186
  WTLGD 27

5001 194, 259, 329, 386, 404, 525, 555, 599, 629, 806
Monty Python and the Holy Grail
  TIAI 183
  H 106
  ML 109
Monty Python's Flying Circus
  H 106, 301, 302
"Mood Indigo" (music)
  SOTA 295
Moody, James
  5001 155
Moody, Jim
  5001 46
Moody, King
  5001 32
Moody, Ron
  GS 202
  DIM 180
  5001 543, 796
Moon for the Misbegotten, A (stage)
  H 70
  ML 292
Moon in the Gutter, The (*La Lune dans le caniveau*)
  SOTA 45-49
  H 136
  5001 (2nd ed)
Moon Is Down, The
  ILIATM 320
  GS 219
Moon, Keith
  5001 709
"Moon Sickness" (story)
  H 123-124
Moon's Our Home, The
  KKBB 363
  RK 17
  5001 (2nd ed)
Moondog
  5001 130
"Moondog Rock 'n' Roll Party" (radio)
  WTLGD 421
Mooney, Michael M.
  5001 334
Mooney, Paul
  H 144
  5001 381
Moonraker
  SOTA 4
  5001
Moonstruck
  H 423-425
  ML 150
  5001 (2nd ed)
"Moonstruck" (story), see "Moon Sickness"
Moonwebs (book)
  TIAI 262
Moore, Alan
  ML 159
Moore, Archie
  5001 121, 260
Moore, Brian
  H 410
  5001 431, 782
Moore, Colleen
  KKBB 325

RK 15, 21, 36, 69
5001 552, 594
Moore, Demi
  SOTA 132
  H 177, 178
  5001 2, 80
Moore, Dennie
  5001 26, 490, 738, 739
Moore, Dickie
  5001 82, 326, 464, 557
Moore, Dudley
  GS 63
  TIAI 99, 231, 232, 333, 370, 462, 463
  SOTA 153, 154-155, 200, 304, 305, 306,
    341
  H 39
  5001 36, 59, 60, 441, 478, 761, 806
Moore, Eva
  5001 542
Moore, Gar
  5001 562
Moore, Grace
  5001 397, 407, 439
Moore, Joanna
  5001 334, 784
Moore, Juanita
  5001 809
Moore, Kenny
  TIAI 304
  5001 576
Moore, Mary Tyler
  DIM 61
  R 85
  WTLGD 224
  TIAI 78, 80, 81
  H 150-151
  5001 386, 553, 763
Moore, Matt
  5001 613
Moore, Michael
  ML dir., *Roger & Me*, 242
  5001 636
Moore, Owen
  5001 672, 707
Moore, Pauline
  5001 860
Moore, Richard
  5001 656
Moore, Robin
  DIM 316
  5001 267
Moore, Roger
  R 359-360
  TIAI 11
  SOTA 4, 5, 368
  5001 256, 291, 462, 495, 538, 703, 815
Moore, Terry
  WTLGD 291
  5001 148, 168, 479
Moore, Victor
  5001 668, 865
Moorehead, Agnes
  KKBB 178, 199, 248, 304
  5001 19, 138, 173, 201, 346, 381, 384, 451,
    614, 627, 679, 683, 726
Morales, Esai
  TIAI 474

H 341
  5001 46, 48
Morales, Jacobo
  5001 809
Morales, Santos
  5001 98
Moran, Dolores
  5001 457, 542
Moran, Frank C.
  5001 302, 726
Moran, Gussie
  KKBB 330
  5001 569
Moran, Jim
  DIM 325
  5001 371
Moran, Polly
  KKBB 228
  5001 6, 337, 680
Moran, Tony
  5001 314
Morandi, Georgio
  ILIATM 192
Morandini, Morando
  5001 61
Moranis, Rick
  SOTA 193
  H 188, 248, 249
  ML 165, 328
  5001 143, 284, 427
Morante, Laura
  TIAI 313
  5001 787
Moravia, Alberto
  DIM 270
  5001 152, 779, 801
More American Graffiti
  TIAI 33, 209
More, Kenneth
  KKBB 270, 328
  DIM 197
  5001 281, 435, 528, 565
More, Sir Thomas
  KKBB 154
More Than a Miracle (C'Era una Volta)
  R 257
  5001
More the Merrier, The
  H 378
  5001
Moreau, Gustave
  WTLGD 471
Moreau, Jeanne
  ILIATM 181, 217, 220-221
  KKBB 81, 202, 235, 260, 296-297, 307
  GS 108, 264, 275
  DIM 12, 115, 162, 226, 227, 308-310, 419
  R 19, 278, 344
  WTLGD 56, 94, 143-147, 155, 218,
    230-233, 456, 461; dir., *Lumière*,
    230-233
  SOTA 183
  H 41, 44, 176, 435
  ML 60, 95
  5001 13, 55, 56, 215, 235, 268, 291, 385,
    411, 420, 443, 466, 488, 495, 536, 789,
    818

Moreland, Mantan
  SOTA 11
  5001 113
Morell, André
  5001 53, 102, 435, 449
Morelli, Rina
  KKBB 237
  SOTA 51
  5001 62, 364, 417
Moreno, Antonio
  5001 161, 662
Moreno, Belita
  5001 492
Moreno, Marguerite
  KKBB 280
  5001 320, 572
Moreno, Rita
  ILIATM 139
  GS 278
  DIM 284
  SOTA 47
  5001 120, 466, 526, 683, 726, 777, 828
Moretti, Michele
  5001 268
Morfogen, George
  SOTA 351
  5001 325
Morgan! (English title: *Morgan--A Suitable Case
  for Treatment*)
  KKBB 20-23, 25, 31
  GS 124
  DIM 152
  WTLGD 258
  H 46, 49, 195
  5001
Morgan, Al
  KKBB 277
  5001 303
Morgan, Dennis
  5001 305, 318, 336, 400, 750
Morgan, Donald M.
  TIAI 100
  5001 810
Morgan, Frank
  5001 30, 48, 91, 106, 106, 294, 305, 314,
    340, 413, 518, 641, 677, 726, 736, 767,
    783, 833, 834, 856
Morgan, Helen
  TIAI 329
  5001 288, 679
Morgan, Henry
  5001 690
Morgan, Henry (later Harry)
  KKBB 328
  5001 287, 331, 363, 559, 677, 745
Morgan, J. P.
  RK 64
Morgan, Jaye P.
  5001 16
Morgan, Michèle
  ILIATM 135
  KKBB 169, 332, 335, 356
  GS 72
  DIM 259
  5001 63, 234, 300, 553, 590, 739
Morgan, Ralph
  5001 391, 464, 593, 617

Morgan, Russ
  KKBB 277
  5001 303
Morgan, Stafford
  5001 141
Morgan, Terence
  5001 21, 315
Morgan--A Suitable Case for Treatment, see
  Morgan!
Mori, Masayuki
  ILIATM 163
  KKBB 337
  5001 47, 354, 616, 802
Mori, Toshia
  5001 75
Moriarty, Cathy
  TIAI 107, 108
  5001 612
Moriarty, Michael
  R 247, 432-433, 435
  H 17
  5001 50, 408, 562, 624
Morin, Edgar
  5001 137
Morishige, Hisaya
  KKBB 246
  5001 124
Morison, Patricia
  5001 406, 694, 843
Morita, Yoshimitsu (Pat)
  H 308
Morituri
  KKBB 194
Moritz, Louisa
  5001 181, 549, 793, 808
"Mork and Mindy" (TV)
  SOTA 309
Morlay, Gaby
  5001 285, 489, 585
Morley, Annabel
  KKBB 327
  5001 558
Morley, Christopher
  5001 267, 400
Morley, Karen
  5001 35, 469, 555, 595, 657
Morley, Robert
  KKBB 229, 236, 265, 299, 327
  DIM 318
  WTLGD 482-483, 485
  5001 9, 20, 55, 57, 163, 167, 243, 440, 453,
    465, 558, 694, 781, 836
Morner, Stanley
  5001 305
Morning After, The
  H 243-246
  5001 (2nd ed)
Morning Glory
  5001
Morocco
  KKBB 59, 240, 360
  GS 113
  ML 48
  5001
Moroder, Giorgio
  WTLGD 496
  TIAI 188, 335

SOTA 6, 101
  5001 125, 250, 477, 479, 658
Morphett, Tony
  WTLGD 534
  5001 412
Morrell, David
  SOTA 375
  5001 615
Morricone, Ennio
  R 215
  WTLGD 331
  H 321
  5001 55, 61, 110, 124, 134, 229, 239, 247,
    266, 296, 369, 429, 530, 549, 729, 759,
    808
Morris, Adrian
  5001 578
Morris, Anita
  H 159
  5001 3, 647
Morris, Chester
  DIM 161
  5001 193, 620
Morris, David
  WTLGD 253
Morris, Desmond
  TIAI 308
  5001 607, 608
Morris, Garrett
  WTLGD 188
  5001 25, 118, 832
Morris, Glenn
  5001 744
Morris, Haviland
  5001 684
Morris, Howard
  R 128-129
  TIAI 215
  5001 331, 537, 702, 747
Morris, Ivan
  ILIATM 226
  5001 245
Morris, Jeff
  TIAI 301
  5001 92
Morris, John
  WTLGD 100
Morris, Oswald
  ILIATM 63, 209
  KKBB 311, 322, 327
  R 112
  WTLGD 108, 190, 338, 475
  5001 57, 222, 223, 388, 434, 461, 490, 494,
    500, 543, 556, 601, 603, 667, 686
Morris, Richard
  5001 763
Morris, Wayne
  5001 393, 570
Morrison, Jim
  SOTA 263
Morrison, Van
  5001 411
Morriss, Frank
  TIAI 486
  5001 87
Morrissey, Eamon
  H 334

5001 211
Morrissey, Paul
  DIM 153-156; dir., *Trash*, 153-157; *Flesh*,
    153, 157
  R 235, 291
  SOTA 262
  5001 326, 479, 627, 788, 848
Morros, Boris
  5001 741, 856
Morrow, Jo
  KKBB 327
  5001 556
Morrow, Vic
  ILIATM 46
  WTLGD 558
  SOTA 19-20
  5001 79, 797
Morse, Helen
  WTLGD 553
  TIAI 158, 159
  5001 10, 113
Morse, Robert
  KKBB 299
  H 300
  5001 310, 440
Morse, Susan E.
  5001 865
Morse, Wayne
  DIM 43
Morte d'Arthur, Le (book)
  TIAI 184
Mortifee, Jane
  5001 506
Mortimer, Caroline
  R 347
Mortimer, Chapman
  5001 622
Mortimer, John
  ILIATM 165
  DIM 73
  H 142
  5001 365, 381
Mortimer, Penelope
  5001 602
Morton, Gary
  R 377
  5001 417, 592
Morton, Joe
  H 136-137
  5001 165, 295, 791
Morton, Rob (pseud.)
  SOTA 167
  5001 738
Moschin, Gaston (also Gastone)
  5001 152, 290
Moscovitch, Maurice
  KKBB 369
  5001 359, 841
Moscow, David
  5001 68
Moscow on the Hudson
  SOTA 155-160
  H 103, 105, 188, 264, 421
Mosel, Tad
  5001 19, 808
Moses, Grandma
  DIM 180

Mosher, John
5001 459
Mosjoukine, Ivan
DIM 246, 248
Moskvin, Andrei
KKBB 289
5001 375
Mosley, Nicholas
5001 3, 37
Moss, Arnold
KKBB 367
5001 276, 818
Moss, Jack
5001 384
Most, The
DIM 109-110
"Most Beautiful Woman in Town, The" (short story)
TIAI 466
Most Dangerous Game, The
TIAI 257
5001
Mostel, Joshua
H 275
5001 150, 320, 397, 610, 706
Mostel, Zero
KKBB 138
GS 67
DIM 329
R 281
WTLGD 171
H 275
ML 93
5001 220, 270, 272, 301, 490, 564, 600, 601
Moten, Etta
KKBB 273
5001 253, 291
Mother (Mat')
KKBB 312:n
GS 45
R 210
5001
Mother and the Whore, The (La Maman et la putain)
R 289-293
5001
Motion Picture Academy of Arts and Sciences
DIM 61, 136, 260
Motion Picture and the Teaching of English, The (book)
DIM 145
Motion Picture Association of America (M.P.A.A.)
DIM 92, 145, 171: Rating Board, 250
Motown Records
WTLGD 60, 469
Mott, Ernie
5001 532
Mouchet, Catherine
H 255, 256
5001 753
Mouchette
TIAI 403
5001
Moulin, Charles
5001 48
Moulin Rouge

ILIATM 47, 298-299
5001 (2nd ed)
Mouloudji
5001 720
Mount, Peggy
KKBB 294
5001 861
Mountain Man (book)
R 87
Moura, Edgar
5001 342
Mourir à Madrid, see *To Die in Madrid*
Mourir d'aimer, see *To Die of Love*
Mourning Becomes Electra
5001
Mouse That Roared, The
5001
Moussy, Marcel
5001 676
Moustache
5001 472
Move
TIAI 21
Movie (periodical)
ILIATM 295, 303, 306-307, 310, 316, 318-319
Movie Movie
WTLGD 501-505
TIAI 345
5001
Movin, Lisbeth
KKBB 254
5001 176
Movita
505
Mowat, Farley
SOTA 98
5001 Farley, 519
Mowbray, Alan
5001 25, 97, 184, 468, 509, 545, 563, 580, 637, 705, 781, 782, 825
Mowbray, Malcolm
SOTA 340-342
ML dir., *Out Cold*, 91-93; *A Private Function*, 91
5001 556, 598
Moyzich, L. C.
5001 247
Mozart and Salieri (stage)
SOTA 250
Mozart, Constanze
SOTA 252
Mozart, Wolfgang Amadeus
KKBB 306
DIM 188, 292
WTLGD 72-76, 459, 460, 461
TIAI 469
SOTA 249-253
H 144, 383
5001 165, 216, 283, 456
Ms. (periodical)
TIAI 379
MTM Enterprises
H 150
MTV
SOTA 211, 267
Mucha, Alphonse

WTLGD 205
Mudd, Roger
R 286
Mudie, Leonard
5001 501
Mudrick, Marvin
ML 154
Mudrick Transcribed (book)
ML 154
Mueller-Stahl, Armin
ML 239-42, 279-82
5001 40, 504
Muerte de un Ciclista, see *Death of a Cyclist*
Muggeridge, Malcolm
5001 357
Muhich, Donald F.
5001 88, 89, 199
Muir, Esther
5001 174, 340
Muir, Georgette
WTLGD 416
Muir, Geraldine
H 368, 370
5001 340
Muir, Jean
5001 542
Mujeres al Borde de un Ataque de Nervios, see *Women on the Verge of a Nervous Breakdown*
Mukherjee, Madhabi
5001 452
Muldaur, Geoff
H 106
Muldowney, Jack
SOTA 79-80
Muldowney, Shirley
SOTA 79-83
5001 323
Mulhall, Jack
KKBB 325
5001 32, 106, 552, 837, 856
Mulhearn, Thomas
TIAI 152
5001 259
Mullavey, Greg
5001 89
Mullen, Barbara
5001 379, 769
Müller, Filip
H 84
Muller, Jorge
WTLGD 386
Müller, Robby
TIAI 42
SOTA 212-213
H 221, 222
5001 22, 51, 200, 340, 624
Mulligan, Gerry
ML 123
5001 379
Mulligan, Richard
DIM 215
5001 68, 309, 424, 478, 690
Mulligan, Robert
KKBB 283; dir., *Inside Daisy Clover*, 283
GS dir., *Inside Daisy Clover*, 73; *The Stalking Moon*, 248-253; *To Kill a*

Mockingbird, 249
DIM dir., *Up the Down Staircase*, 23;
    Summer of '42, 321, 391
WTLGD 445-447, 505-507; dir., *To Kill a*
    Mockingbird, 368, 446; *Bloodbrothers*,
    445-447, 495; *Summer of '42*, 446;
    Same Time, Next Year, 505-507
5001 84, 365, 651, 776, 777, 808
Mumford, Lewis
KKBB 63
Mummy, The
KKBB 219
5001
Munch, Edvard
DIM 410
R 90, 91
H 87
Munchausen, Karl Friedrich Hieronymus, Baron
    von
ML 106
Mundin, Herbert
KKBB 228
5001 8, 26, 127, 505
Mundy, Meg
TIAI 81
5001 230, 553
Muni, Paul
ILIATM 62, 85
KKBB 283
GS 97, 243
RK 20
R 208, 377
WTLGD 206
TIAI 390
SOTA 100-101, 103
H 374
ML 321
5001 27, 293, 348, 384, 657, 704
Munk, Andrzej
ILIATM 153; dir., *Eroica*, 148, 153
DIM 205
Munk, Kaj
KKBB 325
5001 552
Munro
5001
Munro, James
5001 364
Munsey, Frank
RK 67
Munshin, Jules
5001 546, 681, 740
Munson, Ona
5001 671
Murat, Jean
KKBB 245
5001 121, 309
Murch, Walter
5001 770, 804
Murder
5001
Murder at the Vanities
5001
Murder by Contract
5001
Murder by Death
WTLGD 188

Murder by Decree
5001
Murder, He Says
KKBB 232
R 404
5001
H 291
Murder, My Sweet
KKBB 313:n
5001
Murder on the Orient Express
R 390-392
WTLGD 192, 194, 463
5001
Murders in the Rue Morgue, The
KKBB 219
Murdock, George
TIAI 295
5001 676
Mure di Malapurga, Le, see *The Walls of*
    Malapaga
Murfin, Jane
5001 201, 595, 674, 830, 847
Muriel
ILIATM 20, 23
KKBB 164
Murmur of the Heart (*La Souffle au coeur*)
DIM 305-310, 426
R 339
5001
H 437
Murnau, F(red) W.
ILIATM 6, 302; dir., *Nosferatu*, 6
KKBB 319, 356-357, 365; dir., *Nosferatu*,
    319, 356-357, 365; co-dir., *Tabu*,
    356-357; dir., *Faust*, 357; *The Last*
    Laugh, 357; *Sunrise*, 357
GS dir., *The Last Laugh*, 265
RK 76
DIM 87
TIAI 2
ML dir., *Nosferatu*, 151
5001 409, 534, 729, 740
Murney, Christopher
H 300
5001 664
Murphy, Audie
KKBB 336, 360
DIM 296
5001 185, 608, 619, 776
Murphy, Charles F.
RK 61
Murphy, Dennis
GS 240-241
Murphy, Dudley
KKBB 262; dir., *The Emperor Jones*, 262
5001 201, 217, 650
Murphy, Eddie
TIAI 437-438, 439, 440
SOTA 12, 13, 14, 122, 192, 287, 288
5001 66, 261, 786
Murphy, Fred
5001 177, 219, 790
Murphy, Geoff
SOTA 240-246; dir., *Utu*, 240-246; *Goodbye*
    Pork Pie, 244
5001 810

Murphy, George
WTLGD 13
5001 106, 106, 256, 714, 762, 778
Murphy, Mary
5001 838
Murphy, Matt "Guitar"
TIAI 26
Murphy, Michael
R 265, 448
WTLGD 170, 410
TIAI 454
H 182
5001 35, 39, 270, 417, 445, 469, 516-517,
    651, 750, 807, 831, 854
Murphy, Patrick
R 232
Murphy, Richard
5001 92, 151, 564
Murphy, Rosemary
R 285
WTLGD 305
5001 32, 261, 386, 666, 777, 822
Murphy, Walter
WTLGD 368
Murphy's War
R 318
Murray, Bill
TIAI 177, 224-225, 226, 432
SOTA 122, 192, 193-194
H 249, 310, 311, 421, 456
ML 38-42, 164-165
5001 284, 427, 660, 723, 780
Murray, Brian Doyle, see Doyle-Murray, Brian
Murray, Don
5001 8, 219, 317, 449, 574
Murray, Jan
TIAI 216
Murray, John
5001 640, 713
Murray, Julia
5001 264
Murray, Mae
5001 680
Murray, Stephen
5001 451, 605
Murray, Tom
5001 292
Murray, William
WTLGD 114-115
Murrow, Edward R.
WTLGD 220
5001 654
Murry, Middleton
R 49
Mus, Paul
DIM 44
Musante, Tony
SOTA 204
5001 185, 410, 589
Muse, Clarence
5001 78, 112, 118, 157, 253, 326, 437, 524,
    679, 728
Musgrove, Gertrude
5001 623, 659
Music Box
ML 239-42
5001 (2nd ed)

179

Music Lovers, The
  DIM 238-243
  R 48, 49, 50, 51
  5001
Music Man, The
  TIAI 333
  5001
Music Room, The (Jalsaghar)
  ILIATM 251
  5001
Musil, Robert von
  H 61
Musmanno, Michael A.
  KKBB 294
  5001 410
Musolino, Vincenzo
  5001 798
Musselman, M. M.
  5001 101
Musso, Jeff
  KKBB 335; dir., The Puritan, 335
  5001 603
Mussolini, Benito
  DIM 116, 270, 273, 364
  WTLGD 137, 178, 310, 311, 312
Mussolini, Vittorio
  DIM 116
Musuraca, Nicholas
  5001 125, 140, 293, 351, 557, 628
Muti, Ornella
  TIAI 125, 126, 467-468
  SOTA 237
  H 385
  5001 250, 734, 742
Mutiny on the Bounty (1935)
  WTLGD 15
  5001
Mutiny on the Bounty (1963)
  ILIATM 234
  KKBB 193
  DIM 177
Mutrux, Floyd
  WTLGD 421-424
  5001 22
Muybridge, Eadweard
  TIAI 105
Mvusi, Linda
  H 475
  5001 849
My American Cousin
  5001 (2nd ed)
My Apprenticeship (V Lyudyakh; also known as
    Out in the World; part of The Donskoi
    Trilogy)
  5001
My Beautiful Laundrette and the Rainbow Sign
    (book)
  H 391
My Beautiful Laundrette (movie)
  H 118-122, 128, 387, 389, 391
  5001 (2nd ed)
My Bodyguard
  TIAI 399
My Brilliant Career
  TIAI 60-61
  SOTA 292, 302
  H 432, 433, 434

5001 (2nd ed)
My Brother Talks to Horses
  5001 (2nd ed)
My Darling Clemintine
  ILIATM 242
  WTLGD 328
My Dinner with André
  TIAI 286-288, 415
  SOTA 122
  H 364
  5001
My Early Life (book)
  R 16
My Fair Lady
  KKBB 90
  GS 108, 200
  DIM 328
  WTLGD 8, 177
  H 467
  5001
My Favorite Wife
  WTLGD 3, 18, 19
  SOTA 222
  5001
My Favorite Year
  TIAI 394-398
  5001 (2nd ed)
My Friend Flicka
  KKBB 180-181, 185
  5001
My Gal Sal
  5001
"My Girl" (music)
  H 389, 391
My Heart's in the Highlands (stage)
  KKBB 98
My Left Foot
  ML 178-82, 324
  5001 (2nd ed)
My Life and Hard Times (book)
  RK 18
My Life to Live (Vivre sa vie)
  ILIATM 15
  KKBB 128-129
  GS 27
  DIM 281
  TIAI 104
My Little Chickadee
  KKBB 313-314:n
  WTLGD 414
  5001
My Man and I
  TIAI 357
My Man Godfrey
  KKBB 20
  WTLGD 141, 236
  H 195, 372
  5001
"My Man" (music)
  WTLGD 244
My Name Is Ivan
  ILIATM 15
My Sister Eileen
  5001
My Sister, My Love (Syskonbadd 1782)
  5001
My Six Convicts

KKBB 203
My Uncle Antoine (Mon Oncle Antoine)
  R 6
  TIAI 421, 423
  5001 (2nd ed)
My Universities (Moi Universiteti; part of The
    Donskoi Trilogy)
  5001
"My Way" (music)
  TIAI 97, 201
Myerovich, Alvin
  ML 282
Myers, Carmel
  KKBB 355
  5001 63, 734
Myers, David
  WTLGD 287
  5001 411, 770, 827
Myers, Henry
  5001 185
Myers, Stanley
  5001 183
Myerson, Alan
  R 119-120
  5001 273, 713
Myerson, Bess
  WTLGD 495
Myhers, John
  TIAI 216
Myra Breckinridge
  DIM 147, 151
Myrtil, Odette
  5001 196
Mystère Koumiko, Le, see The Koumiko Mystery
Mystère Picasso, Le (The Mystery of Picasso)
  KKBB 315:n
  5001
"Mysteries of Love" (song)
  H 206
Mysterious Island, The
  5001
Mysterious Rhinestone Cowboy, The (music)
  TIAI 205
Mysterious Rhinestone Cowboy Rides Agains as
    the Longhaired Redneck, The (music)
  TIAI 205
Mystery of Kaspar Hauser, The (Jeder für Sich
    und Gott Gegen Alle; also known as
    Every Man For Himself and God
    Against All)
  WTLGD 51-55
  5001
Mystery of Picasso, The, see Le Mystère Picasso
Mystery of the Wax Museum, The
  5001

N

Nabokov, Nicolas
  5001 720
Nabokov, Vladimir
  ILIATM 24, 204, 246
  KKBB 53, 269
  H 168

5001 430
Nabors, Jim
  TIAI 374, 375
  5001 64
Nachts, Wenn der Teufel Kam, see *The Devil*
    Strikes at Night
Naciala, see *The Début*
Nadelman, Elie
  R 243
Nadine
  H 352-353
  5001 (2nd ed)
Nagel, Conrad
  RK 48
  5001 19, 194, 337
Nagy, Bill
  5001 4
Naidu, Ajay
  H 263, 264
  5001 783
Naish, J. Carrol
  5001 30, 58, 83, 118, 130, 140, 345, 393,
    429, 631, 650, 698, 751, 771, 777
Naismith, Laurence
  5001 116, 443, 491, 528, 628
Nakadai, Tatsuya
  TIAI 137
  H 89, 91
  5001 389, 615
Nakano, Desmond
  5001 95
Naked and the Dead, The
  GS 10
  5001
Naked Ape, The (book)
  TIAI 308
Naked City, The
  TIAI 111
  5001
Naked Civil Servant, The (TV)
  WTLGD 498
Naked Edge, The
  5001
Naked Jungle, The
  GS 37
Naked Lunch, The (book)
  ILIATM 238
  DIM 173
Naked Night, The (Gycklarnas Afton; English
    title: *Sawdust and Tinsel*; French title:
    La Nuit des forains)
  KKBB 315:n
  R 90
  TIAI 87
  5001
Naked Runner, The
  GS 94
  R 40
  5001 (2nd ed)
Naked Truth, The, see *Your Past Is Showing*
Naldi, Nita
  5001 587
Namath, Joe
  DIM 173-174
  WTLGD 359
  5001 127
Nance, John

5001 51, 87, 207, 223
Naniwa, Cheiko
  KKBB 246
  5001 124
Nanny, The
  5001
Nanook
  5001 515
Nanook of the North
  ILIATM 248
  KKBB 180, 185, 316:n, 324, 357
  5001
Napier, Alan
  5001 125, 184, 369, 372, 807
Napier, Charles
  WTLGD 321, 322
  TIAI 77
  H 231
  5001 139, 615, 738
Napoleon I (Bonaparte)
  DIM 348
  WTLGD 25, 380-382
Napoleon III
  WTLGD 55
Napoléon (Napoléon vu par Abel Gance)
  ILIATM 277
  WTLGD 324
  TIAI 142-151
  5001
Napoléon vu par Abel Gance, see *Napoléon*
Napoli Milionaria, see *Millionaires of Naples*
Nära Livet, see *Brink of Life*
Nardini, Tom
  KKBB 29
  5001 124
Narita, Hiro
  SOTA 99
  5001 519
Narizzano, Silvio
  KKBB 22; dir., *Georgy Girl*, 20, 22-23, 31,
    142
  5001 282
Narrow Margin, The
  5001 (2nd ed)
Nash, Marilyn
  5001 494
Nash, Mary
  5001 143, 210, 580, 856
Nash, N. Richard
  KKBB 337
  5001 614
Nash, Ogden
  5001 245, 550, 674
Nashville
  R 446-452
  WTLGD 136, 143, 202, 204, 227, 259, 267,
    276, 284, 322, 400, 441, 445
  TIAI 33, 227, 417
  SOTA 268
  H 1, 2, 217, 218, 219
  5001
Nastasia Filipovna, see *The Idiot* (1958)
Nasty Habits
  WTLGD 262-266
  TIAI 415
  5001
Nat, Marie-José

R 421
  5001 816
Nathan, George Jean
  R 197
Nathan, Robert
  GS 38
  5001 141, 590
Nathan, Stephan
  5001 857
Nathenson, Zoe
  5001 493
Natica Jackson (TV)
  ML 188
Nation, The (periodical)
  RK 36
National Ballet of Canada
  WTLGD 495
National Broadcasting Company (NBC)
  WTLGD 149, 284, 486
  TIAI 13, 394
National Catholic Office for Motion Pictures
  KKBB 96
National Council of Teachers of English
  DIM 145
National Educational Television
  DIM 20, 319, 320
National Enquirer (periodical)
  WTLGD 209
  TIAI 3, 290
  SOTA 308
National Film Board of Canada
  R 123
National Geographic (periodical)
  WTLGD 513
  TIAI 29, 308
  H 79
National Lampoon's Animal House (Animal
    House)
  WTLGD 428, 429, 509
  TIAI 26, 69
  SOTA 12
  H 153
National Velvet
  KKBB 180, 185, 285, 316:n
  5001
Native Son (stage)
  RK 37, 38, 60
Natkin, Rick
  5001 98
Natoli, Piero
  TIAI 420
  5001 415
Nattlek, see *Night Games*
Natural, The
  SOTA 169-173
  H 173
  ML 72, 280
  5001 (2nd ed)
"Natural Woman, A" (music)
  SOTA 69
  H 294
Natwick, Mildred
  ML 62
  5001 37, 52, 171, 218, 355, 433, 608, 672,
    856
Naughton, Bill
  5001 13

Naughton, Edmund
    5001 445
Naughton, James
    ML 35
    5001 295
Naughty Marietta
    5001
Nava, Gregory
    SOTA 130-132
    5001 533
Navigator, The
    WTLGD 136
    5001
Nazareth, Christine
    5001 309
Nazarin
    GS 225, 258, 261
    5001
Nazimova, Alla
    WTLGD 335-336
    5001 83, 224, 650, 683
Nazzari, Amedeo
    KKBB 318
    5001 529
NBC, see National Broadcasting Company
Neagle, Anna
    DIM 16
    5001 75, 370
Neal, Billie
    H 222
    5001 200
Neal, Patricia
    ILIATM 88, 140
    KKBB 184
    5001 99, 232, 262, 344
Neal, Tom
    5001 31
Neame, Ronald
    KKBB 276, 282, 307, 335; dir., *Man with a
        Million*, 185, 307; *The Horse's Mouth*,
        282; *The Promoter*, 335; *Gambit*, 364
    GS 181; dir., *The Prime of Miss Jean
        Brodie*, 288
    DIM 196; dir., *The Prime of Miss Jean
        Brodie*, 187; *Scrooge*, 196-197
    5001 276, 302, 341, 349, 461, 543, 591,
        595, 601, 660, 794
Near Dark
    H 454
    5001 (2nd ed)
Near, Laurel
    5001 224
Nebenzal, Harold
    5001 837
Née, Louis
    5001 409
"Need a New Sun Rising" (music)
    WTLGD 400
Needham, Hal
    WTLGD 430
Neenan, Audrie J.
    5001 725
Neeson, Liam
    H 393
    ML 33, 36-37, 43, 44
    5001 295, 333, 733
Neff, Hildegarde, see Knef, Hildegard

Neff, Walter
    5001 198
Neff, William
    5001 352
Negishi, Akemi
    5001 24
Négret, François
    H 437
    5001 38
Negri, Pola
    5001 446, 694, 754
Negro Ensemble Company
    WTLGD 188
    H 212
Negulesco, Jean
    5001 345, 382, 469, 774
Neider, Charles
    5001 549
Neil, Hildegard
    R 203-204
    5001 221
Neill, Bill
    TIAI 192
Neill, Roy William
    5001 312
Neill, Sam
    H 44
    ML 31, 33
    5001 166, 506, 507, 587
Neko to Shozo to Futari no Onna, see *A Cat and
        Two Women*
Nelligan, Kate
    H 69-70, 71-72
    5001 214
Nelson, Barry
    5001 12, 344, 382, 577, 669, 674
Nelson, Craig Richard
    5001 609
Nelson, Craig T.
    TIAI 352
    SOTA 109, 277
    5001 395, 588, 681
Nelson, Judd
    SOTA 347, 348
    5001 99
Nelson, Novella
    5001 156
Nelson, Peter
    H 411
    5001 431
Nelson, Prince Rogers, see Prince
Nelson, Ralph
    GS dir., *Charly*, 151; *Soldier in the Rain*,
        169
    DIM dir., *Charly*, 59; *Requiem for a
        Heavyweight*, 352
    5001 132, 239, 837
Nelson, Ricky
    WTLGD 291
    5001 630
Nelson, Robert
    GS 149
Nelson, Ruth
    WTLGD 261, 444
    5001 345, 392
Nelson, Tracy
    H 103

    5001 199
Nelson, Willie
    TIAI 41, 42, 43, 44, 45, 188, 191, 371, 372,
        373
    H 7, 8, 10
    5001 50, 51, 339, 695, 756
Neptune's Daughter
    TIAI 357
Nero
    DIM 127
Nero, Franco
    WTLGD 140
    5001 116
Neron, Claude
    WTLGD 154
    5001 450
Nesbitt, Cathleen
    5001 78, 184, 386, 605
Nesmith, Michael
    SOTA 212
    5001 624
Ness, Eliot
    H 318, 319, 320, 321-323
"Nessun dorma" (music)
    ML 103
Nest, The
    SOTA 127
Nettleton, Lois
    5001 64
Network
    WTLGD 219-224
    TIAI 244
    5001
Neumann, Kurt
    5001 252
Neumeier, Edward
    H 344
    5001 635
Nevada Smith
    KKBB 39-40
    5001
Nevard, Peter
    5001 309
Nevelson, Louise
    WTLGD 465
Never Cry Wolf
    SOTA 97-100
    5001 (2nd ed)
Never Give a Sucker an Even Break
    KKBB 185, 314
    TIAI 99
    5001
Never Let Go
    WTLGD 238
Never on Sunday
    ILIATM 141
    DIM 248
    5001
Neville, Edgar
    5001 249
Neville, John
    ML 107-109
    5001 6, 72
New Centurions, The
    R 441
    WTLGD 206
New Land, The (Nybyggarna; The Settlers)

R 7, 9, 181-182, 346
  TIAI 477
  5001
New Leaf, A
  DIM 269
  R 71
  5001
New, Nancy
  SOTA 210
  5001 94
New Order
  H 135
New Orleans Funeral and Ragtime Band
  5001 686
New Republic (periodical)
  RK 51
  ILIATM 205
"New Show, The" (TV)
  SOTA 142
New Statesman (periodical)
  KKBB 278
"New Sun in the Sky" (music)
  WTLGD 177
"New World" Symphony (music)
  TIAI 284
New York American
  RK 5
New York *Daily News*
  KKBB 140
  RK 44
New York Film Bulletin (periodical)
  ILIATM 311
New York Film Festival
  DIM 8, 20, 146, 272
  WTLGD 39, 43, 46, 51, 54, 55, 143, 294,
    299, 325, 356, 442, 446, 454, 536
  TIAI 72, 245, 400, 401
  SOTA 68, 234, 260, 360
  H 372
New York Film Critics Award
  RK 44
New York Giants
  ML 126
New York *Herald Tribune*
  ILIATM 32, 68
  RK 43-44
New York Journal-American
  RK 65, 80
New York magazine
  WTLGD 367
  H 251, 293
New York Mirror
  RK 19
New York, New York
  WTLGD 269, 389, 434, 490
  TIAI 109, 110, 297, 391, 457, 460
  SOTA 47, 166, 167, 219
  H 228
  5001
New York Philharmonic Orchestra
  5001 654
New York Post
  KKBB 140
  RK 44
  SOTA 240
  H 459
New York Review of Sex & Politics (periodical)

DIM 57
New York Review of Books, The (periodical)
  TIAI 247
New York State Council on the Arts
  H 212
New York Stories
  ML 100-105, 270
  5001 (2nd ed)
New York Telegraph
  RK 68
New York Times, The
  ILIATM 14, 16, 204, 246, 331
  KKBB 26, 140, 153, 206-207, 233, 236, 370
  RK 10, 11, 12, 17, 29, 35, 43, 44, 65
  DIM 8, 56, 92, 145, 150, 337, 340
  WTLGD 42, 136, 139 153
  TIAI 10, 74, 139, 418, 434, 443
  SOTA 107, 258, 274, 276, 336, 351
  H 25, 70, 81, 88, 116, 175, 188, 215, 258,
    276, 289, 362
New York University film school
  H 183, 213, 229, 251, 268
New York World
  RK 10, 11, 63, 65
New York *World Journal Tribune*
  KKBB 140
New York *World-Telegram*
  KKBB 303
New Yorker, The (periodical)
  ILIATM 153, 325
  KKBB 192, 205
  RK 10, 11, 12, 25, 39, 56, 83
  DIM 293, 308, 418
  WTLGD 12, 439
  TIAI 178
  SOTA 325, 336
  H 457, 458
Newbern, George
  H 448
  5001 738
Newell, Mike
  H 29-31, 283-284; dir., *Dance with a
    Stranger*, 29-31, 45, 283; *The Good
    Father*, 283-284
  5001 170, 294
Newhart, Bob
  SOTA 273
  H 40
  5001 126
Newley, Anthony
  KKBB 322
  GS 39, 40
  R 404
  5001 543, 840
Newman, Alfred
  5001 157, 200, 311, 346, 392, 851
Newman, David
  KKBB 48, 52, 54, 59-61
  DIM 229, 230
  R 12, 14
  WTLGD 261
  TIAI 223, 412, 427
  SOTA 11, 225, 249
  5001 46, 91, 380, 673, 715, 731, 752, 831
Newman, Joy
  H 275
  5001 610

Newman, Laraine
  WTLGD 423
  5001 23
Newman, Leslie
  TIAI 223
  SOTA 11
  5001 731
Newman, Nanette
  DIM 26, 322, 323
  5001 431, 450, 714, 832
Newman, Paul
  ILIATM 79-80, 83, 89, 91, 223
  KKBB 39, 60, 279
  GS 56-57; dir., *Rachel, Rachel*, 128, 196
  DIM 6, 7, 46-47, 110, 173, 174, 182, 200,
    350, 351, 401, 402
  R 76, 98-100, 177, 208, 244-245, 302,
    317-318, 322, 406-407, 433, 467; dir.,
    Rachel, Rachel, 74, 222-223; *The Effect
    of Gamma Rays on Man-in-the-Moon
    Marigolds*, 74-76
  WTLGD 30, 274-277, 442, 549-551
  TIAI 78, 151-152, 153, 155, 288-289, 290,
    321, 390, 440, 441; dir., *Rachel, Rachel*,
    78
  SOTA 170; dir., *The Shadow Box* (TV),
    279-280
  H 223, 224, 225, 226, 227, 348
  ML 207-208, 222-25
  5001 2, 50, 80, 110, 124, 146, 212, 238,
    259, 320, 344, 346, 347, 416, 421, 432,
    600, 609, 616, 686, 715, 734, 782, 785,
    813, 851
Newman, Phyllis
  5001 111
Newman, Randy
  SOTA 171, 172
  ML 324
  5001 518
Newman, Scott
  R 407
Newman, Walter
  WTLGD 445
  5001 4, 84, 124, 462
Newmar, Julie
  5001 667
Newmeyer, Julie, see Julie Newmar
Newsfront
  WTLGD 536
Newsweek (periodical)
  RK 12, 42, 80
  DIM 154
  WTLGD 529
  TIAI 89, 264, 413, 434
  H 146, 147, 182, 303
Newton, Robert
  KKBB 321, 322, 350
  5001 25, 56, 328, 378, 453, 539, 543
Next Man, The
  WTLGD 206
  5001
Next Stop, Greenwich Village
  WTLGD 127-131, 173, 411, 412, 413
  TIAI 320
  H 248-249
  5001
"Next Time, The" (story)

KKBB 112
Next Time We Live, see *Next Time We Love*
Next Time We Love (also known as *Next Time We Live*)
  RK 20
  5001 (2nd ed)
Ney, Marie
  5001 378
Ney, Richard
  5001 486
Ngo Dinh Diem
  DIM 44
Ngor, Haing S.
  SOTA 275
  5001 394
Nhu, Madame
  DIM 44
  5001 360
Niagara
  R 154
  5001
Nibelungen Saga (*Kriemhild's Revenge*;
    Siegfried)
  R 148
  TIAI 186
  5001
Niblo, Fred
  5001 63
Niblo, Fred Jr.
  5001 243
Nicaragua (book)
  SOTA 73
Nicholas and Alexandra
  DIM 366-369
  R 15, 221, 237
  WTLGD 278, 452
  5001
Nicholas Brothers
  SOTA 294, 296
  5001 551, 583, 716, 728, 774
Nicholas, Denise
  WTLGD 66
  5001 418
Nicholas Nickleby
  H 412
  5001
Nicholas, Paul
  WTLGD 84
  5001 424
Nicholls, Allan
  WTLGD 276, 444
  5001 517, 686, 768, 791
Nichols, Barbara
  KKBB 356
  5001 513, 562, 736
Nichols, Dandy
  5001 75
Nichols, Dudley
  KKBB 241
  5001 11, 25, 104, 119, 256, 327, 346, 362,
    433, 457, 467, 500, 583, 659, 672, 704,
    713
Nichols, John
  DIM 32
  TIAI 311
  5001 486, 714
Nichols, Mike

GS dir., *The Graduate*, 14, 97, 124-127,
    198, 274, 276; *Who's Afraid of Virginia
    Woolf?*, 229
DIM 10, 73, 215, 282, 369; dir., *The
    Graduate*, 9, 10, 152, 283, 395;
    Catch-22, 146, 215, 256, 282, 283;
    Carnal Knowledge, 282-285, 348;
    Who's Afraid of Virginia Woolf?, 405,
    406
R 246, 454; dir., *Carnal Knowledge*, 161;
    The Day of the Dolphin, 245-246; *Catch
    22*, 294; *The Graduate*, 309, 444-445
WTLGD 272; dir., *The Fortune*, 87; *The
    Graduate*, 165, 173, 554; *Who's Afraid
    of Virginia Woolf?*, 178
SOTA 106-111; dir., *Silkwood*, 106-111, 325
H 176, 189-192; dir., *Carnal Knowledge*,
    176-177, 190; *Heartburn*, 189-192; *The
    Graduate*, 300
ML dir., *The Day of the Dolphin*, 211;
    Heartburn, 275; *Postcards from the
    Edge*, 273-76; *Working Girl*, 63-66, 274,
    275
5001 52, 120, 125, 175, 260, 299, 325, 591,
    592, 681, 848
Nichols, Peter
  5001 282, 321
Nicholson, Jack
  DIM 251, 283, 284, 347, 350; dir., *Drive,
    He Said*, 294, 323, 350
  R 46, 272-275, 311, 442
  WTLGD 85, 87-88, 196, 199, 218, 507-510;
    dir., *Goin' South*, 507-510; *Drive, He
    Said*, 508
  TIAI 1, 3, 130, 179-180, 181, 280, 282, 300,
    301; dir., *Goin' South*, 3, 75
  SOTA 94, 96, 170, 322, 376-377
  H 189, 192, 314, 323-324, 325, 419, 420,
    421, 481
  ML 29, 118, 159-64
  5001 54, 92, 105, 120, 135, 210, 260, 290,
    323, 325, 371, 396, 407, 411, 427, 549,
    592, 600, 621, 629, 674, 677, 724, 748,
    749, 790, 799, 843
Nickelodeon
  WTLGD 248, 490
  5001 (2nd ed)
Nickles, M. A.
  H 355
  5001 315
Nickson, Julia
  5001 615
Nicoletti, Susi
  KKBB 251
  5001 151
Nicolson, Robert
  5001 832
Niebuhr, Dr. Reinhold
  ILIATM 205, 207
Niehaus, Lennie
  ML 4-5
Nielsen, Asta
  5001 384, 563
Nielsen, Leslie
  KKBB 266
  R 72
  TIAI 51

  5001 12, 258, 591
Nierenberg, George T.
  TIAI 470-473; dir., *Say Amen, Somebody*,
    470-473
  5001 655
Niesen, Gertrude
  5001 762
Nietzsche, Friedrich
  KKBB 298
  ML 192
Night and Day
  WTLGD 22, 25, 26
  5001
Night and the City
  KKBB 316:n
  5001
Night at the Opera, A
  KKBB 185, 317:n, 320
  RK 24, 27, 66
  R 392
  5001
Night Flight
  KKBB 285
Night Games (*Nattelek*)
  KKBB 103-104
  5001 (2nd ed)
Night in an English Music Hall, A (group)
  KKBB 274
Night in Casablanca, A
  5001
"Night Life" (music)
  H 8
Night Must Fall
  5001
Night Nurse
  5001
Night of the Following Day, The
  GS 277-278
  DIM 59
  5001
Night of the Hunter, The
  KKBB 317:n
  5001
Night of the Iguana, The
  KKBB 221, 343
  TIAI 418
  5001
Night of the Living Dead (1968)
  R 189
  TIAI 147, 197, 200
  SOTA 232, 324
  H 69
  5001
Night of the Shooting Stars, The (*La Notte di
    San Lorenzo*)
  TIAI 446-451
  SOTA 127
  H 122, 123, 124, 268, 340, 369
  ML 166
  5001 (2nd ed)
Night People
  ILIATM 319-331
  5001 (2nd ed)
Night Porter, The
  R 342-345
  5001
Night Shift

TIAI 392-394
SOTA 142, 143
H 263, 273
ML 112
5001 (2nd ed)
Night They Raided Minsky's, The
GS 237-239
DIM 83
5001
Night to Remember, A
5001 (2nd ed)
Night Train
KKBB 364
GS 202
Nightcomers, The
DIM 422
5001
Nighthawks (painting)
TIAI 273
Nightingale, Maxine
WTLGD 273
5001 685
Nightmare Alley
5001
"Nightmare at 20,000 Feet" (TV)
SOTA 22
Nights of Cabiria (*Le Notti di Cabiria*)
ILIATM 149, 265
KKBB 298, 318:n, 368
TIAI 251
H 63
5001
Nightwood (book)
ML 304
Nijinsky, Vaslav
WTLGD 335
Nikki (stage)
WTLGD 13, 14
Nilsson, Anna Q.
KKBB 354
5001 730
Nilsson, Harry
TIAI 123
5001 589
Nilsson, Leopoldo Torre, see Torre Nilsson,
 Leopoldo
Nilsson, Maj-Britt
KKBB 353
5001 664, 726
Nilsson, Rob
5001 680, 681
Nimitz, Chester
SOTA 119
Nimoy, Leonard
WTLGD 522
TIAI 356, 358, 359
SOTA 196-198
ML dir., *The Good Mother*, 33-37
5001 295, 368, 707, 708
Ninchi, Annibale
5001 213
Ninchi, Carlo
5001 59
Nine Days of a Queen (also known as *Tudor
 Rose*)
5001
Nine to Five

TIAI 162-164, 373
SOTA 192
H 243
5001
1900 (*Novecento*)
WTLGD 323-333
TIAI 174, 175
H 396, 398
5001
1941
TIAI 98, 100, 208, 211
SOTA 140, 164, 177
ML 226
5001 (2nd ed)
1984
H 279
1984 (book)
DIM 28, 373
H 106-107
"1999" (music)
SOTA 213
Ninotchka (1939)
ILIATM 154
KKBB 243, 318:n
TIAI 403
5001
Nissen, Greta
5001 328
Nitzsche, Jack
5001 167
Niven, David
DIM 269
WTLGD 20, 465
ML 75
5001 44, 51, 87, 123, 130, 174, 181, 196,
 597, 777, 851
Niven, Kip
5001 452
Nixon, Cynthia
H 172
5001 463
Nixon, Marni
5001 697, 828
Nixon, Richard M.
DIM 44, 112, 162, 299
WTLGD 62, 177, 262-265, 269
H 1-4
Nkrumah, Prime Minister
5001 654
No Exit (stage)
ILIATM 12
No Funny Business
GS 164
No Man's Land (stage)
WTLGD 258
SOTA 371
No Maps on My Taps
TIAI 472
"No Matter What Happens" (music)
SOTA 86
No Minor Vices
5001
No Orchids for Miss Blandish (book)
KKBB 147
No Time for Comedy
WTLGD 26
5001

No Way Out
H 355-358
5001 (2nd ed)
No Way to Treat a Lady
GS 74
DIM 314
"No Wonder" (music)
SOTA 87
Nobi, see *Fires on the Plain*
Nobody's Fool
H 236
Noël, Bernard
5001 467
Noel, Magali
KKBB 301, 338, 339
DIM 65
5001 214, 240, 440, 618, 630, 791, 862
Noël-Noël
5001 268
Noiret, Philippe
KKBB 370
DIM 80
R 215
WTLGD 484
TIAI 317, 319, 442, 443, 444
5001 158, 267, 644, 753, 764, 781, 836, 864
Nolan, Doris
R 347
5001 336
Nolan, Jeanette
5001 318, 793, 800
Nolan, Kathleen
R 107, 108
Nolan, Lewis Edward
GS 146, 147
Nolan, Lloyd
H 113, 115
5001 12, 88, 316, 405
Nolde, Emil
GS 187
TIAI 140
Nollier, Claude
KKBB 333
5001 388, 436, 500, 593
Nolte, Nick
TIAI 437, 438, 439, 440
SOTA 71, 72-73, 75, 78, 287
H 103, 105, 106, 381, 382
ML 89-90, 100-103, 270, 307-308
5001 199, 227, 261, 521, 606, 766, 805, 826
"Non, Je Ne Regrette Rien" (music)
H 482
"Non nobis domine" (music)
ML 212, 215
None but the Lonely Heart
WTLGD 22-25, 493
5001 (2nd ed)
Noonan, John Ford
WTLGD 130
5001 521
Noonan, Tommy
5001 707
Nordhoff, Charles
5001 346, 505
Nordin, Birgit
WTLGD 74
Norma (music)

TIAI 173, 176
Norma Jean (book)
  R 152, 153
Norma Rae
  TIAI 383
  SOTA 57
Norman, Gertrude
  5001 307
Norman, Marc
  WTLGD 113
  5001 394, 863
Norman, Marsha
  H 1, 97
Norman, Zack
  5001 638
Normand, Mabel
  5001 831
Normington, John
  SOTA 341
  5001 598
Noro, Line
  KKBB 356
  5001 575, 739
Norris, Patricia
  5001 87
Norris, William J.
  H 67
  5001 618
Norte, El
  SOTA 130-132
  5001 (2nd ed)
North, Alex
  ILIATM 137
  TIAI 222
  SOTA 200, 379
  5001 16, 121, 177, 201, 484, 600, 614, 699,
    722, 806
North by Northwest
  ILIATM 294
  KKBB 318-319:n
  WTLGD 3, 25, 30, 352, 373
  H 117
  ML 247
  5001
North Dallas Forty
  TIAI 195, 439
  SOTA 145
North, Edmund H.
  5001 249, 359, 570
North, John Ringling
  5001 305
North, Sheree
  5001 131, 677
North Star, The (also known as *Armored Attack*)
  ILIATM 324
  5001
North to Alaska
  ILIATM 297
Northup, Harry
  WTLGD 134, 321
  5001 16, 86, 139, 473, 745, 810
Northwest Passage
  5001
Norton, Alex
  5001 149
Norton, B. W. L.
  5001 155

Norton, Barry
  5001 192
Norton, Bill L.
  5001 138
Norton, Edgar
  5001 693
Norton, William
  5001 656
Nosferatu
  ILIATM 6
  KKBB 319:n, 356-357, 365
  R 111
  ML 151
  5001
Not as a Stranger
  ILIATM 45
  KKBB 204-205
"Not the Nine O'Clock News" (TV)
  ML 272
Not Tonight, Henry
  ILIATM 8
Notes from Underground (book)
  ILIATM 256
  WTLGD 132
Nothing but the Best
  5001
Nothing in Common
  H 199-202
  5001 (2nd ed)
Nothing Sacred
  KKBB 319-320:n, 341
  RK 19
  WTLGD 141
  5001
Notorious
  KKBB 320:n, 348
  GS 113
  WTLGD 3, 25, 26, 29, 30
  5001
Notte di San Lorenzo, La, see *Night of the*
  Shooting Stars, The
Notte, La
  ILIATM 12, 20, 24, 179-184, 188, 192-196,
    220
  GS 47
  DIM 113
  WTLGD 233
  H 41, 44, 176
  5001
Notti di Cabiria, Le, see *Nights of Cabiria*
Nous la Liberté, A, see *A Nous la Liberté*
Novak, Kim
  WTLGD 223-224
  TIAI 108
  H 229
  5001 301, 399, 417, 462, 540, 562
Novarro, Ramon
  5001 63, 327
Novecento, see *1900*
Novello, Don
  ML 103
Novotna, Jarmila
  5001 661
Now, Voyager
  WTLGD 233
  ML 35, 275
  5001

"Nowhere to Run" (music)
  WTLGD 559
Noyce, Phil
  WTLGD 536
Ntshona, Winston
  TIAI 168
  ML 185
  5001 205
Nugent, Edward
  5001 11, 262, 525, 556
Nugent, Elliott
  5001 807
Nugent, Frank S.
  TIAI 154
  5001 259, 488, 608, 662, 673, 800
Nuit américaine, La, see *Day for Night*
Nuit de Varennes, La
  TIAI 469-470
  5001 (2nd ed)
Nuit des forains, La, see *The Naked Night*
Numéro deux
  SOTA 230
Nun's Story, The
  ILIATM 24, 305
  KKBB 169, 176
  DIM 421
  WTLGD 159, 305
  ML 247
Nunn, Alice
  H 59
  5001 573
Nunn, Larry
  5001 722
Nuremburg Trials
  WTLGD 175-177
Nureyev, Rudolf
  WTLGD 333-336
  SOTA 126, 367
  5001 811
Nussbaum, Mike
  5001 759
Nutcracker, The Motion Picture
  H 240-243
  5001 (2nd ed)
Nutty Professor, The
  ILIATM 26
  5001
Nuytten, Bruno
  WTLGD 293
  TIAI 21
  5001 108, 268, 291, 379, 792
Nyby, Christian
  5001 758
Nybyggarna, see *The New Land*
Nye, Carrie
  5001 309
Nye, Louis
  5001 723
Nykvist, Sven
  GS 220
  DIM 162
  R 90
  WTLGD 59, 75, 389, 391, 478
  TIAI 48, 179, 488
  H 430
  ML 13, 104, 200
  5001 31, 40, 77, 161, 162, 236, 246, 410,

450, 576, 592, 666, 670, 706, 734, 804, 840
Nyman, Lena
  WTLGD 476-477, 479, 480
  5001 40, 348
Nyswaner, Ron
  SOTA 168, 290
  5001 486, 738

O

O Cangaceiro, see *Cangaceiro, O*
O.K. Nero!
  TIAI 215
Oakie, Jack
  KKBB 7, 185
  RK 15
  5001 15, 327, 355, 441, 481, 502, 547, 566, 692, 774, 839
Oakland Raiders
  WTLGD 214
Oakland, Simon
  5001 109, 828
Oasis, The (book)
  KKBB 79
Oates, Joyce Carol
  DIM 32
  WTLGD 209, 317
  H 132, 261
  5001 689
Oates, Warren
  DIM 229, 323
  R 135-136, 303
  WTLGD 116
  TIAI 225, 301, 485
  5001 47, 87, 92, 360, 531, 677, 723, 752, 757, 838
Oatis, William
  ILIATM 320
O'Bannon, Dan
  TIAI 485
  5001 87
Obchod na Korze, see *The Shop on Main Street*
Ober, Philip
  5001 215, 269, 331, 533, 802
Oberon, Merle
  5001 184, 193, 223, 253, 341, 554, 599, 659, 751, 753, 851
Oblong, Harold
  R 369
  5001 579
Oboler, Arch
  5001 224
O'Brian, Hugh
  5001 677, 752
O'Brien, Conor Cruise
  R 22
O'Brien, Dave
  5001 255, 399
O'Brien, Edmond
  KKBB 42, 156, 234, 235, 291
  WTLGD 44
  5001 30, 51, 73-74, 199, 237, 345, 394, 461, 834, 838

O'Brien, Edna
  DIM 405-408
  WTLGD 59
  H 70
  5001 852
O'Brien, George
  WTLGD 46
  5001 259, 672, 729
O'Brien, Jack
  H 351
O'Brien, Jim
  ML dir., *The Dressmaker*, 45-47; *The Jewel in the Crown*, 46
  5001 204
O'Brien, Kenneth
  TIAI 116
  5001 355
O'Brien, Margaret
  KKBB 185
  TIAI 333
  5001 117, 327, 446
O'Brien, Maria
  WTLGD 44
  5001 688
O'Brien-Moore, Erin
  5001 77, 306
O'Brien, Pat
  KKBB 348
  RK 13, 20
  DIM 45
  TIAI 241, 265
  5001 23, 27, 91, 243, 359, 409, 542, 612, 691, 782
O'Brien, Robert
  5001 406
O'Brien, Virginia
  5001 321, 404, 563, 675
Observer (periodical)
  ILIATM 17, 118, 201, 204
  WTLGD 509
Obsession
  WTLGD 184, 209, 210, 211, 212, 420
  TIAI 228
  SOTA 263
Ocasek, Ric
  H 393, 443
  5001 313, 449
O'Casey, Sean
  5001 858
Occupe-toi d'Amélie, see *Oh, Amelia!*
Ochs, Phil
  WTLGD 226
Ochsenknecht, Uwe
  H 194
  5001 475
O'Connell, Arthur
  KKBB 325
  DIM 249
  R 71
  5001 237, 411, 551, 591, 593, 691, 711, 752
O'Connell, Eddie
  H 158
  5001 3
O'Connell, Helen
  5001 349
O'Connell, Hugh
  5001 294

O'Connell, Jerry
  H 197
  5001 705
O'Connell, L. W.
  5001 657
O'Connor, Carroll
  R 357-358
  5001 196, 322, 414, 466, 588
O'Connor, Derrick
  H 369
  5001 340
O'Connor, Donald
  ILIATM 145
  KKBB 185
  R 130, 193
  TIAI 265
  5001 58, 115, 254, 612, 683, 752
O'Connor, Edwin
  5001 408
O'Connor, Glynnis
  TIAI 70, 71
  5001 764
O'Connor, Kevin J.
  5001 574
O'Connor, Robert E.
  5001 809
O'Connor, Una
  KKBB 249
  5001 7, 8, 52, 102, 117, 127, 128, 143, 363, 369, 616, 660, 733, 844
O'Conor, Hugh
  ML 179
  5001 509
October (*Octyabr'*; also known as *Ten Days That Shook the World*)
  ILIATM 32, 285
  KKBB 357-358:n
  TIAI 279
  5001
Octopussy
  SOTA 3-5
  5001 (2nd ed)
O'Day, Anita
  5001 379
Odd Couple, The
  GS 94
  DIM 233
  R 68
Odd Man Out
  ILIATM 47, 207, 297
  KKBB 321:n, 350
  GS 202
  5001
Odd Obsession, see *Kagi*
O'Dea, Denis
  KKBB 321
  5001 491, 522, 539, 804
Odets, Clifford
  KKBB 33, 238, 356
  R 117-118, 155
  WTLGD 14, 22-25, 403, 489, 493, 494; dir., *None but the Lonely Heart*, 22-25, 493; *The Story on Page One*, 23
  5001 71, 140, 157, 292, 345, 532, 680, 736
Odier, Daniel, see Delacorta
Odlum, Floyd
  RK 7

O'Donnell, Cathy
  KKBB 48
  R 268
  5001 63, 65, 186, 754
O'Donoghue, Michael
  ML 38
  5001 660
Odyssey (book)
  WTLGD 436, 555
Oedipus Rex
  ILIATM 108
  KKBB 56, 321-322:n
  GS 241
  DIM 304
  WTLGD 436
  5001
Oedipus Wrecks
  ML 103-105
Oeil pour oeil, see *An Eye for an Eye*
Of Human Bondage
  ILIATM 37
  KKBB 158
  H 30
  5001
Of Mice and Men
  DIM 4
  WTLGD 447, 489
  5001
"Of This Time, of That Place" (story)
  DIM 32
O'Ferrall, George More
  5001 435
Offenbach, Jacques
  5001 741
Officer and a Gentleman, An
  TIAI 381-383
  SOTA 6, 95, 146, 169
  H 134
  ML 306
  5001 (2nd ed)
Offner, Mortimer
  5001 607, 739
O'Flaherty, Liam
  KKBB 335
  5001 362, 603
Ogden Stiers, David, see under Stiers
Ogier, Bulle
  R 42
  5001 24, 192
Oh, Amelia! (*Occupe-toi d'Amélie*; also known
    as *Look After Amelia*)
  KKBB 320-321:n
  GS 211
  5001
Oh, God!
  WTLGD 505
  5001
"Oh, What a Beautiful Mornin'" (music)
  SOTA 56
Oh! What a Lovely War
  DIM 14-17
  5001
O'Halloran, Jack
  TIAI 224
  5001 731
Ohana, Claudia
  SOTA 183

  5001 224
O'Hanlon, James
  5001 114
O'Hara, Catherine
  H 39, 189-190, 455, 456
  ML 88
  5001 9, 61, 325
O'Hara, Jill
  5001 582
O'Hara, John
  GS 179
  RK 10, 12, 17, 42-43
  5001 110, 322, 562
O'Hara, Mary
  5001 508
O'Hara, Maureen
  KKBB 327
  5001 169, 342, 345, 378, 556, 608, 630,
    631, 684
O'Hara, Shirley
  5001 839
O'Herlihy, Dan
  KKBB 228-229, 282, 320
  H 405
  ML 117
  5001 8, 177, 338, 346, 539, 635
O'Herlihy, Gavan
  SOTA 10
  H 474
  5001 731, 840
"Ohoopee River Bottomland" (music)
  TIAI 206
O'Horgan, Tom
  DIM 54-57; dir., *Futz*, 54-57, 59, 112, 148,
    241
  R 371-373
Oil for the Lamps of China
  5001
Oiseaux vont mourir au Pérou, Les, see *Birds in
    Peru*
Ojeda, Manuel
  SOTA 164
  5001 638
Okada, Eiji
  5001 334, 802, 853
O'Keefe, Dennis
  5001 357
O'Keefe, Michael
  TIAI 51, 52
  5001 303, 371
O'Kelly, Tim
  5001 743
Oklahoma!
  GS 237
  DIM 29, 409, 413
  WTLGD 353
Oktyabr', see *October*
Okumoto, Yoji
  ML 84-85
  5001 792
Oland, Warner
  GS 114
  5001 192, 671
Olbrychski, Daniel
  5001 804
Old Acquaintance (remade as *Rich and Famous*)
  WTLGD 343, 344

  TIAI 247
  5001
Old Dark House, The
  WTLGD 211
  5001
"Old MacDonald Had a Farm" (music)
  SOTA 244
Old Maid, The
  5001
Old Man and the Sea, The
  WTLGD 280
Older, Fremont, Mrs.
  RK 57
Oldfield, Mike
  SOTA 278
  5001 395
Oldman, Gary
  H 295, 296, 297
  5001 595
O'Leary, William
  H 481
  5001 109
Oliansky, Joel
  TIAI 132-133; dir., *The Competition*,
    132-133
  ML 2
  5001 73, 150
Olin, Lena
  H 428, 430, 431
  ML 230-34
  5001 219, 803
Olin, Stig
  KKBB 353
  5001 727
Olive Trees of Justice, The
  KKBB 14
Oliver, Barret
  H 5
  5001 144
Oliver, Edna May
  KKBB 225, 340
  5001 15, 137, 160, 205, 428, 595, 638, 641,
    663, 717, 741
Oliver, Rochelle
  WTLGD 130
  5001 521
Oliver, Sy
  5001 675
Oliver!
  GS 200-205
  DIM 359
  R 219
  5001
Oliver Twist
  KKBB 322:n, 350
  GS 203-204
  5001
Olivia, Marie-Claire
  5001 583, 620
Olivia, see *Pit of Loneliness*
Olivier, Laurence
  ILIATM 71, 118-120, 168, 280-281, 283;
    dir., *Henry V*, 120, 283; *Hamlet*,
    280-281; *Richard III*, 281
  KKBB 57, 142, 173-175, 225, 334, 362; dir.,
    Henry V, 174, 200; *Hamlet*, 174;
    Richard III, 174; *The Prince and the*

Showgirl, 334
GS 136, 164, 183
RK 51
DIM 15, 37, 86, 149, 159, 195, 368, 374
R 76-77, 112, 130, 474; dir., *The Prince and the Showgirl*, 155
WTLGD 26, 148-151, 157, 173, 190-192, 336, 409, 451-453, 506, 530, 553
TIAI 174, 457
H 319
ML 162, 179, 182; dir., *Henry V*, 213-16; *Richard III*, 179, 182
5001 36, 61, 66, 96, 97, 121, 187, 193, 221, 244, 315, 328, 404, 464, 523, 541, 554, 595, 596, 606, 618, 628, 639, 667, 686, 699, 851
O'Loughlin, Gerald S.
5001 244
Olsen, Moroni
5001 11, 30, 143, 240, 468, 591, 642
Olson, James
DIM 276
TIAI 266
5001 26, 612, 719
Olson, Nancy
KKBB 354
R 364
5001 730
Olvidados, Los (originally released in U.S. as *The Young and the Damned*)
ILIATM 285, 340
KKBB 322-323:n
DIM 376
TIAI 250
5001
Olympiad (also known as *Olympia*)
ILIATM 287
KKBB 323:n
5001
O'Malley, Rex
5001 116, 478
Oman, Paul
5001 75
O'Mara, Ellen
5001 808
Omen, The
SOTA 357
Omen, Judd
H 59
5001 573
On a Clear Day You Can See Forever
DIM 185
R 388
WTLGD 193
On an Island with You
TIAI 357
On Approval
ILIATM 289
KKBB 30, 323-324:n
DIM 194
WTLGD 264
5001
On Golden Pond
TIAI 269-272, 418
SOTA 246
H 5, 243
5001

On Her Majesty's Secret Service
DIM 85-86, 389
R 360
5001 (2nd ed)
On the Avenue
KKBB 234
WTLGD 29
5001
On the Beach
ILIATM 177
KKBB 206-207
TIAI 495
5001
On the Bowery
KKBB 324:n
5001
On the Riviera
KKBB 234
"On the Road Again" (music)
TIAI 42
On the Town
ILIATM 278
KKBB 287-288
GS 263
5001
On the Waterfront
ILIATM 47-55, 57, 60, 93
KKBB 93, 191, 223, 350
DIM 152, 338, 421, 426
WTLGD 213, 447
TIAI 110, 229, 322
5001
On with the Show
KKBB 309
DIM 380
WTLGD 503, 504
5001
"Once in a Lifetime" (music)
SOTA 267
Once in a Lifetime
GS 68, 238
RK 28
WTLGD 248
5001
Once in Paris
WTLGD 546-547
5001
Once Is Not Enough
5001
Once Upon a Honeymoon
WTLGD 20
5001
Once Upon a Time
WTLGD 22
Once Upon a Time in America
SOTA 359-364
H 14-15, 320
5001 (2nd ed)
Once Upon a Time in the West
WTLGD 331
SOTA 244, 360
Ondra, Anny
5001 79
Ondricek, J.
5001 367
Ondrícek, Miroslav
SOTA 109, 252

H 117
5001 274, 355, 681, 849
One A.M.
ILIATM 276
One Day in the Life of Ivan Denisovich (book)
R 101
One Flew Over the Cuckoo's Nest
WTLGD 84-90, 200
TIAI 77, 179, 292
5001
ML 113, 249, 320
"One for My Baby (And One More for the Road)" (music)
H 311
One from the Heart
TIAI 296-300, 314, 328, 329, 354, 460
SOTA 46, 47, 230, 296
H 220, 471
ML 309
5001
One Hundred Years of Solitude (book)
SOTA 182
One Magic Christmas
H 99
One Mo' Time (stage)
TIAI 274
One Plus One
DIM 168, 209
One Sings, the Other Doesn't (L'Une chante l'autre pas)
WTLGD 339-342
H 152
5001
One Touch of Venus
5001
"One Trip Across" (story)
KKBB 360
One, Two, Three
ILIATM 150-155
WTLGD 221
5001
One Way Passage
KKBB 213
One Wild Moment
SOTA 133
One-Eyed Jacks
5001
O'Neal, Cynthia
DIM 283, 284
5001 120
O'Neal, Frederick
5001 583
O'Neal, Griffin
TIAI 349, 354
5001 224
O'Neal, Patrick
DIM 105
R 87, 445
ML 101
5001 244, 606, 714, 825
O'Neal, Ron
5001 730
O'Neal, Ryan
DIM 219, 296, 353, 431-433
R 135-136, 163, 466
WTLGD 102-105, 141, 248
TIAI 240

H 362, 363
5001 53, 204, 523, 689, 757, 784, 831
O'Neal, Tatum
R 163, 299
WTLGD 248
5001 517, 523
O'Neal twins
TIAI 472
5001 656
O'Neil, Barbara
5001 351, 713, 832
O'Neil, George
5001 366
O'Neil, Nance
5001 137, 403
O'Neil, Sally
WTLGD 504
5001 55, 547
O'Neill, Bernadette
H 335
5001 211
O'Neill, Eugene
ILIATM 84
KKBB 53, 70, 85, 262
GS 232
DIM 170, 208
R 195-200
TIAI 118, 413
SOTA 331
H 70, 306
ML 292
5001 11, 28, 217, 353, 432, 433, 500, 726
O'Neill, Henry
5001 238, 243, 253, 286, 306, 380, 382,
384, 391, 542, 783, 833
O'Neill, Jennifer
WTLGD 540-541
5001 364, 631, 724
O'Neill, Pat
5001 309
Only Angels Have Wings
ILIATM 305
KKBB 59
WTLGD 3, 4, 18, 30
SOTA 62
Only Game in Town, The
DIM 122-123, 407
TIAI 412
Only Two Can Play
WTLGD 245-246
Ontiveros, Lupe
5001 533
Ontkean, Michael
WTLGD 274, 277
TIAI 46
5001 592, 686, 839
Ooka, Shohei
ILIATM 226
5001 245
Open City (Roma, Città Aperta)
ILIATM 290
KKBB 269, 324:n, 342
DIM 65
R 33, 211
5001
Operation Mad Ball
KKBB 324-325:n

DIM 94
5001
Operation Petticoat
WTLGD 21, 26
Operation Sidewinder (stage)
WTLGD 188
Operations Abolition
GS 149
Ophuls, Marcel
DIM 427, 428, 430; dir., The Sorrow and
the Pity, 426-430
R 21-25; dir., A Sense of Loss, 21-25; The
Sorrow and the Pity, 21, 336, 338, 339
WTLGD 175-177; dir., The Sorrow and the
Pity, 96, 176; The Memory of Justice,
175-177; A Sense of Loss, 177
H 86
5001 475, 665, 696
Ophuls, Max
ILIATM 97-101, 235, 298; dir., The
Earrings of Madame De..., 97-101, 298;
La Ronde, 97-98, 100-101; Le Plaisir,
98, 298; Liebelei, 100; Vendetta (part),
100; Letter from an Unknown Woman,
100; Caught, 100, 235; The Reckless
Moment, 100
KKBB 16, 219, 296; dir., Letter from an
Unknown Woman, 296; Caught, 296
GS 6
DIM 279; dir., The Earrings of Madame
de..., 279, 362
R 33, 356; dir., The Earrings of Madame
de..., 420, 440
WTLGD 153, 177, 324, 358, 541; dir., Le
Plaisir, 358; The Earrings of Madame
De..., 541
TIAI 156
SOTA 55
5001 126, 208, 228, 419, 430, 585
Oppenheimer (TV)
ML 207
Oppenheimer, George
5001 7, 106, 175, 421
Oppenheimer, J. Robert
ILIATM 328
ML 207-208
O'Quinn, Terry
H 261, 262
5001 78, 714
Orbach, Jerry
H 116, 346
5001 162, 190, 273, 277, 596, 692
ML 201
Orbison, Roy
H 206
Orchestra Rehearsal
H 63
Orchestra Wives
SOTA 296
5001
Orchestral Manoeuvres in the Dark
H 135
Orchids and Ermine
KKBB 325:n
5001
Orczy, Baroness
5001 659

Orders to Kill
5001
Ordet
KKBB 325-326:n
TIAI 403
5001
Ordinary People
TIAI 78-82, 207, 383
SOTA 40, 97, 314
H 76
ML 71
5001
O'Reilly, Erin
5001 88
Orfeo ed Euridice (music)
WTLGD 541
Orff, Carl
R 303
TIAI 182, 384
5001 47, 228
Organic Theater
H 67, 68
Orgueilleux, Les (also known as The Proud and
the Beautiful)
KKBB 335:n
DIM 259
5001
Original Sin, The, see Der Apfel Ist Ab
Orion Pictures
H 21
Orlovsky, Julius
5001 472
Ormonde, Czenzi
5001 720
Ormrod, Peter
H dir., Eat the Peach, 334-336
5001 211
Ormsby, Alan
TIAI 336
H 263
5001 125, 783
Ornitz, Arthur
R 358
WTLGD 131, 412
Ornstein, Bruce
5001 655
Oro di Napoli, L', see The Gold of Naples
O'Rourke, Frank
5001 301, 601
O'Rourke, Heather
TIAI 352
5001 588
O'Rourke, Patricia
5001 386
Oroz, Alfredo
H 268
5001 342
Orphans of the Storm
DIM 319
TIAI 146
5001
Orphée, see Orpheus
Orpheus (Orphée)
ILIATM 7, 275, 286, 292
KKBB 43, 114, 239, 326-327:n
TIAI 335
5001

Orr, Mary
  5001 16
Orry-Kelly
  WTLGD 12
Orsini, Umberto
  5001 128, 169
Ortega, Kenny
  H 347
  5001 190
Orton Diaries, The (book)
  H 295
Orton, Joe
  SOTA 341
  H 295-298
Orwell, George
  ILIATM 10, 17
  KKBB 146-147
  DIM 125, 126, 373
  WTLGD 102, 105
  TIAI 182
  H 106-107, 279
  ML 110
Osborn, John Jay, Jr.
  R 190
  5001 564
Osborn, Paul
  5001 210, 446, 855, 859
Osborne, John
  ILIATM 63, 69-71, 200
  DIM 90, 162
  WTLGD 148-152, 256
  TIAI 126, 461
  H 42-43
  ML 162
  5001 221, 246, 250, 283, 434, 778
Oscar, The
  KKBB 134-135
  GS 18
  DIM 182, 259
  R 276
  5001
Oscarsson, Per
  DIM 249
  5001 170, 345, 411, 510
O'Shea, Michael
  5001 373, 405, 490
O'Shea, Milo
  KKBB 169
  GS 173
  TIAI 440
  5001 50, 202, 604, 639, 803, 813
O'Shea, Tessie
  5001 60, 647
Osmond, Cliff
  5001 260, 399
Osmond, Donny
  TIAI 115
O'Steen, Sam
  WTLGD 165-167; dir., *Sparkle*, 165-167,
    188; *Queen of the Stardust Ballroom*
    (TV movie), 165
  5001 135, 643, 699
Ossessione
  R 33
Osterwald, Bibi
  5001 244
Ostre Sledovane Vlaky, see *Closely Watched*

Trains
O'Sullivan, Maureen
  H 113, 115
  5001 28, 52, 175, 186, 316, 387, 574, 595,
    744, 758
Oswald, Lee Harvey
  KKBB 151
  DIM 207
Oswald, Marianne
  5001 441
Otchi Tchornyia, see *Dark Eyes*
"Otchi Tchornyia" (music)
  H 372
Othello
  KKBB 173-175, 198
  DIM 159
  SOTA 114
  5001
Other Side of Midnight, The
  WTLGD 304
  TIAI 176
"Other Son, The" (story)
  H 123
Ottiano, Rafaela
  KKBB 275
  5001 186, 299, 472, 672
O'Toole, Annette
  WTLGD 44, 150
  TIAI 336, 439
  SOTA 10
  5001 125, 261, 688, 731
O'Toole, Peter
  KKBB 69, 133
  GS 175
  DIM 37-38, 40-41, 415
  R 77-78, 115
  TIAI 23, 63, 65, 66, 69, 396, 397, 398
  H 188, 395-396, 398-399
  ML 43-44, 45
  5001 67, 123, 143, 297, 333, 343, 408, 415,
    423, 434, 458, 508, 724, 805, 830
Our Blushing Brides
  5001
Our Daily Bread
  5001
Our Dancing Mothers
  GS 127
Our Gang comedy series
  WTLGD 67, 164-165, 189
  TIAI 263, 264
  H 58
Our Hitler
  TIAI 299
Our Man Flint
  KKBB 8
  5001 (2nd ed)
Our Man in Havana
  KKBB 327:n
  GS 202
  WTLGD 465
  5001
Our Modern Maidens
  5001
Our Town
  KKBB 105, 226
  DIM 76
  R 116

H 205
5001
Our Winning Season
  SOTA 232
Oursler, Fulton (Anthony Abbott)
  5001 92
Oury, Gerard
  5001 600
Ousdal, Sverre Anker
  5001 252
  TIAI 477
Ouspenskaya, Maria
  RK 29
  TIAI 194
  5001 153, 169, 196, 397, 672, 824
Out Cold
  ML 91-93
  5001 (2nd ed)
Out in the World, see *My Apprenticeship*
Out of Africa
  H 76-80, 173
  5001 (2nd ed)
Out of the Past
  SOTA 145
  5001
Out-of-Towners, The
  WTLGD 264
  TIAI 415
Outback
  DIM 415-417
  5001
Outcast of the Islands, An
  ILIATM 47, 297
  KKBB 321, 327-328:n
  GS 202
  5001
Outland
  TIAI 213, 217-220
  5001
Outlaw Josey Wales, The
  WTLGD 254
Outlaw, The
  5001
Outrage, The
  GS 151
Outrageous Fortune
  H 272-274, 484
  5001 (2nd ed)
Outrageous!
  WTLGD 316
  TIAI 176
Outsiders, The
  TIAI 399
  SOTA 47, 296
  H 220, 317, 348
  ML 309, 311
Over 21
  5001
Over the Edge
  TIAI 399
"Over the Rainbow" (music)
  DIM 227
Overall, Park
  ML 56
  5001 486
Overman, Lynne
  KKBB 341

5001 426, 590, 645, 647, 700, 793
Overton, Frank
  5001 777
Ovid
  H 142
Owen, Catherine Dale
  RK 23 (ill.)
Owen, Meg Wynn
  WTLGD 382
  5001 206
Owen, Reginald
  KKBB 249
  5001 60, 143, 153, 238, 294, 305, 440, 446,
    486, 517, 540, 583, 586, 616, 641, 642,
    741, 767, 825, 833, 846, 847
Owen, Seena
  5001 367
Owen, Sid
  5001 627
Owens, Jesse
  KKBB 323
  5001 544
Owens, Patricia
  5001 252
Owens, Rochelle
  DIM 54, 55
Owl and the Pussycat, The
  DIM 183-185, 314, 351
  R 162
  H 228
  5001
Owsley, Monroe
  5001 647, 746-747
Ox-Bow Incident, The
  ILIATM 241
  KKBB 276, 328:n
  GS 53
  5001
Oz books
  H 473
Oz, Frank
  H 81, 247-250; dir., Little Shop of Horrors
    (1986), 247-250
  ML dir., Dirty Rotten Scoundrels, 74-77
  5001 191, 428
Ozu, Yasujiro
  SOTA 381
  H 471

P

P.J.
  GS 207
Paar, Jack
  R 454-455
Pabst, G. W.
  ILIATM 116; dir., The Threepenny Opera,
    116
  KKBB 259, 290, 294, 302; dir., Don
    Quixote, 259-260; Kameradschaft, 290;
    The Last Ten Days, 294; The Three
    Penny Opera, 302, 340
  GS 3
  RK 76

WTLGD 324, 389; dir., Joyless Street, 389
  5001 197, 384, 390, 410, 563, 834
Pachelbel
  TIAI 78
Pacific Heights
  ML 276-78
  5001 (2nd ed)
Pacific Northwest Ballet
  H 241
  5001 537
Pacino, Al
  DIM 422-424
  R 228-229, 397, 400-401
  WTLGD 198-199, 274, 302-304, 335, 369,
    526
  TIAI 368, 370, 463, 475
  SOTA 100, 102-103, 104, 106
  H 94, 95, 183
  ML 310-14
  5001 39, 89, 196, 289, 290, 563, 627, 657,
    666
Pack, David
  H 65
  5001 835
Padamsee, Alyque
  TIAI 433
  5001 277
Padilla, José
  TIAI 158
  5001 17
Padovani, Lea
  KKBB 264
  5001 229
Padre Padrone
  WTLGD 298-302
  TIAI 60, 446, 447
  SOTA 127
  H 122, 124, 340
  5001
Paes, Dira
  H 20
  5001 216
Paese Sera (Rome newspaper)
  TIAI 420
Pagan, Antone
  TIAI 225-226
Paganini, Nicollo
  WTLGD 175
  5001 694
Pagano, Ernest
  5001 119, 819, 857
Page, Anita
  5001 105, 555, 556
Page, Anthony
  5001 406
Page, Elizabeth
  5001 343
Page, Gale
  5001 263, 754
Page, Geneviève
  KKBB 10, 264
  DIM 187
  5001 235, 472, 599, 694
Page, Geraldine
  ILIATM 138-139
  GS 91, 169
  R 86, 476

WTLGD 263-264, 437-440
  SOTA 201, 204
  H 66, 92-93, 411
  5001 176, 366, 517, 577, 589, 726, 734,
    785, 790, 835
Page, Joy
  KKBB 242, 245
  5001 109, 122
Page, Joy Ann
  5001 398
Page, Patti
  5001 215
Paget, Alfred
  5001 367
Paget, Debra
  KKBB 184, 241-242
  5001 74, 107, 747
Pagliacci (music)
  H 320, 323
Pagni, Eros
  5001 437
Pagnol, Marcel
  ILIATM 111, 113
  KKBB 140, 170, 233, 279; dir., The
    Well-Digger's Daughter, 110; Harvest,
    140, 279-280; The Baker's Wife, 233,
    262, 279
  GS 9
  R 95
  WTLGD trilogy--Marius (dir., A. Korda),
    Fanny (dir., M. Allégret), César (dir.,
    Pagnol), 144
  H 329, 330; dir., Harvest (1937), 330; The
    Baker's Wife, 330; César, 330
  5001 47, 127, 236, 320, 379, 465, 781, 827
Paich, Marty
  SOTA 285
  5001 490
Paige, Carol
  5001 857
Paige, Janis
  5001 681
Paige, Mabel
  5001 382, 502
Paine, John
  5001 196
Paint Your Wagon
  DIM 26-31, 328
  R 388
Painted Bird, The (book)
  R 121
  WTLGD 301
  H 414
Paisan
  R 211
  TIAI 450
  5001
Paiva, Nestor
  5001 161, 416
Pakula, Alan J.
  DIM 32, 34, 281, 282; dir., The Sterile
    Cuckoo, 31-34; Klute, 281-282, 285,
    314, 352, 426
  WTLGD 304, 485-488; dir., The Parallax
    View, 42; All the President's Men, 266;
    Comes a Horseman, 485-488; Klute,
    486

TIAI 435-436; dir., *All the President's Men*,
  23, 74; *Klute*, 29, 31; *Starting Over*,
  248; *Sophie's Choice*, 435-436, 494
5001 148, 365, 400, 695, 696, 714, 808
Pal, George
  GS dir., *The Time Machine*, 36
  5001 185, 593, 773
Pal Joey
  GS 100
  DIM 409
  TIAI 195
  5001
"Pal Joey" (short stories)
  GS 165
Palance, Holly
  H 111
  5001 65
Palance, Jack
  KKBB 238, 334, 347
  GS 167
  DIM 162
  ML 124, 160
  5001 54, 70, 495, 564, 601, 671
Palance, Walter Jack, see Palance, Jack
Palcy, Euzhan
  ML dir., *A Dry White Season*, 184-85; *Sugar
    Cane Alley*, 85
  5001 205
Pale Rider
  H 14-17
  5001 (2nd ed)
Paleface, The
  R 281
Palevsky, Max
  WTLGD 271
  5001 271
Paley, Grace
  5001 480
Paley, Natalie
  5001 738
Palin, Michael
  SOTA 341
  H 109
  ML 91
  5001 98, 598-599, 772
"Palladium, The" (comic routine)
  DIM 382
Pallenberg, Anita
  GS 173
  5001 50
Pallenberg, Rosco
  TIAI 183
  H 19
  5001 216, 227
Pallette, Eugene
  KKBB 228, 270
  5001 101, 116, 245, 278, 284, 307, 326,
    367, 391, 404, 466, 489, 509, 671, 713,
    714, 741, 781, 806, 817, 850
Palm Beach Story
  KKBB 363
  5001
Palme, Olof
  5001 348
Palme, Ulf
  5001 203, 485
Palmer, Betsy

5001 488
Palmer, Gretchen
  5001 165
Palmer, Lilli
  GS 19
  WTLGD 453
  5001 97, 531, 662, 663, 769
Palmer, Patrick
  5001 197, 353
Palumbo, Dennis
  TIAI 395
  5001 508
Paluzzi, Luciana
  5001 769
Pampanini, Silvana
  KKBB 303
  5001 449
Pan, Hermes
  KKBB 234
  R 56, 57
  5001 83, 252, 254, 399, 436, 562, 767, 827
Panama Hattie
  5001 (2nd ed)
Panama, Norman
  KKBB 292; co-dir., *Knock on Wood*, 292
  WTLGD 21, 147-148; dir., *I Will, I
    Will...For Now*, 147-148, 316, 317
  5001 352, 402, 633, 750
Panavision
  WTLGD 458, 513
  TIAI 36, 59, 84, 384
  H 321
Pandora and the Flying Dutchman
  GS 171
  WTLGD 393
  TIAI 392
  5001
Pandora's Box (Die Büchse der Pandora)
  RK 76
  5001
Panfilov, Gleb
  DIM 311; dir., *The Début*, 311
  5001 182
Pangborn, Franklin
  ILIATM 201
  KKBB 299, 313, 314
  5001 87, 119, 210, 248, 253, 313, 358, 509,
    536, 562, 703, 726, 782, 819
Panic in Needle Park, The
  DIM 305, 314
  WTLGD 335
  5001
Panic in the Streets
  5001
Panique
  KKBB 142, 328:n
  5001
Pankin, Stuart
  H 374
  5001 239
Pankow, John
  H 300
  5001 664
Panofsky, Erwin
  GS 189-190
Pantages, Lloyd
  RK 23 (ill.)

Pantoliano, Joe
  H 414
  5001 48, 217, 298, 473, 632
Paoli, Dennis
  H 67
  5001 618
Paoli, Gino
  5001 61
"Papa Legba" (music)
  H 219
Papamoskou, Tatiana
  WTLGD 378-379
  5001 370
Papandreou, George
  DIM 64
Papas, Irene
  KKBB 160
  GS 55, 56, 247
  DIM 65, 96, 302-303, 305
  WTLGD 378-379
  SOTA 182, 183
  H 450, 451
  5001 29, 31, 214, 224, 332, 370, 791, 825,
    862, 865
Pape, Paul
  5001 655
Paper Chase, The
  R 190-192, 194
  ML 154
  5001
Paper Moon
  R 163, 466
  WTLGD 248
Paperback Hero
  5001
Papillon
  R 237-239, 312
  WTLGD 279, 452
  5001
Papousek, J.
  5001 367
Papp, Joseph
  R 296
  TIAI 174, 463
Paradine Case, The
  5001
Paradise Alley
  WTLGD 488-493
Paradise Lagoon (The Admirable Crichton)
  5001
Parallax View, The
  WTLGD 42
Paramore, Edward A.
  5001 75, 765
Paramount on Parade
  5001
Paramount Pictures
  RK 7, 9, 12, 17, 24, 26, 29
  DIM 84, 132, 173, 182, 216, 217, 420
  R 314, 447
  WTLGD 6, 7, 12, 13, 14, 15, 18, 20, 21, 27,
    269, 321, 323, 502, 554
  TIAI 194, 208
  H 187
Parély, Mila
  KKBB 236, 343
  5001 59, 586, 647

Parent, Gail
  R 429-432
  5001 673
Parent Trap, The
  ILIATM 232-233
Parenthood
  ML 193
Parents
  ML 93-95
  5001 (2nd ed)
Parents terribles, Les (also known as *The Storm Within*)
  ILIATM 343
  KKBB 329:n
  GS 228
  H 98
  5001
Parfitt, Judy
  H 361
  5001 316, 471
Paris Does Strange Things, see *Eléna et les hommes*
Paris, Jerry
  5001 467, 513, 707
Paris Review (periodical)
  DIM 327
Parker, Alan
  WTLGD 163-165, 496-501; dir., *Bugsy Malone*, 163-165; *Midnight Express*, 496-501
  TIAI 290-295; dir., *Midnight Express*, 20, 122, 188, 290; *Fame*, 30, 290; *Shoot the Moon*, 290-295, 343; *Bugsy Malone*, 290
  SOTA 316-319; dir., *Fame*, 35, 139; *Shoot the Moon*, 58, 200; *Midnight Express*, 284; *Birdy*, 316-319
  H 286-287, 432; dir., *Midnight Express*, 35, 157, 180, 251; *Angel Heart*, 286-287; *Shoot the Moon*, 378, 432
  ML dir., *Birdy*, 151; *Midnight Express*, 53; *Mississippi Burning*, 53-56
  5001 27, 74, 108, 479, 486, 676
Parker, Albert
  5001 77
Parker, Austin
  5001 768
Parker, Bonnie
  KKBB 48-58, 61-62
Parker, Cecil
  KKBB 257, 293, 306, 328-329, 350
  5001 114, 185, 362, 406, 407, 457, 541, 565, 710, 804
Parker, Cecilia
  5001 11, 438, 518
Parker, Chan
  ML 4
Parker, Charlie
  DIM 310
  ML 1-5, 123
  5001 153
Parker, Claire
  5001 789
Parker, Debi
  SOTA 119
  5001 804
Parker, Dorothy

  RK 10, 12, 17, 21
  DIM 327, 333
  WTLGD 305
  5001 496, 688, 706, 733, 736, 786
Parker, Eleanor
  KKBB 134
  5001 186, 462, 540, 554, 697
Parker, Jean
  KKBB 270
  5001 284, 428
Parker, Lara
  5001 330
Parker, Lottie Blair
  5001 824
Parker, Sachi
  5001 715
Parker, Sarah Jessica
  ML 328
  5001 256
Parker, Suzy
  5001 271
Parker, Col. Tom
  TIAI 202
Parker, Willard
  5001 398, 686, 829
Parkes, Walter F.
  TIAI 495
  5001 823
Parkins, Barbara
  DIM 105
Parks, Bert
  WTLGD 43
Parks, Gordon Jr.
  5001 730
Parks, Larry
  5001 200
Parks, Michael
  5001 67, 317
Parks, Rosa
  ML 54
Parlo, Dita
  5001 37, 300
Parrish, Helen
  5001 753
Parrish, Leslie
  5001 462
Parrish, Maxfield
  WTLGD 327
  H 479
Parrish, Robert
  5001 123
Parrott, Ursula
  5001 194, 522
Parry, Natasha
  5001 494, 639
Parslow, Ray
  R 204
  5001 221
Parsonnet, Marion
  5001 356
Parsons, Clive
  5001 365
Parsons, Estelle
  GS 169
  DIM 170, 199
  5001 91, 351, 352, 800
Parsons, Louella

  RK 6, 7, 21, 22 (ill.), 24, 32, 40, 45, 68, 69
Partie de campagne, Une, see *A Day in the Country*
Partisan Review
  KKBB 267
Partner (Il Sosia)
  DIM 272-273
  5001
Parton, Dolly
  TIAI 162, 163-164, 373, 374, 375
  5001 64, 530
Partos, Frank
  5001 760, 807
"Partridge Family, The" (TV)
  WTLGD 347
Party, The
  GS 158
  SOTA 305
  5001
Pas si méchant que ça, see *The Wonderful Crook*
Pascal, Gabriel
  5001 25, 114, 453, 605
Pascual, Cristina S.
  H 467
  5001 172
Pasdar, Adrian
  5001 519
Pasolini, Pier Paolo
  KKBB 133, 237, 253; dir., *The Gospel According to Saint Matthew*, 133; *Accatone*, 253
  GS 7
  DIM 8, 263; dir., *Pigpen*, 59
  5001 62, 298, 748
Pasqualino Settebellezze, see *Seven Beauties*
Pass the Ammo
  H 452-454
  5001 (2nd ed)
Passage to India, A
  SOTA 299-304, 380
  H 127, 433
  5001 (2nd ed)
Passages from Finnegans Wake
  5001
Passenger, The
  WTLGD 51, 87, 201
  TIAI 5, 452
Passer, Ivan
  DIM 351; dir., *Born to Win*, 314, 351-352, 402, 426
  R 356-359; dir., *Law and Disorder*, 356-359; *Born to Win*, 357; *Intimate Lighting*, 357
  5001 94, 167, 367, 414
Passion de Jeanne d'Arc, see *The Passion of Joan of Arc*
Passion of Anna, The
  WTLGD 390, 478
  TIAI 488
Passion of Joan of Arc, The (La Passion de Jeanne d'Arc)
  ILIATM 277
  KKBB 254, 259, 325, 329:n
  DIM 419
  WTLGD 519
  TIAI 148
  H 325

5001
Passport to Pimlico
  KKBB 330:n
  5001
Pasternak, Boris
  5001 195
Pasternak, Joe
  5001 25, 173, 245, 248, 373, 439, 764, 765,
    768, 777
Pasteur, Louis
  WTLGD 206
Pat and Mike
  ILIATM 81, 304
  KKBB 330:n
  GS 177
  DIM 184
  TIAI 429
  5001
Pat Garrett and Billy the Kid
  5001
Patch of Blue, A
  GS 54
  R 432
Pate, Michael
  5001 247, 627, 664
Paterson, Bill
  SOTA 268, 269, 271, 277, 342
  H 279
  5001 7, 148, 183, 395, 599, 842
Paterson, Neil
  5001 640
Paterson, Pat
  5001 354
Pathé, Charles
  KKBB 320
*Pather Panchali (Song of the Road; The Lament
  of the Path; etc.; see also The Apu
  Trilogy)*
  ILIATM 248-250
  SOTA 98, 380
  5001
Paths of Glory
  ILIATM 209
  KKBB 231
  TIAI 2
  5001
Patinkin, Mandy
  SOTA 43, 44, 87, 90
  H 379
  5001 172, 597, 612, 855
Patkin, Max
  H 481-482
  5001 109
Patrick, Gail
  5001 36, 502, 508, 509, 647, 703, 741, 825
Patrick, John
  5001 418, 718, 745
Patrick, Lee
  KKBB 305
  WTLGD 122
  5001 76, 454, 536, 559, 683, 726
Patrick, Nigel
  KKBB 240, 241, 331
  5001 100, 107, 304, 563, 581, 614, 779
Patrick, Vincent
  SOTA 201
  5001 589

Patrizi, Stefano
  5001 154
Patroni Griffi, Giuseppe
  ILIATM 20; dir., *Il Mare*, 12, 20-21
Patsy, The
  RK 69
Patterson, Elizabeth
  KKBB 286
  5001 72, 87, 313, 329, 333, 368, 510, 562,
    685, 744, 777, 778
Patterson, Frank
  H 404, 406
  5001 177
Patterson, James
  5001 360
Patterson, Neva
  5001 174, 184
Patterson, Dr. Paige
  H 441
Patton
  DIM 97-100, 368
  R 238
  WTLGD 452
  5001
Patton, Gen. George
  DIM 97-99, 318
Patton, George S. III
  DIM 45
Patton, Mark
  TIAI 417
  5001 148
Patton, Will
  H 356, 357
  ML 308
  5001 184, 227, 532
Patty Hearst
  ML 8-11
  5001 (2nd ed)
Patucci, Tony
  5001 754
Paul, Alexandra
  H 156
  5001 213
Paul, Richard
  H 454
Paul, Steven
  5001 317
Pauline at the Beach (Pauline à la plage)
  SOTA 37-39
  5001 (2nd ed)
Pauling, Linus
  KKBB 207
Paull, Lawrence G.
  SOTA 164
  5001 45, 638
Paulsen, Albert
  TIAI 169
  5001 231, 462, 521
Pauw, Josse De, see De Pauw, Josse
Pavan, Marisa
  5001 642
Pavarotti, Luciano
  TIAI 113
Pavese, Cesare
  DIM 113
Pavlova, Anna
  WTLGD 494

Pawnbroker, The
  KKBB 82, 88, 146, 160-161, 163
  GS 75
  5001
Paxinou, Katina
  KKBB 251
  H 71, 451
  5001 152, 256, 500, 635
Paxton, Bill
  H 452, 454
  5001 518, 567
Paxton, John
  KKBB 253, 313
  5001 144, 164, 402, 503, 546, 839
Paxton, Tom
  WTLGD 226
Pay Day (1922)
  DIM 194
Payday (1973)
  R 122-125, 312, 326
  5001
Payment on Demand
  5001
Payne, Bruce
  H 159
  5001 3
Payne, Cynthia ("Mme. Cyn")
  H 301, 331
  5001 577
Payne, John
  DIM 159
  5001 303, 327, 623, 728, 774, 827
Payton-Wright, Pamela
  5001 625
PBS (Public Broadcasting System)
  H 441, 442
PBS American Playhouse (TV)
  H 351
Peace Corps
  DIM 220, 258
Peaker, E. J.
  5001 16
"Peanuts" (comic strip)
  RK 60
  DIM 91
Pearce, Alice
  5001 399, 546
Pearce, Richard
  SOTA 234-237; dir., *Country*, 234-237, 319;
    Heartland, 236; *Threshold*, 236
  5001 157, 768
Pearl, Jack
  5001 337
*Pearls of the Crown, The (Les Perles de la
  couronne)*
  KKBB 301
  5001
Pearson, Humphrey
  5001 547
Pearson, Jesse
  5001 111
Pearson, Peter
  5001 564
Peau douce, Le
  KKBB 356
*Peccato che Sia una Canaglia, see Too Bad
  She's Bad*

Peck, Gregory
  ILIATM 46, 177, 224, 320, 322, 325-327
  KKBB 44, 134, 185, 190, 206, 307, 348
  GS 185, 223, 226, 248, 250, 252
  DIM 63, 86, 199, 200, 353
  R 112, 456
  WTLGD 281, 368, 451, 453
  TIAI 382
  SOTA 248, 361
  5001 97, 206, 343, 351, 392, 461, 467, 490,
    527, 546, 565, 636, 701, 776, 777, 854,
    855
Peckinpah, Sam
  KKBB 14, 40, 197, 286; dir., *Ride the High
    Country*, 14, 40-41; *Major Dundee*, 14
  GS 252; dir., *Ride the High Country*, 75
  DIM 133-135, 148, 279, 393-398; dir., *The
    Wild Bunch*, 133-134, 149, 393; *The
    Ballad of Cable Hogue*, 279; *Major
    Dundee*, 358, 393; *Ride the High
    Country*, 393; *Straw Dogs*, 393-399, 426
  R 45, 318, 330, 471; dir., *The Getaway*,
    78-79, 135, 310; *The Wild Bunch*, 162;
    Junior Bonner, 285
  WTLGD 89, 112-119, 238, 324, 418, 421,
    428, 431, 432-434, 437, 557; dir., *The
    Wild Bunch*, 89, 113, 118, 418, 431;
    The Getaway, 112, 557; *The Killer Elite*,
    112-119, 557; *Bring Me the Head of
    Alfredo Garcia*, 114; *Ride the High
    Country*, 117, 260; *Convoy*, 427, 428,
    430, 432-434; *Cross of Iron*, 433
  TIAI 42, 65, 127, 168, 260, 333; dir., *The
    Wild Bunch*, 168; *Junior Bonner*, 333
  SOTA 72, 78, 330; dir., *Straw Dogs*, 72;
    The Wild Bunch, 164; *Ride the High
    Country*, 330
  H 35; dir., *The Wild Bunch*, 322, 424
  5001 48, 154, 283, 368, 393, 569, 629, 721,
    821, 837, 838
Péclet, Georges
  5001 300
Pedestrian, The (Der Fussgänger)
  5001
Pedi, Tom
  R 201
  5001 354, 514, 711
Pee-wee's Big Adventure
  H 58-61, 456
  ML 159, 184, 299
  5001 (2nd ed)
Peel, Dave
  5001 517
Peer Gynt (stage)
  ILIATM 277
Peerce, Larry
  DIM 4, 260-262; dir., *Goodbye, Columbus*,
    4, 32, 218, 260; *The Sporting Club*,
    261-263
  WTLGD 91
  SOTA 310
  5001 37, 665, 703
Peggy Sue Got Married
  H 219-221, 305
  5001 (2nd ed)
Pelayo, Sylvie
  KKBB 264

5001 235
Pelikan, Lisa
  WTLGD 307
  5001 386, 738
Pelissier, Anthony
  KKBB 339; dir., *The Rocking Horse Winner*,
    291, 339
  5001 635, 778
Pellegrin, Raymond
  ILIATM 174
  5001 815
Pellicer, Pina
  5001 549
Peña, Elizabeth
  H 103, 105, 341-342
  5001 48, 199
Pena, Ralph
  5001 462
Pender, Bob
  WTLGD 10, 11, 12
Pendergrass, Teddy
  SOTA 288
  5001 136
Pendleton, Austin
  R 135, 426
  5001 270, 679, 757, 831
Pendleton, Nat
  5001 31, 37, 71, 278, 341, 357, 374, 463,
    534, 678, 680, 758
Penhaligon, Susan
  WTLGD 263, 265
  5001 517
Penn & Teller Get Killed
  ML 183-84
  5001 (2nd ed)
Penn and Teller
  5001 574
Penn, Arthur
  KKBB 52-55, 59-61, 152-153; dir., *The
    Chase*, 21, 60, 151-153; *Bonnie and
    Clyde*, 47-63; *The Miracle Worker*, 55,
    60, 143; *The Left Handed Gun*, 55, 60;
    Mickey One, 60
  GS 252; dir., *Bonnie and Clyde*, 79, 82, 105,
    168, 194
  DIM 5, 135, 212-216; dir., *Alice's
    Restaurant*, 5, 6, 197, 212, 215; *Bonnie
    and Clyde*, 6, 152, 170, 173, 212; *Little
    Big Man*, 212-216, 236, 252
  R 12; dir., *Bonnie and Clyde*, 12-13, 154,
    161, 256, 270, 283, 309, 403, 441; *Little
    Big Man*, 162, 309; *Alice's Restaurant*,
    309
  WTLGD 431; dir., *Bonnie and Clyde*, 52,
    261, 431; *Alice's Restaurant*, 411; *The
    Missouri Breaks*, 427; *Little Big Man*,
    554
  TIAI 260, 283-286; dir., *Bonnie and Clyde*,
    279, 281, 282, 284, 286, 295; *Four
    Friends*, 283-286; *The Missouri Breaks*,
    283; *Alice's Restaurant*, 284; *Little Big
    Man*, 284
  H 73-75; dir., *Four Friends*, 70; *Target*, 73-
    75
  ML dir., *Bonnie and Clyde*, 191, 196, 198;
    Penn & Teller Get Killed, 183-84
  5001 91, 132, 264, 416, 424, 483, 574, 743

Penn, Christopher
  SOTA 139-140
  5001 256, 562
Penn, Irving
  WTLGD 307
Penn, Sean
  TIAI 408, 473, 474
  SOTA 151-152, 153, 314-315
  H 460, 463
  ML 168-77
  5001 46, 124, 147, 233, 238, 610
Pennebaker, D. A.
  GS 12-15
Penner, Joe
  5001 97
Penney, Edward
  5001 48
Pennies from Heaven (1936)
  5001
Pennies from Heaven (1981)
  TIAI 272-278
  SOTA 2, 337
  ML 82
  H 52
  5001
Pennington, Michael
  5001 316
Penny Serenade
  R 85
  WTLGD 20, 21
  SOTA 93
  5001
Penny, Sydney
  5001 562
Penthouse (periodical)
  WTLGD 358
Pentimento, A Book of Portraits (book)
  R 219
  WTLGD 305-310
Penzer, Jean
  WTLGD 460
  5001 283, 363, 843
People (periodical)
  SOTA 69, 335
"People Like Us" (music)
  H 218
People on Sunday
  KKBB 257
People Will Talk
  WTLGD 22
Peoples, David
  TIAI 361
  5001 80
Pépé le Moko (remade as *Casbah*)
  KKBB 244
  R 238
  WTLGD 126-127, 233
  H 308
  5001
Peploe, Clare
  H 449-452; dir., *High Season*, 449-452; 476;
    Couples and Robbers, 452
  5001 332, 863
Peploe, Mark
  H 395, 397, 398, 450, 452
  ML 304, 306
  5001 332, 408

Peppard, George
  ILIATM 141
  5001 86, 99, 121, 343, 719
Pepper, Art
  5001 692
Pepper, Barbara
  5001 258, 399, 464, 503, 555, 736, 755
Pepusch, John
  ILIATM 116
Pera, Marília
  TIAI 251, 252
  5001 584
Percy, Edward
  5001 403
Percy, Esmé
  5001 114, 501, 605
Pereira, Hal
  5001 198
Perelman, S. J.
  RK 10, 83
  SOTA 177
  5001 341, 493, 550
Peretz, Susan
  TIAI 77
  5001 197
Perez, José
  WTLGD 297
  5001 679, 715
Perfect Friday
  DIM 193
  5001
Performance
  DIM 156, 209
  R 234
Performing Garage, The (club)
  H 285
Pergand, Louis
  5001 309
Pergialis, Notis
  KKBB 271
  5001 286
Périer, François
  KKBB 265, 318, 326
  DIM 65
  R 214
  5001 247, 282, 529, 554, 712, 739, 862
Perils of Priscilla, The
  SOTA 98
Périnal, Georges
  KKBB 239
  5001 1, 83, 234, 435, 481, 623, 756, 759
Period of Adjustment
  DIM 281
Perkins, Anthony, see Tony Perkins
Perkins, Elizabeth
  H 177, 178, 483
  ML 280-82
  5001 2, 40, 68
Perkins, Maxwell
  SOTA 57
Perkins, Millie
  ILIATM 66
  5001 629, 677, 838
Perkins, Osgood
  5001 657, 744
Perkins, Tony (Anthony)
  KKBB 206, 346

GS 169
DIM 182, 348
R 45-46, 390, 392
WTLGD 60-61
5001 5, 126, 129, 268, 421, 453, 503, 546,
  578, 587, 594, 661, 789, 851
Perkins, V. F.
  ILIATM 308
Perlberg, William
  RK 30
  5001 157, 293
Perles de la couronne, Les, see The Pearls of the
  Crown
Perlich, Max
  ML 198
  5001 205
Perlman, Ron
  TIAI 307, 309
  5001 607
Perón, Juan
  DIM 257-258
Perrey, Mireille
  5001 482
Perrin, François
  5001 685
Perrin, Jacques
  WTLGD 97
  5001 700
Perrine, Valerie
  R 165, 372, 377
  WTLGD 526
  TIAI 223, 300, 301
  5001 92, 407, 417, 730
Perron, Clément
  5001 510
Perry, Eleanor
  5001 174
Perry, Felton
  5001 452, 822
Perry, Frank
  DIM 182; dir., Diary of a Mad Housewife,
    314, 348, 383, 384; Doc, 349
  R 45-46; dir., Play It As It Lays, 43-46;
    Diary of a Mad Housewife, 45; David
    and Lisa, 444
  WTLGD 90-93; dir., The Swimmer, 37;
    Rancho Deluxe, 90-93, 95; Play It As It
    Lays, 285; David and Lisa, 358
  TIAI 233-237; dir., Mommie Dearest,
    233-237
  H 36-38; dir., Compromising Positions, 36-
    38, 482
  5001 150, 174, 458, 492, 587, 616
Perry, George Sessions
  5001 698
Perry, Hart
  WTLGD 250
Perry, Joan
  5001 474
Perry, Natasha
  KKBB 312
Persky, Lester
  5001 223
Persky, Lisa Jane
  TIAI 52
  H 359
  5001 70, 303

Persoff, Nehemiah
  KKBB 346, 348
  SOTA 87, 90
  5001 546, 593, 661, 691, 819, 855
Persona
  KKBB 171-172
  GS 214, 216
  R 90, 94
  WTLGD 478
  TIAI 492
  5001
Personal Best
  TIAI 302-307
  5001
Personal History
  RK 26
Personal Services
  H 301-302, 331
  5001 (2nd ed)
Persson, Jorgen
  5001 216
Pertwee, Michael
  KKBB 294-295
  5001 167, 272, 413, 779, 861
Perugia, Luciano
  DIM 183
Pesci, Joe
  TIAI 108
  ML 266-70
  5001 297, 548, 612
Pescow, Donna
  5001 655
Pétain, Henri Philippe, Marshal
  DIM 427, 429
  WTLGD 97
Pete 'n' Tillie
  R 84-87
  WTLGD 170
  5001
Peter (pseud.)
  H 90
Peter and the Wolf (music)
  WTLGD 76
Peter Ibbetson
  5001
Peter Pan (stage)
  H 473
Peter, Paul, and Mary
  GS 148
Peters, Brock
  5001 77, 120, 571, 777
Peters, Bernadette
  R 354
  TIAI 273, 274, 276, 278, 345
  SOTA 337
  H 249
  5001 29, 433, 574
Peters, Charlie
  SOTA 133
  5001 80
Peters, Clarke
  5001 493
Peters, House
  5001 618
Peters, Jean
  KKBB 367
  5001 522, 581, 818

Peters, Jon
  WTLGD 241
Peters, Julie
  5001 840
Peters, Susan
  5001 616, 653
Peters, Werner
  KKBB 258, 340
  5001 187, 643
Petersen, Don
  5001 743
Petersen, Tommy
  TIAI 383
Petersen, William L.
  ML 96, 97, 98
  5001 159
Petersen, Wolfgang
  5001 92
Peterson, Dorothy
  5001 11, 257, 357, 780, 845
Petit, Roland
  R 339
  H 65
  5001 168, 287, 317, 835
Petit Soldat, Le
  5001
Petitclerc, Denne Bart
  WTLGD 281-282
  5001 372
Petri, Elio
  GS dir., We Still Kill the Old Way, 56, 96
  DIM 220-222; dir., We Still Kill the Old
    Way, 221; Investigation of a Citizen
    Above Suspicion, 221-222
  5001 368, 747, 825
Petrie, Daniel
  WTLGD 409-410; dir., A Raisin in the Sun,
    178; The Betsy, 409-410, 530; Sybil (TV
    movie), 267
  TIAI 117-119, 151-155; dir., Resurrection,
    117-119, 153; Fort Apache, The Bronx,
    151-155, 288, 289, 412, 441; Sybil (TV
    movie), 153, 289; Eleanor and Franklin
    (TV movie), 153; Lifeguard, 153; The
    Betsy, 153
  H 411; dir., The Dollmaker (TV), 243
  5001 66, 259, 422, 624
Petrie, Daniel Jr.
  SOTA 287
  H 358
  5001 66, 70
Petrified Forest, The
  KKBB 332
  TIAI 176
  H 59, 136-137
  5001
Petronius
  DIM 129
  5001 240
Pettet, Joanna
  KKBB 90
  5001 123, 309
Pettitt, Peggy
  R 60, 61
  5001 77
Petty, Tom
  H 393

5001 449
Petulia
  GS 92, 117-121
  DIM 4
  R 236, 348, 451
  TIAI 64
  SOTA 9
Pevney, Joseph
  5001 458
Peyton Place
  ILIATM 33
  GS 154
  DIM 294
  R 106-107
  WTLGD 210
"Peyton Place" (TV)
  KKBB 7
  DIM 219, 295
Pfeiffer, Michelle
  SOTA 101, 102, 356, 357
  H 162, 324, 325
  ML 48-52, 58, 59, 61, 187-90
  5001 171, 232, 406, 658, 735, 748, 843
Pflug, Jo Ann
  5001 469
Phaedra
  GS 169
  WTLGD 61
  5001
Pham Van Dong
  DIM 45
Phantom Baron, The (Le Baron fantôme)
  5001
Phantom India
  DIM 309
  R 339
  TIAI 434
Phantom Lady
  KKBB 257
  5001
Phantom of the Opera, The (1925)
  KKBB 330-331:n
  R 367
  TIAI 82
  ML 161
  5001
Phantom of the Opera, The (1943)
  5001
Phantom of the Paradise
  R 366-371
  WTLGD 208
  TIAI 99, 201, 212
  SOTA 264
  ML 317
  5001
Phantom President, The
  5001
Phèdre
  5001
Phelan, Anna Hamilton
  ML 6
  5001 298
Phenix City Story, The
  R 284
Philadelphia Story, The
  ILIATM 304
  KKBB 241

GS 177
RK 20, 59
DIM 261
WTLGD 3, 18, 28
5001
Philbin, Mary
  KKBB 331
  5001 460, 579
Philip, John Van Ness
  SOTA 210
  5001 94
Philipe, Gérard
  KKBB 257, 264, 296, 333, 335
  GS 73
  DIM 259, 419
  ML 60
  5001 59, 187, 235, 300, 354, 420, 494, 553,
    593, 619
Philips, Mary
  5001 404, 415, 464
Phillips, Arlene
  TIAI 344
  5001 29
Phillips, Chynna
  ML 136
  5001 656
Phillips, David Graham
  5001 733
Phillips, Julia
  5001 715
Phillips, Leslie
  5001 418, 657
Phillips, Lou Diamond
  H 341, 342
  5001 48
Phillips, Mackenzie
  R 193, 426, 428
  5001 611
Phillips, Michael
  5001 715
Phillips, Michelle
  WTLGD 336
  5001 409, 811
Phillips, Nancie
  5001 442
Phillips, Nicholas
  ML 40
Phillips, Sandra Reaves
  5001 644
Phillips, Sian
  DIM 38, 41
  R 115
  SOTA 286
  5001 207, 297, 805, 812, 859
Philpotts, Ambrosine
  5001 229, 640, 794
Phippeny, Robert
  5001 526
Phipps, Nicholas
  KKBB 243
  5001 118, 449
Phipps, Thomas
  RK 31
Phoenix, River
  H 197
  ML 146
  5001 350, 361, 705

Phoenix (periodical
  H 109
Piaf, Edith
  DIM 383
  H 482
Pialat, Maurice
  H 151
Picardo, Robert
  5001 364
Picasso, Pablo
  ILIATM 32, 217-218, 281
  KKBB 114, 315
  DIM 267
  TIAI 84
  5001 511
Piccoli, Michel
  GS 73
  DIM 80
  R 42, 214
  WTLGD 153-154, 155, 366
  TIAI 176, 177, 419, 420
  SOTA 325, 366, 367
  5001 38, 63, 161, 171, 192, 267, 310, 415,
    449, 450, 481, 751, 781, 815
Piccolo, Ottavia
  5001 449
Piccone, Ugo
  5001 567
Pichel, Irving
  KKBB 290
  5001 23, 141, 185, 253, 333, 357, 380, 446,
    488, 499, 672, 778
Pick-up Artist, The
  H 370-372
  5001 (2nd ed)
Pickens, Slim
  ILIATM 19
  WTLGD 93
  TIAI 43, 44
  5001 48, 81, 160, 283, 340, 343, 531, 549,
    569, 616, 728, 839
Picker, David
  TIAI 14
Pickford, Mary
  WTLGD 11
  H 22
Pickles, Carolyn
  5001 10
Pickles, Vivian
  5001 319, 728
Pickup on South Street
  TIAI 460
  5001
Pickup, Ronald
  H 73
  5001 214
Pickwick Papers. The
  KKBB 331:n
  DIM 54
  5001
Picnic at Hanging Rock
  TIAI 455
Picnic on the Grass (*Le Déjeuner sur l'herbe*)
  5001
Picon, Molly
  DIM 331
  5001 242

Picture of Dorian Gray, The
  KKBB 146, 148
  GS 103
  R 367
  5001
Picture Snatcher
  5001 (2nd ed)
Pidgeon, Walter
  KKBB 233, 266
  GS 136
  DIM 262
  5001 8, 46, 84, 257, 272, 342, 446, 457,
    481, 486, 635, 678, 779, 833
"Piece of Sky, A" (music)
  SOTA 86
Piedmont, Leon (pseud.)
  SOTA 334
  5001 473
Piéplu, Claude
  R 42
  5001 192
Piéral, Pierre
  5001 225, 819-820
Pierce-Roberts, Tony
  H 129
  5001 640
Pierre (book)
  ILIATM 237
Pierrot le fou
  KKBB 130
  GS 277
  TIAI 102
  SOTA 229, 230
  5001 (2nd ed)
Pierson, Dori
  H 484
  5001 68
Pierson, Frank R.
  DIM 117, 118; dir., *The Looking Glass War*,
    117-119
  WTLGD 199, 241-244; dir., *A Star Is Born*
    (1976), 240-244, 434; *The Looking
    Glass War*, 242
  5001 25, 124, 196, 317, 707
Pierson, Tom
  WTLGD 550
  5001 609
Pietrek, Nicholas
  SOTA 372
Pig across Paris, see Four Bags Full
Pigeons
  5001
Pigpen
  DIM 59
Pigs
  SOTA 98
Pigskin Parade
  R 354
  5001
Pike, Robert L.
  5001 109
Pilbeam, Nova
  5001 460, 529, 858
Pileggi, Nicholas
  ML 265, 266
  5001 297
Pillar of Fire (dance)

WTLGD 346
Pillow Talk
  ILIATM 41
  GS 18
Pinal, Silvia
  GS 258
  5001 682
Pinchot, Bronson
  SOTA 288
  H 38-39
  5001 9, 66, 249
Pine, Larry
  5001 202
Pinelli, Tullio
  KKBB 368
  H 140
  5001 14, 67, 286, 386, 482, 836
Pinero, Arthur Wing
  5001 218
Piñero, Miguel
  WTLGD 295-298
  TIAI 153, 154
  5001 260, 679
Pinewood Studios
  WTLGD 190
Pink Panther pictures
  SOTA 154, 305
Pink Panther Strikes Again, The
  WTLGD 245-246
  5001
Pink Panther, The
  ILIATM 25
  WTLGD 245
Pinky
  5001 (2nd ed)
Pinocchio
  ML 107
Pinochet, Augusto, General
  WTLGD 386
Pinon, Dominique
  SOTA 46
  5001 193, 495
Pinoteau, Claude
  WTLGD 152
  5001 685
Pinter, Harold
  KKBB 11, 105-109
  GS 171, 211-212
  DIM 10, 223
  R 219
  WTLGD 94, 216-219, 258
  TIAI 238, 239, 240
  SOTA 14-15
  H 45, 97, 98, 130, 131, 179
  ML 319
  5001 3, 75, 267, 338, 411, 602, 795
Pinvidic, Margo
  5001 342
Piovani, Nicola
  TIAI 451
  H 124, 141, 339
  5001 286, 295, 391, 527
Piper, Evelyn
  5001 515
Pippin
  R 462
Pirandello, Luigi

ILIATM 101, 118
DIM 207
H 122, 123, 124, 125
5001 380, 390, 773
Piranha
TIAI 194
Pirate, The
5001
Pirosh, Robert
5001 175
Pirro, Ugo
DIM 221
Pisan Cantos, The
WTLGD 119
Pisanello, Il
DIM 265
Piscopo, Joe
H 153, 154-155
5001 841
Pisier, Marie-France
WTLGD 145
5001 159, 268, 716
Pistek, Theodor
5001 812
Pit of Loneliness (Olivia)
GS 207
5001
Pitagora, Paola
GS 6
5001 247
Pitchford, Dean
SOTA 139
5001 255
Pitoëff, Sacha
5001 412, 600
Pitoniak, Anne
5001 342, 732
Pitts, ZaSu
ILIATM 139
DIM 31
5001 44, 107, 309, 338, 421, 547, 647
Pixote
TIAI 248-252, 474
H 25, 267
5001
Pizer, Larry
R 369
TIAI 212
5001 126, 579
*Pizza Triangle, The (Dramma della Gelosia; also
    known as A Drama of Jealousy)*
DIM 193-195
WTLGD 311
H 372
5001
Place in the Sun, A
ILIATM 81
KKBB 331-332:n
WTLGD 178, 304, 479
5001
Place, Mary Kay
TIAI 94
SOTA 69, 70
H 132
5001 69, 521, 598, 689
Places in the Heart
SOTA 246-249, 319

H 50
5001 (2nd ed)
Placido, Michele
TIAI 317, 319, 419
5001 68, 415, 764
Plainsman, The
KKBB 185
Plaisir, Le
ILIATM 98, 298
WTLGD 358
5001
Plana, Tony
TIAI 383
H 182
5001 540, 651
Planck, Robert
5001 555, 847
Planer, Franz
KKBB 205
5001 99, 133, 228, 248, 419, 470, 637
Planes, Trains and Automobiles
H 421
Planet of the Apes
GS 36-38, 92, 100
DIM 98, 368
R 237
TIAI 309
5001
Plath, Sylvia
H 30
Platinum Blonde
RK 20
5001
Platoon
H 250-254, 305, 353
ML 251
5001 (2nd ed)
Platt, Edward
5001 331
Platt, Louise
5001 700, 704
Platt, Marc
5001 200, 667
Platt, Oliver
5001 250, 592
Plautus, Titus Maccius
KKBB 138
DIM 219
H 484
5001 272
Play
ILIATM 23
Play Dirty
TIAI 111
Play It Again, Sam
R 240-241
WTLGD 371
Play It As It Lays
DIM 250-251
R 43-46
WTLGD 285
SOTA 362
5001
Play It As It Lays (book)
WTLGD 114
Playboy (periodical)
KKBB 297

DIM 282
WTLGD 114, 374, 398, 437
TIAI 215, 374
SOTA 91, 92
Plaza Suite
R 260
Pleasence, Donald
DIM 26, 415
WTLGD 48, 217, 547
5001 237, 314, 325, 364, 393, 411, 434,
    450, 541, 558, 695, 770, 839, 857
Pleasure Garden, The
5001
Plein Soleil, see *Purple Noon*
Plenty
H 41-45, 46
5001 (2nd ed)
Pleshette, John
5001 478, 690
Pleshette, Suzanne
5001 74, 355, 487, 519
Plimpton, George
GS 17
5001 631
Plimpton, Martha
ML 13, 14
5001 31, 298
Plimpton, Shelley
DIM 197
Plowright, Joan
WTLGD 337
H 94, 95
ML 45, 46, 280-82
5001 40, 204, 222, 223, 350, 627
Plumed Serpent, The (book)
DIM 138
Plummer, Amanda
TIAI 212, 213, 214, 381
SOTA 42, 43
H 393
5001 126, 172, 448, 849
Plummer, Christopher
KKBB 178, 283
DIM 24, 25
WTLGD 65, 111
TIAI 169, 171, 172, 214, 490
SOTA 231, 233, 234
H 265
5001 151, 203, 231, 365, 461, 502, 646, 697
Plunkett, Walter
5001 607, 767
Plutarch
5001 667
Plymouth Adventure
WTLGD 178
PM (periodical)
RK 39, 41, 44
Pocket Money
TIAI 21
Pocketful of Miracles
GS 176
SOTA 123
H 154
ML 28
Podell, Rick
H 199
5001 535

200

Podromines, Joan
  5001 82-83
Poe, Edgar Allan
  KKBB 147
  TIAI 455
  SOTA 34, 237
  H 61
  5001 41
Poe, James
  KKBB 238
  DIM 70
  5001 71, 726, 755, 785
Pogson, Kathryn
  5001 98
Pogue, Charles Edward
  H 210
  5001 252
Pohlmann, Eric
  5001 229
Poil de carotte
  KKBB 243-244
  5001
Poindexter, Buster (pseud.), see Johansen, David
Point Blank
  KKBB 63
  GS 166
  R 278
  TIAI 315
  5001
Pointe courte, La
  WTLGD 341
Pointer, Priscilla
  H 208
  5001 87, 340, 478, 492
Pointer Sisters
  WTLGD 188
  5001 118
Poiret, Jean
  KKBB 301
  TIAI 165
  ML 90
  5001 440, 441
Poitier, Sidney
  ILIATM 91
  KKBB 144-145, 205-206, 261, 284
  GS 40, 50, 109, 110, 185, 242
  DIM 75
  WTLGD 66-68; dir., *Let's Do It Again*,
    66-68; *Buck and the Preacher*, 67; *Up-
    town Saturday Night*, 67
  SOTA 273
  5001 79, 212, 360, 418, 539, 777, 837
Polanski, Roman
  KKBB 150
  DIM 399-401; dir., *Macbeth*, 399-401
  R 311-312, 352, 356, 441; dir., *Repulsion*,
    80; *Rosemary's Baby*, 189, 248, 443;
    Chinatown, 311, 314, 352, 441-442, 473
  WTLGD 208, 301, 435; dir., *Chinatown*, 87,
    118, 125, 165; *Rosemary's Baby*, 165,
    421, 435
  TIAI 35, 38, 134-137, 364; dir., *Tess*,
    134-137; *Chinatown*, 242, 302, 364
  H 446-447; dir., *Rosemary's Baby*, 211;
    Chinatown, 314, 364; *Frantic*, 446-447
  5001 135, 265, 266, 444, 450, 624, 643,
    749, 799

Polglase, Van Nest
  R 56
  5001 139, 311
Police, The (group)
  SOTA 284
politics (periodical)
  ILIATM 184
Politics of Experience, The (book)
  R 392
Polito, Lina
  WTLGD 136
  5001 18-19, 437
Polito, Sol
  5001 262, 291
Polk, Oscar
  5001 306
Poll, Martin
  5001 423, 692
Pollack, Sydney
  KKBB 144; dir., *The Slender Thread*,
    143-145
  GS dir., *The Scalphunters*, 89-90, 92
  DIM 70; dir., *They Shoot Horses, Don't
    They?*, 68-72, 76, 281; *The
    Scalphunters*, 299
  R 88, 175, 178, 470-471; dir., *The
    Scalphunters*, 61; *Jeremiah Johnson*,
    87-88, 98-99, 282; *They Shoot Horses,
    Don't They?*, 161, 185, 309; *The Way
    We Were*, 175-178, 200, 461, 470; *The
    Yakuza*, 442, 464, 469-471; *Tell Them
    Willie Boy Is Here*, 19, 87
  WTLGD 42-43, 196, 302-304; dir., *The Way
    We Were*, 3, 209, 236, 304; *Three Days
    of the Condor*, 42-43, 113, 303; *The
    Yakuza*, 196; *Bobby Deerfield*, 302-304,
    305; *They Shoot Horses, Don't They?*,
    304
  TIAI 288-290, 428-432; dir., *The Electric
    Horseman*, 42; *Absence of Malice*,
    288-290; *They Shoot Horses, Don't
    They?*, 293; *Tootsie*, 428-432
  SOTA 70, 222; dir., *Tootsie*, 16, 70, 193,
    222, 234; *Absence of Malice*, 78; *They
    Shoot Horses, Don't They?*, 81; *The
    Electric Horseman*, 157
  H 76-80; dir., *Out of Africa*, 76-80, 173;
    They Shoot Horses, Don't They? 149,
    243; *The Electric Horseman*, 243
  5001 2, 89, 379, 557, 656, 755, 765, 780,
    825, 853
Pollak, Kevin
  ML 281, 328
  5001 40
Pollan, Tracy
  5001 103
Pollard, Michael J.
  DIM 173
  WTLGD 52
  TIAI 77
  ML 41, 191
  5001 91, 425, 660, 723, 837
Pollard, Snub
  5001 458, 724
Polley, Sarah
  ML 108
  5001 6

Polo, Danny
  5001 75
Polonah, Rui
  H 18
  5001 216
Polonsky, Abraham
  DIM 77; dir., *Tell Them Willie Boy Is Here*,
    76-78
  5001 746
Poltergeist
  TIAI 351-353, 358
  5001 (2nd ed)
Polyvision
  TIAI 143, 147
Pom-Pom Girls, The
  SOTA 232
  H 261
Pommer, Erich
  5001 56, 113, 378
Poncela, Eusebio
  H 288, 290, 468
  5001 414, 470
Ponicsan, Darryl
  R 259, 273, 275
  5001 138, 408
Pons, Maurice
  KKBB 311
  5001 489
Pontecorvo, Bruno
  R 211
Pontecorvo, Gillo
  GS dir., *The Battle of Algiers*, 96
  DIM 175-177; dir., *Burn!*, 175-180; *The
    Battle of Algiers*, 176
  R 210-214, 315; dir., *The Battle of Algiers*,
    209-214, 315; *Burn!*, 209-213, 315
  WTLGD 324; dir., *The Battle of Algiers*,
    524
  SOTA 74; dir., *The Battle of Algiers*, 74,
    278; *Burn!*, 74
  5001 54, 55, 109, 804
Ponti, Carlo
  5001 89, 195, 497, 863
Poole, Roy
  5001 668, 808
Poor Cow
  GS 25-28
  5001
Pop. 1280 (book)
  TIAI 443
Popcorn
  DIM 58-59
  5001
Pope of Greenwich Village, The
  SOTA 201-206
  5001 (2nd ed)
Popescu, Peter
  WTLGD 534
  5001 412
Popeye
  TIAI 119-124, 455
  SOTA 284
  5001
  H 421
Poppe, Nils
  KKBB 346
  5001 669

Poppy
  5001
Popular Mechanics (periodical)
  WTLGD 348
Popwell, Albert
  5001 141, 725
Porcasi, Paul
  5001 253, 281, 313, 407, 472, 498, 734
Porel, Marc
  WTLGD 541
  5001 364
Porgy and Bess (music)
  DIM 333
Port of Shadows (*Quai des brumes*)
  ILIATM 48, 135, 298
  KKBB 332:n
  WTLGD 126
  5001
Portal, Louise
  H 238
  5001 182
Porte des lilas (*Gates of Paris*)
  ILIATM 290
  5001
Porter, Cole
  GS 163
  DIM 328
  R 464
  WTLGD 22, 26, 191
  TIAI 47
  H 277
  5001 32, 37, 93, 106, 398, 399, 418, 523,
    563, 583, 641, 681, 692, 706, 857
Porter, Don
  5001 261, 455
Porter, Katherine Anne
  KKBB 209-213
  5001 675
Porter, William Sydney, see Henry, O.
Portman, Eric
  5001 145, 514, 832
Portnow, Richard
  H 282
  5001 773
Portnoy's Complaint
  DIM 219
  R 476
  WTLGD 128
Portrait of a Lady (book)
  ILIATM 170
Portrait of Jason
  GS 100
  5001
Portrait of Jennie
  5001
Poseidon Adventure, The
  R 71-72, 318, 347, 364, 406
  5001
Possessed
  KKBB 285
  5001
Possessed, The (book)
  GS 80
Post, Ted
  R 251-256
  5001 452
Posta, Adrienne

GS 64-65, 70, 80
Postcards from the Edge
  ML 273-76
  5001 (2nd ed)
Poster, Steven
  5001 692
Postlethwaite, Peter
  ML 45
  5001 204
Postman Always Rings Twice, The (1946)
  KKBB 332-333:n
  TIAI 255
  5001
Postman Always Rings Twice, The (1981)
  TIAI 178-182, 190, 191
  SOTA 234
  5001
Pot-Bouille (also known as *Lovers of Paris* and
    The House of Lovers)
  KKBB 333:n
  5001
Potemkin (*Bronenosets Potyomkin*; also known
    as *The Battleship Potemkin*)
  ILIATM 32, 109-110, 276
  KKBB 55, 273, 333-334:n, 357-358
  R 210
  H 322
  5001
Potter, Charles
  5001 842
Potter, Dennis
  TIAI 274, 276
  H 52, 53
  ML 189
  5001 202, 574
Potter, H. C.
  5001 238, 488, 662, 678, 717, 766
Potter, Madeleine
  SOTA 210
  5001 94
Potter, Martin
  DIM 130
  5001 240
Potter, Maureen
  5001 803
Potts, Annie
  TIAI 425, 426
  SOTA 193
  H 134, 453
  ML 47, 165
  5001 156, 284, 324, 567, 594
Potts, Nell
  R 75
  5001 212
Poujouly, Georges
  ILIATM 112
  5001 215, 257
Pound, Ezra
  DIM 36
Pound, Homer Shakespear
  DIM 36
Pounder, C. C. H.
  5001 592
Povah, Phyllis
  5001 467, 569, 847
Powell, Andrew
  5001 406

Powell, Bill
  5001 192
Powell, Bud
  ML 1
Powell, Dick
  KKBB 233, 273, 313, 341
  RK 13, 15
  DIM 284
  R 186, 262, 474
  WTLGD 501, 503-504
  5001 46, 81, 136, 220, 255, 262, 291, 503,
    545
Powell, Dilys
  KKBB 272
Powell, Eleanor
  5001 93, 105, 105, 106, 349, 404, 641, 675,
    764
Powell, Jane
  5001 173, 646, 667, 765
Powell, Marykay
  H 149
  5001 816
Powell, Michael
  ILIATM 286; dir., *Tales of Hoffmann*, 286
  GS dir., *The Red Shoes*, 105-106
  5001 349, 621, 741, 756
Powell, William
  KKBB 358
  GS 111
  WTLGD 8, 141
  5001 9, 30, 116, 225, 238, 263, 304, 306,
    391, 420, 421, 463, 488, 509, 566, 665,
    669, 721, 758, 865
Power, The
  5001
Power and the Glory, The
  RK 36, 50, 75
  5001
Power, Hartley
  KKBB 255
  5001 178, 461, 636
Power, Tyrone
  KKBB 190
  RK 20
  DIM 177
  R 114
  WTLGD 49
  TIAI 381
  H 53
  5001 13, 83, 359, 465, 466, 529, 617, 642,
    663, 844
Power, Tyrone Jr.
  H 6
  5001 144
Powers, Leslie Ann
  H 443
  5001 313
Powers, Marie
  KKBB 308
  5001 473
Powers, Tom
  5001 26-27, 86, 185, 198, 594, 808
Practically Yours
  5001
Pradal, Bruno
  DIM 419
  5001 775

202

Pramoj, Kukrit
5001 802
Pran, Dith
SOTA 274-279
Prather, Joan
WTLGD 44
5001 688
Pratolini, Vasco
5001 562
Pratt, Anthony
TIAI 187
5001 227
Pratt, Purnell
5001 123, 299, 547, 657
Pratt, Roger
H 166
ML 89, 163
5001 54, 331, 493
Prayer for the Dying, A
H 369, 384
ML 139
Preiss, Jeff
ML 124
5001 418
Preisser, June
R 193
5001 42, 722
Préjean, Albert
KKBB 287
5001 373, 698
Preminger, Ingo
5001 469
Preminger, Michael
H 199
5001 535
Preminger, Otto
ILIATM 130, 298, 303, 305-306; dir., *The
Cardinal*, 9; *Advise and Consent*, 294,
306; *Laura*, 298; *Whirlpool*, 298;
Carmen Jones, 306; *Anatomy of a
Murder*, 306; *Centennial Summer*, 306;
Forever Amber, 306; *That Lady in
Ermine*, 306; *The Thirteenth Letter*, 306;
River of No Return, 308
KKBB 349; dir., *The Cardinal*, 134
GS 208; dir., *Advise and Consent*, 207
DIM 383, 384; dir., *Hurry Sundown*, 59;
Such Good Friends, 383-384
5001 8, 119, 155, 234, 258, 413, 461, 646,
705, 724, 832
Prenom: Carmen, see *First Name: Carmen*
Prentiss, Paula
KKBB 69
R 444
5001 94, 125, 714, 830, 850
Préparez vos mouchoirs, see *Get Out Your
Handkerchiefs*
Preservation Hall Jazz Band (group)
5001 686
President's Analyst, The
GS 94
DIM 10
5001
Presle, Micheline
KKBB 257, 265
5001 187, 247, 600
Presley, Elvis

ILIATM 208
WTLGD 422
TIAI 28, 201, 204, 258, 323
SOTA 369
H 249, 334, 343
5001 211, 377, 393, 761, 762
Presnell, Harve
DIM 28
5001 286
Pressburger, Arnold
5001 672
Pressburger, Emeric
ILIATM 286; dir., *Tales of Hoffmann*, 286
GS 105-106
5001 349, 621, 741
Pressman, Edward R.
5001 684, 794
Pressman, Michael
TIAI 69-71; dir., *Those Lips, Those Eyes*,
69-71
5001 95, 764
Presson Allen, Jay, see Allen, Jay Presson
Presson, Jason
H 479
5001 405
Preston, J. A.
5001 90
Preston, Robert
KKBB 184
R 73, 298
WTLGD 362
TIAI 333, 334
5001 19, 57, 101, 134, 343, 455, 504, 665,
690, 761, 814
Pretty Baby
WTLGD 427
TIAI 176, 177, 392
Pretty in Pink
H 133-135
5001 (2nd ed)
Pretty Maids All in a Row
DIM 225
Pretty Poison
GS 168-170
SOTA 225
5001
Pretty Woman
ML 327
Preu, Dana
H 230-231
5001 693
Prévert, Jacques
KKBB 140, 247, 332
5001 75-76, 133, 383, 441, 590, 817, 819
Prévert, Marcel
ILIATM 298
Prévert, Pierre
5001 10, 236, 819
Previn, André
DIM 27
5001 365, 369
Previn, Dory
5001 365
Prevost, Marie
5001 316, 403
Price, Dennis
KKBB 292, 294

5001 357, 395, 450, 794, 814, 861
Price, George
KKBB 277
Price, Leontyne
GS 99
Price, Lonny
H 348
5001 190
Price, Nancy
KKBB 350
ML 326
5001 349, 710
Price, Richard
WTLGD 445
SOTA 201
H 223, 225, 227
ML 101, 102
5001 84, 146, 521
Price, Stanley
5001 291
Price, Vincent
ML 298, 300
5001 252, 369, 392, 413, 415, 600, 646,
747, 767, 808
Price, Zella Jackson
TIAI 472
5001 656
Prick Up Your Ears
H 295-298
5001 (2nd ed)
Pride and Prejudice
5001
Pride and the Passion, The
KKBB 205
WTLGD 25
Pride of the Yankees
RK 79
Priest, The
TIAI 59
Priestley, J. B.
KKBB 209, 293
5001 378, 408, 542
Priestly, Jack
GS 74
Prim, Suzy
KKBB 302
5001 442
Prima della Rivoluzione, see *Before the
Revolution*
Prima, Louis
5001 642
Prime of Miss Jean Brodie, The
GS 286-288
DIM 187
ML 154
5001
Primus, Barry
DIM 252, 350
TIAI 290
5001 2, 68, 521, 604, 641
Prince (Prince Rogers Nelson)
SOTA 213, 214, 215, 216, 217
5001 54, 603, 604
Prince and the Showgirl, The
KKBB 334:n
R 155
5001

Prince, Clayton
  H 443
  5001 313
Prince, Harold
  WTLGD 424
  TIAI 216
  5001 427
Prince of Foxes
  KKBB 196, 197
Prince of Homburg, The
  TIAI 70
Prince of the City
  SOTA 42
  5001
Prince, Peter
  H 283
  5001 294
Prince, William
  5001 179, 280, 324
Princess and Curdie, The (book)
  TIAI 349
Princess and the Pirate, The
  5001
Princess and the Goblin, The (book)
  TIAI 349
Princess Bride, The
  H 378-380
  ML 39
  5001 (2nd ed)
Principal, Victoria
  R 386
  5001 421
Pringle, Aileen
  RK 23 (ill.)
Prison
  KKBB 171
Prisoner, The
  DIM 201, 203
  5001
Prisoner of Second Avenue, The
  R 454-457
  WTLGD 150
  5001
Prisoner of Zenda, The
  ILIATM 322
  WTLGD 49, 50
  TIAI 138
  5001
Pritchett, Paula
  5001 130
Pritchett, V. S.
  KKBB 210
Private Affairs of Bel Ami, The
  5001
Private Benjamin
  TIAI 92-95, 163, 226
  SOTA 166, 167, 344
  5001
Private Function, A
  SOTA 340-342
  H 411
  5001 (2nd ed)
Private Life of Don Juan, The
  5001
Private Life of Henry VIII, The
  DIM 95
  5001

Private Life of Sherlock Holmes, The
  DIM 186-187
  5001
Private Lives
  GS 164
  5001
Private Lives of Elizabeth and Essex, The
  5001
Private Worlds
  KKBB 249
Privilege
  GS 14, 157
Prize, The
  ILIATM 26
  KKBB 319
  5001 (2nd ed)
Prizzi's Honor
  SOTA 375-379
  ML 75, 265, 283
  5001 (2nd ed)
Procès de Jeanne d'Arc, see *Trial of Joan of Arc*
Prochnik, Leon
  5001 134
Prochnow, Jürgen
  SOTA 285
  ML 185
  5001 92, 205, 207
Prodigal, The
  ILIATM 45, 60
Producers, The
  GS 66-68, 78, 94
  DIM 348
  R 281, 370, 404
  WTLGD 375
  5001
Professionals, The
  KKBB 334:n
  GS 62
  DIM 229
  5001
Professor Unrath (book)
  KKBB 239-240
Proffitt, Nicholas
  H 303
  5001 279
Profumo, John
  ML 129-32
Prokofiev, Sergei
  KKBB 289
  TIAI 133
  5001 13, 341, 375
Promise at Dawn
  DIM 245-248
  5001
Promise Her Anything
  R 248
Promoter, The (also known as *The Card*)
  KKBB 335:n
  5001
Prophet, The (book)
  DIM 337
Proser, Chip
  SOTA 162
  H 336
  5001 353, 364
Prosky, Robert
  TIAI 189

  H 273
  5001 105, 518, 559, 756, 759
Prosperi, Franco
  R 66
  5001 237
Proud and the Beautiful, The, see *Les Orgueilleux*
Prouse, Derek
  ILIATM 86
Proust, Marcel
  DIM 265, 365
  WTLGD 40, 231
  SOTA 237, 254
  H 61, 138
  5001 734
Prouty, Jed
  5001 105
Prouty, Olive Higgins
  5001 536, 713
Proval, David
  R 170
  5001 473
"Prove Me Wrong" (music)
  H 65
Providence
  WTLGD 255-259
  5001
Provine, Dorothy
  KKBB 49
Prud'homme, Cameron
  KKBB 337
  5001 614
Prud'hon, Pierre Paul
  WTLGD 381
Pryce, Jonathan
  H 107, 108
  ML 107
  5001 7, 98, 819
Pryor, Nicholas
  WTLGD 44
  5001 632, 688
Pryor, Richard
  R 40, 222, 280
  WTLGD 188, 189, 246-247, 406-407, 473, 475, 531-532
  TIAI 206, 217, 323-326, 437, 438, 440
  SOTA 7, 8, 11-12, 123, 215, 217
  H 144-148, 292, 421; dir., *Jo Jo Dancer, Your Life Is Calling*, 144-148
  5001 73, 81, 85, 115, 118, 381, 406, 628, 682, 691, 731, 838, 844
Pryor, Roger
  5001 62
Psych-Out
  TIAI 64
Psychedelic Furs (group)
  H 135
Psycho
  GS 88, 168
  DIM 316
  R 248, 367
  WTLGD 209, 373, 436
  TIAI 37, 40
"Psycho Killer" (music)
  SOTA 266
Pu Yi
  H 394-398

Public Broadcasting System, see PBS
Public Enemy. The
    KKBB 51-52, 338
    GS 243
    SOTA 101, 103
    5001
Public Eye. The
    R 221
    5001 (2nd ed)
Puccini, Giacomo
    SOTA 278, 379
    H 129
    ML 103
    5001 600
Pucholt, Vladimir
    5001 441
Pudovkin, V. I.
    ILIATM 281
    KKBB 253, 312; dir., *Mother*, 312
    GS dir., *Mother*, 45
    R 209
    WTLGD 324
    5001 499
Puente, Tito
    5001 610
Pugh, Willard
    H 83
    5001 146, 449
Puglia, Frank
    5001 122, 280, 536, 751
Pugni in Tasca, I, see *Fists in the Pocket*
Puig, Manuel
    H 24-25, 26, 27, 28-29, 269, 289
    5001 399
Pulitzer, Joseph
    RK 21, 63, 64, 67
Pull My Daisy
    GS 16
    SOTA 261
Pullman, Bill
    ML 69-70
    5001 3, 647
Pulman, Jack
    5001 393
Pulp
    TIAI 125
Pulver, Lilo
    5001 550
Pulver, Liselotte
    KKBB 251
    5001 151
Pumping Iron
    5001
Pumpkin Eater. The
    KKBB 108, 143
    DIM 292
    R 16
    H 411
    5001 (2nd ed)
Punch (periodical)
    WTLGD 483
Punch, Angela
    TIAI 56
Punchline
    ML 16-20
Punsley, Bernard
    5001 177

Purcell, Gertrude
    5001 185, 254, 356, 645
Purcell, Henry
    DIM 377
Purcell, Noel
    KKBB 298
    5001 424, 443
Puri, Amrish
    SOTA 176
    5001 362
Puritain, Le, see *The Puritan*
Puritan, The (*Le Puritain*)
    KKBB 335:n
    5001
Purple Noon (*Plein Soleil*)
    GS 242
    WTLGD 313
    H 446
    5001
Purple Rain
    SOTA 213-217
    5001 (2nd ed)
Purple Rain (album)
    SOTA 213, 215
Purple Rose of Cairo, The
    SOTA 335-340
    H 228
    5001 (2nd ed)
Pursall, David
    5001 20
Pursuit of D. B. Cooper, The
    SOTA 72, 73
Purtell, Bob
    H 433
    5001 333
Purviance, Edna
    KKBB 317
    5001 392, 494
Purvis, Jack
    ML 108
    5001 7, 772
Pushkin, Aleksandr
    SOTA 250-251
"Puss in Boots" (stage)
    TIAI 86
Pusser, Buford
    R 283-287
    WTLGD 422
"Put the Blame on Mame" (music)
    ML 190
Putnam, Nina Wilcox
    5001 501
Putney Swope
    DIM 154
    H 186
"Puttin' on the Ritz" (music)
    WTLGD 100, 375
    ML 113
Puttnam, David
    TIAI 246
    SOTA 277-279
    5001 131, 395, 429, 709
Puzo, Mario
    DIM 420-421
    R 398
    TIAI 223
    ML 309

    5001 209, 289, 290, 731
Puzzle of a Downfall Child
    DIM 250-253
    5001
Pygmalion
    R 422
    5001
Pyle, Denver
    WTLGD 283
    5001 91, 416
Pylon (book)
    KKBB 357
Pynchon, Thomas
    SOTA 219
    H 61
Pyne, Daniel
    ML 276
    5001 561
Pyriev, Ivan
    5001 354

Q

Q & A
    5001 (2nd ed)
Q Planes (also known as *Clouds Over Europe*)
    5001
Quadflieg, Will
    5001 430
Quai des brumes, see *Port of Shadows*
Quai des Orfèvres (also known as *Jenny Lamour*)
    5001
Quaid, Dennis
    TIAI 156, 157, 196
    SOTA 65, 231, 232, 233
    H 261, 336, 337, 358, 394
    5001 17, 69, 127, 203, 363, 592, 630, 733
Quaid, Randy
    R 273
    WTLGD 226, 229, 497-498
    H 98, 99
    ML 29, 91-95, 274
    5001 34, 95, 255, 408, 479, 556, 566, 831
Qualen, John
    KKBB 245, 276, 281
    5001 27, 34, 122, 156, 301, 317, 335, 433, 474, 535, 555, 600, 662, 782-783, 837
Quality Street
    KKBB 241, 336:n
    5001
Quan, Ke Huy
    SOTA 176, 181
    5001 298, 362
Quan, Stella
    5001 533
Quartermaine, Leon
    5001 36
Quartetto Basileus, Il, see *Basileus Quartet*
Quatre Nuits d'un rêveur, see *Four Nights of a Dreamer*
Quayle, Anna
    GS 227
    WTLGD 190

5001 667
Quayle, Anthony
    KKBB 369
    DIM 97
    5001 29, 315, 415, 502, 844, 850
Que He Hecho Yo Para Merecer Esto, see *What Have I Done to Deserve This!*
Que la bête meure, see *This Man Must Die*
"Qué Pasa, U.S.A.?" (TV)
    SOTA 103
Que Viva Mexico, see *Time in the Sun*
Queen (group)
    TIAI 125
    5001 250
Queen, The
    GS 100
    DIM 197
    5001
Queen Christina
    R 346
Queen Kelly
    ILIATM 109
Queen of the Stardust Ballroom (TV)
    WTLGD 165
Queimada!, see *Burn!*
Quenaud, Daniel
    R 452
    5001 102
Queneau, Raymond
    KKBB 312, 370
    GS 9
    DIM 308
    5001 494, 864
Quentin, Patrick
    5001 78
Quest for Fire
    TIAI 307-309
    ML 209
    5001
Questel, Mae
    ML 103-104
    5001 521
Quick, Diana
    WTLGD 382
    5001 206
Quiet American, The
    KKBB 336:n
    5001
"Quiet Life" (music)
    H 159
Quiet Man, The
    5001
Quiet One, The
    ILIATM 285
Quigley, Godfrey
    WTLGD 105
    5001 53
Quillan, Eddie
    KKBB 276
    5001 103, 107, 248, 301, 448, 505, 860
Quiller Memorandum, The
    KKBB 10-11
Quilley, Denis
    R 390
    5001 503
Quilligan, Veronica
    WTLGD 84

5001 424
Quine, Richard
    KKBB 252, 325; dir., *Operation Mad Ball*, 324-325
    5001 42, 156, 256, 341, 510, 551, 691
Quinlan, Kathleen
    SOTA 21, 281
    5001 361, 421, 797
Quinn, Aidan
    H 349, 351
    ML 115-17, 280-82
    5001 40, 165, 184, 704
Quinn, Aileen
    TIAI 344, 345
    5001 29
Quinn, Anthony
    KKBB 160, 328, 351, 367
    GS 46, 182
    DIM 34-35, 59, 150, 246, 247, 329, 423
    R 96, 272
    WTLGD 31, 196
    5001 83, 98, 317, 327, 415, 443, 452, 464, 560, 664, 717, 818, 865
Quinn, Gordon
    DIM 207
Quinn, J. C.
    5001 51
Quinn, Pat
    WTLGD 411
    5001 807, 863
Quinn, Roseann
    WTLGD 317
Quintero, José
    ILIATM 140
    H 410-411
    5001 637
Quintet
    WTLGD 548-551
    5001 (2nd ed)
Quo Vadis?
    ILIATM 25, 322
    KKBB 232

R

R.K.O.
    RK 3-4, 6-7, 33-34, 35, 36, 41, 42, 43, 44, 46, 47, 53, 59, 74, 75, 81, 82
    WTLGD 7
R.P.M.
    DIM 150
Rabal, Francisco
    5001 518
Rabe, David
    H 97
    ML 167, 174-75
    5001 124
Rabelais, François
    DIM 124
    WTLGD 457
Rabier, Jean
    DIM 403
    5001 56, 67, 95, 129, 140, 241
Racette, Francine

WTLGD 232-233
    H 437
    5001 38, 443
Rachel, Rachel
    GS 128, 196
    R 74, 222
    TIAI 78
Rachmaninov, Sergei
    5001 102
Racine, Jean
    5001 24, 578, 580
Racing Form (periodical)
    WTLGD 87
Racing With the Moon
    SOTA 151-153, 315
    ML 190
    5001 (2nd ed)
Rackin, Martin
    KKBB 41
    5001 220
Raddatz, Carl
    KKBB 340
    5001 643
Radford, Basil
    KKBB 255, 293, 330
    5001 178, 406, 568, 771, 858
Radha
    5001 632
Radiguet, Raymond
    KKBB 124, 249, 257
    5001 186
Radio City Music Hall
    RK 6, 45
    DIM 42, 80, 91, 92, 324, 383, 390, 391
    TIAI 297
Radio Days
    H 274-278
    5001 (2nd ed)
Radner, Gilda
    WTLGD 422
    5001 408
Radnitz, Robert B.
    R 316
    5001 164
Rado, James
    DIM 31
    5001 423
Radosh, Ronald
    SOTA 41, 44
Rafelson, Bob
    DIM dir., *Five Easy Pieces*, 152, 153, 231, 251, 252
    R 413; dir., *Five Easy Pieces*, 46, 162, 221, 224, 303, 309, 413; *The King of Marvin Gardens*, 272
    TIAI 21, 175, 178-182; dir., *The King of Marvin Gardens*, 175; *The Postman Always Rings Twice*, 178-182, 190, 191
    H 270-272; dir., *Black Widow*, 270-272, 303, 462
    5001 78, 108, 323, 396, 592
Rafelson, Toby Carr
    R 413
    TIAI 76
    5001 92
Rafferty and the Gold Dust Twins
    R 426-428

WTLGD 423
5001
Rafferty, Chips
  5001 558, 729
Rafferty, Frances
  5001 286
Raffin, Deborah
  5001 260-261, 548
Raffles (character)
  GS 111
Raffoul, François
  DIM 247
Raft, George
  ILIATM 292-293
  KKBB 348
  WTLGD 30
  SOTA 103, 298
  5001 78, 90, 123, 208, 226, 254, 355, 464,
    647, 657, 691, 697, 699, 754, 856
Rage of Paris, The
  5001
Raggedy Man
  TIAI 350, 354, 372
  SOTA 91, 204
  H 149, 234
  5001 (2nd ed)
Ragghianti, Marie
  H 54-56
Raging Bull
  TIAI 106-112, 190, 191, 457, 460
  SOTA 103
  ML 265, 266, 267, 269
  5001
Ragland, Rags
  5001 25, 117, 286, 563
Ragni, Gerome
  DIM 31
  5001 423
Ragno, Joseph
  5001 414
Ragtime
  WTLGD 121, 164, 248
  TIAI 263-266
  SOTA 87
  5001
Ragtime (book)
  SOTA 25
RAI (TV network)
  TIAI 316
Raiders of the Lost Ark
  TIAI 207-212, 348, 351, 386-387, 389, 481
  SOTA 4, 116, 163, 176, 177, 179, 182, 217
  ML 147-48
  5001
Railsback, Steve
  TIAI 63, 66, 68
  5001 724
Raimondi, Ruggero
  SOTA 254, 256
  5001 76
Raimu
  KKBB 170, 233, 244, 262
  DIM 329
  WTLGD 154, 513
  H 330
  5001 47, 120, 127, 225, 236, 465, 719, 827
Rain

ILIATM 139
KKBB 343
RK 70
TIAI 96
5001
Rain, Douglas
  5001 800
Rain Man
  ML 78-82, 282, 320, 324
  5001 (2nd ed)
Rain People, The
  DIM 59
  WTLGD 82
  H 303
  5001
Rainbow, The
  ML 137-40
  5001 (2nd ed)
Raine, Norman Reilly
  5001 8, 243
Rainer Dart, Iris, see Dart, Iris Rainer
Rainer, Luise
  DIM 73
  ML 142
  5001 69, 293, 304
Raines, Cristina
  R 448
  WTLGD 382-383
  5001 206, 517
Raines, Ella
  5001 108, 313, 578, 665, 733
Rainger, Ralph
  5001 508
Rainmaker, The
  KKBB 336-337:n
  WTLGD 37
  TIAI 173
  5001
Rains Came, The
  KKBB 285
Rains, Claude
  KKBB 185, 228, 245, 320
  R 419
  WTLGD 527
  TIAI 194
  5001 8, 27, 31, 114, 122, 162, 182, 263,
    329, 369, 384, 397, 415, 489, 536, 579,
    660, 755
Raise the Titanic
  TIAI 73, 114
Raisin in the Sun, A
  GS 102
  WTLGD 178
Raising Arizona
  H 290-292, 420, 481
  ML 82, 150
  5001 (2nd ed)
Rake's Progress, The (music)
  TIAI 413
Raksin, David
  KKBB 363
  5001 46, 259, 278, 414, 800
Rall, Tommy
  TIAI 275
  5001 369, 398, 574, 667
Ralli, Giovanna
  KKBB 270

5001 281
Rally Round the Flag, Boys!
  GS 169
Ralph, Jessie
  KKBB 243
  5001 9, 116, 118, 205, 293, 484
Ralston, Esther
  RK 13
Rambaldi, Carlo
  TIAI 350
  5001 207, 225
Rambeau, Marjorie
  5001 458, 464, 777, 782
Rambo: First Blood Part II
  SOTA 374-375
  H 10, 96, 193, 344, 353
  5001 (2nd ed)
Rambova, Natacha
  WTLGD 335-336
  5001 650
Rameau, Hans
  5001 824
Rameau, Paul H.
  5001 446
Ramer, Henry
  5001 34
Ramis, Harold
  TIAI 225
  SOTA 192
  H 186-189; dir., Club Paradise, 186-189,
    421
  ML 164, 165
  5001 43, 45, 143, 284, 723
Rampage
  R 284
Rampling, Charlotte
  R 277-278, 343-344
  TIAI 89, 441
  H 287
  5001 27, 169, 282, 527, 685, 709, 813, 863
Ramsay, Peggy
  H 295, 298
Ramsey, Anne
  H 382
  5001 298, 826
Ramsey, Remak
  5001 270
Ran
  H 89-92, 473
  5001 (2nd ed)
Rancho Deluxe
  WTLGD 90-93, 95
  5001
Rancho Notorious
  5001
Rand, Ayn
  H 20
  5001 262
Rand, Corey
  5001 718
Rand, Sally
  SOTA 66
  5001 90
Randall, Tony
  GS 102
  R 328
  TIAI 11

5001 20, 441
Randell, Ron
  5001 399
Randion
  5001 266
Randolph, Jane
  5001 125
Randolph, John
  GS 170
  DIM 229
  SOTA 378, 379
  5001 396, 427, 595, 600, 663, 752
Random Harvest
  SOTA 110, 332
  5001
Rankin, Gil
  5001 479
Ransohoff, Martin
  KKBB 343-344
  GS 222
Ransom, Tim
  ML 45
  5001 204
Ransome, Prunella
  DIM 67
  5001 457
Rapf, Harry
  5001 105, 107, 353
Raphael, Frederic
  KKBB 159
  H 45
  5001 173, 237, 534, 798
Raphaelson, Samson
  RK 10
  5001 26, 107, 306, 326, 677, 792
Raphel, Jerome
  5001 153
Rapp, Larry
  5001 548
Rappaport, David
  5001 772
Rappeneau, Paul
  5001 813
Rapper, Irving
  ILIATM 313; dir., *Rhapsody in Blue*, 47
  5001 155, 182, 536
Rasch, Albertina
  5001 555, 641, 736
Rasche, David
  H 392-393
  5001 448
Rascoe, Judith
  5001 219
Rashomon
  ILIATM 120, 122, 244
  KKBB 246, 337:n
  RK 4
  TIAI 141
  SOTA 161, 204
  H 91
  5001
Rasp, Fritz
  5001 477
Rasputin
  DIM 366-368
Rasputin and the Empress
  5001

Rasumny, Mikhail
  5001 28, 256, 672, 761
Ratcliff, Sandy
  5001 825
Rathbone, Basil
  KKBB 184, 228
  GS 109, 207
  R 134
  WTLGD 49, 99
  TIAI 427
  5001 8, 28, 54, 116, 117, 174, 278, 341,
    355, 409, 438, 466, 638, 693, 741, 785,
    828
Ratoff, Gregory
  KKBB 230; dir., *Black Magic*, 196
  5001 16, 303, 357, 366, 547, 642, 692, 830
Rattigan, Terence
  KKBB 240, 265, 334
  DIM 38-39
  SOTA 15
  5001 100, 104, 107, 243, 297, 596
Rauch, Earl Mac
  SOTA 217, 218-219, 220
  5001 7, 521
Raucher, Herman
  GS 40
Ravalec, Blanche
  5001 496
Ravel, Maurice
  KKBB 246
  TIAI 141, 196
  5001 90
Raven, Simon
  5001 545
Raven, The, see *Le Corbeau*
Ravenscroft, Christopher
  ML 214
  5001 329
Ravetch, Irving (see also Frank, Harriet Jr.)
  ILIATM 90-91
  DIM 76, 390
  R 294, 296, 297
  5001 153, 160, 344, 432, 622
Raw Deal
  H 169-171, 353
  5001 (2nd ed)
"Rawhide" (TV)
  TIAI 26
Rawlings, Margaret
  5001 636
Rawlings, Marjorie Kinnan
  SOTA 55-59
  5001 163, 855
Rawlins, David
  WTLGD 368
Rawlins, John
  5001 34
Ray, Aldo
  KKBB 330
  DIM 173
  5001 467, 475, 485, 513, 569, 593, 827
Ray, Andrew
  KKBB 369
  5001 844
Ray, Charles
  GS 126
Ray, Johnnie

5001 752
Ray, Michel
  5001 193
Ray, Nicholas
  ILIATM 307; dir., *55 Days at Peking*, 8, 10;
    Rebel Without a Cause, 33
  KKBB 49; dir., *Rebel Without a Cause*, 21,
    223; *They Live By Night*, 48-49
  WTLGD 314-315; dir., *Rebel Without a
    Cause*, 84, 314, 447; *King of Kings*, 398
  5001 22, 358, 401, 618, 619, 754, 757
Ray, Satyajit
  ILIATM 245-255; dir., Apu Trilogy, 148,
    245, 248, 250-251, 255; *Devi*, 245, 251,
    253-255; *Pather Panchali*, 248-250;
    Aparajito, 248, 250, 290; *The World of
    Apu*, 248, 250; *The Music Room*, 251;
    Two Daughters, 251
  KKBB 219
  R 6, 140-143; dir., *Days and Nights in the
    Forest*, 140-143; *The World of Apu*, 141
  WTLGD 68-72; dir., *Distant Thunder*,
    68-72; *Devi*, 69; *Two Daughters*, 69;
    Charulata, 69; *Days and Nights in the
    Forest*, 69; Apu trilogy, 70
  TIAI 151, 434, 435
  SOTA 301, 380-382; dir., *Pather Panchali*,
    98, 380; *The Home and the World
    (Ghare-Baire)*, 380-382; *The World of
    Apu*, 380
  H 432; dir., *Days and Nights in the Forest*,
    432; *The Home and the World*, 432
  5001 32, 176, 186, 192, 337, 390, 452, 505,
    569, 798, 850
Ray, Ted
  5001 778
Raye, Martha
  ILIATM 196
  KKBB 184
  WTLGD 428
  H 187
  5001 36, 68, 97, 494
Rayfiel, David
  H 245
  5001 498, 644, 765
Raymond, Cyril
  5001 102
Raymond, Gary
  5001 433
Raymond, Gene
  5001 65, 253, 620, 865
Rayner, D. A.
  5001 Commander, 220
Razor's Edge, The (1946)
  GS 194
  5001
Razor's Edge, The (1984)
  H 271
Razumov
  5001
Razzia sur la chnouf
  KKBB 337-338:n
  DIM 316
  5001
Re-Animator
  H 67-69

208

5001 (2nd ed)
Read, Barbara
  5001 768
Reader's Digest (periodical)
  RK 63
  DIM 253
  WTLGD 54, 204
Reading, Bertice
  SOTA 46
  5001 495
"Ready to Begin Again" (music)
  TIAI 96
Reagan, Ronald
  DIM 296
  H 4, 442
  ML 244
  5001 173, 394, 397, 653, 762
Real Life
  SOTA 344
Real Paper (periodical)
  TIAI 190
Real Thing, The (stage)
  H 189
Realist Fantasy, The (book)
  H 61
Réalités (periodical)
  WTLGD 201
Rear Window
  ILIATM 297
  R 195
  SOTA 188, 264
Rebecca
  WTLGD 373
  SOTA 111
  5001
Rebel Without a Cause
  ILIATM 33
  KKBB 21, 223
  DIM 152
  R 194
  WTLGD 84, 314, 447
  SOTA 140, 347
  5001
Reckless Moment, The
  ILIATM 100
Reckoning, The
  DIM 89
  WTLGD 188
"Recordar" (music)
  TIAI 410
Red and the Black, The (Le Rouge et le noir)
  ILIATM 67
  5001
Red Badge of Courage, The
  KKBB 131
  ML 249
  5001
Red Balloon, The (Le Ballon rouge)
  KKBB 180
  5001
Red Dawn (stage)
  H 348
Red Desert (Il Deserto Rosso)
  KKBB 23-25, 93, 189
  DIM 116, 252
  WTLGD 413
  5001

Red Dust (1932)
  H 228
  5001
Red, Eric
  5001 519
Red Inn, The (L'Auberge rouge)
  5001
Red Mill, The
  RK 69
  TIAI 70
Red River
  ILIATM 318
  KKBB 338:n
  DIM 297
  5001
Red Shoes, The
  GS 105-106
  WTLGD 344, 347
  TIAI 338
  ML 22
  5001
"Red-Headed League, The" (story)
  WTLGD 192
Red-Headed Woman
  5001 (2nd ed)
Redbone, Leon
  5001 227
Redbook (periodical)
  TIAI 236
Redd, Freddie
  5001 153
Redd, Mary-Robin
  5001 309
Redding, Otis
  H 134, 349
Reddy, Helen
  R 364
  5001 12
Redeker, Quinn K.
  WTLGD 518
Redfield, William
  DIM 269
  5001 153, 237, 520, 549, 582, 724
Redford, Robert
  KKBB 151, 283
  DIM 6, 7, 45, 47, 77, 78, 88, 173, 174, 231,
    347, 401-403
  R 87-88, 100, 175-178, 201, 244-245, 302,
    317, 319, 322, 466-468
  WTLGD 3, 42, 199, 209, 210, 236
  TIAI 16, 20, 24-25, 42, 78-82; dir., *Ordinary
    People*, 78-82, 207, 383
  SOTA 169-170, 171, 240; dir., *Ordinary
    People*, 40, 97, 314
  H 77, 78, 79, 173, 174; dir., *Ordinary
    People*, 76
  5001 52, 107, 110, 132, 304, 341, 365, 379,
    416, 425, 517, 553, 557, 715, 746, 765,
    825
Redglare, Rockets
  5001 185, 200
Redgrave, Corin
  5001 457, 541
Redgrave, Lynn
  KKBB 22
  5001 68, 282
Redgrave, Michael

ILIATM 164
  KKBB 254-255, 292, 293, 336, 350
  WTLGD 432, 511
  TIAI 237
  SOTA 22
  5001 107, 178, 235, 358, 365, 379, 398,
    406, 500, 523, 541, 608, 710, 769, 859
Redgrave, Vanessa
  KKBB 35
  GS 147, 234-235
  DIM 195, 302
  R 391
  WTLGD 190, 192, 194, 305-309, 551-553
  TIAI 411
  SOTA 167, 209
  H 43, 45, 46, 47, 295, 298
  ML 10
  5001 10, 85, 94, 116, 131, 385, 468, 497,
    503, 541, 595, 660, 667, 791, 829
Redman, Joyce
  5001 555, 778
Redmond Hicks, Tommy, see Hicks, Tommy
    Redmond
Redmond, Liam
  5001 193
Redon, Jean
  5001 230
Reds
  TIAI 278-283, 314, 334
  SOTA 24
  5001
Redwing, Rodric
  5001 392
Redwood, Vicky
  5001 452
Reed, Alan
  KKBB 367
  5001 818
Reed, Barry
  TIAI 440
  5001 813
Reed, Carol
  ILIATM 297, 303; dir., *The Stars Look
    Down*, 47, 297; *Odd Man Out*, 47, 207,
    297; *An Outcast of the Islands*, 47, 297;
    The Fallen Idol, 297; *The Third Man*,
    297; *The Man Between*, 303
  KKBB 10-11, 290-291, 321, 327, 349-350,
    358, 364; dir., *The Third Man*, 10-11,
    198, 258, 321, 358-359; *The Man
    Between*, 10-11; *A Kid for Two
    Farthings*, 263, 290-291; *Odd Man Out*,
    321, 350; *The Stars Look Down*, 321,
    349-351; *The Fallen Idol*, 321; *An
    Outcast of the Islands*, 321, 327-328;
    Our Man in Havana, 327; *Trapeze*, 348;
    Night Train, 364
  GS 181; dir., *The Fallen Idol*, 202; *A Kid
    for Two Farthings*, 202; *The Man
    Between*, 202; *Night Train*, 202; *Odd
    Man Out*, 202; *Oliver!*, 200-205; *Our
    Man in Havana*, 202; *An Outcast of the
    Islands*, 202; *The Stars Look Down*,
    202; *The Third Man*, 202
  WTLGD 414, 556; dir., *Our Man in
    Havana*, 465; *The Third Man*, 555
  TIAI 153, 328; dir., *The Third Man*, 156

5001 11, 234, 392, 398, 456, 539, 543, 556, 558, 602, 710, 760, 787
Reed, Donna
  KKBB 184
  5001 269, 305, 344, 374, 581, 669
Reed, Jerry
  SOTA 16, 18
  5001 732, 851
Reed, Jimmy
  H 458
Reed, Oliver
  GS 202
  DIM 139, 141, 142
  R 218
  WTLGD 50
  ML 109
  5001 7, 543, 645, 767, 790, 847
Reed, Pamela
  TIAI 75, 172, 260
  SOTA 65
  H 111
  5001 65, 231, 474, 630
Reed, Phillip
  5001 400, 542
Reed, Robert
  5001 706
Reed, Tom
  5001 702
Reed, Tracy
  WTLGD 189
  5001 118
"Reelin' and Rockin'" (music)
  WTLGD 423
Rees, Roger
  5001 706
Reese, Barbara
  5001 342
Reese, Florence
  WTLGD 252
Reese, John
  5001 131
Reeve, Christopher
  WTLGD 524, 527, 528
  TIAI 223-224, 326, 327
  SOTA 8, 10, 11, 39, 210
  H 71, 293, 294, 447, 448, 449
  5001 94, 181, 721, 722, 730, 731, 738
Reeve, Geoffrey
  SOTA 371
  5001 677
Reeves, George
  5001 616
Reeves, Keanu
  H 315
  5001 350, 632
Reeves, Steve
  KKBB 133
  5001 38
Reeves, Theodore
  5001 517
Reflections in a Golden Eye
  GS 30, 31, 33-34
  DIM 17, 422
  5001
"Reflections on Extasy" (article)
  KKBB 260
Regain, see Harvest

Regalbuto, Joe
  H 170
  5001 617
Regan, Phil
  5001 288, 359, 736, 767
Reggiani, Aldo
  5001 729
Reggiani, Serge
  KKBB 245
  WTLGD 153
  SOTA 52
  5001 123, 417, 441, 664, 815
Regine
  WTLGD 190
  5001 667
Règle du jeu, La, see The Rules of the Game
Reich, Wilhelm
  KKBB 40
Reid, Beryl
  GS 206
  5001 706
Reid, Carl Benton
  5001 359, 534
Reid, Fiona
  5001 738
Reid, Kate
  DIM 276
  TIAI 173, 175
  5001 26, 38, 223, 582
Reid, P. R.
  5001 145
Reifenstahl, Leni
  5001 834
Reilly, Jane
  5001 568
Reilly, John C.
  5001 124
Reiman, Walter
  5001 113
Reiner, Carl
  DIM 60-62, 185-186; dir., Enter Laughing, 10, 61; The Comic, 60-62; Where's Poppa?, 185-186, 314, 351, 402
  R 128-129, 131; dir., Where's Poppa?, 383
  TIAI 394; dir., The Jerk, 195
  SOTA 1-3, 220-224; dir., The Man with Two Brains, 1-3, 222; Dead Men Don't Wear Plaid, 2; The Jerk, 2, 3; All of Me, 220-224, 265
  ML 327; dir., Dead Men Don't Wear Plaid, 183
  5001 17, 149, 178, 310, 462, 541, 647, 747, 832
Reiner, Rob
  H 197-199, 378-380; dir., Stand by Me, 197-199; The Princess Bride, 378-380
  5001 592, 596, 705, 832
Reinhardt, Elizabeth
  5001 143, 413
Reinhardt, Gottfried
  5001 304, 619
Reinhardt, Max
  ILIATM 287; dir., A Midsummer Night's Dream, 287
  KKBB 71, 367; co-dir., A Midsummer Night's Dream, 348
  WTLGD 177

Reinhold, Judge
  TIAI 408
  SOTA 189, 288
  5001 66, 238, 307, 647
Reiniger, Scott
  5001 174
Reinking, Ann
  WTLGD 501-513
  TIAI 345
  SOTA 304, 305
  5001 29, 478, 501
Reis, Irving
  5001 17, 44, 233
Reisch, Walter
  KKBB 267, 318
  5001 279, 304, 470, 490, 522, 531, 774
Reiser, Paul
  TIAI 322
  5001 15, 66, 190
Reisman, Philip Jr.
  5001 19
Reisz, Karel
  ILIATM 63; dir., Saturday Night and Sunday Morning, 63, 68, 74-77, 165, 260
  KKBB 23, 285; dir., Morgan!, 20-23, 25, 31; Saturday Night and Sunday Morning, 311
  DIM dir., Morgan!, 152
  R 349-351
  WTLGD 417; dir., Morgan!, 258; Isadora, 307; The Gambler, 417; Who'll Stop the Rain, 432, 448
  TIAI 212, 237-241; dir., Saturday Night and Sunday Morning, 84; Isadora, 212; The French Lieutenant's Woman, 237-241; Who'll Stop the Rain, 439
  SOTA 72; dir., Who'll Stop the Rain, 362
  H 48-51; dir., Morgan!, 46, 49, 195; Sweet Dreams, 48-51, 234, 342; Saturday Night and Sunday Morning, 49; Isadora, 49; The Gambler, 49; Who'll Stop the Rain, 49; The French Lieutenant's Woman, 49, 162
  ML dir., Everybody Wins, 306-308
  5001 226, 267, 276, 497, 525, 654, 735
Reitman, Ivan
  TIAI 224-226; dir., Stripes, 224-226; Meatballs, 225
  SOTA 192-194; dir., Ghostbusters, 192-194; Stripes, 192, 193; Meatballs, 192
  H 172-175; dir., Legal Eagles, 172-175, 176, 299; Ghostbusters, 174
  ML dir., Ghostbusters, 164; Ghostbusters II, 164-65; Twins, 81
  5001 284, 416, 723
Reivers, The
  DIM 75-76
  5001
Rekert, Winston
  TIAI 426
  5001 324
Relativity
  R 323
Relph, George
  5001 243
Remar, James

TIAI 439
SOTA 295
5001 156, 202, 205, 261, 823
Remarque, Erich Maria
KKBB 230, 294
WTLGD 302
5001 18, 89, 410, 689, 765
Rembrandt
5001
Remember the Day
5001
Remembrance of Things Past (book)
ILIATM 201
R 148
WTLGD 40
SOTA 237
Remick, Lee
WTLGD 140
TIAI 132
5001 150, 185, 232, 433
Remington, Frederic
RK 64
Remsen, Bert
R 270
WTLGD 30, 443
SOTA 247
5001 121, 361, 445, 517, 585, 757
Rémy, Albert
5001 676
Renaldo & Clara
WTLGD 397-401
5001
Renaldo, Duncan
5001 700
Renant, Simone
KKBB 297
5001 420, 607
Renard, Jacques
5001 499
Renard, Jules
5001 588
Renard, Maurice
5001 445
Renaud, Madeleine
5001 585
Rennie, James
5001 536
Rennie, Michael
KKBB 184
5001 114, 184, 247, 341
Reno, Kelly
TIAI 349
5001 78
Renoir, Claude
ILIATM 104
KKBB 312, 315, 343
DIM 25, 135
WTLGD 457-458
5001 6, 82, 175, 214, 241, 293, 300, 441, 450, 495, 511, 632, 703
Renoir, Jean
ILIATM 22, 68, 101-104, 108-111, 188, 193-194, 222, 247-248, 255, 289, 300, 302, 318; dir., *La Grande Illusion*, 22, 108-111, 226, 283; *The Golden Coach*, 101-104; *The River*, 104, 248; *A Day in the Country*, 111; *The Rules of the*

Game, 111, 193-194; *Madame Bovary*, 289
KKBB 16, 76, 140-142, 150, 197, 254, 302, 341-343, 346; dir., *The Rules of the Game*, 33, 141, 254, 341-343; *The Golden Coach*, 55; *Boudu Saved from Drowning*, 140-142, 343; *A Day in the Country*, 140, 254, 342; *La Grande Illusion*, 140, 206, 254, 279, 342, 349; *The Crime of Mr. Lange*, 141; *La Chienne*, 142; *The Lower Depths*, 302; *The River*, 346
GS 50, 61, 97, 143; dir., *The Golden Coach*, 239
RK 53, 76
DIM 149, 238, 425; dir., *Grand Illusion*, 430
R 6, 19, 33, 142, 269-270, 350; dir., *La Chienne*, 33; *La Bête Humaine*, 33; *La Grande Illusion*, 238; *A Day in the Country*, 269; *The Rules of the Game*, 310, 440
WTLGD 59, 115, 180, 181, 182, 302, 322, 336, 350; dir., *A Day in the Country*, 59; *Boudu Saved from Drowning*, 180, 455; *Rules of the Game*, 181; *The Lower Depths*, 181
TIAI 71, 72, 76, 145, 151, 368, 449; dir., *A Day in the Country*, 368; *Grand Illusion*, 449
SOTA 85
H 74, 103, 430; dir., *The Lower Depths*, 74; *Boudu Saved from Drowning*, 103; *The Rules of the Game*, 430
5001 66, 95, 175, 189, 199, 214, 293, 300, 442, 446, 581, 632, 647, 659, 698, 846
Renoir, Pierre
KKBB 247
5001 133, 446
Renoir, Pierre Auguste
WTLGD 340
Renzelli, Gastone
5001 63
Repo Man
SOTA 211-213, 262, 348
ML 198
5001 (2nd ed)
Report to the Commissioner
R 432-435
5001
Republic Pictures
DIM 107
WTLGD 291, 379
Repulsion
R 80
5001
Requiem (music)
SOTA 252
"Requiem" (story)
H 124
Requiem for a Heavyweight
DIM 352
Resnais, Alain
ILIATM 20-21, 23, 31, 186-189, 194; dir., *Last Year at Marienbad*, 11, 17, 20-21, 24, 179, 181-183, 186-190, 192-196, 220, 265; *Muriel*, 20, 23; *Hiroshima Mon Amour*, 24, 31-35, 42

KKBB 163-166, 222, 343, 370; dir., *Last Year at Marienbad*, 31, 35, 94, 109, 119, 164, 189, 342, 363; *La Guerre est Finie*, 162-166; *Muriel*, 164
GS 120
DIM dir., *La Guerre Est Finie*, 64; *Last Year at Marienbad*, 244
R 236, 417-420; dir., *La Guerre Est Finie*, 212, 215; *Stavisky*, 416-420; *Last Year at Marienbad*, 419
WTLGD 255-259; dir., *Last Year at Marienbad*, 201, 257, 258; *Providence*, 255-259; *Hiroshima, Mon Amour*, 292
5001 310, 334, 412, 601, 712, 864
Resnick, Patricia
WTLGD 444
TIAI 162
5001 530, 609
Resnik, Muriel
5001 32
Resurrection (1931)
5001
Resurrection (1980)
TIAI 117-119, 153
5001
Retour de Don Camillo, Le, see *The Little World of Don Camillo*
Rettig, Tommy
5001 144, 248, 564
Retton, Mary Lou
ML 40
Return of a Man Called Horse, The
WTLGD 197-198
5001
Return of the Native, The (book)
ILIATM 169
Return of the Pink Panther, The
WTLGD 245, 246
Return of the Jedi
TIAI 481-485
SOTA 9
H 450
5001 (2nd ed)
Return of the Secaucus 7
SOTA 70, 71
Return of the Soldier, The
SOTA 330-333, 371
5001 (2nd ed)
Return to Oz
ML 219
Reubens, Paul, see Herman, Pee-Wee
Reve, Gerard
SOTA 195
5001 265
Revel, Harry
5001 828
Revere, Anne
KKBB 316
DIM 391
5001 233, 234, 259, 392, 517, 542, 623, 758
Reversal of Fortune
ML 287-89
Revill, Clive
R 389
5001 110, 244, 599, 866
Reville, Alma
KKBB 293, 359

5001 406, 502, 565, 761
Revolt of Mamie Stover, The
    5001
Revolution
    H 94-96
    5001 (2nd ed)
Revon, Bernard
    5001 716
Revueltos, Rosaura
    ILIATM 339, 344
    5001 650
Rey, Alejandro
    SOTA 157, 158
    5001 499
Rey, Antonia
    5001 842
Rey, Fernando
    DIM 316
    R 42
    WTLGD 137, 364-366, 549-550
    TIAI 411
    5001 6, 192, 235, 267, 609, 667, 751, 819
Reynolds, Burt
    R 294, 352-355, 464-466
    WTLGD 106-107, 124-127, 200, 246, 248,
        323, 358-362, 375, 430
    TIAI 11, 374, 445, 446; dir., *The End*, 214
    SOTA 153, 238, 288, 368-369; dir., *Stick*,
        368-369
    H 447, 448, 449
    ML 191-92
    5001 37, 64, 100, 346, 433, 442, 523, 665,
        714, 738, 851
Reynolds, Debbie
    KKBB 178, 185
    DIM 141
    TIAI 357
    ML 274
    5001 126, 287, 343, 386, 683, 766
Reynolds, Freddy
    TIAI 56, 58
    5001 129
Reynolds, Gene
    5001 157, 360, 438, 653
Reynolds, Jonathan
    SOTA 305
    H 448
    5001 478, 738
Reynolds, Marjorie
    5001 482
Reynolds, Naida
    TIAI 77
Reynolds, William
    5001 697
Rhames, Ving
    ML 11
    5001 124, 571
Rhapsody in Blue
    ILIATM 47
Rhinoceros
    KKBB 20
    WTLGD 520
    ML 93
Rhoades, Barbara
    5001 296
"Rhoda" (TV)
    R 429

Rhoden, Harold
    TIAI 72
Rhodes, Christopher
    5001 145
Rhodes, Cynthia
    SOTA 36
    H 347, 348
    5001 190, 712
Rhodes, Earl
    H 101
    5001 860
Rhodes, Erik
    R 56
    5001 281
Rhone, Trevor D.
    R 126
Rhys-Davies, John
    TIAI 209
    5001 361-362, 613
Rhys, Jean
    TIAI 294
Rhys, Paul
    ML 289-94
Ribeiro, Milton
    5001 117
Ribovska, Malka
    5001 670
Rice Edwards, Sebastian
    H 367, 370
    5001 340
Rice, Elmer
    KKBB 251
    DIM 312
    5001 156
Rice, Florence
    5001 37, 106, 736
Rice, Joan
    5001 167, 717
Rice, Ron
    ILIATM 317
Rice-Davies, Mandy
    ML 130-33
    5001 3
Rich and Famous
    TIAI 247-248
    SOTA 89
    5001
Rich, Buddy
    5001 675
Rich, Claude
    5001 712
Rich, David Lowell
    5001 447
Rich, Irene
    5001 26, 259
Rich, Ron
    5001 260
Richard, Cliff
    KKBB 263
    5001 229
Richard, Edmond
    5001 789
Richard II (stage)
    KKBB 201
Richard III
    ILIATM 281
    KKBB 50, 174

    WTLGD 377, 378
    5001
Richard, Jean
    5001 214
Richard, Jean-Louis
    5001 100
Richard Pryor Live in Concert
    TIAI 96, 323, 325, 326
    H 145
    5001 (2nd ed)
Richard Pryor Live on the Sunset Strip
    TIAI 323-326
    H 145
    5001 (2nd ed)
"Richard Pryor Show, The" (TV)
    H 146
Richard the Lionhearted
    GS 175
Richards, Addison
    5001 11
Richards, Ann
    5001 696
Richards, Beah
    WTLGD 60
    ML 197
    5001 205, 360, 453
Richards, Dick
    R 426-428; dir., *Rafferty and the Gold Dust
        Twins*, 426-428; *The Culpepper Cattle
        Co.*, 428
    WTLGD 304; dir., *Rafferty and the Gold
        Dust Twins*, 423
    TIAI 428, 429
    5001 503, 611
Richards, Evan
    H 104
    5001 199
Richards, Jeff
    5001 667
Richards, Sylvia
    5001 591, 646
Richardson, Henry Hobson
    SOTA 292
Richardson, Ian
    5001 98
Richardson, J. P., see Big Bopper, The
Richardson, Joely
    H 47
    5001 829
Richardson, Lee
    SOTA 377
    5001 600, 606
Richardson, Miranda
    H 29, 30, 414
    5001 170, 217
Richardson, Natasha
    ML 9, 10, 208
    5001 239, 571
Richardson, Ralph
    KKBB 57, 106, 201, 240, 298, 327
    DIM 17, 37, 118
    R 112, 314
    WTLGD 77
    TIAI 221-222, 397
    SOTA 149-150, 371
    H 306
    5001 59, 100, 138, 193, 195, 201, 234, 235,

308, 327, 404, 432, 459, 541, 556, 558, 606, 628, 759, 772
Richardson, Robert
H 183
ML 250
5001 93, 587, 651
Richardson, Samuel
H 61
Richardson, Tony
ILIATM 62-63, 70-71, 123, 196-197, 199-200, 257-258; dir., *The Loneliness of the Long Distance Runner*, 16, 256-261; *Look Back in Anger*, 63, 67-71, 74, 197; *The Entertainer*, 63, 68, 70-71, 74, 197; *A Taste of Honey*, 196-201
KKBB 167, 244, 298, 299-301; dir., *The Entertainer*, 142, 174; *A Taste of Honey*, 158; *Mademoiselle*, 167; *The Loneliness of the Long Distance Runner*, 244; *Look Back in Anger*, 263, 276, 311; *The Loved One*, 299-301
GS dir., *The Charge of the Light Brigade*, 145-148; *The Entertainer*, 136; *The Loneliness of the Long Distance Runner*, 120; *Look Back in Anger*, 150; *Tom Jones*, 120
DIM 4, 15, 89, 90, 99, 213, 308; dir., *The Loved One*, 4; *The Charge of the Light Brigade*, 15, 17, 99, 213, 215; *Laughter in the Dark*, 41, 89; *Hamlet*, 89-91; *A Taste of Honey*, 187; *Tom Jones*, 308
WTLGD 60, 148, 151; dir., *Tom Jones*, 103; *The Entertainer*, 148-151
TIAI 300-302; dir., *The Border*, 300-302
5001 92, 130, 221, 315, 434, 440, 778
Richert, William
5001 414
Richest Girl in the World, The
KKBB 363
5001 (2nd ed)
Richie, Donald
ILIATM 121, 161
Richler, Mordecai
R 316-317
WTLGD 270
ML 98
5001 33, 271, 640
Richman, Arthur
5001 41
Richman, Mark
5001 719
Richmond, Bill
5001 537
Richmond, Tony
5001 709
Richter, Conrad
5001 661
Richter, Hans
R 261
Richter, W. D. (Rick)
R 133
WTLGD 520, 522
TIAI 156
SOTA 217-220
5001 7, 17, 108, 368, 687
Richthoven, A. E. V.

DIM 19
Rickles, Don
R 352, 376
5001 852
Rickman, Thomas
5001 851
Rickshaw Man
ILIATM 290
Ridby, Edward
5001 398
Ride in the Whirlwind
5001 (2nd ed)
Ride the High Country
KKBB 14, 40-41
GS 62
DIM 393
WTLGD 117, 260
SOTA 330
5001
Ride the Pink Horse
5001
Ridgely, John
5001 11, 591
Ridgely, Robert
TIAI 77
Ridges, Stanley
KKBB 369
5001 11, 208, 243, 405, 445, 591, 774, 841
Ridiculous Theatrical Company
WTLGD 504
H 67, 398
Riefenstahl, Leni
ILIATM 287; dir., *Triumph of the Will*, 287; *Olympiad*, 287
KKBB 323; dir., *Olympiad*, 323; *Triumph of the Will*, 323
DIM 28, 207; dir., *Triumph of the Will*, 207
R 211
WTLGD 324
TIAI 338
5001 81, 544, 696
Riegert, Peter
TIAI 464
5001 429
Riesman, David
ILIATM 321
KKBB 350
Riesner, Charles
5001 71, 292, 337, 712
Riesner, Dean
DIM 386
R 206
WTLGD 254
SOTA 307
5001 131, 191, 221, 710
Rif, Vladimir
SOTA 155
Riffraff
DIM 227
5001
Rififi (Du Rififi chez les hommes)
KKBB 316, 338-339:n
GS 183
DIM 248
TIAI 189
5001
"Rifleman, The" (TV)

WTLGD 114
Rigby, Edward
KKBB 350
5001 710
Rigby, Terence
R 221
5001 338
Rigg, Diana
DIM 85, 378
WTLGD 220, 302, 424
5001 341, 427, 545
Riggs, Lynn
5001 278
Riggs, Rita
TIAI 117
"Right Back Where We Started From" (music)
WTLGD 273
Right Stuff, The
SOTA 61-68, 233
H 98, 337, 432
ML 72, 116
5001 (2nd ed)
Rigoletto (music)
DIM 273
WTLGD 326
Rikards, Ron
R 224
Riley, Jack
R 187
TIAI 216
SOTA 111
5001 331, 432, 445, 775
Riley, Larry
SOTA 273
5001 691
Riley, Terry
TIAI 253
Rilke, Rainer Maria
DIM 251
H 470, 473
ML 14, 15
Rilla, Walter
KKBB 251
5001 151, 694
Rilla, Wolf
5001 815
Rimbaud, Arthur
SOTA 375
Rimsky-Korsakov, Nikolai
SOTA 250
Rin Tin Tin
RK 15
Ring, Cyril
5001 144
Ringwald, Molly
TIAI 389, 391
SOTA 173, 174, 347, 348
H 133, 134, 135, 331, 370, 371
5001 99, 580, 594, 684, 746
Ringwood, Bob
ML 161
5001 54
Rintels, David W.
ML 207
Rio Bravo
ILIATM 318
KKBB 59

5001
Rio Grande
5001
Rio Lobo
5001
Rio Rita
WTLGD 13
5001
Rioli, Riccardo
ILIATM 104
KKBB 235
5001 52, 293
Riot
5001
Riot on Sunset Strip
GS 64
Rioux, Geneviève
H 238
5001 182
Ripley, Arthur
5001 433
Ripley, Clements
5001 380
Ripley, Heather
GS 227
Ripley's Game (book)
WTLGD 312
Riscoe, Arthur
5001 398
Risdon, Elisabeth
5001 161, 332, 464, 634
Riskin, Robert
RK 30
5001 23, 373, 436, 473, 483, 487, 586, 758,
836
Risky Business
SOTA 39-41, 122
5001 (2nd ed)
Rispal, Jacques
WTLGD 97
5001 403
Ritchard, Cyril
R 97
5001 79
Ritchie, Michael
DIM 46, 47; dir., *Downhill Racer*, 45-47,
173
WTLGD 43-45, 248, 334, 358-363; dir.,
Smile, 43-45, 150, 321, 361; *Downhill
Racer*, 44; *The Candidate*, 44, 45, 362;
The Bad News Bears, 248, 361;
Semi-Tough, 358-363
TIAI 76, 77, 95-97; dir., *Smile*, 77-78;
Divine Madness, 95-97
SOTA 15-18, 159; dir., *The Survivors*,
15-18, 159; *Smile*, 16; *Downhill Racer*,
16; *The Bad News Bears*, 16;
Semi-Tough, 16
H 59, 217, 422; dir., *Smile*, 59; *The
Survivors*, 421, 422; *Semi-Tough*, 448
5001 193, 251, 665, 688, 732
Riton
WTLGD 460-462
5001 283
Ritt, Martin
ILIATM 90-91; dir., *Hud*, 24, 79-94; *The
Long Hot Summer*, 91; *Hemingway's*

Adventures of a Young Man, 91, 222-
225; *Edge of the City*, 91
KKBB 70, 261; dir., *Hombre*, 39; *Edge of
the City*, 261
GS dir., *The Brotherhood*, 243-247
DIM 103, 104, 158, 159; dir., *The Long, Hot
Summer*, 76; *The Molly Maquires*, 103-
104, 159; *The Great White Hope*,
158-161; *Hud*, 173, 294-295
R 3-7, 84-87, 293-298; dir., *Sounder*, 307,
61, 263, 296; *Pete 'n' Tillie*, 84-87;
Conrack, 293-298, 312
WTLGD 170-172; dir., *The Front*, 170-172;
Hud, 170; *The Long, Hot Summer*, 170;
The Spy Who Came in from the Cold,
170; *The Molly Maquires*, 170; *Pete 'n'
Tillie*, 170; *Sounder*, 170; *Conrack*, 170
SOTA 55-59; dir., *Cross Creek*, 55-59;
Norma Rae, 56
5001 153, 164, 212, 270, 304, 344, 432,
491, 492, 577, 697
Rittau, Gunther
5001 477
Ritter, John
TIAI 11
Ritter, Thelma
KKBB 230
R 284
5001 16, 73, 168, 343, 419, 484, 490, 581,
774
Ritz Brothers
KKBB 31
5001 545, 717
Ritz, Harry
KKBB 31
DIM 352
R 130, 132
WTLGD 29, 522
H 483
5001 545
Riva, Emmanuèle
ILIATM 34
DIM 419
TIAI 442
5001 334, 753
Riva, J. Michael
SOTA 219
ML 41
5001 7, 147, 297, 660
River, The (1951)
ILIATM 104, 248
KKBB 346
5001
River, The (1984)
SOTA 319
River of No Return
ILIATM 308
River's Edge
H 315-318
ML 118
5001 (2nd ed)
Rivera, Chita
5001 734
Rivero, Jorge
5001 631
Rivers, Fernand
5001 191

Rivers, Larry
TIAI 237, 463
5001 442
Rivet, Gilberte
R 336
5001 403
Rivette, Jacques
KKBB 360
5001 24
Rivkin, Allen
5001 238, 582
Roach, Hal
KKBB 273
WTLGD 17, 509
5001 137, 292, 540, 781, 782, 825
Roach, Janet
SOTA 379
5001 600
Road series (Crosby and Hope)
WTLGD 66
SOTA 5, 177
H 309, 310
Road to Mandalay, The
RK 10
Road to Morocco, The
SOTA 180
5001
Road to Singapore
5001
Road to Utopia
5001
Road Warrior, The (*Mad Max 2*)
TIAI 384-389, 456
SOTA 22
5001 (2nd ed)
"Roamin' in the Gloamin'" (music)
TIAI 463
Roaring Twenties, The
5001
Roarke, Adam
R 45
5001 587, 724
Robards, Jason Sr.
5001 165, 238, 372
Robards, Jason Jr.
KKBB 86, 190, 298
GS 239
R 196, 198
WTLGD 305, 309, 485-487
TIAI 73-74, 231, 404
SOTA 361
H 459
ML 36
5001 32, 48, 103, 148, 295, 385, 432, 474,
528, 569
Robards, Sam
5001 124, 746
Robbe-Grillet, Alain
ILIATM 21, 186, 189-190
DIM 418
5001 412
Robbie, Seymour
DIM 173; dir., *C. C. and Company*, 173-174
5001 127
Robbins, Gale
5001 114, 766
Robbins, Harold

DIM 133-136, 151, 420
WTLGD 409
5001 6, 66, 121, 519
Robbins, Jerome
ILIATM 142, 144
DIM 332
H 160
5001 828
Robbins, Matthew
R 301
TIAI 220-223; dir., *Dragonslayer*, 220-223;
Corvette Summer, 221
5001 73, 155, 201, 725
Robbins, Michael
5001 582
Robbins, Oliver
TIAI 352
Robbins, Tim
H 480-481
ML 141-44
5001 109, 484, 485, 780
Robbins, Tod
5001 266
Robbins, Tom
H 393
5001 449
Robe, The
ILIATM 329
KKBB 147, 220
Rober, Richard
5001 243
Robert, Jean-Denis
5001 450
Robert, Yves
WTLGD 97, 152; dir., *Salut l'Ariste*, 152,
153
5001 651, 700
Roberta
R 55, 57
TIAI 39
Roberti, Lyda
RK 15
5001 393, 481
Roberts, Alice
5001 563
Roberts, Ben
5001 458, 834
Roberts, Christian
5001 777
Roberts, Doris
WTLGD 81
5001 427
Roberts, E. B.
5001 259
Roberts, Eric
TIAI 372
SOTA 91, 202, 203-204
5001 589, 611, 706
Roberts, Hermese E.
DIM 217
Roberts, Judith
5001 224
Roberts, Julia
ML 326-27
5001 250
Roberts, Kenneth
5001 534

Roberts, Marguerite
5001 201, 224, 340, 660-661, 865
Roberts, Meade
5001 723, 726
Roberts, Rachel
DIM 260
R 390, 391
H 411
5001 196, 503, 654, 762
Roberts, Roy
5001 220
Roberts, Tanya
WTLGD 416
SOTA 222, 368
5001 673, 815
Roberts, Tony
TIAI 366, 368
H 277
5001 316, 387, 479, 610, 707
Roberts, William
R 166
5001 407, 452
Robertson, Cliff
GS 150-151
R 432
WTLGD 42
SOTA 263
5001 40, 64, 132, 339, 458, 513, 706, 765
Robertson, Jenny
H 481
5001 109
Robertson, Pat
H 438
Robertson, Robbie
H 227
5001 121, 146, 411
Robertson, Willard
5001 11, 195, 542, 726, 837, 856
Robeson, Paul
KKBB 173-174, 262
SOTA 43
5001 172, 217, 652, 679, 741, 742
Robespierre, Maximilien Marie Isidore
WTLGD 294
Robey, George
KKBB 259
5001 197, 328
Robin and Marian (1976)
WTLGD 157-160
5001
Robin, Dany
5001 336, 781
Robin Hood (1922)
5001
Robin, Leo
5001 32, 184, 278, 498, 508
Robins, Oliver
5001 588
Robinson, Amy
R 170
H 41
5001 473
Robinson, Andy
R 206
5001 131, 191
Robinson, Bill
SOTA 294

5001 716
Robinson, Bruce
WTLGD 55
SOTA 275
ML 207
5001 239, 395
Robinson, Casey
KKBB 288, 345
WTLGD 13
5001 118, 155, 374, 397, 536, 543, 654, 785
Robinson, Clarence
5001 716
Robinson, Dar
SOTA 369
5001 714
Robinson, Dewey
5001 58, 82, 302, 313, 672, 726
Robinson, Earl
5001 381, 822
Robinson, Edward G.
ILIATM 62
KKBB 190, 364, 368
GS 243
DIM 424
R 135-136, 327-328
SOTA 103
H 165
5001 17, 51, 198, 251, 392, 393, 425, 464,
600, 659, 686, 694, 719, 741, 742, 747,
771, 800, 801, 836, 845
Robinson, Frank M.
5001 593
Robinson, Jay
R 440
5001 671
Robinson, Joe
KKBB 291
5001 393
Robinson, Julia Anne
5001 396
Robinson, Laura
H 448
5001 738
Robinson, Madeleine
5001 416, 789
Robinson, Marilynne
H 406-407, 408, 409
5001 342
Robinson, Phil Alden
SOTA 221
ML dir., *Field of Dreams*, 126-28
5001 18, 242
RoboCop
H 343-345
5001 (2nd ed)
Robson, Flora
KKBB 340, 345
5001 114, 244, 639, 653, 660, 851, 859
Robson, Greer
TIAI 343
5001 688
Robson, Mark
KKBB 203, 247, 248, 319; dir., *Champion*,
203; *Home of the Brave*, 203, 284; *The
Prize*, 319
GS dir., *Valley of the Dolls*, 61
RK 41

DIM dir., *Peyton Place*, 294; *Happy Birthday, Wanda June*, 369
R 106-107, 385; dir., *Happy Birthday, Wanda June*, 81, 106; *Limbo*, 106-110; *Earthquake*, 364, 384-387; *Inn of the Sixth Happiness*, 391
5001 125, 139, 209, 317, 372, 384, 600
Robson, May
  KKBB 241
  WTLGD 29
  5001 8, 28, 104, 107, 263, 370, 620, 707, 755, 837
Robson, Wayne
  SOTA 31
  5001 308
Roc, Patricia
  5001 459
Rocco, Alex
  R 428
  TIAI 65
  5001 267, 269, 289, 405, 611, 715, 724
Rocco and His Brothers
  R 145
  5001 (2nd ed)
Rocha, Glauber
  SOTA 355
Rochard, Henri
  5001 352
Roche, Eugene
  WTLGD 260-261
  5001 156, 412
Roché, Henri-Pierre
  ILIATM 217
  R 19, 20
  5001 385, 798
Rochefort, Jean
  WTLGD 457-458, 461, 484
  5001 122, 241, 363, 651, 836
Rochester, see Anderson, Eddie
"Rock Around the Clock" (music)
  WTLGD 554
  H 481-482
Rock, Monti III
  5001 655
Rockabye
  5001
Rockefeller, John D.
  RK 6
Rockefeller, Nelson
  RK 3, 6, 7
Rockettes (dance group)
  KKBB 340
Rocking Horse Winner, The
  KKBB 291, 339:n
  5001
Rockoff, Al
  SOTA 275, 276, 277
Rockwell, Norman
  WTLGD 512
  TIAI 270
Rocky
  WTLGD 213-216, 369, 412, 488, 490, 491, 492, 493, 495
  TIAI 346
  SOTA 6, 35, 36, 169, 325
  H 308
  5001

Rocky II
  TIAI 13, 346
  SOTA 6, 35, 169
Rocky III
  TIAI 346-347
  SOTA 6, 35, 169
  5001 (2nd ed)
Rocky IV
  H 95
Roco, Bembol
  TIAI 454
  5001 854
Rodd, Marcia
  DIM 254
  WTLGD 322-323
  H 274
  5001 139, 427, 786
Rodeo
  SOTA 98
Rodgers and Hart, see Rodgers, Richard and Hart, Lorenz
Rodgers, Anton
  5001 191
Rodgers, Ilona
  SOTA 242
  5001 810
Rodgers, Richard
  ILIATM 143
  KKBB 234
  H 115
  5001 42, 97, 226, 314, 350, 463, 562, 580, 697, 711, 848
Rodin, Auguste
  DIM 422
  TIAI 267
Rodman, Howard
  R 206
  5001 131
Rodney, John
  5001 392
Rodway, Norman
  KKBB 201
  5001 235
Roebuck, Daniel
  H 315
  5001 632
Roeg, Nicolas
  R 233-237; dir., *Don't Look Now*, 233-237; co-dir., *Performance*, 234
  WTLGD 200-201, 434, 533, 535; dir., *The Man Who Fell to Earth*, 200-201; *Don't Look Now*, 200, 434, 533; *Walkabout*, 535
  TIAI 452
  H 286, 287
  ML 301
  5001 198, 237, 272, 459, 535, 842
Roehm, Ernst
  DIM 86
Roeves, Maurice
  KKBB 169
  R 17
  5001 803, 860
Roger & Me
  ML 242-45
  5001 (2nd ed)
Roger Rabbit, see *The Framing of Roger Rabbit*

Rogers, Buddy
  5001 566
Rogers, Gamble
  TIAI 206
Rogers, Ginger
  ILIATM 24, 81, 145, 278
  KKBB 234, 252, 273, 341
  GS 134, 190
  RK 53
  DIM 28, 184, 272, 296, 346, 409
  R 56-58
  WTLGD 20, 31, 171, 370, 450
  TIAI 276
  SOTA 110-111, 178
  H 138, 141, 229
  ML 63
  5001 44, 78, 119, 253, 254, 262, 280, 291, 322, 356, 400, 404, 443, 453, 494, 548, 645, 703, 717, 741, 778, 818, 819, 855
Rogers, Howard Emmett
  5001 256, 421, 744
Rogers, Jean
  TIAI 124
Rogers, Lela
  5001 453
Rogers, Mimi
  H 293, 386
  5001 692
Rogers, Paul
  KKBB 327
  DIM 118
  R 220
  5001 2, 72, 338, 556
Rogers, Roy
  R 447
Rogers, Sandy
  5001 255
Rogers, Shorty
  5001 462
Rogers, Wayne
  WTLGD 546
  5001 547, 851
Rogers, Will
  KKBB 273
  5001 292, 384, 711, 712, 713, 728
Rogosin, Lionel
  KKBB 324; dir., *On the Bowery*, 324
  5001 148, 546
Rohmer, Eric
  DIM 265-267; dir., *Claire's Knee*, 264-267, 275, 280
  R 9-12, 83; dir., *Chloe in the Afternoon*, 9-12; *Claire's Knee*, 9-12
  WTLGD 59, 169, 184-187; dir., *Claire's Knee*, 59, 186, 304; *The Marquis of O...*, 184-187
  TIAI 400-401; dir., *Le Beau Mariage*, 400-401; *Claire's Knee*, 400
  SOTA 34, 37-39; dir., *Pauline at the Beach*, 37-39; *Le Beau Mariage*, 37
  5001 58, 136, 140, 467, 571
Rohmer, Sax
  5001 469
Röhrig, Walter
  5001 113
Roiphe, Anne Richardson
  R 82-83, 222-224

5001 809
Roizman, Owen
    5001 267, 625, 765
Roland, Gilbert
    KKBB 233, 242
    WTLGD 281
    TIAI 371, 373
    5001 46, 51, 109, 372, 384, 660, 672
Rolfe, Guy
    5001 20, 375
Rolle, Esther
    ML 235
    5001 141, 205
Rolling Stone (periodical)
    WTLGD 467
    TIAI 247
Rolling Stones (group)
    DIM 58, 208-210
    WTLGD 266
    TIAI 26, 202
    SOTA 69
    5001 589
Rollins, Howard E. Jr.
    TIAI 265
    SOTA 272, 273
    5001 612, 690, 691
Rollins, Sonny
    5001 14
Rollover
    H 243
Rolston, Mark
    H 381
    5001 826
Roma (Fellini), see *Fellini's Roma*
Roma, Città Aperta, see *Open City*
Romagnoli, Mario
    5001 240
Romains, Jules
    5001 194, 819
Roman Holiday
    KKBB 185, 252
    DIM 381
    WTLGD 157, 345
    5001
Roman, Lawrence
    R 275
Roman, Ruth
    KKBB 352
    5001 67, 720
Roman Scandals
    TIAI 215
    5001
Roman Spring of Mrs. Stone, The
    ILIATM 139-140
    KKBB 57
    5001
Romance, Viviane
    KKBB 328, 335
    5001 564, 603
Romancing the Stone
    SOTA 163-165
    H 12, 273
    5001 (2nd ed)
Romand, Béatrice
    DIM 265
    WTLGD 93
    TIAI 400

5001 58, 140, 751
Romanovs
    DIM 366-368
Romantic Comedy
    SOTA 129, 168
Romantic Englishwoman, The
    WTLGD 93-95
    5001
Romanus, Richard
    R 170
    WTLGD 123
    5001 473
Romanus, Robert
    TIAI 408
    5001 238
Romberg, Sigmund
    R 55
    TIAI 113
    5001 472, 641, 808
Rome, Harold
    5001 42
Romeo and Juliet (1936)
    ILIATM 305
    5001
Romeo and Juliet (1954)
    ILIATM 281
    KKBB 339-340:n
    5001
Romeo and Juliet (1968)
    GS 153-158, 279
    DIM 18, 182, 219
    R 17
    TIAI 28
    SOTA 226
    5001
Romeo and Juliet (stage)
    ILIATM 142
    KKBB 288, 369
    WTLGD 345
Romero, Cesar
    5001 58, 187, 294, 322, 552, 741, 758, 827
Romero, George A.
    TIAI 147, 197-201, 384, 386; dir., *Night of the Living Dead*, 147, 197, 200; *Knightriders*, 197-201; *Dawn of the Dead*, 198, 200
    SOTA 232, 324
    H 69
    5001 174, 401, 526
Ronald, James
    5001 733
Ronde, La
    ILIATM 97-98, 100-101
Rondi, Brunello
    5001 386
Ronet, Maurice
    DIM 54, 308
    5001 74, 129, 215, 241, 323, 603
Roof, The
    ILIATM 285
    DIM 361
Rooker, Michael
    5001 504
Rooks, Conrad
    5001 130
Room at the Top
    ILIATM 63, 67-68, 75, 78, 165

KKBB 245, 263, 311
    DIM 142
    TIAI 84
    SOTA 114
    H 411
    5001
Room for One More
    WTLGD 21, 23
Room Service
    SOTA 112
    5001
Room with a View, A
    H 125-130, 359, 361
    5001 (2nd ed)
Rooney, Frank
    5001 839
Rooney, Mickey
    KKBB 185, 316, 325
    DIM 60
    R 193, 474
    WTLGD 465
    5001 11, 42, 78, 99, 106, 118, 128, 149, 286, 344, 438, 463, 517, 551, 552, 722, 726, 727, 764, 848
Roosevelt, Eleanor
    KKBB 229
Roosevelt, Franklin Delano
    KKBB 81, 95, 359
    DIM 204
    WTLGD 15
Rooster Cogburn
    WTLGD 62-64, 197
    5001
Root, Lynn
    5001 113, 233, 685
Root, Wells
    5001 771
Roots (TV)
    WTLGD 267, 269
Roots of Heaven, The
    ILIATM 299
    KKBB 131, 198
Rope
    KKBB 48
    DIM 401
Ropes, Bradford
    5001 261, 288
Roque, Tex
    SOTA 79, 81
Roquevert, Noel
    KKBB 259, 264
Roquevert, Noël
    5001 122, 188, 235, 388, 720
Rosal, Maia
    H 241
Rosalie
    WTLGD 12
    5001
Rosario, see Antonio and Rosario
Rosay, Françoise
    KKBB 169, 244, 245
    5001 76, 120, 121, 573, 620, 643
Rose, The
    TIAI 42, 77, 95, 96, 229, 292
    H 272
    ML 73
    5001

Rose, Billy
R 390, 457-458, 462-463
Rose, George
DIM 269
5001 322, 520, 528
Rose, Helen
5001 46
Rose, Jack
WTLGD 21
Rose, Jamie
SOTA 353
5001 325, 771
Rose, Louisa
5001 684
Rose Marie
ILIATM 321
TIAI 70
5001
Rose of Washington Square
5001
Rose, Reginald
WTLGD 450
5001 692, 795
Rose, Ruth
5001 672
Rose Tattoo, The
KKBB 27
WTLGD 37
TIAI 173, 174
5001
Rose, William
KKBB 270, 293
5001 281, 330, 407, 647
Roseland
WTLGD 356-358
5001
Rosemary (Das Mädchen Rosemarie)
KKBB 340:n
5001
Rosemary's Baby
GS 150
R 189, 248, 443
WTLGD 165, 421, 435
H 211
5001 (2nd ed)
Rosemond, Clinton
5001 293
Rosenberg, Arthur
5001 167
Rosenberg File, The (book)
SOTA 41, 44
Rosenberg, Harold
SOTA 41
Rosenberg, Jeanne
5001 78
Rosenberg, Julius and Ethel
SOTA 41, 44
Rosenberg, Stuart
DIM 181-182; dir., *WUSA*, 181-182; *Cool Hand Luke*, 181; *The April Fools*, 182
R 260; dir., *The Laughing Policeman*, 232, 253, 260, 365; *Cool Hand Luke*, 261, 354
TIAI 20-25; dir., *The Amityville Horror*, 16, 21, 351, 424; *Brubaker*, 20-25; *The April Fools*, 21; *Move*, 21; *WUSA*, 21; *Pocket Money*, 21; *The Laughing*

Policeman, 21; *The Drowning Pool*, 21; *Voyage of the Damned*, 21; *Love and Bullets*, 21; *Cool Hand Luke*, 21, 78
SOTA 201-206; dir., *The Pope of Greenwich Village*, 201-206; *Brubaker*, 217
5001 34, 108, 413, 589, 819, 851
Rosenbloom, Maxie (Slapsy)
KKBB 320
5001 69, 208, 254, 535
Rosenblum, Ralph
KKBB 95-96
DIM 351
5001 686
Rosener, George
5001 195
Rosenfield, Maurice and Lois
5001 50
Rosenman, Leonard
KKBB 261
WTLGD 228
5001 96, 144, 210, 212, 619
Rosenthal, Harry
5001 302, 726
Rosenthal, Jack
SOTA 89
5001 855
Rosenthal, Laurence
5001 625
Rosenthal, Rick
TIAI 473-475; dir., *Bad Boys*, 473-475
5001 46
Rosette
SOTA 38
5001 571
Rosher, Charles
5001 679, 729, 855
Rosher, Charles Jr. (Chuck)
WTLGD 261, 441
SOTA 282
5001 361, 665
Rosi, Francesco
KKBB 118-120; dir., *The Moment of Truth*, 118-120; *Salvatore Giuliano*, 118; *Hands Across the City*, 118
GS dir., *The Moment of Truth*, 96
DIM 171; dir., *The Moment of Truth*, 171
R 125, 209, 211; dir., *The Moment of Truth*, 125; *The Mattei Affair*, 202, 207, 209; *Salvatore Giuliano*, 211; *More Than a Miracle*, 257
WTLGD 324
TIAI 60, 314-320; dir., *Christ Stopped at Eboli*, 60, 315, 316; *Three Brothers*, 314-320; *The Mattei Affair*, 315, 316, 317; *Illustrious Corpses*, 315, 316; *Salvatore Giuliano*, 316; *Lucky Luciano*, 316
SOTA 226, 253-257; dir., *Three Brothers*, 226; *Bizet's Carmen*, 226, 253-257
H 61
5001 63, 76, 492, 496, 497, 651, 749, 764
Rosier de Madame Husson, Le (He, later released as *The Virgin Man*)
5001
Rosing, Bodil
5001 407
Rosny, J. H. Sr.

TIAI 308
5001 608
Rosqui, Tom
5001 160, 290
Ross, Annie
SOTA 8
5001 731
Ross, Anthony
5001 92, 157, 399
Ross, Arthur
5001 161
Ross, Diana
R 36-40
WTLGD 60-61, 140, 469-473, 475-476
SOTA 218-219
H 146
5001 406, 452, 844
Ross, Frank
5001 186, 497
Ross, Gary
H 482
5001 67
Ross, Gaylen
5001 174
Ross, Harold
RK 12, 18, 72, 80
Ross, Herbert
DIM 38, 183, 185, 311; dir., *Goodbye, Mr. Chips*, 38-41; *The Owl and the Pussycat*, 183-185, 314, 351; *T. R. Baskin*, 311-313
R 180, 457-463; dir., *T. R. Baskin*, 117; *The Owl and the Pussycat*, 162; *The Last of Sheila*, 163; *Play It Again, Sam*, 241-243; *Funny Lady*, 457-463
WTLGD 76-79, 190-192, 343-347, 376-378, 487, 529-533; dir., *The Sunshine Boys*, 76-69, 532; *The Seven-Per-Cent Solution*, 190-192; *Funny Lady*, 242; *The Turning Point*, 343-347, 368, 506; *Play It Again, Sam*, 371; *The Goodbye Girl*, 376-378, 466, 532; *California Suite*, 529-533
TIAI 272-278; dir., *Goodbye, Mr. Chips* (1969), 65; *Funny Lady*, 190; *Pennies from Heaven*, 272-278; *The Sunshine Boys*, 276; *The Turning Point*, 276; *The Goodbye Girl*, 276; *The Seven-Per-Cent Solution*, 276, 335, 359
SOTA 139-141; dir., *Pennies from Heaven*, 2, 337; *The Turning Point*, 89; *Footloose*, 139-141, 169, 220
H 298-301; dir., *Pennies from Heaven*, 52; *The Turning Point*, 64; *The Sunshine Boys*, 138; *The Owl and the Pussycat*, 228; *California Suite*, 243; *The Secret of My Success*, 298-301; *The Goodbye Girl*, 350
5001 115, 119, 255, 272, 296, 297, 365, 559, 574-575, 664, 667, 730, 786, 794
Ross, Katharine
DIM 6, 77
R 443
5001 66, 110, 277, 299, 487, 714, 746, 819
Ross, Leonard
5001 19
Ross, Lillian Bos

5001 863
Ross, Shirley
5001 68, 463
Ross, Ted
WTLGD 472, 473
5001 36, 844
Ross, Tiny
5001 772
Rossellini, Isabella
WTLGD 194
H 66, 204, 205, 207, 362, 363
ML 96-99
5001 87, 159, 470, 784, 835
Rossellini, Roberto
ILIATM 287; dir., *Open City*, 290
KKBB 268-270, 324; dir., *Il Generale Della Rovere*, 268-270; *Open City*, 269, 324, 342
GS 219
DIM 361; dir., *Open City*, 65
WTLGD 103
TIAI 450; dir., *Paisan*, 450
H 66
5001 119, 281, 482, 551, 561, 562, 820
Rossen, Carol
5001 35
Rossen, Robert
KKBB 242, 308; dir., *Lilith*, 57; *The Brave Bulls*, 120, 242
DIM dir., *The Hustler*, 47; *All the King's Men*, 63
H 223, 226
5001 19, 72, 88, 98, 109, 155, 347, 422, 466, 634, 718, 821
Rossetti, Christina
H 53
Rossetti, Dante Gabriel
DIM 239
H 53
Rossi, Franco
KKBB 231; dir., *Amici per la Pelle*, 231
5001 23
Rossi, Leo
SOTA 80
5001 78, 323
Rossi, Lucca
H 129
5001 640
Rossif, Frédéric
5001 775
Rossington, Norman
5001 654
Rossini, Gioacchino
DIM 377
SOTA 153, 379
5001 600, 806
Rossiter, Leonard
5001 53, 582, 800, 819, 832
Rossner, Judith
WTLGD 317-320
5001 434
Rosson, Hal
5001 206
Rosson, Harold
5001 619, 683
Rossovich, Rick
H 313

5001 645, 780
Rostand, Edmond
H 312, 314
Rostand, Maurice
5001 107
Rosten, Norman
R 153
Rósza, Miklós
WTLGD 257
Rota, Nino
KKBB 368
GS 156
DIM 422
R 346, 401
SOTA 54
5001 2, 213, 290, 386, 418, 437, 603, 635, 639, 661, 818, 836
Roth, Bobby
SOTA 349-353; dir., *Heartbreakers*, 349-353; *The Boss' Son*, 351
5001 325
Roth, Eric
H 394
5001 733
Roth, Lillian
SOTA 216
5001 28, 338, 356, 447, 566
Roth, Philip
RK 17
DIM 260, 364
WTLGD 128
Roth, Richard
5001 386
Roth, Tim
H 121
ML 289-94
5001 849
Rotha, Paul
ILIATM 270-271
Rothko, Mark
H 173
Rothman, Michael
WTLGD 322
5001 139
Rotunno, Giuseppe
R 26
WTLGD 393
SOTA 54
ML 110
5001 6, 19, 67, 117, 219, 241, 418, 437, 458, 546, 635, 719
Rouch, Jean
KKBB 129
GS 4
5001 137
Roud, Richard
ILIATM 20
DIM 80
Roudenko, Vladimir
TIAI 142
5001 515
Roue, La
TIAI 147
Rouge et le noir, Le, see *The Red and the Black*
Rougeul, Jean
5001 213
Rouleau, Eric

5001 700
Rouleau, Raymond
5001 441
Roulien, Raul
5001 253
'Round Midnight
5001 (2nd ed)
Round the Town (stage)
RK 10
Roundtree, Richard
R 385
5001 209
Rounseville, Robert
5001 741
Rourke, Mickey
TIAI 256, 321
SOTA 202-203, 204
H 31, 32, 183, 286, 287, 383, 384
ML 193
5001 27, 51, 90, 190, 382, 589, 854
Rouse, Russel
5001 554
Rousseau, Jean Jacques
WTLGD 180
Roussel, Myriem
SOTA 228
Roussel, Nathalie
R 422
5001 816
Rousselot, Philippe
H 256
ML 58, 210
5001 171, 193, 216, 495, 752
Roustabout
H 334
Routledge, Patricia
5001 761
Rouvel, Catherine
5001 581
Rouverol, Jean
5001 417
Roux, Jacques
KKBB 298
5001 424
Rowan, Dan
GS 58
Rowe, Nicholas
H 100
5001 860
Rowland Doroff, Sarah, see Doroff, Sarah Rowland
Rowland, Roy
KKBB 203; dir., *The 5000 Fingers of Dr. T.*, 203
5001 248, 337
Rowlands, Gena
R 392-396, 411
TIAI 390, 392
ML 12-16
5001 31, 233, 331, 482, 746, 846
Rowsell, Arthur
ML 94
Roxanne
H 312-314, 408
5001 (2nd ed)
Roxie Hart
KKBB 219, 341:n

R 302
ML 315
5001
Royal Court Theatre
H 120
Royal Family of Broadway, The
TIAI 338
5001
Royal Flash
WTLGD 49-51
5001
Royal Family, The
RK 18
Royal Hunt of the Sun, The
DIM 24-25
WTLGD 227
SOTA 250
5001
Royal Scandal, A
5001
Royal Shakespeare Company
H 166
Royal Wedding
5001
Royle, Selena
5001 169, 321, 327, 523, 726
Rózsa, Miklós
KKBB 348
5001 198, 199, 376, 443, 599, 602, 701,
756, 772
Rozyki, Chris
TIAI 466
5001 429
Rub, Christian
5001 542, 741
Rubel, Marc
H 484
5001 69
Ruben, Aaron
5001 149
Ruben, J. Walter
5001 329, 629
Ruben, Joseph
SOTA 231-234; dir., *Dreamscape*, 231-234;
The Sister-in-Law, 232; *The Pom-Pom
Girls*, 232; *Joyride*, 232; *Our Winning
Season*, 232
H 260-263; dir., *The Stepfather*, 260-263;
Dreamscape, 261, 263; *The Pom-Pom
Girls*, 261
ML dir., *Dreamscape*, 83, 327; *Sleeping with
the Enemy*, 326-27; *The Stepfather*, 82,
83, 85, 327; *True Believer*, 83-86, 327
5001 203, 714, 792
Rubens, Alma
5001 679
Rubens, Bernice
ML 21
5001 447
Rubens, Peter Paul
DIM 407
Rubenstein, Zelda
TIAI 353
Rubes, Jan
5001 844
Rubie, Les
5001 487

Rubin, Benny
5001 288, 329
Rubin, Daniel
5001 192
Rubin, Theodore Isaac
5001 174
Rubinek, Saul
TIAI 262, 422
SOTA 147
H 162, 163
5001 10, 111, 735, 770
Rubinstein, Anton
DIM 240
Rubinstein, Arthur
5001 254
Rubinstein, John
5001 97, 172, 692, 863
Rubinstein, Nicholas
DIM 240
Rubinstein, Zelda
5001 588, 684
Rubirosa, Porfirio
DIM 136, 420
Ruby Gentry
5001
Ruby, Harry
RK 83
5001 28, 206, 341, 391, 393, 766
Ruby, Jack
KKBB 151
Rudd, Paul
5001 66
Ruddy, Albert S.
5001 426
Rudley, Herbert
5001 822
Rudolph, Alan
WTLGD 283-285
SOTA 288-290, 351; dir., *Choose Me*,
288-290; *Welcome to L. A.*, 288
H 7-11, 136-137, 392-393; dir., *Songwriter*,
7-11, 136; *Choose Me*, 9, 136, 137;
Trouble in Mind, 136-137; *Made in
Heaven*, 392-393
5001 136, 448, 695, 791, 827
Ruehl, Mercedes
H 300
5001 68, 664
Rufus
WTLGD 180
5001 224
Ruggles, Charles
KKBB 241
5001 32, 48, 104, 369, 446, 507, 532, 647,
792
Ruggles of Red Gap
5001
Ruggles, Wesley
WTLGD 17; dir., *I'm No Angel*, 6, 17; *True
Confession*, 141; *Cimarron* (1931), 145
5001 90, 137, 338, 351, 357, 369, 780, 793
Rugoff, Don
DIM 153-154, 321
Ruhmann, Heinz
5001 675
Rule, Janice
DIM 260

WTLGD 548
5001 132, 195, 486
Rules of the Game, The (La Règle du jeu)
ILIATM 111, 193-194
KKBB 33, 141, 254, 341-343:n
RK 4
R 310, 440
WTLGD 181
H 430
5001
Rumann, Sig
KKBB 318, 349
R 131, 241
5001 75, 175, 260, 287, 472, 524, 531, 535,
646, 689, 705, 774, 825, 850
Rumba
5001 (2nd ed)
Rumble Fish
TIAI 399
SOTA 104, 120, 296, 310
H 136, 220, 462
ML 198, 309
Run Run Shaw
GS 152
Runacre, Jenny
DIM 222
WTLGD 382
5001 206
Runaway Romany
RK 69
Running
TIAI 11
Running, Jumping and Standing Still Film, The
DIM 17
Runyon, Damon
SOTA 122-123
H 154
ML 28
5001 311, 426, 686
Ruocheng, Ying, see Ying, Ruocheng
Ruscha, Ed
5001 136
Rush, Barbara
5001 859
Rush, Deborah
SOTA 337
H 36-37
5001 68, 150, 604
Rush, Richard
DIM 150-151; dir., *Getting Straight*,
149-151, 236; *The Savage Seven*, 150
TIAI 62-69; dir., *The Stunt Man*, 62-69;
Psycho-Out, 64; *Hell's Angels on
Wheels*, 64; *The Savage Seven*, 64;
Getting Straight, 64; *Freebie and the
Bean*, 64
SOTA 11
5001 266, 724
Rushton, Jared
H 483
5001 68, 405
Rusk, Dean
DIM 43
Ruskin, Harry
5001 592
Ruskin, John
SOTA 373

H 53
Russell, Bertrand
    ILIATM 289
Russell, Cecilia
    WTLGD 218
Russell, Chuck
    SOTA 232
    5001 203
Russell, Craig
    TIAI 96
Russell, Dora
    5001 621
Russell, Gail
    H 243
    5001 26, 807
Russell, Harold
    5001 65
Russell, Jane
    SOTA 368
    5001 93, 558, 626
Russell, John
    5001 562
Russell, Ken
    DIM 138-142, 238-243, 340, 379-383; dir.,
        Women in Love, 138-142, 239; *The
        Music Lovers*, 238-243; *The Devils*, 315;
        The Boy Friend, 379-383
    R 47-49, 111-112; dir., *Savage Messiah*,
        46-52; *The Music Lovers*, 48-51; *The
        Devils*, 49; *Women in Love*, 51
    WTLGD 49, 83-84, 139, 200, 204, 333-336,
        554; dir., *Lisztomania*, 83-84; *Tommy*,
        83, 200; *Savage Messiah*, 83; *The
        Devils*, 83; *Valentino* (1977), 333-336;
        The Boy Friend, 333, 503
    TIAI 127-132; dir., *Altered States*, 127-132;
        Women in Love, 214
    SOTA 252
    H 286; dir., *Women in Love*, 129
    ML dir., *The Lair of the White Worm*, 139;
        The Rainbow, 137-40; *Women in Love*,
        137, 138
    5001 20, 72, 96, 424, 504, 613, 614, 655,
        811, 812, 847
Russell, Kurt
    TIAI 97, 99
    SOTA 107, 108, 110, 165, 168, 334, 335
    H 110, 111, 112
    ML 48-52
    5001 65, 472, 681, 738, 748, 759, 810
Russell, Leon
    WTLGD 244
    5001 339
Russell, Nipsey
    WTLGD 472-473
    5001 844
Russell, Ray
    5001 852
Russell, Robert
    5001 497
Russell, Rosalind
    KKBB 281
    GS 134
    RK 20, 48
    DIM 346, 406
    R 97, 299
    WTLGD 4

H 151, 352, 448, 449
5001 123, 134, 138, 225, 259, 311, 335,
    455, 500, 510, 525, 531, 532, 763, 829,
    847
Russell, Shirley
    SOTA 333
    5001 10, 96, 626, 847
Russell, Theresa
    H 270, 271, 272
    5001 78, 411, 718
Russell, Vivian
    ML 138
    5001 614
Russell, Willy
    SOTA 84
    5001 212
Russian Roulette
    WTLGD 123
Russianoff, Dr. Penelope
    WTLGD 411
*Russians Are Coming, The Russians Are Coming,
    The*
    DIM 330
    R 301, 427, 441
    5001 (2nd ed)
Russier, Gabrielle
    DIM 418, 419
Russo, Aaron
    H 153
Russo, Gianni
    5001 289, 290
Russo, James
    5001 66
Rutherford, Ann
    5001 7, 438, 551, 595, 663
Rutherford, Margaret
    KKBB 142, 202, 278, 294, 330
    WTLGD 465
    5001 81, 167, 235, 317, 357, 358, 568
Ruthless People
    H 179-180, 272, 484
    5001 (2nd ed)
Ruttenberg, Joseph
    5001 273, 486
Ruysdael, Basil
    5001 144, 583
Ryan, Elaine
    5001 42
Ryan, Fran
    TIAI 260
    5001 557
Ryan, Frank
    5001 117
Ryan, J. M.
    DIM 121
    5001 442
Ryan, Kathleen
    KKBB 321
    5001 539
Ryan, Madge
    WTLGD 484
    5001 836
Ryan, Meg
    H 336, 337
    5001 364, 780
Ryan, Mitchell
    DIM 162

5001 269, 452, 495
Ryan, Patrick
    5001 343
Ryan, Peggy
    R 193
    5001 254
Ryan, Robert
    ILIATM 235-236
    KKBB 233, 253, 296, 334
    R 197-198, 209
    5001 47, 72, 126, 140, 164, 228, 353, 475,
        601, 666, 685, 838, 846
Ryan, Sheila
    5001 278
Ryan's Daughter
    DIM 188-193, 218
    R 110, 113, 432
    5001
Rydell, Bobby
    5001 111
Rydell, Mark
    GS dir., *The Fox*, 30-35
    DIM 75, 390, 393; dir., *The Fox*, 59; *The
        Reivers*, 75-76; *The Cowboys*, 390-393,
        398
    R 187, 258; dir., *Cinderella Liberty*,
        259-260, 273; *The Cowboys*, 259
    WTLGD 377; dir., *Cinderella Liberty*, 377;
        Harry and Walter Go to New York, 490
    TIAI 269-272; dir., *The Rose*, 42, 77, 95, 96,
        229, 292; *On Golden Pond*, 269-272,
        418
    ML 20; dir., *The Rose*, 73
    5001 138, 160, 265, 432, 545, 603, 622, 641
Ryder, Winona
    H 457
    ML 118-20, 299
    5001 61, 326
Ryerson, Florence
    5001 116, 123
Ryskind, Morrie
    KKBB 317
    RK 18, 66
    5001 28, 144, 509, 524, 575, 640, 703

S

S.O.B.
    TIAI 331, 332, 333
    5001
S.O.S. Iceberg (*S.O.S. Eisberg*)
    5001
Saadia
    GS 171
Saarinen, Eero
    WTLGD 147
Sabatini, Rafael
    5001 118
Sabela, Simon
    R 359-360
    5001 291
Sabotage (also known as *The Woman Alone*)
    5001
Saboteur

ILIATM 294
5001
Sabouret, Marie
  KKBB 339
  5001 630
Sabrina
  5001
Sabu
  KKBB 184, 185
  WTLGD 334
  SOTA 180
  5001 34, 143, 386, 756, 835
Sacco and Vanzetti
  R 208, 215
Sacha, Claude
  5001 641
Sacher-Masoch, Leopold van, see van
     Sacher-Masoch, Leopold
Sackheim, William
  TIAI 132
  5001 150
Sackler, Howard
  DIM 158-160
  WTLGD 203
  5001 304
Sacks, Michael
  R 300
  5001 725
Sacks, Oliver
  H 376
  ML 318-20
Sade (singer)
  H 159
  5001 3
Sade, Marquis de
  WTLGD 497
Sadler's Wells Chorus
  5001 741
Safe Place. A
  R 46, 222
Safer, Morley
  DIM 45
Saga of Gösta Berling. The
  5001
Sagan, Leontine
  KKBB 303; dir., *Mädchen in Uniform*, 303
  5001 448
Sager, Carole Bayer
  5001 703
Sahara
  5001
Sahl, Mort
  DIM 10
  R 228
Saidy, Fred
  5001 349
"Sail with Me" (music)
  TIAI 123
Saint, Eva Marie
  KKBB 9, 319, 344
  GS 248, 249
  DIM 121, 122
  R 328
  WTLGD 3
  TIAI 294
  H 199, 200, 201
  5001 16, 116, 442, 533, 535, 546, 614, 647,

653, 750
St. Clair, Malcolm
  5001 116
St-Cyr, Lili
  5001 513
St. Denis, Ruth
  H 339
St. Dennis, Madelon
  5001 180
"St. Elsewhere" (TV)
  SOTA 272
Saint-Exupéry, Antoine de
  R 387-388
  WTLGD 302, 304
  5001 427
St. Francis of Assisi
  DIM 183
Saint-Gaudens, Augustus
  ML 256, 262
St. Gerard, Michael
  H 443
  5001 313
Saint Jack
  TIAI 42
St. Jacques, Raymond
  5001 487, 809
Saint James, Susan
  5001 437
"St. James Infirmary" (music)
  WTLGD 536
St. John, Howard
  5001 720
St. John, Jill
  5001 189, 554, 637
St. John, Marco
  WTLGD 207
  5001 521, 771
St. Johns, Adela Rogers
  KKBB 343
  RK 48, 69
  WTLGD 240
  5001 266, 830
St. Joseph, Ellis
  5001 251
St. Laurent, Cecil
  5001 430
St. Laurent, Michael
  5001 641
Saint Laurent, Yves
  WTLGD 258
St. Louis Blues
  5001 (2nd ed)
Saint-Simon, Lucile
  5001 91
St. Theresa of Lisieux, see Theresa of Lisieux,
    St.
St. Urbain's Horseman (book)
  R 317
Sainte-Beuve, Charles Augustin de
  WTLGD 59, 309
Sainte-Marie, Buffy
  DIM 175
  SOTA 110
Saire, David
  5001 436
Saire, Rebecca
  SOTA 372

5001 677
Sakall, S. Z.
  KKBB 245
  5001 48, 122, 186, 751, 853
Sakamoto, Ryuichi
  5001 408
Saks, Gene
  R 299; dir., *The Odd Couple*, 68; *Mame*,
    298-299, 313
  TIAI 463
  H 258-260; dir., *Barefoot in the Park*, 173;
    Brighton Beach Memoirs, 258-260
  5001 52, 103, 113, 442, 455, 597
Sakuma, Yoshiko
  SOTA 327
  5001 454
Salaire de la peur, Le, see *The Wages of Fear*
Salacrou, Armand
  5001 59
Salaman, Chloe
  TIAI 221
  5001 201
Salamanca, J. P.
  5001 422
Salammbô (music)
  GS 7
  TIAI 183
Sale, Charles (Chic)
  5001 857
Sale, Richard
  5001 554, 718, 771
Sale, Virginia
  R 134
Salem, Pamela
  5001 304
Sales, Grover
  ML 2
Salesman
  DIM 208
Salieri, Antonio
  SOTA 249-253
Salinger, Diane
  H 245
  5001 498, 573
Salinger, J. D.
  ILIATM 10
  RK 17
  WTLGD 217
  H 130
  ML 126
Salisbury, Harrison
  DIM 44
  R 104
Salkind, Alexander and Ilya
  SOTA 11
  5001 731
Salmi, Albert
  ML 192
  5001 100
Salome
  WTLGD 335
  5001
Salome, Lou Andreas, see Andreas-Salomé, Lou
Salou, Louis
  KKBB 247
  GS 115
  5001 133, 441

"Salsation" (music)
  WTLGD 368
Salt, Jennifer
  R 195
  5001 330, 479, 684
Salt of the Earth
  ILIATM 331-346
  5001 (2nd ed)
Salt, Waldo
  R 228, 230, 472, 475, 476
  WTLGD 404
  5001 150, 176, 277, 479, 666, 678
Salten, Felix
  5001 49
Salter, James
  DIM 46
  5001 768
Salto nel Vuoto, see *Leap Into the Void*
Saltzman, Harry
  5001 189, 545
Salut l'artiste
  WTLGD 152, 153
  5001
Salvador
  H 180-185, 251, 254
  ML 84
  5001 (2nd ed)
Salvatore Giuliano
  KKBB 118
  R 211
  TIAI 316
  5001
Salvatori, Renato
  KKBB 238
  DIM 65
  R 452
  5001 69, 102, 110, 635, 862
Same Time, Next Year
  WTLGD 505-507
  TIAI 47
  ML 201
  5001
Sammy and Rosie Get Laid
  H 387-391
  5001 (2nd ed)
Samoilova, Tatiana
  5001 160
Sampson, Robert
  H 68
  5001 618
Sampson, Will
  WTLGD 88
  5001 549
Samson and Delilah
  5001
Samuel, Lester
  5001 75
Samuels, Lesser
  5001 4
San Francisco Actors Workshop
  H 381
San Francisco *Chronicle*
  ILIATM 128
  H 441
San Francisco *Examiner*
  ILIATM 129
  RK 35, 63

San Francisco Film Festival
  DIM 113
San Juan, Olga
  WTLGD 44
  5001 58, 550
San Miniato, July 1944
  TIAI 448
San Pietro, see *The Battle of San Pietro*
San Quentin Drama Group
  H 381-382
San Simeon
  RK 6, 8, 21, 24, 35, 38, 58, 68, 72
Sanborn, David
  ML 40
Sanchez, Jaime
  5001 571, 838
Sanchez, Marcelino
  WTLGD 557
  5001 823
Sanchez, Rodolfo
  5001 400, 584
Sand, Bob
  H 263
  5001 783
Sand, Paul
  DIM 401-403
  5001 341
Sand Pebbles, The
  KKBB 8-9, 59
  R 150
Sanda, Dominique
  DIM 162, 163, 271, 274, 363-365, 413
  R 34
  WTLGD 326, 328, 330
  5001 152, 154, 246, 279, 530, 843
Sandburg, Carl
  DIM 74
  5001 275
Sander, Otto
  H 470
  5001 841
Sanders, Denis
  5001 513
Sanders, George
  KKBB 230
  DIM 105
  R 76, 77, 359
  5001 16, 75, 115, 233, 258, 259, 284, 329,
     376, 457, 459, 581, 598, 618, 652, 741,
     750, 784, 815, 820
Sanders, Lawrence
  5001 25
Sanders of the River
  5001
Sanders, Terry
  5001 513
Sanderson, Sybil
  RK 67
Sanderson, William
  TIAI 364
  5001 80, 611
Sandino, Augusto César
  SOTA 74
Sandler, Barry
  WTLGD 141-142
  5001 275
Sandlund, Debra

H 362, 363
5001 784
Sandpiper, The
  KKBB 28, 143, 221, 343-344:n
  5001
Sandrelli, Stefania
  DIM 271
  R 258
  WTLGD 326, 328, 330
  5001 14, 152, 530, 567
Sandrich, Mark
  5001 119, 254, 281, 846
Sands, Diana
  DIM 260
  R 274
  5001 196, 407
Sands, Johnny
  5001 44
Sands, Julian
  SOTA 277
  H 127
  5001 34, 395, 640
"Sanford and Son" (TV)
  R 136
  WTLGD 150
Sanford, Erskine
  5001 65, 138
Sanford, John
  5001 340
Sang d'un poète, Le, see *The Blood of a Poet*
Sangster, Jimmy
  5001 515
Sans mobile apparent, see *Without Apparent
  Motive*
Sans toit ni loi, see *Vagabond*
Sansom, Ken
  R 186
  5001 432
Santa Fe Trail
  5001
Santana, Arnaldo
  SOTA 102
  5001 658
Santell, Alfred
  KKBB 325, 369; dir., *Orchids and Ermine*,
    325; *Winterset*, 369
  5001 322, 552, 841
Santley, Joseph
  5001 144
Santoni, Reni
  DIM 387
  5001 46, 178, 191, 311
Santos, Joe
  5001 269, 277, 564, 863
Sapara, Adé
  ML 115
  5001 165
Saper, Jack
  5001 4
Saperstein, David
  H 5
  5001 144
Sapphire
  ILIATM 66, 77
Sappho
  DIM 36
Saraband

SOTA 253
Sarafian, Richard C.
    DIM 358; dir., *Man in the Wilderness*, 357-359
    WTLGD 206-207
    H 9
    5001 457, 521, 695
Sarandon, Chris
    WTLGD 198-199
    SOTA 203
    H 379
    5001 196, 258, 597
Sarandon, Susan
    R 424, 469
    WTLGD 447
    TIAI 173, 176, 389, 391-392
    SOTA 289
    H 36, 37, 324-325, 480, 482
    ML 185
    5001 38, 109, 150, 205, 270, 304, 746, 843
Sarasohn, Lane
    5001 309
Saratoga Trunk
    KKBB 345:n, 348
    GS 103
    5001
Sarde, Philippe
    TIAI 308
    ML 210
    5001 463, 607
Sargent, Alvin
    DIM 32
    R 74, 178
    WTLGD 302, 305
    TIAI 81
    5001 89, 276, 352, 385, 553, 714, 718
Sargent, Dick
    WTLGD 545
Sargent, Herbert
    5001 111
Sargent, Joseph
    R 365-366
    ML dir., *Day One*, 207
    5001 740
Sarne, Michael
    GS dir., *Joanna*, 193-195, 199
    DIM 151; dir., *Myra Breckinridge*, 147, 151; *Joanna*, 151
Sarner, Arlene
    H 220
    5001 574
Sarnoff, David
    RK 6
Saroyan, Lucy
    5001 86
Saroyan, William
    ILIATM 215
    RK 41, 47
    WTLGD 271
    5001 344
Sarraute, Nathalie
    DIM 418
    H 152
Sarrazin, Michael
    DIM 71
    5001 755
Sarris, Andrew

ILIATM 215, 292-319
Sartain, Gailard
    ML 224
    5001 80
Sartov, Hendrik
    ILIATM 345
    5001 553, 658
Sartre, Jean-Paul
    ILIATM 22
    KKBB 335
    WTLGD 39
    H 86
    5001 190, 553
Sasame Yuki, see *The Makioka Sisters*
Sasek, V.
    5001 367
Sassard, Jacqueline
    KKBB 107
    GS 148
    5001 3, 67
Satan Bug, The
    GS 223
Satan Met a Lady
    KKBB 305
"Satan's Alley" (music)
    ML 73
Satchidananda, Swami
    5001 130
Satchmo the Great
    5001
Satie, Erik
    DIM 308
    R 303
    ML 12
    5001 47
Sato, Reiko
    5001 802
Satta Flores, Stefano
    WTLGD 484
    5001 836
Saturday Evening Post (periodical)
    ILIATM 222, 294
    RK 10, 25, 47, 63, 84
    WTLGD 68
    TIAI 270
    SOTA 177-178, 235
Saturday Night and Sunday Morning
    ILIATM 63, 68, 74-77, 165, 260
    KKBB 311
    TIAI 84
    H 49
    5001
Saturday Night Fever
    WTLGD 367-371, 422, 470, 554
    TIAI 30, 31, 33, 227, 229
    SOTA 35, 36, 376
    H 169, 349
    5001
"Saturday Night Live" (TV)
    WTLGD 188
    TIAI 26, 224, 254, 437
    H 132, 154, 186, 187, 337, 371
    ML 38, 42, 165, 183
Saturday Review (periodical)
    ILIATM 31, 177, 184, 230
    KKBB 206
    DIM 36, 377

Saul, Oscar
    5001 722
Saunders, John Monk
    WTLGD 13, 14
Saunders, Phillip
    5001 794
Saura, Carlos
    DIM 263-264; dir., *The Garden of Delights*, 263-264
    TIAI 409-411; dir., *Sweet Hours*, 409-411; *Elisa, Vida Mia*, 411
    H 469
    5001 278, 735
Sautet, Claude
    R 95-96
    WTLGD 152-155; dir., *Vincent, François, Paul, and the Others*, 152-155; *César and Rosalie*, 153
    TIAI 423; dir., *César and Rosalie*, 423
    5001 128, 230, 449, 450, 816
Sauve qui peut/La Vie, see *Every Man for Himself*
Savage, Ann
    5001 829
Savage, Archie
    5001 106, 119
Savage, Brad
    WTLGD 282
    5001 372
Savage Is Loose, The
    R 379, 382-384
    5001
Savage, John
    WTLGD 512-519
    TIAI 214
    H 182, 184
    5001 126, 183, 651
Savage Messiah
    R 46-52
    WTLGD 83
    5001
Savage, Peter
    TIAI 107
Savage Seven, The
    GS 91
    DIM 150
    TIAI 64
Savalas, Telly
    KKBB 145
    5001 58, 74, 545, 656, 860
Savant, Doug
    H 445
    5001 469
Save the Tiger
    R 116-119
    WTLGD 124, 269
    5001
Saville, Victor
    5001 75, 226, 306, 847
Savin, Lee
    5001 77
Savini, Tom
    TIAI 198
    5001 401
Savoir, Alfred
    5001 87
Sawdust and Tinsel, see *The Naked Night*

Sawyer, Joe
   KKBB 276, 291
   5001 301, 363, 394, 433, 578
Saxon, John
   5001 33, 221
Say Amen, Somebody
   TIAI 470-473
   5001 (2nd ed)
Say Anything
   ML 133-36
   5001 (2nd ed)
Sayers, Dorothy
   H 296
Sayles, John
   TIAI 192, 193, 194
   SOTA 70, 71
   H 213, 231; dir., *The Brother from Another
      Planet*, 213
   ML 191,192
   5001 99, 344, 693
Sayn-Wittgenstein, Carolyne
   WTLGD 83
Sayonara
   KKBB 194
   R 432
   TIAI 357
Sayre, Joel
   WTLGD 18
   5001 30, 310
Scacchi, Greta
   H 278, 339
   5001 183, 295
Scales, Prunella
   5001 97
Scalphunters, The
   GS 89-90, 92
   DIM 299
   R 61
   5001
Scandal
   ML 129-33
   5001 (2nd ed)
Scandal Sheet
   RK 20
Scandale, Le, see *The Champagne Murders*
Scarface (1932)
   KKBB 113, 338
   GS 243, 246
   R 208
   SOTA 100-101, 102, 103, 104
   ML 268
   5001
Scarface (1983)
   SOTA 100-106
   H 33, 34, 117, 157, 180, 251
   5001 (2nd ed)
Scarfiotti, Ferdinando
   TIAI 335
   SOTA 104
   H 395
   5001 125, 180, 408, 410, 658
Scarlet Empress, The
   5001
Scarlet Letter, The
   KKBB 345:n
   5001
Scarlet Pimpernel, The

   5001
Scarlet Street
   5001
Scarwid, Diana
   TIAI 235, 236
   SOTA 110
   5001 492, 681
Scavarda, Aldo
   5001 41, 61
Sceicco Bianco, Lo, see *The White Sheik*
Scenes from a Marriage
   WTLGD 76, 390, 478
   TIAI 78, 291
Scenes from the Class Struggle in Beverly Hills
   5001 (2nd ed)
Schaal, Wendy
   5001 364
Schaefer, George
   KKBB 198
   DIM 260; dir., *Doctors' Wives*, 259, 260,
      262
   5001 195
Schaefer, George J.
   RK 3-4, 5, 6-7, 31, 33-34, 35, 41, 46, 67
Schaefer, Jack
   5001 495, 671
Schaefer, Natalie
   5001 261, 572
Schaeffer, Rebecca
   5001 659
Schaffner, Franklin J.
   GS 94; dir., *Planet of the Apes*, 37, 38
   DIM 98, 367, 368; dir., *Patton*, 97-100, 368;
      Planet of the Apes, 98, 368; *Nicholas
      and Alexandra*, 366-369; *The War Lord*,
      368
   R 238-240; dir., *Nicholas and Alexandra*,
      15, 220, 237; *The Stripper*, 76; *Papillon*,
      237-239, 312; *The War Lord*, 238;
      Planet of the Apes, 238; *Patton*, 238;
      Anne of the Thousand Days, 387
   WTLGD 278-283, 451-454; dir., *Islands in
      the Stream*, 278-283, 452, 453; *The Best
      Man*, 278; *Nicholas and Alexandra*, 278,
      452; *Papillon*, 279, 452; *The Boys from
      Brazil*, 451-454, 530; *Patton*, 452
   5001 64, 97, 372, 523, 565, 570, 586, 723
Schanberg, Sydney
   SOTA 274-279
   5001 394
Schary, Dore
   KKBB 49
   WTLGD 125
   5001 44, 47, 106, 701, 754
Schatz, Willy
   5001 430
Schatzberg, Jerry
   DIM 252; dir., *Puzzle of a Downfall Child*,
      250-253; *The Panic in Needle Park*,
      305, 314
   TIAI 40-45; dir., *The Seduction of Joe
      Tynan*, 19, 44; *Honeysuckle Rose*,
      40-45, 372
   H 292-294; dir., *Honeysuckle Rose*, 10;
      Street Smart, 292-294
   5001 339, 564, 604, 721, 722
Schayer, Richard

   5001 501
Scheider, Roy
   R 208, 429
   WTLGD 173, 196
   TIAI 426, 427, 485, 486
   5001 87, 267, 378, 400, 442, 464, 604, 673,
      706, 715
Scheine, Raynor
   ML 194
   5001 382
Schell, Maria
   5001 137, 282, 730, 819
Schell, Maximilian
   KKBB 208
   DIM 162, 163, 262; dir., *First Love*,
      162-163
   5001 246, 384, 386, 573, 781, 859
Schell, Ronnie
   5001 438
Schenck, Nicholas
   RK 5, 7
Schepisi, Fred
   WTLGD 536
   TIAI 54-60, 266-269, 370-373; dir., *The
      Chant of Jimmie Blacksmith*, 54-60, 267,
      268, 269, 371; *The Priest*, 59; *Libido*,
      59; *The Devil's Playground*, 59,
      266-269, 371; *Barbarosa*, 370-373
   SOTA 160-163; dir., *Barbarosa*, 30; *Iceman*,
      160-163; *The Chant of Jimmie Black-
      smith*, 243
   H 41-45, 312-314; dir., *Barbarosa*, 10;
      Iceman, 34; *Plenty*, 41-45, 46; *Roxanne*,
      312-314, 408
   ML dir., *A Cry in the Dark*, 30-33
   5001 50, 51, 129, 166, 188, 353, 587, 644
Schepps, Shawn
   SOTA 152
   5001 610
Schertzinger, Victor
   5001 75, 439, 480, 633, 693
Scheybal, Vladek
   5001 72
Schiaffino, Rosanna
   KKBB 364
   5001 801
Schiaparelli
   5001 605
Schiavelli, Vincent
   5001 7, 549
Schickele, David
   5001 160
Schickele, Peter
   5001 160, 273
Schiele, Egon
   DIM 242, 410
   WTLGD 388
Schierbeck, Poul
   5001 176
Schiffer, Michael
   H 462
   5001 147
Schiffman, Suzanne
   WTLGD 355
Schifrin, Lalo
   GS 34, 247, 272
   DIM 182, 386

R 205-206
TIAI 196
SOTA 334
5001 95, 109, 127, 131, 191, 221, 327, 473,
    770, 851
Schikaneder
WTLGD 73
Schildkraut, Joseph
5001 141, 165, 278, 354, 465, 488, 553,
    677, 679, 697
Schiller, Danny
H 302
5001 577
Schiller, Joel
5001 695
Schiller, Lawrence
R 151
Schilling, Gus
5001 138, 618
Schilling, William G.
5001 647
Schine, G. David
KKBB 208
DIM 316
Schisgal, Murray
DIM 10
TIAI 429
5001 780
Schlamme, Thomas
ML dir., *Miss Firecracker*, 141-44
5001 484
Schlatter, Charlie
H 459
5001 103
Schlesinger, Arthur Jr.
ILIATM 150, 177, 205
DIM 43
Schlesinger, John
KKBB 159; dir., *Darling*, 158-159
DIM 4, 290, 292, 293, 424; dir., *Midnight
    Cowboy*, 4, 76, 147, 152, 314; *Far from
    the Madding Crowd*, 141; *Darling*, 278;
    Sunday Bloody Sunday, 289-293, 424,
    426
R 326, 471-477; dir., *Midnight Cowboy*, 161,
    172, 185, 239, 293, 309, 326, 475; *Far
    from the Madding Crowd*, 236; *The Day
    of the Locust*, 326, 471-477; *Darling*,
    343, 475
WTLGD 172-175, 215, 404; dir., *Marathon
    Man*, 172-175, 191, 204; *The Day of the
    Locust*, 174, 215; *Midnight Cowboy*,
    175
SOTA 92, 311-315, 318; dir., *Darling*, 92;
    The Falcon and the Snowman, 311-315;
    An Englishman Abroad (TV), 311, 313;
    The Day of the Locust, 315; *Marathon
    Man*, 315
H 45; dir., *Midnight Cowboy*, 24; *Darling*,
    45
ML 167; dir., *Madame Sousatzka*. 20-22;
    Pacific Heights, 276-78
5001 173, 176, 233, 237, 447, 464, 478,
    561, 728
Schlöndorff, Volker
TIAI 237
5001 158, 734

Schmid, Daniel
WTLGD 315
Schmidt, Harvey
SOTA 249
Schmidt, Lars
ILIATM 215-216
Schmitz, Sybille
KKBB 365
5001 812
Schnabel, Stefan
TIAI 462
5001 441, 802
Schnee, Charles
KKBB 233, 338, 363
5001 46, 110, 620, 754, 800
Schnee, Thelma
5001 185
Schneider, Bert
5001 323
Schneider, Maria
R 28, 33-34
WTLGD 365
5001 410
Schneider, Romy
KKBB 69, 167
R 95, 146
5001 37, 89, 128, 443, 449, 789, 830
Schneiderman, George
5001 713
Schnitzler, Arthur
ILIATM 97
Schoedsack, Ernest B.
5001 194, 263, 429, 479, 499
Schoeffling, Michael
SOTA 173
5001 684
Schoelen, Jill
H 261, 262
5001 714
Schofill, John
R 323
Schoenfeld, Bernard C.
5001 578
Schollin, Christina
5001 236
School for Scandal (stage)
RK 11
Schoonmaker, Thelma
5001 146, 297
Schrader, Leonard
R 469
WTLGD 407
H 25
5001 85, 400, 853
Schrader, Paul
R 469
WTLGD 131, 211, 406-409, 543-546; dir.,
    Blue Collar, 406-409, 415, 546;
    Hardcore, 543-546
TIAI 107, 189, 335-336; dir., *American
    Gigolo*, 33, 335, 336; *Cat People*,
    335-336; *Blue Collar*, 335; *Hardcore*,
    335
H 300
ML dir., *Patty Hearst*, 8-11
5001 85, 125, 318, 571, 745, 853
Schramm, David

ML 193-94
5001 382
Schrank, Joseph
5001 113, 141, 686
Schreck, Max
KKBB 319
5001 534
Schreiber, Avery
TIAI 196
5001 127
Schroder, Ricky
TIAI 130
Schroeder, Barbet
TIAI 104
H 383-385; dir., *Barfly*, 383-385, 463
ML dir., *Reversal of Fortune*, 287-89
5001 51
Schroeter, Werner
TIAI 405
Schubert, Franz
WTLGD 459, 461
5001 283, 740
Schuck, John
R 270
H 3
5001 445, 469, 559, 708, 757, 758
Schüfftan, Eugen
5001 130, 230, 347, 422, 477
Schulberg, B. P.
RK 9
WTLGD 14
5001 760
Schulberg, Budd
ILIATM 48
RK 19
R 126
TIAI 110
H 418
5001 232, 546
Schuler, Fred
TIAI 231
5001 36, 842
Schull, Richard B.
5001 25
Schulman, Arnold
GS 238
Schulman, Tom
ML 154
5001 178
Schultz, Dwight
ML 207-208
5001 238
Schultz, Jeff
H 262
5001 714
Schultz, Michael
WTLGD 187-189; dir., *Car Wash*, 187-189;
    Cooley High, 188-189
5001 118
Schulz, Charles M.
5001 97
Schulz, Franz
5001 478
Schulz, Manfred
5001 445
Schumach, Murray
ILIATM 147

Schumacher, Joel
    WTLGD 165, 188, 469-470
    TIAI 160-162; dir., *The Incredible Shrinking*
        Woman, 160-162
    ML dir., *Cousins*, 96-99
    5001 118, 159, 250, 361, 686, 699, 844
Schumann, Robert
    5001 694
Schunzel, Reinhold
    5001 48, 353, 536
Schurr, S. W.
    5001 221
Schuster, Harold
    5001 508
Schuster, Joe
    5001 731
Schutz, Maurice
    5001 568
Schwartz, Arthur
    KKBB 234
    5001 19, 50, 159, 524
Schwartz, Maurice
    5001 242
Schwarzenegger, Arnold
    WTLGD 319, 483
    H 68, 170, 171, 193
    5001 602, 617
Schwarzkopf, Elisabeth
    KKBB 222
Schwerner, Michael
    ML 54
    5001 486
Schygulla, Hanna
    TIAI 469
    5001 477, 537
Sciascia, Leonardo
    GS 55
    DIM 221
    5001 825
Sciorra, Annabella
    ML 263
Scire, Andrea
    KKBB 231
    5001 24
Sciuscià, see *Shoeshine*
Scob, Edith
    5001 230, 481, 753
Scofield, Paul
    KKBB 154-155
    DIM 37, 357, 417, 418
    ML 217
    5001 53, 329, 396, 456
Scola, Ettore
    DIM 194; dir., *The Pizza Triangle*, 193-195
    WTLGD 310-312, 362; dir., *A Special Day*,
        310-312; *The Pizza Triangle*, 311; *We*
        All Loved Each Other So Much, 311
    TIAI 284, 469-470; dir., *We All Loved Each*
        Other So Much, 284; *La Nuit de*
        Varennes, 469-470
    H 374
    5001 537, 584, 700
Scola, Kathryn
    5001 13
Scooler, Zvee
    5001 34
Scopes, John

KKBB 207
Scorpio Rising
    KKBB 19
    DIM 87
    R 174
    WTLGD 368
Scorsese, Martin
    R 167-175, 300, 330, 408-416; dir., *Mean*
        Streets, 167-175, 256, 268, 302, 310,
        315, 320, 329, 399, 414, 415; *Who's*
        That Knocking at My Door?, 173;
        Boxcar Bertha, 173; *Alice Doesn't Live*
        Here Anymore, 408-416
    WTLGD 90, 131-135, 146, 202, 203, 273,
        277, 324, 420, 421, 434, 543; dir., *Taxi*
        Driver, 131-135, 143, 202, 203, 209,
        211, 277, 415, 427, 434, 523, 543;
        Mean Streets, 132, 202, 420, 434, 446,
        447; *Alice Doesn't Live Here Any More*,
        132, 229, 415; *New York, New York*,
        269, 389, 434, 490; *The Last Waltz*,
        427, 434, 523
    TIAI 35, 106-112, 456-461; dir., *Raging*
        Bull, 106-112, 190, 191, 457, 460; *New*
        York, New York, 109, 110, 297, 391,
        457, 460; *Mean Streets*, 109, 153, 457,
        460; *Taxi Driver*, 109, 110, 457, 460;
        Alice Doesn't Live Here Anymore, 109;
        The King of Comedy, 456-461
    SOTA 47, 48, 166, 202, 203; dir., *New York,*
        New York, 47, 166, 167, 219; *Raging*
        Bull, 103; *The King of Comedy*, 123;
        Mean Streets, 201, 204; *Taxi Driver*,
        344
    H 38-41, 223-228, 251; dir., *After Hours*,
        38-41, 226; *The King of Comedy*, 38,
        41, 227; *Taxi Driver*, 41, 227; *Alice*
        Doesn't Live Here Anymore, 49; *The*
        Color of Money, 223-228; *Mean Streets*,
        227; *The Last Waltz*, 227; *New York,*
        New York, 228
    ML 105; dir., *After Hours*, 151; *GoodFellas*,
        265-70, 286-87; *The Last Temptation of*
        Christ, 102; *Life Lessons*, 100-103;
        Raging Bull, 265, 266, 267, 269
    5001 9, 15, 146, 297, 396, 411, 473, 520,
        521, 612, 644, 744, 745, 762
Scortia, Thomas M.
    5001 785
Scott, Adrian
    KKBB 253
    5001 164, 488
Scott, Alan
    R 233
Scott, Allan
    5001 119, 248, 443, 607, 623
Scott, Campbell
    ML 302
Scott, Cedric
    WTLGD 443
Scott, Donovan
    TIAI 232
    SOTA 225
    5001 673, 866
Scott, Douglas
    5001 366

Scott, Elliot
    TIAI 222
    5001 201
Scott, George C.
    KKBB 134, 298
    GS 75, 121
    DIM 97-99, 350, 378, 379, 426
    R 165, 245-246, 264, 318, 348, 379,
        382-384, 429
    WTLGD 120, 122, 196, 220, 278, 281, 282,
        502-503, 543-545
    H 226
    5001 67, 175, 318, 334, 341, 347, 372, 410,
        423, 500, 570, 655
Scott, Gordon
    5001 744
Scott, Hazel
    5001 106, 349, 692
Scott, Janette
    5001 188
Scott, John
    R 205
Scott, Judson
    TIAI 358
    5001 707
Scott, Lizabeth
    DIM 313
    5001 179, 718
Scott, Lois
    WTLGD 250-252
Scott, Maggie
    TIAI 168
Scott, Margaretta
    KKBB 293
    5001 406, 759, 831
Scott, Martha
    R 364
    WTLGD 344
    5001 63, 343, 556, 747, 794
Scott, Pippa
    5001 662
Scott, Randolph
    ILIATM 45
    WTLGD 19, 51
    SOTA 9
    5001 254, 333, 508, 629, 672, 702
Scott, Ridley
    WTLGD 380-383
    TIAI 360-365; dir., *Alien*, 10, 13, 19, 169,
        192; *Blade Runner*, 360-365
    SOTA 30, 188; dir., *The Duellists*, 30; *Blade*
        Runner, 141, 358; *Alien*, 188
    H 192, 386-387; dir., *Blade Runner*, 108,
        344; *Alien*, 192, 194; *Someone to Watch*
        Over Me, 386-387
    5001 15, 79, 206, 692, 759
Scott, Tony
    H 168-169; dir., *Top Gun*, 168-169, 172,
        225, 246, 299
    5001 780
Scott, Walter
    5001 376
Scott, Zachary
    5001 249, 469, 480, 698
Scourby, Alexander
    5001 70, 285
Scoundrel Time (book)

WTLGD 308
Screen Stories (periodical)
   DIM 216
Screen Writers Guild
   RK 27, 28, 38, 39
Scrooge
   DIM 196-197
   5001
Scrooged
   ML 38-42
   5001 (2nd ed)
SCTV
   SOTA 142, 143
   H 186, 187, 310, 337, 455
   ML 271
Sea Gull, The
   GS 230-236
   TIAI 174
   SOTA 127
   5001
Sea Hawk, The
   KKBB 185
   5001
"Sea Hunt" (TV)
   KKBB 183
Sea of Grass, The
   5001
Sea Wall, The (*Barrage contre le Pacifique*; also
    known as *This Angry Age*)
   KKBB 345-346:n
   5001
Seacat, Sandra
   5001 157
Seagrove, Jenny
   TIAI 464
   5001 429
Seale, John
   ML 7
   5001 844
Seales, Franklyn
   5001 698
Seance on a Wet Afternoon
   R 237
Search for the Nile, The (TV)
   TIAI 481
Search, The
   5001
Searchers, The
   WTLGD 544
   H 18
   5001
Searle, Ronald
   KKBB 278
   5001 317
Sears, Heather
   5001 640, 695
Sears, Zelda
   5001 733
Season in Hell, A
   SOTA 375
Seaton, George
   DIM 136; dir., *Airport*, 132, 136-137, 147,
    173, 220, 233, 294; *Miracle on 34th
    Street*, 136; *Little Boy Lost*, 136; *The
    Country Girl*, 136; *The Counterfeit
    Traitor*, 136
   5001 12, 157, 175, 425, 763

Sebastian
   GS 19-24
   5001
Sebastian, Dorothy
   5001 555, 845
Seberg, Jean
   ILIATM 128, 130-131
   KKBB 129, 265
   DIM 27-29, 137
   R 215, 302
   H 229
   5001 12, 74, 100, 244, 247, 267, 422, 500
Secombe, Harry
   5001 59, 543, 694
Second Chorus
   5001
Second City
   DIM 10
   TIAI 196, 225, 394
   5001 723
Second Fiddle
   5001
Second World War, see World War II
Seconds
   5001
Secret Agent
   GS 223
   5001
Secret Ceremony
   GS 171
   DIM 407
   R 235
   WTLGD 95
Secret Glass, The (book)
   ML 46
Secret Honor
   H 1-4, 96
   5001 (2nd ed)
Secret Life of Walter Mitty, The
   5001
Secret of My Success, The
   H 298-301
   5001 (2nd ed)
Secret of NIMH, The
   ML 228
Secret of Santa Vittoria, The
   DIM 34-35
   5001
Secret People
   5001
Secret Sharer, The
   5001 (2nd ed)
Secret War of Harry Frigg, The
   GS 56-58
Secrets of a Soul
   RK 76
Secrets of Women (*Kvinnors Väntan*)
   ILIATM 105-106
   5001 (2nd ed)
Section Spéciale, see *Special Section*
Seddon, Jack
   5001 20
Sedgwick, Edward
   5001 579
Sedgwick, Kyra
   5001 93
Seduced and Abandoned

R 258
Seduction of Joe Tynan, The
   TIAI 19, 44
Seems Like Old Times
   SOTA 166
Seff, Manuel
   5001 81, 255, 292
Segal, Alex
   5001 19
Segal, Erich
   DIM 216-219, 415
   5001 843
Segal, George
   KKBB 10, 213
   GS 53, 74, 89-90
   DIM 120-122, 183-186, 351-353, 401, 402,
    426
   R 204, 310, 350, 357
   WTLGD 122-123, 269-271, 482-484
   TIAI 48
   SOTA 369
   H 208
   5001 76, 88, 94, 111, 271, 341, 442, 559,
    675, 715, 748, 831, 832, 836
Segall, Bernardo
   DIM 122
   5001 442
Segall, Harry
   5001 329, 494
Segar, Elzie
   TIAI 120
Seger, Bob
   SOTA 39
Seidel, Toscha
   5001 366
Seidelman, Susan
   SOTA 354-355; dir., *Desperately Seeking
    Susan*, 354-355; *Smithereens*, 354, 355
   H 40
   5001 184
Seigner, Emmanuelle
   H 446
   5001 266
Seigner, Louis
   WTLGD 97
   5001 96, 586, 700
Seippel, Edda
   WTLGD 187
   5001 467
Seiter, William A.
   5001 33, 356, 496, 550, 628, 640, 808
Seitz, George B.
   5001 438
Seitz, John
   5001 198, 258
Seize the Day (book)
   GS 57
Seizure
   H 183
Sekaryongo
   5001 397
Selby, David
   R 82
   5001 627, 809
Selby, Nicholas
   5001 444
Seldes, George

RK 10
Seldes, Gilbert
   RK 44, 49
Seldes, Marian
   WTLGD 415
Self, William
   5001 759
Sellars, Elizabeth
   KKBB 235
   5001 52, 184, 449
Selleck, Tom
   SOTA 70, 164
Sellers, Peter
   ILIATM 64, 205-207
   KKBB 69, 293, 294
   GS 158
   R 69, 403-404
   WTLGD 238, 245-246, 247, 465
   TIAI 484
   SOTA 154, 301, 305
   H 9
   5001 9, 55, 123, 350, 357, 399, 407, 430,
      450, 500, 567, 582, 597, 752, 781, 830,
      850, 861
Selling of the Pentagon, The (TV)
   RK 11
Sellner, Gustav Rudolf
   5001 573
Seltzer, David
   ML dir., *Punchline*, 16-20
   5001 603
Seltzer, Will
   WTLGD 321
   5001 139
Selwart, Tonio
   5001 52, 534
Selwyn, Edgar
   KKBB 253
   5001 128, 170
Selznick, David O.
   5001 8, 206, 278, 356, 362, 366, 428, 448,
      463, 536, 565, 590, 598, 618, 683, 701,
      707, 741, 781, 830, 859
Sembène, Ousmane
   5001 216
Semi-Tough
   WTLGD 358-363
   SOTA 16
   H 448
   5001
Sémianko, Michel
   5001 136
Semler, Dean
   ML 297
Semon, Larry
   WTLGD 471
Semple, Lorenzo Jr.
   GS 168
   DIM 261
   R 238
   WTLGD 234-239
   TIAI 125
   SOTA 225
   5001 250, 395, 565, 594, 673, 765
Semple, Roberta
   RK 83
Semprun, Jorge

KKBB 164-165
DIM 64, 202
R 211-212, 215, 417, 418, 419
WTLGD 96-97
5001 151, 310, 712, 862
Senator Was Indiscreet, The
   5001
Sendak, Maurice
   H 240, 241, 242, 243
   5001 537
Seneca
   5001 578
Seneca, Joe
   H 143, 144
   5001 164
Sennett Bathing Beauties
   KKBB 273
   5001 292
Sennett, Mack
   ILIATM 26, 151, 227
   KKBB 29, 30, 117, 273, 370
   RK 14
   DIM 195
   WTLGD 17, 416
   TIAI 144
   SOTA 102
   H 195
   5001 292
Sense of Loss, A
   R 21-25
   WTLGD 177
   5001
Senso
   R 33
Separate Peace, A
   5001
Separate Tables
   TIAI 173
September
   H 425-427
   ML 13
   5001 (2nd ed)
"September Song" (music)
   TIAI 74
Serafin, Enzo
   5001 820
Serato, Massimo
   R 234
Serban, Andrei
   TIAI 213
Serengeti Shall Not Die
   KKBB 182-183, 185
Seresin, Michael
   TIAI 295
   SOTA 317
   5001 27, 74, 676
Sergeant, The
   GS 240-242
Sergent, Glenna
   5001 13
Serial
   TIAI 395
Serling, Rod
   GS 36, 95
   R 87
   WTLGD 357
   TIAI 110

SOTA 18, 19, 20
5001 586, 797
Serna, Assumpta
   TIAI 410
   H 468, 469
   5001 470, 735
Serna, Pepe
   5001 592
Serpent's Egg, The
   WTLGD 388-392
   TIAI 488
   H 137
   5001
Serpico
   R 227-232, 435
   WTLGD 206, 223, 369
   TIAI 368
   H 169
   5001
Serpico, Frank
   R 227-232
   5001 666
Serrano, Julieta
   H 467, 469
   ML 24
   5001 172, 470, 848
Serrault, Michel
   KKBB 259, 301
   WTLGD 459
   TIAI 164-165, 166, 167, 313
   5001 114, 188, 283, 441
Serre, Henri
   ILIATM 217
   5001 385, 700
Serrone, Christopher
   5001 297
Servais, Jean
   KKBB 339
   5001 323, 630, 750
Servant, The
   KKBB 107-108
   R 220, 343
   SOTA 303
   H 45
Service, Robert W.
   5001 702
"Sesame Street" (TV)
   WTLGD 469
Set-Up, The
   ILIATM 235
   R 149
   TIAI 107
   5001
Seth, Roshan
   TIAI 433
   H 119
   5001 277, 506, 568
Setlowe, Rick
   DIM 113
Settlers, The, see *The New Land*
Setzer, Brian
   H 342
   5001 48
Seuss, see Dr. Seuss
Sevareid, Eric
   WTLGD 221
Seven Beauties (*Pasqualino Settebellezze*)

WTLGD 136-140
5001
Seven Brides for Seven Brothers
KKBB 29
DIM 29
SOTA 320
5001
Seven Chances
5001
Seven Days in May
KKBB 83
GS 95, 208
DIM 199
Seven Deadly Sins, The
KKBB 169
Seven Faces of Dr. Lao, The
GS 102
Seven Gothic Tales (book)
H 77, 78
Seven-Per-Cent Solution, The
WTLGD 190-192
TIAI 276, 355, 359
5001
Seven Samurai, The (Shichi-Nin No Samurai;
The Magnificent Seven [1954])
ILIATM 119-124, 244
DIM 248
WTLGD 113
TIAI 139
H 90
5001
Seven Sinners
5001
Seven Women
KKBB 143
Seven Year Itch, The
TIAI 330
5001
Seven Years' War
WTLGD 104
Seventeen (book)
R 194
1776
R 53-55
5001
Seventh Cross, The
ML 236
Seventh Heaven
ILIATM 197
SOTA 307
Seventh Seal, The (Det Sjunde Inseglet)
ILIATM 107, 148, 176, 245, 288
KKBB 326, 346:n, 347, 369
GS 138, 216
DIM 17, 18
WTLGD 74
TIAI 183, 484
5001
Seventh Veil, The
KKBB 346-347:n
RK 59
5001
Sexual Perversity in Chicago (stage)
H 176-177, 178, 179
Seyler, Athene
ILIATM 119
5001 62, 599, 664

Seymour, Clarine
5001 793
Seymour, Dan
KKBB 360
5001 70, 101, 122, 345, 382, 392, 524, 616
Seymour, James
5001 255, 262, 291
Seymour, Jane
ML 21
Seyrig, Delphine
ILIATM 181, 188
KKBB 109
R 42, 419
5001 3, 192, 412, 481, 716
Shaber, David
WTLGD 559
TIAI 69
5001 764
Shackleton, Robert
KKBB 367
5001 831
Shadix, Glenn
5001 61
Shadow Box, The (TV)
SOTA 279-280
Shadow of a Doubt
H 263
5001
Shadow of the Thin Man
5001
"Shadow, The" (radio)
RK 56, 79
Shadow Warrior, The, see *Kagemusha*
Shadows
ILIATM 73
GS 16, 195-196, 197
DIM 223
Shaffer, Anthony
R 76-77
WTLGD 338, 463-465
SOTA 250
5001 180, 686
Shaffer, Paul
ML 40
Shaffer, Peter
DIM 24
WTLGD 337-339
SOTA 249, 250, 251
5001 21, 223, 602, 646
Shaft
DIM 314, 316
R 5, 65
Shagan, Steve
R 116-119
WTLGD 124-127
5001 346, 655, 819
Shakar, Martin
5001 655
"Shake Your Tailfeathers" (music)
TIAI 26
Shakespeare Wallah
DIM 195
Shakespeare, William
ILIATM 142, 154, 169, 244-245, 277,
280-282, 318, 327
KKBB 50, 91, 200-202, 266, 339, 352
GS 153-154, 157, 174

DIM 24, 49, 90, 127, 181, 354, 356, 357,
399, 400
WTLGD 149, 232, 264, 274, 277, 303, 330,
337, 350, 377, 436, 439, 473
TIAI 110, 127, 389, 390
SOTA 115, 241, 242, 244, 305
H 89, 90, 91, 451
ML 212, 216
5001 36, 235, 257, 296, 315, 328, 396, 444,
628, 639, 746, 795, 828
Shalako
5001
Shame (Skammen)
GS 214-221
DIM 17, 298
R 89, 346
WTLGD 71, 391, 478
TIAI 492
5001
Shameless Old Lady, The (La Vieille Dame
indigne)
KKBB 110-111
5001
Shampoo
R 436-442
WTLGD 230, 404
TIAI 98, 279, 302, 303, 305, 306
SOTA 77
H 451
5001
Shamroy, Leon
GS 38
5001 760
Shan, M. C.
ML 328
Shane
ILIATM 82-83, 240-241
KKBB 347:n, 368
WTLGD 40
TIAI 20, 385
H 15, 17, 308
5001
Shange, Ntozake
TIAI 127
Shanghai Express
KKBB 59, 364
GS 113-114
5001
Shanghai Gesture, The
KKBB 43, 364
5001
Shank, Bud
5001 462
Shankar, Ravi
5001 33, 130, 132, 569, 850
Shankley, Amelia
H 52
5001 202
Shanley, John Patrick
H 424, 425
5001 496
Shanley, Robert
5001 762
Shannon, Harry
5001 767, 784
Shapiro, Ken
R 384

5001 309
Shapiro, Melvin
5001 724
Shapiro, Stanley
GS 18
WTLGD 21
ML 75
5001 191, 441
Sharaff, Irene
KKBB 344
5001 829, 856
Sharif, Omar
KKBB 136
GS 29, 134-136, 167, 268-271
DIM 190, 248, 249
R 257, 348, 459, 461
WTLGD 246
5001 195, 272, 385, 411, 415, 471, 496,
497, 511, 582, 642
Sharkey, Ray
WTLGD 536-537
TIAI 46, 114, 115, 116
H 154
5001 354, 659, 839, 842
Sharp, Alan
DIM 353
5001 410
Sharp, Margery
KKBB 248
5001 143
Sharp, Vanessa
H 240
Sharpe, Cornelia
WTLGD 206-207
5001 521
Shatner, William
TIAI 355, 357, 358, 360
SOTA 197
5001 384, 707, 708
Shaughnessy, Mickey
5001 269, 377
Shavelson, Melville
WTLGD 21; dir., *Houseboat*, 21, 23
5001 123
Shaver, Helen
H 223, 226
5001 146
Shaw, Annabel
5001 310
Shaw, Artie
5001 662
Shaw, David
5001 356
Shaw, Fiona
ML 181
5001 509
Shaw, George Bernard
RK 5, 72
DIM 84, 156
WTLGD 22, 39, 136, 530, 540
SOTA 40, 259
ML 192
5001 25, 114, 187, 453, 605, 804
Shaw, Irwin
KKBB 346, 364
5001 661, 742, 801, 859
Shaw, Lyn

5001 309
Shaw, Martin
5001 444
Shaw, Oscar
5001 144
Shaw, Robert
DIM 24, 119
R 17, 365
WTLGD 158, 159, 195-196, 203
5001 75, 270, 378, 456, 634, 646, 715, 741,
860
Shaw, Robert Gould
ML 256-62
Shaw, Run Run, see Run Run Shaw
Shaw, Sebastian
H 450
5001 332
Shaw, Stan
TIAI 52
5001 73, 97, 303
Shaw, Wini
5001 292, 359
Shawcross, Hartley
WTLGD 176
Shawn, Dick
GS 67
R 370
5001 438, 601
Shawn, Ted
H 339
5001 288
Shawn, Wallace
TIAI 90, 286, 288, 462, 463
SOTA 122, 210
H 266, 276, 295, 297, 379
5001 60, 94, 441, 478, 507, 595, 597, 610,
659
Shayne, Konstantin
5001 248, 533, 719
She
WTLGD 209
5001
She Done Him Wrong
ILIATM 81
KKBB 314
WTLGD 3, 6
5001
She Married Her Boss
5001
She Wore a Yellow Ribbon
ILIATM 242
5001
She's Gotta Have It
H 212-215
5001 (2nd ed)
"She's Like the Wind" (music)
H 349
Shea, John
TIAI 310, 311
5001 486
Shean, Al
5001 779, 865
Shear, Barry
5001 838
Shearer, Moira
5001 621, 741
Shearer, Norma (Mrs. Irving Thalberg)

KKBB 285, 340
RK 24, 70
DIM 137, 157, 216-217
WTLGD 142, 403
5001 52, 193, 224, 266, 329, 337, 354, 465,
599, 638, 825, 847
Shebib, Don
DIM 171; dir., *Goin' Down the Road*,
171-172
TIAI 424-426; dir., *Heartaches*, 424-426;
Goin' Down the Road, 425
5001 290, 324
Sheean, Vincent
RK 26
Sheedy, Ally
TIAI 474, 475, 493, 494
SOTA 347, 348-349
5001 46, 99, 678, 796, 823
Sheehan, Winfield
5001 127
Sheehy, Gail
ML 16
Sheekman, Arthur
5001 115, 493
Sheen, Charlie
H 251, 252
5001 586
Sheen, Martin
R 302, 304
TIAI 433
H 252
5001 47, 125-126, 277
Sheen, Ruth
ML 87, 88-89
5001 331
Sheena
SOTA 224-226
5001 (2nd ed)
Sheik, The
WTLGD 138, 242
ML 303
Sheila Levine Is Dead and Living in New York
R 429-432
5001
Sheinberg, Sid
ML 107
Sheldon, Edward
5001 694
Sheldon, Sidney
WTLGD 21; dir., *Dream Wife*, 21, 23
TIAI 391
5001 30, 44
Shellen, Stephen
H 262
5001 714
Shelley, Mary
R 405
5001 101, 265
Shelley, Percy Bysshe
KKBB 223
Sheltering Sky, The
ML 301-306
Shelton, Deborah
5001 90
Shelton, Marla
5001 705
Shelton, Ron

SOTA 73, 77
H 110, 112, 480-482; dir., *Bull Durham,*
   480-482
ML dir., *Blaze,* 221-25; *Bull Durham,* 143,
   333, 334
5001 65, 80, 108, 805
Shenar, Paul
   H 170, 266
   5001 60, 617, 658
Shentall, Susan
   KKBB 339
   5001 639
Shepard, Alan
   SOTA 65
Shepard, Sam
   WTLGD 188, 397, 400
   TIAI 118, 127
   SOTA 61, 62, 66, 235, 236
   H 96-100, 236, 377
   5001 43, 157, 162, 177, 254, 611, 625, 630,
   863
Shepherd, Cybill
   DIM 296
   R 68, 70, 464-465
   WTLGD 131, 133
   SOTA 344
   5001 37, 324, 406, 410, 745
Shepherd, Richard
   5001 12
Shepperd, John, see Strudwick, Shepperd
Shepperton Studios
   H 368
Sheridan, Ann
   5001 27, 77, 352, 397, 459, 750, 754, 755,
   782
Sheridan, Dinah
   KKBB 270
   5001 100, 281
Sheridan, Jim
   ML dir., *My Left Foot,* 178-82, 324
   5001 509
Sheridan, Margaret
   5001 759
Sheriff, Paul
   5001 500
Sherlock Jr.
   SOTA 337, 340
   5001
Sherman, Hiram
   5001 691
Sherman, Lowell
   WTLGD 240; dir., *She Done Him Wrong,* 3,
   6
   5001 305, 403, 498, 672, 824, 830
Sherman, Richard
   5001 13, 256, 359, 717
Sherman, Vincent
   5001 4, 7, 19, 156, 169, 318, 542
Sherriff, R. C.
   KKBB 321
   5001 369, 539, 542
Sherwin, David
   GS 285
   5001 355
Sherwood, Madeleine
   5001 43, 125
Sherwood, Robert E.

KKBB 270, 332
RK 10, 41
5001 65, 284, 354, 577, 578, 618, 637, 659,
   785, 824
Shevelove, Burt
   KKBB 138
   5001 272
Sheybal, Vladek
   DIM 380
   5001 96, 123, 270, 364, 841, 847
Shibata, George
   5001 802
Shichi-Nin No Samurai, see *The Seven Samurai*
Shields, Arthur
   5001 155, 205, 392, 517, 608, 632, 672
Shields, Brooke
   TIAI 28, 29
   5001 86, 219
Shigeta, James
   5001 252, 436
Shima, Koji
   SOTA 327
   5001 454
Shimura, Takashi
   ILIATM 123
   KKBB 337
   5001 47, 356, 616, 668, 769
Shindo, Kaneto
   KKBB 286-287; dir., *The Island,* 286-287
   5001 371
Shingleton, Wilfred
   5001 302
Shining, The
   TIAI 1-7, 179
   SOTA 322
   5001
Shining Hour, The
   5001
Ship Ahoy
   5001
Ship of Fools
   KKBB 209-213
   WTLGD 120
   5001
Ship to India, A
   R 341
Shire, David
   WTLGD 368
   5001 334, 655
Shire, Talia
   R 401
   WTLGD 214-215, 369, 492
   TIAI 347
   ML 310, 313-14
   5001 289, 290, 636
Shirelles (group)
   H 349
Shirin, Moti
   5001 425
Shirley, Anne
   KKBB 313
   5001 503, 713, 815
Shivas, Mark
   ILIATM 306, 308
Shoah
   H 83-88
   5001 (2nd ed)

"Shoah": An Oral History of the Holocaust
   (book)
   H 84
Shoeless Joe (book)
   ML 126
Shoemaker, Ann
   KKBB 230
   5001 15, 260, 713, 722
Shoes of the Fisherman, The
   GS 181-183
Shoeshine (Sciuscià)
   ILIATM 110, 114-116, 149, 290
   KKBB 198, 269, 366
   DIM 361, 362
   TIAI 250
   ML 166
   5001
Shook, Warner
   TIAI 199
   5001 401
Shoot the Moon
   TIAI 290-295, 343
   SOTA 58, 200
   H 378, 432
   5001
Shoot the Piano Player (Tirez sur le pianiste)
   ILIATM 25, 210-216, 222, 312
   KKBB 54, 81, 150, 356
   GS 82
   DIM 92, 243
   ML 186
   5001
Shooting, The
   5001
Shooting Party, The
   SOTA 369-373
   5001 (2nd ed)
Shootist, The
   WTLGD 197
   TIAI 413
   5001
Shop Around the Corner, The
   WTLGD 370
   SOTA 281
   H 372
   5001
Shop on Main Street, The (Obchod na Korze)
   KKBB 110
   GS 98
   5001
Shopworn Angel, The
   5001
Shor, Daniel
   5001 480
Shore, Dinah
   5001 254, 541, 750, 772
Shore, Sig
   R 64
Short, Bobby
   5001 316
Short Circuit
   H 349
   5001 (2nd ed)
Short Eyes
   WTLGD 295-298
   5001
Short Introduction to the History of Human

Stupidity. A (book)
ML 244
Short, Martin
H 336, 337-338
ML 90
5001 363, 766
Short-Timers, The (book)
H 325
Shostakovich, Dmitri
5001 764
Shot in the Dark, A
WTLGD 246
Shoulder Arms
DIM 93
Show (periodical)
ILIATM 16, 205, 264
Show Boat (1936)
ILIATM 322
5001
Show Boat (1951)
5001
Show Business Illustrated (periodical)
ILIATM 164
Show People
RK 69
5001 (2nd ed)
Show-Off, The (stage)
RK 18
Showalter, Max
KKBB 299
5001 25, 435, 610
Showtime (TV)
TIAI 413
Shrake, Bud
H 8, 9, 10, 136
5001 695
Shryack, Dennis
WTLGD 380
H 15, 16, 17
5001 280, 562
Shubert, Lee and Jacob J.
WTLGD 12, 13, 14, 15
Shue, Elizabeth
ML 227
5001 45
Shuftan, Eugen
ILIATM 7
Shull, Richard B.
R 134
TIAI 462
SOTA 143, 154
5001 260, 400, 441, 687, 702, 806
Shulman, Arnold
5001 528
Shulman, Irving
5001 618
Shumlin, Herman
KKBB 251; dir., *Confidential Agent*, 251;
Watch on the Rhine, 251
5001 152, 824
Shuster, Joe
WTLGD 525
Shute, Nevil
KKBB 207
5001 546
Shyer, Charles
TIAI 94

H 377-378; dir., *Irreconcilable Differences*,
273; *Baby Boom*, 377-378
5001 42, 598
Sibirskaya, Nadia
KKBB 352
5001 476
Sibley, Antoinette
WTLGD 347
5001 795
Sickner, Roy N.
5001 838
Sid and Nancy
H 295, 389
Side Street Story, see *Millionaires of Naples*
"Sidestep" (music)
TIAI 374, 375
Sidney, George
5001 25, 30, 54, 111, 321, 399, 562, 679,
764, 767
Sidney, Sylvia
KKBB 49, 332
R 224
WTLGD 6, 419
H 390, 457
5001 23, 61, 139, 177, 273, 446, 584, 649,
727, 760, 787, 856, 857
Sieber, Maria
5001 658
Siegel, Donald (Don)
ILIATM 313
KKBB 286, 360; dir., *Invasion of the Body
Snatchers*, 286; *The Gun Runners*, 360
DIM 386; dir., *Invasion of the Body
Snatchers*, 275; *Dirty Harry*, 385-388,
392, 398
R 205-207, 254, 471; dir., *Dirty Harry*, 100,
206-207, 254-256, 260, 283, 288, 310;
Invasion of the Body Snatchers, 109,
304, 442; *Charlie Varrick*, 205-207,
365; *Madigan*, 206
WTLGD 197, 520, 524; dir., *Dirty Harry*,
125, 126, 253-254; *The Shootist*, 197;
The Invasion of the Body Snatchers
(1956), 520, 524
TIAI 411-413; dir., *Jinxed!*, 411-413; *The
Shootist*, 413; *Escape from Alcatraz*,
413; *Dirty Harry*, 437, 444
SOTA 240; dir., *The Invasion of the Body
Snatchers* (1956), 187; *Dirty Harry*, 240
H 211
5001 4, 131, 191, 368, 380, 394, 677, 776
Siegel, Jerry
WTLGD 525
5001 731
Siegfried, see *Nibelungen Saga*
Siemaszko, Casey
ML 191-92
5001 100, 279
Sigal, Clancy
ILIATM 23
Sight and Sound (periodical)
ILIATM 63-65, 72, 271, 310, 316
KKBB 228
Sign of the Cross, The
KKBB 68
DIM 131
5001

Signal 7
5001 (2nd ed)
Signorelli, Tom
H 371
5001 581
Signoret, Simone
KKBB 213, 245, 258
GS 233, 235-236
DIM 142, 202, 204
R 33, 96
WTLGD 120
H 411
ML 21
5001 123, 151, 188, 277, 383, 640, 660, 675
Signs of Life
GS 215
WTLGD 54
Sikking, James B.
TIAI 219
5001 558
Silence, The
ILIATM 22-23
KKBB 128
GS 214
DIM 59
R 89, 92, 94
WTLGD 389
TIAI 488
Silencers, The
KKBB 8
R 63, 284
5001
Silent Movie
WTLGD 246, 371, 373, 374, 375, 505
Silent Partner, The
H 265
Silent Running
R 216
WTLGD 350, 512
Silent World, The
KKBB 185
DIM 307
Silent Years, The
DIM 319-321
Siletti, Mario
5001 210, 220
Silk Stockings (1957)
5001
Silkwood
SOTA 106-111, 325
5001 (2nd ed)
Silkwood, Karen
SOTA 106-110
5001 681
Silliphant, Stirling
KKBB 144
GS 150, 151
DIM 151
R 72, 406
WTLGD 113, 254
5001 132, 221, 360, 394, 466, 591, 785
Sillitoe, Alan
ILIATM 63, 77, 256-258, 260-261
5001 654
Silva, Henry
5001 462, 818
Silva, Trinidad

5001 147, 533
Silvain
KKBB 329
5001 568
Silver, Borah
5001 86
Silver Chalice, The
KKBB 279
Silver, Joan Micklin
R 109
WTLGD 79-82
5001 329
Silver, Joe
5001 34, 738, 857
Silver, Ron
TIAI 463
SOTA 109
ML 229-34, 287-89
5001 64, 219, 442, 681
Silver Streak
WTLGD 246-248, 269
TIAI 163
5001
Silvera, Frank
KKBB 367
5001 311, 394, 809, 818
Silverado
H 13-14
5001 (2nd ed)
Silverheels, Jay
5001 392
Silverman, Fred
TIAI 10
Silverman, Jonathan
H 258
5001 104
Silverman, Mark
H 291
5001 615
Silvers, Phil
KKBB 138, 341
R 130
5001 20, 159, 272, 310, 404, 508, 645, 727,
    778
Silvers, Sid
5001 93, 106, 256
Silverstein, Elliot
KKBB 30, 295; dir., *Cat Ballou*, 29-30; *The
    Happening*, 295
5001 124, 317, 625, 779
Silverstein, Shel
ML 27
5001 759
Silvestre, Armando
5001 656
Silvia Gutierrez, Zaide
SOTA 130
Sim, Alastair
KKBB 265, 277, 278, 294
WTLGD 50
5001 254, 306, 317, 413, 645, 826
Sim, Gerald
5001 166
Simcoe, Ben
5001 502
Simenon, Georges
KKBB 328

5001 459, 465, 564, 719
Simmons, Jean
ILIATM 313
KKBB 276, 282
GS 22
WTLGD 65
TIAI 29
5001 5, 19, 25, 86, 114, 184, 215, 301, 311,
    315, 317, 337, 487, 699
Simmons, Kendrick,
ML 4
Simmons, Richard Alan
5001 685
Simms, Ginny
WTLGD 26
5001 106, 523
Simms, Hilda
5001 78
Simon
TIAI 462
Simon & Garfunkel
DIM 23
5001 299
Simon, Carly
R 309
H 191
ML 63
5001 325, 703, 848
Simon, Charles
5001 864
Simon, Danny
R 131
TIAI 394
Simon del Desierto, see *Simon of the Desert*
Simon, François
WTLGD 231
SOTA 125
5001 53, 443
Simon, Frank
5001 607
Simon, Melvin
5001 438, 692, 866
Simon, Michel
KKBB 142, 328, 332
GS 50-51
R 33
H 103
5001 37, 59, 76, 95, 564, 568, 590, 592
Simon, Miklos
TIAI 286
5001 264
Simon, Neil
R 68-70, 131, 453, 454-456
WTLGD 76-79, 376-378, 466, 529-533
TIAI 394, 395, 445
SOTA 129, 358
H 138, 258-260
5001 9, 25, 52, 103, 115, 296, 324, 431,
    597, 707, 730, 734
Simon of the Desert (*Simon del Desierto*)
GS 255-262
5001
Simon, Paul
TIAI 90, 130
Simon, Roger L.
WTLGD 467-469
5001 70, 219

Simon, S. Sylvan
5001 631
Simon, Simone
KKBB 246
WTLGD 522
5001 66, 125, 166, 167, 583, 585
Simonton, Ida Vera
5001 833
Simpson, Claire
5001 587
Simpson, Don
H 168
5001 66, 780
Simpson, Helen
5001 804
Simpson, O. J.
R 406
5001 785
Simpson, Russell
KKBB 276
5001 301, 728, 733, 777
Sims, Joan
KKBB 295
5001 861
Sinatra, Frank
ILIATM 49, 57, 211
KKBB 44, 184, 205, 222, 298
GS 263
DIM 209, 271, 420
R 319, 352
WTLGD 21, 41, 373
TIAI 195, 323, 357
SOTA 205, 307
H 3, 311
5001 25, 123, 185, 263, 269, 311, 424, 461,
    462, 514, 546, 548, 554, 562, 633, 675,
    714, 740, 772, 858
Sinatra, Nancy
5001 837
Since You Went Away
WTLGD 178
5001
Sinclair, Andrew
R 114-116
5001 805
Sinclair, John Gordon
TIAI 466
Sinclair, Madge
R 295-296
WTLGD 147, 267
5001 153, 155, 352, 708
Sinden, Donald
5001 491
Singapore Sue
WTLGD 13, 14
Singer, Alexander
KKBB 250; dir., *A Cold Wind in August*,
    249-250
5001 145
Singer, Isaac Bashevis
SOTA 85, 86, 87, 88, 89, 373
ML 229, 232, 233
5001 219, 855
Singer, Lori
SOTA 139, 140, 315
H 137
5001 233, 256, 791

Singer Midgets (group)
  WTLGD 165
Singin' in the Rain
  ILIATM 24, 81, 142, 145, 278
  KKBB 185, 232, 234
  GS 59, 237, 238
  RK 28
  DIM 209, 322
  R 241
  WTLGD 79
  TIAI 407
  SOTA 338
  H 174
  5001
"Singin' in the Rain" (music)
  WTLGD 79
  ML 18-19
Singing Detective. The (TV)
  ML 82, 132
Singing Nun. The
  KKBB 176, 178
  GS 117
  TIAI 357
Singleton, Penny
  5001 9
Singleton, Zutty
  5001 716
Sinners in the Sun
  WTLGD 6
Sinoël
  5001 819
Siodmak, Curt
  5001 369
Siodmak, Robert
  ILIATM 224, 313; dir., *The Crimson Pirate*,
    24, 81; *The Killers*, 224
  KKBB 252, 257, 291, 349; dir., *The
    Crimson Pirate*, 180, 252, 257, 297; *The
    Devil Strikes at Night*, 257-258; *The
    Spiral Staircase*, 257, 349; *The Suspect*,
    257; *Phantom Lady*, 257; *The Killers*,
    257, 291; *People on Sunday*, 257
  R 356
  5001 136, 143, 163, 187, 243, 394, 578,
    701, 733
Siriaque
  5001 397
Sirico, Tony
  H 371
Sirk, Douglas
  ILIATM 303, 305
  KKBB 357; dir., *Tarnished Angels*, 357
  WTLGD 443; dir., *Magnificent Obsession*
    (1954), 443; *All That Heaven Allows*,
    443
  5001 19, 744, 850
Sister-in-Law. The
  SOTA 232
Sisters
  R 189, 195, 368
  5001
Sisters. The
  TIAI 35, 424
  5001
Sisters of Darkness, see *Dark Habits*
Sitting Pretty
  5001

Sitwell, Osbert
  R 440
Sixteen Candles
  SOTA 173-175, 347, 348
  H 133, 135, 372
  5001 (2nd ed)
"16 Millimeter Earrings" (music)
  H 173
"60 Minutes" (TV)
  ML 31, 33
Sjöberg, Alf
  5001 485, 782
Sjöman, Vilgot
  5001 348, 510
Sjöström, Victor
  ILIATM 206; dir., *The Wind*, 206
  KKBB 345, 369; dir., *The Scarlet Letter*,
    345
  R 224
  5001 658, 659, 839
Sjöwall, Maj
  R 260
  5001 413
Sjunde Inseglet. Det, see *The Seventh Seal*
Skaaren, Warren
  H 456-457
  ML 159
  5001 54, 61
"Skag" (TV)
  TIAI 258
Skala, Lilia
  WTLGD 358
  5001 115, 132, 642, 675
Skammen, see *Shame*
Skarsgard, Stellan
  5001 804
"Skating in Central Park" (music)
  DIM 219
Skelton, Red
  R 130
  TIAI 96
  SOTA 1
  5001 54, 322, 349, 404, 563, 675, 764, 766,
    865
Skelton, Richard, see Skelton, Red
Skerritt, Tom
  DIM 94
  WTLGD 346
  5001 469, 780, 794, 808
Ski Bum, The
  DIM 345
  5001
Skin. The
  KKBB 252
Skin Game. The
  DIM 299-300, 426
  5001
Skinner, Cornelia Otis
  R 92
  5001 807
Skippy
  TIAI 121
Skipworth, Alison
  GS 94
  SOTA 338
  5001 15, 59, 123, 170, 187, 355, 694
Sklar, Michael

5001 788
Skobline, Irene
  5001 158
Skoda, Albin
  KKBB 294
  5001 410
Skolimowski, Jerzy
  H 66
  5001 835
*Sky Above, The Mud Below, The (Le Ciel et la
  boue)*
  KKBB 347-348:n
  5001
Sky's the Limit, The
  5001
Skye, Ione
  H 316
  ML 133-35
  5001 632, 656
Skyjacked
  R 65
  WTLGD 238
Slack, Freddie
  5001 254, 685
Slade, Bernard
  WTLGD 505-507
  TIAI 127
  5001 651, 652
Slansky, Rudolph
  DIM 201, 202, 204
Slap, The (La Gifle)
  WTLGD 152
  5001
Slap Shot
  WTLGD 273-278
  TIAI 151, 288, 289, 441
  5001
Slate, Jeremy
  5001 93
Slater, Christian
  ML 118
  5001 326
Slater, Helen
  H 298, 299
  5001 647, 664
Slater, John
  5001 569
Slaughter, Frank G.
  5001 196
Slaughterhouse-Five
  R 318
  TIAI 380
  SOTA 253
Sleep, Wayne
  WTLGD 540
  5001 304
Sleeper
  R 240-244
  WTLGD 188
  TIAI 161, 462
  5001
Sleeper, Martha
  5001 447, 555, 747
Sleeping Car Murder, The
  DIM 64
  R 391
  WTLGD 95

235

Sleeping Dogs
TIAI 341, 342
Sleeping Prince, The (stage)
KKBB 334
Sleeping with the Enemy
ML 326-27
Slender Thread, The
KKBB 143-145
GS 50
Slesinger, Tess
5001 169, 293, 623
Sleuth
R 76-77
WTLGD 26, 338
TIAI 326
SOTA 250
5001
Slezak, Walter
WTLGD 20, 138
5001 115, 421, 548, 583, 596, 714
Slick, Grace
DIM 85, 210
"Slide Some Oil to Me" (music)
WTLGD 473
Slight Case of Murder, A
SOTA 123
H 154
5001
Slim and Clem
5001 809
Slither
R 133-135, 427
WTLGD 46
TIAI 156
SOTA 217
5001
Sloane, Everett
KKBB 199, 238, 248
5001 71, 138, 220, 384, 443, 475
Sloane, Olive
5001 167
Slocombe, Douglas
WTLGD 265, 304, 352
5001 86, 386, 423, 504, 517, 613, 788
Sloman, Roger
TIAI 282
Slovo, Joe
H 475
Slovo, Shawn
H 475
5001 849
Slow Dancing in the Big City
WTLGD 488-489, 493-496
5001
Sly Fox (stage)
WTLGD 264, 281, 503
Small Change (*L'Argent de poche*)
WTLGD 167-170
5001
Small, Marya
WTLGD 87
5001 549
Small, Michael
WTLGD 486
5001 401, 605, 743
Small, Neva
DIM 332

5001 242
Smalls, Charlie
WTLGD 472
5001 844
Smart, Ralph
5001 21, 167
Smash Palace
TIAI 341-343
SOTA 184, 242
H 54, 165
5001 (2nd ed)
Smash-Up (originally called *Smash-Up--The Story of a Woman*)
5001
Smeaton, Bruce
TIAI 59, 373
SOTA 161
H 43
5001 51, 215, 353, 587, 645
Smight, Jack
KKBB 279; dir., *Harper*, 279
GS dir., *Harper*, 57; *No Way to Treat a Lady*, 74; *The Secret War of Harry Frigg*, 57
R 363-365
5001 12, 320
Smile
WTLGD 43-45, 150, 321, 361
TIAI 77-78
SOTA 16
H 59
5001
Smiler with the Knife, The (book)
RK 34
Smiles of a Summer Night (*Sommarnattens Leende*)
ILIATM 22, 105-107, 148, 274
KKBB 171, 342, 353
GS 73, 211, 216
R 437-438, 440
WTLGD 74, 424
TIAI 365
5001
Smilin' Through
WTLGD 514
SOTA 173
Smith, Alexis
5001 282, 336, 523, 548
Smith, Art
5001 359
Smith, Bessie
R 39
WTLGD 107
H 144
5001 644, 650
Smith, C. Aubrey
KKBB 163, 249
WTLGD 465
SOTA 150
5001 25, 31, 48, 91, 130, 134, 141, 143, 251, 278, 346, 428, 446, 597, 618, 638, 658, 792, 824, 834
Smith, Charles Martin
SOTA 98-99
H 319, 322
5001 519, 710, 807
Smith, David

WTLGD 280
Smith, Dodie
5001 807
Smith, Ethel
5001 54
Smith, Fred
RK 84
Smith, Howard
5001 519
Smith, Jack
ILIATM 19; dir., *Flaming Creatures*, 19
Smith, Kate
5001 762
Smith, Kent
KKBB 247, 349
5001 125, 166, 167, 169, 262, 277, 701
Smith, Kurtwood
ML 85, 155
5001 179, 635, 792
Smith, Lane
H 381
5001 86, 585, 826
Smith, Leila
5001 139
Smith, Leonard
5001 855
Smith, Lewis
SOTA 218
5001 7, 698
Smith, Liz
ML 44
SOTA 341, 342
5001 333, 599
Smith, Lois
WTLGD 130
TIAI 118, 285, 286
5001 78, 210, 264, 521, 625
Smith, Madolyn
TIAI 32, 33
SOTA 222, 224
5001 17, 809
Smith, Maggie
KKBB 173
GS 286-288
DIM 15
R 97
WTLGD 464, 529-532
SOTA 341, 342
H 127, 128, 409-410, 411, 412
ML 14, 76, 91, 154, 300
5001 115, 181, 339, 431, 541, 555, 595, 599, 602, 603, 640, 788, 859
Smith, Mel
H 379
ML dir., *The Tall Guy*, 270-72; Smith and Jones, 271
5001 597, 742
Smith, Muriel
5001 500
Smith, Oliver
5001 311
Smith, Patti
WTLGD 493
Smith, Paul L.
WTLGD 497-498
TIAI 122
SOTA 284

5001 207, 479, 589
Smith, Pete
  GS 238
  5001 463
Smith, Priscilla
  5001 371
Smith, Queenie
  5001 679
Smith, Rebecca Dianna
  R 429
  5001 673
Smith, Roger
  ML 242-45
  5001 127
Smith, Terrence Lore
  R 135
  5001 757
Smith, Thorne
  5001 350, 781
Smith, W. Eugene
  R 469
Smith, Wallace
  5001 280
Smith, Wilbur
  5001 291
Smith, William
  5001 127
Smith, Willie Mae Ford
  TIAI 471-472
  5001 655
Smithereens
  SOTA 354, 355
Smokey and the Bandit
  TIAI 200
Smoktunovski, Innokenti
  5001 172
Smoldering Fires
  GS 127
Smolinski, Aaron
  5001 730
Smooth Talk
  H 131-133, 206
  5001 (2nd ed)
Smordoni, Rinaldo
  ILIATM 115
Smultronstallet, see Wild Strawberries
Sneider, Vern J.
  5001 745
Snider, Paul
  SOTA 91, 92
Snodgress, Carrie
  WTLGD 421
  TIAI 38
  H 16, 17
  5001 273, 562
"Snow Frolic" (music)
  DIM 219
Snow White and the Seven Dwarfs
  GS 191
  SOTA 191
  H 473
Snows of Kilimanjaro, The
  ILIATM 224
  WTLGD 281
Snyder, Arlen Dean
  5001 325
Snyder, John

ML 86
So Big
  ILIATM 143
  WTLGD 145
So Ends Our Night
  5001
So Fine
  TIAI 240-241
  5001
"So Long, Dearie" (music)
  DIM 83
So Proudly We Hail
  R 107
So This Is New York
  5001
So This Is Paris
  TIAI 150
"Soap" (TV)
  SOTA 94
Sobieski, Carol
  TIAI 344
  5001 29
Sobocinski, Witold
  5001 266
Socialist Revolution (periodical)
  WTLGD 387
Söderberg, Hjalmar
  ILIATM 107
Soeteman, Gerard
  SOTA 195
  5001 264
Sofaer, Abraham
  5001 323
Soffel, Kate
  SOTA 290-293
Sofonova, Elena
  H 373, 374
  5001 172
Soft Skin, The
  R 20
Sohnker, Hans
  KKBB 264
  5001 243
Soho News (periodical)
  H 232
Soil, see Earth
Sokol, Marilyn
  5001 296
Sokoloff, Vladimir
  KKBB 302
  5001 82, 153, 256, 442, 452, 488, 700
Solanas, Fernando
  DIM 257, 258; dir., The Hour of the
    Furnaces, 257-259
  5001 342
Soldier in the Rain
  GS 169
Soldier of Fortune (periodical)
  SOTA 375
Soldier of Orange
  SOTA 194, 358
  H 343
Soldier's Play, A (stage)
  SOTA 271
Soldier's Story, A
  SOTA 271-274
  5001 (2nd ed)

Soles, P. J.
  TIAI 94
  5001 314, 598, 723, 735
Soles, Steven
  WTLGD 400
Solid Gold Cadillac, The
  5001
Solinas, Franco
  DIM 176
  R 210-213
  WTLGD 396
  5001 54, 110, 487, 488
Soliti Ignoti, I, see The Big Deal on Madonna
    Street
Solms, Kenny
  R 429
  5001 673
Solo, Robert
  TIAI 474
  5001 46
Sologne, Madeleine
  5001 225
Solomon, Maribeth
  5001 768
Solt, Andrew
  TIAI 201-204; co-dir., This is Elvis, 201-204

  5001 359, 761, 762, 832
Solzhenitsyn, Alexander
  R 101-105
  5001 245
Sombert, Claire
  5001 369
Sombrero
  TIAI 357
Some Call It Loving
  R 222
  5001
Some Came Running
  H 307
Some Like It Hot
  ILIATM 39, 151, 206
  KKBB 348:n
  R 426
  WTLGD 3, 29
  TIAI 67, 331, 332, 429
  5001
Somebody Killed Her Husband
  WTLGD 450-451
  5001
Somebody Up There Likes Me
  ILIATM 143
  R 149
  WTLGD 213
Someone to Watch Over Me
  H 386-387
  5001 (2nd ed)
Something to Shout About
  5001
Something to Sing About
  5001
Something Wild
  H 228-232, 285
  ML 64, 277
  5001 (2nd ed)
Sommarlek, see Summer Interlude
Sommarnattens Leende, see Smiles of a Summer

Night
Sommer, Elke
  5001 554, 600
Sommer, Josef
  TIAI 290, 426, 427
  SOTA 109
  5001 2, 258, 353, 361, 681, 696, 715, 743,
    844
Sondergaard, Gale
  KKBB 296
  R 92
  5001 28, 31, 136, 312, 384, 419, 466, 625
Sondheim, Stephen
  ILIATM 143
  KKBB 138
  R 417
  WTLGD 190, 424
  TIAI 216
  ML 274
  5001 272, 311, 427, 667, 712, 828
Son of Frankenstein
  5001
Son of Fury
  DIM 177
Song of Bernadette, The
  R 77
  WTLGD 57
Song of Love
  KKBB 285, 353
Song of Norway
  DIM 187, 242, 359
  WTLGD 205, 424
  5001
Song of Songs
  R 291
  5001
Song of the Road, see *Pather Panchale*
Song of the South
  SOTA 20
  H 81, 82
Song to Remember, A
  ILIATM 47
  KKBB 68
  DIM 187, 240
  SOTA 250
"Song to the Moon" (music)
  ML 238
Song Without End
  DIM 187
  5001 (2nd ed)
Songwriter
  H 7-11, 136
  5001 (2nd ed)
Sonnenfeld, Barry
  SOTA 325
  5001 84, 150, 615
Sons and Lovers
  ILIATM 63, 68, 72-75, 165
  DIM 142
  WTLGD 301
  H 306
  5001
Sons of the Pioneers
  5001 631
Sontag, Susan
  ILIATM 19

DIM 18, 35, 36; dir., *Duet for Cannibals*,
    35-36
  R 118
  SOTA 24
  5001 206
Soo, Jack
  5001 252
Sophie's Choice
  TIAI 435-436, 494
  5001 (2nd ed)
Sophocles
  KKBB 321
  5001 539
Sordi, Alberto
  KKBB 366, 368
  TIAI 313
  5001 817, 835
Sorel, Cecile
  5001 572
Sorel, Jean
  ILIATM 172
  5001 815
Sorok Pervyi, see *The Forty-First*
Sorrow and the Pity, The
  DIM 426-430
  R 21, 23, 336, 338-339
  WTLGD 96, 176
  H 86
  ML 202
  5001
Sorry, Wrong Number
  5001
Sorvino, Paul
  WTLGD 147, 148, 446-447, 493-495
  TIAI 282
  ML 266-70
  5001 84, 176, 276, 297, 352, 541, 564, 621,
    687, 832
Sosia, Il, see *Partner*
Sothern, Ann
  5001 65, 253, 404, 419, 563, 786, 848
Souffle au coeur, La, see *Murmur of the Heart*
Soul, David
  5001 452
Souls at Sea
  5001
Sound Barrier, The, see *Breaking the Sound
    Barrier*
Sound of Music, The
  KKBB 163, 176-178
  GS 60, 117, 162, 201
  DIM 27, 84, 187, 219, 328, 330, 390
  R 150
  WTLGD 120, 470
  TIAI 13
  H 401
  5001
Sounder
  R 3-7, 61, 263, 296
  WTLGD 170
  5001
Sourire, Soeur
  KKBB 178
Sous les toits de Paris (*Under the Roofs of Paris*)
  5001 (2nd ed)
Soutendijk, Renée
  SOTA 195

5001 258, 264
"South American Way" (music)
  H 275
South Pacific
  ILIATM 144, 233
  DIM 409
  TIAI 299
South Riding
  TIAI 221
Southern Comfort
  TIAI 257-261, 438
  H 143
  5001
Southern, Eve
  5001 498
Southern, Terry
  KKBB 300
  GS 173, 223, 224, 257
  DIM 9, 111, 123, 218
  R 28
  WTLGD 353
  SOTA 73
  5001 117, 123, 210, 218, 440, 450
Southerner, The
  5001
Souvenir d'en France, see *French Provincial*
Souza, Steven E. de, see de Souza, Steven E.
Sowards, Jack B.
  TIAI 355
  5001 708
Spaak, Catherine
  5001 341
Spaak, Charles
  KKBB 244
  5001 121, 300, 388
"Space Seed" (TV)
  TIAI 356, 357, 358
Spacehunter
  SOTA 173
  H 371
Spacek, Sissy
  R 302, 304
  WTLGD 208-212, 283, 442, 467
  TIAI 38, 135-136, 310, 311, 312, 349, 372
  SOTA 37, 91
  H 54, 55, 148, 149, 206, 233, 234
  5001 47, 122, 162, 464, 485, 611, 816, 827
Spacey, Kevin
  ML 65, 206
  5001 168, 849
Spader, James
  5001 43, 594
Spaeth, Merrie
  5001 850
Spain (book)
  SOTA 255
Spain, Fay
  5001 290
Spanish Civil War
  WTLGD 125, 281, 466, 467
Spano, Vincent
  H 338, 339
  5001 294
Spark, Muriel
  GS 286, 288
  WTLGD 149, 262-266
  5001 517

Sparkle
  WTLGD 165-167, 188
  SOTA 296
  5001 (2nd ed)
Sparks, Ned
  KKBB 273
  5001 15, 81, 116, 262, 291, 358
Spartacus
  5001
Sparv, Camilla
  DIM 45, 47
Spawn of the North
  5001
Speaking in Tongues (music)
  SOTA 267
Special Day, A (Una Giornata Particolare)
  WTLGD 310-312
  5001
Special Section (Section Spéciale)
  WTLGD 96-98
  5001
Specter of the Rose
  KKBB 143, 234
  GS 157
  TIAI 132
  5001
Spector, Phil
  5001 211
Speer, Albert
  DIM 428
  WTLGD 176
Spellbound
  KKBB 348:n
  WTLGD 372
  TIAI 461
  5001
Spence, Bruce
  TIAI 386
  5001 634
Spence, Ralph
  5001 160, 552
Spencer, Douglas
  5001 759
Spencer, Kenneth
  5001 113
Spencer, Scott
  SOTA 263
  5001 219
Spenser, Jeremy
  5001 637
Sperber, Wendie Jo
  5001 45, 531
Sperling, Milton
  5001 220, 303
Spetters
  SOTA 195
Spewack, Bella
  5001 399, 508
Spewack, Samuel
  5001 399, 508
Spider's Strategem, The (Strategia del Ragno)
  DIM 273
  WTLGD 146, 326
  5001
Spiegel, Sam (S. P. Eagle)
  ILIATM 48
  KKBB 152-153

  DIM 366, 369
  R 316
  WTLGD 216
  H 364, 365, 366
  5001 9, 132, 411, 415, 719, 741
Spiegelgass, Leonard
  5001 311
Spielberg, Anne
  H 482
  5001 67
Spielberg, David
  5001 414
Spielberg, Steven
  R 300-303, 330
  WTLGD 195, 203-204, 348-354, 420, 421;
    dir., *Jaws*, 40, 123, 156, 195, 203, 208,
    349, 350, 352, 427, 520; *Close
    Encounters of the Third Kind*, 269,
    348-354, 420, 513; *Duel* (TV), 349; *The
    Sugarland Express*, 349
  TIAI 53-54, 98, 100, 207-212, 213, 222,
    265, 347-351, 352, 353, 380, 386, 387,
    493; dir., *Close Encounters of the Third
    Kind*, 53, 54, 98, 208, 211, 222, 347,
    348, 351, 493; *Close Encounters of the
    Third Kind, Special Edition*, 53-54;
    1941, 98, 100, 211; *Jaws*, 195, 427;
    Raiders of the Lost Ark, 207-212, 348,
    351, 386, 387, 389, 481; *The Sugarland
    Express*, 221; *E.T. The Extra-
    Terrestrial*, 347-351, 358, 380, 493
  SOTA 18, 19, 20, 22, 164, 175-182, 188,
    190, 326; dir., *Raiders of the Lost Ark*,
    4, 116, 163, 176, 177, 179, 182, 217;
    Twilight Zone--The Movie (co-dir.),
    18-23; *Jaws*, 22, 182; *E.T. the
    Extra-Terrestrial*, 57, 163, 182, 188;
    1941, 140, 164, 177; *Indiana Jones and
    the Temple of Doom*, 175-182, 234;
    Close Encounters of the Third Kind, 182
  H 12, 80-83, 101, 413-416, 479; dir., *Close
    Encounters of the Third Kind*, 6; *E.T.
    The Extra-Terrestrial*, 45, 74, 83, 464;
    The Color Purple, 80-83, 414; *Indiana
    Jones and the Temple of Doom*, 101;
    Empire of the Sun, 413-416
  ML dir., *Always*, 245-48; *The Color Purple*,
    147; *Empire of the Sun*, 147; *E.T.*, 107-
    108; *Indiana Jones and the Last
    Crusade*, 145-149; *Indiana Jones and
    the Temple of Doom*, 148, 149; *The
    Mission*, 191; *1941*, 226; *Raiders of the
    Lost Ark*, 147-48; cod-dir., *Twilight
    Zone---The Movie*, 147
  5001 21, 142, 146, 217, 225, 297, 361, 362,
    364, 378, 530, 588, 612, 725, 797
Spiesser, Jacques
  5001 685
Spigelgass, Leonard
  5001 19, 352
Spike Jones and His City Slickers (group)
  5001 750
Spikings, Barry
  5001 460
Spillane, Mickey
  KKBB 234

  R 46
  WTLGD 549
  5001 49
Spinell, Joe
  WTLGD 215
  H 371
  5001 290, 745
Spinetti, Victor
  R 115, 389
  5001 711, 767, 805, 819
Spiral Staircase, The
  KKBB 257, 349:n
  5001
Spivak, Charlie
  5001 254
Spivy, Madame
  5001 17, 462, 724
Splash
  SOTA 141-145, 157, 163, 265
  H 6
  5001 (2nd ed)
Splendor in the Grass
  ILIATM 137-138
  KKBB 93
  R 76, 393
  WTLGD 210
  TIAI 284
  SOTA 347
  5001
Splet, Alan R.
  SOTA 100
  H 207
  5001 87, 224
Spolin, Viola
  5001 13
Split, The
  GS 181, 183-185
Spoilers, The
  5001
Sporting Club, The
  DIM 261-263
  WTLGD 91
  5001
Sporting Life, This, see under *This*
Spottiswoode, Roger
  TIAI 438
  SOTA 71-78; dir., *Under Fire*, 71-78, 119;
    Terror Train, 72; *The Pursuit of D. B.
    Cooper*, 72, 73
  H 110-113, 422, 481; dir., *Under Fire*, 73,
    112, 183, 481; *The Best of Times*, 110-
    113, 300, 421, 422, 481
  5001 65, 261, 721, 804
Spradlin, G. D.
  R 402
  5001 290, 495, 839
Spring, Howard
  5001 235
Springer, Gary
  5001 197
Springsteen, Bruce
  SOTA 215
"Springtime for Hitler" (music)
  WTLGD 375
Spy Who Came in from the Cold, The
  WTLGD 170
Spy Who Loved Me, The

WTLGD 395, 520
TIAI 195
5001
Squier, Billy
5001 478
Squire, Ronald
KKBB 307, 339
5001 21, 461, 635
Sragow, Michael
TIAI 95
ML 189
Stack, Robert
KKBB 242, 357
TIAI 51
SOTA 117
H 185, 322
5001 12, 109, 173, 245, 530, 744, 774, 804,
850
Stacpoole, Henry de Vere
5001 86
Stadlen, Lewis J.
R 230
5001 813
Stafford, Frederick
DIM 80
5001 780
Stage Door
KKBB 88, 273
R 97
5001
Stage Door Canteen
5001
Stage Struck
KKBB 70
Stagecoach (1939)
KKBB 41
GS 62
RK 76
R 282
5001
Stagecoach (1966)
KKBB 41
Stahl, John M.
5001 44, 337, 358, 392, 415, 452
Staiola, Enzo
5001 52
Stairway to Heaven
DIM 16
TIAI 299
Stakeout
H 349-351
ML 116
5001 (2nd ed)
Stakeout on Dope Street
R 330
Stalag 17
ILIATM 17, 47
KKBB 194, 349:n
5001
Stalin, Joseph
KKBB 289, 334
RK 26, 50; Stalinism, 26, 28
DIM 112, 201, 369; anti-Stalinism, 203
WTLGD 170
Stalking Moon, The
GS 248-253
Stallings, Laurence

RK 18, 70
5001 386, 673, 680, 728, 779
Stallone, Frank
H 383
5001 51
Stallone, Sylvester
WTLGD 213-216, 319, 369, 488-493, 495;
dir., *Paradise Alley*, 488-493
TIAI 346-347; dir., *Rocky II*, 13, 346; *Rocky
III*, 346-347
SOTA 34-37, 116, 374, 375; dir., *Rocky II*,
6, 35, 169; *Rocky III*, 6, 35, 169;
Staying Alive, 34-37, 169
H 72, 95, 96, 193; dir., *Rocky IV*, 95
ML dir., *Staying Alive*, 73
5001 181, 615, 635, 636, 712
Stamp, Terence
ILIATM 235-236
GS 26
TIAI 224
H 120, 173, 174
5001 72, 145, 237, 416, 482, 589, 730, 731,
748
Stand by Me
H 197-199
5001 (2nd ed)
"Stand by Me" (music)
TIAI 32
Stand-In
5001
Stander, Lionel
KKBB 299, 364
WTLGD 123
5001 76, 170, 277, 353, 356, 440, 474, 487,
521, 531, 700, 707, 806
Standiford, Jim
H 148
5001 816
Standing, Sir Guy
KKBB 163
5001 428
Stang, Arnold
DIM 348
5001 462
Stangertz, Göran
TIAI 477
5001 252
Stanislavski, Constantin
WTLGD 335
Stanley, Florence
5001 260, 559
Stanley, Frank
5001 118, 156
Stanley, Kim
KKBB 272
R 87
WTLGD 219, 223
SOTA 62
5001 289, 630
Stanton, Harry Dean
R 428
WTLGD 93, 397
TIAI 93, 244, 297
SOTA 212
H 97, 99, 134
5001 138, 255, 290, 550, 569, 594, 598,
611, 616, 624, 641, 718, 863

Stanwyck, Barbara
ILIATM 131
KKBB 363
DIM 345
R 186, 368
WTLGD 61, 144
TIAI 256, 425, 456
SOTA 107
5001 30, 48, 75, 140, 198, 243, 251, 257,
292, 336, 403, 404, 405, 445, 473, 478,
483, 525, 528, 696, 713, 718, 746, 774,
775
Staples, the (group)
5001 411
Staples, Pops, see Staples, Roebuck
Staples, Roebuck (Pops)
H 219
5001 794
Stapleton, Jean
5001 808
Stapleton, Maureen
ILIATM 172, 174
DIM 137
R 75, 257, 324
WTLGD 438-440
TIAI 279-280, 282
H 5, 6, 190, 392
5001 12, 111, 144, 325, 366, 448, 621, 815
Stapleton, Oliver
H 120, 297
5001 3, 506, 595
Star!
GS 161-165
DIM 26, 328
R 150, 325
5001
Star, The
5001
Star 80
SOTA 91-92, 204
5001 (2nd ed)
Star Is Born, A (1937)
KKBB 272, 283, 363
R 75
WTLGD 240, 244
5001
Star Is Born, A (1954)
ILIATM 207
KKBB 272
WTLGD 240, 241, 243, 244
TIAI 45, 277
5001
Star Is Born, A (1976)
WTLGD 240-244, 434
5001
"Star-Spangled Banner, The" (music)
DIM 228, 325
WTLGD 273
TIAI 286
Star Spangled Girl
DIM 369
5001
Star Trek--The Motion Picture
TIAI 355, 356
Star Trek II: The Wrath of Khan
TIAI 355-360
SOTA 197-198

5001 (2nd ed)
Star Trek III: The Search for Spock
SOTA 196-198
5001 (2nd ed)
Star Trek IV: The Voyage Home
5001 (2nd ed)
"Star Trek" (TV)
TIAI 114, 356, 359
Star Wars
WTLGD 291, 295, 350, 353, 527
TIAI 8, 182, 208, 211, 212, 308, 389, 481,
482, 485
SOTA 217
5001 (2nd ed)
Star Wars trilogy
SOTA 177
H 473
Stardust
WTLGD 553
5001
Stardust Memories
TIAI 86-92, 365
H 115
5001
Stark, Cecillia
SOTA 262
Stark, Graham
5001 14
Stark, Ray
R 459, 461
WTLGD 123
TIAI 344
5001 29, 76, 115, 238, 272, 296, 559, 622,
628, 730, 825
Starkweather, Charles
R 302
Starling, Lynn
5001 322
Starman
SOTA 306-308
5001 (2nd ed)
Starr, Ben
5001 555
Starr, Blaze
ML 221-25
5001 80
Starr, Ringo
KKBB 117
GS 224
TIAI 1'95, 196, 197, 394
5001 117, 127, 411, 450
Starrett, Charles
GS 185
SOTA 338
5001 469, 645
Starrett, Jack
5001 141
Stars Look Down, The
ILIATM 47, 297
KKBB 321, 349-351:n
GS 202
5001
"Starsky and Hutch" (TV)
WTLGD 200
TIAI 188, 384
Starstruck
SOTA 292

H 432
Start the Revolution Without Me
DIM 123
R 403
H 484
5001
Starting Over
TIAI 248
State Fair (1933)
5001
State Fair (1945)
5001
State of Siege
R 163, 210, 213-215
WTLGD 96
TIAI 312
H 182
State of the Union
5001
Stavisky
R 416-420
5001
"Stay with Me" (music)
TIAI 95, 123
"Stay" (music)
H 349
"Stayin' Alive" (music)
SOTA 36
Staying Alive
SOTA 34-37, 169
ML 73
5001 (2nd ed)
Steadicam
TIAI 1, 36
Steadman, Alison
5001 7
Steagle, The
DIM 314
Steamboat Bill, Jr.
ILIATM 277
TIAI 120
5001
Steamboat Round the Bend
5001
Steegmuller, Francis
DIM 364
TIAI 183
Steel, Anthony
KKBB 294
5001 413
Steel, Dawn
ML 168
Steel Helmet, The
SOTA 181
Steele, Barbara
TIAI 193
5001 78, 213
Steele, Bob
5001 540, 631
Steele, Freddie
5001 258, 313
Steele, Karen
5001 467
Steele, Marjorie
5001 101
Steele, Robert
5001 220

Steele, Tommy
GS 159
5001 244
Steelyard Blues
R 119-120, 245
5001
Steeman, S. A.
5001 607
Steen, Peter
R 102
Steenburgen, Mary
WTLGD 508
TIAI 74, 75, 266, 365, 366-367
SOTA 56, 57
ML 141-44
5001 164, 290, 474, 479, 485, 612, 772
Stefanelli, Simonetta
DIM 424
5001 289
Stefano, Joseph
5001 514
Steibel, Warren
5001 339
Steiger, Rod
ILIATM 51, 159
KKBB 88, 161, 238, 299
GS 74-75, 109-110, 240-242
DIM 330, 348-349
R 187
TIAI 213
5001 4, 70, 126, 195, 317, 360, 440, 467,
546, 571, 616
Stein, Gertrude
ILIATM 217
Stein, John
5001 570
Stein, Joseph
DIM 332
TIAI 394
5001 242
Stein, Margaret Sophie
ML 229-33
5001 219
Stein, Paul L.
5001 482
Steinbeck, John
KKBB 276, 366-367
WTLGD 84, 225, 226
5001 209, 301, 421, 540, 782, 818
Steinberg, Norman
TIAI 395
5001 81, 508
Steiner, Max
KKBB 296, 361
DIM 104
R 346
WTLGD 178, 239
H 82
5001 36, 67, 74, 99, 130, 137, 155, 250,
278, 306, 363, 380, 392, 419, 428, 536,
628, 653, 662, 781, 788
Steinhilber, Budd
5001 273
Stelfox, Shirley
H 302
5001 577
Stella

KKBB 271, 351:n
DIM 246
5001
Stella Dallas
R 75
WTLGD 144-145
TIAI 141
SOTA 111
H 432
5001
Stellman, Martin
H 278
5001 183
Stemmle, R. A.
5001 184
Sten, Anna
5001 689
Stendhal
ILIATM 67
KKBB 124
TIAI 158
5001 61, 619
Step Lively
5001
Stepfather, The
H 260-263
ML 82, 83, 85, 327
5001 (2nd ed)
Stepford Wives, The
R 442-446
5001
Stephan, Aram
5001 268
Stéphane, Nicole
KKBB 262
GS 6
DIM 364
5001 220
Stephens, Harvey
5001 225-226
Stephens, Martin
ILIATM 167
5001 365, 815
Stephens, Robert
GS 288
DIM 186-187
WTLGD 382
H 451
ML 217, 317
5001 206, 329, 332, 497, 595, 599, 788
Stephenson, Henry
5001 72, 118, 130, 153, 428, 505, 524, 543,
620, 628, 760
Stephenson, James
KKBB 295
5001 419, 543, 600
Stephenson, Pamela
SOTA 8
5001 731
Steppat, Ilse
DIM 86
5001 545
"Steptoe and Son" (TV)
WTLGD 150
Sterile Cuckoo, The
DIM 31-34
5001

Sterling, Ford
WTLGD 9
Sterling, Jan
5001 4, 382
Sterling, Robert
5001 382, 679
Sterling, Thomas
5001 339
Stern, Bert
R 151
5001 379
Stern, Daniel
TIAI 320, 485
5001 87, 190, 316
Stern, Isaac
DIM 328, 332
SOTA 125
5001 242, 345
Stern, Leonard
5001 743, 766
Stern, Miroslava
5001 163
Stern, Richard Martin
5001 785
Stern, Sandor
TIAI 16
Stern, Stewart
R 223, 225
5001 409, 618, 727, 802
Sternberg, Josef von, see von Sternberg, Josef
Sterne, Laurence
H 431
Sternhagen, Frances
TIAI 219
H 459
5001 103, 361, 558, 800, 808
Stevenin, Jean-François
WTLGD 168
TIAI 167
5001 197
Stevens, Andrew
WTLGD 419
5001 98, 273
Stevens, Ashton
RK 35
Stevens, Cat
5001 320
Stevens, Craig
5001 345
Stevens, Fisher
5001 679
Stevens, George
ILIATM 241; dir., *Gunga Din*, 24, 241;
Swingtime, 24; *A Place in the Sun*, 81;
Shane, 82-83, 240-241
KKBB 230, 274, 278, 331-332, 336, 347;
dir., *Talk of the Town*, 68; *Gunga Din*,
180, 184, 278; *Alice Adams*, 229-230;
Quality Street, 241, 336; *Woman of the
Year*, 330; *A Place in the Sun*, 331-332;
Shane, 347, 368
GS dir., *Alice Adams*, 177; *The Diary of
Anne Frank*, 210
DIM 122; dir., *The Only Game in Town*,
122-123, 407; *Vivacious Lady*, 184;
Alice Adams, 311
WTLGD 17, 18, 228, 304, 513; dir., *Gunga*

Din, 17, 18, 19, 23, 29, 107; *Penny
Serenade*, 20, 21; *The Talk of the Town*,
22; *Shane*, 40; *Woman of the Year*, 61;
A Place in the Sun, 178, 304, 479; *Alice
Adams*, 209
TIAI 385; dir., *Shane*, 20, 385; *Gunga Din*,
209; *Woman of the Year*, 254; *The Only
Game in Town*, 412; *Giant*, 415, 480
ML 156
5001 14, 30, 284, 292, 310, 351, 391, 497,
575, 584, 607, 671, 742, 815, 818, 831,
845
Stevens, George Jr.
WTLGD 178-179
Stevens, Gösta
5001 366
Stevens, Inger
5001 310
Stevens, K. T.
5001 89
Stevens, Leslie
KKBB 60
5001 416
Stevens, Onslow
KKBB 252
5001 156, 547
Stevens, Robert
H 451
Stevens, Robert, Secretary of the Army
ILIATM 327-328
Stevens, Stella
KKBB 90
GS 18, 22, 24
DIM 28
R 71, 72
WTLGD 248
5001 48, 523, 537, 591, 681
Stevens, Warren
KKBB 234
5001 51
Stevenson, Adlai
KKBB 94
WTLGD 530
Stevenson, Parker
5001 422
Stevenson, Robert (actor)
5001 352
Stevenson, Robert (director)
DIM 360; dir., *Bedknobs and Broomsticks*,
359-360
5001 60, 529
Stevenson, Robert Louis
5001 393
Stevenson, Venetia
5001 724
Stevie
SOTA 332
Steward, Kenny
5001 679
Stewart, Alexandra
WTLGD 82
5001 77, 266
Stewart, Bill
SOTA 76
Stewart, Charlotte
5001 224
Stewart, Donald

TIAI 311
5001 486
Stewart, Donald Ogden
  RK 10
  TIAI 434
  5001 52, 190, 336, 391, 400, 413, 421, 580,
    597, 741, 744, 843, 847
Stewart, Douglas Day
  TIAI 28, 29, 381, 383
  5001 86, 540
Stewart, Elaine
  KKBB 233
  5001 46, 103
Stewart, Fred
  5001 702
Stewart, James
  KKBB 42, 184, 185, 190, 256
  GS 98
  RK 20
  R 186, 195
  WTLGD 4, 5, 178, 227, 451
  ML 127
  5001 9, 93, 107, 185, 287, 305, 343, 353,
    373, 374, 448, 460, 461, 488, 522, 531,
    532, 580, 642, 677, 678, 800, 818, 836,
    837, 865
Stewart, Mel
  R 114
  WTLGD 66
  5001 407, 418, 789
Stewart, Michael
  5001 111
Stewart, Nick
  5001 120
Stewart, Patrick
  ML 328
Stewart, Paul
  KKBB 249
  TIAI 391
  5001 46, 138, 144, 382, 488, 746
Stewart, Rod
  TIAI 148
  H 337
Stewart, Sophie
  5001 36
Stick
  SOTA 368-369
  5001 (2nd ed)
Stickney, Dorothy
  5001 126, 351, 496, 502, 807
Stiers, David Ogden
  ML 13, 69
  5001 3, 31
Stigwood, Robert
  5001 655, 699
Still of the Night
  TIAI 426-428
  5001 (2nd ed)
Stiller, Jerry
  H 352, 443
  5001 313, 513, 517
Stiller, Mauritz
  R 328
  5001 649
Stine, Clifford
  5001 802
Stine, Harold E.

DIM 94
5001 469
Sting (Gordon Sumner)
  SOTA 284
  H 42
  ML 107
  5001 7, 207, 587, 692
Sting, The
  R 244-245, 302, 314-315, 318, 321-322,
    422, 468
  WTLGD 67, 106, 273, 275
  TIAI 390
  H 13
  5001
Stinson, Joseph C.
  5001 725
Stir Crazy
  TIAI 325
Stock, Nigel
  H 100
  5001 423, 860
Stockwell, Dean
  ILIATM 72
  KKBB 250, 298
  H 206, 306
  5001 25, 87, 151, 200, 207, 279, 409, 432,
    695
Stockwell, Guy
  5001 58
Stoddard, Brandon
  R 324-325
Stoker, Bram
  KKBB 319
  5001 201, 534
Stokowski, Leopold
  GS 192
  R 38
  SOTA 154
  5001 236
Stolen Holiday
  R 419
Stolen Kisses (Baisers volés)
  GS 273-276
  DIM 243, 244
  5001 (2nd ed)
Stolen Life, A
  KKBB 350
  WTLGD 504
Stoler, Shirley
  DIM 106
  WTLGD 137, 517
  5001 183, 185, 339, 667
Stoltz, Eric
  ML 136
  5001 656
Stompanato, Johnny
  H 426
Stone, Andrew L.
  DIM 187; dir., *Song of Norway*, 187, 242,
    359
  5001 304, 694, 716
Stone, Arnold M.
  H 2, 3-4
  5001 663
Stone, Christopher
  TIAI 192
  5001 343

Stone, David C.
  5001 314, 480
Stone, Fred
  KKBB 230
  WTLGD 471
  5001 15, 787, 829
Stone, George E.
  5001 137, 262, 425, 462, 581, 692, 856
Stone, Grace Zaring
  5001 75
Stone, Harold J.
  5001 129, 850, 852
Stone, Irving
  5001 11, 443
Stone, James
  5001 52
Stone, Lewis
  KKBB 210, 275
  5001 134, 299, 353, 438, 469, 597, 620,
    711, 733, 845
Stone, Milburn
  5001 581, 728
Stone, Oliver
  WTLGD 496
  SOTA 100, 102, 103, 105
  H 31, 32, 33, 34, 35, 156, 157, 180-185,
    250-254; dir., *Salvador*, 180-185, 251,
    254; *Seizure*, 183; *The Hand*, 183;
    Platoon, 250-254, 305, 353
  ML dir., *Born on the Fourth of July*, 249-55;
    Platoon, 251; *Salvador*, 84
  5001 93, 213, 479, 586, 651, 657, 854
Stone, Peter
  GS 57
  R 54, 366
  WTLGD 482-483
  H 299
  ML 12
  5001 130, 239, 664, 668, 685, 734, 741, 836
Stone, Philip
  TIAI 2
Stone Promotions
  DIM 208
Stone, Robert
  DIM 182
  5001 851
Stone, Virginia
  5001 694
Stones of Florence, The (book)
  KKBB 97
Stong, Phil
  5001 711
Stop Making Sense
  SOTA 265-267, 327
  H 217, 218, 232, 285
  5001 (2nd ed)
Stoppa, Paolo
  KKBB 310
  SOTA 52
  5001 9, 59, 417, 483, 635
Stoppard, Tom
  WTLGD 93, 95
  SOTA 326
  H 107, 414
  5001 98, 217, 638
Stora Äventyret, Det, see *The Great Adventure*
Storaro, Vittorio

R 33
WTLGD 327, 551
TIAI 177, 281, 298, 314
H 310, 395
ML 103, 302, 394
5001 10, 152, 371, 406, 408, 410, 530, 621,
    701
Storch, Arthur
    5001 719
Storch, Larry
    5001 301, 690
Storey, David
    ILIATM 18
    5001 763
Storm, Gale
    DIM 296
Storm Warning
    DIM 296, 297
Storm Within, The, see *Les Parents terribles*
Stormy Monday
    ML 263, 277
Stormy Weather
    5001
Story of a Cheat, The
    KKBB 301
Story of Adèle H., The (*L'Histoire d'Adèle H.*)
    WTLGD 55-60
    5001
Story of Robin Hood, The (1952)
    5001
Story of the Lost Reflection, The (book)
    H 61-63
Story of Vernon and Irene Castle, The
    5001
Story on Page One, The
    WTLGD 23
Stossel, Ludwig
    5001 20, 115, 122, 457
Stothart, Herbert
    5001 201, 294, 505
Stout, Archie
    5001 728
Stout, Rex
    5001 473
Stowe, Madeleine
    H 349, 350
    5001 704, 799
Stowell, Kent
    H 241, 242
    5001 537
Strada, La
    ILIATM 192
    KKBB 318, 351:n
    GS 46
    H 268-269
    5001
Stradling, Harry
    KKBB 245
    5001 26, 121, 366, 581, 605, 722
Stradling, Harry Jr.
    5001 121, 155, 424, 752
Stradner, Rose
    5001 392
Straight Arrow Books
    WTLGD 467
Straight, Beatrice
    WTLGD 221

TIAI 352
5001 219, 519, 588
Straight, Place, and Show
    KKBB 6
    5001
Straight Time
    WTLGD 552
    TIAI 244
    ML 80
    5001
Stranger, The (1946)
    5001
Stranger, The (*Lo Straniero*; 1967)
    GS 30, 35
    DIM 68, 193
    WTLGD 38
    5001
Strange, Billy
    DIM 19
Strange Cargo
    5001
Strange Deception, see *Il Cristo Proibito*
Strange Love of Martha Ivers, The
    5001
Strange, Mark
    5001 371
Strange One, The (also known as *End as a Man*)
    5001
Strange Ones, The, see *Les Enfants terribles*
Stranger Than Paradise
    SOTA 260-263
    H 221, 222
    5001 (2nd ed)
Strangers in the House (*Les Inconnus dans la
    maison*)
    5001
Strangers on a Train
    ILIATM 27, 81, 135
    KKBB 352:n
    GS 242
    DIM 261-262
    WTLGD 313
    H 446
    ML 277
    5001
Straniero, Lo, see *The Stranger* (1967)
Strasberg, Lee
    R 153, 156, 401
    5001 290
Strasberg, Susan
    KKBB 249
    5001 144, 498, 790
Strategia del Ragno, see *The Spider's Stratagem*
Strathairn, David
    TIAI 463
    ML 207
    5001 239, 353, 442
Stratten, Dorothy
    SOTA 91-92
Straus, Émile
    SOTA 254
Strauss, Helen M.
    WTLGD 205
    5001 360
Strauss, Johann
    WTLGD 204
    5001 304

Strauss, Richard
    DIM 239
    TIAI 453
    5001 854
Strauss, Robert
    KKBB 349
    5001 462, 668, 705
Stravinsky, Igor
    DIM 242, 304
    TIAI 413
    5001 236, 720
Stravinsky Portrait, A
    5001
Straw Dogs
    DIM 393-399, 426
    SOTA 72
    5001
Strawberry Statement, The
    DIM 149-151
    WTLGD 297
    5001
Streamers
    WTLGD 447
    H 1, 97
    ML 167
Strecha, J.
    5001 367
Streep, Meryl
    WTLGD 514, 517-518
    TIAI 238, 239, 240, 336, 379, 426-427, 428,
        435, 436
    SOTA 106-107, 108, 110-111, 170, 279,
        280, 281
    H 41, 43-44, 76, 78, 79, 189, 190, 192, 421
    ML 30-33, 273-76
    5001 166, 183, 234, 267, 325, 371, 386,
        557, 587, 591, 681, 695, 696, 715
Street of Chance
    5001
Street of Sorrow, The, see *The Joyless Street*
Street Smart
    H 292-294
    5001 (2nd ed)
Streetcar Named Desire, A (1951)
    ILIATM 47, 82
    KKBB 309, 352-353:n
    GS 229
    R 157
    WTLGD 178
    5001
Streetcar Named Desire, A (stage)
    WTLGD 149
Streetcar Named Desire, A (TV, 1984)
    H 99
Streeter, Edward
    5001 240
Streeter, Tim
    ML 195
    5001 454
Streets of Fire
    H 344
Streisand, Barbra
    GS 133-137
    DIM 80-85, 149, 183-185, 353, 383,
        431-432
    R 38, 82, 84, 175-178, 457-463, 466
    WTLGD 3, 61, 140, 167, 209, 236, 240-244

TIAI 95, 155, 156, 157
SOTA 85-91
H 228; dir., *Yentl*, 379
5001 17, 271, 272, 327, 559, 642, 707, 809,
    825, 831, 855
Strick, Joseph
    KKBB 170; dir., *Ulysses*, 169-170; *The
        Balcony*, 170
    DIM 123-127; dir., *Tropic of Cancer*,
        123-127; *The Balcony*, 124; *Ulysses*,
        124
    R 115; dir., *Ulysses*, 17, 115, 449, 450;
        Tropic of Cancer, 411
    WTLGD 177
    TIAI 467; dir., *Tropic of Cancer*, 467
    5001 791, 803
Strick, Wesley
    ML 84
    5001 34, 792
Strickland, Gail
    5001 804
Stride, John
    5001 444
Strike
    KKBB 358
Strike Up the Band
    5001
Strindberg, August
    ILIATM 219
    DIM 109
    R 29, 90, 93, 94
    WTLGD 156, 480
    TIAI 174, 491
    5001 485
Stripes
    TIAI 224-226
    SOTA 192, 193
    5001
Stripper, The
    R 76
    5001
Stritch, Elaine
    WTLGD 255, 258
    H 426, 427
    5001 601, 666
Strode, Woody
    KKBB 334
    TIAI 383
    SOTA 361-362
    5001 461, 601, 670, 699, 800
Stroheim, Erich von, see von Stroheim
Stroker Ace
    SOTA 153
Stromberg, Hunt
    5001 305, 472, 518, 758
Strong Man, The
    5001
Strong, Michael
    5001 588
Stroud, Don
    5001 277
Strouse, Charles
    GS 237
    5001 29, 91, 111, 528
Stroyberg, Annette
    5001 82, 420
Strudwick, Shepperd

5001 19, 585, 623
Strüss, Karl
    5001 384, 729
Struther, Jan
    5001 486
Struthers, Sally
    R 79
    5001 283
Stryker, Amy
    WTLGD 443
    TIAI 260
Stuart, Aimee
    5001 379
Stuart, Don A. see Campbell, John W. Jr.
Stuart, Gloria
    TIAI 397
    5001 291, 369, 508, 542, 637
Stuart, Mel
    5001 356, 840
Stuart Masterson, Mary, see Masterson, Mary
    Stuart
Stubbs, Levi
    H 249-250
    5001 427
Stubbs, Louise
    R 61
    5001 77
Student Prince, The (stage)
    GS 269
Studs Lonigan
    5001
Stulberg, Gordon
    R 387
Stumar, Charles
    5001 501
Stunt Man, The
    TIAI 62-69, 327, 396
    SOTA 11
    ML 72
    5001
Sturges, John
    ILIATM 296; dir., *The Magnificent Seven*,
        121; *Escape from Fort Bravo*, 296; *Bad
        Day at Black Rock*, 296
    KKBB 233; dir., *Bad Day at Black Rock*,
        233
    GS 94; dir., *Bad Day at Black Rock*, 223;
        Escape from Fort Bravo, 223; *The
        Great Escape*, 223; *Ice Station Zebra*,
        222, 223; *The Satan Bug*, 223
    DIM 86; dir., *Marooned*, 86
    R 275-276
    5001 47, 445, 452, 467, 754
Sturges, Preston
    ILIATM 205, 289; dir., *The Lady Eve*, 24,
        81
    KKBB 219, 363, 364; dir., *Unfaithfully
        Yours*, 219, 364; *The Lady Eve*, 363;
        The Palm Beach Story, 363
    GS 158
    RK 10, 12, 18, 28, 36, 50, 52
    DIM 255
    R 241, 301, 328; dir., *Hail the Conquering
        Hero*, 301; *The Miracle of Morgan's
        Creek*, 301
    WTLGD 13, 20, 213, 321; dir., *The Lady
        Eve*, 8; *Hail the Conquering Hero*, 213

TIAI 76, 87; dir., *Sullivan's Travels*, 87; *The
        Lady Eve*, 456
    SOTA 12, 153, 154, 345, 346; dir., *The
        Lady Eve*, 12, 222; *Unfaithfully Yours*
        (1948), 153, 154
    H 110, 112, 291, 395, 480; dir., *Hail the
        Conquering Hero*, 110; *The Miracle of
        Morgan's Creek*, 110
    ML 315
    5001 58, 71, 136, 210, 268, 294, 302, 313,
        355, 404, 483, 522, 562, 593, 726, 760,
        806
Stuyck, Joris
    SOTA 373
Styne, Jule
    5001 25, 272, 311, 714
Styron, William
    TIAI 435, 436
    5001 695
Su, Cong
    5001 408
Subject Was Roses, The
    GS 159-160
    DIM 122
    R 61
    TIAI 244
Sublett, John William see Bubbles
Subor, Michel
    5001 577, 781
Subterraneans, The
    R 48
Such a Gorgeous Kid Like Me
    R 178
    WTLGD 354, 355
Such Good Friends
    DIM 383-384
    5001
Suchet, David
    SOTA 315
    H 478
    5001 233, 849-850
Sucksdorff, Arne
    KKBB 180, 184, 276; dir., *The Great
        Adventure*, 180, 184, 276
    5001 301
Sudden Impact
    SOTA 120-121, 240
    5001 (2nd ed)
Suddenly, Last Summer
    ILIATM 139
    5001
Sudermann, Hermann
    5001 251, 694, 729
Sugar Cane Alley
    ML 185
Sugarland Express, The
    R 300-303, 305, 315, 438, 474
    WTLGD 349
    TIAI 221
    5001
Suggs in the City (stage)
    R 302
Sul-Te-Wan, Madame
    5001 358, 453
Sullavan, Margaret
    KKBB 363
    RK 17, 65

WTLGD 48, 370
SOTA 281
5001 33, 44, 294, 496, 522, 674, 675, 677,
    678, 689, 764
Sullivan, Annie
    KKBB 55
Sullivan, Barry
    KKBB 233
    DIM 77
    5001 35, 46, 209, 404, 541, 572, 746
Sullivan, Ed
    ILIATM 39
    KKBB 53, 178
    H 3
Sullivan, Francis L.
    KKBB 277, 316, 322
    5001 114, 302, 524, 543
Sullivan, Louis
    5001 808
Sullivan, Sean
    TIAI 177
Sullivan's Travels
    TIAI 87
    5001
Sult, see *Hunger*
Summer and Smoke
    ILIATM 137-139
    5001
Summer, Cid Ricketts
    5001 583
Summer Holiday
    5001
Summer Interlude (*Sommarlek*; also known as
    Illicit Interlude)
    KKBB 171, 353:n
    GS 216
    DIM 252
    R 91
    5001
Summer of '42
    DIM 321:n, 391
    WTLGD 446
Summer Stock
    R 59
    5001
"Summer Wind" (music)
    SOTA 205
Summer Wishes, Winter Dreams
    R 222-227, 453
    5001
Summertime
    KKBB 353-354:n
    GS 23
    WTLGD 487
    5001
"Summertime Blues" (music)
    H 342
"Summertime, Summertime" (music)
    WTLGD 415
Summerville, Slim
    KKBB 231
    5001 18, 777
Sumner, Gordon, see Sting
Sun Also Rises, The
    DIM 217
    WTLGD 280
Sun in the Net, The

R 121
Sun Shines Bright, The
    5001
Sun Valley Serenade
    5001
Sunday Bloody Sunday
    DIM 289-293, 424, 426
    5001
Sunday Times (London), see under London
Sunday Woman (*La Donna della Domenica*)
    5001
Sundays and Cybèle (*Les Dimanches de Ville
    d'Avray*)
    ILIATM 246
    5001
Sundberg, Clinton (J. Clinton)
    5001 30, 296, 488, 777
Sunderland, Scott
    5001 605
Sundman, Per Olof
    TIAI 477
    5001 252
Sundowners, The
    GS 108
    DIM 18
    WTLGD 305
    5001 (2nd ed)
Sundquist, Folke
    5001 839
Sunrise
    KKBB 357
    5001
Sunset Boulevard
    ILIATM 140
    KKBB 354-355:n
    GS 49, 66
    R 364
    5001
Sunshine Boys, The
    WTLGD 76-79, 532
    TIAI 276
    H 138
    5001
Super Fly
    R 63-67
    5001
Superman
    WTLGD 524-528, 540
    TIAI 121, 223, 424
    SOTA 8, 10, 225, 357
    H 344
    5001
Superman II
    TIAI 223-224
    SOTA 8, 225
    5001
Superman III
    SOTA 7-12, 225
    5001 (2nd ed)
Supremes (group)
    R 38-39
    WTLGD 165
    H 248
Surtees, Bruce
    TIAI 48
    5001 88, 562, 771
Surtees, Robert

KKBB 233, 286
WTLGD 345, 505-506
5001 46, 146, 299, 304, 368, 397, 409, 491,
    795
Survivors, The
    SOTA 15-18, 159
    H 421, 422
    5001 (2nd ed)
Susan and God
    5001
Susan Lenox, Her Fall and Rise
    WTLGD 142
    5001
Susann, Jacqueline
    R 322
    WTLGD 224
    5001 548
Suschitzky, Peter
    GS 47
    SOTA 279
    5001 131, 218, 234
Suschitzky, Wolfgang
    5001 283
Susi, Carol Ann
    H 300
    5001 664
Susman, Todd
    5001 707
Suspect (1987)
    H 393-394
    5001 (2nd ed)
Suspect, The (1944)
    KKBB 257
    5001 (2nd ed)
Suspicion
    WTLGD 25
    TIAI 37
Susskind, David
    KKBB 192
    GS 102
    DIM 65
    R 413
    TIAI 112
Sutherland, Donald
    DIM 93, 94, 123, 206, 224-227, 254,
        281-282
    R 119-120, 234, 236, 475
    WTLGD 200, 328-331, 333, 346, 522, 539
    TIAI 78, 81
    H 95, 398, 484
    ML 184-85
    5001 5, 12, 176, 198, 205, 240-241, 304,
        368, 400, 427, 469, 502, 530, 553, 627,
        710, 711, 713, 768
Sutherland, Edward (Eddie)
    5001 97, 254, 566, 590
Sutherland, Kiefer
    H 459
    5001 103, 250, 705
Sutton, Dudley
    ML 139
    5001 614
Sutton, Grady
    KKBB 299, 314
    5001 25, 130, 322, 350, 459, 509, 703, 819
Sutton, John
    5001 369, 572, 767

Sutton, Kay
  5001 119
Suzman, Janet
  DIM 368, 369
  SOTA 31
  ML 185
  5001 202, 205, 522, 819
Suzuki, Hideo
  KKBB 271; dir., *A Girl in the Mist*, 271
  5001 287
Suzy
  WTLGD 15, 27
  5001
Svengali
  KKBB 355:n
  5001
Svenson, Bo
  5001 304, 325
Svierkier, Anna
  KKBB 254
  5001 176
Svoboda, Josef
  SOTA 252
Swaggart, Jimmy
  H 438, 442
Swaim, Bob
  H dir., *Masquerade*, 444-446
  5001 469
Swain, Jon
  SOTA 275, 277
Swain, Mack
  KKBB 273
  R 128
  WTLGD 9
  5001 292, 831
Swan Lake (ballet)
  DIM 235, 243
Swan, The
  SOTA 111
Swanagan, Don
  WTLGD 558-559
  5001 823
Swann in Love (*Un Amour de Swann*)
  SOTA 237
  5001 (2nd ed)
Swanson, Gloria
  KKBB 328, 354-355
  RK 69, 70
  R 364
  5001 12, 485, 565, 730, 831
Swarm, The
  WTLGD 325
Swarthout, Miles Hood
  5001 677
Swayze, Patrick
  SOTA 119
  H 346, 347, 348-349
  5001 190, 804
Sweeney, D. B.
  H 303, 305
  5001 279
Sweeney, Joseph
  5001 795
Sweet Bird of Youth
  5001
Sweet, Blanche
  5001 41, 385

Sweet Charity
  DIM 26, 409
  R 372
  5001
Sweet, Dolph
  TIAI 282
Sweet Dreams
  H 48-51, 234, 342
  5001 (2nd ed)
"Sweet Georgia Brown" (music)
  SOTA 112
Sweet Hours (*Dolces Horas*)
  TIAI 409-411
  H 469
  5001 (2nd ed)
Sweet Liberty
  H 161-164, 167
  5001 (2nd ed)
Sweet November
  GS 38-40
  TIAI 415
Sweet Rosie O'Grady
  5001
Sweet Smell of Success
  ILIATM 24
  KKBB 33, 263, 348, 356:n
  GS 102
  RK 28
  DIM 252, 318
  WTLGD 37, 219
  TIAI 173, 323
  5001
Sweet Sweetback's Baadasssss Song
  R 62, 64
Sweethearts
  5001
Swept Away by an Unusual Destiny in the Blue
    Sea of August (*Travolti da un Insolito*
    Destino nell'Azzuro Mare D'Agosto)
  WTLGD 99, 135-138, 393
  5001
Swenson, Inga
  5001 8, 483
Swerling, Jo
  RK 30
  5001 83, 257, 311, 415, 421, 448, 464, 483,
    586, 747, 829, 836
Swift, Jonathan
  KKBB 120
  DIM 221
  5001 61
Swimmer, The
  WTLGD 37
Swimming to Cambodia
  H 284-286
  5001 (2nd ed)
Swinburne, Nora
  5001 632
Swindlers, The, see *Il Bidone*
Swing Shift
  SOTA 165-169
  5001 (2nd ed)
Swing Time
  ILIATM 24
  R 57, 59
Swink, Robert
  5001 637

Swit, Loretta
  5001 267, 690
Switching Channels
  H 447-449
  5001 (2nd ed)
Syberberg, Hans-Jürgen
  TIAI 299; dir., *Our Hitler*, 299
Sybil (TV)
  WTLGD 267
  TIAI 153, 289
  ML 19
Sydney, Basil
  5001 114, 315, 376
Sydow, Max von, see von Sydow, Max
Sykes, Brenda
  5001 44, 141
Sykes, Eric
  5001 670
Sylbert, Anthea
  WTLGD 307
Sylbert, Paul
  TIAI 228
  5001 44
Sylbert, Richard
  5001 43, 135, 156, 299, 643, 702
Sylvester
  5001 641
Sylvester, Harold
  SOTA 117
  5001 804
Sylvia Scarlett
  WTLGD 7, 201
  SOTA 86
  5001
Sylvie
  KKBB 110
  5001 670
Sylvie and the Phantom (*Sylvie et le fantôme*)
  5001
Sylvie et le fantôme, see *Sylvie and the Phantom*
Sylwan, Kari
  R 89
  5001 161
Symbionese Liberation Army (S.L.A.)
  WTLGD 223
  ML 8-11
Symonds, Robert
  5001 478
Symons, Arthur
  WTLGD 205
"Sympathy for the Devil" (music)
  DIM 210
Symphonie pastorale, La
  KKBB 356:n
  5001
Syms, Sylvia
  KKBB 263, 369
  5001 229, 814, 844
Syrett, Netta
  5001 846
Syskonbadd 1782, see *My Sister, My Love*
Szabó, István
  TIAI 337-340; dir., *Mephisto*, 337-340
  5001 476, 477
Szabo, Laszlo
  5001 20
Szalapski, James

TIAI 204-207; dir., *Heartworn Highways*,
204-207
5001 326
Szarabajka, Keith
5001 465
Sze, Yang
5001 221
Szekely, Hans
5001 184

T

T. R. Baskin
DIM 311-313
R 117
5001
Tabori, George
GS 171
5001 349
Tabu
KKBB 356-357:n
5001
Tacchella, Jean-Claude
5001 159
Tafler, Sydney
GS 211
5001 6, 14, 75, 569
Tafuri, Sara
TIAI 319
Taggart, Rita
H 381
5001 718, 826
Tagore, Rabindranath
ILIATM 249, 251, 253-254
SOTA 380
5001 337, 798
Tagore, Sharmila
ILIATM 254
R 140-143
5001 176, 186, 850
Takakura, Ken
5001 853
Takemitsu, Toru
H 89
5001 615
Take Me Out to the Ball Game
5001
"Take Me to the River" (music)
SOTA 267
"Take My Hand, Precious Lord" (music)
TIAI 471
Take the Money and Run
DIM 13, 60
R 244
Taking of Pelham One Two Three, The
R 365-366
5001
Taking Off
DIM 351
WTLGD 89
TIAI 175
Talbot, Lyle
5001 253, 303, 322, 542, 767, 796
Talbott, Gloria

5001 19
Talchi, Vera
5001 822
Tale of Two Cities, A (1935)
TIAI 358
5001
Tales of Hoffmann
ILIATM 286
TIAI 363
5001
Tales of Manhattan
5001
Tales of Mystery and Imagination (book)
KKBB 147
Tales of Ordinary Madness
TIAI 466-469
H 385, 463
5001 (2nd ed)
Talk of the Town, The
KKBB 68
WTLGD 22
5001
"Talk with Mother, A," see "Conversing with
Mother"
Talking Heads (rock group)
SOTA 265-267
H 216, 217, 218
5001 716, 793, 794
Tall Guy, The
ML 270-272
5001 (2nd ed)
Tallchief, Maria
5001 481
Tallman, Patricia
TIAI 199
5001 401
Talmadge, Constance
5001 367
Tamarind Seed, The
TIAI 332
Tamblyn, Russ (Rusty)
ILIATM 11
5001 240, 321, 409, 667, 828
Taming of the Shrew, The
KKBB 288
GS 105, 153
Tamiroff, Akim
KKBB 361
WTLGD 394
5001 9, 20, 31, 117, 128, 134, 184, 201,
248, 256, 288, 301, 302, 333, 429, 435,
483, 700, 781, 783, 784, 789
Tammes, Fred
SOTA 371
5001 677
Tampopo
H 306-309
5001 (2nd ed)
Tanaka, Kinuyo
5001 802
Tandy, Jessica
TIAI 428
SOTA 210
H 6
ML 235-38
5001 64, 74, 94, 144, 204, 259, 715
Tangerine Dream (group)

SOTA 39, 278
5001 325, 519, 632, 756
Tanizaki, Junichiro
ILIATM 160
KKBB 246
SOTA 327, 329
5001 124, 390, 454
Tanner, Alain
WTLGD 179-183; dir., *Jonah Who Will Be
25 in the Year 2000*, 179-183; *The
Middle of the World*, 180
SOTA 137
5001 383
Tanner, Peter
5001 315
Tapeheads
ML 143
Taplin, Jonathan T.
R 174
5001 473
Taps
TIAI 473
Taradash, Daniel
DIM 260
5001 184, 195, 198, 269, 322
Tarascio, Enzo
5001 152
Target (1985)
H 73-75
5001 (2nd ed)
Targets (1968)
5001
Tarkington, Booth
KKBB 229, 304
5001 14, 451
Tarkovsky, Andrei
H 61, 471, 473
Tarloff, Frank
GS 57
5001 239, 310
Tarnished Angels, The
KKBB 357:n
5001
Tarnished Lady
5001
Tars and Spars (stage)
R 131
Tarso, Ignacio Lopez
5001 806
Tartuffe
RK 76
Tarzan and His Mate (1934)
5001
Tarzan of the Apes (book)
SOTA 148
Tarzan, the Ape Man (1932)
TIAI 483
5001
Tarzan's Greatest Adventure (1959)
WTLGD 238
Tashlin, Frank
H 159
5001 20, 524, 550
Tasker, Robert
5001 195
Taste of Honey, A
ILIATM 196-201

KKBB 158
DIM 187
Tate, Nick
  TIAI 267
  5001 188
Tate, Sharon
  DIM 152, 167, 339
Tati, Jacques
  KKBB 185, 290, 311, 312; dir., *Mr. Hulot's
    Holiday*, 185, 312-313; *Jour de Fête*,
    290; *Mon Oncle*, 311
  DIM 308; dir., *Mr. Hulot's Holiday*, 194;
    Mon Oncle, 245
  R 73-74; dir., *Traffic*, 73-74; *Mon Oncle*, 73;
    Jour de Fête, 73; *Mr. Hulot's Holiday*,
    73
  WTLGD 146, 167
  TIAI 120, 421
  H 195
  ML 134
  5001 383, 487, 492, 493, 786
Tattoli, Elda
  GS 5
  5001 134
Taube, Sven-Bertil
  5001 110
Tauber, Richard
  WTLGD 177
Taurog, Norman
  5001 8, 106, 286, 580, 777, 828, 848
Tavernier, Bertrand
  TIAI 442-445; dir., *Coup de Torchon*,
    442-445; *The Judge and the Assassin*,
    443, 445
  5001 158, 644
Taviani, Paolo and Vittorio
  WTLGD 298-302
  TIAI 60, 446-451; dir., *Padre Padrone*, 60,
    416, 447; *The Night of the Shooting
    Stars*, 446-451; *San Miniato, July 1944*,
    448
  H 122-125, 267, 338-341; dirs., *Kaos*, 122-
    125, 340; *Padre Padrone*, 122, 124,
    340; *The Night of the Shooting Stars*,
    122, 123, 124, 268, 340, 369; *Good
    Morning, Babylon*, 338-341
  5001 294, 390, 527, 561
Tavoularis, Dean
  TIAI 297
  5001 91, 290, 424, 550
Taxi Driver
  WTLGD 131-135, 143, 202, 203, 209, 211,
    277, 415, 427, 434, 523, 543
  TIAI 109, 110, 457, 460
  SOTA 344
  H 41, 227
  5001
"Taxi" (TV)
  SOTA 16, 93, 197
  H 154, 379
  ML 39
Taxman, Tamara
  H 268
Taylor, Beverly
  5001 507
Taylor, Chip
  H 232

5001 693
Taylor, Delores
  DIM 341, 342
  R 378, 381-382
  5001 72, 73, 93, 789
Taylor, Don
  KKBB 349
  5001 240, 357, 514, 705
Taylor, Dub
  H 112
  5001 65, 91, 260, 531, 622, 838
Taylor, Dwight
  R 56
  5001 254, 581, 758
Taylor, Elizabeth
  ILIATM 39, 43, 190
  KKBB 184, 185, 225, 285, 316, 332,
    343-344
  GS 9, 33-34, 41, 171
  DIM 112-123, 296, 297, 405-409
  R 115, 452
  WTLGD 178, 211, 282, 424
  TIAI 487
  SOTA 357
  ML 130
  5001 23, 37, 110, 124, 141, 173, 194, 240,
    285, 375, 421, 427, 517, 584, 585, 614,
    621, 622, 653, 725, 805, 834, 852
Taylor, Erich
  5001 579
Taylor, Estelle
  5001 137
Taylor, Gilbert (Gil)
  TIAI 125
  H 266
  5001 60, 250, 624
Taylor, Holland
  5001 638
Taylor, Kent
  5001 298, 357, 572
Taylor, Libby
  5001 302, 357, 647
Taylor, Lili
  ML 134
  5001 656
Taylor, Linda
  5001 309
Taylor, Lisa
  5001 230
Taylor, Renée
  DIM 369-372
  TIAI 463
  5001 442, 448, 601
Taylor, Robert
  ILIATM 48
  KKBB 44, 184, 190, 243
  GS 185, 285
  R 208
  WTLGD 133
  TIAI 183, 345
  SOTA 358
  ML 80
  5001 105, 105, 116, 224, 298, 329, 375,
    382, 451, 765, 824
Taylor, Rod
  KKBB 185
  WTLGD 157

5001 74, 126, 285, 341, 614, 773, 859, 863
Taylor, Ronnie
  5001 166
Taylor, Samuel
  5001 318, 649, 781
Taylor, Telford
  WTLGD 176
Taylor-Young, Leigh
  H 57
  5001 6, 110, 277, 350, 377, 434
Tchaikovsky, Nina
  DIM 239
Tchaikovsky, Peter Ilych
  DIM 239-243
  TIAI 128
  SOTA 153
  5001 504, 537, 658, 806
Tchaikovsky Violin Concerto (music)
  SOTA 153-154
Tcherina, Ludmilla
  5001 441, 621, 741
Te Kanawa, Kiri, see Kanawa, Kiri Te
Teaching Film Custodians
  DIM 145
Teagarden, Jack
  5001 75, 379
Teahouse of the August Moon, The
  5001
Teal, Ray
  5001 4, 839
Tearle, Conway
  KKBB 253
  5001 170
Tearle, Godfrey
  KKBB 359
  5001 761
Teasdale, Verree
  5001 238, 637, 782
Tebaldi, Renata
  H 424
Téchiné, André
  WTLGD 143-147; dir., *French Provincial*,
    143-147; *Barocco*, 145
  TIAI 21; dir., *French Provincial*, 21
  SOTA 48; dir., *French Provincial*, 48;
    Barocco, 48
  5001 267, 268
Technicolor
  WTLGD 62, 486, 503, 556
Teen Kanya, see *Two Daughters*
Teen Wolf
  H 300
Teenage Mutant Ninja Turtles
  5001 (2nd ed)
Teichmann, Howard
  5001 691
Telephone Book, The
  DIM 325
Tell Me Where It Hurts (TV)
  R 325
Tell, Olive
  5001 658
Tell Them Willie Boy Is Here
  DIM 76-78
  R 19, 87
  5001
Temaner, Gerald

DIM 207
Tempest (1982)
  TIAI 389-392
  SOTA 173
  H 371, 482
  5001 (2nd ed)
Tempest, The (stage)
  KKBB 266
  GS 36
  ML 117
Temple, Julien
  H 157-161; dir., *Absolute Beginners*, 157-161, 389
  5001 3
Temple, Shirley
  KKBB 23
  RK 40
  R 299
  WTLGD 20, 62, 86, 165
  TIAI 210, 345
  H 7, 135
  5001 44, 259, 356, 426, 683
Templeton, Fay
  5001 106
Temps modernes, Les (periodical)
  H 86
Temptations (group)
  H 389
10
  TIAI 196, 331, 332, 333
10:30 P.M. Summer
  KKBB 167-168
Ten Cents a Dance
  5001
Ten Commandments, The
  ILIATM 329
  KKBB 205
  5001
Ten Days That Shook the World, see *October*
Ten Days to Die (book)
  KKBB 294
Ten from Your Show of Shows
  R 127-132
  5001
Ten Little Indians (book)
  R 318
  TIAI 258
Tender Is the Night
  GS 10
Tender Mercies
  TIAI 479-481
  SOTA 246, 280
  H 98
  5001 (2nd ed)
Tender Trap, The
  GS 102
Tendeter, Stacey
  R 20
  5001 798
Tennant, Victoria
  SOTA 221, 223-224
  ML 328
  5001 17
Tenniel, John
  H 54
  5001 202
Tennyson, Alfred Lord

WTLGD 19
H 53
5001 508
Tenth Man, The (stage)
  WTLGD 220
Tenth Month, The (TV)
  TIAI 80
10th Victim, The (*La Decima Vittima*)
  5001
Tenue de soirée, see *Ménage*
Teorema
  DIM 9
  5001
Tepper, William
  DIM 350
Tequila Sunrise
  ML 48-52
  5001 (2nd ed)
"Tequila" (music)
  H 59
Ter Steege, Johanna
  ML 292
Teresa, Mother
  H 441
Terminal Man, The
  TIAI 125
  5001
Terminator, The
  H 68, 170, 193, 344
Termo, Leonard
  5001 854
Terms of Endearment
  SOTA 93-97, 246, 338
  H 76, 200, 300, 416, 418
  5001 (2nd ed)
Terra Trema, La
  R 145
  5001
Terrell, John Canada
  H 213
  5001 674
Terris, Malcolm
  WTLGD 539
  5001 304
Terror Train
  SOTA 72
Terry, Alice
  5001 597
Terry, Ellen
  DIM 84
  WTLGD 206
  H 53
Terry, Nigel
  TIAI 183, 185
  5001 227, 423
Terry, Phillip
  5001 48, 437, 776
Terry, Ruth
  5001 13
Terry, Sonny
  5001 165
Terry, Walter
  5001 249
Terry, William
  5001 704
Terry-Thomas
  KKBB 277, 294, 295

5001 306, 310, 357, 779, 861
Terzieff, Laurent
  5001 481
Tesich, Steve
  TIAI 169, 170-171, 284, 285, 286, 376-377
  H 70-71, 72
  5001 214, 230, 264, 849
Tess
  TIAI 134-137
  5001
Tess of the D'Urbervilles (book)
  TIAI 134, 136-137
Tessier, Robert
  WTLGD 41
  5001 93, 318
Tessier, Valentine
  ILIATM 289
  5001 388, 446
Tessitore, Pete
  TIAI 152
  5001 259
Testament
  SOTA 146
"Testament of Youth" (TV)
  SOTA 371
Tester, Desmond
  KKBB 350
  5001 529, 649, 710
Testori, Giovanni
  5001 635
Tetzel, Joan
  5001 206, 243
Tetzlaff, Ted
  5001 316, 509, 536, 793, 850
Teuber, Andreas
  GS 41
  5001 194
Teufels General, Des, see *The Devil's General*
Tevis, Walter
  H 223
  5001 347, 460
Tewkesbury, Joan
  R 269, 271, 447-448
  5001 516, 757
Tex
  TIAI 398-400
  H 316, 317, 445
  5001 (2nd ed)
"Texas" (music)
  TIAI 205
Thackeray, William Makepeace
  WTLGD 101-103, 105
  5001 52
Thackery, Eugene
  5001 807
Thaïs (music)
  RK 67
Thalberg, Irving
  KKBB 317
  RK 5, 22 (ill.), 24, 26, 27, 70
  DIM 216-217
  R 327-328
  WTLGD 105, 216
  TIAI 99
  5001 52, 293, 472, 505, 524, 638
Thalberg, Irving, Mrs., see Norma Shearer
Than, Joseph

5001 182
Thank Your Lucky Stars
5001
Tharp, Twyla
TIAI 265
SOTA 34, 252-253
H 65
5001 21, 835

That Certain Feeling
5001
That Certain Summer (TV)
R 285
That Certain Woman
DIM 157
That Cold Day in the Park
TIAI 415
5001
That Lady in Ermine
ILIATM 306
That Man from Rio (*L'Homme de Rio*)
5001
That Night in Rio
5001
That Obscure Object of Desire (*Cet Obscur Objet du désir*)
WTLGD 363-367
5001
"That Old Black Magic" (music)
DIM 371
That Sinking Feeling
SOTA 269
H 408
That Touch of Mink
GS 18
WTLGD 21, 31
"That's Amore" (music)
H 310, 424
That's Entertainment
WTLGD 27
That's Entertainment. Part 2
WTLGD 178
"That's Motivation" (music)
H 160
Thatcher, Torin
KKBB 252, 277
5001 163, 302, 322, 402, 459, 649
Thaw, Evelyn Nesbit
RK 67
Thaw, Harry K.
RK 67
Thaw, John
5001 166
Thaxter, Phyllis
WTLGD 527
5001 730
Theatre Arts (periodical)
KKBB 204
Théâtre de la Gare
5001 751
Thelen, Jodi
TIAI 284
5001 264
"Theme from *Love Story*" (music)
DIM 219
Themroc
5001

Theodora Goes Wild
KKBB 68
WTLGD 16
5001
Theodorakis, Mikis
DIM 64
R 230
5001 214, 441, 862, 866
Theodorides, Costa
5001 713
Theory of Film, the Redemption of Physical Reality (book)
ILIATM 269-292
There Was a Crooked Man...
DIM 229-230
R 12, 14
5001
There's A Girl in My Soup
DIM 231, 235
5001
There's No Business Like Show Business
5001
Theresa of Lisieux, St. (The Little Flower of Jesus)
H 255-257
Thérèse
H 255-257
5001 (2nd ed)
Thérèse Desqueyroux
TIAI 442
5001
Thérèse Raquin (TV)
H 69
Théry, Jacques
5001 776, 856
These Three
5001
Thesiger, Ernest
ILIATM 7
KKBB 225, 257, 282, 294, 306
5001 102, 114, 185, 328, 341, 408, 413, 457, 459, 542, 637, 695, 794
Thew, Harvey
5001 672, 787
They All Kissed the Bride
5001
"They Call the Wind Maria" (music)
DIM 28
They Drive by Night
5001
They Knew What They Wanted
TIAI 179
5001
They Live by Night
KKBB 48-49
R 268
5001
They Made Me a Criminal
5001
They Shoot Horses, Don't They?
DIM 68-72, 76, 281
R 161, 185, 309
WTLGD 304
TIAI 293
SOTA 81
5001
H 149, 243

"They'll Never Keep Us Down" (music)
WTLGD 253
Thibault, Olivette
5001 510
Thibeau, Jack
5001 725
Thief
TIAI 187-191
SOTA 146
5001
Thief of Bagdad, The (1924)
DIM 320
R 257
TIAI 210
SOTA 180
5001
Thief of Bagdad, The (1940)
KKBB 185
SOTA 98
ML 107
5001
Thief of Paris, The (*Le Voleur*)
DIM 309
5001
Thief Who Came to Dinner, The
R 135-137
WTLGD 141
5001
Thiele, Herthe
KKBB 303
5001 448
Thiele, Rolf
KKBB 340; dir., *Rosemary*, 340
5001 643
Thieves
WTLGD 271-272
5001
Thieves Like Us
R 276-271, 310
WTLGD 86
TIAI 423
H 1, 3
5001
Thigpen, C. H.
5001 765
Thimble Theatre (comic)
TIAI 120
Thin Man series
H 112
Thin Man, The
ILIATM 81
KKBB 241, 358:n
WTLGD 6, 18
5001
Thin Man Goes Home, The
5001
Thing, The (1951; *The Thing From Another World*)
DIM 275
TIAI 192
5001 (2nd ed)
Thing, The (1982)
5001 (2nd ed)
Thing From Another World, The see *The Thing* (1951)
Things Change
ML 27-29

5001 (2nd ed)
Things to Come
   5001
"Think" (music)
   TIAI 26
Thinnes, Roy
   5001 334
Thirard, Armand
   5001 821
Third Man, The
   ILIATM 297
   KKBB 11, 198, 258, 321, 358-359:n
   GS 202
   DIM 415
   R 173, 174, 187
   WTLGD 555
   TIAI 153
   SOTA 194, 195, 196
   H 155, 279
   5001
Thiriet, Maurice
   5001 817
13 Rue Madeleine
   5001
Thirteenth Letter, The
   ILIATM 306
30 Is a Dangerous Age. Cynthia
   GS 63
   5001
39 Steps. The
   ILIATM 294
   KKBB 206, 319, 352, 359:n
   5001
   H 117
Thirty Years of Fun
   KKBB 185
Thirty-Day Princess
   5001
This Angry Age, see *The Sea Wall*
This Gun For Hire
   5001
This Is Elvis
   TIAI 201-204
   5001
This Is My Beloved (book)
   ILIATM 141
"This Is Not America" (music)
   SOTA 314
"This Is One of Those Moments" (music)
   SOTA 86
This Is the Army
   5001
This Is the Night
   WTLGD 6
"This Is Your Life" (TV)
   ML 141
"This Land Is Your Land" (music)
   WTLGD 226, 228
This Man Must Die (*Que la bête meure*)
   DIM 172
   5001
This Sporting Life
   ILIATM 15-18
   GS 281
   5001 (2nd ed)
This Strange Passion, see *El*
This Thing Called Love

5001
Thoeren, Robert
   KKBB 251
   5001 151
Thom, Robert
   GS 90, 107
   5001 181, 417, 838
Thomas, A. E.
   5001 338
Thomas, Anna
   SOTA 130-132
   5001 533
Thomas, Antony
   H dir., *The Kingdom Come, The Will Be Done*, 438-442
   5001 770
Thomas, Bob
   RK 30
Thomas, Brandon
   5001 831
Thomas Crown Affair, The
   GS 92, 111-115, 117, 166
   R 135, 441
   5001 (2nd ed)
Thomas, D. M.
   SOTA 250
Thomas, David
   WTLGD 358
   5001 642
Thomas, Diane
   SOTA 163
   5001 638
Thomas, Dylan
   ILIATM 20
   KKBB 282
   GS 224
   R 114-116
   WTLGD 339
   SOTA 83
   5001 805
Thomas, Frankie
   5001 453
Thomas, Gordon
   5001 819
Thomas, Henry
   TIAI 349-350
   H 75
   ML 219
   5001 225, 611, 812
Thomas, Hugh
   ML 272
   5001 742
Thomas Indra A.
   ML 238
Thomas, Jameson
   5001 373, 487, 580
Thomas, John
   5001 106
Thomas, Marlo
   WTLGD 271-272
   5001 374, 757
Thomas, Michael
   SOTA 357
   ML 129
   5001 406, 656
Thomas, Philip Michael
   WTLGD 166

5001 699
Thomas, Ralph L.
   TIAI 261-263; dir., *Ticket to Heaven*, 261-263
   5001 771
Thomas, Richard
   TIAI 51
Thomas, Trevor
   SOTA 225
   5001 673
Thomerson, Tim
   SOTA 117
   5001 519, 804
Thompson, Brian
   H 453
Thompson, Caroline
   ML 300
Thompson, Emma
   ML 216, 271
   5001 329, 742
Thompson, Ernest
   TIAI 269, 270, 272
   5001 545
Thompson, Fred
   H 55
Thompson, Fred Dalton
   5001 239, 465, 532
Thompson, Harlan
   5001 358, 580
Thompson, J. Lee
   KKBB 369; dir., *Woman in a Dressing Gown*, 369
   5001 844
Thompson, Jack
   TIAI 55, 159
   5001 114
Thompson, Jim
   TIAI 443
   ML 285-86
   5001 158, 283, 570
Thompson, Kay
   5001 271
Thompson, Lea
   H 11, 13
   ML 227
   5001 45
Thompson, Marshall
   KKBB 183
   5001 141, 794, 848
Thompson, Morton
   5001 507
Thompson, Rob
   WTLGD 46
   5001 325
Thompson, Robert E.
   DIM 70
   5001 755
Thompson, Sada
   R 76
   WTLGD 151
Thompson, Shawn
   H 443
   5001 313
Thompson, Slim
   5001 578
Thomson, Alex
   TIAI 187

ML 45
   5001 227, 333, 617, 854
Thomson, Kenneth
   5001 105
Thomson, Kim
   ML 272
   5001 742
Thomson, R. H.
   TIAI 263
   5001 770
Thomson, Virgil
   KKBB 272
   5001 289
Thorin, Donald
   TIAI 189
   SOTA 146, 214
   5001 604, 756
Thornburg, Newton
   5001 167
Thorndike, Sybil
   KKBB 334
   H 296
   5001 155, 453, 523, 529, 596
Thornton-Sherwood, Madeleine
   5001 625
Thoroughly Modern Millie
   KKBB 172
   5001
Thorp, Raymond W.
   R 87
Thorp, Roderick
   5001 185
Thorpe, Richard
   5001 174, 376, 377, 525, 758, 767, 833
Those Lips, Those Eyes
   TIAI 69-71
   5001
Those Magnificent Men in Their Flying
   Machines
   GS 226
Thousand Clowns, A
   KKBB 23
   GS 38
Thousands Cheer
   5001
Three Amigos!
   H 249
Three Broadway Girls, see *The Greeks Had a*
   Word for Them
Three Brothers (Tre Fratelli)
   TIAI 314-320
   SOTA 226
   5001 (2nd ed)
Three Cases of Murder
   KKBB 198
Three Comrades
   GS 10
   5001
Three Daring Daughters
   5001 (2nd ed)
Three Days of the Condor
   WTLGD 42-43, 113, 303
   5001
Three Faces of Eve, The
   5001
Three for the Show
   5001 (2nd ed)

Three Fugitives
   ML 89-90
   5001 (2nd ed)
Three Guineas (book)
   ILIATM 106
Three in the Attic
   GS 276-277
   5001
Three Little Pigs
   DIM 359
Three Little Words
   5001
Three Musketeers, The (1948)
   5001
Three Musketeers, The (The Queen's Diamonds)
   (1973; also known as *The Four*
   Musketeers)
   R 311-312, 348, 352
   WTLGD 49, 535
   TIAI 215
   SOTA 9
   5001 (2nd ed)
Three Musketeers, The (book)
   WTLGD 18
Three Musketeers, The (stage)
   WTLGD 13
Three on a Match
   5001
Three Sisters, The (stage)
   ILIATM 181
   TIAI 174
Three Smart Girls
   5001
Three Stooges, The
   GS 186
   RK 46
   DIM 31, 180, 198
   WTLGD 160
   TIAI 108
   SOTA 202
   H 272
   ML 183
3 Women
   WTLGD 269, 442, 548
   TIAI 157, 417
   H 136
Threepenny Opera, The
   ILIATM 116
   KKBB 302, 340
   TIAI 275
   SOTA 366
   H 158
Three's a Crowd
   5001
Threshold
   SOTA 236
   5001 (2nd ed)
Throne of Blood (Kumonosu-jo)
   ILIATM 244
   KKBB 200
   GS 157
   DIM 139, 336
   TIAI 140
   SOTA 244
   H 91
   5001 (2nd ed)
Through a Glass Darkly

GS 217
R 44
Thu Le, Thuy, see Le, Thuy Thu
Thulin, Ingrid
   KKBB 103-104, 164, 304, 369
   DIM 86, 87
   R 89, 91-92, 94
   5001 104, 161, 169, 310, 451, 525, 839
Thunder Bird, Chief
   5001 30
Thunder in the East
   R 420
Thunder Rock
   5001
Thunderball
   KKBB 183
   5001
Thunderbolt
   5001
Thunderbolt and Lightfoot
   WTLGD 512
Thundering Sword, The, see *Cartouche*
Thurber, James
   RK 18, 30
   5001 55, 663
Thurman, Uma
   ML 58, 109
   5001 7, 171
Thursday's Children
   5001
Thurston, Harry
   5001 25
THX 1138
   5001
Thy Kingdom Come, Thy Will Be Done
   H 438-442
   5001 (2nd ed)
Ticket to Heaven
   TIAI 261-263
   5001
Ticket to Tomahawk, A
   5001
Ticotin, Rachel
   TIAI 154
   5001 260
Tidy, Frank
   SOTA 28, 30, 334
   5001 307, 472, 735
Tidyman, Ernest
   DIM 316
   R 64, 433
   5001 267
Tierney, Gene
   ILIATM 306
   KKBB 316
   DIM 177
   R 435
   5001 8, 78, 253, 283, 326, 413, 415, 524,
     617, 671, 672, 777, 785, 832
Tierney, Harry
   5001 370
Tierney, Lawrence
   H 362, 363
   5001 36, 305, 600, 784
Tiffin, Pamela
   ILIATM 139
   5001 320, 550, 726

Tiger Bay
  ILIATM 66, 77
Tiger Makes Out, The
  DIM 10
Tiger Shark
  5001
Tighe, June
  5001 386
Tight Little Island (also known as *Whisky
  Galore*)
  5001
Tight Spot
  R 284
Tightrope
  SOTA 238-240
  H 16
  5001 (2nd ed)
Tilbury, Zeffie
  KKBB 276
  5001 184, 301, 777
"Till Death Us Do Part" (TV)
  WTLGD 150
Till, Eric
  GS 181; dir., *Hot Millions*, 106
Till the Clouds Roll By
  5001
Tiller, Nadja
  KKBB 340
  5001 563, 643
Tilly, Jennifer
  ML 44
  5001 232, 333
Tilly, Meg
  TIAI 399
  SOTA 70-71
  H 444, 445-446
  ML 278
  5001 69, 469, 750, 799, 812
Tilton, Martha
  5001 858
Time (periodical)
  ILIATM 8, 20, 32, 37, 53, 73, 77, 90-92,
    133-134, 151-153, 169-171, 202, 204,
    212, 224, 323
  KKBB 33-34, 77, 209, 232
  RK 11, 41, 42, 43, 80
  DIM 8
  WTLGD 281
  TIAI 264, 272, 369
  SOTA 335
Time, The (group)
  SOTA 215, 216
  5001 604
Time After Time
  TIAI 75, 355, 359
  5001 (2nd ed)
Time Bandits
  H 106, 108
  5001
Time for Burning, A
  GS 13
  DIM 207
Time in the Sun (*Que Viva Mexico*)
  5001
Time Machine, The (1960)
  ILIATM 177
  KKBB 185

GS 36
  5001
Time of the Cuckoo, The (stage)
  KKBB 354
Time-Life
  WTLGD 235
Times Gone By
  DIM 362
  5001 (2nd ed)
Tin Men
  H 279-282, 350
  ML 278
  5001 (2nd ed)
Tin Pan Alley
  5001
Tinker, Tailor, Soldier, Spy (TV)
  TIAI 168
  H 169, 353
Tiny Tim
  GS 149
Tiomkin, Dmitri
  KKBB 43, 281
  5001 123, 189, 206, 268, 285, 304, 331,
    436, 489, 590, 620, 630, 669, 700, 759,
    829
Tirez sur le pianiste, see *Shoot the Piano Player*
Tisse, Eduard
  KKBB 289
  5001 13, 375, 773
Tissier, Jean
  5001 285, 720
Tissue, Su
  H 231
  5001 693
Titanic
  5001
Titicut Follies
  GS 166
  DIM 20, 21
  R 163
  5001 (2nd ed)
Tito, Marshal
  DIM 201
To an Early Grave (book)
  GS 51-52
To Be or Not to Be (1942)
  SOTA 111
  5001
To Be or Not to Be (1983)
  SOTA 111-112
  5001 (2nd ed)
To Be Young, Gifted and Black (TV)
  WTLGD 188
To Catch a Thief
  GS 23
  WTLGD 3, 25, 30, 31, 304
  5001
To Damascus (stage)
  ILIATM 277
To Die in Madrid (*Mourir à Madrid*)
  KKBB 163
  5001
To Die of Love (*Mourir d'aimer*)
  DIM 418-419
  5001
To Each His Own
  5001

To Have and Have Not
  ILIATM 24, 81, 214, 300, 304, 324
  KKBB 59, 194, 251, 359-360:n
  DIM 235, 237, 413
  WTLGD 281, 282
  ML 48
  5001
To Kill a Mockingbird
  GS 108, 249
  WTLGD 368, 446
  SOTA 248
  5001
To Live and Die in L.A.
  ML 262
"To Remember," see "Recordar"
To Sir, with Love
  GS 40, 109, 150, 152
  DIM 343
  WTLGD 358
  5001 (2nd ed)
To the Lighthouse (TV)
  ML 214
Toast of New Orleans, The
  5001
Tobacco Road
  KKBB 107
  DIM 155
  5001
Toback, James
  R 349
  WTLGD 414-418
  H 370-372; dir., *The Pick-up Artist*, 370-
    372; *Fingers*, 370; *Exposed*, 370
  5001 244, 276, 581
Tobey, Kenneth
  TIAI 192
  5001 352, 364, 759, 822
Tobias, George
  5001 11, 48, 101, 287, 510, 531, 666, 681,
    754, 762, 782, 853
Tobias, Heather
  ML 88
  5001 331
Tobin, Genevieve
  5001 531, 578, 864
Tobin, Vivian
  5001 680
Tobisch, Lotte
  KKBB 294
  5001 410
Tobolowsky, Stephen
  H 218
  ML 192
  5001 100, 486, 794
Today We Live
  5001
Todd, Ann (Amer)
  5001 366, 623
Todd, Ann (Brit)
  KKBB 240, 241, 346
  5001 100, 449, 565, 669, 759
Todd, Bobby
  5001 33
Todd, Michael
  KKBB 255
Todd, Richard
  5001 717

Todd, Thelma
  KKBB 252
  5001 156, 340, 493
Tofano, Sergio
  5001 567
Toffel, André
  KKBB 335
  5001 553
Together Again
  5001
Togliatti, Palmiro
  KKBB 324
Tognazzi, Riki
  TIAI 313
  5001 787
Tognazzi, Ugo
  GS 173
  TIAI 165, 309, 312, 313, 314
  5001 50, 114, 786
Toho Company
  TIAI 139
Toibin, Niall
  H 335
  5001 211
Tokyo Olympiad
  SOTA 327
Tolan, Michael (Lawrence)
  DIM 73
  5001 220, 381
Toland, Gregg
  KKBB 248, 276
  RK 8, 33, 43, 46, 75-79, 84
  5001 48, 66, 139, 178, 301, 335, 366, 393,
      433, 445, 484, 558, 637, 753, 829, 851
Toler, Sidney
  5001 82, 355, 580, 835
Toles-Bey, John
  H 381
  5001 826
Tolkien, J. R. R.
  DIM 60, 230
Tolkin, Mel
  R 131
Tolstoy, Leo
  WTLGD 325, 328, 386, 541
  H 153
  5001 28, 624
Tom, Dick, and Harry
  5001
Tom Jones
  GS 120
  DIM 308
  WTLGD 103
  5001 (2nd ed)
Tom Tom Club, The
  SOTA 267
Tomb of Ligeia
  R 441
Tombes, Andrew
  5001 473
Tomlin, Lily
  R 449, 451
  WTLGD 250, 259-261, 322
  TIAI 160, 162, 164
  SOTA 221, 222, 223, 224
  H 484
  5001 17, 68, 361, 412, 517, 530

Tomlinson, David
  DIM 359, 360
  5001 60
Tomlinson, John
  SOTA 253
Tommy
  WTLGD 83, 200
"Tomorrow" (music)
  TIAI 344
"Tomorrow Belongs to Me" (music)
  DIM 413
Tomorrow Entertainment
  R 263
Tomorrow Is Forever
  5001
"Tomorrow Night" (music)
  SOTA 86
Tone, Franchot
  KKBB 184, 336
  WTLGD 15, 27, 30, 108
  ML 258
  5001 8, 91, 171, 248, 298, 397, 428, 439,
      459, 505, 578, 607, 733, 765, 778
Tonight at 8:30
  5001
"Tonight Show, The" (TV)
  WTLGD 164
Tonite Let's All Make Love in London
  GS 149
Tonti, Aldo
  5001 124, 482, 622
*Too Bad She's Bad (Peccato che Sia una
    Canaglia)*
  5001
"Too Close to Paradise" (music)
  WTLGD 487
Too Hot to Handle
  RK 59
  5001
Too Late Blues
  GS 195
Too Many Crooks
  KKBB 295
  5001 (2nd ed)
Too Many Husbands
  5001
Toomey, Regis
  KKBB 281
  5001 67, 335, 473, 578, 721
Tootsie
  TIAI 428-432
  SOTA 16, 70, 193, 222, 234
  ML 80, 240
  5001 (2nd ed)
Top Gun
  H 168-169, 172, 225, 246, 299
  5001 (2nd ed)
Top Hat
  ILIATM 24
  DIM 381
  R 56-57
  TIAI 276
Top Secret!
  H 484
Topaz (1969)
  DIM 79-80
  5001

Topaze (1933)
  KKBB 355
  5001
Topkapi
  GS 23
  5001
Topkins, Katherine
  5001 402
Topo, El
  DIM 334-340
  R 98-99, 250
  WTLGD 82
  SOTA 164
  5001
Topol (Chaim Topol)
  DIM 328-330
  R 220
  TIAI 124
  5001 123, 242, 250, 256, 602
Topor, Roland
  5001 734
Topper (1937)
  KKBB 363
  WTLGD 7, 16, 17, 30
  SOTA 221-222
  5001
Topper Returns (1941)
  5001
Topper Takes a Trip (1939)
  WTLGD 18
  5001
Tora! Tora! Tora!
  DIM 147-148
  R 209
Torch Song
  5001
Toriel, Caprice
  5001 502
Tormé, Mel
  TIAI 70
  5001 296, 848
Torment (Hets)
  GS 223
  5001
Torn Curtain
  DIM 79
  5001
Torn, Rip
  DIM 36, 126
  R 122-124, 200
  WTLGD 264, 395
  TIAI 44, 411, 413, 467
  SOTA 57, 58
  H 9, 352
  5001 43, 56, 147, 149, 164, 380, 453, 460,
      513, 517, 572, 695, 734, 791
Torre Nilsson, Leopoldo
  ILIATM 22, 24
  5001 233
Torrence, David
  5001 118, 830
Torrence, Ernest
  R 128
  5001 349, 712
Torres, Edwin
  5001 606
Torrid Zone

5001
Törst
 GS 216
 R 90
Tortilla Flat
 5001
Tosi, Mario
 WTLGD 212, 409
 TIAI 64, 117
 5001 66, 624, 625, 724
Tosi, Piero
 5001 180, 364
Totheroh, Dan
 5001 157, 865
Totheroh, Rollie
 5001 292
Toto Il Buono (book)
 KKBB 310
Totò
 KKBB 238
 WTLGD 311
 SOTA 285
 5001 69, 292, 380, 481
Tottenham, Merle
 5001 525
Totter, Audrey
 5001 121, 404, 592, 666
Touch and Go
 H 263-265
 ML 112
 5001 (2nd ed)
Touch of Class, A
 R 180, 204, 219, 312, 432
 WTLGD 27, 147
Touch of Evil
 ILIATM 277
 KKBB 360-361:n
 WTLGD 394, 420
 TIAI 327
 5001
 ML 270, 317
Touch of Larceny, A
 ILIATM 207
 5001
Touch, The
 DIM 348
 R 418
 WTLGD 390
Touchstone, see Disney Studios
Tough Guys Don't Dance
 H 362-364
 5001 (2nd ed)
Toulouse-Lautrec, Henri de
 DIM 412
 WTLGD 165
 TIAI 95
Toumanova, Tamara
 5001 369, 782
"Tourbillon, Le" (music)
 TIAI 46
Tourneur, Jacques
 KKBB 247; dir., *The Cat People*, 246-247,
  365
 SOTA 145
 5001 125, 557, 741
Tourneur, Maurice
 5001 339, 511, 815, 819

Tournier, Jean
 5001 496, 743
Toussaint, Lorraine
 ML 192
 5001 100
Tout va bien
 5001
Toutain, Roland
 KKBB 343
 5001 647
Tovarich
 5001
Towering Inferno, The
 R 318, 387, 405-407
 WTLGD 106, 121, 238, 325
 5001
Towne, Gene
 5001 226, 335, 705, 857
Towne, Robert (pseud.: P. H. Vazak)
 R 272-273, 311, 438, 441-442, 470
 WTLGD 404
 TIAI 302-307, 423; dir., *Personal Best*,
  302-307
 SOTA 148, 150, 168, 170
 H 371
 ML 29; dir., *Tequila Sunrise*, 48-52
 5001 91, 135, 138, 308, 407, 576, 581, 670,
  738, 748, 799, 853
Towne, Roger
 SOTA 170
 5001 518
Towns, Colin
 ML 151
 5001 812
Townsend, Jill
 5001 667
Townsend, Robert
 SOTA 273
Toy, The
 SOTA 357
Toyoda, Shiro
 KKBB 246; dir., *A Cat and Two Women*,
  246
 5001 124
Toys in the Attic
 5001 (2nd ed)
Tra Donne Sole
 DIM 113
Tracey, Ian
 5001 704
Tracy, Arthur
 TIAI 274-275
Tracy, Lee
 KKBB 341
 RK 20
 R 425
 5001 65, 81, 91, 190, 195
Tracy, Spencer
 KKBB 207-208, 228, 233, 330
 GS 34, 177
 RK 20, 36
 DIM 184, 227, 351, 353
 WTLGD 5, 20, 28, 215
 TIAI 241, 254, 429
 H 73, 365
 ML 185, 246, 258
 5001 5, 47, 69, 118, 184, 240, 273, 343,

  363, 384, 391, 409, 420, 464, 472, 534,
  569, 593, 629, 660, 711, 782, 783, 796,
  808, 809, 843, 845
Tracy, William
 5001 677, 722, 777
Trade Winds
 5001
Trading Places
 SOTA 12-14, 192
 5001 (2nd ed)
Tradition of the New, The (book)
 SOTA 41
Traffic
 R 73-74
 5001 (2nd ed)
Tragedia di un Uomo Ridicolo, La, see *Tragedy
  of a Ridiculous Man*
*Tragedy of a Ridiculous Man (La Tragedia di un
  Uomo Ridicolo)*
 TIAI 309, 312-314
 H 395
 5001
Trail, Armitage
 5001 657
Trail of the Lonesome Pine, The
 5001
Trainor, Mary Ellen
 SOTA 164
 5001 638
Trains
 TIAI 353
Tramont, Jean-Claude
 TIAI 155-158; dir., *All Night Long*, 155-158,
  196, 224; *Focal Point*, 156
 5001 17, 37
Tramp, Tramp, Tramp
 5001
Transamerica
 WTLGD 524
 H 21, 22
Transatlantic
 RK 75
Transatlantic Tunnel
 5001
Trapeze
 KKBB 348
 5001
Trapp Family, see *Von Trapp*
Trash
 DIM 153-157
 SOTA 262
 5001
Trauner, Alexander
 WTLGD 108
 5001 438, 461, 599, 817
Travels with My Aunt
 R 97-98
 WTLGD 19, 194
 5001
Traven, B.
 KKBB 362
 5001 788
Travers, Bill
 KKBB 340
 5001 639, 826
Travers, Henry
 5001 48, 201, 332, 369, 374, 446, 669, 684,

855
Travers, Linden
5001 406
Traversée de Paris, La, see *Four Bags Full*
Travis, Nancy
ML 262, 263
5001 367
Travis, Neil
5001 532
Travis, Richard
5001 459
Travolta, John
WTLGD 210, 367-371
TIAI 31, 32, 33, 226, 227, 228-229, 230
SOTA 35, 36, 263, 376
ML 172, 173
5001 84, 122, 654, 655, 678, 712, 809
Travolti da un Insolito Destino nell'Azzuro Mare d'Agosto, see *Swept Away by an Unusual Destiny in the Blue Sea of August*
Treacher, Arthur
KKBB 316
5001 32, 259, 370, 517
Tree, David
5001 605
Treasure of Sierra Madre, The
ILIATM 25, 299-300
KKBB 131, 134, 305, 361-362:n
GS 20
DIM 298
R 270
WTLGD 26, 110, 178, 509
TIAI 387, 388, 479
ML 287
5001
Tre Fratelli, see *Three Brothers*
Tree Grows in Brooklyn, A
KKBB 185
H 477
Tree, Marietta
5001 484
Tremayne, Les
5001 260
Trent's Last Case
KKBB 196
Trevor, Claire
KKBB 313, 364
5001 177, 340, 392, 503, 704, 723, 801
Trevor, Norman
KKBB 253
5001 170
Tri-Star
H 10, 11, 263
Trial (book)
RK 10
Trial, The
KKBB 199
DIM 220
TIAI 330
5001
Trial of Billy Jack, The
R 378-382, 384
5001
Trial of Joan of Arc (*Procès de Jeanne d'Arc*)
ILIATM 22
5001

Trials of Oscar Wilde, The
ILIATM 43
"Tribal Rites of the New Saturday Night" (article)
WTLGD 367
Trick Baby
R 113-114
5001
Triesault, Ivan
5001 681
Trieste, Leopoldo
KKBB 366, 368
5001 290, 817, 825, 835
Trigere, Pauline
5001 99
Trikonis, Gus
5001 828
Trilling, Diana
R 153
Trilling, Lionel
DIM 32
Trintignant, Jean-Louis
KKBB 126, 297
GS 148
DIM 65, 270-271, 273, 274, 413-415
R 201, 215, 258, 421-422
WTLGD 97
SOTA 38, 74, 77, 78
H 396, 397
5001 67, 152, 267, 420, 456, 537, 728, 805, 816, 843, 862
Trip, The
5001
Trip to Bountiful, The
H 92-93
5001 (2nd ed)
Trip to the Moon, A (book)
KKBB 255
TIAI 124
Triple Echo
R 218-220
5001
Tristan and Isolde (music)
WTLGD 82
Tristan, Dorothy
DIM 111
H 380, 382
5001 218, 400, 458, 826
Tristram Shandy (book)
H 431
Triumph of the Will
ILIATM 287
KKBB 323
DIM 207
R 211
Trivas, Victor
5001 719
Trivers, Barry
5001 829
Troell, Jan
R 7-8, 181-182; dir., *The Emigrants*, 6-9, 181-182, 346; *The New Land*, 7, 181-182, 346
WTLGD 478
TIAI 475-479; dir., *Hurricane* (1979), 73; *The Flight of the Eagle*, 475-479; *The Emigrants*, 477; *The New Land*, 477

5001 216, 251, 346, 520, 863
Trog
5001 (2nd ed)
Trojan Women, The
DIM 300-305
5001
Trollflöjten, see *The Magic Flute*
Tropic of Cancer
DIM 123-127
R 411
WTLGD 455
TIAI 467
H 40
5001
Tropic of Capricorn (book)
ILIATM 214
Trosper, Guy
5001 73, 377, 549
Trotsky, Leon
KKBB 21, 358
DIM 369; Trotskyism, 201
Trotter, John Scott
DIM 91
Trotti, Lamar
KKBB 328
5001 13, 205, 359, 560, 713, 752, 860
Troup, Bobby
5001 331
Trouble in Mind
H 136-137
5001 (2nd ed)
Trouble in Paradise
KKBB 363
RK 26
GS 115
5001 (2nd ed)
Trouble with Angels, The
R 364
Trovatore, Il (music)
KKBB 317
Troy, William
RK 36
Troyanovski, Mark
5001 133
Truck, The (*Le Camion*)
WTLGD 291-295
TIAI 21
5001
Truckline Cafe (stage)
R 31
True Believer
ML 83-86, 327
5001 (2nd ed)
True Confession (1937)
KKBB 362
WTLGD 141
5001
True Confessions (1981)
TIAI 241-245, 457
5001
True Detective (periodical)
DIM 106
True Grit
DIM 149
R 260
WTLGD 62, 64
H 16

257

True Heart Susie
   R 269
   5001
True Stories
   H 215-219
   5001 (2nd ed)
Trueman, Paula
   5001 487
Truex, Ernest
   KKBB 281
   5001 44, 170, 335, 374
Truffaut, François
   ILIATM 24-25, 132, 210-218, 221-222, 247;
      dir., *Shoot the Piano Player*, 25,
      210-216, 222, 312; *The 400 Blows*, 132;
      Jules and Jim, 211-212, 216-222
   KKBB 54, 81, 129, 146-150, 310-311, 356,
      360; dir., *Jules and Jim*, 33, 54, 61, 81,
      125, 150; *Shoot the Piano Player*, 54,
      81, 150, 356; *The 400 Blows*, 81, 129,
      310; *Fahrenheit 451*, 146-150; *The
      Mischief-Makers*, 310-311; *Le Peau
      Douce*, 356
   GS dir., *The Bride Wore Black*, 108, 275;
      Fahrenheit 451, 141; *The 400 Blows*,
      273; *Love at Twenty*, 273; *Shoot the
      Piano Player*, 82; *Stolen Kisses*,
      273-276
   RK 3
   DIM 243-245, 307; dir., *Shoot the Piano
      Player*, 92, 243; *Jules and Jim*, 243; *The
      Wild Child*, 243, 245; *The Bride Wore
      Black*, 243; *Stolen Kisses*, 243, 244; *Bed
      and Board*, 243-245; *The 400 Blows*,
      244, 245, 307
   R 18, 21, 178-180, 243; dir., *Two English
      Girls*, 18-21, 178; *Jules and Jim*, 19, 21;
      The Soft Skin, 20; *Day for Night*,
      178-180; *Such a Gorgeous Kid Like Me*,
      178; *Fahrenheit 451*, 179, 236; *Les
      Mistons*, 291; *The 400 Blows*, 291
   WTLGD 53, 55-60, 82, 167-170, 349, 350,
      354-356, 428; dir., *The Wild Child*, 53,
      350; *The Story of Adèle H.*, 55-60; *Jules
      and Jim*, 56; *The 400 Blows*, 57, 168,
      169; *Two English Girls*, 58; *Small
      Change*, 167-170; *The Man Who Loved
      Women*, 354-356; *Such a Gorgeous Kid
      Like Me*, 354, 355
   TIAI 54, 65, 421, 494; dir., *Jules and Jim*,
      46, 48, 49, 50, 280; *Day for Night*, 65
   SOTA 149; dir., *The Wild Child*, 149; *Jules
      and Jim*, 183
   H 61, 63, 471
   ML dir., *Shoot the Piano Player*. 186
   5001 59, 100, 142, 175, 233, 385, 460, 489,
      676, 687, 715, 716, 717, 739, 798, 819,
      865
Trujillo, Rafael
   DIM 135
Truman, Harry S.
   WTLGD 398
Trumbo, Dalton
   KKBB 40, 344
   GS 209
   R 209, 237-238

   ML 251
   5001 228, 248, 310, 322, 400, 565, 637,
      653, 699
Trumbull, Douglas
   WTLGD 350; dir., *Silent Running*, 350, 512
Truscott, John
   DIM 30
Truslow, Sara
   5001 387
Trustman, Alan R.
   5001 109, 763
Truth About Women, The
   5001
"Truth or Consequences" (TV)
   TIAI 72
"Try a Little Tenderness" (music)
   H 134
Tryon, Tom
   5001 851
Trzcinski, Edmund
   KKBB 349
   5001 705
Tselios, Paris
   H 451
   5001 332
Tubbs, William
   5001 821
Tucci, Maria
   SOTA 44
   5001 172, 783
Tucci, Stanley
   ML 224
Tuchock, Wanda
   5001 733
Tucker
   ML 309
Tucker, Forrest
   5001 116, 528, 829, 855
Tucker, Ken
   TIAI 44
Tucker, Larry
   GS 158
   DIM 9-10, 14, 148, 225-227
   WTLGD 130
   5001 13, 89, 350
Tucker, Michael
   H 275, 282
   5001 610, 773
Tucker, Sophie
   5001 106, 254
Tudor Rose, see *Nine Days a Queen*
Tufts, Sonny
   5001 668
Tugend, Harry
   5001 663, 740
Tuggle, Richard
   SOTA 238-240
   5001 771
Tulli, Marco
   KKBB 236
   5001 57
Tully, Tom
   5001 119, 356, 386, 439, 646
Tunberg, Karl
   5001 551, 808
Tune, Tommy
   DIM 381

   5001 96
Tunes of Glory
   5001
Tupamaros, the
   R 213-214
   WTLGD 96
"Turandot" (music)
   SOTA 278
Turgenev, Ivan Sergeyevich
   DIM 162, 163
   WTLGD 328
   5001 245
Turkel, Joseph
   TIAI 2
   5001 570, 674
Turman, Glynn
   WTLGD 391
   SOTA 189
   5001 307
Turn of the Screw, The (book)
   ILIATM 164-165, 168-169, 171
Turner and Hooch
   ML 193
Turner, Angela
   ML 143
   5001 485
Turner, J. M. W.
   WTLGD 432
   TIAI 84
Turner, Kathleen
   TIAI 256
   SOTA 3, 163, 164, 165, 167, 376, 378
   H 219, 220, 447, 448, 449
   ML 67, 70
   5001 3, 90, 462, 573, 600, 638, 738
Turner, Lana
   KKBB 121-123, 232, 333, 363
   GS 108
   DIM 284
   WTLGD 61, 491
   TIAI 108, 180, 357
   H 426
   5001 46, 305, 340, 382, 438, 447, 592, 767,
      800, 865
Turner, Tina
   WTLGD 83
   H 83
Turning Point, The
   WTLGD 342-347, 368, 506
   TIAI 247, 276
   SOTA 89
   H 64
   5001
Turpin, Ben
   KKBB 273
   5001 160, 292, 481, 831
Turpin, Gerry
   5001 861
"Turtle" (story)
   WTLGD 308
Turtle Diary
   H 130-131, 169
   5001 (2nd ed)
Turturro, John
   5001 146
Tushingham, Rita
   ILIATM 197, 199

KKBB 117
DIM 17
5001 59, 195, 401
Tutin, Dorothy
ILIATM 119
R 51-52
WTLGD 83
SOTA 370, 373
5001 62, 163, 358, 655, 677
Tuttle, Frank
5001 307, 637, 761
Tuttle, Lurene
5001 198, 260, 287, 822
Tutto a Posto e Niente in Ordine, see *All Screwed Up*
Twain, Mark (pseud. of Samuel Clemens)
KKBB 185, 307
DIM 124
WTLGD 327, 517
TIAI 117, 354, 372, 483
SOTA 357, 358
H 408
5001 8, 152, 461, 679, 804
Twelfth Night
5001
Twelve Angry Men
ILIATM 40-41
KKBB 70
5001
Twelve Chairs, The
DIM 180, 226
R 281, 405
WTLGD 375
5001
Twentieth Century
ILIATM 304
KKBB 362:n
GS 67
WTLGD 6, 16, 141
TIAI 65, 240, 338, 396
5001
Twentieth Century-Fox
RK 7
DIM 100, 148
R 123, 151, 154, 318, 387, 407
WTLGD 106
TIAI 10, 13, 69, 138
Twenty Million Sweethearts
DIM 284
20,000 Leagues Under the Sea
GS 167
20,000 Years in Sing Sing
5001
Twice in a Lifetime
H 73, 75-76
5001 (2nd ed)
Twiggy
DIM 59, 380-382
WTLGD 333
H 187, 188
ML 22
5001 96, 143, 447, 589
"Twilight Zone, The" (TV)
SOTA 18-23, 109
Twilight Zone--The Movie
SOTA 18-23, 188, 232, 344
ML 147

5001 (2nd ed)
Twilight's Last Gleaming
5001
Twins
ML 81
Twist, John
5001 30
"Twistin' the Night Away" (music)
H 337
Two Cents Worth of Hope (Due Soldi di Speranza)
5001
Two Daughters (Teen Kanya)
ILIATM 251
WTLGD 69
5001
Two English Girls (Les Deux Anglaises et le continent)
ILIATM 217
R 18-21, 178
5001 (2nd ed)
Two for the Seesaw
R 150
Two for the Road
DIM 10
5001
Two Jakes, The
5001 (2nd ed)
Two Men and a Wardrobe (Dwaj Ludzie z Szafa)
5001
Two of Us, The
GS 49-51
Two or Three Things I Know About Her
TIAI 105
H 9
Two People
R 149-150
5001
Two Rode Together
5001
2001: A Space Odyssey
GS 92, 101, 117, 121-124
RK 62
DIM 131
R 216, 276
WTLGD 103, 140, 350-351, 353
TIAI 1, 7, 125, 196, 307
SOTA 64
H 328
5001 (2nd ed)
Two Weeks in Another Town
KKBB 363-364:n
5001
Two Women (La Ciociara)
ILIATM 283
WTLGD 311
5001 (2nd ed)
Two-Way Stretch
ILIATM 128
Tyler, Anne
ML 67, 69
5001 3
Tyler, Bonnie
5001 478
Tyler, Judy
5001 377
Tyler, Tom

5001 704, 829
Tynan, Kathleen
WTLGD 551
5001 10
Tynan, Kenneth
KKBB 256
5001 444
Tyner, Charles
5001 320
Tyrrell, Susan
R 432
TIAI 467
5001 238, 742, 863
Tyson, Cathy
H 164, 166-167
5001 493
Tyson, Cicely
R 3-5, 263-265
5001 39, 697
Tyzack, Margaret
5001 595, 800, 832
Tzavellas, George
5001 31
Tzelniker, Meier
5001 229

U

U.A., see United Artists
"'Uncanny,' The" (essay)
TIAI 6
U.C.L.A.
DIM 5, 171
H 316
U.S.A. (book)
RK 65, 81
Uccello, Paolo
TIAI 447
H 130
Udet, Ernst
KKBB 258
5001 696, 834
UFA
RK 76
TIAI 406
ML 106
Ugarte, Eduardo
5001 163
Uger, Alan
5001 81
Ugetsu
ILIATM 163
ML 124
5001
Uggams, Leslie
R 61
5001 77, 801
Ugly American, The
KKBB 193
5001
Ugly Dachshund, The
KKBB 179-180
Uher, Stefan
R 120-122

Uhry, Alfred
ML 234, 236, 237
5001 204
Ullman, Tracey
H 44
5001 350, 587
Ullmann, Linn
WTLGD 481
Ullmann, Liv
KKBB 171
GS 219, 221
R 8, 89-94, 138-139, 178, 181-182, 345,
346-347
WTLGD 194, 388-391, 476-481
TIAI 378
SOTA 321, 367
H 426
5001 1, 40, 161, 171, 216, 260, 436, 520,
576, 666, 670, 863
Ulmer, Edgar G.
5001 77, 729
Ulric, Lenore
KKBB 243
5001 116
Ultimo Tango a Parigi, see Last Tango in Paris
Ultra Violet
5001 479
Ulysses
KKBB 169-170, 315
DIM 124
R 17, 115, 449, 450
H 402
5001
Umberto D.
ILIATM 149, 247, 284-285, 290
KKBB 247, 269, 283-284, 310, 364:n
DIM 361
H 267, 268, 269
5001
Umbrellas of Cherbourg, The
GS 194, 263, 265, 266, 267
SOTA 85
Umeki, Miyoshi
5001 252
Un Chant d'Amour
ML 195
Unbearable Lightness of Being, The
H 427-432
ML 166, 233
5001 (2nd ed)
Uncle Tom's Cabin (book)
KKBB 276
Uncle Vanya (stage)
R 438
Uncommon Valor
SOTA 116-120
H 348
5001 (2nd ed)
Unconquered, The (Helen Keller in Her Story)
5001
Under Capricorn
5001
Under Fire
SOTA 71-78, 119
H 73, 112, 183, 481
5001 (2nd ed)
Under Milk Wood

R 114-116
5001
"Under the Boardwalk" (music)
ML 73
Under the Roofs of Paris, see Sous les toits do
Paris
"Under the Sea" (music)
ML 228
Under the Volcano
SOTA 198-201
5001 (2nd ed)
Under the Volcano (book)
ML 301
Undercurrent
KKBB 353
Underdown, Edward
KKBB 236
5001 2, 57
Underworld
RK 9, 16, 49
Une chante l'autre pas, L', see One Sings, the
Other Doesn't
Unfaithfully Yours (1948)
KKBB 219, 364:n
SOTA 153, 154
5001
Unfaithfully Yours (1984)
SOTA 153-155, 344
5001 (2nd ed)
Unfinished Business
5001
Unfinished Woman, An (book)
WTLGD 307
Unger, Gladys
5001 739
Unholy Three, The
5001
Uninvited, The
5001
United Artists (U.A.)
DIM 177
R 446
WTLGD 113, 228, 485, 495, 524
TIAI 13, 14, 114
H 21-24
United Auto Workers
WTLGD 408
United Mine Workers
WTLGD 249-253
United States Information Agency
WTLGD 178, 179
Universal Pictures
RK 17, 67
DIM 91
R 123, 150, 318, 365, 385, 387
WTLGD 62, 64, 119, 121, 469
TIAI 158, 312
H 109
Universal Studios, see Universal Pictures
University of Michigan
H 1
Unlisted Jazz Band (group)
5001 535
Unmarried Woman, An
WTLGD 410-414
TIAI 47, 49, 135
SOTA 108, 135

H 105
5001
Unseen Enemy, An
R 179
Unsworth, Geoffrey
DIM 413
R 277, 390
WTLGD 525, 540
5001 2, 112, 163, 304, 461, 470, 503, 528,
555, 645, 717, 731, 749, 800, 864
Untouchables, The
H 318-323
ML 145, 167
5001 (2nd ed)
"Untouchables, The" (TV)
H 322
Unwed Father (TV)
WTLGD 467
Up in Arms
KKBB 234
DIM 93
Up in Central Park
5001
Up in Smoke
WTLGD 448-450
TIAI 196
SOTA 283
5001
Up the Down Staircase
DIM 23
TIAI 415
5001
Up the Junction
GS 68-70
Up the River
5001
Up the Sandbox
R 82-84, 463
5001
Up Tight
5001
Updike, John
H 324
5001 843
"Upstairs, Downstairs" (TV)
WTLGD 150
Uptown Saturday Night
WTLGD 67
Urban Cowboy
TIAI 31-34, 42, 212, 229, 382
SOTA 95, 222
H 176
5001
"Urban Cowboy, The" (article)
TIAI 30
Urbisci, Rocco
H 144
5001 381
Ure, Mary
DIM 119
5001 433, 695
Urich, Robert
5001 452
Uris, Leon
DIM 79
5001 781
Used Cars

TIAI 97-100
SOTA 164, 212
H 12, 106, 280, 453
ML 226
5001
Usigli, Rodolfo
5001 163
Ustinov, Peter
ILIATM 235-239; dir., *Billy Budd*, 234-239, 316
DIM dir., *Billy Budd*, 170
WTLGD 465, 466
5001 72, 181, 430, 699, 729, 781, 827
Utt, Kenneth
H 231
5001 693
Utu
SOTA 240-246
5001 (2nd ed)
Utvandrarna, see *The Emigrants*
Uytterhoeven, Pierre
5001 456

V

V Lyudyakh, see *My Apprenticeship*
V.I.P.s, The
DIM 136
Vacances de Monsieur Hulot, Les, see *Mr. Hulot's Holiday*
Vaccaro, Brenda
TIAI 233
5001 479, 548, 866
Vadim, Annette Stroyberg
KKBB 297
Vadim, Roger
KKBB 296-297, 365; dir., *Les Liaisons Dangereuses*, 296-297; *Blood and Roses*, 365
GS dir., *Barbarella*, 172, 173
DIM 222, 225; dir., *Pretty Maids All in a Row*, 225
ML dir., *Les Liaisons Dangereuses*, 60
5001 50, 82, 420, 627, 812
Vadnay, Laslo
5001 251
Vagabond (Sans toit ni loi; literally *Without Roof or Law)*
H 151-153
5001 (2nd ed)
Vagabond King, The
TIAI 70
Vague, Vera (Barbara Jo Allen)
5001 106
Vai, Steve
5001 165
Vail, Lester
5001 169
Vailland, Roger
5001 82
Vajda, Ernest
5001 52, 107, 309, 846
Vajda, Ladislaus
5001 563

Valberg, Y.
5001 510
Valdez, Luis
H 341-343; dir., *La Bamba*, 341-343; *Zoot Suit*, 341
5001 48
Valens, Ritchie
H 341-343
5001 48
Valentine, Joseph
5001 591, 669
Valentino (1951)
WTLGD 140
Valentino (1977)
WTLGD 333-336
5001
Valentino, Rudolph
KKBB 285
RK 15
WTLGD 138, 140, 333-336, 357
TIAI 33, 128
ML 303
5001 83, 811
Valère, Simone
5001 59
Valerie, Jeanne
KKBB 297
5001 416, 420
Valk, Frederick
KKBB 255, 327
5001 145, 178, 558, 769
Vallee, Rudy
KKBB 364
SOTA 338
5001 44, 58, 288, 351, 562, 663, 690, 806
Valley Girl
SOTA 318
H 132, 134
Valley of the Dolls
KKBB 147
GS 61
Valley of the Kings
ILIATM 55
Valli, Alida
ILIATM 7
KKBB 346, 358
DIM 415
5001 230, 308, 530, 565, 661, 701, 760
Valli, Romolo
WTLGD 326
SOTA 52
5001 180, 417
Valli, Virginia
5001 587
Vallone, Raf
ILIATM 172, 174
KKBB 253, 279
GS 169
R 470
ML 310-11
5001 163, 319, 519, 578, 801, 815
Valmont
ML 217-20
5001 (2nd ed)
Valseuses, Les, see *Going Places*
Vampire's Kiss
ML 150-52

5001 (2nd ed)
Vampyr
ILIATM 6, 275
KKBB 325, 365:n, 368
5001
Van, Bobby
5001 398, 436
Vanbrugh, Violet
5001 605
Vance, Courtney B.
H 353
5001 315
Vance, Ethel
5001 224
Van Cleef, Lee
5001 296, 331, 859
Van Der Vlis, Diana
5001 852
Van Devere, Trish
DIM 185
R 383
WTLGD 503
5001 176, 410, 501, 655, 832
Van Dine, S. S.
5001 116, 123, 278, 298, 306, 391
van Druten, John
KKBB 267
WTLGD 343
5001 279, 348, 351, 443, 525, 542, 627
Van Dyke, Conny
5001 851
Van Dyke, Dick
GS 226
DIM 60
5001 111, 149
Van Dyke, W. S.
KKBB 358; dir., *The Thin Man*, 241, 358
5001 9, 31, 75, 259, 350, 367, 374, 440, 463, 465, 518, 597, 641, 642, 669, 736, 744, 758
Vaneck, Pierre
5001 224, 323
Vanel, Charles
KKBB 165, 259
TIAI 316, 318
5001 188, 764, 775, 821
Van Every, Dale
5001 118
Van Eyck, Peter
KKBB 165, 340
5001 248, 527, 643, 670, 821
Van Fleet, Jo
KKBB 346
5001 210, 277, 350, 357, 642, 661
Vangelis
TIAI 362
SOTA 172, 186, 278
ML 12
5001 96, 131
Vangelo Secondo Matteo, Il, see *The Gospel According to St. Matthew*
Van Gogh, Vincent and Theo
ML 289-94
Van Hamel, Martine
5001 795
Van Hamme, Jean
TIAI 329

5001 193
Van Heusen, Jimmy
5001 152
Van Houten, Micheline
H 464
Vanishing Point
H 9
Vanity Fair (periodical)
RK 10
Vanlint, Derek
TIAI 222
5001 201
Van Ness Philip, John, see Philip, John Van Ness
Van Nest Polglase, see Polglase, Van Nest
Van Pallandt, Nina
R 187-188
WTLGD 444, 550
5001 167, 432, 609
Van Patten, Dick
WTLGD 372
5001 132, 331
Van Patten, Joyce
GS 158
R 261
SOTA 313
5001 91, 233, 350, 455
Van Peebles, Mario
5001 325
Van Riper, Kay
5001 42
Van Ronkel, Rip
5001 331
van Runkle, Theadora
DIM 52
R 298
van Sacher-Masoch, Leopold
DIM 312
Van Sant, Gus
ML dir., *Drugstore Cowboy*, 195-98; *Mala Noche*, 195, 198
5001 205, 454
Van Sloan, Edward
5001 201, 265, 501, 658
Van Tilburg Clark, Walter, see Clark, Walter Van Tilburg
Van Upp, Virginia
5001 159, 590, 778, 856
Van Valkenburgh, Deborah
WTLGD 558
5001 823
Van Vooren, Monique
5001 285
Van Zandt, Philip
5001 138, 818
Van Zandt, Townes
TIAI 204, 206
5001 326
Varconi, Victor
5001 717, 718
Varda, Agnès
GS dir.,"Cleo from 5 to 7," 27
DIM 30; dir., *Lions Love*, 30-31
WTLGD 339-342; dir., *One Sings, the Other Doesn't*, 339-342; *La Pointe Courte*, 341; *Le Bonheur*, 341-342; *Cleo from 5 to 7*, 342

H 151-153; dir., *Vagabond* (*Sans Toit ni Loi*), 151-153; *One Sings, the Other Doesn't*, 152; *Le Bonheur*, 152
5001 140, 161, 423, 550, 811
Varden, Evelyn
KKBB 317
5001 184, 526, 583
Varden, Norma
5001 517, 665, 834, 844
Varhol, Michael
H 60
5001 573
Variété, see *Variety* (film)
Variety (periodical)
ILIATM 9-10, 69, 177-178, 204, 233, 246
KKBB 41, 354
RK 41, 43, 80
DIM 113, 124, 219, 322
SOTA 160
Variety (*Variété*; also known as *Vaudeville*)
KKBB 315
RK 76
H 247, 363, 372
5001
Variety Lights (*Luci del Varietà*)
KKBB 365:n
5001
Varsi, Diane
KKBB 250
GS 91, 107
5001 151, 838
Vartan, Sylvie
KKBB 128
Vassilikos, Vassili
DIM 63
5001 862
Vaudeville, see *Variety* (film)
Vaughan-Hughes, Gerald
WTLGD 382
5001 662
Vaughan, Peter
5001 772
Vaughn, Robert
GS 166
DIM 262
SOTA 8, 9, 11
5001 109, 452, 482, 690, 731, 785
Vazak, P. H., see Towne, Robert
Veber, Francis
ML dir., *Three Fugitives*, 89-90
5001 766
Vega, Isela
WTLGD 116
5001 51
Vega, Tata
H 83
5001 147
"Vega$" (TV)
TIAI 188
Veidt, Conrad
KKBB 185, 221, 242, 245, 289, 367
H 27
ML 161
5001 19, 113, 122, 224, 445, 460, 756, 824, 846
Veiller, Anthony
KKBB 291, 298

5001 329, 394, 424, 500, 703, 712, 719, 815, 841, 846
Veiller, Bayard
5001 35
Velasco, Manuela
5001 414
Velez, Lupe
5001 337, 624
Venable, Evelyn
KKBB 230
5001 15
Venanzo, Gianni di, see di Vananzo, Gianni
Vendetta
ILIATM 100
Venice Film Festival
H 152
Venice Observed (book)
KKBB 97
Venora, Diane
H 117
ML 3, 4
5001 73, 274, 371
Ventura, Lino
5001 215, 685
Venuta, Benay
5001 30
Vera-Ellen, 115
5001 546, 766, 767, 848
Verdi, Giuseppe
WTLGD 326-327, 328, 332
TIAI 451
SOTA 54, 379
H 330
5001 600, 694
Verdict, The
TIAI 440-441
SOTA 42
H 226, 321
5001 (2nd ed)
Verdon, Gwen
TIAI 344
H 6
5001 144, 156, 513
Verea, Lisette
5001 524
Vereen, Ben
R 462
WTLGD 267
Verhoeven, Paul
SOTA 194-196; dir., *The 4th Man*, 194-196; *Soldier of Orange*, 194, 358; *Spetters*, 195
H 343-345; dir., *RoboCop*, 343-345; *Soldier of Orange*, 343; *The 4th Man*, 343, 344; *Flesh & Blood*, 345
5001 264, 634
Vérité, La
ILIATM 37-38
Verley, Bernard
R 9
5001 136
Verne, Jules
KKBB 255-256
5001 179, 511
Verne, Kaaren
5001 20, 397, 447, 675
Verneau, Janine

5001 140
Vernette, Tevaite
  SOTA 186
  5001 96
Verneuil, Louis
  5001 182, 793
Vernon, Anne
  KKBB 270
  5001 281
Vernon, Bobby
  5001 831
Vernon, Howard
  5001 20
Vernon, John
  R 205
  WTLGD 310
  5001 131, 191, 588, 746, 781
Vernon, Richard
  5001 582
Vernon, Wally
  5001 13
Versois, Odile
  5001 122
Vertès, Marcel
  5001 500, 756
Vertigo
  ILIATM 297
  WTLGD 372, 373
  SOTA 264
Vertue, Beryl
  WTLGD 149, 150
Verushka
  5001 85
Very British Coup, A (TV)
  ML 328
Very Private Affair, A (*Vie privée*)
  DIM 308
  5001
"Vesti la giubba" (music)
  H 320
Vestoff, Virginia
  R 54
  5001 668
Veterans of Foreign Wars
  RK 41
Vetsera, Maria
  GS 270
Viacom
  TIAI 413
Viaggio in Italia, see *A Voyage to Italy*
Vickers, Martha
  KKBB 239
  WTLGD 262
  5001 71, 457
Victim
  ILIATM 201-203
  R 343
  5001
Victor, Henry
  5001 266
Victor/Victoria
  TIAI 331-335
  5001 (2nd ed)
Victoria of England
  WTLGD 98, 107-108
Victory
  5001

Victory March
  SOTA 137
Vidal, Gore
  KKBB 60
  R 27, 30
  TIAI 112
  5001 63, 64, 126, 144, 241, 416, 725
Vidal, Henri
  5001 590
Vidor, Charles
  5001 159, 285, 317, 403, 439, 469, 559,
    694, 778
Vidor, Florence
  5001 15
Vidor, King
  KKBB 131; dir.,"War and Peace, "131; "The
    Fountainhead," 143; "Duel in the Sun,"
    143
  RK 22 (ill.), 24, 70
  5001 67, 74, 128, 138, 206, 262, 534, 555,
    646, 680, 713
"Vie en Rose, La" (music)
  H 482
Vie privée, see *A Very Private Affair*
Vieille Dame indigne, La, see *The Shameless Old
  Lady*
Vieira, Asia
  ML 37
  5001 295
Vierde Man, De, see *The 4th Man*
Vierny, Sacha
  5001 412, 712
Viertel, Peter
  KKBB 229
  R 316
  H 364, 366
  5001 9, 318
Viertel, Salka
  5001 28, 153
Vigard, Kristen
  5001 732
Vietnam
  DIM 14, 42-45, 147, 163, 179, 215, 216,
    249, 415
  R 100, 105-107, 109, 161, 163, 165, 310
  WTLGD 84, 175-177, 195, 315, 402-405,
    431, 432, 437, 483, 499, 507, 512-519,
    554
  H 36, 250-253, 325-329, 421-423
  ML 166-177
View from the Bridge, A
  ILIATM 172-175
  KKBB 70
  5001
View to a Kill, A
  SOTA 368
  5001 (2nd ed)
Vigard, Kristen
  SOTA 18
Vigil in the Night
  5001
Vigny, Benno
  5001 498
Vigo, Jean
  KKBB 93, 140; dir., *Zero for Conduct*, 93,
    140, 301; *L'Atalante*,93, 140, 142
  GS 50; dir., *Zero for Conduct*, 281-286

R 33
  WTLGD 59, 455; dir., *L'Atalante*, 59; *Zero
    for Conduct*, 455
  TIAI 144, 250; dir., *Zero for Conduct*, 144,
    250
  5001 37, 865
Vigoda, Abe
  5001 289, 290
Viguerie, Richard
  H 437
Vikings, The
  GS 167
Viktor und Viktoria
  TIAI 331, 332
Vilbert, Henri
  KKBB 333
  5001 593
Villa Rides
  R 441
Village of the Damned
  GS 90
  TIAI 145
  5001
Village Voice (periodical)
  KKBB 28
  WTLGD 138, 375
  SOTA 91
  H 71, 298, 391
Villalobos, Reynaldo
  5001 80
Villalpando, David
  SOTA 130
  5001 533
Villard, Frank
  5001 285
Villechaize, Hervé
  5001 277, 462
Villella, Edward
  GS 70
Villiers, James
  SOTA 200
  5001 20, 515, 535, 624, 806
Villon, François
  R 119
  WTLGD 492
Vilmorin, Louise de, see de Vilmorin, Louise
Vincent & Theo
  ML 289-94
Vincent de Paul
  KKBB 312
Vincent, François, Paul, and the Others (*Vincent,
    François, Paul, et les autres*)
  WTLGD 152-155
  5001
Vincent, François, Paul, et les autres, see
    Vincent, François, Paul, and the Others
Vincent, Frank
  TIAI 108
Vincenzoni, Luciano
  H 169
  5001 617
Vincze, Ernest
  WTLGD 356
Vinegar, Leroy
  5001 692
Viner, Fanny
  5001 294

Vinson, Helen
  KKBB 283
  5001 348, 359, 391, 594, 758, 782
Vint, Alan
  5001 564
Vinton, Bobby
  H 207
Violent Four, The
  GS 96-97
"Violetera, La" (music)
  TIAI 158
Violets are Blue
  H 148-150, 151
  5001 (2nd ed)
Violons du bal, Les
  R 420-422
  5001
Virgin Man, The, see *Le Rosier de Madame
    Husson*
Virgin Spring, The
  TIAI 488
"Virginales" (story)
  KKBB 311
Virginia (stage)
  H 70
Virginian, The
  5001
Viridiana
  ILIATM 15, 17
  GS 255-256, 258, 260
Visconti, Luchino
  ILIATM 264; dir., *The Leopard*, 264
  GS dir., *The Stranger*, 30, 35
  DIM 86, 87, 271, 272; dir., *The Damned*,
    86-88, 271, 272, 274; *The Stranger*, 68,
    193
  R 33, 144-148; dir., *Senso*, 33; *Ossessione*,
    33; *Ludwig*, 144-149; *Rocco and His
    Brothers*, 145; *The Damned*, 145, 148,
    342-343, 345; *La Terra Trema*, 145;
    Death in Venice, 147, 148, 205, 343
  WTLGD 35-40, 324, 330, 513, 540-542;
    dir., *Conversation Piece*, 35-40; *Ludwig*,
    35; *Death in Venice*, 36, 38, 541; *The
    Leopard*, 37, 104, 330; *Bellissima*, 38;
    The Stranger, 38; *The Damned*, 330;
    The Innocent, 540-542
  TIAI 174, 465; dir., *The Leopard*, 174, 465
  SOTA 50-55, 226, 356; dir., *The Leopard*,
    50-55; *Death in Venice*, 126, 226
  H 82
  5001 62, 63, 89, 154, 168, 180, 364, 417,
    443, 592, 635, 719, 749
Viskin, Roberto
  5001 781
Visiteurs du soir, Les (*The Devil's Envoys*)
  5001
Visitors, The
  ML 167
Viskningar och Rop, see *Cries and Whispers*
Vitale, Enzo
  5001 667
Vitelloni, I (released in U.S. as *The Young and
    the Passionate*)
  KKBB 366:n
  R 169, 171-172
  WTLGD 136

TIAI 252, 320
5001
Vitold, Michel
  SOTA 126, 127
  5001 53, 151
Vitti, Monica
  ILIATM 188
  GS 136
  DIM 194, 195
  R 363
  5001 41, 211, 237, 536, 584, 619
Viva
  DIM 31
  R 113
  5001 138, 423, 479
Viva Maria!
  GS 90
  DIM 309
  R 341
  5001 (2nd ed)
Viva Villa!
  RK 20
Viva Zapata!
  KKBB 366-367:n
  DIM 175
  5001
Vivacious Lady
  DIM 184
  5001
Vivaldi, Antonio
  TIAI 253
  5001 220, 293
Vivre sa vie, see *My Life to Live*
Vlachos, Anestis
  KKBB 271
  5001 286
Vlad, Roman
  KKBB 311-312, 340
  5001 494, 639, 823
Vlady, Marina
  KKBB 202
  SOTA 228
  H 9
  5001 235
Vogel, Mitch
  DIM 75
  5001 622
Vogeler, Robert
  ILIATM 320
Vogler, Karl Michael
  5001 570
Vogue (periodical)
  KKBB 32
  H 247
Voice in the Wind
  GS 157
Voie lactée, La, see *The Milky Way*
Voight, Jon
  R 221, 239, 260, 293-295, 297, 312
  WTLGD 175, 402-405, 517
  5001 16, 125, 149, 153, 478, 479
Voleur, Le, see *The Thief of Paris*
Volonte, Gian Maria
  GS 55, 56, 97
  DIM 221
  R 207-208, 215
  TIAI 316

5001 267, 369, 825
Volpone
  TIAI 97, 99
  SOTA 34, 342
  H 485
  5001
Von Braun, Wernher
  KKBB 213
Von Bülow, Claus
  ML 287-89
Von Bülow, Sunny
  ML 288, 289
Von Eltz, Theodore
  5001 263, 451, 703, 733
Von Fritsch, Gunther
  5001 167
von Harbou, Thea
  5001 444, 477
von Kleist, Heinrich
  WTLGD 184-187
  TIAI 70, 265
  5001 467
von Meck, Mme.
  DIM 239, 240
von Musil, Robert, see Musil, Robert von
von Seyffertitz, Gustav
  5001 116, 192, 671, 693
von Sternberg, Josef
  ILIATM 188, 248
  KKBB 16, 43, 59, 219, 239-240, 302, 364;
    dir., *Shanghai Gesture*, 43, 364;
    Morocco, 59, 240, 360; *Shanghai
    Express*, 59, 364; *The Blue Angel*,
    239-240, 264; *The Last Command*, 240;
    Crime and Punishment, 262, 302; *An
    American Tragedy*, 332; *Docks of New
    York*, 360
  GS 113; dir., *The Blue Angel*, 264; *Morocco*,
    113; *Shanghai Express*, 113
  RK 9, 13, 16, 47, 49
  R 33, 149
  WTLGD 365; dir., *The Blue Angel*, 37; *The
    Devil Is a Woman*, 365
  TIAI 363, 364
  SOTA 214, 374; dir., *Anatahan*, 374
  5001 23, 24, 82, 85, 161, 187, 192, 206,
    223, 397, 498, 584, 658, 671, 769, 813
von Stroheim, Erich
  ILIATM 108-110
  KKBB 16, 132, 349, 354-355; dir., *Greed*,
    131
  RK 47
  R 149, 328
  WTLGD 324
  5001 81, 248, 255, 300, 302, 367, 534, 689,
    730
von Stroheim, Erich Jr.
  5001 801
von Sydow, Max
  KKBB 10, 135-136, 303-304, 346
  GS 219, 221, 235
  DIM 105
  R 8, 181-182, 248-250
  WTLGD 42, 390
  TIAI 124, 126, 183, 476, 477
  SOTA 231, 233
  H 113, 115

5001 104, 203, 207, 216, 228, 229, 250,
  252, 316, 322, 451, 520, 669, 670, 765,
  819, 839
Von Trapp Family
  KKBB 177
von Trotta, Margarethe
  5001 158
Vonnegut, Kurt Jr.
  DIM 230
  TIAI 376
  SOTA 316
  H 130
  5001 45, 317
Vorkapich, Slavko
  5001 162, 294, 472, 489
Voskovec, George
  R 201
  TIAI 372
  5001 51, 354, 458, 487, 795
Vosper, Frank
  5001 438
Voutsinas, Andreas
  TIAI 215
Voyage of the Damned
  WTLGD 452
  TIAI 21
  5001
Voyage Surprise
  5001
Voyage to Italy, A (Viaggio in Italia)
  5001
Voyagis, Yorgo
  SOTA 259
  5001 425
Vredens Dag, see Day of Wrath
Vuillard, Édouard
  H 331
Vukotic, Milena
  5001 192, 495
Vuolo, Tito
  5001 220, 249
Vye, Murvyn
  5001 581
Vynalez Zkazy, see The Deadly Invention

W

W. W. and the Dixie Dancekings
  WTLGD 360
  5001
Wachsfigurenkabinett, see Waxworks
Wada, Natto
  ILIATM 225-226
  5001 245
Wade, Kevin
  ML 65
  5001 849
Wademant, Annette
  5001 209
Wager, Anthony
  KKBB 276
  5001 235, 301
Wages of Fear, The (Le Salaire de la peur)
  KKBB 165-166, 315

5001
Waggner, George
  TIAI 193; dir., The Wolf Man, 193, 194
  5001 143, 312, 835
Wagner, Bruce
  5001 659
Wagner, Cosima
  WTLGD 84
Wagner, Fritz Arno
  5001 444
Wagner, Jane
  TIAI 161, 162; dir., Moment by Moment, 32
  5001 361
Wagner, Lindsay
  R 149-150, 190, 192
  5001 564, 799
Wagner, Richard
  R 145
  WTLGD 49, 83, 84, 137, 234, 315, 515
  TIAI 182, 278
  SOTA 153
  H 211, 344
  5001 228, 694, 806
Wagner, Robert
  DIM 47
  R 318, 406
  TIAI 13
  ML 121
  5001 320, 774, 785
Wagoner, David
  TIAI 353
  5001 225
Wagonmaster
  DIM 296
Wahl, Ken
  TIAI 152, 411, 412
  5001 259, 380
Wahlöö, Per
  R 260
  5001 413
Wainwright, James
  5001 732
Waite, Genevieve
  GS 195
Waite, Ric
  TIAI 301, 399
  SOTA 120
  5001 92, 261, 749, 804
Waites, Thomas
  5001 823
"Waitin' Around to Die" (music)
  TIAI 206
Waiting for Godot (stage)
  H 381
Waits, Tom
  TIAI 296, 299
  SOTA 230, 288
  H 221, 222, 421
  5001 200, 371, 550, 759
Wakeford, Kent
  R 174
  5001 473
Wakhévitch, Georges
  5001 62, 472, 817
Walas, Chris
  5001 307
Walbrook, Anton

WTLGD 344
  5001 280, 430, 470, 621
Walburn, Raymond
  5001 93, 106, 157, 313, 333, 487, 711, 736
Wald, Jerry
  R 155
  5001 4, 7, 20, 249, 318, 359, 382, 392, 464,
    591, 634, 782
Wald, Malvin
  5001 514
Waldekranz, Rune
  ILIATM 107
Waldman, Frank
  WTLGD 245
  5001 567, 582
Waldman, Tom
  5001 567
Waldron, Mal
  5001 155
Walk in the Sun, A
  5001
Walk with Love and Death, A
  DIM 17-18
  5001
Walkabout
  WTLGD 535
Walken, Christopher
  WTLGD 130, 357-358, 512-519
  TIAI 113, 167, 168, 275, 276
  SOTA 368
  5001 25, 183, 197, 521, 574, 642, 815
Walker, Alice
  H 80, 81, 82
  5001 146
Walker, Arnetia
  5001 659
Walker, Cheryl
  5001 704
Walker, Clint
  5001 301
Walker, David
  5001 826
Walker, Gertrude
  5001 169
Walker, Hal
  5001 633
Walker, Helen
  KKBB 249
  5001 143, 503, 529
Walker, Jimmie
  WTLGD 66-67
  5001 12, 418
Walker, Mayor Jimmy
  5001 288
Walker, Joseph
  5001 75, 257, 404, 483
Walker, Kathryn
  5001 686
Walker, Kim
  ML 119, 135
  5001 326, 656
Walker, Nancy
  5001 64, 106, 261, 286
Walker, Nella
  5001 359, 400, 649, 713, 768, 792
Walker, Robert
  ILIATM 135

KKBB 352
DIM 261
ML 277
5001 141, 446, 550, 660, 683, 720, 772
Walker, Robert Jr.
5001 211, 317
Walker, Sara
H 408
5001 342
Walker, Tippy
5001 850
Walker, Zena
5001 204
Walking Tall
R 282-288, 310, 313-314
WTLGD 200, 422
TIAI 384
5001
Wall, Bob
5001 221
Wallace, Anzac
SOTA 241, 244
5001 810
Wallace, Dee
TIAI 192, 350
5001 225, 343
Wallace, Earl W.
SOTA 320
5001 844
Wallace, Edgar
5001 652
Wallace, Irving
DIM 420
5001 129, 600
Wallace, Jean
5001 459
Wallace, Lew
5001 63
Wallace, Morgan
5001 299, 809
Wallace, Pamela
5001 844
Wallace, Richard
KKBB 370; dir., *The Little Minister*, 241;
The Young in Heart, 369-370
5001 426, 859
Wallach, Eli
KKBB 232
GS 18, 22
R 259
WTLGD 265, 502
ML 312
5001 43, 138, 296, 343, 434, 452, 484, 501,
517, 799
Wallach, Roberta
R 74
5001 212
Wallant, Edward Lewis
5001 571
Waller, Fats
DIM 85
WTLGD 473
5001 716
Wållgren, Gunn
TIAI 487, 492
5001 236
Wållgren, Pernilla

TIAI 492
5001 236
Wallis, Hal B.
KKBB 245
R 316
WTLGD 62-63
5001 8, 20, 29, 52, 112, 122, 148, 243, 306,
348, 468, 602, 614, 634, 640, 654, 683,
719, 726
Wallis, J. H.
5001 845
Wallis, Shani
GS 202
5001 543
*Walls of Malapaga, The (Au-delà des grilles; Le
Mure di Malapurga)*
5001
Wally, La (music)
TIAI 330
Walsh, David M.
WTLGD 529
5001 157, 495, 559, 686, 141
Walsh, J. T.
H 282, 422
ML 51
5001 168, 295, 748, 773
Walsh, Joey
R 350
5001 204, 317
Walsh, Kay
KKBB 282, 293-294, 322
5001 341, 360, 408, 451, 543, 778, 794
Walsh, M. Emmet
TIAI 22, 244
SOTA 204, 323, 325
H 112
5001 37, 45, 65, 83, 108, 251, 589, 686,
718, 831
Walsh, Maurice
5001 608
Walsh, Raoul
ILIATM 292-294, 301, 315-316, 318; dir.,
Every Night at Eight, 292-293; *High
Sierra*, 293-294
DIM 78
5001 36, 226, 282, 332, 400, 457, 464, 472,
513, 627, 634, 753, 756, 834
Walska, Ganna
RK 66
Walston, Ray
TIAI 123, 409
5001 238, 399, 589, 682, 715
Walt Disney Studios, see Disney Studios
Walter, Harriet
5001 294, 795
Walter, Jessica
KKBB 10
SOTA 310-311
5001 111, 249, 422
Walter, Patricia
5001 632
Walter, Tracey
SOTA 212
H 231
ML 278
5001 561, 611, 624
Walters, Barbara

WTLGD 303
Walters, Charles
5001 30, 210, 287, 296, 422, 727, 782
Walters, Julie
SOTA 83, 84
H 301, 302
5001 212, 576, 577, 595
Walthall, Henry B.
KKBB 345
5001 41, 112, 186, 262, 385, 472, 658, 741
Walthall, Wade
H 241
Walton, Douglas
5001 102, 157, 468, 505, 717
Walton, Tony
R 391
WTLGD 474, 475
5001 96, 272, 388, 503
Walton, William
5001 315, 328, 454, 628
"Waltons, The" (TV)
R 225, 226
WTLGD 446
H 197
Waltz of the Toreadors
WTLGD 238
Wanamaker, Sam
TIAI 93, 133
H 170
5001 43, 150, 598, 617, 819
Wand, Betty
5001 828
"Wand'rin' Star" (music)
DIM 29
Wanda
DIM 267-269
5001
Wanderers, The
TIAI 152, 211, 412
SOTA 63
Wanger, Walter
RK 11, 26
5001 34, 75, 82, 226, 258, 335, 433, 496,
704, 705, 786, 787
Wannberg, Ken
WTLGD 261-262
War and Peace (book)
ILIATM 281
WTLGD 325
SOTA 89
War and Peace
KKBB 131
War Brides
WTLGD 335
War Lord, The
DIM 368
R 238
"War of the Worlds, The" (radio)
RK 3, 39-40, 55
SOTA 218
War Wagon, The
KKBB 42-45
Warburton, John
KKBB 251
5001 127, 152, 654, 834
Ward, David S.
R 120, 245

5001 715
Ward, Douglas Turner
WTLGD 188
Ward, Fred
SOTA 66, 67, 109, 117, 120, 166
H 484-485
5001 68, 630, 681, 698, 738, 804
Ward, Mackenzie
5001 36
Ward, Rachel
SOTA 145, 146, 147
5001 10, 178
Ward, Richard
TIAI 21
5001 108
Ward, Robert
TIAI 213
5001 126
Ward, Sela
H 200
5001 535
Ward, Simon
R 15
5001 767, 860
Ward, Sophie
H 101
5001 860
Ward, Stephen
ML 129-32
Ward, Warwick
5001 812
Warden, Jack
KKBB 261
GS 52
R 436, 439, 442
WTLGD 466
TIAI 97, 240, 440
SOTA 77
H 426
ML 308
5001 34, 111, 181, 212, 227, 666, 670, 689,
703, 795, 810, 813
Warden, Jonathan
5001 307
Ware, Darrell
5001 322, 551
Ware, Herta
H 7
5001 144
Warfield, Marlene
WTLGD 223
5001 381
Warfield, William
5001 435, 679
WarGames
TIAI 493-495
H 349
5001 (2nd ed)
Warhol, Andy
KKBB 28, 32
GS 12; dir., *The Chelsea Girls*, 196-197
DIM 13, 31, 153-157, 197; dir., *Lonesome
Cowboys*, 153; *The Chelsea Girls*, 154
R 151, 235, 291; dir., *Andy Warhol's
Frankenstein*, 311
WTLGD 82
TIAI 298, 457

5001 26, 788, 847, 848
Warm, Hermann
5001 113
Warnecke, Gordon
H 118
5001 506
Warner Brothers
RK 5, 7, 8, 70, 80
DIM 105, 299, 343, 390
R 64-66, 123, 145, 187, 254, 318, 407
WTLGD 162, 205, 241, 489, 501, 502, 504,
537
TIAI 21, 290, 342, 452, 474
SOTA 184, 295-296
H 41, 175, 176
ML 167
Warner, David
KKBB 20
GS 210, 235
DIM 89, 193, 395
WTLGD 255, 258
SOTA 3
H 46, 195
5001 48, 248, 267, 462, 497, 575, 601, 660,
721, 772, 778
Warner, H. B.
ILIATM 66
KKBB 354
5001 298, 374, 436, 489, 730, 741, 747
Warner, Jack
KKBB 265, 293
DIM 119
5001 243, 407, 779
Warner, Jack L.
5001 244, 668
Warner, Steven
R 388-389
5001 427
Warnock, Craig
5001 772
Warren, Annette
5001 679
Warren, Harry
KKBB 273
5001 255, 262, 278, 288, 291, 292, 321,
637, 726, 727, 736, 827, 856
Warren, Jennifer
WTLGD 277
5001 686
Warren, Lesley Ann
TIAI 332, 335
SOTA 289
H 8, 9-10, 11, 482
5001 136, 695, 814
Warren, Mike
5001 141
Warren, Robert Penn
5001 19
Warrender, Harold
KKBB 253
5001 175, 376
Warrick, Ruth
RK 54
5001 138, 301, 384
Warriors, The
WTLGD 554-559
TIAI 259

SOTA 233
H 143
5001
Warshow, Robert
GS 244, 245
DIM 425
SOTA 41, 105
Wartime (book)
ML 170
Warui Yatsu Hodo Yoku Nemuru, see *The Bad
Sleep Well*
Warwick, Robert
5001 7, 8, 195, 302, 359, 694, 726
Washbourne, Mona
5001 59, 145
Washburn, Deric
WTLGD 518
TIAI 301
5001 92, 183
Washington, Denzel
SOTA 272
H 399, 400, 401
ML 257-62
5001 165, 288, 691
Washington, Dinah
5001 379
Washington, Fredi
5001 358
Washington, Hazel
5001 358
Washington, Kenny
5001 583
Washington, "Walkin' Blacksmith"
TIAI 206
Wass, Ted
SOTA 225
5001 673
Wasserman, Dale
R 78
5001 458, 487, 822
Wasserman, Lew
R 387
Wasson, Craig
TIAI 284
SOTA 263, 265
5001 89, 98, 264
Waste Land, The (poem)
H 389
Watanabe, Gedde
5001 684
Watch on the Rhine
KKBB 251
5001
Water Is Wide, The (book)
R 294, 296
Water of the Hills, The (book)
H 329
Watergate
R 161, 163, 310, 314
WTLGD 86, 96, 205, 262-266, 315, 369
Waterhouse, Keith
GS 54
5001 832
Waterloo
DIM 348
R 15, 476
Waterloo Bridge

5001
Waterman, Dennis
  GS 70
Waterman, Juanita
  5001 166
Waters, Daniel
  ML 118
  5001 326
Waters, Ethel
  KKBB 309
  SOTA 294
  H 305
  5001 112, 474, 547, 583, 704, 741, 742
Waters, John
  H 231, 442-444; dir., *Hairspray*, 442-444
  ML 64
  5001 313, 693
Waters, Muddy
  5001 411
Waterston, Sam
  R 247
  WTLGD 90, 92, 95, 439
  SOTA 275, 276
  H 116, 425, 426, 427
  ML 199, 203, 207
  5001 162, 316, 366, 387, 394, 615, 666
Watkin, David
  GS 145
  R 221
  WTLGD 158
  TIAI 246
  SOTA 90
  H 65, 66, 80, 424, 445
  5001 59, 96, 126, 130, 131, 219, 338, 343,
    401, 469, 496, 557, 634, 767, 835, 855
Watkins, Maurine
  KKBB 341
  5001 421, 645, 808
Watling, Jack
  5001 515, 804
Watson and Webber
  DIM 242; dirs., *Lot in Sodom*, 55, 242
Watson, Doc
  SOTA 247
  5001 585
Watson, James S.
  5001 Dr., 437
Watson, Lucile
  5001 278, 448, 736, 758, 768, 778, 824,
    846, 847
Watson, Minor
  5001 67, 101, 243, 705
Watson, Wylie
  5001 729
Wattis, Richard
  KKBB 334
  5001 596
Watts, Alan
  H 285
Watts, Deborah
  5001 402
Wattstax
  H 145
Waugh, Evelyn
  KKBB 300
  WTLGD 266
  5001 440

Waves, The (book)
  ILIATM 149
Waxman, Al
  H 448
  5001 738
Waxman, Franz
  5001 118, 565, 585, 591, 618, 765
Waxworks (Wachsfigurenkabinett)
  KKBB 289, 367:n
  5001
Way Down East (1920)
  ILIATM 199
  GS 45
  TIAI 134
  5001
Way of All Flesh, The
  KKBB 240
Way Out West
  KKBB 274
  5001
Way We Were, The
  R 175-178, 200, 461, 470
  WTLGD 3, 209, 236, 304
  5001
Way West, The
  KKBB 39, 42-43, 45
Wayborn, Kristina
  SOTA 4
  5001 539
Wayne, Carol
  SOTA 350
  5001 325
Wayne, David
  KKBB 228
  DIM 276
  5001 6, 26, 270, 591, 765
Wayne, John
  ILIATM 45, 48, 240
  KKBB 42-46, 338
  DIM 174, 229, 350, 390-393
  R 253, 259-260, 275-276
  WTLGD 62-64, 196-197, 430, 451, 544, 545
  TIAI 23, 388, 438, 439
  SOTA 9, 117-118, 238, 239, 375
  H 16, 118
  5001 26, 116, 123, 159, 214, 259, 343, 433,
    445, 461, 608, 620, 630, 631, 640, 661,
    668, 672, 677, 702, 704
Wayne, Naunton
  KKBB 255, 293, 330
  5001 178, 406, 568
Wayne, Patrick
  5001 662, 728
We All Loved Each Other So Much
  WTLGD 311
  TIAI 284
We Still Kill the Old Way (A Ciascuno il Suo)
  GS 55-56, 96
  DIM 221
  5001
"We Three Kings of Orient Are" (music)
  ML 40
We Were Dancing
  5001 (2nd ed)
We're No Angels
  5001
We're Not Dressing

H 187
5001
Weathers, Carl
  WTLGD 213-214
  TIAI 346
  5001 636
Weaver, Dennis
  5001 784
Weaver, Doodles
  5001 116
Weaver, Fritz
  R 73
  TIAI 494
  5001 70, 176, 464
Weaver, Jacki
  TIAI 159
  5001 114
Weaver, John
  5001 8
Weaver, Marjorie
  5001 860
Weaver, Sigourney
  TIAI 169, 170, 171, 452, 453, 456
  SOTA 167, 193, 194
  H 193, 194
  ML 5-7, 63, 165
  5001 15, 230, 284, 298, 849, 854
Web of Passion, see *Léda*
Webb, Alan
  KKBB 201
  DIM 357, 368
  WTLGD 382, 539
  5001 206, 235, 304, 396, 602, 847
Webb, Charles
  5001 299
Webb, Clifton
  RK 17
  5001 413, 528, 617, 684, 774
Webb, Jack
  KKBB 355
  5001 475, 730
Webb, James R.
  5001 343
Webb, Millard
  5001 288
Webb, Roy
  5001 536
Webber, Melville
  5001 437
Webber, Robert
  WTLGD 116
  5001 320, 598, 690, 723, 795
Webber, Timothy
  SOTA 30
Weber, André
  WTLGD 365
Weber, Bruce
  ML dir., *Broken Noses*, 122, 124; *Let's Get
    Lost*, 121-26
  5001 418
Weber, Fred
  TIAI 36
Weber, Joe
  5001 422
Weber, Pierre
  KKBB 303
  5001 449

Weber, Steven
  H 354
  5001 315
Webster, Paul Francis
  5001 114
Webster, Tony
  R 131
Wechsler, Lazar
  5001 661
Wedding, A
  WTLGD 440-445
Wedding Party, The
  WTLGD 210
Wedding Present
  RK 20, 48
Wedekind, Frank
  5001 563
Wedgeworth, Ann
  R 358
  WTLGD 322-323
  H 49, 51, 274, 392
  ML 143
  5001 50, 139, 414, 448, 485, 735
Wednesday's Child (also known as *Family Life*)
  R 394
  5001
Wee Geordie (also known as *Geordie*)
  5001
Weeds
  H 380-383
  5001 (2nd ed)
Weekend
  GS 138-144, 220
  DIM 253, 298, 404
  R 269
  WTLGD 456
  SOTA 212, 227
  5001
Weekend in Havana
  5001
Weeks, Geoffrey
  5001 221
Weeks, Michelle
  H 250
  5001 427
Wehe, Oliver
  5001 224
Weidler, Virginia
  5001 42, 580, 779, 847
Weidman, Jerome
  5001 169
Weil, Simone
  DIM 430
  WTLGD 523
  SOTA 107
Weill, Kurt
  ILIATM 116
  KKBB 340
  GS 163
  DIM 410
  TIAI 96
  SOTA 366
  H 158
  ML 15, 284
  5001 404, 550, 706, 856
Weiman, Rita
  5001 591

Weinberger, Ed
  SOTA 129
  5001 431
Weincke, Jan
  5001 574
Weingarten, Isabelle
  R 289, 291
  5001 264, 499
Weingarten, Lawrence
  5001 48, 569, 779, 843
Weingrod, Herschel
  SOTA 12
  5001 786
Weintraub, Fred
  5001 221
Weintraub, Sandra
  R 413
Weir, Peter
  WTLGD 533-536
  TIAI 451-456; dir., *The Year of Living Dangerously*, 451-456; *Gallipoli*, 454, 455, 456; *The Last Wave*, 455; *Picnic at Hanging Rock*, 455
  SOTA 74, 319-323; dir., *The Year of Living Dangerously*, 74; *Witness*, 319-323
  H 20; dir., *The Last Wave*, 20; *The Year of Living Dangerously*, 183; *Witness*, 479
  ML dir., *Dead Poets Society*, 153-57, 323; *Gallipoli*, 157
  5001 178, 276, 412, 804, 844, 854
Weiss, Robert K.
  5001 88
Weisse Hölle vom Piz Palü, Die, see *The White Hell of Pitz Palu*
Weissmuller, Johnny
  5001 288, 744
Weist, Dianne
  5001 361
Welch, Bo
  5001 61
Welch, Margaret
  H 131
  5001 689
Welch, Raquel
  KKBB 156
  R 62, 352, 444
  H 6
  5001 60, 237, 450, 767
Welch, Tahnee
  H 6
  5001 144
"Welcome Back, Kotter" (TV)
  WTLGD 369
Welcome to L.A.
  WTLGD 283-285
  TIAI 299
  SOTA 288
  5001
Weld, Tuesday
  KKBB 298
  GS 169, 224
  DIM 199, 223
  R 44, 46, 303
  WTLGD 210, 236, 285, 319
  TIAI 188, 191, 369
  SOTA 362, 363
  5001 39, 352, 434, 435, 548, 587, 594, 756

Welfare
  WTLGD 219
Well-Digger's Daughter, The (*La Fille du puisatier*)
  KKBB 110
  5001
Welland, Colin
  TIAI 245
  H 75, 76
  ML 185
  5001 131, 205, 796
Weller, Michael
  TIAI 265
  5001 612
Weller, Peter
  TIAI 294
  SOTA 217
  H 343, 344
  5001 7, 387, 634, 676
Welles, Beatrice
  KKBB 202
  5001 235
Welles, Gwen
  R 452
  5001 517
Welles, Orson
  ILIATM 110, 115, 119, 277; dir., *Citizen Kane*, 24, 110, 288; *The Magnificent Ambersons*, 251; *Touch of Evil*, 277
  KKBB 11, 16, 58, 124, 132, 155, 175, 196-202, 219, 225, 233, 247-248, 250, 304, 322, 358-359, 360-361; dir., *Citizen Kane*, 33, 124, 197, 199, 232, 247-248, 304; *Othello*, 175, 198; *Falstaff*, 197, 200-202; *The Magnificent Ambersons*, 197, 199, 219, 304; *Macbeth*, 198, 200; *The Trial*, 199; *Touch of Evil*, 360-361
  GS dir., *Citizen Kane*, 7, 60, 161-162, 164
  RK 3-4, 5, 7, 8, 24, 28, 29, 31-33, 33-35, 36-40, 41-42, 43-44, 44-47, 48-51, 52-54, 55-56, 58, 59, 61-63, 65, 66, 67, 71, 73-75, 76, 77, 80, 81, 83, 84
  DIM 105; dir., *Citizen Kane*, 252
  R 149, 352; dir., *Citizen Kane*, 179, 202
  WTLGD 23, 104, 146, 272, 324, 414, 420, 421; dir., *Citizen Kane*, 104; *Touch of Evil*, 394, 420
  TIAI 35, 144, 151, 187, 330, 331, 338, 457; dir., *Falstaff*, 187; *Citizen Kane*, 315, 340; *Touch of Evil*, 327; *The Trial*, 330
  SOTA 35, 218, 326; dir., *Citizen Kane*, 24, 179, 216
  H 330; dir., *Citizen Kane*, 295, 415
  ML 297; dir., *Chimes at Midnight*, 163, 215; *Touch of Evil*, 270, 317
  5001 49, 123, 125, 138, 151, 235, 254, 383, 432, 435, 451, 456, 490, 719, 760, 778, 783, 784, 788, 789, 819
Welles, Terri
  5001 434
Welles, Virginia Nicholson
  RK 21, 37
Wellman, Maggie
  WTLGD 91
Wellman, William
  KKBB 51, 320, 328, 341; dir., *The Public*

Enemy, 51-52, 338; *Goodbye, My Lady*, 180; *Beau Geste*, 184; *Roxie Hart*, 219, 341; *Yellow Sky*, 266; *A Star is Born* (1937), 272, 363; *The Ox-Bow Incident*, 276, 328; *Nothing Sacred*, 319-320, 341
RK 13, 75
5001 57, 405, 422, 525, 535, 560, 602, 645, 706, 815, 837
Wellman, William Jr.
5001 93
Wells, Brember
5001 542
Wells, Claudia
5001 45
Wells, George
5001 727, 740, 766, 777
Wells, H. G.
KKBB 253-254, 255, 309
GS 36
RK 55
WTLGD 193
ML 163, 185
5001 175, 178, 369, 398, 459, 477, 759, 773
Wells, Hubert
SOTA 225
Wells, Jacqueline, see Bishop, Julie
Wells, John
5001 761
Wells, Vernon
TIAI 385
5001 634
Welsh, Kenneth
ML 13
5001 31
Wenders, Wim
WTLGD 312-316
TIAI 42; dir., *The American Friend*, 42
H dir., *Wings of Desire*, 470-473
5001 22, 841
Wendkos, Paul
5001 311
Wendt, Elizabeth
KKBB 290
5001 390
Wendt, George
5001 203, 251
Wentz, Robert
TIAI 77
Wepper, Fritz
DIM 412
5001 112
Werfel, Franz
5001 384
Werner, Oskar
ILIATM 217
KKBB 148-149, 213, 294
GS 183
TIAI 43
5001 233, 366, 385, 410, 430, 675, 819
Wernicke, Otto
5001 444
Wertmüller, Lina
DIM 183
WTLGD 135-140, 392-394; dir., *Swept Away by an Unusual Destiny in the Blue Sea of August*, 99, 135-138, 393; *Seven Beauties*, 136-140; *The Lizards*, 136;

Love and Anarchy, 136; *All Screwed Up*, 138; *The End of the World in Our Usual Bed in a Night Full of Rain*, 392-394
SOTA 365
5001 18, 218, 429, 437, 666, 667, 737
Wesley, Richard
WTLGD 66
Wessely, Paula
5001 470
Wesson, Dick
5001 114, 185
West, Claudine
5001 52, 293, 309, 834
West, Jessamyn
5001 268
West, Judi
5001 260
West, Julian (pseud. of Nicolas de Gunzburg)
KKBB 365
5001 812
West, Lockwood
SOTA 113
5001 60, 204
West, Mae
KKBB 313-314
GS 94, 223
RK 26
DIM 183
R 405
WTLGD 3, 5, 6, 304, 414
TIAI 121, 162, 255
H 228
5001 62, 357, 400, 509, 672
West, Martin
KKBB 299
5001 435
West, Nathanael
GS 10
RK 9
DIM 68
R 186-187, 325-326, 471, 472-476
5001 176
West, Rebecca
SOTA 330, 331, 332
5001 621, 626
West Side Story
ILIATM 10, 141-147, 278
GS 108, 153, 154, 162, 237
DIM 328, 409
R 150
WTLGD 120, 369, 370, 440
5001
H 160
West, Tegan
H 354
5001 315
West, Timothy
5001 10
Westcott, Helen
5001 7, 724
Westerner, The
R 99
5001
"Westerner, The" (TV)
WTLGD 114
Westlake, Donald E.

DIM 401
H 261, 262, 263
ML 284, 286
5001 714
Westley, Helen
5001 13, 422, 679, 864
Westman, Nydia
5001 428
Westmoreland, Gen. William C.
WTLGD 516
Weston, Jack
DIM 269
H 310, 311, 346, 348
5001 34, 113, 190, 371, 763
Weston, Robert R.
5001 66
Westworld
R 215-217
WTLGD 395, 538
TIAI 254
H 68, 344
5001
Wetherby
H 43, 45-48
5001 (2nd ed)
Wexler, Haskell
GS 114, 115
DIM dir., *Medium Cool*, 117
WTLGD 228, 278, 381, 403
TIAI 324
H 461, 478
ML 90
5001 22, 64, 95, 147, 150, 177, 360, 440, 549, 628, 724, 763, 766
Wexler, Norman
R 228, 230, 231
WTLGD 223, 353, 369
H 169
5001 617, 654, 666
Wexley, John
5001 27
Weymouth, Tina
SOTA 266
WGBH-TV
H 441
Whale, James
WTLGD 211; dir., *The Man in the Iron Mask* (1939), 49; *The Old Dark House*, 211; *The Bride of Frankenstein*, 211
SOTA 161
5001 101, 265, 328, 369, 542, 679, 693
Whaley, Frank
5001 93
Whalley, Joanne (Whalley-Kilmer, Joanne)
H 474
ML 129-32
5001 656, 840
Wharton, Anne
WTLGD 449
Wharton, Edith
5001 542
Wharton, William (pseud.)
ML 204
SOTA 316
5001 74, 168
What a Way to Go!
TIAI 436

What a Woman!
5001
What Did You Do in the War, Daddy?
KKBB 18
R 248
What Ever Happened to Baby Jane?
ILIATM 8, 14, 294, 303
GS 208
TIAI 234
What Every Woman Knows
ILIATM 106
5001
What Have I Done to Deserve This! (Que He Hecho Yo Para Merecer Esto)
SOTA 364-366
H 141, 288, 467
5001 (2nd ed)
What Is Cinema? (Vol. II) (book)
DIM 366
"What Is This Thing Called Love?" (music)
TIAI 47
What Makes Sammy Run?
H 418
What Price Glory
DIM 93
H 304
What Price Hollywood
WTLGD 240
5001
"What Will You Do When Jesus Comes?" (music)
WTLGD 398
"What Would I Do If I Could Feel?" (music)
WTLGD 473
"What'll I Do?" (music)
H 427
What's New Pussycat?
KKBB 29, 69, 298
5001
What's Up, Doc?
DIM 431-433
R 281, 466
WTLGD 248
TIAI 240
5001
What's Up, Tiger Lily?
5001
Wheaton, Wil
H 197
5001 705
Wheeler, Bert
5001 160, 391
Wheeler, Charles F.
5001 65
Wheeler, Hugh
DIM 412
WTLGD 424
5001 112, 427, 788
Wheeler, Lyle
5001 859
Wheeler-Nicholson, Dana
5001 251
Wheelis, Allen
5001 160
Whelan, Arleen
5001 665, 728, 860
Whelan, Tim

5001 193, 606, 714, 756
When Comedy Was King
KKBB 185
5001
"When Doves Cry" (music)
SOTA 215
"When I Paint My Masterpiece" (music)
WTLGD 397
When I Think of Russia (TV)
SOTA 155
When Knighthood Was in Flower
RK 68
"When the Red, Red Robin Comes Bob, Bob, Bobbin' Along" (music)
TIAI 262
When You're in Love
WTLGD 6
"Where Are You Going, Where Have You Been?" (story)
WTLGD 209
H 132
"Where Have All the Flowers Gone?" (music)
WTLGD 177
Where the Wild Things Are (book)
ML 228
Where's Charley?
KKBB 185, 234, 367-368:n
5001
Where's Poppa?
DIM 185-186, 314, 351, 402
R 383
WTLGD 503
5001
"Which Side Are You On?" (music)
WTLGD 252-253
"Whiffenpoof Song, The" (music)
SOTA 338
Whipper, Leigh
KKBB 328
5001 540, 560, 833
Whirlpool
ILIATM 298
5001
Whisky Galore, see *Tight Little Island*
Whisperers, The
DIM 323
5001
Whistle Down the Wind
5001
Whitaker, Forest
H 225, 253, 423
ML 2, 3-4, 193
5001 73, 146, 295, 382, 587, 704
Whitcraft, Elizabeth
H 287
5001 27
White, Alice
5001 582
White, Betty
5001 8
White Cargo
SOTA 351
5001
White, Carol
GS 26
R 222
5001 248, 588, 691

White Cliffs of Dover, The
KKBB 285
5001
White, David
DIM 151
White Dawn, The
WTLGD 199, 523
SOTA 63
White, Ethel Lina
5001 406
White Heat
SOTA 106
5001
White Hell of Pitz Palu, The (Die Weisse Hölle vom Piz Palü)
KKBB 258
5001
White Horse, Chief
5001 704
White Hunter, Black Heart (book)
KKBB 229
R 317
H 364, 366
White Line Fever
WTLGD 200
White, Lionel
GS 277
5001 394, 526, 582
White Mane (Crin blanc)
KKBB 180, 185, 291
5001
White, Marjorie
5001 387
"White Negro, The" (essay)
WTLGD 134
White Nights
H 64-67
5001 (2nd ed)
White, Onna
GS 202
R 298
5001 304, 455, 543
White, Patrick
TIAI 59
White, Pearl
DIM 184
White, Ruth
DIM 76
5001 123, 132, 479, 622, 777, 808
White, Sammy
5001 569
White Savage
5001
White Sheik, The (Lo Sceicco Bianco)
KKBB 366, 368:n
5001
White Sox
ML 126
White, Stanford
RK 67
White, T. H.
5001 115
White, Welker
ML 268
5001 297
White, Wilfred Hyde, see Hyde-White, Wilfred
Whitehall, Richard

ILIATM 89
Whitehead, Paxton
  H 186
  5001 45
Whitehead, Peter
  GS dir., *Tonite Let's All Make Love in London*, 149
Whitelaw, Billie
  H 361
  ML 45, 46, 47
  5001 131, 204, 471, 711
Whiteman, Paul
  5001 722
Whitemore, Hugh
  SOTA 332, 333
  5001 626
Whitfield, Norman
  WTLGD 187
  5001 118
Whiting, Leonard
  GS 154
  DIM 24
  5001 639, 646
Whiting, Richard
  5001 32
Whitlock, Albert J.
  WTLGD 121
  TIAI 215
  5001 331, 334, 335
Whitman, Stuart
  ILIATM 157-159
Whitman, Walt
  DIM 274
  WTLGD 225, 421
  TIAI 435
  SOTA 299, 300
  H 222
Whitmore, James
  DIM 147
  R 207
  WTLGD 392
  H 303
  5001 37, 311, 399, 586
Whitmore, James Jr.
  TIAI 260
  5001 98
Whitney, Peter
  5001 48, 360, 502
Whittingham, Jack
  5001 193, 606
Whitton, Margaret
  H 112, 298, 300, 421
  5001 43, 65, 371, 664
Whittum, Kevin
  H 439
Whitty, Dame May
  KKBB 267, 293
  5001 153, 251, 279, 406, 446, 486, 525, 833
"Who Am I?" (music)
  DIM 371
Who Framed Roger Rabbit?
  ML 146, 226
Who Is Harry Kellerman and Why Is He Saying Those Terrible Things About Me?
  DIM 314, 323
  TIAI 244
Who Is Killing the Great Chefs of Europe?

WTLGD 482-485
H 299
5001
Who'll Stop the Rain
  WTLGD 432, 448
  TIAI 439
  SOTA 362
  H 49
Who's Afraid of Virginia Woolf?
  KKBB 23, 212
  GS 229
  DIM 405, 406
  WTLGD 178
Who's Been Sleeping in My Bed?
  ILIATM 26
  R 86
Who's That Knocking at My Door?
  R 174
"Whole Lotta Shakin' Goin' On" (music)
  TIAI 452
Whole Town's Talking, The
  KKBB 368:n
  GS 62
  5001
Whorf, Richard
  5001 88, 136, 391, 772, 853
Whose Life Is It, Anyway? (stage)
  TIAI 80
Why Are We in Vietnam? (book)
  GS 31
  H 362
"Why Do Fools Fall in Love?" (music)
  TIAI 389
Why Israel?
  H 86
Wiazemsky, Anne
  GS 80
  5001 38, 135
Wibberley, Leonard
  5001 500
Wicked Dreams of Paula Schultz, The
  GS 9
Wickes, Mary
  5001 5, 592
Wicki, Bernhard
  5001 102, 171
Wicking, Christopher
  H 159
  5001 3
Widdoes, Kathleen
  GS 235
  5001 309, 660
Widerberg, Bo
  DIM 41-42; dir., *Elvira Madigan*, 7, 41, 154, 365; *Adalen 31*, 40-42, 104
  5001 5, 216, 381
Widmark, Richard
  KKBB 43, 208, 249, 316
  R 390
  WTLGD 395
  SOTA 146, 233
  5001 10, 144, 147, 198, 200, 343, 384, 399, 503, 524, 564, 581, 798, 800
Wieck, Dorothea
  KKBB 303
  GS 45
  5001 448

Wiene, Robert
  KKBB 243; dir., *The Cabinet of Dr. Caligari*, 242-243, 310, 317, 367
  5001 113, 445
Wiesenfeld, Joe
  TIAI 422
  5001 111
Wiesenthal, Simon
  WTLGD 451-452
Wiest, Dianne
  SOTA 281, 282, 338
  H 113, 114, 275, 425, 426, 427, 459
  ML 193, 298-300
  5001 103, 234, 256, 316, 604, 610, 666
Wife Versus Secretary
  KKBB 285
  5001
Wifstrand, Naima
  ILIATM 107
  KKBB 304, 369
  5001 451, 525, 688, 839
Wiggins, Russell
  R 110
Wightman, Bob
  WTLGD 558-559
  5001 823
Wilby Conspiracy, The
  5001 (2nd ed)
Wilby, James
  H 360
  5001 471
Wilcox, Collin
  5001 777
Wilcox, Fred M.
  KKBB 266; dir., *Lassie Come Home*, 180, 184; *Forbidden Planet*, 266
  5001 258, 765
Wilcox, Herbert
  5001 370
Wilcox, John
  KKBB 328
  5001 558
Wilcox, Shannon
  TIAI 301
  5001 92
Wilcox-Horne, Collin
  DIM 157
  5001 44
Wilcoxon, Henry
  5001 140, 165, 305, 355, 457, 486, 652, 697, 747
Wild 90
  GS 9-17, 196
  R 30
  WTLGD 399
  H 362
Wild Angels, The
  KKBB 19, 21
  GS 91-92
  DIM 84
  5001
Wild Boys of the Road
  5001
Wild Bunch, The
  DIM 133-134, 149, 393
  R 162
  WTLGD 89, 113, 117, 118, 418, 431

TIAI 168
SOTA 164
H 322, 424
5001
Wild Child, The
DIM 243, 245
WTLGD 53, 350
SOTA 149
Wild Duck, The (stage)
TIAI 174
Wild in the Streets
GS 89, 90-92, 105, 107
5001
Wild, Jack
GS 202
5001 543
Wild Man of Borneo, The (stage)
RK 10
Wild One, The
ILIATM 58-59, 68
KKBB 190, 204, 366
DIM 152
R 120, 470
WTLGD 84, 320, 368, 455, 557
5001
Wild Palms, The (book)
ILIATM 127
R 271
Wild Party, The
5001
Wild Strawberries (*Smultronstallet*)
KKBB 280, 368-369
GS 216
DIM 252
R 223-225
WTLGD 74, 76, 258
TIAI 491
ML 12, 14
5001
"Wild Thing" (music)
H 232
Wilde, Cornel
DIM 62, 240, 242
5001 56, 149, 259, 305, 332, 415
Wilde, Hagar
KKBB 241
5001 104, 119, 352
Wilde, Marty
5001 709
Wilde, Oscar
ILIATM 174
GS 193
WTLGD 482
SOTA 370
ML 129
5001 117, 251, 358, 581
Wilder, Billy
ILIATM 151-155, 303; dir., *Irma la Douce*,
10, 14; *Some Like It Hot*, 39, 151, 206;
The Apartment, 41, 151; *Stalag 17*, 47;
Double Indemnity, 81, 129, 131, 160;
Sunset Boulevard, 140; *One, Two,
Three*, 150-155; *Ace in the Hole*, 153
KKBB 257, 318, 348, 349, 355; dir., *Stalag
17*, 194, 349; *Double Indemnity*, 219,
352; *Some Like It Hot*, 348; *Sunset
Boulevard*, 354-355

DIM 186-187; dir., *The Private Life of
Sherlock Holmes*, 186-187
R 422-426; dir., *Double Indemnity*, 135-136,
184, 186, 412; *Sunset Boulevard*, 364;
The Front Page, 422-426; *The Fortune
Cookie*, 425; *Some Like It Hot*, 426
WTLGD 183; dir., *Some Like It Hot*, 3, 29;
The Front Page, 150; *Double Indemnity*,
207, 262; *One, Two, Three*, 221
TIAI 14, 19; dir., *Some Like It Hot*, 67, 331,
332, 429; *Double Indemnity*, 256
5001 4, 48, 87, 123, 187, 198, 248, 258,
260, 270, 370, 399, 437, 438, 453, 478,
531, 550, 551, 599, 649, 668, 692, 705,
730, 844
Wilder, Gene
GS 67, 78
DIM 123
R 280-281, 389, 403-405
WTLGD 98-101, 247-248, 371; dir., *The
Adventure of Sherlock Holmes' Younger
Brother*, 98-101
H 69, 291, 455, 484
5001 6, 80, 91, 427, 601, 682, 710, 711,
836, 840, 850, 859
Wilder, Robert
5001 249, 850
Wilder, Sally
5001 249
Wilder, Thornton
ILIATM 101
GS 179
H 263
5001 556, 669
Wilder, Yvonne
5001 84
Wilding, Michael
5001 287, 360, 398, 514, 782, 804
Wildman, John
5001 506
Wilhelm, Wolfgang
5001 351, 664
Wilhoite, Kathleen
ML 308
5001 227
Wilkins, June
5001 44
Wilkosz, George
5001 518
Will Penny
5001
"Will You Love Me Tomorrow?" (music)
H 349
Willard
R 286
WTLGD 297
William Randolph Hearst, American (book)
RK 57
William, Warren
KKBB 273
5001 116, 140, 245, 291, 298, 358, 455, 767
Williams, Adam
5001 533
Williams, Andy
KKBB 360
5001 776
Williams, Barbara

5001 381
Williams, Ben Ames
5001 415
Williams, Billy
DIM 408
WTLGD 60
H 54
5001 72, 202, 214, 463, 614, 728, 819, 841,
847, 852
Williams, Billy Dee
R 36-37, 40
TIAI 482
5001 73, 218, 406, 453, 626
Williams, Brook
5001 606
Williams, Cara
5001 92, 196
Williams, Cindy
R 192-193
5001 788
Williams, Clarence III
SOTA 216
5001 155, 604
Williams, Cootie
5001 62
Williams, Dick
5001 25
Williams, Dick Anthony
5001 279
Williams, Emlyn
KKBB 350
R 3
5001 138, 155, 226, 376, 378, 453, 525,
710, 845
Williams, Esther
WTLGD 371
TIAI 357
SOTA 321
5001 54, 481, 740, 865
Williams, Gordon M.
5001 721
Williams, Grant
KKBB 184
5001 360
Williams, Guinn
5001 243, 856, 857, 858
Williams, Hal
TIAI 94
5001 598
Williams, Harcourt
5001 104, 315, 328, 636
Williams, Heathcote
H 332
5001 842
Williams, Hugh
5001 851
Williams, JoBeth
SOTA 69
5001 69, 588
Williams, John
KKBB 259
R 184
WTLGD 352, 419, 525
TIAI 210, 348, 482
SOTA 181
H 416
ML 71, 148, 250, 251

5001 3, 93, 138, 160, 189, 217, 218, 362,
    378, 432, 531, 564, 591, 613, 626, 649,
    691, 725, 731, 775
Williams, Kay
  5001 5
Williams, Maurice, see Maurice Williams and
    the Zodiacs
Williams, Paul
  R 367-368, 370
  WTLGD 164, 244
  5001 108, 179, 440, 579, 707
Williams, Rhys
  5001 155, 237, 282
Williams, Richard
  GS 146
  R 390
  5001 131, 503
Williams, Robert
  5001 586
Williams, Robin
  WTLGD 491
  TIAI 120, 123, 124, 377, 379
  SOTA 15, 16, 17, 18, 156, 158, 159, 190,
    304
  H 110, 111, 112, 113, 187, 188, 189, 264,
    300, 421, 422, 423, 456
  ML 17, 109, 153-56, 321-26
  5001 7, 65, 143, 178, 295, 499, 589, 731,
    732, 849
Williams, Samm-Art
  5001 84
Williams, Tennessee
  ILIATM 90, 139-140
  KKBB 27-28, 58, 103, 232, 352-353
  R 74, 154, 199, 246
  WTLGD 113-114, 169, 297, 310, 414
  TIAI 110, 175, 413, 415
  H 29, 233, 236, 239
  5001 43, 44, 124, 526, 637, 642, 722, 725,
    726, 734
Williams, Treat
  H 132
  5001 531, 548, 596, 689
Williams, Vanessa
  H 371
  5001 581
Williams, Zack
  5001 264
Williamson, David
  TIAI 454
  5001 276, 854
Williamson, Fred
  5001 469
Williamson, Nicol
  DIM 37, 88-91
  WTLGD 158, 159, 190-192
  TIAI 183, 184
  SOTA 114
  H 271, 465
  5001 78, 227, 315, 634, 667, 837
Willie & Phil
  TIAI 46-51, 392
  5001
"Willie Brown Blues" (music)
  H 144
Willingham, Calder
  R 269

5001 299, 424, 549, 570, 719, 757
Willis, Bruce
  ML 316-17
Willis, Gordon
  DIM 112, 122, 254
  R 13, 83, 401
  WTLGD 412, 485-487
  TIAI 88, 277, 278
  SOTA 338, 339
  H 371, 460
  5001 103, 148, 218, 289, 290, 366, 401,
    407, 427, 442, 479, 564, 574, 581, 604,
    809, 865
Willis, Ted
  KKBB 369
  5001 844
"Willkommen" (music)
  DIM 410
Willm, Pierre-Richard
  KKBB 244
  5001 120
Willman, Noel
  5001 4, 195
Willmer, Catherine
  5001 847
Willow
  H 473-474
  5001 (2nd ed)
Wills, Chill
  5001 32, 285, 321, 329, 340, 415, 569, 631,
    829, 855
Willson, Meredith
  5001 504
Willy Wonka and the Chocolate Factory
  5001
Wilmer, Douglas
  WTLGD 99
Wilson, Angus
  ILIATM 213
  DIM 150
Wilson, Carey
  KKBB 325
  5001 35, 502, 505, 552
Wilson, Dooley
  KKBB 245
  5001 122, 716
Wilson, Edmund
  ILIATM 168, 170
  R 182, 186, 188, 477
  WTLGD 272
  TIAI 179
Wilson, Eileen
  5001 550
Wilson, Elizabeth
  KKBB 272
  5001 289, 299, 361, 427, 458, 597
Wilson, Flip
  DIM 85, 149, 363
  5001 116
Wilson, Forrest
  5001 81
Wilson, Georges
  5001 382, 497, 685
Wilson, Harry Leon
  5001 646
Wilson, Ian
  H 333

5001 842
Wilson, Jackie
  H 342
Wilson, Janis
  5001 536
Wilson, Julie
  5001 719
Wilson, Larry
  H 456-457
  5001 61
Wilson, Larry Jon
  TIAI 206
Wilson, Lester
  WTLGD 368
  5001 655
Wilson, Lisle
  5001 684
Wilson, Margery
  5001 367
Wilson, Marie
  H 228
  5001 598, 768
Wilson, Michael
  5001 102, 247, 268, 584, 586, 651, 653
Wilson, Michael G.
  KKBB 331-332, 344
  GS 36
  SOTA 4, 368
  5001 257, 539, 815
Wilson, Mitchell
  5001 846
Wilson, Richard
  RK 8, 34, 39, 58
  5001 766
Wilson, Robert
  ML 79, 80
Wilson, S. S.
  5001 679
Wilson, Sandy
  DIM 379, 380, 382
  5001 96, 505
Wilson, Scott
  GS 102
  SOTA 65
  ML 193
  5001 360, 382, 630
Wilson, Stuart
  H 47
  5001 829
Wilson, Thomas F.
  ML 226
  5001 45
Wilson, Trey
  H 481
  ML 143
  5001 109, 485, 615
Wilton, Penelope
  5001 267
Wimperis, Arthur
  5001 606
Winchell, Walter
  KKBB 341
  RK 48
Wind and the Lion, The
  WTLGD 42
  5001
Wind, The

ILIATM 206
Windom, William
5001 185, 777
Windsor, Barbara
5001 96
Windsor, Duke of
WTLGD 27
Windsor, Marie
KKBB 291
5001 58, 394, 516
Windust, Bretaigne
5001 101, 220, 386
Windy Day
DIM 91
Winesburg, Ohio (short stories)
H 198
ML 118
Winfield, Paul
R 3, 5, 262, 296
WTLGD 124
TIAI 358
H 175, 176
5001 153, 346, 480, 697, 707, 798
Winfrey, Oprah
H 83
5001 146
Wing, Toby
5001 262
Winger, Debra
TIAI 31, 33, 382, 383
SOTA 94-95, 107, 338, 348
H 46, 173, 174-175, 176, 270, 271-272, 393
ML 302-308
5001 78, 227, 416, 448, 480, 540, 748, 809
Wings in the Dark
WTLGD 6
Wings of Desire (original title: *Der Himmel über Berlin*)
H 469-473
ML 39, 163
5001 (2nd ed)
Wings of the Dove, The (book)
ILIATM 282
SOTA 206
Winkler, Henry
WTLGD 467
TIAI 393-394
5001 527, 528
Winkler, Irwin
5001 39, 612, 627, 630, 636, 644, 793
Winkless, Terence H.
TIAI 192
5001 344
Winn, Kitty
DIM 305
5001 229, 563
Winner, Michael
GS 181
5001 71, 529
Winning
WTLGD 275
Winninger, Charles
KKBB 45, 256, 320
5001 42, 106, 185, 525, 535, 679, 711, 728, 768, 865
Winningham, Mare
H 392

5001 448, 768
Winsloe, Christa
KKBB 303
5001 448
Winslow, George
5001 494
Winsor, Kathleen
5001 258
Winsten, Archer
RK 44
Winston, S. K.
5001 187
Winter Carnival
GS 10
Winter, Jonathan
5001 440
Winter, Keith
5001 674
Winter Kills
H 364
Winter Light
TIAI 488
Winter Soldier
WTLGD 251
Winters, Jonathan
KKBB 299
GS 40-41
DIM 85, 329-330
R 128, 131, 243, 403
WTLGD 506
5001 647
Winters, Shelley
ILIATM 208
KKBB 238, 279, 317, 332
GS 91
DIM 109
R 72, 432
WTLGD 128, 131, 479
ML 95
5001 14, 71, 88, 129, 141, 185, 199, 320, 348, 430, 521, 526, 584, 585, 591, 656, 690, 838, 860
Winterset
KKBB 369:n
R 345
WTLGD 489
5001
Winterton, Peter
5001 784
Winwood, Estelle
KKBB 336
R 97
5001 116, 277, 287, 484, 601, 607
Wir Wunderkinder. see *Aren't We Wonderful*
Wisconsin Death Trip (book)
SOTA 30-31
Wisdom, Norman
GS 239
5001 528
Wise Guys
H 153-155
5001 (2nd ed)
Wise, Robert
ILIATM 10, 142; dir., *The Haunting*, 10-13; *West Side Story*, 10, 141-147, 278; *I Want to Live*, 35, 143; *So Big*, 143; *Executive Suite*, 143, 323; *Somebody Up*

There Likes Me, 143; *The Set-Up*, 235
KKBB 8, 50, 178, 248, 304; dir., *The Sand Pebbles*, 8-9, 59; *I Want to Live!*, 50; *The Sound of Music*, 163, 176-178; *The Day the Earth Stood Still*, 184
GS dir., *The Sound of Music*, 60, 117, 162, 201; *Star!*, 161-165; *West Side Story*, 108, 153, 154, 162, 237
RK 41, 46
DIM 275, 276; dir., *Star!*, 26, 328; *The Sound of Music*, 27, 84, 187, 219, 328, 330, 390; *The Andromeda Strain*, 275-276; *West Side Story*, 328, 409
R 149-150; dir., *I Want to Live!*, 111, 149; *Two People*, 149-150; *The Body Snatcher*, 149; *The Set-Up*, 149; *Executive Suite*, 149; *Somebody Up There Likes Me*, 149; *West Side Story*, 150; *Two for the Seesaw*, 150; *The Haunting*, 150; *The Sound of Music*, 150; *The Sand Pebbles*, 150; *Star!*, 150, 325; *The Andromeda Strain*, 150
WTLGD 119-122; dir., *The Hindenburg*, 119-122; *West Side Story*, 120, 369, 370, 440; *The Sound of Music*, 120, 470; *Somebody Up There Likes Me*, 213; *The Curse of the Cat People*, 547
5001 26, 44, 139, 167, 321, 334, 451, 666, 697, 706, 799, 828
Wiseguy (book)
ML 265
"Wiseguy" (TV)
ML 206
Wiseman, Fred
DIM 20, 24, 101, 207, 295; dir., *Law and Order*, 20, 23, 207; *High School*, 20-24; *Titicut Follies*, 20, 21; *Hospital*, 101-102
R 163, 330; dir., *Titicut Follies*, 163; *High School*, 163
WTLGD 43, 219; dir., *High School*, 43; *Welfare*, 219
TIAI 205; dir., *Essene*, 205
5001 155, 332, 388, 774
Wiseman, Joseph
KKBB 367
GS 53, 239
5001 33, 66, 111, 186, 528, 818
Wiseman, Thomas
WTLGD 93
5001 638
Wish You Were Here
H 331-333
5001 (2nd ed)
Witch's Milk (book)
R 85
Witches, The
5001 (2nd ed)
Witches of Eastwick, The
H 323-325, 482
5001 (2nd ed)
Witcombe, Eleanor
TIAI 61
5001 283, 506
Withers, Googie
KKBB 255, 293, 316, 323-324

5001 178, 379, 406, 524, 544
Withers, Grant
  5001 631, 728
Withers, Jane
  WTLGD 178
  5001 285, 533
Witherspoon, Cora
  KKBB 336
  5001 420, 545, 559, 607
Without Apparent Motive (Sans mobile apparent)
  DIM 413-415
  R 201, 258
  5001
Without Love
  KKBB 330
  5001
Without Roof or Law, see Vagabond
Withrow, Glenn
  H 454
  5001 567
Witliff, William D.
  TIAI 372
  SOTA 234
Witness
  SOTA 319-323
  H 479
  5001 (2nd ed)
Witness for the Prosecution
  5001
Witnesses, The (book)
  H 265
Witt, Alicia Roanne
  SOTA 286
  5001 207
Wittgenstein, Carolyne Sayn, see
    Sayn-Wittgenstein, Carolyne
Wittliff, William D.
  5001 50, 78, 157, 611
Witts, Max Morgan
  5001 819
Wixted, Michael-James
  WTLGD 279, 282
  5001 372
Wiz, The
  WTLGD 469-476, 556
  SOTA 217
  5001
Wizard of Oz, The (book), see The Wonderful
    Wizard of Oz
Wizard of Oz, The (1939)
  ILIATM 145
  KKBB 234
  R 389
  WTLGD 210, 349, 354, 471, 472, 473, 474
  TIAI 126, 292, 483
  SOTA 177
  ML 107
Wjingaarden, Jip
  ML 293, 294
WNET (Channel 13)
  DIM 319, 320
Wodehouse, P. G.
  TIAI 230
  5001 679
Wohl, Burton
  KKBB 250
  5001 145, 631

Wolf, Dick
  H 445
  5001 469
Wolf Man, The
  TIAI 193, 194
Wolf, Rita
  H 120
  5001 506
Wolfe, Ian
  5001 5, 52, 260, 505, 616, 618, 748, 754,
    770, 844
Wolfe, Thomas
  TIAI 435
  ML 181
Wolfe, Tom
  R 164, 165
  SOTA 61, 62, 66, 67
  H 391
  ML 315, 317
  5001 407, 630
Wolff, Frank
  5001 22, 38
Wolff, Ruth
  R 346
  WTLGD 205
  5001 1, 360
Wolfit, Donald
  KKBB 331
  SOTA 114, 200
  5001 415, 581, 640
Wolfman Jack (pseud.)
  H 250
Wolfson, P. J.
  5001 445, 582, 753, 763, 819
Wolheim, Louis
  KKBB 231
  H 304
  5001 18, 553
Wolk, Emil
  ML 272
Wolper, David L.
  TIAI 202
  5001 762, 840
Wolsey, Cardinal
  DIM 97
Woman Accused, The
  WTLGD 6
Woman Alone, The, see Sabotage
Woman in a Dressing Gown
  KKBB 369:n
  5001
Woman in the Painting, The, see Amici per la
    Pelle
Woman in the Window, The
  5001
"Woman in the Moon, The" (music)
  WTLGD 243
Woman Like Satan, A
  WTLGD 365
Woman of Affairs, A
  KKBB 285
  DIM 364, 365
  5001 (2nd ed)
Woman of Dolwyn (also known as The Last Days
    of Dolwyn)
  5001
Woman of the Rock

RK 82, 83
Woman of the Year
  KKBB 330
  WTLGD 61
  TIAI 254
  H 83
  5001
Woman on the Beach, The
  5001
Woman Rebels, A
  5001
Woman Under the Influence, A
  R 392-396, 411
  5001
Woman's Face, A
  ILIATM 305
  ML 193
  5001
Women, The
  DIM 137
  5001
Women in Love
  DIM 138-142, 239
  R 51
  TIAI 214
  H 129
  ML 137, 138
  5001
Women in Revolt
  5001
Women of the World
  R 66
Women on the Verge of a Nervous Breakdown
    (Mujeres al Borde de un Ataque de
    Nervios)
  H 466
  ML 23-27
  5001 (2nd ed)
Women's Wear (periodical)
  RK 10
Wonderful Crook, The (Pas si méchant que ça)
  WTLGD 285-287
  5001
Wonderful Night, A
  WTLGD 13
Wonderful Wizard of Oz, The (book)
  WTLGD 470, 471
  H 39
Wong, Anna May
  GS 54
  5001 671, 756
Wong, James
  5001 11
Wood, Charles
  GS 145-146, 147
  DIM 17
  R 18
  5001 130, 343, 401
Wood, Christopher
  5001 496, 703
Wood, Elijah
  ML 279-82
  5001 40
Wood, Helen
  5001 287
Wood, John
  WTLGD 451

TIAI 494
SOTA 337, 338, 356, 358
H 190
5001 325, 406, 604, 692, 823
Wood, Lana
   5001 661
Wood, Natalie
   ILIATM 138, 145-146
   KKBB 41, 283
   GS 73
   DIM 11-13
   R 393, 422, 429
   WTLGD 433
   ML 121
   5001 89, 284, 311, 365, 618, 662, 702, 705,
      778, 828
Wood, Peggy
   5001 697
Wood, Robin
   R 141
Wood, Sam
   KKBB 275, 317, 345; dir., *Madame X*
      (1937), 121; *A Day at the Races*, 184; *A*
      Night at the Opera, 185, 317, 320;
      Goodbye, Mr. Chips, 275; *Saratoga*
      Trunk, 345, 348
   5001 175, 186, 256, 296, 336, 397, 400,
      524, 556, 654
Woodard, Alfre
   SOTA 56, 58
   ML 40, 142, 144
   5001 164, 485, 660
Woodbury, Joan
   5001 318
Woodhouse, Barbara
   TIAI 383
   SOTA 4
Woodlawn, Holly
   DIM 155-157
   5001 788, 847
Woodley, Richard
   R 65
Woods, Aubrey
   5001 523
Woods, Donald
   H 399-401
   5001 253, 524, 741, 824
Woods, Harry M.
   5001 226
Woods, James
   WTLGD 183
   TIAI 171
   SOTA 145, 146, 361
   H 180-181, 183, 185, 251
   ML 83-86
   5001 10, 12, 231, 548, 651, 792
Woodstock
   DIM 208
Woodstock
   WTLGD 83
   H 227
Woodward, Joanne
   ILIATM 91
   DIM 59, 181, 182
   R 74-76, 222, 224
   5001 212, 244, 432, 723, 727, 765, 851
Woodward, W. E.

5001 225
Wooland, Norman
   5001 315, 375, 449, 628
Wooldridge, Susan
   H 369
   5001 340
Woolf, Edgar Allan
   5001 107, 123
Woolf, John
   5001 543
Woolf, Virginia
   ILIATM 106, 149
   DIM 36, 188, 291
   WTLGD 205, 551
   TIAI 134
   H 70, 389
Woollcott, Alexander
   KKBB 275, 358
   RK 14
   WTLGD 482
   5001 296, 459
Woolley, Monty
   5001 334, 337, 398, 459, 478, 523, 535,
      683, 765
Woolsey, Judge John M.
   KKBB 170
Woolsey, Robert
   5001 160, 391
Worden, Hank
   5001 662
Words After Speech: A Comparative Study of
   Romanticism and Symbolism (book)
   H 61
Words and Music
   5001
Working Girl
   ML 63-66, 274, 275
   5001 (2nd ed)
Workman, Nimrod
   WTLGD 252
World According to Garp, The
   TIAI 376-381
   SOTA 22
   H 421
   5001 (2nd ed)
World Apart, A
   H 475-478
   ML 72
   5001 (2nd ed)
"World in Action" (TV)
   H 476
World of Apu, The (*Apur Sansar*; see also *The*
   Apu Trilogy)
   ILIATM 248, 250
   R 141
   SOTA 380
   5001
World of Henry Orient, The
   5001 (2nd ed)
World Première
   5001
World War I
   DIM 15, 189, 368, 429
   WTLGD 326, 329, 553
World War II
   DIM 40, 45, 86, 99, 100, 146, 216, 359,
      427, 429

WTLGD 20, 22, 24, 58, 69, 97, 118, 126,
   136-139, 144, 149, 150, 175-177, 199,
   279, 310, 325, 326, 328, 330-332, 371,
   396, 402, 405, 451-454, 485, 489, 516
   H 367-370
World Without Sun
   KKBB 185
World's Greatest Lover, The
   5001
Worlock, Frederic
   5001 199
Woronov, Mary
   TIAI 424
   5001 78, 211, 659
Worth
   5001 605
Worth, Irene
   DIM 369
   TIAI 169, 172, 326, 327
   5001 181, 231, 552, 664
Worts, George F.
   5001 580
Woton's Wake
   R 368
Would-Be Gentleman, The, see *Le Bourgeois*
   Gentilhomme
Wound and the Bow, The (book)
   WTLGD 272
Wounded Knee
   WTLGD 175
Wozzeck
   R 145
WR--Misterije Organizma, see *WR--Mysteries of*
   the Organism
WR--Mysteries of the Organism (*WR--Misterije*
   Organizma)
   5001
Wray, Fay
   KKBB 43, 184, 249
   WTLGD 13, 14, 235
   5001 144, 194, 263, 499, 512, 566, 628, 769
Wray, John
   KKBB 231
   5001 18, 195
Wrecking Crew, The
   R 284
Wren, Percival C.
   5001 58
Wright, Amy
   ML 69
   5001 3, 183, 485
Wright, Dorsey
   5001 823
Wright, Frank Lloyd
   SOTA 197
   5001 808
Wright, Jenny
   5001 518
Wright, Jenny Lee
   DIM 222
Wright, Max
   TIAI 280
   5001 621, 783
Wright, Richard
   RK 37
Wright, Robert
   5001 694

Wright, Robin
 H 379
 5001 597
Wright, Samuel E.
 ML 4
 5001 73, 426
Wright, Steven
 5001 184
Wright, Teresa
 KKBB 304
 WTLGD 357
 TIAI 69
 ML 34, 37
 5001 5, 65, 295, 426, 475, 486, 642, 669
Wright, Will
 5001 86
Wrightsman, Stan
 5001 88
Writers Guild of America
 H 299
Written on the Wind
 5001
Wrong Man, The
 5001
Wrye, Donald
 WTLGD 149-152; dir., *The Entertainer*
  (1976, TV), 149-152, 254
Wu Jun Mimei, see Mimei, Wu Jun
Wuhl, Robert
 H 481
 ML 224
 5001 54, 80, 109
Wunderlich, Fritz
 WTLGD 75
Wunsch, Robert J.
 5001 686
Wurlitzer, Rudolph
 5001 569
WUSA
 DIM 181-182
 TIAI 21
 5001
Wuthering Heights (1939)
 RK 76
 WTLGD 146
 5001
Wyatt, Jane
 5001 92, 436, 531, 533, 708
Wyatt, Tessa
 R 204
 5001 221
Wycherly, Margaret
 5001 391, 616, 814-815, 834, 855
Wyeth, Andrew
 WTLGD 527
Wyler, William
 ILIATM 175-176; dir., *The Best Years of*
  Our Lives, 81; *The Children's Hour*,
  175-176; *Ben-Hur*, 119, 190
 KKBB 252, 289, 296; dir., *Funny Girl*, 23;
  Dead End, 61; *Roman Holiday*, 185,
  252; *Friendly Persuasion*, 194; *Mrs.*
  Miniver, 221, 304; *Counsellor-at-Law*,
  251-252; *The Little Foxes*, 252; *The*
  Best Years of Our Lives, 252; *The*
  Desperate Hours, 252; *Jezebel*, 289-290;
  The Letter, 295-296

GS dir., *Funny Girl*, 133-137; *The Letter*, 62
 DIM 381; dir., *How to Steal a Million*, 37;
  Roman Holiday, 381
 R 459; dir., *Funny Girl*, 38, 177, 457, 459,
  460, 462; *The Westerner*, 99; *The Best*
  Years of Our Lives, 364; *Jezebel*, 431
 WTLGD 146, 228, 506; dir., *Wuthering*
  Heights, 146; *Roman Holiday*, 157, 345;
  Funny Girl, 346; *The Best Years of Our*
  Lives, 405; *The Little Foxes*, 478
 H 444
 ML 156
 5001 63, 65, 121, 133, 145, 156, 178, 186,
  196, 268, 272, 294, 327, 343, 366, 380,
  419, 426, 486, 636, 637, 753, 829, 851
Wylie, I. A. R.
 5001 391, 819, 859
Wylie, Philip
 5001 369
Wyman, Jane
 KKBB 185, 285
 5001 19, 381, 437, 451, 509, 523, 854
Wymark, Patrick
 5001 163, 624
Wyndham, John
 5001 815
Wyngarde, Peter
 5001 365
Wynn, Ed
 KKBB 277
 R 16
 H 302
 5001 302, 704
Wynn, Keenan
 KKBB 277
 GS 102, 159
 R 450
 5001 30, 64, 116, 141, 244, 256, 287, 303,
  387, 399, 442, 517, 588, 646, 766, 767,
  843, 865
Wynn, Nan
 5001 159, 858
Wynn, Tracy Keenan
 R 265
 5001 39
Wynter, Dana
 KKBB 286
 DIM 137
 5001 12, 368, 424
Wynyard, Diana
 5001 127, 280, 398, 617

X

X--The Man with the X-Ray Eyes
 5001
X Y & Zee (English title *Zee and Co.*)
 DIM 405-409
 5001
Xenophon
 WTLGD 555, 556, 557
 5001 823

Y

"Ya Got Trouble" (music)
 TIAI 333
Yablans, Frank
 R 320
 WTLGD 269
 TIAI 236
 5001 492
Yablonski, Joseph A.
 WTLGD 249, 252
Yacht Club Boys (group)
 5001 582
Yafa, Stephen
 5001 766
Yakovlev, Yuri
 5001 354
Yakusho, Koji
 H 307
 5001 743
Yakuza, The
 R 442, 464, 469-471
 WTLGD 196, 303
 5001
Yamada, Isuzu
 ILIATM 244
 KKBB 246
 H 91
 5001 124, 769
Yamashta, Stomu
 TIAI 392
 5001 746
Yamazaki, Tsutomu
 TIAI 137
 H 307
 5001 743
Yankee Doodle Dandy
 5001
Yanne, Jean
 GS 139
 DIM 172, 404
 5001 95, 762, 827
Yarborough, Norman
 WTLGD 250, 252
Yared, Gabriel
 ML 292
Yarrow, Peter
 GS 148
Yates, Cassie
 WTLGD 433
 SOTA 154
 5001 155, 806
Yates, Peter
 GS dir., *Bullitt*, 165-166
 DIM 73, 402, 403; dir., *John and Mary*,
  72-73; *Bullitt*, 162, 316, 402; *The Hot*
  Rock, 401-403
 R 317-318; dir., *Bullitt*, 161, 260, 317; *The*
  Friends of Eddie Coyle, 317, 470; *The*
  Hot Rock, 317; *John and Mary*, 317;
  Murphy's War, 317; *For Pete's Sake*,
  318, 328, 459
 TIAI 8, 169-172, 285; dir., *Breaking Away*,
  8, 12-13, 169, 196, 285; *Eyewitness*,
  169-172, 327; *The Deep*, 439

SOTA 113-116; dir., *The Dresser*, 113-116, 200; *Breaking Away*, 309
H 69-73, 393-394; dir., *Eleni*, 69-73; *Breaking Away*, 70; *Eyewitness*, 70; *John and Mary*, 177; *Suspect*, 393-394
5001 109, 204, 214, 230, 269, 341, 381, 695, 733

Yeager, Chuck
SOTA 61, 62, 64, 65, 66, 67
5001 630

Year of Living Dangerously, The
TIAI 451-456
SOTA 74
H 183
5001 (2nd ed)

Year of the Dragon
H 31-36, 157, 180, 183, 251
5001 (2nd ed)

Yearling, The
KKBB 180, 185, 285-286
SOTA 57, 59
5001

Yeats-Brown, Francis
5001 429

Yeats, William Butler
KKBB 199, 321-322
5001 539

Yelland, David
5001 131

Yellow Sky
KKBB 266

Yellow Submarine
GS 187-192
RK 72
5001

Yentl
SOTA 85-91
H 379
5001 (2nd ed)

"Yentl, the Yeshiva Boy" (story)
SOTA 85, 86, 87, 88, 89

"Yes, Yes!" (music)
TIAI 276

Yesterday and Today
KKBB 303

Yesterday, Today, and Tomorrow (stage)
DIM 362

"Yesterday When I Was Young" (music)
WTLGD 125

Yeux sans visage, Les, see *Eyes Without a Face*

Yevtushenko, Yevgeni
5001 348

Yi, Pu, see Pu Yi

Ying, Angela Mao
5001 221

Ying, Ruocheng
H 397
5001 408

Yñiguez, Richard
5001 95

Yojimbo
ILIATM 239-245, 316
WTLGD 523, 556
H 308
5001

Yolanda and the Thief
TIAI 131

5001

Yordan, Philip
DIM 24
5001 475, 646, 724

Yordanoff, Wladimir
ML 292

York, Dick
KKBB 325
5001 363, 551

York, Michael
GS 155, 156
DIM 67, 412
R 138, 203-204, 390
WTLGD 65
5001 3, 112, 151, 221, 436, 503, 639, 767

York, Rebecca
WTLGD 502
5001 501

York, Susannah
GS 19, 24, 208
DIM 69, 189, 405, 406, 408
R 80-81, 359
WTLGD 65, 528
5001 151, 291, 317, 358, 435, 456, 541, 662, 730, 755, 778, 794, 852

Yorkin, Bud
DIM 123; dir., *Start the Revolution Without Me*, 123
R 135-137; dir., *The Thief Who Came to Dinner*, 135-137; *Start the Revolution Without Me*, 403
H 75-76; dir., *Twice in a Lifetime*, 73, 75-76; *Start the Revolution Without Me*, 484
5001 711, 757, 796

Yoshinaga, Sayuri
SOTA 327
5001 454

Yoshioka, Adele
5001 452

Yost, Daniel
ML 195
5001 205

Yost, Dorothy
5001 717

Yothers, Tina
TIAI 295
5001 676

You and Me
5001

"You and Me" (music)
TIAI 333

You Are What You Eat
GS 148-149

"You Can't Win" (music)
WTLGD 472

"You Don't Know Me" (music)
ML 275

"You Don't Own Me" (music)
H 349

You Light Up My Life
5001

You Only Live Once
ILIATM 299
KKBB 49-52, 54
5001

You Only Live Twice

GS 122
5001 (2nd ed)

"You Send Me" (music)
H 50

"You'd Be So Nice to Come Home To" (music)
H 277

You'll Never Get Rich
5001

"You're a Policeman" (music)
H 454

"You're in Paradise Now" (music)
H 454

"You're the Top" (music)
DIM 432
WTLGD 26

Youmans, Vincent
5001 253

Young, Alan
5001 26, 773

Young and Innocent (also known as *The Girl Was Young*)
5001

Young and the Damned, The, see *Los Olvidados*

Young and the Passionate, The, see *I Vitelloni*

Young at Heart
ILIATM 57-58
5001

Young, Barbara Eda, see Eda-Young, Barbara

Young, Burt
R 350
WTLGD 115, 117-118, 214-215
TIAI 347
SOTA 204
5001 45, 135, 155, 276, 394, 548, 589, 636, 798

Young, Carleton
5001 287, 533, 688

Young Cassidy
5001

Young, Dalene
SOTA 58
5001 164

Young Doctors, The
R 284

Young Doctors in Love
SOTA 310

Young Frankenstein
R 403-405
WTLGD 99-100, 371, 373, 375
TIAI 215, 224
SOTA 2, 286
H 69
ML 113
5001

Young, Freddie
DIM 368
R 112
5001 114, 195, 376, 415, 435, 436, 443, 491, 523, 648, 857

Young, Gig
DIM 70
WTLGD 115-118
5001 11, 184, 334, 394, 542, 755, 767, 782, 858

Young Girls of Rochefort, The
GS 100, 265, 266
TIAI 47, 255

279

Young, Harold
  5001 659
Young in Heart, The
  KKBB 369-370:n
  5001
Young, Janis
  5001 442
Young, Lee
  5001 349, 723
Young Lions, The
  DIM 249
  R 120
  5001
Young, Loretta
  GS 239
  RK 20
  DIM 73
  WTLGD 215
  SOTA 337
  5001 165, 237, 464, 586, 719, 814, 865
Young Mr. Lincoln
  KKBB 61
  5001
Young, Ned
  5001 377
Young, Neil
  H 393
  5001 411, 449
Young, Otis
  R 273, 274
  5001 408
Young, Rida Johnson
  5001 518
Young, Robert
  KKBB 253
  WTLGD 8
  5001 117, 164, 218, 351, 393, 404, 534,
    663, 674, 684, 736, 765, 778
Young, Robert M.
  WTLGD 295-298
  5001 679
Young, Roland
  KKBB 363, 369-370
  SOTA 221, 222
  5001 25, 248, 309, 322, 334, 370, 447, 459,
    580, 647, 741, 753, 781, 782, 859
Young, Ruth
  ML 125
Young Savages, The
  TIAI 173
  5001
Young Scarface, see *Brighton Rock*
Young, Sean
  TIAI 363
  SOTA 286
  H 355, 356
  ML 96, 97, 98
  5001 80, 159, 207, 532, 723
Young Sherlock Holmes
  H 100-102
  5001 (2nd ed)
Young, Snooky
  5001 88
Young, Stark
  R 84
Young, Steve
  TIAI 204, 205

  5001 326
Young, Terence
  GS 181; dir., *Mayerling*, 271
  5001 270, 472, 545, 769
Young, Victor
  5001 243, 558, 728, 807
Young, Waldemar
  5001 141, 184, 476, 590, 680
Young Winston
  R 15-18
  5001
"Young Woman's Blues" (music)
  WTLGD 107
Youngblood Hawke
  WTLGD 393
Youngman, Henny
  TIAI 215
Youngs, Jim
  5001 256
Youngson, Robert
  KKBB 184, 185, 274
  5001 292, 831
Your Past Is Showing (also known as *The Naked
    Truth*)
  KKBB 294-295
  WTLGD 246
  5001
"Your Show of Shows" (TV)
  WTLGD 374
  TIAI 394
  R 127, 129-132
Yourcenar, Marguerite
  5001 158
Youskevitch, Igor
  5001 369
Yukl, Joe
  5001 287
Yule, Joe
  5001 106
Yulin, Harris
  DIM 112
  SOTA 102
  ML 13
  5001 31, 218, 284, 658
Yung, Victor Sen
  5001 4, 419, 771
Yurick, Sol
  WTLGD 555-559
  5001 823
Yurka, Blanche
  5001 698, 741, 760
Yust, Larry
  R 113-114
  5001 789
Yuzna, Brian
  5001 618

Z

Z
  DIM 63-67, 152, 154, 200, 202, 204, 316,
    317, 319
  R 209, 211-212, 214
  WTLGD 95, 97

  H 54
  5001
Zabriskie, Grace
  H 359
  5001 70, 205
Zabriskie Point
  DIM 113-117, 131, 211
  R 107, 304, 326
  WTLGD 421
  H 452
  5001
Zachariah
  5001
Zadora, Pia
  H 363, 443
  5001 313
Zaentz, Saul
  WTLGD 86
  H 432
  5001 22, 549, 572, 804
Zafiriou, Eleni
  KKBB 271
  5001 286
Zaharias, Mildred Didrikson "Babe"
  KKBB 330
  5001 569
Zaillian, Steven
  SOTA 313
  ML 320, 326
  5001 233
Zaks, Jerry
  5001 559
Zampa, Luigi
  5001 380
Zampi, Mario
  KKBB 294-295; dir., *Laughter in Paradise*,
    294; *Your Past is Showing*, 294-295;
    Too Many Crooks, 295
  5001 413, 779, 861
Zandy's Bride
  5001
Zanetti, Eugenio
  5001 251
Zanuck, Darryl F.
  DIM 83, 151
  R 155
  5001 129, 583, 642, 713, 818
Zanuck, Harrison
  5001 725
Zanuck, Richard D.
  5001 378, 715, 726, 743, 813
Zapponi, Bernardino
  5001 240
Zardoz
  R 276-280
  TIAI 184
  5001
Zaslow, Michael
  5001 857
Zavattini, Cesare
  ILIATM 115
  KKBB 247, 269, 310, 364
  DIM 361-362
  R 452
  SOTA 26
  5001 9, 63, 67, 102, 133, 362, 483, 676,
    801, 803, 823

Zaza
  5001
Zazie (also known as *Zazie dans le Métro*)
  KKBB 370:n
  DIM 308, 309
  R 341
  TIAI 327
  5001
Zbyszko, Stanislaus
  KKBB 316
  5001 524
Zee and Co., see *X Y & Zee*
Zeffirelli, Franco
  GS dir., *Romeo and Juliet* (1968), 153-158,
    279; *The Taming of the Shrew*, 105-106,
    153
  DIM 182, 183, 272; dir., *Romeo and Juliet*,
    18, 182, 219; *Brother Sun and Sister
    Moon* (projected), 182-183
  R 17
  TIAI 28, 113, 114; dir., *Romeo and Juliet*,
    28; *The Champ* (1979), 113
  SOTA 226, 254; dir., *Romeo and Juliet*, 226
  5001 63, 219, 639, 749
Zeitlin, Denny
  WTLGD 523
  5001 368
Zelig
  SOTA 23-27
  ML 202
  5001 (2nd ed)
Zelniker, Michael
  ML 4
  5001 73
Zeman, Karel
  ILIATM 275; dir., *Invention of Destruction*,
    275
  KKBB 180, 255-256; dir., *The Deadly
    Invention*, 180, 184, 255-256
  GS 192
  ML 106
  5001 179
Zemeckis, Robert
  TIAI 97-100; dir., *Used Cars*, 97-100; *I
    Wanna Hold Your Hand*, 98
  SOTA 163-165, 212; dir., *Romancing the
    Stone*, 163-165; *I Wanna Hold Your
    Hand*, 164; *Used Cars*, 164, 212
  H 11-13, 280; dir., *Back to the Future*, 11-
    13, 74, 220, 300; *Used Cars*, 12, 106,
    280, 454; *Romancing the Stone*, 12, 273
  ML dir., *Back to the Future*, 226, 227; *Back
    to the Future Part II*, 225-227; *I Wanna
    Hold Your Hand*, 226; *Who Framed
    Roger Rabbit?*, 146, 226
  5001 45, 530, 638, 810
Zemlya, see *Earth*
Zen and the Art of Motorcycle Maintenance
  R 388
Zerbe, Anthony
  WTLGD 63, 492
  5001 413, 421, 492, 565, 794, 839
Zéro de conduite, see *Zero for Conduct*
Zero for Conduct (*Zéro de conduite*)
  ILIATM 222
  KKBB 93, 140, 301
  GS 281-286

  WTLGD 455
  TIAI 144, 250
  5001
Zetterling, Mai
  KKBB 103-104, 292; dir., *Night Games*,
    103-104
  5001 402, 525, 782, 794, 842
Zetterlund, Monica
  R 181
  5001 520
Zieff, Howard
  R 133-135
  WTLGD 45-49; dir., *Hearts of the West*,
    45-49; *Slither*, 46
  TIAI 92-95; dir., *Private Benjamin*, 92-95,
    163, 226; *Slither*, 156
  SOTA 153-155; dir., *Unfaithfully Yours*
    (1984), 153-155, 344; *Private Benjamin*,
    166, 167, 344; *Slither*, 217
  ML 112-114; dir., *The Dream Team*
  5001 202, 325, 598, 686, 806
Ziegfeld, Florenz (Flo)
  GS 136
  RK 69
  R 462
  WTLGD 12, 15
  5001 288, 641, 679
Ziegfeld Follies
  KKBB 222
  5001
Ziegfeld Follies
  WTLGD 474
"Ziegfeld Follies of 1916" (stage)
  RK 69
Ziegfeld Girl
  5001
Zimbalist, Efrem Jr.
  R 364
  5001 129, 338
Zimbalist, Sam
  5001 397, 783
Zimmer, Sonia
  TIAI 423
  5001 111
Zimmerman, Paul
  TIAI 459, 460
  5001 396
Zindel, Paul
  R 74, 83, 299
  H 233
  5001 212, 455, 809
Zinnemann, Fred
  ILIATM 303, 305; dir., *From Here to
    Eternity*, 25, 47, 49, 54, 93, 305; *The
    Nun's Story*, 25, 305; *The Men*, 47; *The
    Member of the Wedding*, 47; *High
    Noon*, 242
  KKBB 154-155, 169, 176, 203, 231, 257,
    281, 309; dir., *High Noon*, 40, 151-152,
    194, 203, 219, 280-281; *A Man for All
    Seasons*, 50, 154-155; *The Nun's Story*,
    169, 176; *The Men*, 203; *The Member of
    the Wedding*, 203, 308-309
  GS 170; dir., *A Man for All Seasons*, 108,
    174; *The Sundowners*, 108
  DIM 176; dir., *Oklahoma!*, 29, 409, 413;
    The Sundowners, 18; *A Man for All

  Seasons*, 95; *Behold a Pale Horse*, 176;
    The Men, 322; *High Noon*, 387; *From
    Here to Eternity*, 421; *The Nun's Story*,
    421
  R 330; dir., *A Man for All Seasons*, 110; *The
    Day of the Jackal*, 214
  WTLGD 304-310; dir., *From Here to
    Eternity*, 41, 305; *The Nun's Story*, 159,
    305; *Julia*, 304-310; *The Sundowners*,
    305; *A Man for All Seasons*, 305, 309;
    Oklahoma!, 353
  5001 18, 187, 269, 331, 385, 456, 474, 475,
    507, 661, 729
Zinner, Peter
  5001 183
Zionism
  DIM 201
Zito, Stephen
  TIAI 353
  5001 225
Zobda, Frances
  5001 673
Zoetrope Studios
  TIAI 299, 354
  SOTA 29
Zoffoli, Marta
  TIAI 318
Zola, Émile
  KKBB 333
  DIM 267
  WTLGD 206, 340
  H 330
  5001 66, 282, 344, 592, 593
Zola, Jean-Pierre
  5001 493
Zolotow, Maurice
  ILIATM 37
  R 153
Zolotow, Sam
  RK 11
Zoo in Budapest
  5001
Zoot Suit
  H 341
Zorba the Greek
  KKBB 160
  DIM 35, 246
  5001
Zorina
  5001 254
Zorro, the Gay Blade
  TIAI 232-233
  5001
Zouzou
  R 9
  5001 136
Zsigmond, Vilmos
  R 80, 187, 259, 300
  WTLGD 352, 442, 445, 513
  TIAI 112, 228, 301
  5001 85, 92, 138, 183, 358, 411, 432, 445,
    641, 685, 725, 799, 843
Zucco, George
  KKBB 251
  5001 152, 153, 245, 345, 446, 459, 583,
    641, 697
Zucker, David and Jerry

Introduction to a
Selected Bibliography

There are a number of scholarly articles about Pauline Kael cited in the following bibliography. A common theme among some of them is that Pauline Kael has no aesthetic, no theory of film, and no set of standards she uses to measure a film against. Perhaps this is because Kael approaches each film she sees with a fresh eye, hoping to be astonished and delighted. What some perceive as a fault, may also be seen as an advantage Kael has over those with rigid theories of film. Kael is free to say what she thinks about the films she critiques without the added baggage of making sure it fits into some ideological framework. A typical Kael review grabs you, makes a powerful statement, and then seems to contradict or question it. In reading Kael, and reading about Kael, the reader will find that she has become famous for her slanginess, her eroticism, her insistence that judging film by literary standards is absurd, her willingness to insert profanity and vulgarity into serious criticism, her heavy reliance on asides and parenthetical comments, her insistence that most male filmmakers don't understand women, her willingness to attack actors based upon their looks, and her willingness to attack the work of creative people who are her friends.

However, the essence of Kael's literary charm cannot be found in the details of her writing. Her essays and criticisms are better than the sentences that comprise them. When reading her, look at the forest and forget the trees. Notice the big picture. She is not a didact who wants to tell you what to think. She is an impressionist telling you what she feels.

Of Kael's book *Reeling*, Susan Brownmiller opened her review in the *Chicago Tribune* in April 1976, like this: "*New Yorker* columnist Pauline Kael is famous for the cluttered pocketbook approach to movie criticism. She doesn't actually review a film in the strictest sense; she writes around and about it, by energetically dumping the contents of her interesting and impressive mind on the table in front of you, alongside the coffee and cake...."

The best we've seen on Pauline Kael, and listed in this bibliography, include interviews with Ray Sawhill and Polly Frost in *Interview* magazine, a long, detailed piece in *New York Woman* by Phillip Lopate, and the interview by Marc Smirnoff in the *Oxford American*. Keep in mind that Sawhill and Frost are close Kael friends.

Scholars, some of them, have faulted Kael for being too enthusiastic about movies, for liking too many of them, for liking movies they hated, and for having pet directors who can do no wrong in her eyes. There may be truth in all these criticisms. Kael is not exempt from saying questionable things, from liking what we may think is awful, from praising what most conceive as terrible, and from panning what touches many of us. What you will discover about Kael from the following selected bibliography of articles and books written by Kael's friends and critics is that she is considered by many the most influential movie critic of our time and that she is among the best writers about the film industry.

A Selected Bibliography

Adachi, Ken. "Is She the Best Critic in the World?" *Sunday Star* [Toronto], 11 May 1980, p. D14.

Adler, Renata. "The Perils of Pauline." Rev. of *When the Lights Go Down*, by Pauline Kael. *The New York Review of Books*, 14 August 1980, pp. 30-35.

Aitken, Will. "The Erotics of Pauline Kael." *Christopher Street*, June 1980, pp. 60-61.

Albert, Hollis. "Raising Kael." *Saturday Review*, 24 April 1971, pp. 48-49, 60-61.

Allen, Bruce. "Going to the Movies with Pauline Kael." Rev. of *Taking It All In*, by Pauline Kael. *The Christian Science Monitor*, 6 June 1984.

Ambuter, Jean. "She Found It at the Movies: Pauline Kael." *The Herald*, 28 November - 4 December 1971, p. 19.

Aufderheide, Pat. "How Pauline Kael Outgrew Hollywood." Rev. of *Taking It All In*, by Pauline Kael. *Reader, Los Angeles's Free Weekly*, 31 August 1984, pp. 18-19.

Aufderheide, Pat. "Pauline Kael on the New Hollywood." *In These Times* [Chicago], 7-13 May 1980, pp. 12, 23.

Aufderheide, Pat. "When the Lights Come Up." *In These Times* [Chicago], 7-13 May 1980, pp. 12-13, 23.

Barra, Allen. "A Critic of Influence." *New York Newsday*, 8 April 1991, pp. 50-51.

Barra, Allen. "Pauline Kael's Last Picture Show." *The San Francisco Bay Guardian*, 28 August 1991, pp. 29-31.

Barra, Allen. "Queen of the Screen." *The Hartford Advocate*, 22 August 1991, pp. 12, 15.

Barra, Allen. "The Farewells of Pauline." *The Riverfront Times*, 18-24 September 1991, pp. 24-26.

Baumbach, Jonathan. "The Kael Book of World Records." Rev. of *Reeling*, by Pauline Kael. *Partisan Review*, 1976, pp. 447-451.

Benson, Sheila. "Kael as a Voice of Reason." *Los Angeles Times*, Part VI, 26 June 1980, pp. 1, 6.

Benson, Sheila. "The Critic's Critic." *Pacific Sun*, 11-17 July 1980, pp. 5-6.

Berendt, John. "Critic Power." *Mainliner*, March 1977, pp. 29-31.

Boone, William. "Pauline Kael: Criticism in Search of Understanding." *Writing*, April 1984, pp. 21-22.

Brennan, Mary. "Perils of Pauline." *Seattle Weekly*, 4 April 1990, pp. 47-49.

Brownmiller, Susan. "Kael's Movie Criticism, 'Cluttered Pocketbook' Style." Rev. of *Reeling*, by Pauline Kael. *Chicago Tribune*, 4 April 1976.

Brustein, Robert. "Pauline Kael, Still Going Steady." Rev. of *Reeling*, by Pauline Kael. *The New York Times Book Review*, 4 April 1976, pp. 1-2.

Butler, Marilyn. "Reviewers." Rev. of *When the Lights Go Down*, by Pauline Kael. *London Review of Books*, 22 January - 4 February 1981, pp. 23-24.

Callenbach, Ernest. Rev. of *Kiss Kiss Bang Bang*, by Pauline Kael. *Film Quarterly*, Summer 1968, p. 54.

Carney, Raymond. "Writing in the Dark: Film Criticism Today." *Chicago Review*, Summer 1983, pp. 89-110.

Carson, Tom. "Citizen Kael." *Sight and Sound*, June 1991, pp. 22-23.

Christiansen, Richard. "Peerless Pauline, the Critic Terrific." *Chicago Daily News*, 13-14 July 1974, Panorama, pp. 2-3.

Coleman, John. "Rosebud Revisited." Rev. of *The Citizen Kane Book*, by Pauline Kael. *New Statesman*, 21 January 1972, pp. 82-83.

Croce, Arlene. "Getting a Fix on the Environment." Rev. of *Kiss Kiss Bang Bang*, by Pauline Kael. *National Review*, 4 June 1968, pp. 560-562.

Davidson, Sara. "A Carping of Critics." *Boston Sunday Globe*, 2 March 1969, pp. 16-19, 22-23.

Ebert, Roger. "Greatest American Film?" *Chicago Sunday Sun-Times Book Week*, 31 October 1971, pp. 1-2.

Ephron, Nora. "Back at the Movies." *New York Post*, 11 May 1966, p. 47.

Farber, Stephen. "The Power of Movie Critics." *American Scholar*, Summer 1976, pp. 419-423.

Feeney, Mark. "The Pearls of Pauline." *The Boston Globe Magazine*, 11 June 1989, pp. 18-19, 47-54.

Fox, Laura J. "The Woman Behind the Myth." *Valley News*, 4 May 1980, pp. 10-11, 21.

French, Philip. "The Exuberant Road to Xanadu." Rev. of *The Citizen Kane Book*, by Pauline Kael, Herman J. Mankiewicz, and Orson Welles. *The Times* [London], 17 January 1972, p. 5.

Fulford, Robert. "Pauline's Progress." *The Montreal Star*, 8 August 1973, p. E1.

Garcia, Jane. "Kael Force." *Movieline*, 14 July 1989, pp. 28-29, 52.

Geracimos, Ann. "Portrait of a Woman Reading." *The Washington Post Book World*, 23 February 1969, p. 17.

Gelman, Richard. "Pauline Kael Lost It All at the Movies." *The Village Voice*, 7 June 1976, pp. 40-41.

Green, Randall. "A Conversation with Pauline Kael." *New York Arts Journal*, 23, pp. 4-9.

Haber, Joyce. "The Education of Pauline Kael, Part 1." *The Toronto Sun*, 23 September 1974, p. 23.

Haber, Joyce. "The Education of Pauline Kael, Part 2." *The Toronto Sun*, 24 September 1974, p. 23.

Harding, William J. Rev. of *Going Steady*, by Pauline Kael. *The Daily Planet* [Philadelphia], 20 July 1971, p. 12.

Kael, Pauline. *Deeper into Movies*. Boston: Atlantic-Little, Brown, 1973.

Kael, Pauline. *5001 Nights at the Movies*. New York: Henry Holt, 1982.

Kael, Pauline. *5001 Nights at the Movies*. 2nd ed. New York: Henry Holt, 1991.

Kael, Pauline. *Going Steady*. Boston: Atlantic-Little, Brown, 1968.

Kael, Pauline. *Hooked*. New York: A William Abrahams Book/E. P. Dutton, 1989.

Kael, Pauline. *I Lost It at the Movies*. Boston: Atlantic-Little, Brown, 1965.

Kael, Pauline. "Incredible Shrinking Hollywood." *Holiday*, March 1966, pp. 86-92, 130-34.

Kael, Pauline. *Kiss Kiss Bang Bang*. Boston: Atlantic-Little, Brown, 1968.

Kael, Pauline. *Movie Love: Complete Review 1988-1991*. New York: A William Abrahams Book/ E. P. Dutton, 1991.

Kael, Pauline. "Old Movies Never Die." *Mademoiselle*, July 1965, pp. 63, 122-125.

Kael, Pauline. "Raising Kane." In *The Citizen Kane Book*. Boston: Atlantic-Little, Brown, 1971.

Kael, Pauline. *Reeling*. Boston: Atlantic-Little, Brown, 1976.

Kael, Pauline. *State of the Art*. New York: A William Abrahams Book/E. P. Dutton, 1985.

Kael, Pauline. *Taking It All In*. New York: Holt, Rinehart & Winston, 1984.

Kael, Pauline. *When the Lights Go Down*. New York: Holt, Rinehart & Winston, 1975.

Kasindorf, Jeanie. "Inside Hollywood: True Tales of Critics, Scripts and Long, Long Lunches." *New West*, 26 March 1979, pp. 17-23.

Katovsky, William R. "My Dinner with Pauline." *Arrival*, Spring 1987, pp. 18-21.

Kerr, Walter. "Bitchy to a Purpose." Rev. of *Kiss Kiss Bang Bang*, by Pauline Kael. *The New York Times Book Review*, 5 May 1968, p. 4.

Kilday, Gregg. "Hot Fun in the Summer Cinema." *Los Angeles Times*, Part IV, 25 September 1978, p. 8.

Kleinberg, Seymour. "You'll Find Her at the Movies." Rev. of *Deeper Into Movies*, by Pauline Kael. *The Nation*, 2 September 1973, pp. 186-187.

Koué, Don. "Citizen Kael: Criticism with a Touch of Class." *California Monthly*, December 1974, pp. 1, 8.

Lambert, Brian. "Pauline Kael, Everybody's Critic." *Twin Cities Reader*, 24-30 August 1988, p. 17.

Landau, Jon. "Loose Ends: Kael, Sarris, Simon & Violence." *The Phoenix* [Boston], 2 February 1972, pp. 32-33.

Leary, Richard. "...and Leary Razes Kael." *Columbia Daily Spectator*, 11 May 1971, pp. 4-5.

Lee, Betty. "Confessions of a Movie Critic: It Takes a Film to Shut Her Up." *The Globe and Mail* [Toronto], Entertainment/Travel, 11 August 1973, p. 1.

Leonard, John. "Pauline Kael Is Better Than Movies." Rev. of *Going Steady*, by Pauline Kael. *New York Times*, 12 February 1970, p. 35.

Leonard, John. "Reeling from Swamp Gas: Film Critics Review Film Critics Reviewing Film Critics." *More*, November 1976, pp. 32-34.

Loercher, Diana. "Wanting to Love the Movies." Rev. of *Going Steady*, by Pauline Kael. *The Christian Science Monitor*, 21 May 1970, p. 9.

Loevy, Diana. "'Hiss Hiss, Bang, Bang!'" *Home Video*, November 1980, pp. 54-59.

Lopate, Phillip. "The Lady in the Dark." *New York Woman*, November 1989, pp. 100-107.

Lynch, F. Dennis. "Pauline Kael's Critical Theories." *Journal of the University Film Association*, 1970, pp. 35-38.

Macklin, F. A. "Pauline Kael: Tangents Become Theses." Rev. of *Kiss Kiss Bang Bang*, by Pauline Kael. *Commonweal*, 28 June 1968, pp. 444-45.

Malcolm, Derek. "Work of a Genius, But...." Rev. of *The Citizen Kane Book*, by Pauline Kael. *The Guardian*, 29 January 1972, p. 19.

Malko, George. "Pauline Kael Wants People to Go to the Movies: A Profile." *Audience*, January-February 1972, pp. 38-48.

Maloff, Saul. "The Pleasure and Perils of Pauline." Rev. of *Kiss Kiss Bang Bang*, by Pauline Kael. *Chicago Sun-Times Book Week*, 12 May 1968, pp. 1, 11.

Marcus, Greil. "Making Sense of the Movies." Rev. of *Reeling*, by Pauline Kael. *Rolling Stone*, 6 May 1976, p. 95.

Marcus, Greil. "The Critics' Inquisition." *Rolling Stone*, 4 September 1980, pp. 26-27.

Maslin, Janet. "Critic Gives Up Long Lines for Long Books." *The Berkshire Eagle*, 16 March 1991, p. B10.

McCabe, Bruce. "Why Pauline Kael Went to Hollywood." *The Boston Globe*, 11 April 1980, p. 25.

McKenna, Kristine. "Pauline Kael: An Interview." *Reader, Los Angeles's Free Weekly*, 3 September 1982, pp. 1, 6-9, 18.

McMurtry, Larry. "Once More to the Screening Room." Rev. of *When the Lights Go Down*, by Pauline Kael. *American Film*, June 1980, pp. 66-67.

Morgenstern, Joe. "The Moviegoer." *Newsweek*, 23 February 1970, pp. 100-101.

Nobile, Philip. "Adler vs. Kael." *New York*, 11 August 1980, pp. 26-29.

O'Toole, Lawrence. "Assayer of the Silver Screen." *Maclean's*, 14 July 1980, pp. 8-11.

Olmert, Michael. "The True Story About 'Citizen Kane'." Rev. of "Raising Kane," by Pauline Kael. *Chicago Tribune Book World*, 31 October 1971, pp. 4, 12.

"Pauline Kael on the Current Cinema." *The Pennsylvania Gazette*, December 1988, pp. 32-36.

"Pauline Kael Talks About Violence, Sex, Eroticism and Women & Men in the Movies." *Mademoiselle*, July 1972, pp. 132-33, 173-78.

Podhoretz, John. "She Lost It at the Movies." *The American Scholar*, Winter 1989, pp. 117-22.

Powers, John. "Pauline Kael and the Rise and Fall of the Movies." *LA Weekly*, 5-11 April 1991, pp. 16-23.

Quinn, Anthony. "So Farewell, Queen of Spleen." *The Independent on Sunday*, 24 March 1991, p. 17.

Rea, Steven. "Married to the Movies." *Applause*, December 1988, pp. 22-24, 60.

Reed, Rex. "Sideshow: Pauline Pompous." *Sunday News Leisure*, 11 April 1976, pp. 7-8.

Samuels, Charles T. "No One in Film Reviewing Is So Utterly Unsentimental." Rev. of *Going Steady*, by Pauline Kael. *The New York Times Book Review*, 22 February 1970, pp. 6-7, 36.

Sarris, Andrew. "Sarris vs. Kael: The Queen Bee of Film Criticism." *The Village Voice*, 2-8 July 1980, pp. 1, 30-31, 70.

Sarris, Andrew. "Why Doesn't Richard Gilman Love Pauline Kael Anymore?" *The Village Voice*, 21 June 1976, pp. 121-22.

Sawhill, Ray, and Polly Frost. "Kaeleidoscope." *Interview*, April 1989, pp. 98-101, 130.

Schickel, Richard. "A Way of Seeing a Picture." Rev. of *I Lost It at the Movies*, by Pauline Kael. *New York Times Book Review*, 14 March 1965, sec. 7, p. 6.

Schiff, Stephen. "The Critics Talk Shop." *The Boston Phoenix*, 22 April 1980, pp. 4, 16-18.

Schrader, Paul. "Matthew Arnold in LA." *The Spectacle*, 10 May 1968, pp. 3-4.

Seligman, Craig. "Tribute: Pauline Kael." *Image*, 1 July 1990, pp. 24-26.

Sheed, Wilfrid. "The Good Word: Kael vs. Sarris vs. Simon." *The New York Times Book Review*, 7 March 1971, pp. 2, 42.

Sklar, Robert. "'The Good Ones Never Make You Feel Virtuous'." Rev. of *Hooked*, by Pauline Kael. *The New York Times Book Review*, 19 March 1989, p. 7.

Smirnoff, Marc. "Pauline Kael: The Critic Wore Cowboy Boots." *The Oxford American*, Spring 1992, pp. 40-51.

Sragow, Michael. "Fear of Kael: Why the Critics Who Attack Her Are Wrong." *Los Angeles Herald Examiner*, 22 August 1980, pp. D-7, D-32.

Sragow, Michael. "Passion of a Critic: Kael on Mediocrity, Risk and the American Movies." *San Francisco Examiner*, 18 December 1985.

Sragow, Michael. "Pauline Kael: She Got It at the Movies." Rev. of *5001 Nights at the Movies: Expanded for the '90s with 800 New Reviews*, by Pauline Kael. *San Francisco Examiner*, 2 June 1991.

Sragow, Michael. "The D.H. Lawrence of Movie Criticism." *Los Angles Herald Examiner*, 29 April 1980, pp. B1, B4.

Sragow, Michael. "The Merits of Pauline." Rev. of *Reeling*, by Pauline Kael. *The Real Paper* [Boston], 13 November 1976, pp. 8, 13.

Sragow, Michael. "Script Mining: Sam Raphaelson's Screen Gems." *The Boston Phoenix*, sec. 3, 25 April 1983, pp. 2, 10.

Sragow, Michael. "The Valedictory of an Inspired Critic of the Movies." Rev. of *Movie Love*, by Pauline Kael. *The Boston Globe*, 8 September 1991, pp. A15-A16.

Staggs, Sam. "Did She Lose It at the Movies?" *Mandate*, May 1983, pp. 10-13, 29, 80.

Thomson, David. "Frenzy in the Dark: The Perils of Pauline." *The Real Paper* [Boston], 28 July 1979. pp. 23-25.

Tynan, Kenneth. "The Road to Xanadu." Rev. of *The Citizen Kane Book*, by Pauline Kael. *The Observer Review*, 16 January 1972, p. 34.

Vineberg, Steve. "Critical Fervor," *The Threepenny Review*, Summer 1992, pp. 25-27.

Warren, Elaine Warren. "Movie Critic Dean Pauline Kael Calls 'em as She Sees 'em." *Los Angeles Herald Examiner*, 20 April 1984, pp. 6-7.

Welles, Orson. "The Creation of 'Citizen Kane'." *The Times* [London], 17 November 1971.

Wilmington, Michael. "Critical Differences." *L.A. Style*, August 1991, pp. 60-62.

Wolcott, James. "Renata Adler Sat in My Drink." *The Village Voice*, 6-12 August 1980, p. 55.

Wood, Michael. "At Home in the Dark." Rev. of *When the Lights Go Down*, by Pauline Kael. *New York Times Book Review*, 6 April 1980, pp. 3, 20.

Young, Toby. "A Tribute to Pauline Kael." *The Modern Review*, Autumn 1991, p. 27.